Ukraine

THIS EDITION WRITTEN AND RESEARCHED BY

Marc Di Duca, Leonid Ragozin

PLAN YOUR TRIP

ON THE ROAD

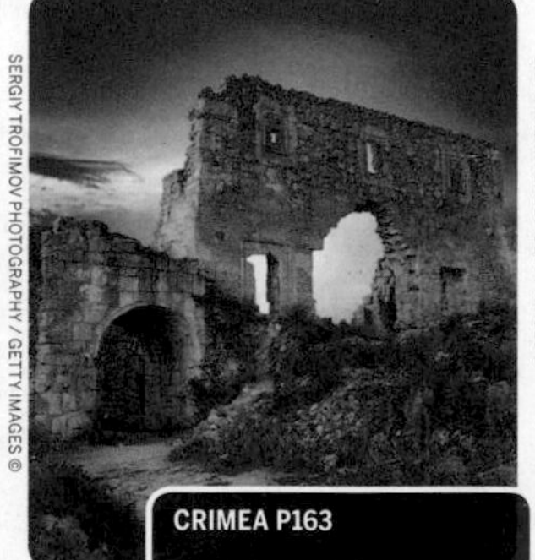
SERGIY TROFIMOV PHOTOGRAPHY / GETTY IMAGES ©

CRIMEA P163

MORDOLFF / GETTY IMAGES ©

THE CARPATHIANS P122

GRAHAM LAWRENCE / GETTY IMAGES ©

Contents

KYIV P32

UNDERSTAND

SURVIVAL GUIDE

SPECIAL FEATURES

Welcome to Ukraine

Big, diverse and largely undiscovered, Ukraine is one of Europe's last genuine travel frontiers, a poor nation rich in colourful tradition, warm-hearted people and off-the-map experiences.

Big & Diverse

Ukraine is big. In fact it's Europe's biggest country (not counting Russia, which isn't entirely in Europe) and packs a lot of diversity into its borders. You can be clambering around the Carpathians in search of Hutsul festivities, sipping Eastern Europe's best coffee in sophisticated Lviv and partying on a subtropical Crimean beach all in a few days. Ukrainians are also a diverse crowd; from the wired sophisticates of Kyiv's business quarters to the Donbas miner, the Crimean Tatar cook and the Hungarian-speaking bus drivers of Uzhhorod, few countries boast such a mixed population.

Hospitable Hosts

Despite their often glum reticence and initial distrust of strangers, the Euro 2012 football championships proved what travellers to the country have known for years – that Ukrainians are, when given the chance, one of Europe's most open and hospitable people. Break down that reserve and you'll soon be slurping *borshch* in someone's Soviet-era kitchen, listening to a fellow train passenger's life story or being taken on an impromptu tour of a town's sights by the guy you asked for directions.

Outdoor Fun

A diverse landscape obviously throws up a whole bunch of outdoorsy activities. How about cave exploring, hiking or beach fun in Crimea, mountain biking or hill walking in the Carpathians, bird spotting in the Danube Delta or water sports on the Kyiv Sea? But if the idea of burning calories on hill and wave has you fleeing for the sofa, rest assured that most Ukrainians have never tried any of the above, but love nothing more than wandering their country's vast forests, foraging for berries and mushrooms or picnicking by a meandering river. So why not join them?

Living History

Some claim history ended around 1989, but not in Ukraine. The country is passing through a choppy period in its post-independence story and one which is fascinating to watch (from a safe distance perhaps). History is all around you wherever you go in this vast land, whether it be among the Gothic churches of Lviv, the Stalinist facades of Kyiv, the remnants of the once-animated Jewish culture of West Ukraine or the more recent Soviet high-rises just about anywhere.

Why I Love Ukraine

By Marc Di Duca, Author

Is it the feeling of being Elsewhere but still in Europe, the bizarre Soviet legacy, the country's raw history, the unexpected travel experiences, the openness of locals or the stories tall and true of life under postwar communism? Or is it the star-dusted, blacker-than-black nights in Myrhorod, the *Nutcracker* at the opera house in snow-bound Kyiv, empty churches on rainy autumn Wednesdays in Lviv, or the endless bus journeys across the steppe in the company of Gogol and Kurkov? I suppose it's all the above and volumes more that have me returning to this magical Slavic hinterland time and time again.

For more about our authors, see page 288

Above: Women performing a traditional Ukrainian folk dance

Ukraine

BELARUS
Babrujsk
POLAND
Brest
Pinsk
Homel
Makrany
Novy
Yarylovichy
Shatsky
National
Park
Lublin
Okopy
Nowe
Kovel
Sarni
VOLYN
REGION
RIVNE
REGION
Ovruch
Chornobyl
Lviv
Join the crowds on the city's central piazza (p95)
Lutsk
Rivne
Korets
Korosten
POLISSYA
Kyivske
Reservoir
(Kyiv Sea)
Chervonohrad
Dubno
Novohrad
Volynsky
Rzeszów
Zhovkva
Kremenets
Shepetivka
Zhulyany
Airport
Kyiv
Shehyni
Lviv
Olesko
Pochayiv
Zhytomyr
Boryspil
International
Airport
LVIV
REGION
Berdychiv
Drohobych
Ternopil
Bila
Tserkva
Stry
Khmelnytsky
TERNOPIL REGION
Vinnytsya
Vyšné Nemecké
Ivano-
Frankivsk
Chortkiv
Uzhhorod
Nemyriv
Mukacheve
Yaremcha
Kamyanets-
Podilsky
PODILLYA
Kolomyya
Mogyliv-
Podilsky
Uman
Carpathian NP
Tatariv
Kosiv
Khotyn
Yasinya
Bukovel
Rakhiv
Chernivtsi
Briceni
Siret
Pervomaysk
The Carpathians
Bike and hike Ukraine's relaxing uplands (p122)
Kamyanets-Podilsky
Wander this town atop a rock island (p79)
Balta
Duba
Kolomyya
An engaging base for Carpathian exploration (p131)
MOLDOVA
Berezivka
Cluj-
Napoca
Chişinău
Tylukulsky
lyman
Tiraspol
Kuchurhan
Odesa
Beach parties by the Black Sea (p146)
Odesa
Ilychevsk
Bilhorod-
Dnistrovsky
Dnistrovsky
lyman
Sibiu
ROMANIA
Lake
Sasyk
Bolhrad
oz Kytay
oz Katlabukh
oz Kahul
Vylkovo
Izmayil
Brăila
oz Yalpuh
Dunaysky
NP
Piteşti
Danube Delta
Bird spotting and watery vistas (p161)
Bucharest
Black Sea
(Chorne More)
29°E
30°E
31°E

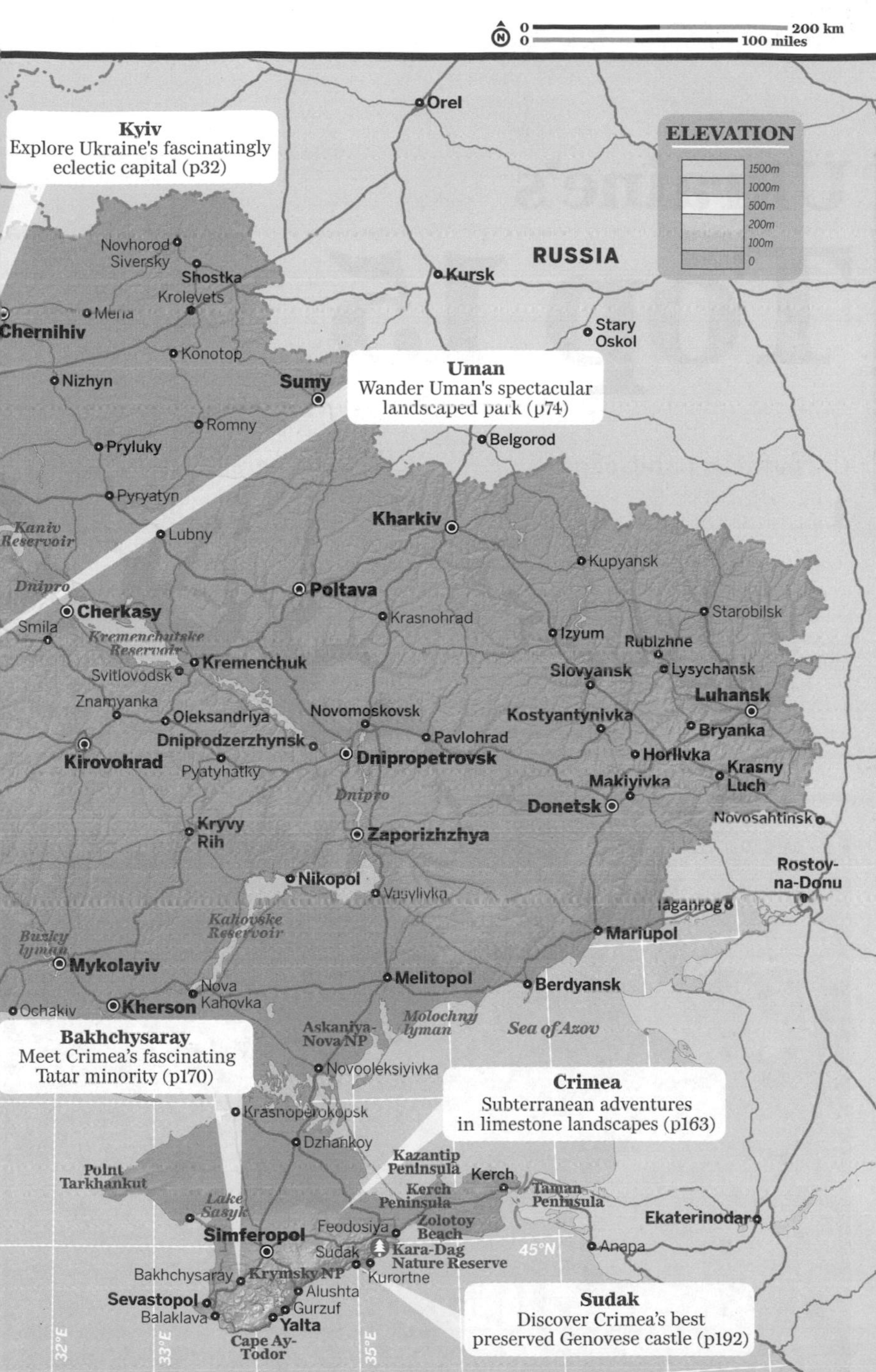

0 200 km
0 100 miles
Kyiv
Explore Ukraine's fascinatingly eclectic capital (p32)
Uman
Wander Uman's spectacular landscaped park (p74)
Bakhchysaray
Meet Crimea's fascinating Tatar minority (p170)
Crimea
Subterranean adventures in limestone landscapes (p163)
Sudak
Discover Crimea's best preserved Genovese castle (p192)
ELEVATION
1500m
1000m
500m
200m
100m
0
RUSSIA
Orel
Kursk
Stary Oskol
Belgorod
Novhorod Siversky
Shostka
Krolevets
Mena
Chernihiv
Konotop
Nizhyn
Sumy
Romny
Pryluky
Pyryatyn
Lubny
Kaniv Reservoir
Dnipro
Cherkasy
Smila
Kremenchutske Reservoir
Kremenchuk
Svitlovodsk
Znamyanka
Oleksandriya
Kirovohrad
Dniprodzerzhynsk
Pyatyhatky
Poltava
Krasnohrad
Kharkiv
Kupyansk
Starobilsk
Izyum
Rubizhne
Slovyansk
Lysychansk
Luhansk
Kostyantynivka
Bryanka
Horlivka
Krasny Luch
Makiyivka
Donetsk
Novosahtinsk
Novomoskovsk
Pavlohrad
Dnipropetrovsk
Dnipro
Zaporizhzhya
Kryvy Rih
Nikopol
Vasylivka
Kahovske Reservoir
Buzky lyman
Mykolayiv
Kherson
Ochakiv
Nova Kahovka
Melitopol
Berdyansk
Mariupol
Taganrog
Rostov-na-Donu
Askaniya-Nova NP
Molochny lyman
Sea of Azov
Novooleksiyivka
Krasnoperokopsk
Dzhankoy
Point Tarkhankut
Lake Sasyk
Simferopol
Feodosiya
Kazantip Peninsula
Kerch Peninsula
Kerch
Taman Peninsula
Zolotoy Beach
Kara-Dag Nature Reserve
Sudak
Kurortne
Anapa
Ekaterinodar
45°N
Bakhchysaray
Krymsky NP
Alushta
Sevastopol
Balaklava
Gurzuf
Yalta
Cape Ay-Todor
32°E
33°E
35°E

Ukraine's Top 15

Carpathian Landscapes

1 By and large Ukraine is as flat as a topographically challenged *blin* (pancake), which makes its bumpy bits all the more special. Ukraine's slice of the Carpathian arc barely reaches over 2000m, but its soothing wooded slopes, rough stony trails, flower-filled upland pastures and wide, snaking valleys make this prime hiking, biking and skiing territory. Needless to say, the Carpathians (p122) are home to Ukraine's highest peak, Mt Hoverla, a fairly easy trek from nearby villages, as well as several ski resorts.

Kyevo-Pecherska Lavra, Kyiv

2 Discover the mysteries of Eastern Orthodoxy and descend into catacombs to see mummies of much-revered saints on an excursion to the holy of holies for all eastern Slavs. Founded as a cave monastery in 1051, the *lavra* (p43) is packed with golden-domed churches, baroque edifices and orchards. Religious ceremonies take place in lavishly decorated, icon-filled interiors, accompanied by beautiful choir singing and attended by flocks of pilgrims and monks. Obscure museums in the grounds are dedicated to Scythian gold and micro-miniatures and decorative arts.

1

2

Sheshory (ArtPole) Festival

3 Think Woodstock meets Burning Man and you have Sheshory (p22), an annual four-day gathering of musicians and artists from all over Eastern Europe. For the first few years the event was held in the Carpathian village of Sheshory, but has since gone walkabout, and now the action can take place anywhere in the country's rural west. If your experience of Ukraine has been mostly scowling receptionists and devious taxi drivers, the hippy spirit of the Sheshory Festival comes as a very pleasant surprise.

Andriyivsky Uzviz, Kyiv

4 The apostle Andrew is said to have climbed this steep ascent to erect a cross and prophesise the rise of Kyiv. Today it's the haunt of artists, who install their canvases on this cobbled Montmartre-like street, which – in true decadent style – Kyivites call Andrew's Descent (p42). Packed with souvenir stands selling all sorts of junk, the uzviz has heaps of bohemian charm and is great for people-watching. Here Russian writer Mikhail Bulgakov wrote *The White Guard*, perhaps the best novel about Kyiv and its people; his house is now a museum. Near right: St Andrew's Church (p42) atop Andriyivsky uzviz

3

VADYM ILKOV / ARTPOLE

ULANA SWITUCHA / ALAMY ©

MARTIN MOOS / GETTY IMAGES ©

Kolomyya

5 With its traveller-friendly places to stay, two fascinating museums and effortless access to the surrounding forested hills, Kolomyya (p131) is one of the best bases from which to scale the heights of the Carpathian Mountains. The town's central Pysanky Museum, housed in a giant Easter egg, is the obvious highlight, but aimless wandering also bears fruit in the shape of some twirling Art Nouveau architecture from the town's Austro-Hungarian days. Top right: Pysanky Museum (p131), Kolomyya

Kamyanets-Podilsky

6 Ringed by the dramatic gorge of the Smotrych River, there are few more eye-pleasing spots in Ukraine than this Podillyan town (p79). A stroll from the new bridge takes you through the cobbled quarters of this once-divided community, past beautifully renovated churches, crumbling palaces and forgotten pieces of the once beefy defences, to the town's impossibly picturesque fortress, surely one of the highlights of any visit to Ukraine. The best thing? Outside high season you may have the place entirely to yourself. Bottom right: Kamyanets-Podilsky Fortress (p80)

Pyrohovo Museum of Folk Architecture, Kyiv

7 You can safely claim you've seen all of Ukraine after a visit to Pyrohovo (p48) – a large chunk of countryside just outside Kyiv filled with traditional wooden architecture representing all parts of the country. Whole churches, windmills, shops and houses were brought here from their original villages, providing a wonderful backdrop for folk festivals, which frequently take place on the grounds. Here Transcarpathia is walking distance from the Poltava region, although it might require a bit of footwork.

Colourful Markets

8 In the market for a 5L jar of gherkins, a Lada gearbox, a kilo of pig fat or a bottle of fake-brand perfume? You'll probably find them all, plus almost everything else under the sun, at Ukraine's amazing bazaars. They're the best spots to source seasonal fruit and veg, and if you're looking to pack a picnic, these are the places to get supplies. The biggest and best can be found in Odesa (p157), Kharkiv (p213), Kyiv (p59) and Chernivtsi (p138). Top right: Porcelain eggs in a souvenir market, Dnipropetrovsk

MARTIN MOOS / GETTY IMAGES ©

MARTIN MOOS / GETTY IMAGES ©

MATTHEW SHALVATIS / GETTY IMAGES ©

Lviv's Historical Centre

9 Lviv is the beating cultural heart of Ukraine, and the main square, pl Rynok (p96), is the bustling heart of Lviv. Plonked in the middle is the huge *ratusha* (town hall), around which mill clutches of camera-toting tourists and quick-footed locals. The aroma of freshly milled coffee beans wafts across the square from the city's legendary coffeehouses, and summer tables tumble out across the Habsburg-era cobbles as old Soviet-era trams rumble past. Take a seat, order a coffee and take it all in.

Sofiyivka Park, Uman

10 Forget boxes of chocolates, bouquets of roses or even diamond rings – how about wowing your loved one with a gift measuring 150 hectares, complete with grottoes, water features and an entire town's worth of architectural follies? That was the grandiose way one 18th-century Polish magnate chose to express adoration for his wife, Sofia, and the legacy of his devotion is this amazing landscaped park (p74) intended to resemble the countryside of Sofia's native land. Her response – an affair with his son.

Danube Delta Biosphere Reserve

11 The Danube Delta Biosphere Reserve (p161), Europe's largest wetland, is located in Ukraine's far southwest where the Danube dumps water and silt into the Black Sea. Few make the effort to reach this far-flung wedge of fertile territory (few Ukrainians have been there), but those who do are rewarded with astoundingly beautiful scenery, colourful birdlife, and serene evenings in drowsy Vylkovo, fancifully nicknamed the 'Ukrainian Venice' thanks to its network of canals.

Below: Great White Pelican, Danube Delta

Odesa's Nightlife

12 By day Odesa's museums, parks, beaches and, of course, the celebrated Potemkin Steps provide ample distraction, but it's at night that the city really comes alive. With its imaginatively styled dance temples and chill-out zones just steps from the Black Sea, Arkadia Beach is the place to strut and pose until the wee summer hours. But Odesa (p146) also has a stomping alternative scene, with several hip venues serving up cool ales to the sound of guitar-happy indie bands and local DJs.

11

DANITA DELIMONT / GETTY IMAGES ©

12

ALLOVER PHOTOGRAPHY / ALAMY ©

KEREN SU / GETTY IMAGES ©

HOLGER LEUE / GETTY IMAGES ©

HANS NELEMAN / GETTY IMAGES ©

Crimean Cave Cities

13 It was not breathtaking views but the need to protect themselves from bloodthirsty nomads that prompted ancient Crimeans to carve dwellings out of limestone atop high plateaus. Goths, Alans, Feodorites – these long-forgotten peoples come to life when you hear the story of Mangup-Kale (p175). Another cave city, Chufut-Kale (p172), the Jewish fortress, remains the Zion of Karaites – a small Turkic group that has managed to preserve its unique culture and religion, rooted in Judaism, for centuries. Top left: Uspensky Monastery (p172)

Bakhchysaray's Crimean Tatar Culture

14 Back from a 50-year exile, Crimean Tatars are busy turning their capital Bakhchysaray (p170) into what its name means – garden city. Family-run guesthouses provide some of the best (and cheapest) accommodation in Crimea, while their Asian-influenced food is now served across the peninsula. Ancient crafts, such as embroidery and filigree, are being revived by small cooperatives. Tatars are wonderful hosts, eager to spread the word about their unique culture. Top right: Crimean Tatar women in traditional dress

Sudak's Crumbling Castle

15 Once a far-flung corner of the Roman Empire, Crimea was rediscovered by medieval Genovese traders, who came here to link up with caravans bringing silk and spices from the Orient. Trade outposts were protected by mighty fortresses, most of which were razed by the Mongols. But at least one remains intact. Imagine yourself as a knight or doge when you climb the Consul's Tower and look down the vertiginous cliff from the wall of Sudak's Genovese Fortress (p192), waiting for white sails to appear on the horizon.

Need to Know

For more information, see Survival Guide (p253)

Currency
Hryvnya (uah; *hriv*-nya)

Language
Ukrainian and Russian

Money
ATMs widespread, even in small towns. Credit cards accepted at most hotels but only upmarket restaurants.

Visas
Generally not needed for stays of up to 90 days.

Mobile Phones
Local SIM cards can be used in European and Australian phones. US and other phones aren't compatible; consider a cheap Ukrainian mobile.

Time
East European Time (GMT/UTC plus two hours)

When to Go

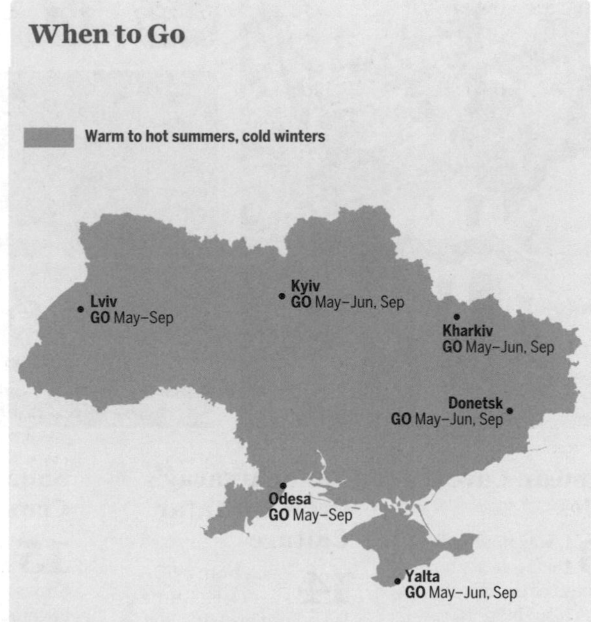

High Season
(Jul–Aug)

➡ Expect stifling heat and humidity as well as heavy thunderstorms.

➡ Accommodation rates rise in Crimea but fall in the Carpathians.

➡ Cities empty as people head for the coast and their country cottages.

Shoulder Season
(May–Jun & Sep–Oct)

➡ Travel now to dodge the extreme temperatures of summer or winter.

➡ Spring can be chilly, but it's a pleasant time to be in blossoming Kyiv.

➡ Visit Crimea in autumn and avoid the summer crowds.

Low Season
(Nov–Apr)

➡ Expect temperatures well below zero, heavy snowfalls and hard frosts.

➡ The Carpathians skiing season runs November to March.

➡ Book ahead for New Year and early January.

Websites

Lonely Planet (www.lonelyplanet.com/ukraine) Info, hotel bookings, traveller forum and more.

Brama (www.brama.com) The most useful gateway site.

Ukraine.com (www.ukraine.com) Gateway site with news and lots of background info.

Ukraine Encyclopedia (www.encyclopediaofukraine.com) One of the largest sources of info on Ukraine.

Travel to Ukraine (www.traveltoukraine.org) Official state tourism website.

Important Numbers

When calling within a city, leave off the city code. When calling abroad from landlines, dial ☎0 then wait for another tone before pressing ☎0 again.

Country code	☎38
International access code	☎00
General emergency number	☎112

Exchange Rates

Australia	A$1	7.45uah
Canada	C$1	7.72uah
Europe	€1	11.16uah
Japan	¥100	8.01uah
New Zealand	NZ$1	6.73uah
Poland	1zł	2.66uah
Russia	R10	2.47uah
UK	UK£1	13.46uah
US	US$1	8.21uah

For current exchange rates see www.xe.com.

Daily Costs

Budget: Less than 250uah

- 100km of bus travel: 30uah
- Cafeteria-style meal: from 30uah
- Dorm beds: 70–150uah

Midrange: 250uah–1000uah

- Double room with breakfast in a good hotel: 400–800uah
- Three-course dinner in a restaurant with waiters: under 100uah
- 100km of travel by express train: 70uah

Top end: More than 1000uah

- Double room in a comfortable, European standard hotel: from 800uah
- Taxis between cities: per kilometre 2–3uah
- English-speaking guide and driver per day: 400–600uah

Opening Hours

Opening hours are consistent throughout the year with very few seasonal variations.

Banks 9am–5pm Monday to Friday

Restaurants 11am–11pm

Cafes 9am–10pm

Bars and Clubs 10pm–3am

Shops 9am–9pm

Arriving in Ukraine

Boryspil International Airport (Kyiv; p264) Regular round-the-clock bus services leave from outside the terminal to the main train station. Taxis cost 200uah to 300uah to the city centre (around 40 minutes). An express train planned for the Euro 2012 football championships may still be built.

Lviv International Airport (p264) Take trolleybus 9 to the university or bus 48 to the corner of vul Doroshenka and pr Svobody. Taxis cost around 50uah to the city centre (15 minutes).

Getting Around

Getting around Ukraine isn't as difficult as it may first appear. Bus is the best way to cover distances of up to around 100km; after that let the train, probably a sleeper, take the strain. Detailed bus timetables can be found at www.bus.com.ua. **Ukrainian Railways** (www.uz.gov.ua) has an online timetable and you can even book tickets on the web.

Train Cheap but slow; best for overnight journeys between big cities. Some new express trains link Ukraine's biggest cities during the day.

Bus Very cheap with regular services but normally packed to bursting and unbearably hot in summer.

Car Only advisable for the main routes between the biggest cities and for tours such as the Gogol Circuit.

For much more on **getting around**, see p268

If You Like...

Folk Culture

Traditional folk culture has boomed since independence with new festivals and events added to an ever-growing calendar.

Hutsul Celebrations Hutsul festivals, weddings and red-letter days are the best times to see the culture of the Carpathians' Hutsul people in all its woolly glory. (p135)

Pyrohovo Museum of Folk Architecture This is the best open-air museum in the country highlighting local crafts and customs. (p48)

Bakhchysaray Head here to track down traditional Crimean Tatar culture and some delicious ethnic food. (p170)

Kosiv Craft Market Ukraine's biggest traditional craft market is the place to pick up genuine handmade souvenirs. (p133)

Beaches

Ukraine has more than its fair share of sun-kissed sand and shingle to keep that tan glowing.

Truhaniv Island Barbecuing and river bathing in central Kyiv as well as welcome relief from the summer city heat. (p52)

Odesa The southern metropolis has several popular Black Sea beaches, and the further from the city you get, the less crowded they become. (p150)

Cape Fiolent Descend 800 steps from a clifftop monastery to access one of Crimea's most attractive beaches. (p177)

Balaklava Join the charge of the sun brigade on some of southern Crimea's most gobsmacking strands. (p182)

Churches

Stalin did his levelling best to destroy Ukraine's stock of wonderful churches, but somehow many survived.

Kyevo-Pecherska Lavra This gathering of golden domes is Ukraine's holiest site. (p43)

Carpathian wooden churches Ukraine's timber places of worship were recently added to Unesco's list of World Heritage Sites. (p90)

St Sophia's Cathedral Kyiv's most atmospheric place of worship. (p37)

St Andrew's Church Many a 19th-century aristocratic wedding took place in this magnificent chunk of baroque architecture. (p42)

Chernihiv The town's collection of exquisite church buildings has earned it Unesco recognition. (p202)

Pochayiv This golden-domed huddle of churches and monastery buildings can be seen for miles around. (p115)

Soviet Architecture

Will Ukraine's Lenin statues, brutish war memorials, plinthed tanks and Stalin monuments be carted off to a nostalgia museum? Probably no time soon!

Rodina Mat This 62m-tall titanium goddess wields sword and shield high above the Dnipro River. (p47)

Derzhprom This megalomaniac's dream in concrete even manages to dominate the world's second-largest square. (p209)

Kyiv Metro Some of Kyiv's metro stations are proof that the Soviets did sometimes create things of ornate beauty. (p92)

IF YOU LIKE... CAVES

Crimea has whole subterranean cities of them, buried deep below the peninsula's limestone plateau. (p175)

Friendship of Nations Monument A huge Soviet realist monument under a tin rainbow in Kyiv. (p38)

Jewish Sites

Cemeteries, former synagogues, 19th-century *shtetls* (villages) and tombs can be found across Ukraine but the holocaust left few Jews to tend to them.

Uman The tomb of Rabbi Nachman draws thousands of pilgrims at Jewish New Year. (p75)

Berdychiv The highlight here is the tomb of Levi Yitzhak set amid toppling, Hebrew-inscribed graves. (p73)

Sharhorod One of the region's best preserved *shtetls*. (p79)

Dnipropetrovsk Check out east Ukraine's best Jewish museum. (p220)

Museums

Most of Ukraine's museums are threadbare, underfunded affairs; however, there are some quirky exceptions.

Museum of One Street Relates the story of Kyiv's Andriyivsky uzviz in a delightful jumble of knick-knacks. (p42)

Korolyov Cosmonaut Museum A blast off from the Soviet space program past. (p72)

Nuclear Missile Museum See how close the world was to obliteration at this former nuclear missile launch site. (p78)

Chornobyl Museum Tells the horrific story of the world's worst nuclear disaster. (p43)

Pysanky Museum The yoke's on you if you miss this folksy museum housed in a huge painted egg. (p131)

(Top) Mosaic in Uspensky Monastery (p172), Crimea
(Bottom) Friendship of Nations Monument (p49), Kiev

Month by Month

TOP EVENTS

Carnival Humorina, April

Ivan Kupala, July

Sheshory (ArtPole) Festival, August

Koktebel International Jazz Festival, September

New Year's Eve, December

January

Winter bites cold in January and you'll have to wrap up pretty snugly to do any sightseeing. However, this is a great time to snap on skis in the Carpathian Mountains.

Orthodox Christmas

Only revived nationally since independence, Ukrainians celebrate Orthodox Christmas according to the old Julian Calendar on 7 January. On Christmas Eve families gather for the 12-course meal of Svyata Vecherya (Holy Supper).

Old New Year's Eve

Not only do Ukrainians get to celebrate two Christmases (Catholic and Orthodox), they also get two stabs at New Year – according to the Julian Calendar Orthodox New Year falls on 13 January.

Epiphany

Across Ukraine during 18–19 January, deranged individuals can be seen leaping into icy rivers to celebrate the arrival of Christianity in Kyivan Rus. Kyiv sees the biggest event with scores of men braving the numbing waters of the Dnipro River.

April

Things begin to warm up along the southern coast, but inland you'll still need those chunky Hutsul woollen socks. Visit Kyiv at the end of the month when thousands of chestnut trees begin to bloom.

Carnival Humorina

Odesa's biggest annual fiesta is a one-day street parade on 1 April. Floats, music, dancing and lots of food flood the streets to celebrate the city's status as Ukrainian capital of humour.

Orthodox Easter

Falling two weeks after Catholic Easter, colourful Orthodox *paskha* arrives in April two years out of three. This is more of a religious festival than in the West, with churchgoers taking baskets of *pysanky* (painted eggs) and specially baked loaves to be blessed by priests.

May

Ukraine is most definitely a shoulder-season destination and May is the first of those shoulders. Colour returns to the snow-bleached land, the last river ice fades and the first seedlings nudge through Ukraine's black soil.

Lviv City Day

Early May is the time to be in Lviv when the city celebrates its 'day' as well as a number of other festivals that take place to coincide with the long May holidays.

Kamyanets-Podilsky Days

Mid-May sees street parties, concerts, choirs, parades, exhibitions and sporting events take over the rock-island town of Kamyanets-Podilsky.

(Top) Independence Day (p22) celebrations in Kyiv
(Bottom) Traditional fair in Velyki Sorochyntsi (p206)

Kyiv Day

A colourful spring celebration and festival in honour of the capital city held on the last weekend of May. The day of fun events comes to an end around 10pm with a huge firework display over the Dnipro.

July

Alas, most visitors arrive in the hottest months of the year when travel becomes a sweaty ordeal. Give Crimea a wide berth at this time of year and head instead for the cooler Carpathians.

Ivan Kupala

An exhilarating pagan celebration of midsummer involving fire jumping, maypole dancing, fortune-telling, wreath floating and strong overtones of sex. Celebrated 7 July, head for the countryside for the real heathen deal.

Kazantip

The huge, seaside Kazantip rave festival (p170; www.kazantip.com) kicks off in late July and runs for five weeks, into August. It's held in Popovka north of Yevpatoriya and attracts over 100,000 party people.

Kraina Mriy Festival

This free festival of ethnic music (p53; www.krainamriy.com) attracts traditional musicians from across the world. Performances take place on several stages erected in the park next to Kyiv's Kyevo-Pecherska Lavra.

August

Crowded and superheated, Crimea is still the place to avoid during August. Colossal sunflower fields are a gobsmacking sight across Ukraine's agricultural heartlands this month, and by the end the harvest is in full swing.

✩ Festival 'Under the Rock'

Held in the tiny village of Pidkamin (meaning 'under the rock'), this popular ethnic music, jazzy-type festival (p116) is held around a huge hilltop rock formation. It's one of the most popular festivals in the west with a tent city and loads of side events.

✩ Independence Day

On the 24th, cities across the land lay on festivals and parades with performances and special events. But the place to be is Kyiv's maydan Nezalezhnosti (Independence Sq), which bops to an evening pop concert followed by a mega firework show.

Sheshory (ArtPole) Festival

A huge range of folk and art events take place as part of the country's most talked-about festival (www.artpolefest.org). The roving event was held near Ivano-Frankivsk in 2013; check the website for this year's destination and program.

September

Temperatures mellow out, people return to the cities and everyday life resumes in the hazy light of the Ukrainian autumn. By far the best time to travel and to gorge on Ukraine's legendary fruit and veg.

✩ Koktebel International Jazz Festival

In mid-September international jazz stars join locals at this cool festival (http://jazz.koktebel.info) after Crimea's summertime crush has passed. Over 20,000 fans swamp tiny Koktebel to tap feet in rhythm with almost 200 musicians, making this one of Ukraine's largest music festivals.

✩ Gogolfest

The biggest festival of the autumn in Kyiv, Gogolfest (p53) takes place at various venues across the capital. The week-long festival includes art, theatre, music, cinema, workshops and kid's events.

Lviv Coffee Festival

Disciples of the bean should go west to Ukraine's caffeine capital for the country's only coffee festival (www.coffeefest.lviv.ua). Highlights of the three-day event include the presentation of an award for 'Lviv coffeehouse of the year', various concerts and coffee-themed tours.

October

Comfortable temperatures give way to chilly days, falling leaves and the first frosts. Ukrainians head out to their country cottages and gardens to wind up the season and lock up for the long winter.

✩ Kyiv International Film Festival Molodist

Late October sees Kyiv host this superb film festival (www.molodist.com), a great opportunity to check out new cinematic talent from Ukraine and other countries. Running for over four decades, it's recognised as one of Eastern Europe's top film events.

December

End-of-year commercialism is yet to take off in a big way here, so if you're looking to flee the Christmas shopping blues, decidedly un-festive and very chilly Ukraine could be the antidote.

Catholic Christmas

On 25 December Catholic Ukrainians celebrate the first of two Christmases the country marks every year. However, for most people, especially in the predominantly Orthodox and Russian-speaking areas, this is just an ordinary working day.

New Year's Eve

This is by far the biggest bash of the year and if you think you've seen it all on New Year's Eve, you haven't been to Kyiv. Needless to say, gallons of *horilka* (vodka) and cheap bubbly are involved.

Itineraries

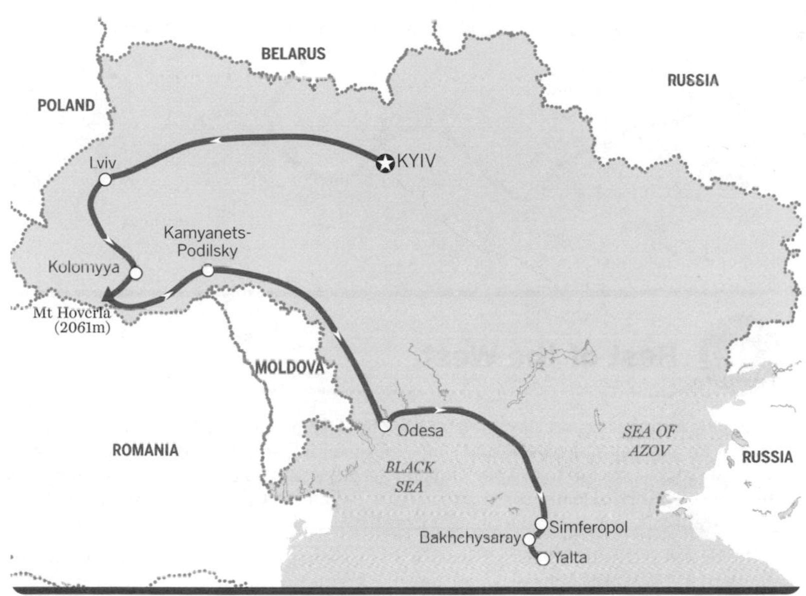

Essential Ukraine

The quintessential Ukrainian experience kicks off in **Kyiv**, the cradle of Slavic civilisation. Three days are just enough to absorb the mix of gold-domed Orthodox churches, monumental Stalinist architecture, leafy parks and raucous nightlife.

From Kyiv catch an overnight sleeper train to the former Habsburg city of **Lviv**. With its Italianate buildings and Austrian-style cafes, it's a cosy contrast to the Soviet capital.

From there, it's a simple ride south to **Kolomyya**, a great base from which to explore the Carpathian Mountains and perhaps climb **Mt Hoverla**, Ukraine's highest peak. A short road journey from here brings you to dramatic **Kamyanets-Podilsky**, where the medieval Old Town perches atop a tall rock in the middle of a river loop.

Next stop, **Odesa**, famous for the Potemkin Steps and weekend clubbing at Arkadia Beach. Then take an overnight train to **Simferopol**, before heading to the Crimean Tatar capital of **Bakhchysaray**, with its captivating Khans' Palace and cave city of Chufut-Kale.

Then head south to kitschy **Yalta**, a handy base for exploring Crimea's southern coast.

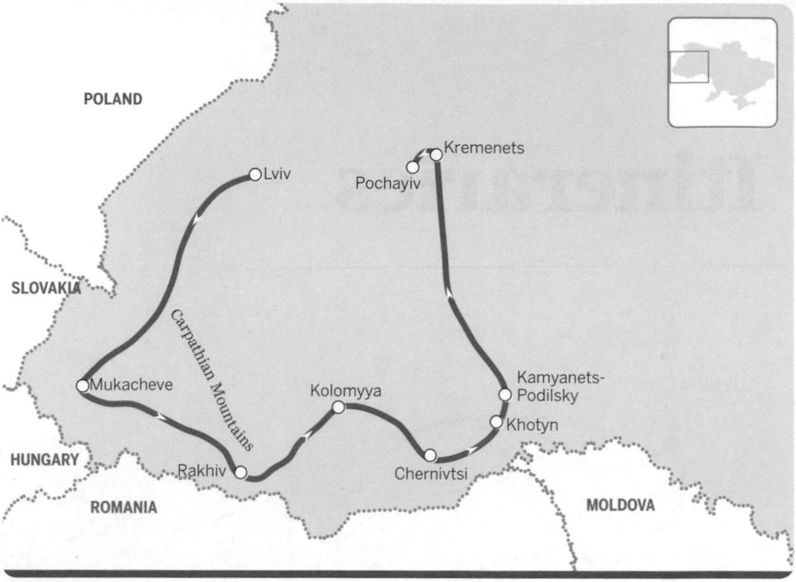

Best of the West

Launch your loop around Ukraine's far west in **Lviv**, an eastern outpost of central Europe with a strong cafe culture and some gobsmacking architecture that make it one of Ukraine's top stops for any visitor. Outside the city centre the Lychakivske Cemetery is a must-see. The city also has some of the country's wackiest restaurants, with the Masonic Restaurant and Dim Lehend topping a zany list.

If you can tear yourself away from Lviv's European charms, hop on board a slow train south to low-key **Mukacheve**, where one of Ukraine's most dramatic hilltop castles awaits. From here it's into soothingly forested mountain country, the Carpathians to be exact. Ukraine's wedge of the Carpathian arc is etched with long broad valleys, and a great place to start your exploration is **Rakhiv**. Here you can have your first brush with Hutsul culture and head off into the hills for some exhilarating hiking and biking, before picking your way north along the A265 road linking resort villages, ski centres and hiking bases en route. Call a halt at quaint **Kolomyya**, a superb launch pad for more hikes. The town also has two intriguing museums, including the famous Pysanky Museum housed in a giant Easter egg. It also boasts one of the best places to stay in all Ukraine in the shape of the On the Corner guesthouse.

Consider short stops at energetic **Chernivtsi**, to visit the psychedelic university building, and the spectacular **Khotyn** fortress on the banks of the wide Dnister River, before you next unpack your bags in the show-stopping island town of **Kamyanets-Podilsky**. One of Ukraine's must-see attractions, the town is as historically fascinating as it is dramatically situated, in a loop of the Smotrych River.

A long haul by bus across giant fields of sunflowers and sugar beet via off-the-beaten-track Ternopil delivers you to picturesque **Kremenets**, another town boasting a superb fortress as well as an eerie Cossack cemetery. From here it's a short *marshrutka* (fixed-route minibus) hop to the polished golden domes of **Pochayiv**, Ukraine's second most important monastery after Kyiv's Kyevo-Pecherska Lavra. Lviv is a four-hour bus ride away.

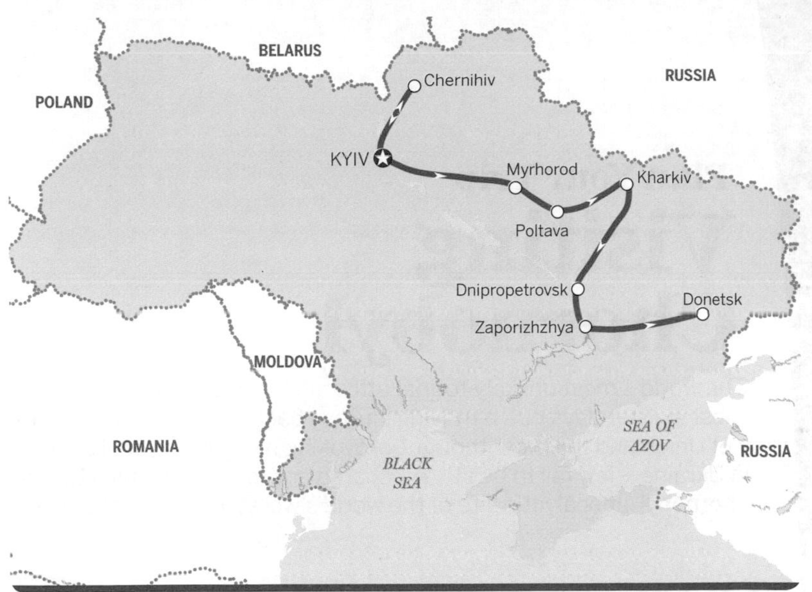

Best of the East

This venture into the less-frequented east begins with a quick jump north from Kyiv to atmospheric **Chernihiv**, with its amazing Unesco-listed collection of monasteries and cathedrals. Most make this a day trip from the capital but staying the night gives more time to appreciate the wonderful collection of ancient church buildings.

Unless you're up for some slow and complicated train journeys, backtrack to the capital and jump aboard an express train heading east – first stop the spa town of **Myrhorod**. Gogol was born nearby, and the town and surrounding area feature in many of his tales. Get off the beaten track in these parts by spending a couple of days on the Gogol Circuit, which visits many sites associated with the author. Local guesthouses can put you up for a few hryvnya.

Reboard the express for the short trip to **Poltava**, a pleasant, park-dotted place and the scene of a key battle in Ukrainian history. Designed as a kind of mini–St Petersburg, this grand city contrasts with the surrounding bucolic scenery and is well worth half a day's exploration. The final stop of the express is **Kharkiv**, a huge student city. Essential viewing here is the world's second-largest city square, which is dominated by the mammoth, Stalinist-era Derzhprom building.

From Kharkiv it's a smooth roll south to another of Ukraine's eastern megacities – **Dnipropetrovsk** – still a major centre for Ukraine's rocket and aviation industries (so be careful what you aim your camera at!). Take a stroll by the Dnipro River before continuing south to **Zaporizhzhya**, an ugly industrial city but also the location of Khortytsya Island, where the Ukrainian Cossacks once gathered at the *sich* (fort). This is the best place in the country to learn about the Cossacks, their way of life and their influence on the country's history. From the banks of the Dnipro, catch a bus or train to **Donetsk**, the power base of the east. The main industry is still coal mining, but among the slag heaps you'll also glimpse Eastern Europe's most cutting-edge football stadium, a Euro 2012 venue. Donetsk is an overnight bus or train journey back to Kyiv.

Plan Your Trip

Visiting Chornobyl

The world's most unlikely tourist attraction, one of dark tourism's most sinister days out, a moving journey back to the days of the Soviet Union and the most thought-provoking nine hours you'll spend in Ukraine – few fail to be stirred, scared and/or angered by a tour to Chornobyl, apocalyptic site of the world's worst nuclear accident.

Need to Know

Where?

Chornobyl is located 110km north of Kyiv city centre as the crow flies, around two hours' drive.

How?

You can only realistically visit Chornobyl as part of guided tour from Kyiv. You must book around 10 days prior to give the authorities time to run security checks.

When?

You can visit any time of year; however, as most of the tour takes place out of doors, warmer months are better.

How Long?

Tour groups leave Kyiv early morning, returning in the early evening.

Who?

To join a tour you must be over 18 years of age (no children are allowed into the exclusion zones).

How Much?

Expect to pay US$150 to $500 per person, depending on the number of people in your party and which tour company you choose.

The Accident

In perhaps the blackest of ironies in history, the world's worst nuclear catastrophe was the result of an unnecessary safety test. On the night of 25 April 1986, reactor No 4 at the Chornobyl power plant was due to be shut down for regular maintenance. Workers decided to use the opportunity to see if, in the event of a shutdown, enough electricity remained in the grid to power the reactor core cooling systems, and turned off the emergency cooling mechanism. For various reasons, including a design flaw, operational errors and flouted safety procedures, the result was a power surge, a steam explosion and a full-blown nuclear explosion. At 1.26am on 26 April 1986, the reactor blew its 500-tonne top and spewed tonnes of radioactive material mainly over Belarus, and Ukraine. Some material also wafted over Sweden, whose scientists were the first to alert the world.

The ensuing evacuation and clean-up cost billions of dollars and was a contributing factor in the collapse of the Soviet Union.

The Tour

The day begins at a meeting point in central Kyiv (Maydan Nezalezhnosti, main train station). Passports are checked, remaining payments are made and Geiger counters hired. Then it's into the minibus for the two-hour drive to the exclusion zone, during which you'll probably be shown a documentary film about the disaster.

Having arrived at the Dytyatky checkpoint (30km from the reactor) papers and passports are rechecked and the official guide joins the group. After the 10km checkpoint (more checks) itineraries vary from agency to agency, but all trips include a photo op near reactor No 4, a stroll around the eerie ghost town of Pripyat with its spooky fairground, abandoned school, swimming pool and hotel, and lunch in Chornobyl town (all the ingredients are brought from Kyiv).

The official state-employed guides really know their stuff, and where to find hotspots caused by buried bits of radioactive something. These send the Geiger counter readout crazy (and tour participants into slightly nervous oohs and aahs).

Different people react in different ways to the tour. Whether it be the sight of reactor No 4, or the plight of the 'liquidators', the nonchalance of the Soviet authorities or the tragedy of the model Soviet town of Pripyat that leaves the biggest impression, you're likely to be in a pensive mood by the time you reach the two checkpoints again. Here simple radiation checks are carried out before the journey back to Kyiv.

Is it Dangerous?

The simple answer is – no. Well, not unless you go wandering off into undergrowth for too long, bring back a few Soviet-era souvenirs from Pripyat, or feast on forest berries and mushrooms (all activities strictly forbidden, by the way). By all accounts you are exposed to twice the amount of radiation on a trans-Atlantic flight than you are during an entire day at Chornobyl and, somewhat ironically, radiation levels are actually higher on maydan Nezalezhnosti, from where some tours depart, than in most of the exclusion zone! If you're worried about radiation, hire a Geiger counter from your tour agency.

Tour Agencies

Agencies should provide transfers to the exclusion zone, transport around it, an English-speaking guide, and the necessary permits and insurance as a minimum. Some charge extra for lunch and most will rent you a Geiger counter for around US$10 a day. Agencies include:

Soloeast (Map p38; ☎279 3505; www.tourkiev.com; vul Prorizna 10, office 105; ⏰9am-6pm Mon-Fri; Ⓜ Khreshchatyk) Online booking and credit card payment.

Tour2Chernobyl (Map p38; ☎096 785 4363; www.tour2chernobyl.com; vul Khreshchatyk 19A, Kyiv; ⏰9am-6pm; Ⓜ Khreshchatyk) Popular agency with online booking facility.

SAM (Map p38; ☎238 6957; www.sam.ua; vul Ivana Franka 40B; ⏰9am-7pm Mon-Fri, 10am-4pm Sat; Ⓜ Universytet) Long-established agency.

New Logic (Map p38; ☎206 2200; www.newlogic.ua; vul Mikhaylivska 6A; Ⓜ Teatralna) Well run, though the website is slightly out of date.

Chernobylwel.come (☎00421-902 654 876; www.chernobylwel.com; Halkova 1, Bratislava, Slovakia) Probably the only agency to run two-day tours with an overnight stay in Chornobyl town.

CHORNOBYL DOS & DON'TS

- Do remember your passport – you won't be allowed on the bus without it.
- Don't wear shorts, short-sleeved T-shirts or sandals.
- Do take bottled water and a snack as lunch is sometimes served very late in the day.
- Do bring mosquito repellent between April and October.
- Don't take photos of anything you're told not to by the guides, especially around checkpoints.
- Don't pocket 'souvenirs' from the buildings in Pripyat – much of the junk strewn around the place is radioactive.
- Don't eat berries, mushrooms or anything else you may find growing in the forests around Chornobyl, and never drink any water except in the lunch canteen.

Regions at a Glance

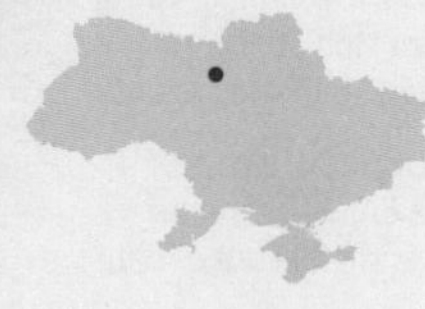

Kyiv

History
Architecture
Walks

Kyivan Rus

One of those places 'where it all started', Kyiv is the cradle of all things Russian, Ukrainian and Belarusian. While visiting St Sophia's Cathedral or the Kyevo-Pecherska Lavra, you'll be stepping on stones that remember the arrival of the Viking princes and Greek bishops who shaped East Slavic civilisation.

Eclectic Cityscape

Early medieval monasteries, Polish-influenced baroque, Russian Art Nouveau, Stalinist bombast, drab Soviet constructivism and post-Soviet kitsch – Kyiv's architecture is a charmingly incongruous cocktail of epochs and styles.

Riverside Promenades

You might feel as if you are flying above the mind-bogglingly wide Dnipro when you observe it from the hilly right bank. Here, a chain of parks forms a long green belt separating Kyiv's centre from the river.

p32

Central Ukraine

Jewish Heritage
Architecture
Museums

Jewish Sites

The Nazis and post-Soviet emigration emptied Central Ukraine's cities of Jews, but many a crooked, Hebrew-inscribed gravestone and cracked synagogue remain. The region is also the birthplace of Hasidism, its founders' tombs attracting a stream of pilgrims every year.

Architectural Landscape

Central Ukraine boasts one of the country's most spectacular castles at Kamyanets-Podilsky, but there are many other fortresses and mansions. Zhytomyr flaunts a stern Soviet style while Uman wows with its romantically landscaped Sofiyivka Park.

Quirky Museums

What do an embalmed doctor, a real nuclear missile launch site and assorted junk from the space race have in common? Well, Central Ukraine has museums dedicated to them all – surely the most fascinating collection in the country.

p70

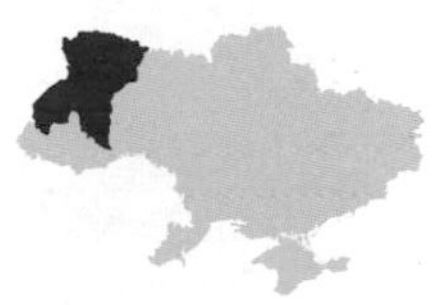

Lviv & Western Ukraine

Architecture
Coffee
Castles

Architectural Style

From the handsome austerity of Gothic churches to box-ugly Soviet apartment blocks, Lviv is a textbook of European architectural styles from the last seven centuries. Echoes of the past can be found in towns and villages across the region.

Cafe Culture

Lviv has a distinct Central European coffeehouse tradition that sets it firmly apart from the rest of Ukraine. One of the city's delights is visiting its many intimate, bean-perfumed coffeehouses, sampling the country's best doses of Arabica.

Castles & Fortresses

No other region of Ukraine possesses such a large number of castles, fortresses, chateaux and mansions. When they ruled the roost, the Polish nobility converted many crumbling medieval castles into noble baroque residences. In a strange way their current shabby state just adds to the magic.

p93

The Carpathians

Outdoor Fun
Landscapes
Food

Boot & Bike

The mountains are becoming a mecca for more adventurous outdoorsy types with routes for both knobbly tyre and treaded boot criss-crossing the forested ranges. Cycling and hiking trails have been marked out in places, but on the whole the going is delightfully rough and uncharted.

Moving Mountainscapes

Only Crimea can rival the Carpathians for mountain vistas and peak-top views. Carpeted in thick forest, the Carpathians are generally more soothing than dramatic, but some of the views out across the valleys are spectacular.

Carpathian Menu

The mountain-dwelling Hutsuls have a traditional diet dominated by the ingredients they fish, pluck and forage from the Carpathians' bountiful rivers and forests. But star of the food show in these parts is the delicious local cheese, made in special huts high up in the mountains.

p122

Odesa & Southern Ukraine

Nightlife
Beaches
Wildlife

Seaside Clubbing

Odesa's nightlife comes a close second to the capital's, with bars, clubs and music venues to suit every taste and hairstyle. The blingy beachside megaclubs attract the glitterati for nights of see-and-be-seen clubbing, but the city centre hides more low-key spots for an alternative crowd.

Black Sea Fun

The Black Sea's sand-fringed shores attract once-a-year holidaymakers from across the former USSR, who tan until crisp before wallowing in the tepid waters. Not the cleanest beaches in the world, but the further out of the city you go, the better they get.

Ukrainian Safari

Southern Ukraine is a magnet for wildlife spotters with two unique areas teeming with winged and hooved critters. Go on safari around the Askaniya Nova Reserve, where zebra, camels and Przewalski horses roam free, or venture into the Danube Delta.

p145

Crimea

Mountains
Palaces
Battlefields

Stunning Landscapes

A chain of plateaus with near-vertical slopes looms above the Black Sea, which is almost always a stunning shade of sapphire. Looking like cream topping on a cake, their limestone hats hide ancient cave cities and bizarrely eroded forms. Spring transforms them into flower-filled Oriental tapestries.

Royal Retreats

Russian aristocrats squandered fortunes here on the whimsical creations of fin de siècle architects. These monuments of imperial decadence dot the Crimean coast, surrounded by lush parks and memories of the last Romanovs.

Crimean War

The Crimean War was fought on some of the world's most picturesque battlefields. After checking out a landscape that remembers Florence Nightingale and the Charge of the Light Brigade, plunge into a turquoise sea or discover that Balaklava is more about seafood than dodgy head gear.

p163

Eastern Ukraine

Cossacks
Quirky Donbass
Village Life

Cossack Stronghold

Wondering about the Cossacks? Spend a day on the island of Khortytsya in Zaporizhzhya, the site of their main stronghold known as the Sich. History aside, the place is beautiful with its rocky cliffs and rapids, and Dniproges Dam looming in the distance.

Caves & Mines

There are some gems lurking behind those heaps of mining slag – a particularly cute Orthodox cave monastery and a mindboggling salt mine. Besides, the escapist culture of Britain-obsessed Donetsk has produced some great places to eat and have fun.

Northern Countryside

It's Ukrainian to the core, complete with sunflowers, pumpkins and villagers that seem to have walked out of Nikolai Gogol's books. Tourist infrastructure is embryonic here, so be the first to discover it!

p201

On the Road

Lviv & Western Ukraine
p93
Kyiv
p32
Central Ukraine
p70
The Carpathians
p122
Eastern Ukraine
p201
Odesa & Southern Ukraine
p145
Crimea
p163

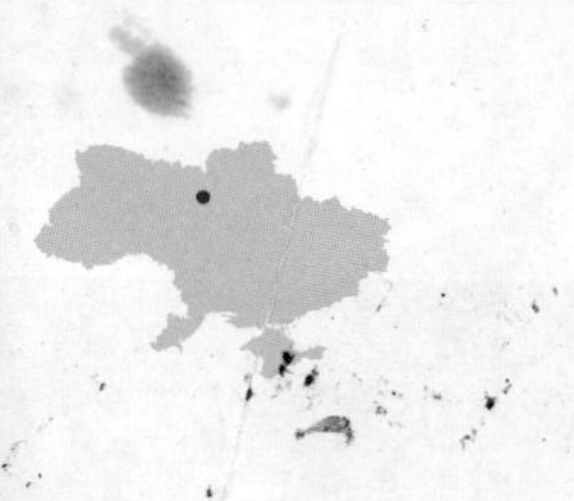

Kyiv Київ

☎044 / POP 2.9 MILLION

Includes ➡

Best Places to Eat

- Under Wonder (p57)
- Arbequina (p56)
- Harbuzyk (p58)
- Kanapa (p58)
- Kyivska Perepichka (p56)

Best Places to Stay

- Rented Apartment (p55)
- 11 Mirrors (p54)
- Sunflower B&B Hotel (p53)
- Hyatt Regency Kyiv (p54)
- Central Station Hostel (p54)

Why Go?

In the beginning there was Kyiv. Long before Ukraine and Russia came into being, its inhabitants had already been striding up and down the green hills, idling hot afternoons away on the Dnipro River and promenading along Kreshchatyk – then a stream, now the main avenue. From here, East Slavic civilisation spread all the way to Alaska.

But thanks to its many reincarnations, there are few signs of ageing on Kyiv's face. Wearing its latest national capital's hat, it reveals itself as a young and humorous gentleman, elegant on the eating/drinking front, but prone to kitsch when it comes to urban development.

It has a fair few must-sees, mostly related to the glorious Kyivan Rus past, as well as both charming and disturbingly eclectic architecture. But its main asset is the residents – a merry, tongue-in-cheek and perfectly bilingual lot, whose distinct urban identity outweighs their ethnic allegiance.

When to Go

Kyiv

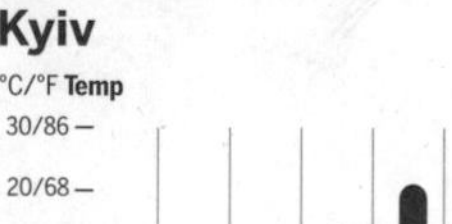

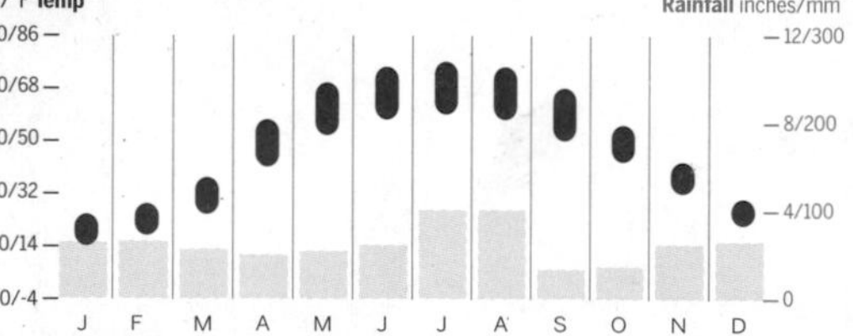

Jan Party on New Year's night, then repent at an Orthodox Christmas service a week later.

May Frolic in Kyiv's two botanical gardens, where just about every tree is blossoming.

Jul Witness ancient rites and enjoy great music during the Ivan Kupala festival.

History

Legend has it that three Slavic brothers and their sister founded Kyiv. The eldest, Kyi, gave the city its name. The names of brothers Shchek, Khoriv and sister Lybid now appear in its topography. An iconic statue of the four siblings – the Foundation of Kyiv Monument (Пам'ятник засновникам Київу) – stands on the banks of the Dnipro River.

Four hundred years later the city really started to prosper, after Vikings from Novgorod took control. Circa 864 two Novgorod warlords Askold and Dir settled in Kyiv after a failed raid on Constantinople. Novgorod's new prince Oleh journeyed to Kyiv in 882, dispatched the two Vikings and declared himself ruler. This was the beginning of Kyivan Rus ('Rus' being the Slavic name for the red-haired Scandinavians). The city thrived on river trade, sending furs, honey and slaves to pay for luxury goods from Constantinople. Within 100 years its empire stretched from the Volga to the Danube and to Novgorod.

In 989 Kyivan prince Volodymyr decided to forge a closer alliance with Constantinople, marrying the emperor's daughter and adopting Orthodox Christianity. Kyiv's pagan idols were destroyed and its people driven into the Dnipro for a mass baptism.

Under Volodymyr's son, Yaroslav the Wise (1017–54), Kyiv became a cultural and political centre in the Byzantine mold. St Sophia's Cathedral was built to proclaim the glory of both God and city. However, by the 12th century, Kyiv's economic prowess had begun to wane, with power shifting to northeast principalities (near today's Moscow).

In 1240 Mongol raiders sacked Kyiv. Citizens fled or took refuge wherever they could, including the roof of the Desyatynna Church, which collapsed under the weight.

The city shrank to the riverside district of Podil, which remained its centre for centuries. Only when Ukraine formally passed into Russian hands at the end of the 18th century did Kyiv again grow in importance. The city went through an enormous boom at the turn of the 20th century when it was essentially the third imperial capital after St Petersburg and Moscow. Many new mansions were erected at this time, including the remarkable House of Chimeras.

During the chaos following the Bolshevik Revolution, Kyiv was the site of frequent battles between Red and White Russian forces, Ukrainian nationalists, and German and Polish armies. Author Mikhail Bulgakov captured the era's uncertainty in his first novel, *The White Guard*. The home in which he wrote this book is now a museum.

In August 1941 German troops captured Kyiv and more than half a million Soviet soldiers were caught or killed. The entire city suffered terribly. Germans massacred about 100,000 at Babyn Yar and 80% of the city's inhabitants were homeless by the time the Red Army retook Kyiv on 6 November 1943.

The postwar years saw rapid industrialisation and the construction of unsightly suburbs. During the late 1980s nationalistic and democratic movements from western Ukraine began to catch on in the capital. Throughout the presidency of Leonid Kuchma, Kyiv and its young population increasingly became a base of opposition politics. During the Orange Revolution of 2004, activists from around Ukraine poured into the capital to demonstrate on maydan Nezalezhnosti (Independence Sq) and outside the parliament building. In the 2010 presidential elections, two-thirds of voters in Kyiv supported Orange Revolution leader Yulia Tymoshenko, although she still lost to Viktor Yanukovych.

Sights

Some of Kyiv's main attractions are half-day adventures and not always terribly central. So, rather than plunging right in, it's highly recommended you warm up with an initial stroll.

City Centre

★**Maydan Nezalezhnosti** SQUARE
(майдан Незалежності; Independence Sq; Map p38; Ⓜ Maydan Nezalezhnosti) Be it celebration or revolution, whenever Ukrainians want a get-together – and they very often do – Independence Sq is the nation's meeting point. This is a new phenomena and so is the name of this huge fountain-filled space flanked by Stalin-era buildings and presided over by a kitschy post-Soviet statue of a winged female atop the **Independence Column**.

Nothing of note happened here until pro-independence students set up a tent camp in the early 1990s, when it was still called October Revolution Sq. After the USSR collapsed, the urge for change was so strong that even the perfectly normal Ukrainian word *ploshcha* – square – sounded too Russian. That's when the word *maydan*, related

Kyiv Highlights

❶ Stroll up and down **Khreshchatyk** (p36) munching on a hotdog from **Kyivska Perepichka** (p56).

❷ Admire the beauty of Orthodox ritual and meet the mummies at **Kyevo-Pecherska Lavra** (p43).

❸ Get as close to the earth's core as you can while riding a train in Kyiv's **metro** (p66), the world's deepest.

❹ Share a few beers and *horilka* (vodka) shots with local bohemians in a smoke-filled dive, such as **Palata No.6** (p60).

❺ Step on the rugged cobblestones of **Andriyivsky uzviz** (p42), inhale its Parisian air and sample some quality

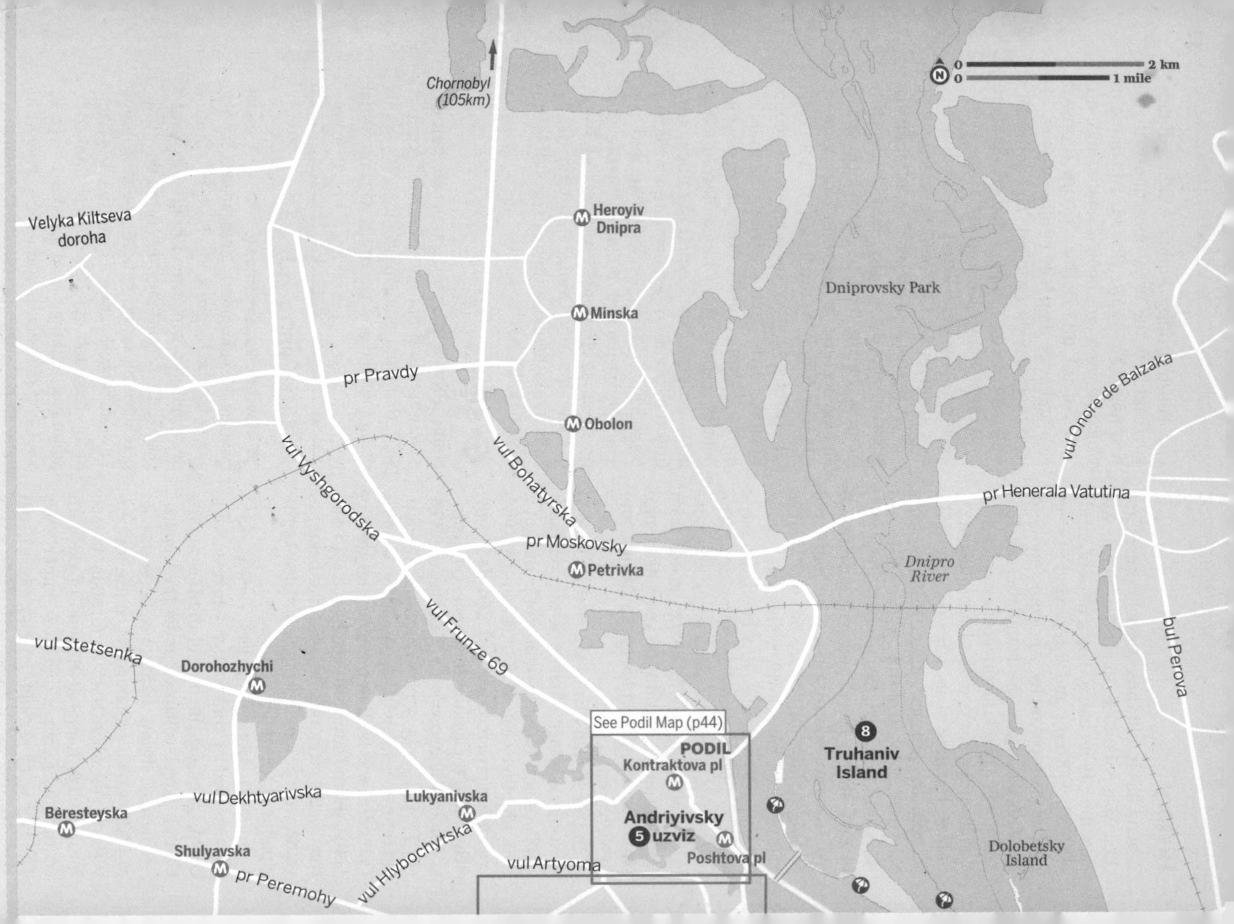

French food in one of its cafes.

6 Explore all of Ukraine in one day at the open-air **Pyrohovo Museum of Folk Architecture** (p48).

7 Visit the fantastic motley collection of wooden houses in **Pereyaslav-Khmelnytsky** (p68).

8 Plunge into the Dnipro River or go cycling at **Truhaniv Island** (p52).

9 Meet new friends and embark on a pub crawl from one of Kyiv's lovely **hostels** (p53).

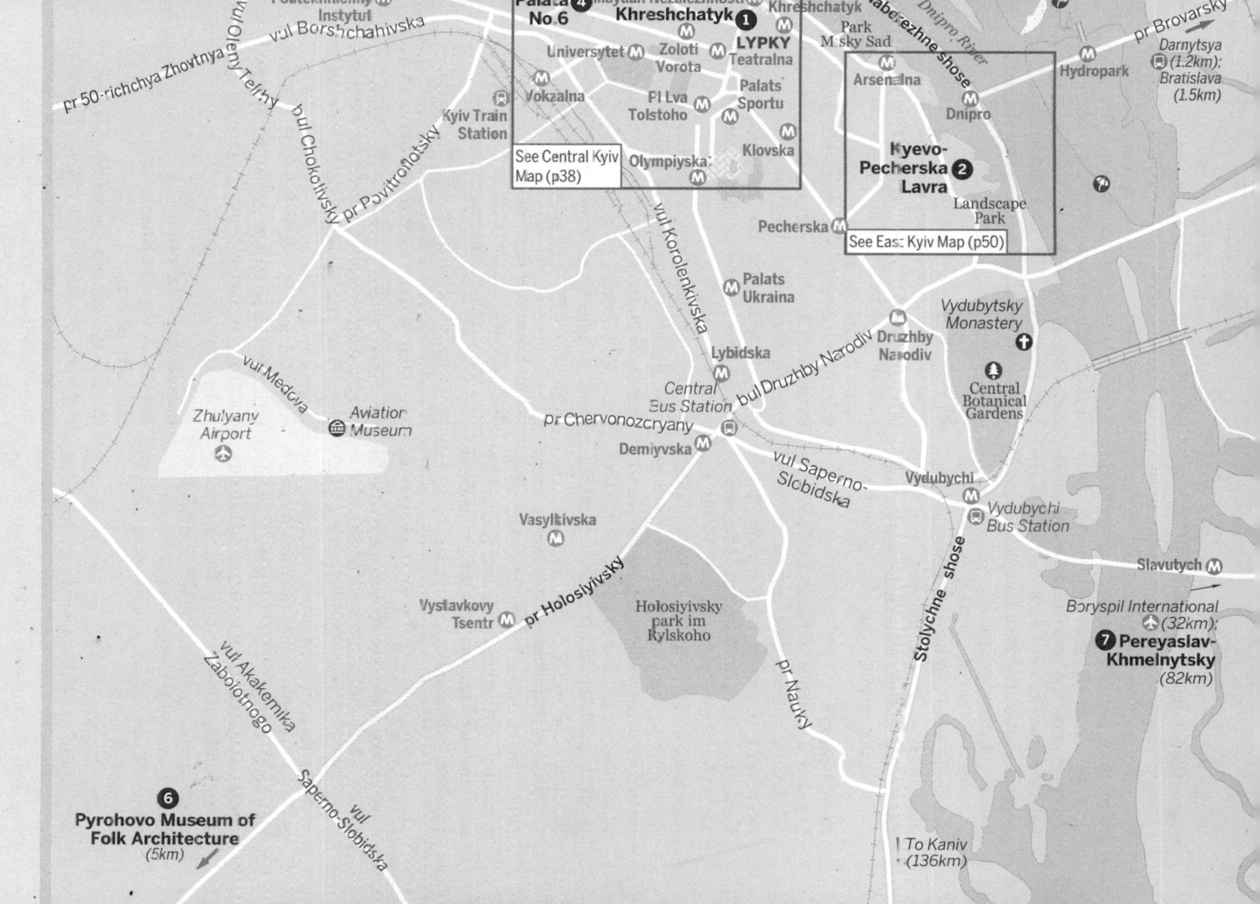

to the Arabic *medina,* was salvaged from the nation's linguistic attic and put into use.

Since then it's been a mindboggling succession of festivals and protests. The Orange Revolution put Maydan into the spotlight in 2004 – check out **graffiti** preserved from that period on the Post Office Column. Global TV networks were back for the Eurovision song contest and the Euro 2012 football (soccer) championships.

Come to Maydan during the weekend. Get some snacks in the underground shopping mall, sit by the fountain and watch Ukrainians in their own element. Will they start singing or mutinying? You never know.

Khreshchatyk STREET

(Хрещатик; Map p38; Ⓜ Khreshchatyk) Always filled with promenading crowds, the city's main drag is named after a river, which these days runs underneath, enclosed in an underground pipe. During WWII the retreating Soviet army mined the buildings here, turning them into deadly booby traps for any German soldiers setting foot inside. Most places exploded or caught fire, which is why it had to be rebuilt in the current Stalinesque style.

Khreshchatyk is at its best during weekends, when it's closed to traffic and becomes a giant pedestrian zone. Getting gussied up and strolling Khreshchatyk is Kyivans' No 1 pastime.

House of Chimeras NOTABLE BUILDING

(Map p38; vul Bankova 10; Ⓜ Khreshchatyk) Hard to say which other national president has a bunch of otherworldish creatures peering into his window, but the Ukrainian one does for his office is face-to-face with Kyiv's weirdest edifice. The 'chimeras', which cover every patch of architect Wladislaw Horodecki's creation, are in fact depictions of his exotic hunting trophies – elephants, rhinos, crocodiles, lions and whatever you name. He kept many prototypes inside – in the stuffed form.

The Art Nouveau house, which he built for himself in 1903, is placed on a high cliff so it appears as a six-storey structure on one side and three-storey on the other. The 'chimeras' are here not only to decorate, but also to advertise the revolutionary building material – concrete, of which Horodecki was a huge fan. Many locals say that the house is best admired at night, when spooky creatures seem ready to come alive and jump down from the roof.

Getting inside is tough, the Ukrainian presidency being the main obstacle, since the house is used as a reception office for fellow leaders. Tours are conducted once a week, at best. Companies that offer them include **Prime Tour** (☎ 207 1244; http://primetour.ua/en; vul Shchekavytska 30/39) and Interesny Kiev (p64). If you do enter, about the first thing you'll see is a fireplace shaped as an octopus.

St Volodymyr's Cathedral CHURCH

(Map p38; bul Tarasa Shevchenka 20; Ⓜ Universytet) Although not one of Kyiv's most important churches, St Volodymyr's Cathedral arguably has the prettiest interior. Built in the late 19th century to mark 900 years of Orthodox Christianity in the city, its yellow exterior and seven blue domes conform to standard Byzantine style. However, inside it breaks new ground by displaying Art Nouveau influences.

Huge murals, flecked with golden accents, include a painting of Volodymyr the Great's baptism into Orthodox Christianity in Chersoneses (now Khersones) and of Kyiv's citizens being herded into the Dnipro River for a mass baptism soon afterwards.

Fomin Botanical Gardens GARDENS

(Map p38; Ⓜ Universytet) FREE Lying behind the Universytet metro station building, the landscaped gardens are best visited in spring when just about everything there is blooming. A short walk to the left from the entrance, you'll find a leaning apron-clad bronze figure wielding something that looks like a bow. This strange-looking monument is dedicated to the professors and students who died defending Kyiv in WWII. Students cynically call it 'monument to the deceased botanist' – 'botanist' being the Russian slang word for nerd.

Museums & Galleries

Bohdan & Varvara Khanenko Museum of Arts MUSEUM

(Музей художнього мистецтва Богдана та Варвари Ханенко; Map p38; www.khanenkomuseum.kiev.ua; vul Tereshchenkivska 15/17; adult/student 30/15uah, last Wed of month free, tour in English per group 250uah; ⏲ 10.30am-5.30pm Wed-Sun, to 2pm last Wed of month; Ⓜ Pl Lva Tolstoho) Kyiv's most impressive collection of European art boasts Bosch, Velázquez and Rubens among the many masters represented, but they are only part of the attraction. The house, with its frescoed ceilings and intricately carved woodwork, alone is

KYIV IN...

Two Days

Stroll down the main boulevard, vul Khreshchatyk, from **Bessarabsky Rynok** (p59) market to **maydan Nezalezhnosti** (p33). Head up to **Zoloti Vorota** (p41) for a drink on the terrace before moving on to **St Sophia's Cathedral** (p37) and **St Michael's Monastery** (p40). Catch the funicular down to **Podil**, visit the **Chornobyl Museum** (p43) and then walk up **Andriyivsky uzviz**. Dine at **Kanapa** (p58).

Arrive early on the second day at the Kyevo-Pecherska Lavra, before visiting **Rodina Mat** (p47) and the **Museum of the Great Patriotic War** (p48). Return to the city centre on Kyiv's astonishingly deep **metro**. Wander around **Shevchenko Park** and sample *blyny* (pancakes) from the **O'Panas Blyny Stand** (p58). Check out the **Bohdan & Varvara Khanenko Museum of Arts**, then rest up before hitting a few bars and clubs.

Four Days

Follow the two-day itinerary and on the third day visit the **Pyrohovo Museum of Folk Architecture** (p48). Visit **Babyn Yar** (p50) and a few more museums. In summer head to the beach at **Truhaniv Island** (p52).

worth the price of admission. All the better that it's packed with priceless antique furniture, ancient Greek sculptures, porcelain ceramics and dazzling paintings, such as a version of Hieronymus Bosch's *Temptation of St Anthony*. The museum's climax is on the top floor: four rare religious icons from the 6th and 7th centuries. Even if icons aren't your thing, it's hard not to be moved by these primitive Byzantine treasures. And we've only described the 'Western' wing. The 'Eastern' wing has Buddhist, Chinese and Islamic art.

★ PinchukArtCentre GALLERY

(Map p38; www.pinchukartcentre.org; Arena Entertainment Complex, vul Baseyna 2A; ⌚ noon-9pm Tue-Sun; Ⓜ Pl Lva Tolstoho or Teatralna) FREE The rotating exhibits at this world-class gallery feature elite names in the world of European contemporary art and design, all financed by billionaire mogul Viktor Pinchuk. Works by world giants like Antony Gormley, Damian Hirst and Ai Weiwei have exhibited here. Don't miss the view of Kyiv's roofs from the excellent coffeeshop on the top floor. The oligarch-style security at the door and inside the gallery can be a little off-putting, but you may regard them as modern art objects.

Russian Art Museum MUSEUM

(Музей російського мистецтва; Map p38; www.kmrm.com.ua; vul Tereshchenkivska 9; adult/student 30/10uah, tour in English per group 250uah; ⌚ 11am-7pm Tue & Fri, 10am-6pm Wed, Sat & Sun; Ⓜ Teatralna or Pl Lva Tolstoho) With 2000 paintings, it is the largest collection of Russian artwork outside Moscow and St Petersburg.

Taras Shevchenko Memorial House Museum MUSEUM

(Літературно-Меморіальний Будинок-музей Тараса Шевченка; Map p38; prov Tarasa Shevchenka 8A; admission 7uah; ⌚ 10am-6pm Wed-Sun, noon-8pm Tue; Ⓜ Maydan Nezalezhnosti) A beautifully restored, 19th-century wooden house where the man who dominates the Ukrainian literary pantheon once lived. You can see drawings he made on ethnological expeditions of Ukraine, which inspired his nationalism.

Water Museum MUSEUM

(Музей води; Map p38; vul Grushevskoho 1V; tour adult/child 30/25uah; ⌚ 10am-5pm; Ⓜ Maydan Nezalezhnosti) Inside a historic water pump, this Danish-funded museum is a fun place, especially for children. On the obligatory tour, you're taken on a walk through a rainwater collector, allowed to sit on a giant toilet or stand inside a bubble, and introduced to a yellow fish called Vasily.

Old Town

★ St Sophia's Cathedral CHURCH

(Map p38; pl Sofiyska; admission grounds/cathedral/bell tower 3/53/13uah; ⌚ grounds 9am-7pm, cathedral 10am-6pm Thu-Tue, 10am-5pm Wed; Ⓜ Maydan Nezalezhnosti) The interior is the most astounding aspect of Kyiv's oldest standing church, St Sophia's Cathedral. Many of the mosaics and frescoes are original, dating back to 1017–31, when the cathedral was built to celebrate Prince Yaroslav's victory in protecting Kyiv from the Pechenegs (Tribal Raiders). While equally

Central Kyiv

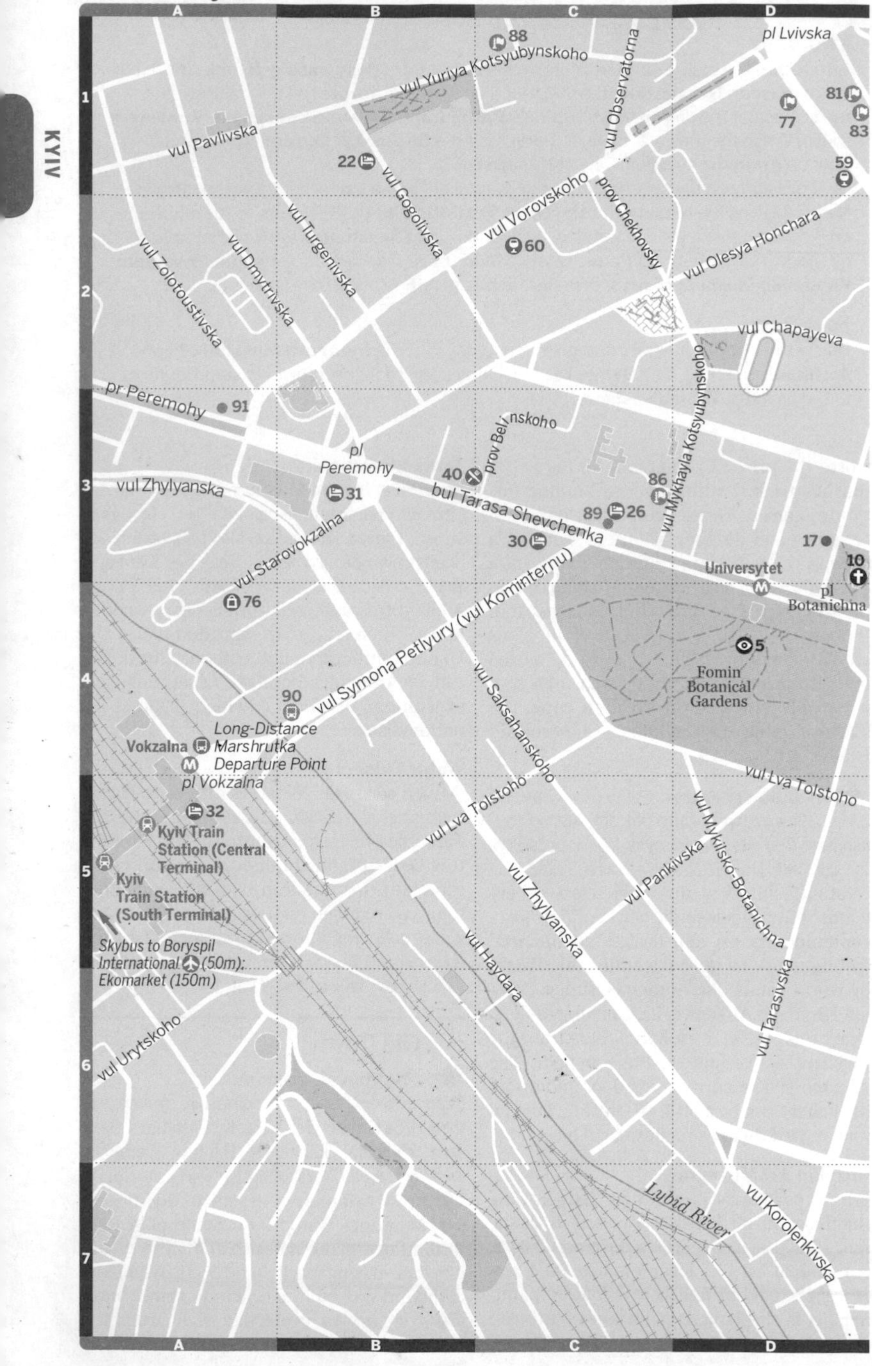

A B C D

1 2 3 4 5 6 7

vul Yuriya Kotsyubynskoho
88
pl Lvivska
vul Observatorna
81
77
83
59
vul Pavlivska
22
vul Gogolivska
vul Vorovskoho
prov Chekhovsky
vul Turgenivska
vul Dmytrivska
vul Zolotoustivska
60
vul Olesya Honchara
vul Chapayeva
vul Mykhayla Kotsyubynskoho
pr Peremohy
91
prov Bel…nskoho
pl Peremohy
40
86
vul Zhylyanska
31
bul Tarasa Shevchenka
89
26
30
17
10
vul Starovokzalna
Universytet
pl Botanichna
76
vul Symona Petlyury (vul Kominternu)
5
Fomin Botanical Gardens
vul Saksahanskoho
90
Long-Distance Marshrutka Departure Point
Vokzalna
pl Vokzalna
vul Lva Tolstoho
32
Kyiv Train Station (Central Terminal)
Kyiv Train Station (South Terminal)
vul Mykilsko-Botanichna
vul Pankivska
vul Zhylyanska
Skybus to Boryspil International (50m); Ekomarket (150m)
vul Haydara
vul Tarasivska
vul Urytskoho
Lybid River
vul Korolenkivska

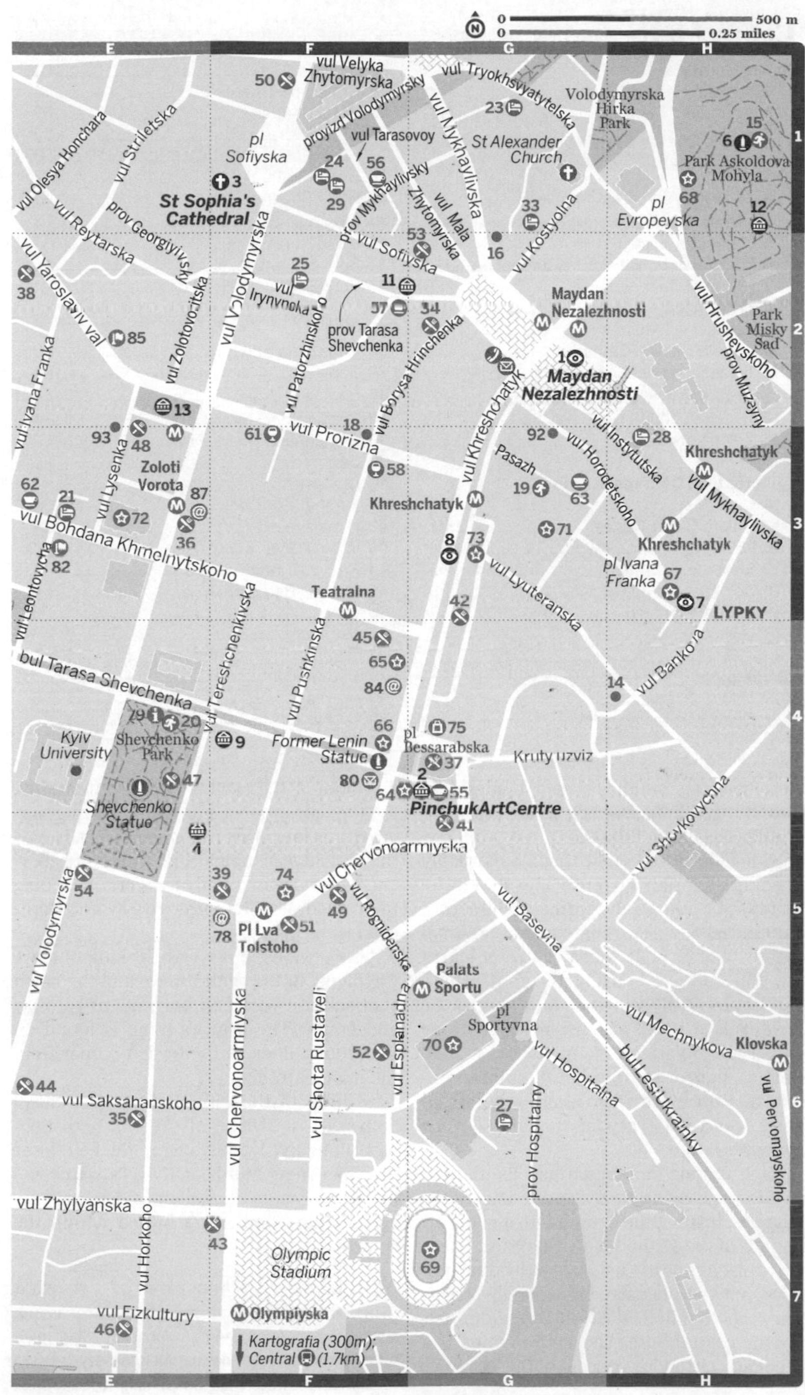
0 500 m
0 0.25 miles
E
F
G
H
1
2
3
4
5
6
7
vul Velyka Zhytomyrska
vul Tryokhsvyatytelska
Volodymyrska Hirka Park
proyizd Volodymyrsky
vul Tarasovoy
pl Sofiyska
St Sophia's Cathedral
St Alexander Church
Park Askoldova Mohyla
pl Evropeyska
vul Striletska
vul Olesya Honchara
vul Reytarska
prov Georgiyivsky
vul Yaroslaviv val
vul Volodymyrska
vul Zolotovoritska
vul Patorzhinskoho
vul Irynynska
prov Mykhaylivsky
vul Mykhaylivska
vul Mala Zhytomyrska
vul Sofiyska
vul Kostyolna
prov Tarasa Shevchenka
vul Borysa Hrinchenka
Maydan Nezalezhnosti
vul Hrushevskoho
prov Muzeyny
Park Misky Sad
vul Ivana Franka
vul Prorizna
vul Khreshchatyk
vul Instytutska
vul Horodetskoho
Pasazh
Zoloti Vorota
vul Lysenka
Khreshchatyk
vul Mykhaylivska
vul Bohdana Khmelnytskoho
vul Leontovycha
pl Ivana Franka
LYPKY
vul Lyuteranska
Teatralna
vul Tereshchenkivska
vul Pushkinska
vul Bankova
bul Tarasa Shevchenka
Kyiv University
Shevchenko Park
Shevchenko Statue
Former Lenin Statue
pl Bessarabska
Kruty uzviz
PinchukArtCentre
vul Shovkovychna
vul Chervonoarmiyska
vul Rognidenska
vul Basevna
Pl Lva Tolstoho
Palats Sportu
pl Sportyvna
vul Mechnykova
Klovska
bul Lesi Ukrainky
vul Hospitalna
vul Esplanadna
vul Shota Rustaveli
vul Chervonoarmiyska
prov Hospitalny
vul Pervomayskoho
vul Saksahanskoho
vul Zhylyanska
vul Horkoho
Olympic Stadium
vul Fizkultury
Olympiyska
Kartografia (300m); Central (1.7km)
KYIV

Central Kyiv

Top Sights
1 Maydan Nezalezhnosti G2
2 PinchukArtCentre G4
3 St Sophia's Cathedral F1

Sights
4 Bohdan & Varvara Khanenko Museum of Arts E5
5 Fomin Botanical Gardens D4
6 Friendship of Nations Monument H1
7 House of Chimeras H3
8 Khreshchatyk G3
9 Russian Art Museum F4
10 St Volodymyr's Cathedral D3
11 Taras Shevchenko Memorial House Museum F2
12 Water Museum H1
13 Zoloti Vorota E2

Activities, Courses & Tours
14 Chervona Ruta H4
15 Dnipro Cable Trolley H1
16 New Logic G2
17 SAM D3
18 SoloEast Travel F3
19 Tour2Chernobyl G3
20 veliki.ua E4

Sleeping
21 11 Mirrors E3
22 Central Station Hostel B1
23 Gintama Hotel G1
24 Grata Apartments F1
25 Hotel Bontiak F2
26 Hotel Express C3
27 Hotel Rus G6
28 Hotel Ukraine H3
29 Hyatt Regency Kyiv F1
30 Ibis C3
31 Lybid Hotel B3
32 Service Centre A5
33 Sunflower B&B Hotel G1

Eating
34 Arbequina G2
35 Babel E6
36 Barkas E3
37 Bessarabsky Rynok G4
38 Bulochnaya Yaroslavna E2
39 Concord F5
40 Dio Long B3
41 Furshet Gourmet G5
42 Himalaya G3
43 Imbir F7
44 Knaypa Sinoval E6
45 Kyivska Perepichka F4
Linas ..... (see 37)
46 Megamarket E7
47 O'Panas Blyny Stand E4
48 Osteria Pantagruel E3
49 Pervak F5
50 Spotykach F1

attractive, the building's gold domes and 76m-tall wedding-cake bell tower are 18th-century baroque additions.

Named after the great Hagia Sofia (Holy Wisdom) Temple (currently mosque) in Istanbul, St Sophia's Byzantine architecture announced the new religious and political authority of Kyiv. It was a centre of learning and culture, housing the first school and library in Kyivan Rus. Adjacent to the Royal Palace, it was also where coronations and other royal ceremonies were staged, treaties signed and foreign dignitaries received. Prince Yaroslav himself is buried here, or at least everyone thought so until a few years ago.

Each mosaic and fresco had its allotted position according to Byzantine decorative schemes, turning the church into a giant 3D symbol of the Orthodox world order. There are explanations in English of individual mosaics, but the one that immediately strikes you is the 6m-high **Virgin Orans** dominating the central apse. The Virgin Orans is a peculiarly Orthodox concept of the Virgin as a symbol of the earthly church interceding for the salvation of humanity. Having survived this long, this particular Orans is now thought indestructible by Orthodox believers. (Unesco was slightly less certain, adding the cathedral to its protective World Heritage List in 1990.)

Less obvious, but worth seeking out, are fragments in the central nave and the north stairwell of two group portraits of Yaroslav and family. The prince's tomb is found on the ground floor, in the far left corner from the main entrance.

In front of the cathedral complex on pl Sofiyska is a **statue** of Cossack hero Bohdan Khmelnytsky. Just before the bell tower lies the ornate **tomb** of Kyiv Patriarch Volodymyr Romanyuk. Religious disputes prevented him from being buried within the complex.

★St Michael's Monastery MONASTERY
(Михайлівський Золотоверхий Монастир; Mykhaylivsky Zolotoverkhy Monastyr; Map p44; http://www.archangel.kiev.ua; vul Tryokhsvyatytelska 6; admission free, museum 14uah; ⌚8am-8pm,

51	Under Wonder	F5
52	Varenichnaya #1	F6
53	Walter's	G2
54	Zheltok	E5

Drinking & Nightlife

	Banka	(see 54)
55	Chashka	G4
56	Experiment 12	F1
57	Kaffa	F2
58	Kupidon	F3
59	La Bodeguita del Medio	D1
60	Palata No.6	C2
61	Pub Trallebus	F3
62	Repriza	E3
63	Wolkonsky	G3

Entertainment

64	Arena Night Club	F4
65	Art Club 44	F4
66	Bibique	F4
	Divan	(see 37)
67	Ivan Franko National Academic Drama Theatre	H3
68	National Philharmonic	H1
69	Olympic Stadium	G7
70	Palats Sportu	G6
71	Pomada	G3
72	Taras Shevchenko National Opera Theatre	E3
73	Theatre Box Office	G3
74	Theatre Box Office	F5

Shopping

	Bessarabsky Rynok	(see 37)
	Experiment 12	(see 56)
75	Roshen	G4
76	Roshen	A4

Information

77	Canadian Embassy	D1
78	Chasopys	F5
79	Coffee Tram	E4
80	DHL International	F4
81	French Embassy	D1
82	German Embassy	E3
83	Hungarian Embassy	D1
	New Logic	(see 16)
84	Oscar Internet Centre	F4
85	Polish Embassy	E2
86	Romanian Embassy	C3
87	Tsiferblat	E3
88	US Embassy	C1

Transport

89	Advance Train Ticket Office	C3
90	Avtonstantsiya Kyiv	B4
91	Kiy Avia	A3
92	Kiy Avia	G3
93	Ukraine International Airlines	E3

museum 10am-7pm Tue-Sun; M Poshtova pl) Looking from St Sophia's past the Bohdan Khmelnytsky statue, it's impossible to ignore the gold-domed blue church at the other end of proyizd Volodymyrsky. This is St Michael's Gold-Domed Monastery, named after Kyiv's patron saint. As the impossibly shiny cupolas imply, this is a fresh (2001) copy of the original St Michael's (1108), which was torn down by the Soviets in 1937.

The church's fascinating history is explained in great detail (in Ukrainian and English placards) in a **museum** (Map p44; admission 9uah; ⏲10am-6pm Tue-Sun, ticket office 10am-5pm) in the monastery's bell tower. The museum also explains the sad history of the neighbouring Tryokhsvyatytelska Church, destroyed by the Soviets in 1934. They then added insult to injury by building the gargantuan **Ministry of Foreign Affairs** (Міністерство закордонних справ; Map p44; pl Mykhaylivska 1) on the site.

Heading around the left of the church to the rear, you'll find the quaint **funicular** (tickets 1.50uah; ⏲7am-10pm, weekends & holidays 8am-11pm; S Poshtova pl) that runs down a steep hillside to the river terminal in the mercantile district of Podil. Although in summer trees partially obscure your view, this is still the most fun public-transport ride in town.

Zoloti Vorota HISTORIC BUILDING

(Golden Gate; Map p38; vul Volodymyrska; admission 10uah; M Zoloti Vorota) Part of Kyiv's fortifications during the rule of Yaroslav the Wise, the famous Zoloti Vorota sounds much better than it looks, but the summer patio around the fountain out the front is a great place to have a drink. Erected in 1037 and modelled on Constantinople's Golden Gate, this was the main entrance into the ancient city, with ramparts stretching out from both sides. However, the gate was largely destroyed in the 1240 Mongol sacking of Kyiv, and what you see today is a 1982 reconstruction that encloses whatever remains of the original. The statue to the side is of Yaroslav, although people call it 'monument to the Kyiv cake' – you'll understand why when you see it.

Andriyivsky Uzviz

A man walked up the hill, erected a cross and prophesised: 'A great city will stand on this spot'. That legend is in the name of this steep cobbled street, lined with quaint, randomly shaped houses. It translates as Andrew's Descent for the man is Apostle Andrew. Despite multiple stalls selling junk souvenirs, like fake Soviet army hats and *matryoshka* (Russian dolls), the street exudes an almost Parisian, precisely, Monparnasse, air. There are diversions galore along the way, including a few wonderful cafes, restaurants, galleries, craft shops and museums.

Peyzazhna alleya STREET

(Map p44) Starting at the top of Andriyivsky uzviz by the National Museum of Ukrainian History, the alley skirts around a large ravine offering great views of the city. It's always full of people and there is a cluster of modern urban art in its middle section. On warm nights, young Kyivites perch on a stone barrier here to chat over a latte or beer – bottles always wrapped in paper because of the not-so-vigorously enforced ban on drinking alcohol in the street. Many people descend the wooded slope to enjoy stronger booze and more intimate communication.

St Andrew's Church CHURCH

(Map p44; Andriyivsky uzviz; ⌚10am-8pm; Ⓜ Kontraktova pl) Naturally, the stunning gold and blue sight shining at the top of Andriyivsky uzviz is called after Apostle Andrew. Built in 1754 by Italian architect Bartolomeo Rastrelli, who also designed the Winter Palace in St Petersburg, this is a magnificent interpretation of the traditional Ukrainian five-domed, cross-shaped church.

National Museum of Ukrainian History MUSEUM

(Національний музей історії України; Map p44; ☎044 278 2924; vul Volodymyrska 2; admission 18uah; ⌚10am-5pm Thu-Tue; Ⓜ Kontraktova pl) Located more or less at the spot where history began for Kyiv, Ukraine and Russia, this museum has exhibits of archaeological and recent historical interest, including books and currencies.

Bulgakov Museum MUSEUM

(Музей Булгакова; Map p44; ☎425 3188; www.bulgakov.org.ua; Andriyivsky uzviz 13; adult/student & child 30/15uah; ⌚10am-5pm Thu-Tue; Ⓜ Kontraktova pl) The much-loved author of *The Master and Margarita* lived here long before writing his most famous book – between 1906 and 1919. But this building was the model for the Turbin family home in *The White Guard*, his first full-length novel and the best book to read about Kyiv. Substituting for the interiors lost in the Soviet period, designers created a strange and memorable space populated with the author's memories and characters. There are more tourists in Andriyvsky uzviz than the museum can cope, so booking is essential.

Museum of One Street MUSEUM

(Музей однієї вулиці; Map p44; Andriyivsky uzviz 2B; admission 30uah; ⌚noon-6pm Tue-Sun) This museum lays out individual histories of Andriyvsky uzviz buildings. The sheer jumble-sale eclecticism of the collection – showcasing the lives of dressmakers, soldiers, a rabbi, a Syrian-born Orientalist and more – exudes bags of charm.

Podil

The funicular and Andriyivsky uzviz both lead down to this riverside mercantile quarter. An appealing grid of streets lined with quaint lanterns and eclectic turn-of-the-20th-century buildings, it's the antidote to all those Soviet facades that dominate vul Khreshchatyk. Dating back to the earliest settlements, the area grew quickly around the port. Podil was last rebuilt in 1811 after a devastating fire and emerged largely unscathed from WWII. Today it's a buzzing restaurant district.

St Nicholas Naberezhny CHURCH

(Церква Миколи Набережного; Map p44; vul Grygogoria Skovorody 12; Ⓜ Kontraktova pl) Church lovers will find several attractive and historic specimens in Podil, including this church near the river, which is dedicated to sailors and others journeying along the river to do business. Consider coming here if you are taking a cruise of the Dnipro.

Florivsky Monastery CONVENT

(Флорівський жіночий монастир; Map p44; vul Prytytsko Mykilska; Ⓜ Kontraktova pl) This is a 15th-century convent that remained open during the communist era. Pass through the bell tower to the grounds, which contain several attractive churches; there are great views from here of St Andrew's Church. Dress appropriately to enter the grounds.

Pharmacy Museum MUSEUM

(Музей-аптека; Map p44; vul Prytitsko Mykilska 7; adult/student 15/10uah; 9am-5pm; M Kontraktova pl) This excellent museum is set in the premises of an early-19th-century German pharmacy. There are separate rooms dedicated to alchemy and witchcraft.

Church of Mykola Prytysk CHURCH

(Церква Миколи Притиска; Map p44; vul Khoriva 5A; M Kontraktova pl) The Church of Mykola Prytysk survived the 1811 fire that destroyed much of Podil. This 1631 church is the oldest structure in the district and is surrounded by several pastel-coloured brick buildings exhibiting the eclectic style in vogue in Kyiv at the end of the 19th century.

Chornobyl Museum MUSEUM

(Map p44; www.chornobylmuseum.kiev.ua; prov Khoryva 1; admission 10uah, English-language audio guide 50uah; 10am-6pm Mon-Sat; M Kontraktova pl) It's hard to convey the full horror of the world's worst nuclear accident, but the Chornobyl Museum makes a valiant attempt. It is not so much a museum as a shrine to all the firemen, soldiers, engineers, peasants and whole villages that perished in the aftermath of the explosion of Chornobyl power plant reactor No 4, on 26 April 1986. The location in a former fire-squad garage evokes strong associations with 9/11. Chornobyl is indeed Ukraine's Ground Zero.

The exhibits are predominantly in Russian and Ukrainian, but there is plenty here of interest for English speakers, including several videos, distressing photos of the sorts of deformities – in animals and humans – the accident caused, and a few jarred specimens of mutant animals such as an eight-legged baby pig. Front pages of the *New York Times* and *Philadelphia Inquirer* from the days immediately following the accident are on display, and the largest hall contains poignant anti-nuclear posters sent in by artists from around the world on the 20th anniversary of the accident.

The signs above the stairs as you enter represent the 'ghost' cities evacuated from the Chornobyl area in the wake of the disaster. If you wish to see for yourself, it's possible to take a tour to the Chornobyl exclusion zone (p26).

English-language audio guides are available, but they are in short supply.

Lavra Area & Around

Any day and in any weather Arsenalna metro station discharges a steady flow of tourists and pilgrims moving along vul Ivana Mazepy (Sichnevoho Povstannya) towards pl Slavy. Their main magnet is the Kyevo-Pecherska Lavra – the holiest of holy sites in Ukraine and beyond, but there are a few other things to see in its vicinity.

The Lavra is a pleasant 15-minute walk from the metro. On the way back, you can take trolleybus 38 or *marshrutka* (fixed-route minibus) 520 or 406, which will return you to the metro station.

★ **Holodomor Memorial** MEMORIAL

(vul Ivana Mazepy 15A; M Arsenalna) FREE At the far end of Vichnoy Slavy Park, centred around a Soviet-era war memorial, you will find a monument from an entirely different epoch. President Viktor Yushchenko's pet project, it is dedicated to almost four million victims of the famine, artificially induced by Stalin's policy of collectivisation in 1932–33. Inside the round-shaped structure, village household objects are contrasted against bloodthirsty quotes from Bolshevik leaders, such as Lenin's 'We should resolve the Cossack issue by the means of their full extermination; all assets and property to be confiscated'.

★ **Kyevo-Pecherska Lavra** MONASTERY

(Києво-печерська лавра; Caves Monastery; 280 3071; www.lavra.ua; vul Sichnevoho Povstannya 21; upper lavra adult/student & child 50/25uah, lower lavra free; upper lavra 9am-8pm Apr-Sep, to 6pm Oct-Mar, lower lavra sunrise-sunset, caves 8.30am-4.30pm; M Arsenalna) Tourists and Orthodox pilgrims alike flock to the Lavra. It's easy to see why the tourists come. Set on 28 hectares of grassy hills above the Dnipro River, the monastery's tight cluster of gold-domed churches is a feast for the eyes, the hoard of Scythian gold rivals that of the Hermitage in St Petersburg, and the underground labyrinths lined with mummified monks are exotic and intriguing.

For pilgrims the rationale is much simpler. To them, this is the holiest ground in all three East Slavic countries – Ukraine, Russia and Belarus.

A *lavra* is a senior monastery, while *pecherska* means 'of the caves'. The Greek St Antony founded this *lavra* in 1051, after Orthodoxy was adopted as Kyivan Rus' official religion. He and his follower Feodosy

Podil

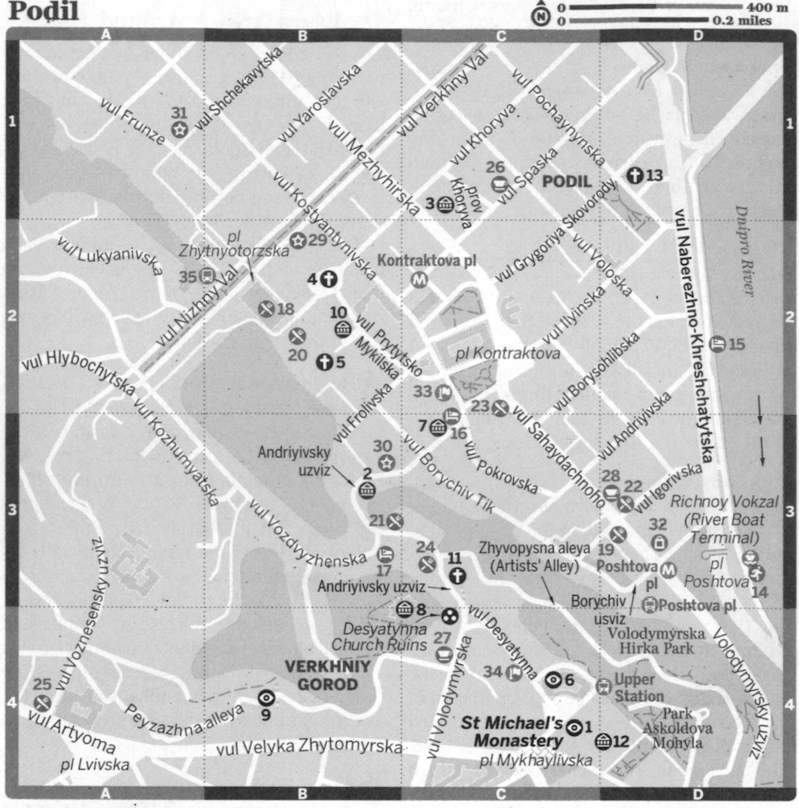

progressively dug out a series of catacombs, where they and other reclusive monks worshipped, studied and lived. When they died their bodies were naturally preserved, without embalming, by the caves' cool temperature and dry atmosphere. The mummies survive even today, confirmation for believers that these were true holy men.

The monastery prospered above ground as well. The Dormition Cathedral was built from 1073 to 1089 as Kyiv's second great Byzantine-inspired church, and the monastery became Kyivan Rus' intellectual centre, producing chronicles and icons and training builders and artists.

Wrecked by the Tatars in 1240, the Lavra went through a series of revivals and disastrous fires before being mostly rebuilt, with its prevailing baroque influences, in the 18th century. It was made a museum in 1926, but partly returned to the Ukrainian Orthodox Church (Moscow Patriarch) in 1988.

The complex is divided into the upper *lavra* (owned by the government and Kyiv Patriarchy) and the lower *lavra* (which belongs to Moscow Patriarchy and contains the caves).

As this is the city's single most fascinating and extensive tourist site, you will need at least half a day to get a decent introduction. Try to avoid the Lavra on weekends, when it gets extremely busy. If you must go, then visit early and head for the caves first.

Entrance to the upper *lavra* is free from 6am to 9am, and for a couple of hours after closing (until sunset). Admission to the upper *lavra* allows access to the churches, but several museums on-site charge additional fees.

The **Upper Lavra Excursion Bureau** (☎280 3071; www.kplavra.kiev.ua), just to the left past the main entrance to the upper *lavra*, sells two-hour guided tours in various languages (500uah per group of up to

Podil

Top Sights
1 St Michael's Monastery C4

Sights
2 Bulgakov Museum B3
3 Chornobyl Museum C1
4 Church of Mykola Prytysk B2
5 Florivsky Monastery B2
6 Ministry of Foreign Affairs C4
7 Museum of One Street C3
8 National Museum of Ukrainian History C4
9 Peyzazhna alleya B4
10 Pharmacy Museum B2
11 St Andrew's Church C3
12 St Michael's Gold-Domed Monastery Museum D4
13 St Nicholas Naberezhny D1

Activities, Courses & Tours
14 Richnoy Vokzal D3

Sleeping
15 Bohdan Khmelnitsky Boatel D2
16 Dream House Hostel C3
17 Vozdvyzhensky Hotel B3

Eating
18 Zhytny Rynok B2
19 Alaverdy D3
20 Harbuzyk B2
21 Kanapa B3
22 Tsymes D3
23 Varenichnaya Katyusha C2
24 Vernisazh C3
25 Vernisazh A4

Drinking & Nightlife
Druzi Cafe .... (see 16)
26 Kaffa C1
27 Kult RA C4
28 Repriza D3

Entertainment
29 Bochka B2
30 Koleso Kafe-Theatre B3
31 Xlib A1

Shopping
32 Kyivsky Vedmedik D3

Information
33 Dutch Embassy C2
34 UK Embassy C4

Transport
35 Podil Bus Station B2

10 people). Book in advance during peak periods. Entrance to the lower *lavra* and the caves is free of charge for pilgrims. Foreign tourists are likely to be asked to join one of the Russian-language tours (26uah, every 20 minutes) that depart from the **Lower Lavra Excursion Bureau** (Екскурсійне бюро нижньої лаври), located near the exit from the upper *lavra*.

To enter the caves, women must wear a headscarf and either a skirt that extends below their knees or, at a pinch, trousers. Trousers are officially forbidden but nowadays a blind eye is frequently turned. Men are obliged to remove their hats, and wearing shorts and T-shirts is forbidden. Men and women will also feel more comfortable donning scarves and doffing hats in the monastery's churches.

➡ Upper Lavra

The main entrance to the upper *lavra* is through the striking **Trinity Gate Church** (Троїцька надбрамна церква; Troitska Nadbramna Tserkva), a well-preserved piece of early-12th-century Rus architecture. Rebuilt in the 18th century, it once doubled as a watchtower and as part of the monastery fortifications. It's well worth going inside to observe its rich frescoes and lavish gilded altar. To access the church, turn left immediately after entering through the main gate. Also in this northwest section of the grounds is the small, late-17th-century **St Nicholas' Church** (Церква Св Миколая), its unique blue dome adorned with golden stars. It's now an administrative building.

Back out on the main path, you can't miss the seven gleaming gold domes of the **Dormition Cathedral** (Успенський собор; Uspensky Sobor), a year-2000 replica of the famous and sacred original. It was blown up during WWII – most probably by Soviet partisans, although pro-Russian historians still blame it on the Nazis. You can enter the church only during services, typically held on Saturday afternoons at 5pm and Sunday mornings at 7am. The big rock in the square between the cathedral and the bell tower is a **fragment** of the original cathedral.

Towering over the cathedral is the 96.5m-tall **Great Bell Tower** (Дзвіниця). Climbing the 174 steps to the top is an essential experience; however, the tower was shut down for renovations in 2005 and was still closed for visitors at the time of research.

Beneath the Great Bell Tower on the south side, the **Museum of Microminiature** (Музей мікромініатюр; admission 20uah; ⌚9am-1.30pm & 2.30-6pm Wed-Mon) provides something even for atheists within this holiest of holies – and, boy, is it popular! Possibly the most orderly queues in unruly Kyiv forms in front of Russian artist Nikolai Siadristy's tiny creations. The world's smallest book (with some verses of Shevchenko), a *balalaika* with strings one-fortieth the width of a human hair and a flea fitted with golden horseshoes are just some of his works of whimsy. Each is so small that microscopes are needed to view them, but you can occupy yourself with the brief English explanations while you wait.

The cluster of buildings just south of the Assumption Cathedral includes the excellent **Museum of Ukrainian Folk & Decorative Arts** (Музей українського фольклору та прикладного мистецтва; admission 20uah; ⌚10am-6pm Mon, Wed & Thu, to 8pm Fri & Sat), which boasts a vast collection of clothes, carpets, jewellery, ceramics and other beautiful items produced by generations of Ukrainian craftsmen. Nearby is the **Refectory Church of St Antony & St Feodosy** (Трапезна церква Св Антонія та Феодосія), sporting the monastery's most famous gold-striped dome (1885–1905). The main domed space is slightly reminiscent of Istanbul's Hagia Sophia, with its ring of small narrow windows along the base of the drum. The interior is beautifully painted with biblical scenes, saints and Art Nouveau patterns. The generously frescoed **refectory** (Трапезна палата) attached to the church is a sight in itself.

The **Historical Treasures Museum** (Музей історичних коштовностей України; admission 30uah; ⌚10am-4.45pm Tue-Sun), behind the Dormition Cathedral, has an astounding collection of precious stones and metal found or made in Ukraine. The highlight is the fabulous hoard of gold jewellery worked for the Scythians by Greek Black Sea colo-

Kyevo-Pecherska Lavra

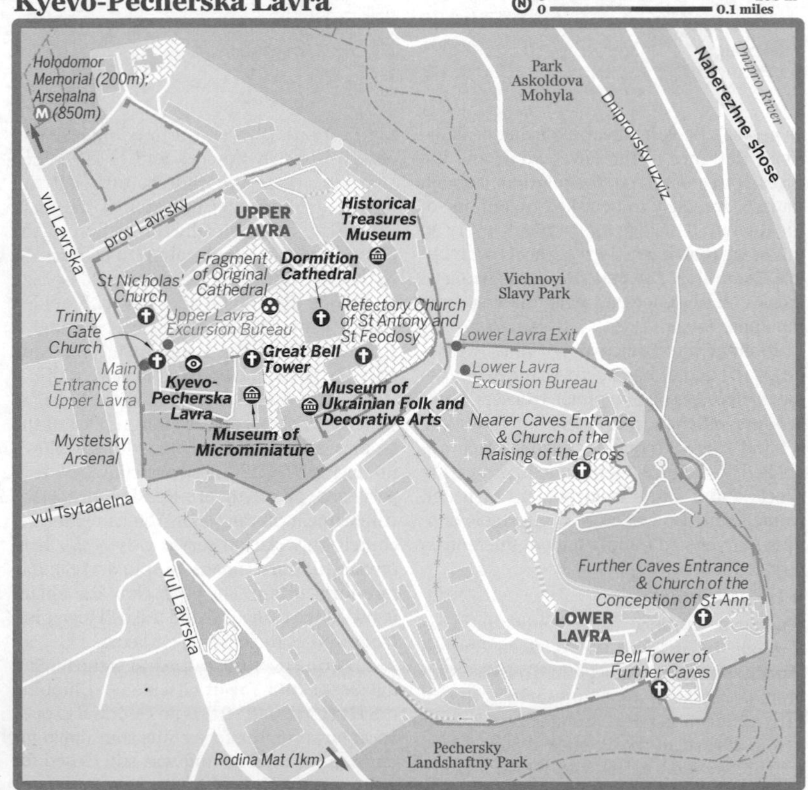

nists. Much of the treasures come from two 4th-century BC burial mounds: the Tolstaya grave in the Dnipropetrovsk region and the Gaimana grave in the Zaporizhzhya region.

To get to the lower *lavra* from the upper *lavra,* find the path behind the Refectory Church of St Antony & St Feodosy and head downhill under the flying buttress.

➡ Upper Lavra

The entrance to the **Nearer Caves** (Вхід у Ближні печери; ⌚8.30am-4.30pm) is inside the **Church of the Raising of the Cross** (Хрестовоздвиженська церква, 1700). Before the stairs head downwards, there's a table selling candles (3uah) to light your way through the dark passages. The use of cameras is forbidden in the caves.

Underground, the mummified monks' bodies, preserved in glass cases, are clothed and you only see the occasional protruding toe or finger. The coffins are arranged in niches in the tunnels, underground dining hall and three **subterranean churches**. Antony, the monastery's founder, and Nestor the Chronicler are just two of the 123 bodies down here. Students consider the latter their patron saint and leave candles near his mummy to have luck at exams. Another notable monk lying here is Ioann the Long-Sufferer, who fought the sin of womanising by half-burying himself in the ground every year for the duration of Lent. As a result, his sinning lower half completely decayed, while his saintly upper half remained intact. Would it be accurate to call him a half-saint, we wonder?

Tourists are only allowed into the first section of the caves, as many areas are cordoned off for Orthodox pilgrims and clergy. Monks frequently guard the entrance to restricted tunnels and are expert at spotting foreigners and nonbelievers.

Visiting the caves when they're not crowded can be a very moving experience. However, their low, narrow passageways are not for the seriously claustrophobic. If you visit on a busy day, it's total chaos down there. The monks' bodies are believed to have healing powers and pilgrims will bow to kiss the feet of one, before quickly diving to the other side of the tunnel to kiss the hand of another. Lost in religious ecstasy or sheer novelty, people wave their lit candles dangerously close to your back and face, particularly if you're a woman wearing a flammable headscarf – you will, frankly, feel more vulnerable than in the mosh pit of a punk-rock concert. It's an experience you will never forget, but if you like to take things calmly, choose a weekday visit.

The **Further Caves** (⌚8.30am-4.30pm) FREE were the original caves built by Antony and Feodosy. Their entrance (Вхід у Дальні печери) is in the **Church of the Conception of St Ann** (Аннозачатіївська церква; 1679), reached from the Nearer Caves by a viaduct. This cave system is also lined with ornamented mummified monks and contains three underground churches. Uphill from the Church of the Conception of St Ann is the seven-domed **Church of the Nativity of the Virgin** (Різдва Богородиці церква; 1696). Rising to the right is the unusual high-baroque **Bell Tower of Further Caves** (Дзвіниця на Дальніх печерах; 1761).

From the Further Caves it's a long walk back up the hill to the **main entrance** (Вхід до Нижньої лаври) on vul Sichnevoho Povstannya, or you can exit (or enter) at the nearby **lower entrance** (Нижній вхід до Нижньої Лаври). There may be taxis waiting at the lower entrance, or you can walk 15 minutes' north along busy Naberezhne shose to the Dnipro metro station.

Mystetsky Arsenal ARTS CENTRE

(Мистецький арсенал; http://artarsenal.in.ua; vul Lavrska 12; ⌚11am-8pm; Ⓜ Arsenalna) Once a storage for gunpowder and harnesses, these days it is a playground for visionary curators – each exhibition becomes an event of national importance. Eclecticism rules – exhibitions feature both new and old art. Unfortunately, the place often closes for months on end in the interim periods between exhibitions. Check its website to see what's on during your visit.

Rodina Mat MEMORIAL

(Батьківщина-мати; vul Lavrska 24; Ⓜ Arsenalna) There's not much to say about Rodina Mat (literally 'Nation's Mother', but formally called the Defence of the Motherland Monument). However, from certain parts of Kyiv it's highly visible and so requires a high-profile explanation. Especially when you're approaching from the left (or east) bank, this 62m-tall statue of a female warrior standing on a 40m-tall podium is liable to loom on the horizon and make you wonder, 'What the hell is that?'

Inaugurated by Soviet leader Leonid Brezhnev in 1981, it was the second and the last Nation's Mother monument erected in the USSR. Although initially designed by the same artist as the iconic Rodina Mat in Volgograd, it completely lacked its appeal and became a subject of ridicule, especially when the communist authorities reduced the size of the sword so that it doesn't rise over the cupolas of Kyevo-Pecherska Lavra. Even if you don't like such Soviet pomposity, don't say too much; you'd be taking on a titanium woman carrying 12 tonnes of shield and sword. You can look straight into her eyes by taking an elevator (200uah) to a platform located at the top of her shield.

The grounds around Rodina Mat are popular for strolling and contain a number of intriguing relics of the communist era, including an eternal flame in memory of WWII victims; various old tanks, helicopters and anti-aircraft guns; and a veritable garden of Soviet realist sculpture in and around the underpass leading towards the Lavra.

Museum of the Great Patriotic War MUSEUM

(www.warmuseum.kiev.ua; vul Lavrska 24; adult/student 40/30uah; ⏲10am-5pm Tue-Sun; Ⓜ Druzhby Narodiv) While the Museum of the Great Patriotic War was built belatedly in 1981 to honour Kyiv's defenders during the 'great patriotic war' of WWII, it seems to be straight out of the 1950s, with gloomy lighting and huge display halls covered in creaky parquet flooring. This is a sombre and sometimes even macabre exhibition, such as in Hall No 6 where you find yourself looking at a pair of gloves made from human skin.

Outside the City Centre

Pyrohovo Museum of Folk Architecture MUSEUM

(http://pirogovo.org.ua; vul Chervonopraporna 1; adult/child 30/15uah; ⏲grounds 10am-9.30pm, village houses till 6pm) Ukraine is dotted with 'open-air' museums like this, full of life-size models of different rustic buildings. However, the Pyrohovo Museum of Folk Architecture, 12km south of Kyiv, is one of the most fun and best maintained.

Two things make it stand out. Firstly, the quaint 17th- to 20th-century wooden churches, cottages, farmsteads and windmills are divided into seven 'villages' representing regional areas of Ukraine. So in just one long afternoon you can journey from the architecture of eastern to western to southern Ukraine.

Walking Tour Eras & Chimeras

START MAYDAN NEZALEZHNOSTI
END BESSARABSKY RYNOK
LENGTH 6KM; THREE HOURS

Set out from **1 maydan Nezalezhnosti** (p33), walking south along cobbled vul Horodetskoho to pl Ivana Franka. Set your sights on Wladislaw Horodecki's bizarre **2 House of Chimeras** (p36) on the hill behind the square. Ascend this hill via a path to the right of the House of Chimeras. At the top you'll be face-to-face with the huge **3 Presidential Administration building** on vul Bankova. Take a right to the corner of vul Lyuteranska and turn left again, pausing at the Art Nouveau facade of the **4 Weeping Widow House** at vul Lyuteranska 23. It is best seen when it rains and water is dripping down the cheeks of the sad female face on the facade. Sometimes the square by the Presidential Administration is closed for official receptions, in which case retreat from pl Ivana Franka to vul Zankovetskoyi and walk left to vul Lyuteranska.

Continue straight and take a left at the next corner onto vul Shovkovychna. Many of Kyiv's aristocrats built mansions in this area, known as Lypky, at the turn of the 20th century. Examples include the neo-Gothic **5 mansion** at vul Shovkovychna 19 and the brown-coloured **6 Chocolate House** next door. Follow vul Shovkovychna until it terminates at the **7 Verkhovna Rada** (Parliament Building).

Cross the street and walk through Park Misky Sad to the right of the Verkhovna Rada. The blue baroque building on your left is **8 Mariyinsky Palace**, based on a design by Italian architect Bartolomeo Rastrelli, who built St Andrew's Church and much of St Petersburg. A former Kyiv residence of the Russian royals, it is now used for official ceremonies attended by the Ukrainian president.

Behind the palace, follow a path leading northwest through the park. Eventually you'll spy **9 Olympic Stadium** (p64), just before crossing the high **10 Devil's Bridge** adorned with hundreds of locks left by newlywed couples who defiantly ignore the

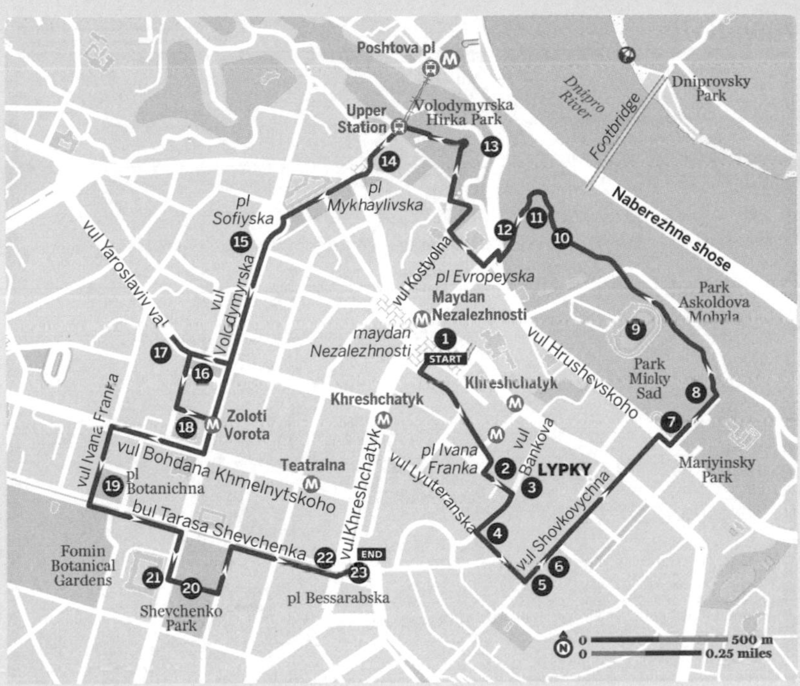

bridge's infernal name. Continue straight until you come to a giant, dull, metal parabola. It is part of the ⓫ **Friendship of Nations Monument** celebrating the 1654 'unification' of Russia and Ukraine.

Descend the hill via a path leading by the ⓬ **National Philharmonic** (p63), and cross pl Evropeyska. On the other side, follow vul Tryokhsvyatytelska uphill, turning right into Volodymyrska Hirka Park beyond the intersection of vul Kostyolna. All trails in here lead to the viewpoint looking down on the ⓭ **statue of Volodymyr the Great** – who brought Christianity to the eastern Slavs in 989 – and out across the Dnipro and the monolithic suburbs beyond.

Continue round the elevated riverbank, past a children's playground to the blue-and-gold ⓮ **St Michael's Monastery**. From pl Mykhaylivska you can see the tall bell tower and gold domes of ⓯ **St Sophia's Cathedral** (p37), which you should now head towards. Turn left into vul Volodymyrska, and two long blocks along, on your right, you'll see ⓰ **Zoloti Vorota** (p41). From here, turn right to vul Yaroslaviv wall and make a quick detour to ⓱ **Karaite Kenasa** built by Wladislaw Horodecki. Karaites are a small Crimean ethnic group who have preserved a peculiar religion mixing Judaism and Turkic paganism. Having lost a massive cupola in the Soviet period, the temple now houses a theatre.

Back on vul Volodymirska walk towards ⓲ **Taras Shevchenko National Opera Theatre** (p63) before turning right into vul Bohdana Khmelnytskoho and, two blocks later, left into vul Ivana Franka. At the end of this road on the left stands ⓳ **St Volodymyr's Cathedral**.

Turning left, you're on bul Tarasa Shevchenka, named after the Ukrainian national poet, Taras Shevchenko. On the right is his ⓴ **statue** in Shevchenko Park. A quick detour will give you a look at ㉑ **Kyiv University**.

At the end of the street once stood Kyiv's last ㉒ **Lenin statue**, famously pulled down and smashed to bits by Euromaidan protesters in late 2013. Until his demise, Lenin looked across thundering vul Khreshchatyk to the wonderfully atmospheric ㉓ **Bessarabsky Rynok** (p59).

East Kyiv

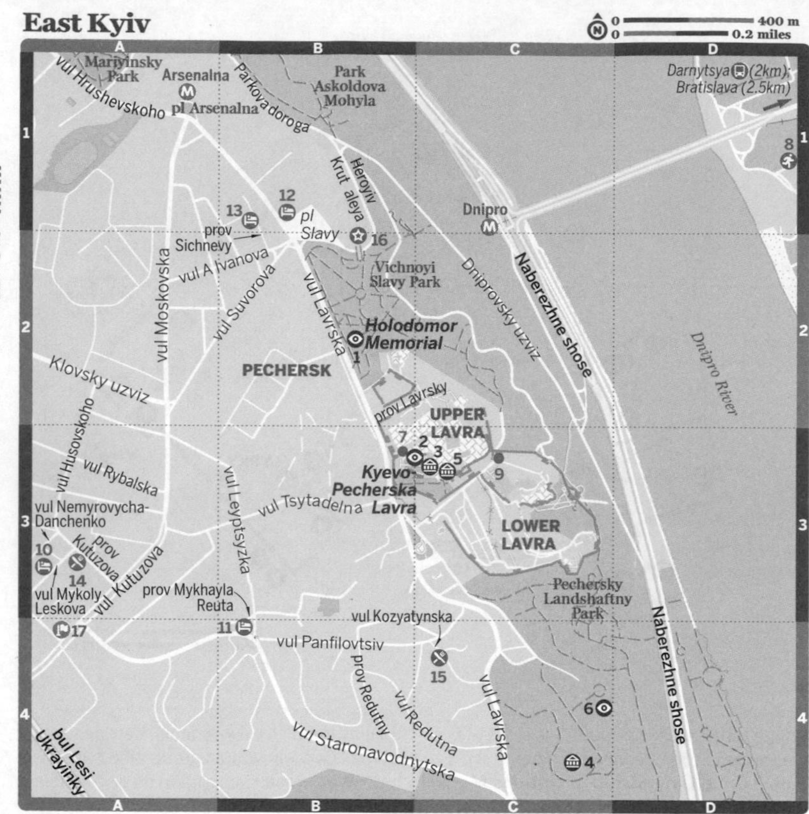

Secondly, in summer workers enact different village roles, carving wood, making pottery, doing embroidery, and driving horses and carts. There are restaurants, pubs and stalls selling barbecued *shashlyk* (shish kebab). The place is perfect for kids.

Throughout the year Pyrohovo hosts various festivals – the biggest is during the countrywide Ivan Kupala festival. Ukrainian musicians play on weekends.

The museum is near Pyrohovo village. From Vystavkovy Tsentr metro station take *marshrutka* 172, which stops right by the entrance. *Marshrutky* 3 and 156, as well as trolleybus 11, stop at the turn-off to the museum. A taxi will cost about 100uah one way.

Babyn Yar MONUMENT

(M Dorohozhychi) On 29 September 1941, Nazi troops rounded up Kyiv's 34,000-strong Jewish population, marched them to the Babyn Yar ravine and massacred them all in the following 48 hours. Victims were shot and buried in the ravine, some of them still alive. Over the next two years, many more people of all ethnic, religious and political backgrounds lost their lives at Babyn Yar when it was turned into a concentration camp, called Syrets after the Kyivan suburb it was located. The total number of people buried here is estimated at 100,000.

Monuments commemorating various groups targeted by the Nazis – among them Russian Orthodox priests, Ukrainian nationalists, Romany people – are scatterred around the unkempt park. Follow the path from vul Melnykova 44, past a TV station, to the secluded spot where you'll find the 1991 Jewish memorial, a menorah, which better marks the actual killing field. From here several paths lead to points overlooking the ravine itself.

South of Dorohozhychi metro stands a striking non-sectarian Soviet-era monument comprised of choking figures as if strug-

East Kyiv

Top Sights
1 Holodomor Memorial............................ B2
2 Kyevo-Pecherska Lavra........................ C3

Sights
Historical Treasures Museum........(see 5)
3 Museum of Microminiature.................. C3
4 Museum of the Great Patriotic War C4
5 Museum of Ukrainian Folk and Decorative Arts C3
6 Rodina Mat... C4

Activities, Courses & Tours
7 Excursion Bureau B3
8 Hydropark... D1
9 Lower Lavra Excursion Bureau............ C3

Sleeping
10 Asteri...A3
11 Black Sea...B4
12 Hotel Salute... B1
13 Sherborne Guest House....................... B1

Eating
14 Barsuk..A3
15 Tsarske Selo..C4

Entertainment
16 Crystal Hall..D2

Information
17 Russian Consulate A4

gling to climb out of their grave. Because of anti-Semitism and their own atrocities, it took decades for the Soviets to recognise the Babin Yar tragedy – the monument was only erected in 1976.

A smaller monument nearby is dedicated to the whopping three million Ukranians, mostly young women, who were used as slave labour in Germany. Many of them died because of terrible conditions and allied bombing raids targeting German industries.

Another monument was erected in 2001 beside Dorohozhychi metro to commemorate the Jewish children who perished at Babyn Yar.

★Central Botanical Gardens PARK
(Центральний Ботанічний Сад; vul Tymiriazivska 1; adult/student 20/10uah) The long, steep hill running along the Dnipro River from Olympic Stadium and Mariyinsky Palace to Rodina Mat continues south for several kilometres, eventually becoming the Central Botanical Gardens. The gardens' fastidiously manicured grounds are criss-crossed by a network of paths leading to hidden viewpoints and churches frozen in time.

The botanical gardens are tricky to reach by public transport. Take trolleybus 14 or bus 62 from Pecherska metro to the final stop.

Vydubytsky Monastery CHURCH
(Видубицький Монастир; vul Vydubytska 40; M Druzhby Narodiv) Few churches appear more frozen in time than those of the Vydubytsky Monastery, nestled into the hill's dense foliage beneath the Central Botanical Gardens. If you found the crowds at the Lavra a little too much to bear – or if you're just into intense serenity – you should not hesitate to come here. The monastery, which is thought to be at least as old as Kyiv, is looking in fine fettle today after centuries of catastrophes followed by years of Soviet neglect. The monastery is home to a small community of monks, who, quite frankly, have chosen a much more monk-friendly place to practise their faith than the increasingly touristy Lavra.

The bucolic church looking down on the monastery from the crest of the hill is the recently restored **Trinity Cathedral** (Троїцький собор).

Aviation Museum MUSEUM
(http://aviamuseum.com.ua; vul Medova 1; admission 50uah, photo 10uah; ⏰10am-7pm Wed-Sun) Soviet aviation might have been a target of ridicule lately, yet it was a mighty industry that outcompeted the Germans in WWII and raced neck-to-neck with the Americans during the Cold War. Located at the far side of Zhulyany airfield, this open-air museum displays dozens of aircraft designed to carry people or tanks, land on ice or water and indeed to bomb the hell out of Western Europe. The museum is about a 1.5km walk along vul Medova from the roundabout in front of Zhulyanya airport's new terminal, or take a taxi.

Activities

Contact details for organisers of regular football, cricket and Ultimate Frisbee games are in the *Kyiv Post* community listings. For lists of bowling alleys, fitness centres, swimming pools, tennis courts and golf ranges, consult *In Your Pocket* or the *Kyiv Business Directory*.

LOCAL KNOWLEDGE

YEVHEN SAFONOV: KYIV EXPERT

Yevhen Safonov is the editor of *Village.ru*, Kyiv edition – a publication reviewing the city's new places and trends.

Only in Kyiv... Mobile coffeeshops – when espressos and lattes are served from the boot of a car.

The Most Enchanting Place Several benches in the Central Botanical Gardens (p51) with the view of Vydubytsky Monastery and the left bank. Best visited in the evening.

Best Place to Get Drunk Peyzazhna alleya.

A Must-Eat in Kyiv *Borshch* at Kanapa (p58).

The Best Season Early autumn.

Richnoy Vokzal CRUISE

(River Port; Map p44; cruise 50uah; Ⓜ Poshtova pl) Cruises leaving from Richnoy Vokzal are a great way to get a totally different perspective on the city – if you can tolerate kitschy music blasted from loudspeakers.

veliki.ua BICYCLE RENTAL

(Map p38; www.veliki.ua; Shevchenko Park; per day from 55uah; Ⓜ Universytet) With its long green belt along the river and forested islands, Kyiv is a good place for cycling. This pan-Ukrainian bicycle-rental co-op runs several outlets around Kyiv, including the one by the Coffee Tram (p64) at Shevchenko Park.

Dnipro Cable Trolley ADVENTURE SPORTS

(Map p38; ride 150uah, student 100uah before 5pm; ⏲10.30am-9.30pm; Ⓜ Maydan Nezalezhnosti) If walking across the bridge to Truhaniv Island seems boring, you can slide down to the beach on the other side of the river in a matter of seconds, defying Nikolay Gogol's famous statement that 'only a rare bird can fly to the middle of the Dnipro'. Located by the Friendship of Nations Monument.

Beaches

Thanks to a dam a few kilometres downstream, the Dnipro around Kyiv is full of islands and beaches, which are packed with sunbathers in summer. Water sports like wake-boarding and sailing are popular summer pursuits, while in winter ice fishers descend on the frozen river en masse and intrepid 'walrus' swimmers take to the frigid bouillabaisse.

Truhaniv Island BEACH

(Ⓜ Poshtova pl) Accessible from central Kyiv via a pedestrian bridge, the island has a long sandy and usually uncrowded beach facing the city. It is forested and criss-crossed by roads and paths – a great place for cycling.

Hydropark BEACH

(Ⓜ Hydropark) The main recreational zone on the Dnipro islands, Hydropark deafens people arriving by metro with terrible pop music blasted from dozens of bars all at the same time. The area around the station is full of tacky entertainment and guys in training suits. But if you venture a bit further, you'll find less crowded beaches and some quirky sights – like a giant outdoor gym and a platform, where elderly Kyivites gather to dance to the tunes of their youth.

Tours

Chervona Ruta CRUISE

(Червона Рута; Map p38; ☎253 6909; www.ruta-cruise.com; vul Lyteranska 24; Ⓜ Khreshchatyk) This is your only port of call if you're interested in Dnipro River and Black Sea cruises. The standard cruise is one week along the Kyiv–Sevastopol–Odesa route. Some cruises go into the Danube Delta.

New Logic TOUR

(Map p38; ☎206 2200; www.newlogic.ua; vul Mikhaylivska 6A; Ⓜ Teatralna) Has great deals on Chornobyl tours for individual tourists. Another office is near **maydan Nezalezhnosti** (Map p38; ☎206 3322; Mykhaylivska 6A; Ⓜ Maydan Nezalezhnosti).

SAM TOUR

(Map p38; ☎238 6957; www.sam.ua; vul Ivana Franka 40B; ⏲9am-7pm Mon-Fri, 10am-4pm Sat; Ⓜ Universytet) The leading inbound operator organises sightseeing tours, hotel bookings, and trips to Chernihiv, Chornobyl and Uman.

SoloEast Travel TOUR

(Map p38; ☎279 3505; www.tourkiev.com; vul Prorizna 10, office 105; ⏲9am-6pm Mon-Fri; Ⓜ Khreshchatyk) Ukrainian-husband-and-Canadian-wife team offering tickets, apartments and tours, including to Chornobyl. Probably the most helpful, friendly travel service in Kyiv, with B&B accommodation just outside the city.

Festivals & Events

Epiphany RELIGIOUS

In January scores of the faithful leap into the Dnipro River at Hydropark and elsewhere to celebrate the baptism of Christ.

Ivan Kupala FESTIVAL

(Іван Купала) On the night of this pagan fest (6 July, but often moved to the nearest weekend), crowds pour into Pyrohovo Museum of Folk Architecture to sing and dance, consume tons of food and – most importantly – jump over fire with your beloved ones.

Kraina Mriy Festival MUSIC

(www.krainamriy.com) VV frontman Oleh Skrypka organises a three-day festival of ethnic music from Ukraine and elsewhere in July during the countrywide Ivan Kupala festival. Over the last years the same festival has also taken place in January around Orthodox Christmas.

Kyiv Days CITY FESTIVAL

This celebration of spring brings musicians and street performers to Andriyivsky uzviz, maydan Nezalezhnosti and other streets of the capital on the last weekend of May.

Baptism of Rus RELIGIOUS

Kyivans plunge into the Dnipro River on 12 August, just as they did in 988 AD on the orders of Prince Volodymyr, who decided that his land should join the Christian world.

Gogolfest ART

A lively festival of modern theatre, music, cinema, architecture and all imaginable kinds of art dedicated to writer Nikolai Gogol takes place in early September. It's new and not necessarily annual.

Kyiv International Film Festival Molodist FILM

(www.molodist.com) An annual event that takes place during the last week of October.

Sleeping

Kyiv's hotel scene can serve as an illustration of the widening gap between the rich and the poor.

All is happy at the extreme budget end. Kyiv has a lovely hostel scene, a typical hostel being a large converted flat sleeping about 20 people. Owners and staff are often fellow travellers who you will find cooking in the kitchen and sleeping on a mat in the common room. There are dozens of hostels listed on international hostel websites.

But if you want to find a normal, centrally located hotel room for US$50 – well, forget it. Prices at pretty much all the decent, semi-decent and even completely indecent establishments start at the equivalent of US$100, with the exception of the hotels located on the left bank of the Dnipro.

Fortunately, rented apartment agencies fill the gap – you can typically get a well-furnished, centrally located apartment for half the price of any dodgy hotel.

But watch for considerable discounts that many good hotels offer during weekends and long holiday periods (22 December to 12 January, 24 April to 11 May and 30 June to 30 August) when business travellers stay home.

City Centre

Hotel Ukraine HOTEL $$

(Готель Україна; Map p38; ☎278 2804; www.ukraine-hotel.kiev.ua; vul Instytutska 4; s/d from 630/800uah; ❄📶; Ⓜ Maydan Nezalezhnosti or Khreshchatyk) This Stalin-era giant presiding over maydan Nezalezhnosti offers the best view of future revolutions, Orange or otherwise. Short on comforts, big on atmosphere, its musty rooms have air-con to protect you from natural and political heat.

★ **Sunflower B&B Hotel** B&B $$$

(Map p38; ☎279 3846; www.sunflowerhotel.kiev.ua; vul Kostyolna 9/41; s/d from 850/1000uah; ❄@📶; Ⓜ Maydan Nezalezhnosti) The name is an oxymoron – it's more B&B than hotel – but we're not complaining. The highlight is the continental breakfast (with a warm pastry) delivered to your room, on request, by English-speaking staff. It's centrally located but nearly impossible to find – calling for a pickup is not a bad idea.

Gintama Hotel LUXURY HOTEL $$$

(Map p38; ☎278 5092; www.gintama.com.ua; vul Tryokhsvyatytelska 9; s/d from1230/1310uah; ❄📶; Ⓜ Maydan Nezalezhnosti) This friendly family-run hotel has an understated style, with smallish, individually decorated rooms tending towards the traditional, but with cleaner lines and fewer florals than usual. The hotel is in a quiet spot just a three-minute walk from maydan Nezalezhnosti.

Hotel Rus HOTEL $$$

(Готель Русь; Map p38; ☎256 4000, 256 4020; www.hotelrus.kiev.ua; vul Hospitalna 4; r from 900uah; ❄@; Ⓜ Palats Sportu) Perched above Olympic Stadium, it is a Soviet-era high-rise hotel transformed into a professionally run establishment. It's a bit of an uphill grind to walk here, but it's perfect if you're in town for a football match.

Hotel Greguar HOTEL $$$
(Грегуар; ☎498 9791, 498 9790; www.greguar.com; vul Chervonoarmiiyska 67/7; s/d from 920/1040uah) What makes this hotel different is the kitchenettes in each of the large comfortable rooms. It's not like Kyiv has any shortage of good inexpensive food, but should you need to cater for yourself – here is a perfect choice. Breakfast isn't included in the rates.

Old Town

Hyatt Regency Kyiv HOTEL $$$
(Map p38; ☎581 1234; http://kiev.regency.hyatt.com; vul Tarasovoy 5; r from 4100uah; P ❄ 🛜 ≋; M Maydan Nezalezhnosti) Other Ukrainian hotels can only dream of having the Hyatt's view of duelling 11th-century churches. Inside, everything is just as perfect, from the fabulous gym to the spacious and eminently comfortable rooms, to its popular panorama bar and Grill Asia restaurant. Western leaders tend to stay here and we've never heard them complain.

11 Mirrors BOUTIQUE HOTEL $$$
(Map p38; ☎581 1111; www.11mirrors-hotel.com; vul Bohdana Khmelnytskoho 34A; r from 2650uah; ❄ 🛜; M Zoloti Vorota) If you want to admire the cupola of St Volodymyr's Cathedral from your bathtub through a one-way transparent wall or perhaps share a sumptous buffet breakfast with boxing champions the Klichko brothers, who are associated with the business, here is your chic place to stay. At 120uah, the breakfast is also a good deal for nonguests.

Hotel Bontiak BOUTIQUE HOTEL $$$
(Map p38; ☎284 0475; http://bontiak.ru; vul Irynynska 5; d from 1100uah; ❄ @ 🛜; M Zoloti Vorota) Flashy new 35-room boutique hotel located equally close to maydan Nezalezhnosti and pl Sofiyska. The stylishly minimalist rooms are generously cut and well equipped, and breakfast is served in your room.

Andriyivsky Uzviz & Podil

Dream House Hostel HOSTEL $
(Map p44; ☎580 2169; www.dream-family.com; Andriyivsky uzviz 2D; dm/d from 110/400uah; ❄ @ 🛜; M Kontraktova pl) Kyiv's most happening hostel is this gleeming new 100-bed affair superbly located at the bottom of Andriyivsky uzviz. An attached cafe-bar, a basement kitchen, a laundry room, keycards, bike hire (160uah per day), and daily events and tours make this a comfortable and engaging base from which to explore the capital.

★Bohdan Khmelnitsky Boatel CRUISE BOAT $
(Ботель Богдан Хмельницький; Map p44; ☎2291919; www.vipteplohid.kiev.ua; vul Naberezhno-Khreshchatytska, moorage 5; r from 350uah, without bathroom 250uah; ⊙Oct-Apr; M Kontraktova pl) The grand dame of the Dnipro River fleet, this paddle boat built in Budapest in 1954 is now permanently moored in Podil. The dark-wood panelling in its corridors and smallish cabins looks immaculate, but it may be stuffy in the summer heat.

Vozdvyzhensky Hotel BOUTIQUE HOTEL $$$
(Готель Воздвиженський; Map p44; ☎531 9900; www.vozdvyzhensky.com; vul Vozdvyzhenska 60; standard s/d 1200/1940uah; ⊖ ❄ @; M Kontraktova pl) Tucked away in a nook just off Andriyivsky uzviz, the Vozdvyzhensky is one of Kyiv's few true boutique hotels. The 29 rooms are all individually designed and boast fine art. The hotel highlight is the rooftop summer terrace, which has views overlooking Podil. Our main gripes are the small standard rooms and the difficulty pronouncing 'Vozdvyzhensky'.

Train Station Area

Central Station Hostel HOSTEL $
(Map p38; ☎093 758 7468; www.kievcentralstation.com; vul Hoholivska 25, apt 11; dm 90-130uah; M Vokzalna) We should thank Ukrainian bureaucracy for leaving the Brazilian owner stranded in Ukraine with an expired visa. Now fully legalised, Aricio runs one of Kyiv's most atmospheric hostels set in converted flats on the upper floors of a charming house in a quiet, leafy neighbourhood. In the evening, Ukrainian and expat friends drop in for a beer, which inevitably results in everyone setting out on a pub crawl. The place is, however, not as close to the train station as its name might lead you to believe.

Ibis HOTEL $$
(Map p38; ☎5912222; www.ibis.com; bul Tarasa Shevchenka 25; r from 790uah; M Universytet) Yes, it is a predictable chain hotel, but it is sparkling new and about the best value you can get for US$100 a night – and the most comfortable bed, too! Otherwise, it is Ibis – with

minimalistically designed, slightly cramped rooms and no minibar.

Hotel Express HOTEL **$$**
(Готель Експрес; Map p38; ☎503 3045, 234 2113; www.expresskiev.com; bul Tarasa Shevchenka 38/40; s/d from 730/930uah; ❄@; Ⓜ Universytet) The Soviet-style Express has a mix of renovated and unrefurbished rooms. The cheapest have tiny beds and lack showers. Prices increase proportionally as amenities and coats of paint are added. Air-con rooms don't cost extra, but you must request them. Prices go down by about 100uah during weekends and in July and August.

Service Centre TRAIN STATION ROOMS **$$**
(Обслуговий центр залізничної станції; Map p38; ☎465 2080; Kyiv train station; s/d 300/600uah; ❄@; Ⓜ Pl Vokzalna) In the station's older Central Terminal, this has a comfortable wi-fi–enabled lounge and clean bright rooms. Head to the right as you exit the Central Terminal.

Lybid Hotel HOTEL **$$$**
(Готель Либідь; Map p38; ☎236 9572; www.hotellybid.com.ua; pl Peremohy 1; s/d from 930/1070uah; ❄@; Ⓜ Universytet) Lybid hails from the same Soviet architectural incubator as many other hotels in Kyiv, but it stands out from its siblings thanks to friendly service and convenient location – a five-minute walk from the train station and metro. All rooms are renovated; they're about 200uah cheaper in July and August and during public holidays.

Lypky & Pechersk

Hotel Salute HOTEL **$$**
(Готель Салют; ☎494 1420; www.salute.kiev.ua; vul Ivana Mazepy 11B; s/d from 650/750uah; ❄@; Ⓜ Arsenalna) Affectionately dubbed 'the grenade', the Salute features psychedelic '70s furniture and a few rooms with exceptional views of the Dnipro. For a converted Soviet hotel it has surprising benefits, like smiling receptionists and a 24-hour business centre.

Black Sea HOTEL **$$**
(Чорне море; ☎364 1054; www.bs-hotel.com.ua; vul Leyptsizka 16A; r from 500uah; ❄; Ⓜ Pecherska) Midrange hotels at mid-European prices are a rare breed in Kyiv these days, so don't expect much from this one. It is clean, friendly and – stretching boundaries a bit – one can call it central. Convenient for Lavra.

Sherborne Guest House BOUTIQUE HOTEL **$$$**
(☎490 9693; www.sherbornehotel.com.ua; prov Sichnevy 9, 1st entrance; apt from 1000uah; ❄@; Ⓜ Arsenalna) An apartment-hotel,

APARTMENTS

Kyiv has dozens of apartment agencies and sorting through them all can be a chore. Most reputable agencies have websites where you can browse their apartments. Booking is best done online or via phone or text message; only a few firms have offices. Most agencies require that you pay the first night's accommodation in advance in order to book.

All of the following have English-speaking representatives and accept credit cards.

Absolut (☎099 214 6480, 541 1740; www.hotelservice.kiev.ua; apt from 400uah) Reasonable, if not great, service.

Best Kiev Apartment (☎067 442 2533, 067 506 1875; www.bestkievapartment.com; apt from 650uah) Smartly renovated apartments.

Grata Apartments (Map p38; ☎238 2603, 468 0757; www.accommodation.kiev.ua; prov Mykhaylivsky 9A, office 3; apt from 500uah) Service-oriented firm has nice range of apartments.

Rentguru (☎098 364 6509, 050 240 2581; www.rentguru.com.ua/en; apt from 300uah) Canadian-educated doctor Valentyn offers some of the cheapest, though not very central, apartments.

Teren Plus (☎289 3949; www.teren.kiev.ua; apt from 500uah) Tried and true.

UARent (☎067 403 6030; www.uarent.com; apt from 450uah) Apartments in prime locations for average price.

UKR Apartments (☎050 311 0309, 234 5637; www.ukr-apartments.kiev.ua; apt from 600uah) Has a wide selection of inexpensive apartments.

this is very salubrious both on the inside and out, with 12 internet-enabled apartments where you can cook for yourself and go about your business unhindered. The reception area is open 24 hours, and there's laptop hire and a zillion other services. Book well in advance, as this place is justifiably popular.

Asteri HOTEL **$$$**
(☎300 1048; http://asteri.kiev.ua; vul Leskova 4; r from 840uah; Ⓜ Pecherska) With breakfast served on the rooftop of a high-rise building, most of which is occupied by tax collectors (oops), this new hotel is good value for money. The only complaint is that the receptionist can be hard to find when you need her most.

Outside the City Centre

Slavutych Hotel HOTEL **$$**
(Готель Славутич; ☎561 1112; www.hotel-slavutich.com; vul Entuziastov 1; renovated s/d 460/560uah, s/d unrenovated without breakfast 330/430uah; ❄@; Ⓜ Druzhby Narodiv) A Soviet high-rise on the left bank of the Dnipro, Slavutych lets you marvel at the golden domes of Kyevo-Pecherska Lavra and Vydubytsky Monastery from its bland, but totally acceptable, rooms. A Korean restaurant on the top floor comes as a bonus. The hotel is a short ride from Druzhby Narodiv metro by any *marshrutka* going across Paton bridge, eg 527.

Hotel Adria HOTEL **$$**
(Готель Адрія; ☎568 457; www.adria.kiev.ua; vul Rayisy Okypnoy 2; s/d 710/770uah; ❄@; Ⓜ Livoberezhna) This Polish outfit occupies several floors of the lower-quality Hotel Tourist on the left bank of the Dnipro. Breakfast costs 100uah extra.

Oselya BOUTIQUE HOTEL **$$$**
(Оселя; ☎258 8281; www.oselya.in.ua; vul Kamenyariv 11; s 710uah, d from 930uah; ❄@📶; Ⓜ Lybidska) Incoveniently located around 5km south of the city centre, just to the east of Zhulyany airport, this superb seven-room family-run hotel has immaculately kept rooms in period style and receives encouraging reviews from travellers for its friendly welcome. The location feels almost rural, but you'll need to arrange a pickup from Lybidska metro station to find it or grab a cab.

Eating

Note that most drinking venues also make fine and often cheaper places to eat, especially if you can't bear to be more than 2m away from a keg at any given time. For further eating options, see the *Kyiv Post, What's On Kiev* or www.chicken.kiev.ua.

Maydan & Khreshchatyk Area

Kyivska Perepichka FAST FOOD **$**
(Київська перепічка; Map p38; vul Bohdana Khmelnytskoho 3; pastry 5.50uah; ⏲9am-9pm Mon-Sat, 11am-9pm Sun; Ⓜ Teatralna) The perpetually long queue moves with lightning speed towards a window where two women hand out pieces of fried dough enclosing a mouthwatering sausage. The place became a local institution long before locals heard 'hot dog' for the first time. An essential Kyiv experience.

Linas ARABIC **$**
(Линас; Map p38; pl Bessarabska 2; mains 30uah; ⏲9am-11pm; Ⓜ Teatralna) A friendly little felafel embassy in the land of *borshch*. Lamb kebab tastes like celery juice after seeing all that lard at Bessarabsky Rynok market next door.

★Arbequina SEAFOOD **$$**
(Map p38; ☎223 9618; vul Borysa Hrinchenka; mains 80-150uah; ⏲9am-11pm; 📶; Ⓜ Maydan Nezalezhnosti) Barcelona meets Odessa in this excellent restaurant a few steps away from Maydan. Food is mostly Spanish – think paella and *fideua* – but the chef successfully experiments with Black Sea fish and East European staples, which results in most unusual dishes, such as Black Sea mullet with buckwheat and anchovy bliny.

Varenichnaya #1 UKRAINIAN **$**
(Вареннична #1; Map p38; vul Esplanadna 28; varenyky 40-90uah; ⏲24hr; 📶; Ⓜ Palats Sportu) Focusing on *varenyky* (Ukrainian dumplings), this place mimics the homey interior of an early-20th-century private apartment. Nearly 25 different *varenyky* fillings are offered. Surely, though, the live piglet in the basket near the door (so cute!) must deter anyone from ordering pork?

Walter's ITALIAN **$$**
(Map p38; ☎279 7911; http://walters.ua; vul Sofiyvska 10; mains 100-150uah, pizza 60-140uah; ⏲noon-11.30pm; 📶; Ⓜ Maydan Nezalezhnosti) In Kiev, there is no shortage of good Italian res-

taurants, but in this one you can hear Italian spoken most of the time, because Walter, the owner, made it a home away from home for expats from the Apennines – a sure sign that nothing can go terribly wrong with your pizza or North Italian meat dishes, which dominate the menu. There are also a few good options for vegetarians.

Himalaya INDIAN **$$**
(Гімалая; Map p38; ☎462 0437; www.kanapa-restaurant.kiev.ua; vul Khreshchatyk 23; mains 75-130uah; 📶; Ⓜ Teatralna) Himalaya has occupied a prime perch overlooking Khreshchatyk for some time, and somehow it just gets better with age. The Indian food is spicier than you expect in these parts and there are many veggie options.

Pl Lva Tolstoho & Olympic Stadium Area

Zheltok INTERNATIONAL **$**
(Желток; Map p38; http://jeltok.com.ua; vul Lva Tolstoho 11; mains 35-65uah; ⌚8.30am-12pm; 📶; Ⓜ Pl Lva Tolstoho) A lighthearted take on American diner – large bowls of salad, burgers, fluffy pancakes and – the pride of the place – homemade cola. The best deal here is a takeway lunch box: pay 35uah, find a bench in Shevchenko Park across the road and enjoy your meal!

Knaypa Sinoval UKRAINIAN **$$**
(Кнайпа Сіновал; Map p38; ☎289 5475; http://sino.com.ua; vul Saksahanskoho 40; mains 40-70uah; Ⓜ Pl Lva Tolstoho) 'Knaypa' (a Galitsian-style pub) suggests this place is about drinking, but we like it most for the hearty Carparthian food, like *banosh* (a West Ukrainian version of polenta) and *halushki* dumplings. Three kinds of Sinoval's own beer go for 18uah a pint.

Pervak UKRAINIAN **$$**
(Первак; Map p38; ☎235 0952; vul Rognidenska 2; mains 70-180uah; ⌚11am-midnight; 📶; Ⓜ Pl Lva Tolstoho) This place masterfully recreates old Kyiv (c 1900) without falling into the schmaltz trap that dogs many a Ukrainian-theme restaurant. The chefs boldly prepare original takes on Ukrainian classics, which are adroitly delivered to tables by waitresses in frilly, cleavage-baring country outfits. There's nightly live music and black-and-white silent movies playing on old Soviet TVs.

Babel SEAFOOD **$$**
(Бабель; Map p38; ☎361 8144; vul Saksahanskoho 33-35; mains 100-140uah; ⌚11am-11pm; 📶; Ⓜ Olympiyska) Odesa's famous son Isaak Babel lived in this house, which is this restaurant's main excuse to exploit the Babel fish pun. The eclectic menu features Black Sea fish and Jewish *forshmak* (herring paste), along with Georgian specialities, such as *khachapuri* cheese pastry and spicy *kharcho* soup.

Imbir VEGETARIAN **$$**
(Имбирь; Ginger; Map p38; ☎287 6180; http://cafeimbir.com; vul Zhylyanska 7; mains 55-80uah; ⌚8am-10pm; 📶✍; Ⓜ Olimpiyska) A slightly sterile place filled with incense and soothing musical sounds, Ginger serves European and Asian vegetarian specialities, as well as smoothies and lassies.

★**Under Wonder** INTERNATIONAL **$$$**
(Map p38; ☎234 2181; www.underwonder.com.ua; vul Chervonoarmiyska 21; mains 100-200uah; ⌚24hr; 📶; Ⓜ Pl Lva Tolstoho) With its multicoloured tinted glass, purple tablecloths, lots of woodwork and racks of old newspapers, this place is a kind of magic. And it only gets better when you order. Chicken stuffed with sundried tomatoes, olives and Bergader cheese, rabbit with foie gras and cream sauce, ravioli nero with salmon – the very sound of the menu items is already mouthwatering. A great central place to land at any time of day or night – it works around the clock and serves great breakfasts.

Concord FUSION **$$$**
(Конкорд; Map p38; ☎229 5512; 8th fl, vul Pushkinska 42/4; mains 250-370uah; 📶; Ⓜ Pl Lva Tolstoho) Concord delivers the entire package: incredible Euro-Asian fusion food, effortlessly slick interior design, impeccable service, and a DJ spinning tunes that everybody else will be playing three months from now. The mouthwatering salads here are like temples to the sultan of sassafras, like shrines to the Raman of radicchio. The views from atop the Donbas Centre are just dressing on the salad.

Old Town

Bulochnaya Yaroslavna PIES **$**
(Булочна Ярославна; Map p38; vul Yaroslaviv val 13; pies 4.50uah; ⌚9am-10pm; Ⓜ Zoloti Vorota) A veteran institution with stand-up tables serves awesome pies with a variety of

fillings – from jam to meat – and hot chocolate. Ignore the basement restaurant – it's overpriced.

O'Panas Blyny Stand UKRAINIAN $

(Блинний кіоск Опанас; Map p38; Shevchenko Park; blyny 10uah; ⏲9am-8pm; Ⓜ Pl Lva Tolstoho) The city's best *blyny* (pancakes) come from a shack in front of the otherwise unspectacular Ukrainian restaurant, O'Panas.

★ **Spotykach** UKRAINIAN $$

(Спотикач; Map p38; ☎586 4095; vul Volodymyrska 16; mains 90-160uah; ⏲11am-midnight; 📶; Ⓜ Zoloti Vorota) A tribute to the 1960s – a happier (and funnier) period of Soviet history – this discreetly stylish retro-Soviet place will make even a hardened dissident shed a tear. Food is October Revolution Day banquet in the Kremlin, but with a Ukrainian twist. The eponymous *spotykach* is vodka-based liquor made with different flavours, from blackcurrant to horseradish. Beware: its name derives from the Russian for 'stumble', which pretty much describes the effect it might cause on the uninitiated.

Barkas SEAFOOD

(Баркас; Map p38; ☎569 5640; vul Volodymyrska 49A; ⏲11am-11pm; 📶; Ⓜ Zoloti Vorota) Fresh from the Black Sea is the fish and fresh from Sevastopol is this Crimean transplant. It's not only about local seafood favourites like *sargan* and *barabulya*. The chef plays with the best Crimean produce, including goat cheese, lamb, 'bull's heart' tomatoes and sweet Yalta onions. The restuarant is hidden in the courtyard of a new business centre.

Dio Long CHINESE $$

(Діо Лонг; Map p38; bul Tarasa Shevchenka 48A; dishes 90-140uah; Ⓜ Universytet) Beijing duck comes in all shapes and sizes in this Chinese expat getaway hiding in a courtyard off bul Tarasa Shevchenka.

Osteria Pantagruel ITALIAN $$$

(Остерія Пантагрюєль; Map p38; ☎278 8142; vul Lysenka 1; mains 85-145uah; 📶; Ⓜ Zoloti Vorota) Homemade pasta, risotto and bruschetta are turned out at this whitewashed cellar restaurant by Zoloti Vorota. The warm months see tables and chairs spill onto the square out the front – probably the best place in Kyiv for a beer on a summer evening. The bronze cat across the road is a monument to Pantyusha, who once lived in the restaurant.

Andriyivsky Uzviz & Podil

Alaverdy EASTERN EUROPEAN $

(Алаверди; Map p44; vul Sahaydachnoho 23/4; mains 20-25uah; Ⓜ Poshtova pl) This unpretentious little affair is the best value of Kyiv's many Georgian restaurants. There's no English menu; if you're stuck order some *suluguni* (Georgian cheese) and anything from the 'hot dishes'; it's all good (unless you're vegetarian).

Harbuzyk UKRAINIAN $$

(Гарбузик; Little Pumpkin; Map p44; vul Khoryva 2V; mains 35-100uah; ⏲11am-11pm; Ⓜ Kontraktova pl) This fun, if slightly hokey, eatery offers a great introduction to Ukrainian food without breaking the bank. Pumpkin is not just in the name, it's all over the menu – from the *mammlyha* (Hutsul polenta-like dish) to fresh pumpkin juice. More unusual items on the drinks list include birch tree sap and *kvas* (drink made from rye bread). And there is plenty of *horilka* (vodka) – pure and pumpkin-free. Set lunch served between 11am and 5pm is a great deal at 43uah.

★ **Kanapa** UKRAINIAN $$

(Канапа; Map p44; ☎425 4548; www.kanapa-restaurant.kiev.ua; Andriyvsky uzviz 19; mains 100uah; ⏲9am-11pm; 📶) Sneak away from the busy *uzviz* and you find yourself in what seems like a treehouse – a wooden terrace perched above the dense canopy of trees underneath. A unique place, Kanapa serves gentrified, 21st-century Ukrainian food, largely made from their own farm's produce. Everything tastes great and you can spend a lot of money here. Our favourite is *okroshka* cold soup made with rhubarb *kvas* and served in a bowl of ice – literally.

Tsymes NON-KOSHER JEWISH $$

(Цимес; Map p44; ☎428 7579; Sahaydachnoho 10/5; mains 95-165uah; ⏲11am-11pm; 📶; Ⓜ Poshtova pl or Kontraktova pl) This small place is tucked into a vaulted cellar with green walls and Chagall-style frescoes. It has an extensive menu of Jewish dishes that hail from all parts of Ukraine. The bill is a laugh – if only in the sense that it comes with a random Jewish joke, although the three-course lunch available from 11am to 4pm on weekdays is also laughably cheap.

Varenichnaya Katyusha EAST EUROPEAN $$

(Варенична Катюша; Map p44; http://katysha.com.ua; vul Sahaydachnoho 41; mains 40-70uah;

WHERE THE STREETS HAVE MORE NAMES

All the confusion over Ukraine bilingualism and the Soviet past is epitomised in the name of one street. Or rather its many names.

It's very likely that you'll find yourself looking for something in Kyiv's Red Army St, which is the main artery in the bustling neighbourhood around the Olympic Stadium. A few restaurants and hotels described in this book are located in the vicinity.

So, Ukrainian-language street signs (and this book as well) call it Chervonoarmiyska, while in real-life conversations with locals it goes under its Russian name – Krasnoarmeyskaya.

However, in 1998 the city council voted to return its old, pre-Soviet name – Velyka Vasilkivska. But due to politcial squabbles the law has never been stamped and enforced. Soviet-era street signs remain unchanged.

Yet, an absolute majority of businesses located here have switched to using the new-old name on their websites, business cards and leaflets. Even the town hall website occasionally joins the trend! But – adding to the confusion – they mostly use the Russian version – Bolshaya Vasilkovskaya.

Fortunately, Ukrainian and Russian are very close languages, so names of most streets sound almost identical. Following are some useful words that cause the most head-scratching:

- Red is *chervony* (червоний) in Ukrainian and *krasny* (красный) in Russian.
- Big is *velyky* (великий) in Ukrainian and *bolshoy* (большой) in Russian.
- October (as in October Revolution) is *zhovten* (жовтень) in Ukrainian and *oktyabr* (октябрь) in Russian.
- Descent is *uzviz* (узвіз) in Ukrainian and *spusk* (спуск) in Russian.

24hr; ; Poshtova pl) Unashamedly playing the Soviet nostalgia card, though without hammers and sickles, this popular chain serves *pelmeni* and *varenyky* – Russian and Ukrainian dumplings – with all imaginable fillings, from blackberries to cabbage and smoked bacon. Conveniently for Podil party animals, it provides fodder round the clock.

Vernisazh FRENCH $$$
(Вернісаж; Map p44; 425 2403; Andriyivsky uzviz 30; mains 120-280uah; Poshtova pl or Kontraktova pl) The atmosphere is arty-farty and the menu eclectic. Dishes exhibit Ukrainian, Thai and French influences and, yes, the chef is talented enough to pull it off. If it's raining, you can kill time admiring the art or thumbing through the colourful coffee-table books. It used to be the city's main Francophone hang-out, but the crowd has largely moved to its new outlet near **pl Lvivska** (Map p44; vul Artyoma 10, cnr vul Smyrnova-Lastochkyna).

Lypky & Pechersk

Tsarske Selo UKRAINIAN $$
(Царське Село; vul Ivana Mazepy 42/1; mains 60-190uah; 11am-1am; ; Arsenalna) A pure bodily delight well deserved by those who descend the spiritual heights of Kyevo-Pecherska Lavra, this rustic-style restaurant serves great Ukrainian staples.

Barsuk PUB $$
(Барсук; http://barsuk.kiev.ua; prov Kutuzova 3A; mains 80-170uah; Pecherska) Tucked away in a small lane opposite Pechersky market, the Badger brings three nouvelle concepts to Kyiv, namely gastropub, organic food and open-view kitchen. The cuisine could be slightly more inventive in a place striving to look progressive, but if you like it, you are welcome to attend cooking classes during weekends.

Self-Catering

Bessarabsky Rynok MARKET $
(Бессарбський ринок; Map p38; pl Bessarabska; 8am-8pm Tue-Sun, to 5pm Mon; Teatralna) The arrangements of colourful fruit, vegetables, meat and flowers in this light-filled hall are works of art and it almost seems a shame to disturb them by buying them – almost, but not quite. The market was built from 1910–12 for traders coming to Kyiv from Bessarabia. Some imported produce is on sale (at a high price).

Zhytny Rynok MARKET

(Житній ринок; Map p44; pl Zhytnyotorzska) It's been here in Podil since the times of the Vikings (though not the current Soviet structure). Like any Ukrainian market, it is always rich in seasonal fruit and vegetables.

Furshet Gourmet SUPERMARKET $$

(Фуршет; Map p38; ☎044 230 9522; basement, Mandarin Plaza Shopping Centre, vul Baseyna 4; ⊙24hr; Ⓜ Pl Lva Tolstoho) An upscale supermarket with imported foods, pre-prepared meals and – what else? – a sushi bar.

Megamarket SUPERMARKET $

(Мегамаркет; Map p38; vul Horkoho 50; ⊙8.30am-11.30pm; Ⓜ Olympiyska) A little outside the city centre, but worth it if size and selection are what you seek.

Ekomarket SUPERMARKET $

(Екомаркет; Europort Shopping Mall, vul Mykoly Lukashevycha 15A; Ⓜ Vokzalna) Convenient for stocking up on food before a train journey.

Drinking & Nightlife

Smoky basement bars dominate the action in Kyiv until late spring, when the drinking masses move outside to summer terraces. Beware of the new law that bans drinking alcohol in the street, or you'll become an easy target for the police.

Kupidon PUB

(Купідон; Cupid; Map p38; vul Pushkinska 1-3/5; ⊙10am-10pm; 📶; Ⓜ Kreshchatyk) Apocalyptically dubbing itself 'the last shelter for the Ukrainian intelligentsia', this is in fact a missionary station spreading Ukrainian culture in the Russian-speaking capital. Siege mentality apart, Cupid is a lovely Lviv-styled *knaypa* (pub) with an attached bookshop – a favourite drinking den for nationalist-leaning and cosmopolitan bohemians alike.

Palata No.6 BAR

(Ward No.6; Map p38; vul Vorovskoho 31A; beer from 12uah, shots 25uah; ⊙noon-2am; 📶; Ⓜ Universytet) For a healthy dose of insanity sneak into this well-hidden bar named after Anton Chekhov's story about life in a madhouse. Dressed in doctors' white robes, stern-looking waiters nurse you with excellent steaks and pour vodka into your glass with giant syringes. A perfect cure for the maddening quotidian.

Pub Trallebus PUB

(Паб Траллебус; Map p38; vul Prorizna 21; ⊙noon-2am; Ⓜ Zoloti Vorota) Ten kinds of draught beer, including unusual Ukrainian brands from Radomyshl, Slavuta and Pirnovo are the main reason we like this place. Add inexpensive food, tables easily accommodating six or more of your drinking buddies plus football on plasma screens and what you get is the formula for a perfect evening.

Kult RA CAFE

(Культ Ра; Map p44; http://kultra.org/; vul Volodymyrska 4; drinks 35-55uah; 📶; Ⓜ Zoloti Vorota) You may treat this place as a teashop, pub, restaurant, music venue or a bookshop, but crucially it is a stronghold of Ukrainian nationalism spiced with New Age mysticism. Who built Babylon? Ancient Ukrainians, who else – say books available in the cellar store. Drinkwise, it makes great herbal teas and its trademark coffee with yolk and cedar nuts. But for better appreciation of Ukraine's role in world history we recommend some shots of excellent *horilka*.

La Bodeguita del Medio BAR

(Map p38; ☎272 6500; vul Yaroslaviv val 21/20; Ⓜ Zoloti Vorota) An outlet of this international Cuban jazz-cafe chain was an instant success in Kyiv, where many Cuban students chose to remain when the USSR called it a day. A mix of Ukrainians and expats gather here to plunge into Buena Vista melancholy induced by outstanding resident and guest performers, while tucking into fajitas and emptying one mojito after another. All Cuban waiters seem to be part-time salsa teachers.

Banka BAR

(Банка; Map p38; ☎098 988 7988; www.bankabar.com.ua; vul Lva Tolstoho 11; shots/cocktails 20/40uah; ⊙noon-1am; Ⓜ Pl Lva Tolstoho) Here is the curious case of Andy Warhol's *32 Campbell Soup Cans* idea taken a bit too far. Designers made the place look like a preserves storage – there are cans everywhere. All drinks are also served in cans or jars (*banka* means both in Ukrainian). But it does fill them with the most invigorating mixtures, including some beer-based cocktails. Naturally, no draught beer, only canned.

Experiment 12 CAFE

(Експеримент 12; Map p38; ☎099 200 6641; http://creativespace12.com; prov Mykhaylivsky 10/2; ⊙11am-11pm; Ⓜ Zoloti Vorota) It feels like somewhere on the Aegean Islands when you sit in their tiny garden surrounded by ramshackle old buildings. A great place for slow conversations and long drinks, this cafe

HIPSTER TIME

Despite politicians' fearmongering, not everything that spreads from Moscow should necessarily cause alarm. One trend that has reached Ukraine can indeed benefit foreign travellers.

Emerging from Russia's *khipstery* culture, these are comfortable, artfully designed environments where one can use wi-fi, consume infinite amounts of free coffee or lemonade, and partake in various community events, while only paying for time – usually an equivalent of one euro per hour or less. They have become known as 'open spaces' or 'anti-cafes'.

For travellers, they replace internet cafes in the age of portable gadgets. You can sit down and browse away in an environment infinitely cosier than your average internet cafe, without getting annoyed looks from waiters, as you often would in a normal cafe.

Besides, these are community centres for hipsters, holding all sorts of events from acoustic concerts, poetry evenings to cooking classes. Finally, most people come here to make new friends without getting drunk in a pub, and many of them speak English.

The trend has already spread to Odesa, Dnipropetrovsk and Lviv. Here are our favourite two in Kyiv:

Chasopys (Часопис; Map p38; www.chasopys.kiev.ua; vul Lva Tolstoho 3; ⌚8am-11.30pm; Ⓜpl Lva Tolstoho) A super-comfortable pay-for-time coworking environment where you can surf the web using your own gadgets or one of the local notebooks. There are many nooks and crannies in this place, which you can choose based on whether you want to be close to other people or left completely alone.

Tsiferblat (Циферблат; Map p38; http://kiev.ziferblat.net/en; vul Volodymyrska 49A; ⌚11am-11pm Sun-Fri, to 6am Sat; ⓂZoloti Vorota) Kyiv's original 'open space' is more artsy and less businesslike than the others. Attracts younger people and essentially becomes a nightlife spot on Saturdays. To find it, enter the courtyard of a new business centre, walk past Barkas restaurant and then down one level.

is part of a community centre for Ukrainian designers. Which brings us to the 'experimental' component – the interior is being redesigned every month by a new artist. Comes with a shop/exhibition of modern Ukrainian design.

Druzi Cafe CAFE
(Map p44; http://druzicafe.com.ua; Andriyvsky uzviz 2D; ⌚8am-12pm; ⓂKontraktova pl) This new place has many virtues. Tucked in a courtyard and invisible from the outside, it is an escape from the crowds on Andriyvsky uzviz. Having escaped, you can choose between coffee, refreshing lemonades and competently mixed cocktails. Food is also available. Finally, it is attached to Dream House hostel – so it's always full of young foreign and ex-Soviet travellers, who engage in table games and long drinking sessions.

Coffeehouses

Dozens of coffeehouses, most of them chains, have sprung up in Kyiv, making it easy to find a cup of real brewed coffee anytime, anywhere.

Kaffa COFFEE
(Каффа; Map p38; prov Tarasa Shevchenka 3; coffee 17-25uah; ⌚9am 10.30pm; ⓂMaydan Nezalezhnosti) The onslaught of Ukrainian and Russian coffee chains has not changed one thing: longstanding Kaffa still serves the most heart-pumping, rich-tasting brew in town. Coffees and teas from all over the world are served in a pot sufficient for two or three punters in a blissfully smoke-free, whitewashed African-inspired interior – all ethnic masks, beads and leather. A Podil outlet is at **vul Grygoriya Skovorody 5** (Map p44).

Chashka COFFEE
(Чашка; Map p38; vul Chervonoarmiyska 1; ⌚8am-11pm; ⓂTeatralna) A very friendly cafe serving lattes with rather experimental local flavours – such as *uzvar* (dried-pear drink) and *khalva* (Turkish sweet). It's kind of works, but regular coffee is also available.

Repriza CAFE
(Реприза; Map p38; vul Bohdana Khmelnytskoho 40/25; coffee 20-30uah, breakfast 45-65uah;

GAME OF ARCHITECTURE

Beautifying Kyiv's skyline was obviously his vocation, but Wladislaw Horodecki had very little time for it. There were so many exciting things to do in Kyiv at the start of the 20th century, like riding first motorcars or taking to the skies in flimsy biplanes built by aspiring aviation engineers. One of them was Igor Sikorsky, a fellow Kyivite, destined to become the father of the US helicopter industry. But Horodecki's main passion was big-game hunting, which took him to Siberia, Central Asia, Afghanistan and Africa. He even authored a book about his exploits in the savannah.

That is why his contribution to Kyiv's cityscape appears relatively modest. But discounting all the storehouses and public toilets the architect designed to fund his adventures, it is fair to say that his creations became Kyiv's architectural icons. Those include the classical-styled National Arts Museum, the neo-Gothic St Nicholas Catholic Cathedral, the Karaite Kenasa on vul Yaroslaviv val and – most famously – House of Chimeras.

He decorated the latter with his hunting trophies and intended to occupy one of the apartments, while renting out the others. But debts were piling up and he had to sell it in 1912. Soon WWI began, followed by the Russian revolution. Horodecki escaped to Poland, but always passionate about travel (and short of funds), he moved to Iran at the age of 65 to build Tehran's train station and shah's palace. He died there in 1930.

These days, Wladislaw Horodecki (or at least his bronze statue) seems to be in no hurry and is always available for a coffee and a chat in the Pasazh. There is a vacant seat by his (also bronze) table, which you are free to take, without worrying that he will dash off to walk his pet monkey on vul Khreshchatyk, as he did a century ago.

(M Zoloti Vorota) Not only does it have good coffee and delectable sandwiches, pastries and cakes, but it also makes a fine, affordable lunch stop. Also has a branch in Podil at **vul Sahaydachnoho 10** (Map p44; M Poshtova pl).

Wolkonsky CAFE
(Волконський; Map p38; www.wolkonsky.com; Pasazh; ⌚8am-10pm; M Khreshchatyk) This pricey French-owned cafe offers superb desserts, breakfast and lunches, as well as a chance to mingle with oligarchs, politicians and their dressed-to-kill partners.

Nightclubs

Arena Night Club CLUB
(Арена Сіті; Map p38; ☎492 0000; Arena Entertainment Complex, vul Baseyna 2A; admission 100-150uah; M Pl Lva Tolstoho or Teatralna) Top-end club.

Bibique DJ
(Map p38; bul Tarasa Shevchenka 2; ⌚6pm-1am Sun-Thu, till 3am Fri & Sat; M Pl Lva Tolstoho or Teatralna) A well-hidden place for those in the know, this DJ bar is good at mixing – both sounds and liquids. Enter Polyana wine store and look for the unmarked glass door on the left. Don't come too early.

☆ Entertainment

Rock

Olympic Stadium hosts a few large outdoor rock concerts and festivals every summer. The main venues for big rock and pop concerts:

Palats Sportu MULTIPURPOSE VENUE
(Палац Спорту; Sports Palace; Map p38; ☎246 7406, reservations 501 2520, schedule 246 7405; pl Sportyvna 1; M Palats Sportu) One of the main venues for rock concerts. It also hosts Ukraine's international basketball and hockey games.

Palats Ukraina CONCERT VENUE
(Палац Україна; Ukraine Palace; ☎247 2476; vul Chervonoarmiyska 103; M Palats Ukraina) A main venue for rock concerts.

Crystal Hall CONCERT VENUE
(☎288 5069; Dniprovsky uzviz 1; M Arsenalna)

Live Music

Check *What's On Kyiv* and the *Kyiv Post* for the latest big thing.

Art Club 44 LIVE MUSIC
(Map p38; www.club44.com.ua; vul Khreshchatyk 44; M Teatralna) With its jazz nights on Tuesdays, Balkan parties on Thursdays and an occasional good gig over the weekend, this

veteran venue, once set by the local nightlife legend – a German called Eric – remains a beacon for more sophisticated night creatures.

Divan CLUB
(Диван; Map p38; ☎235 7366; http://festrest divan.com.ua; pl Bessarabska 2; ⏰12pm-3am; Ⓜ Pl Lva Tolstoho) Best place to check what's up with indie music in Ukraine and Russia. Live concerts pretty much daily. Inside Bessarabsky Rynok market.

Xlib CLUB
(Map p44; www.xlib.com.ua; vul Frunze 12; Ⓜ Kontraktova pl) Kyiv's main alternative stage was closing for reconstruction at the time of writing but it was promising to re-emerge in the same place, though not necessarily under the same name, by this book's publication. Watch out!

Bochka LIVE MUSIC
(Бочка; Map p44; ☎200 0360; http://bochka.ua; vul Verkhny Val 22; Ⓜ Kontraktova pl) You may encounter some major Ukrainian and Russian rock/alternative bands playing in this large busy pub on Friday or Saturday night.

Classical Music & Opera

Tickets to classical music and opera performances are significantly cheaper than in the West. To get a decent seat will usually only set you back about 50uah. Advance tickets and schedules are available at the theatres or at *teatralna kasa* (Театральна Каса; theatre box offices) scattered throughout the city. Handy ones are at **vul Khreshchatyk 21** (Map p38; Ⓜ Khreshchatyk) and **vul Chervonoarmiyska 16** (Map p38; Ⓜ Pl Lva Tolstoho).

Taras Shevchenko National Opera Theatre OPERA
(Map p38; ☎234 7165; www.opera.com.ua; vul Volodymyrska 50; Ⓜ Zoloti Vorota) This is a lavish theatre (opened 1901) and a performance here is a grandiose affair. It is during one of such performances in 1911 that young terrorist Dmitry Bogrov shot progressive prime minister Pyotr Stolypin, which many believe predetermined Russia's plunge into revolutionary chaos. True imbibers of Ukrainian culture should not miss a performance of *Zaporozhets za Dunaem* (Zaporizhzhyans Beyond the Danube), a sort of operatic, purely Ukrainian version of *Fiddler on the Roof.*

National Philharmonic LIVE MUSIC
(Map p38; ☎278 1697; www.filarmonia.com.ua; Volodymyrsky uzviz 2; Ⓜ Maydan Nezalezhnosti) Originally the Kyiv Merchants' Assembly headquarters, this beautiful building is now home to the national orchestra.

House of Organ & Chamber Music CONCERT HALL
(Будинок органної та класичної музики; ☎526 3186; vul Chervonoarmiyska 75; tickets from 10uah; ⏰shows 7.30pm; Ⓜ Olympiyska or Palats Ukraina) Housed in neo-Gothic St Nicholas' Cathedral built by Wladislaw Horodecki.

Theatre

Theatre-going is a major part of Kyiv life, but most performances are in Ukrainian or Russian. The following may be of borderline interest if you're not schooled in Slavic tongues.

Dakh Theatre THEATRE
(☎529 4062; http://dax.com.ua; vul Chervonoarmiyska 136; Ⓜ Lybidska) Simply the coolest thing that's happening on a Ukrainian theatre stage. Look out for perfomances involving *The Dakh Daughters* – a 15-strong 'singing siren' collective which took YouTube by storm with the mock Gothic 'Donbass Roses' clip.

Koleso Kafe-Theatre THEATRE
(Колесо Кафе-Театр; Map p44; ☎044 425 0527; Andriyivsky uzviz 8A; Ⓜ Kontraktova pl) This semi-avant-garde theatre has an informal, cafe-like environment. Performances involve much song and dance as well as food, so understanding the language is not essential.

Ivan Franko National Academic Drama Theatre THEATRE
(Map p38; ☎279 5991; pl Ivana Franka 3; Ⓜ Khreshchatyk) Kyiv's most respected theatre has been going strong since 1888.

Gay & Lesbian Venues

Pomada GAY
(Помада; Lipstick; Map p38; www.pomada-club.com.ua; vul Zankovetskoyi 6; Ⓜ Khreshchatyk) You know Kyiv's come a long way when we can actually publish the names of gay clubs (they used to all be underground). This is lively and centrally located, and it's the one place in town where women pay *more* to get in.

Sport

Besides being one of the main ven rock concerts, Palats Sportu als

Ukraine's international basketball and hockey games.

Olympic Stadium STADIUM
(Олімпійський стадіон; Map p38; vul Chervonoarmiyska 55; Ⓜ Olympiyska) Kiev's new slick football arena hosted the Euro 2012 football (soccer) final. Today it's the home arena of Dynamo (Kyiv). You can visit the arena on a guided tour that takes place every two hours on the hour between 11am and 5pm (adult/child 50/25uah). There is also a shop selling good quality sportwear with Dynamo insignia.

Shopping

Around major sights, especially on Andriyvsky uzviz, there is no shortage of souvenir stalls selling *matryoshka*, Soviet army hats and a million kinds of 'this lousy T-shirt'. A bottle to bring home would be that of *horilka* (vodka), available at any foodstore.

Roshen SOUVENIRS
(Рошен; Map p38; vul Starovokzalna 21; ⌚8am-9pm; Ⓜ Vokzalna) On the sweet-tooth front, there is nothing more symbolic than Kyivsky Tort, a nutty, layered sponge cake sold in circular cardboard cartons. Its main producer has a chain of immaculate shops, including this one by the train station and another outlet at **vul Kreshchatyk 29** (Рошен; Map p38; ⌚8am-10pm). They are filled to the top shelf with all kinds of sweets.

Experiment 12 ARTS & CRAFTS
(Map p38; www.creativespace12.com; prov Mykhaylivsky 10; ⌚10am-7pm; Ⓜ Zoloti Vorota) A showroom of modern Ukrainian design, where you can buy random objects – from lamps to plates or clothes – produced by aspiring Ukrainian artists. Comes with a nice cafe.

Kyivsky Vedmedik CHILDREN
(Київський Ведмедик; Map p44; http://vedmedyk.com.ua; vul Sahaydachnoho 6A; ⌚8am-10pm Mon-Fri, 11am-10pm Sat & Sun; Ⓜ Poshtova pl) This tiny shop, which comes with an even tinier cafe, sells handmade teddy bears, produced by Ukrainian artists. Some bears are just cute, some are dressed as Cossacks, some look like they hail from outlying galaxies.

Petrivka Market MARKET
(Петрівський ринок; pr Moskovsky; ⌚8am-6pm; Ⓜ Petrivka) Locals call it the 'book market', but you can get a vast array of junk here. It's also Kyiv's main receptacle of DVDs, CDs and software of questionable legitimacy.

Kartografia MAPS
(vul Chervonoarmiyska 69; Ⓜ Olympiyska) A good selection of maps can be found in this centrally located shop.

Information

INTERNET ACCESS

The Central Post Office has an efficient internet service. For more internet facilities, see p61.

Oscar Internet Centre (Map p38; 2nd fl, vul Khreshchatyk 48; per hr 20uah; ⌚24hr; Ⓜ Teatralna) VOIP calls to Europe and the US cost 0.85uah per minute.

MEDICAL SERVICES

American Medical Center (☎emergency hotline 044 490 7600; http://amcenters.com; vul Berdychivska 1; ⌚24hr; Ⓜ Lukyanivska) Western-run medical centre with English-speaking doctors.

MONEY

Both ATMs and exchange booths signposted 'обмін валют' *(obmin valyut)* are ubiquitous. Rates offered by exchange booths in hotels are not necessarily worse. Larger banks will cash travellers cheques and give cash advances on credit cards.

POST

Central Post Office (Map p38; vul Khreshchatyk 22; internet per hr 18uah; ⌚8am-9pm Mon-Sat, 9am-7pm Sun, internet 24hr; Ⓜ Maydan Nezalezhnosti) The entrance is on maydan Nezalezhnosti.

DHL International (Map p38; ☎490 2600; www.dhl.com.ua; vul Chervonoarmiyska 2; Ⓜ Pl Lva Tolstoho)

TELEPHONE

Internet cafes often offer VOIP calls or Skype.

Central Telephone Centre (Map p38; vul Khreshchatyk 22; ⌚24hr; Ⓜ Maydan Nezalezhnosti) You can make international calls here or purchase phonecards.

TOURIST INFORMATION

Coffee Tram (Map p38; Shevchenko Park; Ⓜ Universytet) A meek substitute for the non-existent municipal tourist office, this old tram standing in Shevchenko Park offers coffee, bikes for rent and advice on what to do in Kyiv. Staff can set up a walking tour of your choice at 300uah per group.

USEFUL WEBSITES

Go2Kiev (www.go2kiev.com) Usually up-to-date site with events listings and practical information for visitors.

Interesny Kiev (Mysterious Kiev; ☎364 5112; http://mysteriouskiev.com) This website hooks you up with tour guides offering all sorts of walks around the city. It also contains heaps of tourist information about well-known and more unusual sights.

Lonely Planet (www.lonelyplanet.com/ukraine/kyiv) Get inspired with planning advice, author recommendations and travel reviews.

Visit Kyiv (www.visitkyiv.com.ua) Heaps of city-related info.

Getting There & Away

AIR

Most international and domestic flights use Boryspil International Airport (p264), about 35km east of the city, but the small modern **Zhulyany airport** (☎585 7254; www.airport.kiev.ua) is getting increasingly important because of its proximity to the city centre. Budget airline Wizz Air flies from here to about a dozen European destinations, including London, plus to Kutaisi in Georgia.

Ukraine International Airlines (Map p38; ☎234 4528; www.ukraine-international.com; vul Lysenka 4; Ⓜ Maydan Nezalezhnosti) is the main national airline. Dniproavia and Utair Ukraine fly to numerous domestic destinations.

Plane tickets are also sold at **Kiy Avia** (Map p38; www.kiyavia.com; pr Peremohy 2; ⊙8am-9pm Mon-Fri, 8am-8pm Sat, 9am-6pm Sun; Ⓜ Vokzalna). It has another branch at **vul Horodetskoho 4** (Map p38; ☎490 4949; Ⓜ Maydan Nezalezhnosti).

BOAT

Kyiv is the most northerly passenger port on the Dnipro and the usual starting or finishing point of river cruises between May and mid-October; contact Chervona Ruta (p52).

BUS

There are seven bus terminals, but the most useful for long-distance trips is the **Central bus station** (Tsentralny Avtovokzal; pl Moskovska 3), near Demiivska metro station – look out for McDonald's as you exit. Buses for Petrushivka and Trostyanets leave from **Darnytsya bus station** (Автостанція Дарниця; ☎559 4618; pr Gagarina 1; Ⓜ Chernihivska). **Vydubychi bus station** (Автостанція Видубичі; ☎559 4618; vul Naberezhno-Pecherska 10; Ⓜ Vydubychi) is handy for Kaniv. Buses for Zhytomir and Berdychev leave from **Dachna bus station** (pr Peremohi 142).

Long-distance express carriers **Autolux** (☎451 8628; www.autolux.com.ua) and **Gunsel** (☎525 4505; www.gunsel.com.ua) run by far the fastest and most comfortable buses in the business. They have frequent trips to most large regional centres; most go via, or continue to, Boryspil International Airport. You can book on their websites, or buy tickets at the Central bus station or Boryspil airport.

MARSHRUTKA

Many destinations in central and western Ukraine can be reached by private *marshrutky* (fixed-route minibuses) – 15-seat minibuses, which (normally) don't accept standing passengers.

The largest *marshrutka* station – **Avtostantsiya Kyiv** (Map p38; vul Symona Petlyury 32; Ⓜ Vokzalna) – is right by the train station. From here, buses leave for Uman (65uah, three hours, hourly), Rivne (100uah, 3½ hours, half hourly), Ternopyl (130uah, seven hours, six daily), Zhytomir (30uah, 1½ hours) and Vinnitsa (100uah, 3½ hours, four daily).

For Chernihiv, *marshrutky* leave from both Chernihivska and Lisova metro stations (50uah, 1¾ hours, every 15 minutes).

Kharkivska metro station is the point of departure for *marshrutky* to Pereyaslav-Khmelnytsky (30uah, one hour, every 20 minutes) and Cherkasy (50uah, 2½ hours).

TRAIN

You can get pretty much everywhere in the country from Kyiv's modern **train station** (☎503 7005; pl Vokzalna 2; Ⓢ Vokzalna), conveniently located near the city centre at Vokzalna metro station.

Heading west, the quickest way to Lviv is on the daily express day train (270uah, five hours), or there are several overnight passenger trains (200uah, eight to 10 hours). Other popular western destinations include Uzhhorod (230uah, 15½ hours, three daily), Ivano-Frankivsk (150uah, 11 to 13 hours, daily) and Chernivtsi (190uah, 13½ hours, two daily). There's both an overnight and an express train to Kamyanets-Podilsky (70uah, seven to nine hours).

Heading south, there are about four (mostly night) services to Odesa (210uah, eight to 12 hours) and two daily services to Sevastopol (200uah, 17 hours). These and at least one additional train go to Simferopol (180uah, 15 hours).

Eastern destinations are now best served by fast Intercity trains, which depart for Kharkhiv (250uah, 4½ hours, three daily), Dnipropetrovsk (250uah, 5½ hours, two daily) and Donetsk (300uah, seven hours, two daily). Slower (and cheaper) trains are also available.

You can buy tickets at virtually any of the myriad ticket booths in both the **Central Terminal** (Tsentralny Vokzal) and the new, adjacent **South Terminal** (Pivdenniy Vokzal), or at the **advance train ticket office** (Map p38; bul Tarasa Shevchenka 38/40; ⊙7am-9pm; Ⓢ Universytet), a five-minute walk from the station, next to Hotel Express. You can also train tickets from Kiy Avia.

Kyiv Metro

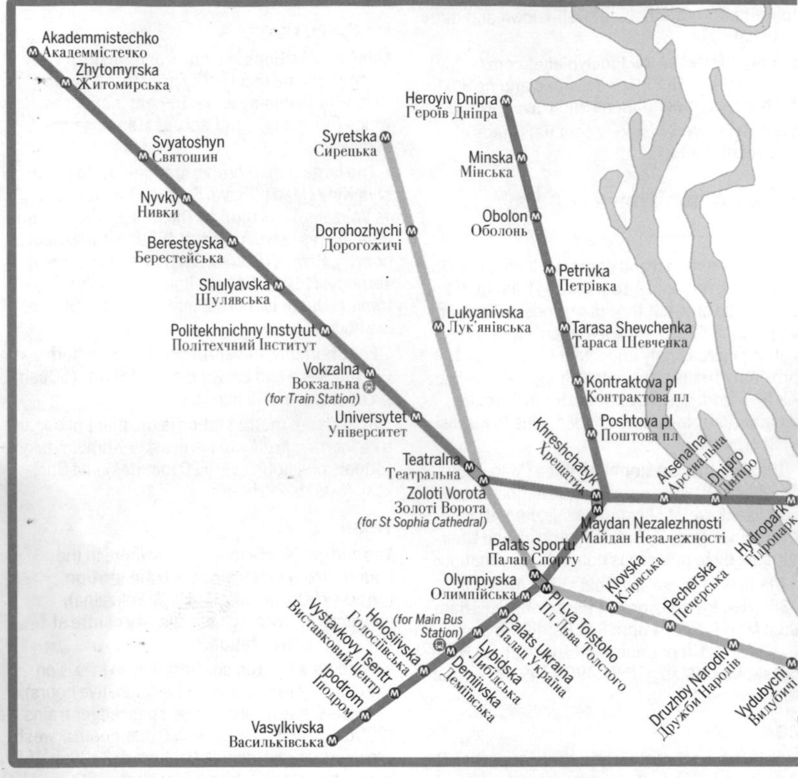

Getting Around

TO/FROM THE AIRPORT

Catching a Skybus is the usual way to Boryspil International Airport (40uah, 45 minutes to one hour). Buses depart from behind Kyiv train station's South Terminal every 15 minutes during the day and half-hourly during the night.

One way to save considerable time on the way to the airport during rush hour is to take the metro to Kharkivska metro station. Skybus stops under the bridge to collect passengers. The same trick works leaving the airport, as all buses stop at Kharkivska metro on their way to the train station.

Taxis into town from the airport cost around 300uah if arranged at the airport taxi desk. Use that price as a benchmark for negotiating with the myriad freelance drivers, which you can bargain down to 200uah. For travelling to the airport from the city it's better to order a taxi by phone.

For Zhulyany airport, take trolleybus 22 from Shulyavska or Dorohozhychi metro stations.

TO/FROM THE TRAIN STATION

The taxi drivers hanging out by the train station can be the biggest rip-off artists in Kyiv, typically charging 100uah for what should be a 40uah ride into the city centre. Avoid them by walking five minutes to bul Tarasa Shevchenka, or better yet, save money by taking the metro.

CAR

All the major car-rental players and various minor ones are represented at both airports and in central Kyiv.

PUBLIC TRANSPORT

Although often crowded, Kyiv's metro is clean, efficient, reliable and easy to use if you read Cyrillic. It is also the world's deepest, requiring escalator rides of seven to eight minutes! Trains run frequently between around 6am and midnight on all three lines. Blue-green plastic tokens *(zhetony)* costing 2uah (good for one ride) are sold by cashiers and token dispensers at metro station entrances. But their days are numbered as the authorites are planning to switch to a

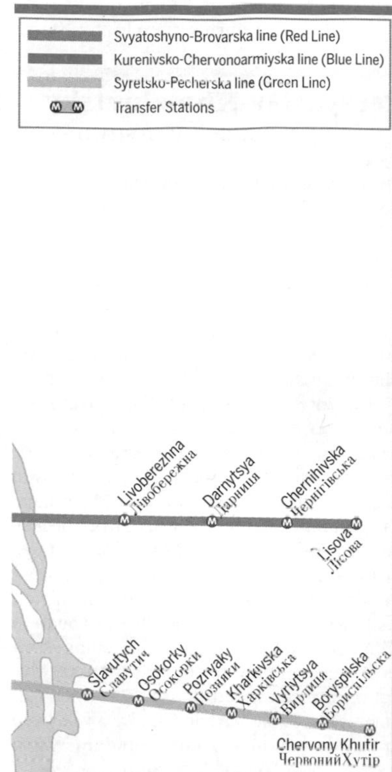

more flexible zone-based system of payment. You can avoid the easy-to-lose tokens by getting a plastic card for 7uah, which can be topped up using terminals also available at every station.

Buses, trolleybuses, trams and many quicker *marshrutky* serve most routes. Tickets for buses, trams and trolleybuses cost 1.5uah and are sold at street kiosks or directly from the driver/conductor. *Marshrutky* rides cost 2.5uah plus.

TAXI

Taxi prices in Kyiv are cheap by world standards. Expect to pay 30uah to 45uah for short (less than 5km) trips within central Kyiv. Locals prefer booking taxis by phone – they arrive fast and you know the price in advance; ask your hotel reception for assistance. To do it yourself, you need to speak some Ukrainian/Russian and know the exact addresses of your departure point and destination – saying something like 'drop me off at Maydan' won't get you anywhere. If you dial a taxi service, they usually hang up and call you back immediately. **Troyka** (☎237 0047, 233 7733) is a reliable call centre working with several taxi companies.

If you flag a taxi in the street – as people still do – always agree on the price before getting inside, unless it is an official metered taxi. Taking standing taxis from outside hotels, as well as train and bus stations, inevitably incurs a much higher price.

AROUND KYIV

Kyiv lies in the heart of the woodsy Polissya region. Outdoor types can have a field day camping, canoeing, fishing and *shashlyking* (BBQ-ing) in the forests that roll northwest and northeast of Kyiv along the Desna and Teteriv Rivers. Life isn't complicated in these parts; people work the land and fish the streams, and when it's time to relax, they head to the woods or, in winter, the *banya* (bathhouse): Some say this region epitomises the 'real Ukraine' and, frankly, it would be hard to argue with that.

Pereyaslav-Khmelnytsky and Kaniv are feasible as a single two-day trip or separate one-day trips, and Bila Tserkva is an easygoing jaunt into small-town Ukraine. Closer to the city, Vyshhorod and the Kyiv Sea make for a half day or longer flit into the sticks. However, in recent years Chornobyl has become a very popular excursion out of Kyiv. For extended details on tours to the site of the world's worst nuclear accident, see Visiting Chornobyl (p26).

Bila Tserkva Біла Церква

☎04563 / POP 211,000

Some 80km south of Kyiv, the drowsy town of Bila Tserkva is an easy and rewarding day trip out of the capital, especially for those who appreciate a little faded aristocratic splendour and a chance to picnic.

Founded by Yaroslav the Wise in 1032 as Yuriev, the town's main claim to historical fame is that Cossack Hetman (Leader) Bohdan Khmelnytsky signed the Treaty of Bila Tserkva with the Polish-Lithuanian commonwealth here in 1651 after defeat in the battle of Bila Tserkva. In the 18th century the estate was owned by the influential Polish Branicki family who created most of the town's places of interest.

Marshrutky from Kyiv deposit arrivals a beeswax candle's throw from the **Spaso-Preobrazhensky Cathedral** (vul Gagarina), which has a much more atmospheric interior than the rather plain 1830s exterior might suggest. The complex is surrounded by attractive gardens and there's a kids' playground in one corner.

A five-minute walk north from the cathedral lies the town's former epicentre, **Torgova pl**, where you can wander the now semi-deserted early-19th-century **covered market** (Torgovy Ryad). Lenin stands nearby, his back turned to this erstwhile snake's nest of capitalism.

Having wandered the rather focus-less centre, you may be wondering why you came – well, board trolleybus 1 or 4 to the Oleksandriya (Олександрія) stop to find out. Bila Tserkva's wonderful **Dendropark Oleksandriya** (Дендропарк Олександрія; entrance on bul Peremohy; admission 10uah; ⏲8am-10pm) is Ukraine's largest landscaped park and almost gives Uman's Sofiyivka a run for its money. However, it's a much less trumpeted attraction with far fewer visitors (most people in Kyiv have never heard of the place). The park derives its name from Aleksandra von Engelhardt, Potemkin's niece and wife of Poland's Crown Hetman (head of the Polish army) Ksawery Branicki, who in the mid-18th century commissioned French garden architects to create the 200-hectare chunk of greenery and fill it with follies, bridges, glades and pieces of sculpture.

Today the park's quietly overgrown woods, wandering sandy pathways and scattered bits of crumbly architecture provide ample opportunity for getting lost and picnicking with the locals. Where Polish silk dresses once rustled and aristocratic canes crunched on gravel paths, now headscarved *babushkas* march entrusted grandchildren on health walks and couples smooch on park benches, but the style and romantic megalomania of the Polish nobility still shines through in faded lustre.

Kartografiya maps of Bila Tserkva (10uah) are available from all news kiosks and include a map of the Dendropark Oleksandriya.

Reaching Bila Tserkva is simple enough – *marshrutky* (25uah, 1¼ hours) line up near Lybidska metro station (to the left of Ocean Plaza facing the building). Some also leave less often from outside Kyiv train station. Heading back, there's a special station dedicated solely to Kyiv-bound *marshrutky* located at the intersection of vuls Gagarina and Knyazya Volodymyra. For a bottom-numbing adventure on the Ukrainian rails, a commuter train (9uah, 2½ hours) leaves Kyiv's train station at 7.16am heading for Myronivka. The return service is at 2.50pm.

Pereyaslav-Khmelnytsky
Переяслав-Хмельницький

☎04567 / POP 28,300

The 'museum city' of Pereyaslav-Khmelnytsky was the hometown and stronghold of Cossack leader Bohdan Khmelnytsky, and also where he signed the infamous agreement accepting Russia's overlordship of Ukraine on 18 January 1654.

Today the whole town, with its 23 museums, has been declared a historical preserve. The highlight is the truly brilliant outdoor **Mid-Dnipro Museum of Folk Architecture & Life** (Музей народної архітектури та побуту Середньої Надніпрянщини ; www.niez-pereyaslav.com.ua; vul Litopisna 2; admission 15uah; ⏲10am-5pm), with around 70 heritage wooden buildings brought here from nearby villages and clustered tightly on 32 hectares of forested land. Some of them are turned into little thematic museums, in which case visitors have to pay another 3uah to 5uah to enter. But you get to see some gems, such as the charmingly retro-Soviet **Bread Museum**; the childhood house of leading Yiddish writer Sholem Aleichem, who was born in Pereslav; and the **Space Museum**, which occupies a wooden village church.

When you arrive at the bus station, it's wise to take a taxi (30uah), which goes via an 8km roundabout route to the park's main entrance. You can then exit through the opposite gate and find your way into town. Alternatively, walk further along vul Bohdana Khmelnytskoho (the city's main street), passing some high-rise blocks on your left, until you see the Lenin statue. Turn right and follow vul Litopisna almost to the end, then turn left before it becomes a dirt track in the fields. It should take about 40 minutes from the station.

The churches and museums in the town centre are clustered near central pl Bohdana Khmelnytskoho. Here you'll find the **Ascension Monastery**, with two prominent churches, and nearby the 17th-century **St Michael's Church**, where an Orthodox church stood even before the Kyivan Rus converted to Christianity in 988.

Pereyaslav-Khmelnytsky is 90km southeast of Kyiv and makes an easy day trip – just catch one of the buses or *marshrutky* that depart every 20 to 40 minutes from outside Kharkivska, Borispilska or Chernihivska metro stations (all 20uah, one to 1½ hours).

From here you may find the odd *marshrutka* heading to Kaniv – a very pleasant 50km ride through Van Gogh–like sunflower- and haystack-filled landscapes and across the giant Kaniv dam on the Dnipro. Taxi drivers charge around 160uah.

Kaniv Канів

☎04736 / POP 26,700

When Taras Shevchenko, Ukraine's national poet, died in 1861, his famous poem *Zapovit* (Testament) requested his fellow countryfolk bury him on a hill overlooking the great Dnipro River where, after rising up and liberating the land, they could 'freely, and with good intent, speak quietly of him'.

Kaniv, 162km down the Dnipro from Kyiv, is the spot they chose. In 1925 the steep and scenic bluff overlooking the river, **Tarasova Hora**, was designated a State Cultural Preserve. On a hill above the mothballed river pier you'll find the poet's tomb, which is crowned with a tremendous statue of the man himself. There is an observation point in front with great views of the river, and 15 hectares of parkland to explore behind the statue. Behind the grave is the huge and surprisingly glitzy **Taras Shevchenko Museum** (Музей Тараса Шевченка; www.shevchenko-museum.com.ua; admission 10uah; 9am-3.45pm Tue-Sun), which prides itself on its interactive touchscreens, glass cases of first editions and big-print engravings of the moustachioed one himself.

Sleeping in Kaniv is a way of combining it with Pereyaslav-Khmelnytsky on a relaxed two-day trip. You can stay in the Spartan hotel **Tarasova Gora** (☎321 10, 322 72; vul Shevchenko 2), which is located right on the historical hill and was built on the orders of Soviet leader Nikita Khrushchev, who came back from a US trip overexcited about panel boards. The much fancier, 13-room **Knyazhya Hora** (☎095 283 3833, 315 88; www.knyazhahora.com.ua; vul Dniprovska 1; r 500-950uah; ❄📶) is located down by the river and offers immaculate, European-standard facilities.

Kaniv is just about doable as a long day trip from Kyiv. Kaniv buses (45uah, 3½ hours, at least hourly) depart from Kyiv's Vydubychi bus station. Tarasova Hora is about 7km south of the bus station. A taxi should cost around 25uah.

Vyshhorod & the Kyiv Sea

Вишгород & Київське море

☎04596 / POP 23,000

A royal residence in Kievan Rus times, the small town of Vyshhorod is at least as old as Kyiv, though today is no more than a dormitory town with a couple of pretty churches. Around 1km east of the town a dam holds back the Kyiv Sea, obviously not a sea at all but a 110km-long, 922 sq km reservoir extending north and supplying the capital with drinking water and some electricity generated by a hydroelectric power plant.

The normally placid waters of the Kyiv Sea are popular with yachtsmen and fishermen, but the forests reaching deep into Polissya and the mile after deserted mile of sandy beach are the real off-the-beaten-track reasons to come. Walks into the endless woods are popular with foraging locals, but the northern end is worryingly close to Chernobyl so be wary of picking mushrooms and berries.

The favourite spot of Princess Olga a millennium ago, royalty has returned to the Vyshhorod area in recent years. About 3km up the coast from the dam rises one of the most controversial buildings in Ukraine – **President Yanukovych's residence**. Home to Soviet bigwigs until 1991, the residence was built on the site of the ancient Mezhyhiriya Monastery, which once overlooked the Dnipro. Yanukovych moved in when serving as prime minister, then, it's alleged, illegally 'privatised' the 137-hectare complex. Since then extensive building work has been taking place to bring the residence up to the standard expected by King Yanyk, with rumours abounding of solid-gold toilets, US$64,000 Lebanese cedar doors and a private zoo packed with exotic animals. It's Ukraine's very own Versailles and, like the palaces of the Arab world's erstwhile despots, a definite future tourist attraction when the day of reckoning comes for the Party of the Regions. You'd be lucky to get anywhere near the place today, however, and even locals need special passes to use the surrounding roads, Ukraine's smoothest and best maintained. Journalists trying to get snaps of the complex are often met by heavily armed special forces.

To reach Vyshhorod take the metro to Heroyiv Dnipra station in far northern Kyiv, from where *marshrutky* leave every few minutes.

Central Ukraine
Центральна Україна

POP 5.5 MILLION

Includes ➡

Best Places to Stay

➡ Reikartz Kamyanets-Podilsky (p83)

➡ Hotel 7 Days (p82)

➡ Reikartz Zhytomyr (p72)

➡ Hetman (p82)

Best Museums

➡ Nuclear Missile Museum (p78)

➡ Korolyov Cosmonaut Museum (p72)

➡ Pirogov Museum (p76)

➡ Podillya Antiquities Museum (p81)

Why Go?

Layered with dark fertile soil, Ukraine's breadbasket heartlands are split between forested Polissya to the north and the endless agricultural flatlands of Podillya to the south. Bucolic outdoor pleasures, some decidedly quirky museums and the show-stopping fortress town of Kamyanets-Podilsky are the odd mix of highlights provided by this often overlooked region.

Overlooked, that is, unless you are a Jewish pilgrim come to visit the tombs of Hasidic masters that dot the region. This was the birthplace of Hasidism and of the Jewish *shtetl* (village), both of which flourished within the Jewish Pale of Settlement, a demarcation line established by Catherine the Great in the 18th century to remove Jews from Russia and define the area they were allowed to inhabit. The Nazis obliterated practically every trace of Jewish culture here, with only the odd hauntingly abandoned Jewish cemetery remaining.

When to Go

Zhytomyr

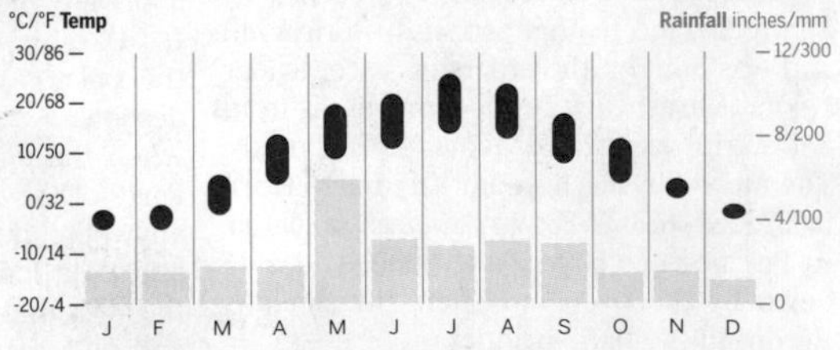

Aug Gaze in awe at central Ukraine's humungous sunflower fields in full bloom.

Sep Pick mushrooms and berries in the vast forests of Polissya.

Oct The most colourful time to visit Uman's romantic Sofiyivka Park.

POLISSYA

The woodsy, river-sliced region radiating out of Kyiv in all directions is known as Polissya. The bulk of the region lies north of Kyiv, extending into Belarus, and sees none of the tourist traffic of southern and western Ukraine. Those who do make it here are usually campers, mountain bikers, rock climbers, mushroom pickers, canoeists and the odd hunter. If you don't fit one of those categories, you might enjoy taking in Zhytomyr's Soviet-era small-town charm or exploring the rich Jewish history of Berdychiv, both west of Kyiv.

Zhytomyr Житомир

☎0412 / POP 277,900

Some 140km west of Kyiv, no other right-bank city evokes the Soviet Union more

Central Ukraine Highlights

1. Lay photographic siege to the medieval island town of **Kamyanets-Podilsky** (p79) and its dramatic fortress.
2. Take a riverside seat in Zhytomer to enjoy the aquatic light and sound show performed by the **Roshen Fountain** (p76), Ukraine's most spectacular water feature.
3. Get all spaced out at Zhytomyr's **Korolyov Cosmonaut Museum** (p72).
4. Amble around Uman's painfully romantic **Sofiyivka Park** (p74).
5. Watch devout Jewish pilgrims revere deceased Hasidic masters in **Berdychiv** (p73), **Uman** (p74) and **Bratslav** (p79).
6. Be careful what buttons you push at the **Nuclear Missile Museum** (p78).

than Zhytomyr. With its well-tended Lenin and Marx monuments, its plinthed tank and wreathed war memorials, wandering old trolleybuses and a fascinatingly nostalgic space museum, Zhytomyr has a kind of time-warped provincial charm that makes it just worth leaving Kyiv to see – but only for a day trip.

Sights & Activities

Korolyov Cosmonaut Museum MUSEUM
(Музей Космонавтики ім. С. П. Корольова; ☎372 653; www.cosmosmuseum.info; vul Dmytrivska 5; admission 10uah; ⏲10am-1pm & 2-5.15pm Tue-Sun) Named after acclaimed Soviet rocket engineer and local lad Sergei Korolyov, this surprisingly well-curated museum is famous across the former Soviet Union. Suitably space-aged music plays and fake stars glimmer as you walk around a dark hall packed with assorted mementos of the Soviet space program, including several satellites, a lunar ranger and an actual Soyuz rocket. More amusing exhibits include black-and-white photos of dogs the Soviets propelled into space, sachets and tubes of real space food (cottage cheese, mashed potato!), and a section on the Soviet space shuttle that literally never got off the ground. All in all, not bad for a country that struggled to produce reliable combustion engines and functional plumbing.

The house where Korolyov was born, now a museum (same hours) dedicated to his life, is directly across the street from the museum, but is of little interest to foreign visitors.

To reach the museum, from maydan Rad head along vul Velika Berdychivska for two blocks until you reach vul Ivana Franka. Turn left here and continue for 400m until you see the museum on your right.

St Sophia's Church CHURCH
(vul Kafedralna) With its distinctive ochre-and-white exterior, double clock towers and lavish interior, this small church dating from 1746 is a must-see for fans of baroque architecture.

Gagarin Park PARK
Flanking the Teteriv River about 1.5km south of the city centre, this park is a hive of activity in the summer months and serves up great views of the river gorge and the forest beyond, accessible via the Berdychivsky bridge over the gorge. To reach the park from maydan Rad, follow bul Stary from ul Velika Berdychivska to its southern terminus (around 1km).

Lenin Statue STATUE
(maydan Soborny) The city's main square is dominated by a giant Lenin apparently emerging from a lump of bedrock. Over two decades since the collapse of the Soviet Union, it's still as well cared for as ever.

Sleeping & Eating

Reikartz Zhytomyr HOTEL $$
(☎255 8910; www.reikartz.com; maydan Zamkovy 5/8; s/d from 480/560uah; ❄📶) Throughout the post-Soviet era Zhytomyr has been in desperate need of European-standard quarters – and now it has them in the shape of a slick Reikartz operation. The latest addition to this home-grown chain offers perfectly appointed rooms in soothingly coordinated fabrics and woods, pin-clean bathrooms and amiable, English-speaking staff, all somewhat in stark contrast to what you may experience outside its doors.

Hotel Ukraina HOTEL $$
(готель Україна; ☎472 999; vul Kyivska 3; s/d 250/400uah) All the rooms here have undergone de-Sovietisation, though the resulting sofa-dominated rooms, bedecked in translucently shimmering synthetic curtains and 'busy' carpetry, could hardly be described as soothingly 21st century. For those looking for a touch of USSR nostalgia, some balconies have views overlooking the Lenin statue on maydan Soborny. Breakfast included.

Chas Poyisty CANTEEN $
(Час Поїсти; pl Peremohy 3; meals around 25uah; ⏲9am-10pm Mon-Fri, 9am-10am Sat & Sun) When it's 'time to eat' (a translation of the name), join the feeding frenzy at this cheap, quick and painless self-service canteen just across from the mounted tank on pl Peremohy. Serves all the usual favourites from across the ex-USSR, plus decent coffees and beers.

Schultz BEER HALL $$
(www.schulz.ua; vul Peremohy 1; mains 40-110uah; ⏲11am-last customer) This underground Ukrainian interpretation of a Czech microbrewery restaurant feels more like an American bar abutting a subterranean chemical plant (no romantic copper brewing vats here). But the service is pleasant, the meat-heavy menu tasty and the commendable wheat beer and dark ale, both brewed on the premises, go down a treat on scorching days.

UKRAINE'S WORLD HERITAGE SITES

There are now seven Unesco World Heritage Sites in Ukraine (http://whc.unesco.org/en/statesparties/ua), although another 15 have been nominated for future consideration, with the town of Kamyanets-Podilsky one of the strongest candidates for inclusion. The six already inscribed on the list include three transnational entries.

The Danube Delta Biosphere Reserve is also part of Unesco's global network of biosphere reserves.

St Sophia's Cathedral and Kyevo-Pecherska Lavra A joint entry from Kyiv.

Lviv Lviv's historic centre made the list in 1998.

Primeval Beech Forests of the Carpathians Consisting of 10 separate patches of forest stretching from Rakhiv into Slovakia.

Struve Geodetic Arc A chain of scientific survey markers (1816–55) in a long arc from Norway to the Black Sea.

Wooden churches of Ukraine and Poland Sixteen old timber churches in the Carpathian Mountains received Unesco protection in 2013.

Residence of Bukovinian and Dalmatian Metropolitans Makes up a large part of the university of Chernivtsi.

Getting There & Away

The simplest way to make Zhytomyr a day trip from Kyiv is to take a (virtually) nonstop *marshrutka* (fixed-route minibus; 40uah, 1½ hours) from outside the main train station. These arrive at and depart from Zhytomyr's bus station, a short trolleybus ride from the city centre. Other *marshrutky* leave from Kyiv's Zhytomyrska metro station (near the western end of the red line) and Dachna bus station but are harder to track down. Most other public buses (frequent) and trains (sporadic) to and from Kyiv take much longer (three to four hours). Heading back to Kyiv, *marshrutky* leave on a rolling basis from right in front of the bus-station building.

Berdychiv Бердичів

☎04143 / POP 86,200

You'd never guess today that this sleepy town on the southern edge of Polissya was once an important intellectual centre and hotbed of Jewish culture. At the turn of the 19th century, Berdychiv's population was more than 80% Jewish. The Nazis took care of that, murdering just about every one of the city's 39,000 Jews and burying them in mass graves on the town's outskirts. These days Berdychiv's Jewish community numbers only several hundred, but the city remains an important pilgrimage site for followers of revered Hasidic master Levi Yitzhak (1740–1810), who is buried in the town's remarkable Jewish cemetery.

The website www.berdichev.org is a good resource for information on the town.

Sights

Jewish Cemetery CEMETERY

(vul Lenina) Levi Yitzhak's mausoleum is in Berdychiv's eerie, overgrown Jewish Cemetery. While the mausoleum itself has been looked after, several-hundred odd boot-shaped tombstones lie hideously askew and virtually hidden by weeds, neglected almost to the point of disbelief. Many tombstones, etched with barely legible Hebrew inscriptions, lie flat on the ground. The graves predate the Nazis by at least several decades, but it was the Nazis who sealed the cemetery's fate by leaving no Jews behind to care for it.

A walk through the cemetery is moving and awe-inspiring. The effect is magnified by the solitude of the place. Despite its sorry state, it has fared better than the many Jewish cemeteries in Ukraine that have been buried and lost forever. It is thus a symbol of defiance and a powerful, important and rare reminder of the country's rich pre-Holocaust Jewish past.

The cemetery is about 15 minutes' walk north of Berdychiv's town centre just beyond where a set of train lines cross the main road to Zhytomyr. The entrance is across from a petrol station.

BERDYCHIV'S KILLING FIELDS

Those who are interested can try to hunt down the two **mass burial sites** that lie outside the town. The first one is about 3km west of the Berdychiv Castle monastery complex on the Khmelnytsky Hwy. A memorial on the right side of the highway commemorates the 18,640 'Soviet citizens' killed here in September 1941 – like all Soviet Holocaust monuments it makes no mention of Jews. The actual burial site, marked by a plaque with Hebrew writing, is hidden under a clump of low-lying trees about 150m into the cow pasture behind the Soviet plaque. A second burial site, where another 18,000 Jews died, is a further 1km towards Khmelnytsky on the left side of the highway. At both sites the Nazis shot their victims in the back of the head and let their slumped bodies fall into pre-dug pits.

Berdychiv Castle MONASTERY
(Soborna pl) The impressive brick-walled complex hogging the horizon as you approach Berdychiv from Khmelnytsky is widely known as the castle *(krepost)*, but it's actually a 17th-century Carmelite monastery. The fortress-like defensive walls and towers were built in the late 18th century. Sadly, it's not open to the public.

St Barbara Church CHURCH
(vul Karalipnika) Berdychiv has links to two great 19th-century literary figures: Joseph Conrad was born in Berdychiv (1857), and Honoré de Balzac (of all people) was married to Polish noblewoman Ewelina Hańska (1850) in this rose-tinted neoclassical church. Look out for the brass plaque celebrating the latter event.

Sleeping

Berdychiv is best visited as a day trip from, or en route to, Vinnytsya or Zhytomyr. If you do want to stay the night there's only one place to bed down, so book ahead if you can.

Hotel Mirabella HOTEL $
(готель Мірабелла; ☎409 70; vul Lenina 20; r standard/deluxe 250/350uah) Well located within walking distance of the Jewish Cemetery, Berdychiv's sole lodgings boast unimaginative rooms with satellite TV hook-up and fridge, an erratic hot-water supply but quite helpful staff.

Getting There & Away

Several buses an hour head this way from Zhytomyr (15uah, one hour), terminating at Berdychiv's Central bus station. However, the station is a long way from anywhere so ask to be dropped off in the town centre. There are buses or *marshrutky* at least every hour to Vinnytsya (31uah, two hours) and Kyiv (60uah, 3½ hours).

PODILLYA

Podillya is the borderland within the country whose name means 'borderland'. Podillya is the bridge between the stolid, Russia-leaning east and the pro-European south. A swing district politically, topographically it's more predictable: flat and agricultural. The iconic image of bright blue sky over vast wheat field (possibly the inspiration for the colours of the Ukrainian flag) is practically inescapable here. But Podillya is not all farms and flatlands. Castle hunters will find business to attend to in the region's southern half, particularly in the 'rock island' city of Kamyanets-Podilsky. And there are a handful of unusual sites, including a Hitler bunker and a missile museum, scattered about the region for those with time, stamina and patience to explore.

Uman Умань

☎04744 / POP 86,900

All roads in Ukraine seem to pass through this central hub, home of relentlessly idyllic Sofiyivka Park and the final resting place of the revered Hasidic Rabbi Nachman of Bratslav. Visiting Uman is a perfect way to break up the journey between Kyiv and Odesa, or in a pinch, the town can be visited as a long day trip from either city. Beyond the park and the tomb, this is one of many places in Ukraine where time seems to have stopped c 1985.

Sights

Sofiyivka Park PARK
(☎322 10; www.sofiyivka.org.ua; vul Sadova; adult/child 25/15uah; ⏲9am-6pm May–mid-Nov) Sofia Pototsky was a legendary beauty, and Uman's stunning park is her husband Count Felix's monument to her physical perfection. Having bought Sofia for two million

zloty from her former husband (she had been sold into slavery at an early age by her parents), the Polish count set to landscaping this 150-hectare site with grottoes, lakes, waterfalls, fountains, pavilions and 500 species of tree. The result, completed in 1802, was Ukraine's answer to Versailles.

A map at the park entrance describes the history of the park in English and points the way to the various highlights, most bearing sentimental names like **Island of Love** and **Grotto of Venus**. The park is such a superlative piece of landscape architecture that you do not need to be a park lover to appreciate it. In summer you can hire boats to traverse the park's many ponds. As it turns out, Sofia broke Felix's heart before he died, having an affair with his son.

Tours of the park are available in English (480uah). However, these are tediously detailed, so only commit if you're really interested. The park is about a 10-minute walk from central Uman, down vul Sadova.

Rabbi Nachman's Tomb TOMB
(vul Pushkina) To visit the tomb of Rabbi Nachman, head towards Sofiyivka Park, and about halfway down vul Sadova, turn right onto vul Pushkina.

Sleeping & Eating

During Rosh Hashana most Uman residents rent out their flats to pilgrims or tourists.

Fortetsya HOTEL $
(готельний комплекс Фортеця; ☎500 41; www.fortecya.biz; vul Chapaeva 52; s 240uah, d 300-330uah; 📶) Located around 100m south of the main vul Radyanska, this relatively freshly hatched hotel complex offering 57 rooms is a welcome alternative to the town's Soviet flea pits. Living quarters are gaudy and cheaply furnished by Western standards, but they're clean and functional, and breakfast is included in the room rate – surprising given the low prices here.

Hotel Sofiyivka HOTEL $
(готель Софіївка; ☎33 527; vul Sadova 53; dm/s/d from 75/200/300uah) This faded number has seen only token renovations since the 1980s, but the location next to the park entrance is a major drawcard. The hilarious price list posted at reception features 'rooms without comfort' (a direct translation of the Russian for 'without bathroom') – perhaps someone should point out this linguistic faux pas (we didn't). The restaurant often heaves with Uman's shaven-headed and short-skirted celebrating weddings to a techno beat.

Shynok Kadubok UKRAINIAN $
(Шинок Кадубок; vul Radyanska 7; mains around 20uah; ⏰noon-11pm; 📶) On the east side of Uman Hotel, this cafe-cum-restaurant serves Ukrainian and Russian classics including tasty *borshch* in a faux rural setting.

Celentano PIZZERIA $
(vul Radyanska 15; pizzas around 25uah; ⏰10am-10pm) Ukraine's ubiquitous pizza chain is a blessing in restaurant-starved Uman.

Getting There & Away

Uman is located 210km south of Kyiv and 280km north of Odesa. Most Autolux and other buses between the two cities stop at Uman's bus station. To and from Kyiv (95uah, three hours), these buses are a better option than private *marshrutky* from the main bus station or train station, as the journey time is around the same. Buses take around four hours to reach Odesa (80uah). There are also regular services to/from Vinnytsya (62uah, three hours, up to three hourly).

PILGRIMS FLOCK TO PODILLYA

Ever since the death of Rabbi Nachman (1772–1810), Jewish pilgrims have flocked to his graveside in Uman every Jewish New Year (Rosh Hashana) to pay homage to this 18th-century sage who founded the Breslov branch of Hasidism.

The rabbi was born in Medzhybizh, made his name in Bratslav (Breslov), near Vinnytsya, and died of tuberculosis in Uman at the young age of 38. On his deathbed, Nachman promised his followers that he would save and protect anyone who came to pray beside his tomb. Today some 20,000 Jews answer his call at Rosh Hashana, and at any time of year you'll find a handful of devout worshippers – male and female – praying at his gravesite.

Pilgrimages also take place to the grave of the Baal Shem Tov (Besht), Rabbi Nachman's grandfather and the founder of Hasidism, in Medzhybizh; to Levi Yitzhak's grave in Berdychiv; and to Bratslav.

Vinnytsya Вінниця

☎0432 / POP 370,100

Straddling a kink in the Pivdenny Buh River, Vinnytsya is a city that's come on in leaps and bounds in recent years. Commendably digestible museums, hotels amid renovation, odd bits of street sculpture, a tourist office, quaint little trams (bought secondhand from Zurich) and the new Roshen Fountain have all made the experience of visiting this regional centre a much more pleasant affair than was the case a decade ago.

The city famously plays host to the embalmed body of a renowned Russian doctor and to one of Hitler's bunkers, but its true appeal lies in its city centre, where several churches, a park and a pleasant pedestrian street compete for the attention of travellers. Vinnytsya is also a convenient jumping-off point for some interesting excursions in southern Podillya.

Sights & Activities

★Roshen Fountain FOUNTAIN

(Фонтан Roshen; www.roshen.com; nab Roshen; shows 9pm May-Oct) FREE Ask any Ukrainian a few years ago what he or she considered Vinnytsya's biggest attraction, and the answer would probably have been the Pirogov Chapel. But not anymore. Since 2011 the Roshen Fountain, set directly in the river, has taken over as the city's must-see and it's easy to see why. Built by the Roshen chocolate company next to its shiny new factory (billionaire owner and Ukrainian Willy Wonka, Petro Poroshenko, was brought up in Vinnytsya), it's the biggest floating fountain in Europe and is a truly amazing spectacle when in full *son-et-lumière* mode. The shows are free, there's ample seating (with special wheelchair areas!) and the acoustics are impressive. Vinnytsya's biggest water feature warms up and flexes it muscles during the day, but it's well worth sticking around until 9pm to see the full spectacle.

The fountain was voted 'Ukrainian Structure of the Year' in 2012.

Pirogov Chapel TOMB

(vul Pyrohova 195; admission 10uah, combined with Pirogov Museum 50uah; 10am-7pm) The second-most famous embalmed corpse in the former Soviet Union (after Lenin in Moscow) rests in the basement of a chapel in the suburb of Pyrohove about 6.5km southwest of central Vinnytsya. Nikolai Pirogov was a Russian medical pioneer who invented a type of cast as well as a revolutionary anaesthesia technique. His wife had him embalmed when he died in Vinnytsya in 1881 and chose the chapel as his final resting place. The body is said to be much better preserved than Lenin's younger corpse. Without question one of Ukraine's oddest sites. Take bus 13 or *marshrutka* 70 or 48.

Pirogov Museum MUSEUM

(vul Pyrohova 155; admission combined with Pirogov Chapel 50uah; 10am-7pm) About 1.5km before you get to the chapel containing Pirogov's body, you can see his house, now a museum. It's actually more interesting than you'd expect, and not just because of the Soviet character of the place (the Soviets claimed Pirogov as a hero many years after his death because his inventions saved countless lives in the world wars). The doctor's anatomical sketches are also quite interesting, and one room remains unchanged from the surgeon's era. Bus 13 or *marshrutka* 70 or 48 pass the entrance on their way to the suburb of Pyrohove.

Regional Museum MUSEUM

(Краэзнавчий музей; www.muzey.vn.ua; vul Soborna 19; admission 10uah; 10am-6pm Tue-Sun) This large and diverse museum is well worth an hour or two for its interesting archaeological artefacts, bug-eyed taxidermy and large WWII exhibition with Soviet propaganda posters galore. Other highlights include a 30,000-year-old mammoth skeleton, pieces of Scythian gold ornament and some Scythian-era stone figures.

Avtomotovelofototeleradio Museum MUSEUM

(Автомотовелофототелерадио музей; vul Soborna 1; admission 10uah; 11am-7pm Tue-Sun) Big name for a small museum but worthwhile for anyone with a wistful soft spot for the days of Soviet mass production. This octagonal building near the main bridge over the river (on the city-centre side) houses some interesting classic cars (Trabant, Zaporozhets, Moskvich, Lada), as well as clunky old Soviet TVs, radios, gramophones, cameras and other assorted junk.

Orange Revolution Monument MONUMENT

(maydan Nezalezhnosti) Vinnytsya's epicentre is maydan Nezalezhnosti (Independence

WEHRWOLF

WWII buffs might fancy a trip out to the remains of Hitler's forward bunker, 8km north of Vinnytsya and 500m to the east of the town of Stryzhavka. Hitler visited this bunker a couple of times (accounts vary) between May 1942 and July 1943. Presumably it was on one of these visits that he ordered the execution of the 15,000 Ukrainian slave labourers who built the complex – he was ostensibly worried that they would spill the beans about the bunker's location. At its peak the Wehrwolf complex consisted of three bunkers and 20 standing structures, complete with swimming pool, movie theatre and casino. The Nazis blew it all up on their retreat in 1944. Today there's not a whole lot to see here besides some large concrete fragments of the bunker in an otherwise empty field – which is arguably more affecting than the typical Soviet monument. To get here take a taxi (for about 60uah return) from Vinnytsya or ask at Vinnytsya's tourist office about tours and guides.

Sq), where major demonstrations and meetings were held during the 2004 Orange Revolution. A rather inconspicuous monument on its western side keeps alive the memory of those heady days.

War Veterans Museum MUSEUM
(admission 3uah; ⏲10am-6pm Tue-Sun) The red-brick clock tower at the end of pedestrian vul Kozytskoho houses an interesting museum, where you'll find tributes to the 167 young local men who made the ultimate sacrifice in the Soviet-Afghan War.

Transfiguration Church CHURCH
(Свято-Преображенський кафедральний собор; vul Soborna 23) This light-yellow, gold-domed church dating from 1758 is worth checking out for its dim and atmospheric painted interior.

Sleeping

Vinnytsya HOTEL $
(готель Вінниця; ☎610 332; vul Soborna 69; s/d from 195/294uah) A member of the once prestigious Savoy group (along with the Ukraina across the road), the Vinnytsya is quite a good deal. Even the cheapest rooms are clean and comfortable, and (in places skin-deep) renovation efforts are in evidence throughout. High ceilings and extras such as a minibar and in-room phones make this place feel decidedly un-Soviet.

Hotel Park HOTEL $$
(Парк Отель; ☎675 844; www.da-lucio.com; vul Hrushevskoho 28; d from 500uah; wi-fi) While Vinnytsya's hotel scene is in flux, the 15 rooms at this small hotel above a pizza place represent the best price-to-quality ratio. Some of the decor is a touch over the top (giraffe-print carpets, lime-green curtains) but everything is well maintained and spotless. Somewhat surprisingly, rates include breakfast. Staff speak little English.

Podillya HOTEL $$
(готель Поділля; ☎592 233; www.vintur.com.ua; vul Pushkina 4; s/d from 250/500uah; wi-fi) The Podillya has been threatening *'remont'* (modernisation) for years but so far has done very little actual de-Sovietisation of its rooms. The 4th floor has been renovated but is overpriced so go for the essentially USSR-era rooms anywhere else, survivable for a night or two. Full and half board available, and a decent tour agency lurks somewhere in the building.

Ukraina Hotel HOTEL $$$
(vul Kozytskoho 36) Occupying an opulent 19th-century Art Nouveau building in a prime location at the maydan Nezalezhnosti end of vul Kozytskoho, this grand old dame was undergoing a comprehensive refit at the time of research. It's set to reopen as sorely needed luxury-end lodgings by the time you read this. When it does, it will be the best place to stay between Kyiv and Lviv.

Eating

For a city of this size there are surprisingly few places to eat in the centre. The highly visible 'golden arches' just off maydan Nezalezhnosti are a blessing here, even if you ain't lovin' it.

Masay Mara CAFE $
(Масай Мара; vul Hrushevskoho 70; mains 15-35uah; ⏲9am-11pm Mon-Fri, 10am-11pm Sat & Sun) One of a handful of places along vul Hrushevskoho, this funky coffeehouse at

WORTH A TRIP

NUCLEAR MISSILE MUSEUM

It's not easy to find, but deep in Ukraine's agricultural heartland, 25km north of Pervomaysk, lies arguably Ukraine's coolest museum. The **Museum of Strategic Missile Forces** (Музей ракетних військ стратегічного призначення; ☎05161-732 18; www.rvsn.com.ua; admission 20uah; ⏰10am-5pm), better known among travellers as the Nuclear Missile Museum, was formerly a nuclear missile launch facility.

The highlight is the journey taking you 12 storeys underground in a Brezhnev-era elevator to the control room (extra 40uah), where you can't help thinking that once upon a time a simple push of a button could have ended civilisation as we know it. You can even sit at the desk of doom, hand hovering over the button, and pretend to take that fateful call on an old Soviet phone.

The facility controlled 10 missiles, each of which lay hidden in subterranean silos near the control room. In the grounds of the museum are four huge decommissioned intercontinental ballistic missiles (ICBM), including a 75ft SS-18 Satan rocket, the Soviets' largest ICBM. There were actually no Satan rockets at this complex and this particular specimen was hauled in from Baikanor, Kazakhstan. Ukraine's facility was for shorter-range missiles targeting Europe.

It's an intriguing museum, but there are no English guides and getting here is a pain. Most take a Mykolayiv- or Koblevo-bound bus from Kyiv to Pervomaysk (125uah, six hours, around 14 daily), then a taxi (60uah to 100uah) from there (if they can find one that has heard of the museum). On the way back some visitors walk back to the main road (P06) and flag down a vehicle heading south to Pervomaysk. The new museum website has maps of the exact location. Otherwise Kyiv's ever-enterprising tour companies (p27) have started running day trips to the museum.

the park gates has an African theme (think cave drawings and lots of rough-hewn wood), but the menu of light meals is firmly Eurasian. The outdoor seating draws a crowd in the evenings, as does the real fire in winter.

Celentano PIZZERIA $
(vul Soborna 43; pizzas around 20uah; ⏰10am-11pm) If you've been in the country a long time, you may have grown weary of Ukrainian-flavoured pizzas, but the Vinnytsya branch also does a good line in pancakes, salads and soups.

Self-Catering

Silpo Supermarket SUPERMARKET
(Сільпо; Sky Park shopping centre, entrances vul Soborna & vul Kozytskoho) There's a good Silpo Supermarket buried deep within the unexpectedly upmarket Sky Park shopping centre.

Shopping

Roshen FOOD
(Soborna 22) As well as selling mouthwatering slabs of chocolate and other tooth-rotting goodies, the Vinnytsya's Roshen shop has a fun mechanical puppet show in the window.

Information

Tourist Office (☎508 585; www.bashnya.vn.ua; Vinnytsya Tower, vul Kozytskoho 20; ⏰10am-7pm) Covering all of Podillya, this freshly minted tourist office can help you get to sights outside the city as well as supplying free maps and other information. Also runs a meet-and-greet service.

Getting There & Away

BUS

From the **Central bus station** (vul Kyivska 8) services fan out in all directions.

Berdychiv 27uah, 1½ hours, at least two hourly
Bratslav 20uah, 1½ hours
Kyiv 99uah, four hours, 10 daily
Uman 58uah, three hours, many daily
Zhytomyr 37uah, 2¾ hours, at least two hourly

For Kyiv you may be better off looking for a shared taxi (90uah, 3½ hours) from in front of the train station.

TRAIN

Vinnytsya is a major stop for many east–west trains, including some international services. Up to 18 passenger trains daily connect Vinnytsya with Kyiv (110uah, around three hours) and there are at least five services to Lviv (140uah, seven hours) and four to Odesa (100uah to 130uah, six to eight hours).

Getting Around

The train station is about 3km east of Vinnytsya's centre and is linked to it by trams 1, 4 and 6 as well as several trolleybuses. If arriving by bus, turn left out of the Central bus station and walk around 100m to pl Zhovtneva, from where any tram will take you into the city centre.

Around Vinnytsya

There are a couple of interesting side trips from Vinnytsya, especially if you are interested in Jewish heritage sites. The village of **Bratslav**, 50km southeast of Vinnytsya, is where Rabbi Nachman lived and wrote most of his teachings before moving to Uman. Several of Nachman's disciples are buried in a shrine-like **cemetery** on a lovely hillside overlooking a river. Jewish pilgrims allege that the graves have healing powers.

Southwest of Vinnytsya is the *shtetl* of **Sharhorod**. The *shtetl* originated in Ukraine and the one in Sharhorod is said be the best-preserved example in the country. But it may not be that way for long. Sharhorod's *shtetl* is dying; its 16th-century **fortress synagogue** (used as a liquor factory in Soviet times) and many of the houses clustered around it have been abandoned to the elements.

Sharhorod also has a sprawling **Jewish cemetery** with thousands of exquisitely carved tombstones, some dating as far back as the 17th century. To get to it, follow the lane to the right of the post office down the hill, bearing left and crossing the creek. Then follow the trail up the hill bearing left and you will see the black cemetery gate marked with three large Stars of David.

The tourist office in Vynnitsya can help you reach all of the above places.

Kamyanets-Podilsky
Кам'янець-Подільський

03849 / POP 103,000

Kamyanets-Podilsky is the sort of place that has writers lunging for their thesauruses in search of superlatives. Even words like 'dramatic', 'stunning' and 'breathtaking' just will not do. Like the Swiss capital of Bern, or Český Krumlov in the Czech Republic, the town is located where a sharp loop in a river has formed a natural moat. However, Kamyanets-Podilsky is much wilder and less commercial than these other places, and attracts a fraction of their visitor numbers.

The wide tree-lined Smotrych River canyon is 40m to 50m deep, leaving the 11th-century Old Town standing clearly apart on a tall, sheer-walled rock 'island'. According to an oft-told legend, when the Turkish Sultan Osman arrived to attack the town in 1621, he asked one of his generals, 'Who has built such a mighty town?' 'Allah', came the reply, to which the Sultan responded, 'Then let Allah himself conquer it', and bid a hasty retreat.

Split-personalitied K-P is really a tale of two cities – the noisy and slightly chaotic Soviet New Town, where most of the hotels are located, and the quieter Old Town, where all of the sights are gathered. Until recently the latter sometimes gave the impression of having been abandoned by the townsfolk c 1950 for the Soviet utopia across the river, but of late the locals have realised there might be money to be made from people called tourists visiting old stuff and the historical quarter has begun to receive a facelift (not always with desirable results). Another worrying phenomenon are the enormous walled *dachi* (cottages) being built by wealthy individuals slap-bang in the centre of town.

History

Named after the stone on which it sits, Kamyanets-Podilsky existed as early as the 11th century as a Kyivan Rus settlement. Like much of western Ukraine, the town spent periods under Lithuanian and Polish rule, with the latter dominating from the 15th to 17th centuries. Unlike much of western Ukraine, however, it fell briefly to the Ottoman Turks, who conquered it with a tremendous army in 1672 and ruled for 27 years. After being returned to Polish rule, Kamyanets-Podilsky was conquered in 1793 by the Russians. They used its fortress as a prison for Ukrainian nationalists. In 1919 the town became the temporary capital of the short-lived Ukrainian National Republic. During WWII the Germans used the Old Town as a Jewish ghetto, where an estimated 85,000 people died. Intensive fighting and air raids destroyed some 70% of the Old Town.

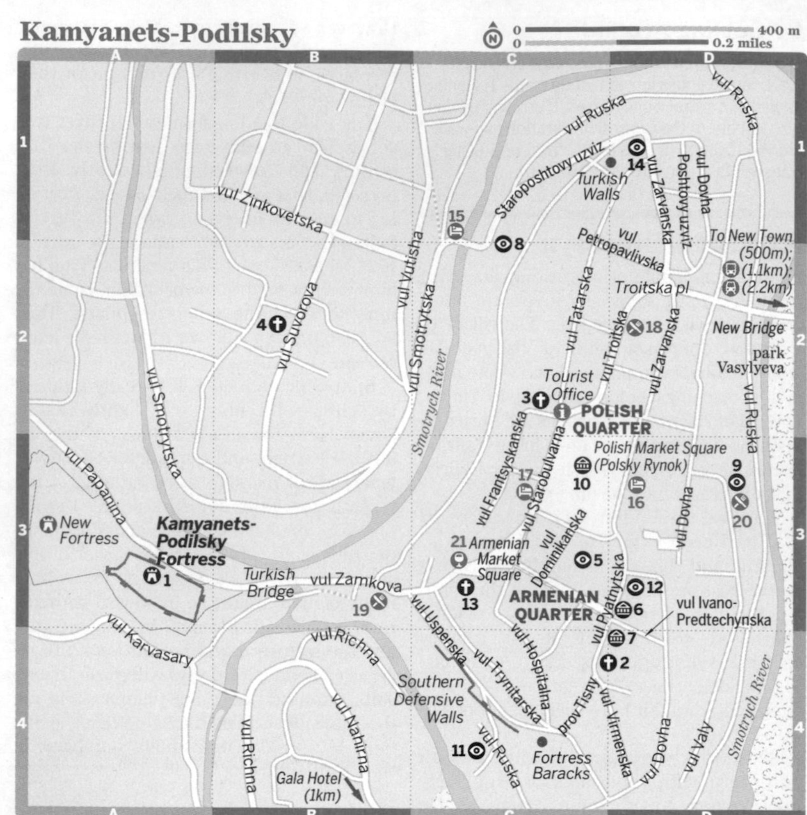

Sights

★Kamyanets-Podilsky Fortress FORTRESS

(adult/child 20/10uah; ⏲9am-8pm Tue-Sun, to 7pm Mon) Built of wood in the 10th to 13th centuries, then redesigned and rebuilt in stone by Italian military engineers in the 16th century, K-P's fortress is a complete mishmash of styles. But the overall impression is breathtaking, and if Ukraine ever gets its act together as a tourist destination, the view from the **Turkish Bridge** leading to the fortress will become one of the country's iconic, front-page vistas. The name of the bridge is slightly misleading, as it's essentially a medieval structure whose arches were filled in and fortified by Turks in the 17th century.

The fortress is in the shape of a polygon, with nine towers of all shapes and sizes linked by a sturdy wall. In the middle of it all is a vast courtyard. The **New East Tower** (1544) is directly to your right as you enter the fortress and contains a well and a huge winch stretching 40m deep through the cliff to bring up water.

Just beyond the New East Tower, an unmarked white building houses a fantastic **museum** that romps through the history of K-P and Ukraine over the last century in a jumble of nostalgia-inducing exhibits. Two revolutions bookend the collections, with the blood-red silken flags of 1917 looking symbolically more potent than the limp orange banners of 2004.

Polish Quarter

Under the medieval Magdeburg Laws, each of the Old Town's four major ethnic groups (Poles, Ukrainians, Armenians and Jews) occupied a different quarter. The focus of the old Polish Quarter is the Polish Market Sq (Polsky Rynok), the Old Town's main piazza

Kamyanets-Podilsky

Top Sights
1 Kamyanets-Podilsky Fortress A3

Sights
2 Armenian Church D4
3 Cathedral of SS Peter & Paul C2
4 Church of St George B2
5 Dominican Monastery C3
6 Picture Gallery D3
7 Podillya Antiquities Museum D4
8 Polish Gate C2
9 Potters' Tower D3
10 Ratusha C3
11 Ruska Gate C4
12 Russian Magistrate D3
13 St Jehoshaphat's Church C3
14 Vitryani (Windy) Gate D1

Sleeping
15 Bilya Richky C1
16 Hetman D3
17 Reikartz Kamyanets-Podilsky C3

Eating
18 Hostynny Dvir D2
19 Kafe Pid Bramoyu B3
20 Stara Fortetsya D3

Drinking & Nightlife
21 Kava Vid Politsmeystera C3

where you'll find the new tourist office and myriad souvenir stalls.

Cathedral of SS Peter & Paul CHURCH
(vul Starobulvarna) Through a small triumphal gate in the northwest corner of Polish Market Sq lies this fascinating cathedral, K-P's busiest place of worship. One feature of the building perfectly illustrates how the Polish and Turkish empires collided in Kamyanets-Podilsky. Built in 1580 by the Catholic Poles, the cathedral was converted into a mosque when the Turks took over in the late 17th century; they even built an adjacent 42m-high minaret. When the town was handed back to the Poles by treaty in 1699, the Turks specifically stipulated that the minaret could not be dismantled. So the Poles topped it with its current 3.5m-tall golden statue of the Virgin Mary instead.

Ratusha HISTORIC BUILDING
(Polsky Rynok) Polish Market Sq is lorded over by the tall 14th-century Ratusha (Town Hall). The renovated peach-hued building now houses three single-room museums that are of limited interest unless you are into coins, medieval justice or the Magdeburg legal system, but there is a decent bar on the ground floor. In front of the Ratusha stands the enclosed **Armenian well** (Вірменська криниця; 1638), which looks more like a baroque chapel than a well.

Dominican Monastery MONASTERY
(vul Dominkanska) Vul Dominikanska cuts south from Polish Market Sq, linking it with the Armenian Quarter. Here you'll find the Dominican Monastery complex, some parts of which date from the 14th century. The buildings suffered serious damage during WWII but are now under constant restoration. The monastery Church of St Nicholas holds services in Ukrainian and Polish throughout the day.

Armenian Quarter

The Armenian Quarter is centred around the quiet Armenian Market Sq, an elongated cobbled expanse to the south of the Polish Quarter. The Armenians are long gone, but the name remains.

Podillya Antiquities Museum MUSEUM
(vul Ivano-Predtechynska 2; admission 5uah; 10am-5pm Tue-Sun, to 4pm Mon) This imaginatively presented museum with English explanations takes visitors through the archaeology of Podillya in six easy steps. You begin in a Stone Age cave and end in a courtyard of sculpted Slavic gods, passing through Trypillian, Scythian and early Slav dwellings along the way. Slavophiles will appreciate the exhibit on the Glagolitic script (forerunner to today's Cyrillic alphabet).

Picture Gallery ART GALLERY
(Картинна галерея; vul Pyatnytska 11; admission 10uah; 10am-5pm Tue-Sun, 1to 4pm Mon) The permanent collections here are of wildly varying quality and some works are in downright wretched condition. But temporary exhibitions lift the mood and if the art on the walls doesn't impress, the elaborate parquet floors will.

Armenian Church CHURCH
(vul Virmenska) Huge, decorative wrought-iron gates keep prying tourists out of this set of 15th-century church ruins, its perimeter still weeping masonry onto the cobbles below.

The reconstructed defensive bell tower is now a small Ukrainian Orthodox chapel.

Russian Magistrate NOTABLE BUILDING
(Російський магістрат; vul Pyatnytska) There are some interesting old buildings on vul Pyatnytska, which branches off Armenian Market Sq. The large structure with a distinctive metal dragon projecting from its facade is the old Russian Magistrate, now the headquarters of **NIAZ Kamyanets** (НІАЗ Камянець; www.niazkamenec.org.ua), the body overseeing K-P's conservation area (which seems to have had limited success of late!).

St Jehoshaphat's Church CHURCH
(vul Starobulvarna) Heading towards the fortress along the main drag through the Old Town, you'll pass this baroque 18th-century Greek Catholic Church (formerly St Trinity's), fronted by sculptures of two saints who appear to be boogieing on down. The interior is disappointingly plain.

Festivals & Events

Kamyanets-Podilsky City Day CITY FESTIVAL
Held in mid-May; features concerts, folk performances, parades, fireworks displays and, of course, acres of souvenir stalls.

Sleeping

Gala Hotel HOTEL $
(383 70; www.gala-hotel.com; vul Lesi Ukrainky 84; d from 300uah;) This is a solid midrange choice with a wide range of rooms – from cupboard-sized twins to deluxe apartments with their own kitchens. It's about 15 minutes' walk south of the New Town.

Hotel 7 Days HOTEL $$
(690 69; www.7dniv.ua; vul Soborna 4; s/d from 240/420uah;) This immensely popular place in the New Town impresses from the moment you walk into the air-conditioned, design-style lobby. Staff speak English, the service is professional, and the room rate includes breakfast plus use of the swimming pool and fitness centre. Despite having 218 comfortable rooms, it's still advisable to book ahead. Bathrooms could do with an update here and there but overall it's a superb place to unzip your pack.

Hetman HOTEL $$
(готель Гетьман; 067 588 2215; www.hetman-hotel.com.ua; Polsky Rynok 8; r/ste from 400/900uah;) The mammoth rooms, great location in a town house on Polish Market Sq and easy-going staff make this atmospheric, 14-room theme hotel worth

AND THERE'S MORE...

Most visitors content themselves with a stroll from the New Bridge to the fortress and back, stopping off at a restaurant or cafe along the way. But if your legs are up to the job, there's so much more to explore in Kamyanets-Podilsky's run-down backstreets and lanes where forgotten chunks of the town's defences lurk.

Looking south from the New Bridge you can spot the 1583 **Potters' Tower** (Гончарська башта), so named because it was looked after by the town's potters. Twelve of these towers once lined the bank of the gorge along the perimeter of the island; seven or eight remain today.

At the northern edge of the Old Town is the still-functioning 16th-century **Vitryani (Windy) Gate** (Вітряні брама), where Peter the Great's hat blew off in 1711. Connected to the gate is the seven-storey stone **Kushnir (Furriers') Tower** (Кушнірська башта), a defensive structure funded by artisans who lived nearby. From the tower, Staroposhtovy uzviz turns southwest and descends steeply into the ravine down to the **Polish Gate** (Польська брама). This gate was named after the historic Polish section of the city, which was located on the other side of the river, built around the hill dominated by the 19th-century Orthodox **Church of St George** (Церква Св Юрія), with its five spires painted a brilliant azure.

Both the Polish Gate and the **Ruska Gate** (Руська брама), on the south side of the isthmus in the old Ruthenian (Ukrainian) Quarter, were built from the 16th to 17th centuries to guard the two most vulnerable entrances into the Old Town. Both gates were ingeniously fashioned with dyke mechanisms that could alter the flow of the Smotrych River and flood the entrances – an impressive engineering feat for the time.

Just across the river from the fortress stands the **Khrestovozdvyzhenska Church** (Хрестовоздвиженська церква), K-P's only remaining timber temple dating from 1799.

LOCAL KNOWLEDGE

QUEEN OF THE CASTLE

Iryna Pustynnikova is Ukraine's original castle hunter. She runs the website http://castles.com.ua and doles out castle-hopping itineraries to anybody who asks. We caught up with Iryna in her hometown, Kamyanets-Podilsky, and asked her to pick the top 10 lesser-known castles in Ukraine.

Czerwonogrod 'It's simply…wow! One hundred years ago the guidebooks called it the most beautiful manor in Poland. For me it's the most beautiful place in the whole country.' From the 14th to 19th centuries; near Nyrkiv, 50km north of Chernivtsi.

Sydoriv Castle 'It looks like an ocean liner sailing through a sea of maize and other vegetables.' Built in the 17th century; near Husyatyn, 60km northwest of Kamyanets-Podilsky.

Kudryntsi Castle 'The landscapes are unbelievable, the ruins are very scenic and vivid, and tourists are rare birds here.' Early 17th century; 22km west of Kamyanets-Podilsky.

Nevytske Castle 'Legend has it this very picturesque castle served as a shelter for Uzhhorod's girls – *nevesta* is the local word for "girl".' Built in the 16th century; 12km north of Uzhhorod.

Hubkiv Castle (Rivne oblast) 'It rises 32m over an area known as "Switzerland on the Sluch River". The views these castle ruins command are simply breathtaking. The fresh air that wafts forth from the surrounding forests inebriates the visitor like a good wine, and heals as well as any medicine.' From the 15th to 16th centuries.

Svirzh Castle 'This picturesque Renaissance castle stands in its own park and is surrounded by water. Watch out for the female ghosts that locals claim wander the grounds.' Built in the 16th century; 55km northeast of Lviv.

Starostynsky Castle 'None other than Batu-Khan (Genghis Khan's grandson, who led the Mongol invasion of Europe) put paid to the first fortress on this hill, overlooking the Dnister River.' Current building from 17th century; 23km north of Ivano-Frankivsk.

Olyka Castle 'In summer, flowers perfume the courtyard of this once noble residence, though today you're more likely to meet white-coated doctors and pale-faced patients rather than the aristocratic Radziwills here, as it's now part of a hospital.' Built between 16th and 18th centuries; halfway between Lutsk and Rivne.

Berezhany Castle 'This mighty, thick walled Renaissance castle is now the haunt of grazing cows and mums with prams, but is still an impressive sight. The Zolota Lypa River grips the castle on two sides.' Built between 16th and 18th centuries; 50km southwest of Ternopil.

Chynadiyeve Castle 'This striking building was once a hunting castle belonging to the Schönborn family. In the 1890s they gave it a pseudo Gothic makeover and transformed it into a grand residence.' Ten kilometres northeast of Mukacheve.

the extra hryvnya. The walls are lined with paintings of all Ukraine's Hetmans (Cossack heads of state), an 11m-long tapestry bearing the words of the national anthem hangs in the stairwell and the Ukrainian restaurant (mains 20uah to 55uah) serves five types of *borshch*.

Reikartz Kamyanets-Podilsky HOTEL $$
(☎916 35; www.reikartz.com; vul Starobulvarna 2; s/d from 650/750uah; ❄📶) K-P's plushest place to achieve REM is this Reikartz rebranded hotel, occupying a former Polish palace right in the thick of the Old Town. Not sure what the Polish *szlachta* (nobility) would make of the deep pile carpets, antique-style furniture and the baths in most rooms, but you'll love them. Bigger price just means bigger room here.

Bilya Richky HOTEL $$
(Біля Річки; ☎097 258 1734; www.hotel-kp.com.ua; vul Onufrievska 5; r 200-400uah; 📶🅿) Occupying an almost rural spot down by the river, a 10-minute walk from the Polish Market Sq, this family-run hotel has just 14 timber-rich rooms where you can rest weary limbs to a soundtrack of birdsong and the

trickle of flowing water. The Polish gate stands opposite and an anonymous chunk of the city's old defences forms part of the grounds. Owners can arrange horse-riding trips, English-language tours of K-P and full board. Breakfast is a very reasonable 15uah to 20uah extra.

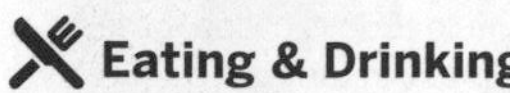

Eating & Drinking

Despite growing visitor numbers, K-P has few places to eat.

★ Kafe Pid Bramoyu UKRAINIAN $
(Кафе під брамою; vul Zamkova 1A; mains 15-45uah; ⌚9am-midnight) Located in the 17th-century casemates near the fortress, this is the town's most characterful place to fill the hole and a real treat in eatery-poor K-P. The small interior flaunts authentic dimly lit period character and is very atmospheric at night. There's a terrace with pretty views, tablecloths are pieces of traditional Ukrainian embroidery and waiting staff are done up in similarly folksy garb. The menu is a run-down of Ukrainian favourites.

Hunska Krytnytsa CANTEEN $
(Ханська критниця; vul Soborna 12; mains 6-18uah; ⌚8am-11pm) No-frills Ukrainian self-service canteen in the New Town serving basic belly fillers. In summer tables tumble out onto pedestrianised vul Soborna.

Hostynny Dvir UKRAINIAN $
(vul Troitska 1; mains 15-40uah; ⌚11am-11pm) Around for longer than anyone can remember remembering, this old favourite has a bearskin spreadeagled on one wall, slow service, a carnivore-friendly menu and a new summer terrace.

Stara Fortetsya UKRAINIAN $
(vul Valy 1; mains 15-40uah; ⌚11am-11pm) If you're after an evening snifter, what better place to enjoy it than out on the balcony of this place, perched dramatically on a 40m cliff over the gorge. The Ukrainian food served indoors is basic and cheap.

Kava Vid Politsmeystera BAR
(Кава від Поліцмейстера; vul Zamkova; ⌚10am-11pm) With cheap Lvivske *pyvo* (beer) on draught and a summer terrace, it's the best place in the Old Town for a drink.

Self-Catering

Yuvileynyy Supermarket SUPERMARKET
(Ювілейний; cnr vul Soborna & vul Lesi Ukrainky) The best supermarket anywhere near the city centre is Yuvileynyy, located in the new town.

Information

Post, Internet & Telephone Office (vul Soborna 9; internet per hr 6uah; ⌚post 9am-6pm Mon-Fri, to 4pm Sat, internet 8.30am-9pm Mon-Fri, 10am-10pm Sat & Sun)

Tourist Office (☎255 33; www.travelk-p.info; Polsky Rynok 18; ⌚9am-6pm) Brand-new English-speaking office with free maps and other information. The website is a work in progress.

Getting There & Away

BUS

Standard connections from Kamyanets-Podilsky:

Chernivtsi 32uah, 2½ hours, half-hourly to hourly

Khotyn 10uah, 45 minutes, at least two hourly

Kyiv 155uah, nine hours, around eight daily

Lviv 100uah, five to seven hours, four daily

Odesa 240uah, 12 hours, three daily (all overnight)

TRAIN

Express trains 173 (80uah, seven hours) and 177 (71uah, seven hours) from Kyiv are the quickest way to reach Kamyanets-Podilsky. They depart the capital at 11.39pm and 4.43pm. Bus is better for all other destinations.

Getting Around

The bus station is within walking distance (two blocks east) of the New Town centre. The train station is 1km north of the bus station. You can take bus/*marshrutka* 1 into the New or Old Towns.

JONATHAN SMITH/GETTY IMAGES ©

Ukrainian Gems

Ukraine may be Europe's biggest country, but that doesn't mean its highlights are thin on the ground. Whether it be man-made gems such as the country's Unesco-listed wooden churches, or nature's grand Crimean opus, there's a lot to point your camera at in Ukraine.

Contents

Above: Swallow's Nest (Lastochkino Gnezdo, p189), Crimea

Cultural Tapestry

Invasion, occupation and settlement from outside have bequeathed Ukraine a patchwork of cultures, from the woolly Hutsul traditions of the Carpathians to the exotic Middle Eastern world of the Crimean Tatars and the colourful Orthodox customs of the Slavic majority.

Pysanky

1 With their flashes of colour, intricate designs and pleasing shape, Ukraine's decorated eggs are an iconic symbol of traditional Slavic folk crafts. Kolomyya's Pysanky Museum (p131), itself housed in a monster egg, is the place to go to admire the egg-decorator's skill.

Slavic Knees-Up

2 Whether it's the on-the-spot jitter of a Hutsul hop, a boot-slapping Russian shindig, the swirling veils and curling hands of Crimean Tatars or the drama of Cossack acrobatics, dance is at the heart of all Ukraine's cultures.

Bandura Players

3 Hey, Mr Bandura Man. *Kobzary* (minstrel-like bards; p250) were the keepers of Ukrainian folklore, travelling from village to village reciting epic poems across the steppe while strumming the 65-string *bandura*. Stalin had them all shot, but the tradition is making a slow comeback.

Taras Shevchenko Statues

4 Chiselled in classic stone, set in 19th-century bronze and moulded in Art Deco concrete, old and young, moustachioed and clean-shaven, statues of the national poet Taras Shevchenko (p251) can be found in almost every city across Ukraine.

Jewish Ukraine

5 Jewish communities were virtually wiped out in the Holocaust and depleted further by post-independence emigration, but remnants of Ukraine's Jewish past can be seen in Berdychiv, Uman, Bratslav and Lviv.

1

3

Clockwise from top
1. Basket of *pysanky* **2.** Traditional folk dancing
3. Musician strumming a *bandura*

Great Outdoors

The Ukrainian steppe, traversed by mighty rivers, rolls on to far-flung horizons. The Carpathians, in the country's west, and the Crimean peninsula, jutting into the Black Sea in the south, provide striking landscapes and show-stopping vistas.

Kara-Dag Nature Reserve

1 Eerie volcanic rock formations on Crimea's east coast (p197) create an otherworldly landscape that can be explored on foot or aboard pleasure boats, which approach from the adjacent Black Sea and sail right through the formations.

Black Sea Coast

2 A balmy Black Sea slaps its tepid waves against almost 2800km of coastline, much of which is hemmed with golden sand or shingle. Odesa (p150) and Crimea (p163) are where most bucket-and-spade fun is to be had.

Snow Fun

3 Popular with Ukraine's steppe dwellers, and enjoying a relatively long winter season, the Carpathian ski resorts are slowly getting their act together. The most developed winter sports centre at Bukovel (p130) is even considering a bid for the 2018 Winter Olympics.

Summer in the Carpathians

4 With soothingly forested peaks and broad valleys, western Ukraine's Carpathian Mountains (p122) are the best place to head for some warm-weather hiking and mountain biking. Trails are faint or unmarked, but locals are working on them.

Mt Hoverla

5 At a mere 2061m, Ukraine's highest peak (p127) hardly has the Himalayas quaking with fear, but it makes up for its modest altitude with some soothing Carpathian vistas. The trails to the top are easy, but get busy in summer.

1

WIN-INITIATIVE / GETTY IMAGES ©

4

YEVGEN TIMASHOV / GETTY IMAGES ©

Clockwise from top left

1. Kara-Dag **2.** Gurzuf beach (p191), Crimea
3. Snowboarders in the Carpathians **4.** Hiker in the Carpathians

SASHA MASLOV / GETTY IMAGES ©

3

Religious Artistry

A highlight of Ukraine is its churches: from the golden domes of Orthodox monasteries to the Gothic arches of western Ukraine and the timber spires of the Carpathians, there's certainly nothing austere about its places of worship.

Inside an Orthodox Church

1 Featuring elaborately carved iconostases, riotously frescoed walls and neck-stiffening high domes, Ukrainian churches will impress you with their colour, atmosphere and scent.

Carpathian Timber Churches

2 If there's one commodity the Carpathians have in ample supply, it's wood! Locals have been cobbling together timber churches since at least the 16th century, and although fire and woodworm have destroyed many, a surprising number still dot the landscape.

Call to Prayer

3 Catherine the Great had many Tatar religious buildings pulled down and Stalin did his best to wipe Islam off the Crimean map, but the Tatar call to prayer has returned in the last two decades, and more mosques and schools are planned.

Onion-Domed Beauty

4 The sight of the gilt onion domes of an Orthodox cathedral or monastery catching the fiery rays of a Ukrainian sunset is one of the strongest images travellers take home from these parts.

Temple Fatigue in Lviv

5 Lviv is said to have over 100 churches – not bad for a city of just over 700,000. The most interesting examples hoist their spires above the city centre, where it's easy to overdose on beautiful church interiors.

MARTIN MOOS / GETTY IMAGES ©

KEREN SU / GETTY IMAGES ©

Clockwise from top

1. Bernardine Church and Monastery (p101) **2.** Carpathian timber church **3.** Dormition Cathedral, Kyevo-Pecherska Lavra (p43)

Soviet Relics

Ukraine may have shaken off its Soviet shackles, but its towns, cities and villages are still peppered with hammers and sickles, great-coated Lenin statues and stern war memorials. These often well-tended sites look like they're here to stay.

Kyiv's Ornate Metro

1 Blasted deep into the rock below the city, Kyiv's metro system (p66) is a time-warped subterranean realm of ornate Stalinist-era stations, brave-new-world frescoes and socialist-realist reliefs.

Defence of the Motherland

2 There are taxi-hailing Lenins, plinthed tanks and brutish Red Army conscripts seemingly emerging from the bedrock, but the queen of Soviet relics must be Kyiv's sword-wielding Rodina Mat (Defence of the Motherland Monument; p47).

Stalin's Back

3 Somewhat incredibly, new Stalin statues were recently erected in several Russian-speaking cities in the south and east of the country. Look out for Joseph Dzhugashvili (Stalin's real name) making an unlikely return in Odesa and Zaporizhzhya, moustache and all.

Nuclear Missile Museum

4 The Cold War is long over and much of Ukraine's military infrastructure has been left to crumble into the steppe. But the fascinating Museum of Strategic Missile Forces (p78) near Pervomaysk is a real missile base preserved in the middle of the Ukrainian countryside.

Kharkiv's Derzhprom Building

5 Proof that big can be quite clever, Kharkiv's mammoth Derzhprom (House of State Industry; p209) used pioneering construction techniques when it was built in the 1920s. Now in a bit of a state, its granite and concrete hulk still dominates the world's second-largest city square.

Right
1. Metro station, Kyiv **2.** Rodina Mat (Defence of the Motherland Monument; p47) Artist: Yevgeny Vuchetich

EKATERINA NOSENKO / GETTY IMAGES ©

1

KEREN SU / GETTY IMAGES ©

2

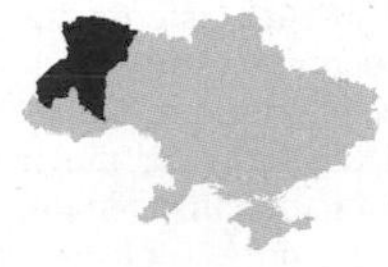

Lviv & Western Ukraine
Львів і Західна Україна

POP 5.85 MILLION / AREA 75,847 SQ KM

Includes ➡

Best Places to Eat & Drink

- ➡ Masonic Restaurant (p109)
- ➡ Dim Lehend (p108)
- ➡ Korona Vitovta (p119)
- ➡ Kupol (p109)
- ➡ Kabinet Cafe (p110)

Best Places to Stay

- ➡ Vintage (p107)
- ➡ Leopolis Hotel (p108)
- ➡ Old City Hostel (p106)
- ➡ Hotel Zaleski (p119)
- ➡ Reikartz Medievale (p107)

Why Go?

More quintessentially Ukrainian than the rest of the country, and distinctly more European, the west is all about its largest city, the Galician capital of Lviv. An emerging tourist magnet, the city is a truly captivating place, rich in historic architecture and with an indulgent coffeehouse culture, but only a fraction of the tourist hordes who choke similar city break destinations such as Kraków and Prague. Piecemeal gentrification has made only small dents in its shabby authenticity.

The Soviets ruled for only 50 years here, making the west the most foreigner-friendly province with less surly 'no-can-do' bureaucracy than in eastern regions. People here speak Ukrainian (rather than Russian) and show greater pride in Ukrainian traditions than elsewhere.

Away from Lviv, the moody Carpathian Mountains are a short hop by bus, as are historic Lutsk, the olde-worlde spa at Truskavets and the golden domes of Pochayiv Monastery.

When to Go

Lviv

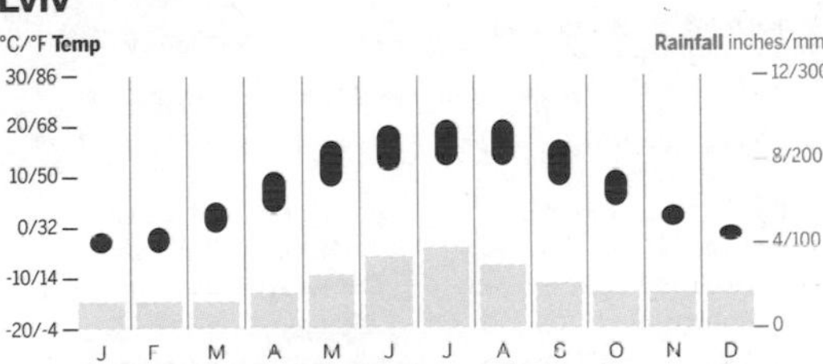

May A great time to be in Lviv with simultaneous festivals filling the early part of the month.

Jul Experience a Ukrainian summer of love at Pidkamin's Ethnofestival.

Aug Pilgrims flock to Pochayiv Monastery during the Feast of the Assumption.

History

Mongols overrunning Kyivan Rus in 1240 never made it as far west as the powerful province of Galicia-Volynia. They did occasionally knock on its door, but the region was largely left to enjoy self-rule under King Roman Mstyslavych, his son Danylo Halytsky and his descendants.

This idyllic state was shattered in the 1340s when Polish troops invaded, but western Ukraine never lost its taste for independence. Several centuries of Polish domination saw the rise of a unique Ruthenian identity, which is the basis for much contemporary Ukrainian nationalism. Many Galician *boyars* (nobles) – often sent from

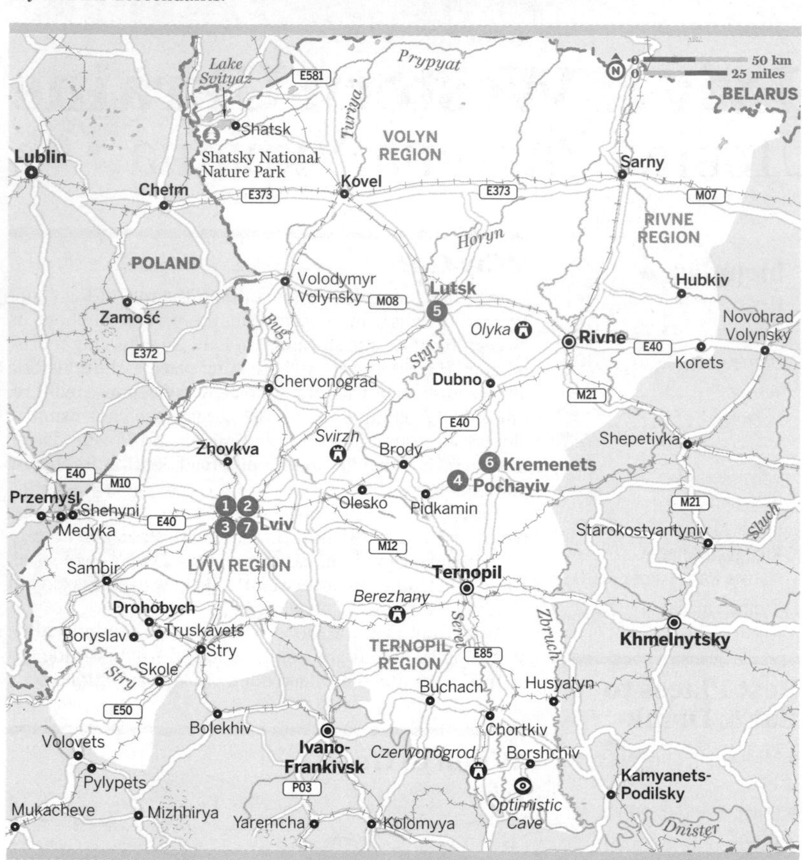

Lviv & Western Ukraine Highlights

1. Do a spot of cobble-surfing in Lviv's **historical centre** (p96), packed with churches, museums and eccentric restaurants.

2. Make a caffeine-and-cake halt at Lviv's **coffeehouses** (p110), some of the best in the country.

3. Pay your respects to Lviv's great and good of yesteryear at the city's amazing **Lychakivske Cemetery** (p101).

4. Join the Orthodox faithful for a pilgrimage to **Pochayiv Monastery** (p115) to find Ukraine's most devout atmosphere.

5. Take a turn around Lutsk's **old quarter** (p118) for a blast from western Ukraine's past.

6. Head uphill to **Kremenets Fortress** (p116) for trip-stopping views of the town's many churches.

7. Catch a **festival** (p102) in Lviv – not difficult as there's something happening almost every day of the year.

Poland, Germany or Hungary – adopted the Polish language and Roman Catholicism. However, the peasants, also known as Ruthenians, remained Orthodox. They were only persuaded to join the new Ukrainian Catholic Church, also known as the Uniate Church, in 1596 (thereby acknowledging the pope's spiritual supremacy) because this church agreed to retain Orthodox forms of worship. Other Ruthenians fled southeast to set up Cossack communities.

In 1772 Galicia became part of the Habsburg Austro-Hungarian Empire and to this day western Ukrainians touchingly remember the Austrians as (relatively) liberal, tolerant rulers. In other parts of the empire separatists suffered under the Austrian yoke, but in Ukraine the Habsburgs allowed Ukrainian nationalism to re-emerge and that made them good guys in this country. Western Ukraine even enjoyed a few days' independence as the Habsburg Empire collapsed at the end of WWI, but it soon found itself again under the dreaded Polish thumb.

Following the outbreak of WWII in September 1939, things went from bad to worse in local eyes. The Red Army marched in and asserted Moscow's control over the region for the first time in history. Finally dispatching the Nazis after bloody battles during WWII, the Soviets hung around until 1991, when the USSR imploded.

LVIV REGION

Lviv Львів

☎032 / pop 700,000

If you've done time in any other region of Ukraine, Lviv (luh-*veev*) will come as a shock. Mysterious and architecturally lovely, this Unesco World Heritage Site is the country's least Soviet and exudes the same authentic central European charm as pre-tourism Prague or Kraków once did. Its quaint cobbles, bean-perfumed coffeehouses and rattling trams are a continent away from the post-Soviet badlands to the east. It's also a place where the candle of Ukrainian national identity burns brightest and where Russian is definitely a minority language.

But the secret is out about Lviv, and those who foresaw a decade ago that the city would become Ukraine's premier tourist attraction are now watching their prediction come true. No other place in the country is more geared up for visitors and no other attracts so many of them. The Euro 2012 football (soccer) championships gave the world a taste of this Ukrainian treat; a successful bid for the 2022 Winter Olympics would be the icing on the cake.

Lviv is on the map and regardless of what the rest of the country may be doing, it has its sights set firmly on the visitor experience. The city has the best range of hotels in the country; hostels, tour agencies, guides and English-language information abound; and local restaurateurs have been letting their imaginations run amok, producing one of Eastern Europe's wackiest list of places to eat. So forget Ukraine's capital of humour, Odesa – you're bound to find infinitely more smiles here in forward-looking Lviv.

History

Lviv has had as many names as it has had rulers. It took its first name from Lev, the son of King Danylo Halytsky, who founded a hilltop fort here on present-day Castle Hill in the 13th century. When the Poles took over 100 years later, the place became known as Lwów, as it still is in Poland. Austrians called it Lemberg between the 18th and 20th centuries, and still do. The Russians, who later christened it Lvov, continue to use this historical name. Most of its names – apart from Lemberg, which has many competing origins – can be traced back to 'lion', and the city has always taken the big cat as its symbol.

Lviv had another set of unwelcome occupiers who also called the place Lemberg – the Nazis. They invaded in 1941 and weren't driven back by the Soviets until 1944. During these three years, 136,000 people are reported to have died in Lviv's Jewish ghetto and nearly 350,000 in nearby concentration camps.

The Galician capital played a major role in the movement that led to Ukrainian independence in 1991. Ukrainian nationalism and the Greek Catholic Church re-emerged here in the late 1980s, and in the early 1990s its people unanimously elected nationalist politicians and staged mass demonstrations. Today it still has its eyes focused firmly on Europe and has been a stronghold for Western-oriented politicians.

Sights

Ploshcha Rynok SQUARE

(Map p104) Thanks to its splendid array of buildings Lviv was declared a Unesco World Heritage Site in 1998, and this old market square lies at its heart. The square was progressively rebuilt after a major fire in the early 16th century destroyed the original. The 19th-century **Ratusha** (Town Hall; Map p104) stands in the middle of the plaza, with fountains featuring Greek gods at each of its corners (you'll see these garbed in traditional Ukrainian embroidered shirts around 24 August, Ukrainian Independence Day). Vista junkies can climb the 65m-high neo-Renaissance **tower** (admission 10uah; ⏲9am-9pm Apr-Oct, shorter hours rest of year), though it's a hard slog to the top. Multilingual signs point the way to the ticket booth on the 4th floor.

Around 40 buildings in various states of repair hem the square's perimeter. Most of these three- and four-storey buildings have uniform dimensions, with three windows per storey overlooking the square. This was the maximum number of windows allowed tax-free, and those buildings with four or more belonged to the extremely wealthy.

House No 4, the **Black Mansion** (Map p104), has one of the most striking facades. Built for an Italian merchant in 1588–89, it features a relief of St Martin on a horse. The **Kornyakt House** (Map p104) at No 6 is named after its original owner, a Greek merchant. An interesting row of sculptured knights along the rooftop cornice makes it a local favourite. Together, Nos 2 and 6 house the largest portion of the Lviv History Museum.

Prospekt Svobody BOULEVARD

(Freedom Ave; Map p104) Just in case it should ever slip your mind that Lviv is Ukraine's most patriotic large city, an enormous **statue of Taras Shevchenko** (Пам'ятник Тарасу Шевченку; Map p104; pr Svobody) rises up in the middle of Prospekt Svobody. A gift from the Ukrainian diaspora in Argentina, the statue of the revered national poet stands beside a wave-shaped relief of religious folk art. In summer the broad pavement in the middle of the *prospekt* is the town's main hang-out and the hub of Lviv life, where homegrown tourists pose for photos at Shevchenko's feet. Locals promenade along the strip of park, kids scoot around in rented electric cars, beggars politely hassle people sitting on the many park benches and wedding parties mill around barking photo instructions.

At the northern end of the boulevard is the 1897–1900 **Solomiya Krushelnytska Lviv Theatre of Opera & Ballet**. At the southern end a **statue of Adam Michiewicz** (Map p104), the Polish poet, stands in pl Mitskevycha.

Latin Cathedral CATHEDRAL

(Map p104; pl Katedralna 1; donation requested) With various chunks dating from between 1370 and 1480, this working cathedral is one of Lviv's most impressive churches. The exterior is most definitely Gothic while the heavily gilded interior, one of the city's highlights, has a more baroque feel with colourfully wreathed pillars hoisting frescoed vaulting and mysterious side chapels glowing in candlelit half light. Services are in four languages including…wait for it…English! If you walk around the cathedral, you'll eventually come to a relief of Pope John Paul II, erected to commemorate his visit to Lviv in 2001.

Dominican Cathedral CHURCH

(Map p104; pl Museyna) Dominating a small square to the east of pl Rynok is one of Lviv's signature sights, the large rococo dome of the Dominican Cathedral. Attached to the cathedral and to the left of the entrance is the **Museum of Religious History** (Map p104; admission 5uah; ⏲10am-6pm Tue-Sun), which was an atheist museum in Soviet times. The exhibition looks at all religions currently active in Ukraine and includes an Ostroh Bible, one of the first complete translations into Old Church Slavonic printed in 1580.

East of the cathedral is a square where you'll see a **statue** of a monk holding a book. This is Federov, who brought printing to Ukraine in the 16th century. Fittingly, there's a secondhand book market here on weekends.

Armenian Cathedral CHURCH

(Map p104; vul Virmenska 7) By some accounts, Lviv has more than 100 churches and it's all too easy to overdose on ornate interiors and golden iconostases, but one church you should not miss is the elegant 1363 Armenian Cathedral. The placid cathedral courtyard is a maze of arched passageways and squat buildings festooned with intricate Caucasian detail. Stepping into the courtyard feels like entering another era. Outside, quaint, cobbled vul Virmenska was once the heart of the old Armenian ('Virmenska' in Ukrainian) Quarter.

Lviv History Museum MUSEUM

(Львівський історичний музей; Map p104; www.lhm.lviv.ua; admission to each branch 10uah; ⏲all branches 10am-5.30pm Thu-Tue) Lviv's main museum is split into three collections dotted around pl Rynok. The best branch is at **No 6** (Map p104). Here you can enjoy the Italian-Renaissance inner courtyard and slide around the exquisitely decorated interior in cloth slippers on the woodcut parquetry floor made from 14 kinds of hardwood. It was here on 22 December 1686 that Poland and Russia signed the treaty that partitioned Ukraine. **No 2**, the Palazzo Bandinelli, covers 19th- and 20th-century history, including two floors dedicated to the Ukrainian nationalist movement. **No 24** (Map p104) expounds on the city's very early

JEWISH LVIV

Jewish sites in Lviv may be more about what's been destroyed than what remains, but a tour through the city's rich Jewish past can still elicit a range of emotions. There were more than 100,000 Jews in Lviv before WWII, not including the several thousand Jewish refugees who arrived from Germany and western Poland before the war. The Nazis murdered nearly all of them at Lviv's Janowska concentration and forced labour camp, and at Belzec, another hideous extermination camp in present-day Poland, where, it is believed, some 600,000 people were killed and only two survived. Today Lviv's Jewish community numbers only about 2000.

Before the tragic events of WWII there were two Jewish districts in Lviv: a wealthy inner district around vuls Staroyevreyska (Old Jewish St), Fedorova and Ruska in the Old Town; and a larger outer district covering a vast area north and west of the Solomiya Krushelnytska Lviv Theatre of Opera and Ballet.

The late-16th-century **Golden Rose Synagogue** (Map p104; vul Staroyevreyska) stood at the heart of the inner district before the Nazis blew it up in 1941. Today there's not much to see at the fenced-off site, and the local Jewish community's plans to rebuild a replica of the synagogue have stalled. Another synagogue once stood in the open lot directly across vul Staroyevreyska.

In the outer district, you'll find the **Jewish Hospital** (Єврейська лікарня; Map p98; vul Rappoporta), one of Lviv's architectural highlights. From afar this Moorish, dome-topped building looks like a mosque, but up close Jewish motifs are evident in the striking, eclectic facade. **Krakivsky Market**, right behind the hospital, was a Jewish cemetery in medieval times. Writer Sholem Aleichem lived not far away, at Kotlyarska 1, in 1906. There's a **plaque** (Map p104) to Aleichem on the side of the building. South of here, on vul Nalyvayka, a few old Yiddish shop signs remain. About 500m north of the Solomiya Krushelnytska Lviv Theatre of Opera and Ballet on pr Chornovola is the **Holocaust memorial** (Map p98), a vaguely cubist statue of a tormented figure looking skyward. The Lviv ghetto began here after most of the city's Jews were killed or deported to Belzec in the 'Great Action' of August 1942. Nazi hunter Simon Wiesenthal was the most famous resident of the ghetto, which was liquidated in June 1943.

The **Yanivskę Cemetery** (Янівське кладовище; Map p98; vul Tarasa Shevchenka), northwest of the city centre, has a large **Jewish section** (Map p98) accessible from vul Yeroshenka (a side street off vul Tarasa Shevchenka). A 15-minute walk west of the cemetery are a plaque and a billboard marking the spot of the **Janowska concentration camp** (vul Vynnytsya, off vul Tarasa Shevchenka), now a prison. About 200m further west on vul Tarasa Shevchenka is **Kleparivska train station**, the last stop before Belzec on the Nazi death train. A plaque commemorates the 500,000 doomed Galician Jews who passed through here.

Artefacts of Lviv's Jewish heritage are scattered around various museums in the Old Town. There's a small Holocaust exhibit in the Lviv History Museum branch at pl Rynok 6, while the Museum of Religious History attached to the Dominican Cathedral has a collection of Jewish relics, and the **Hesed-Arieh Jewish Centre** (Map p98; www.hesed.lviv.ua; vul Kotlyevskoho 30) has a tiny museum on Jews in Galicia. Lviv's only functioning synagogue is the attractive **Beis Aharon V'Yisrael Synagogue** (Map p98; vul Brativ Mikhnovskykh 4), built in 1924.

Lviv

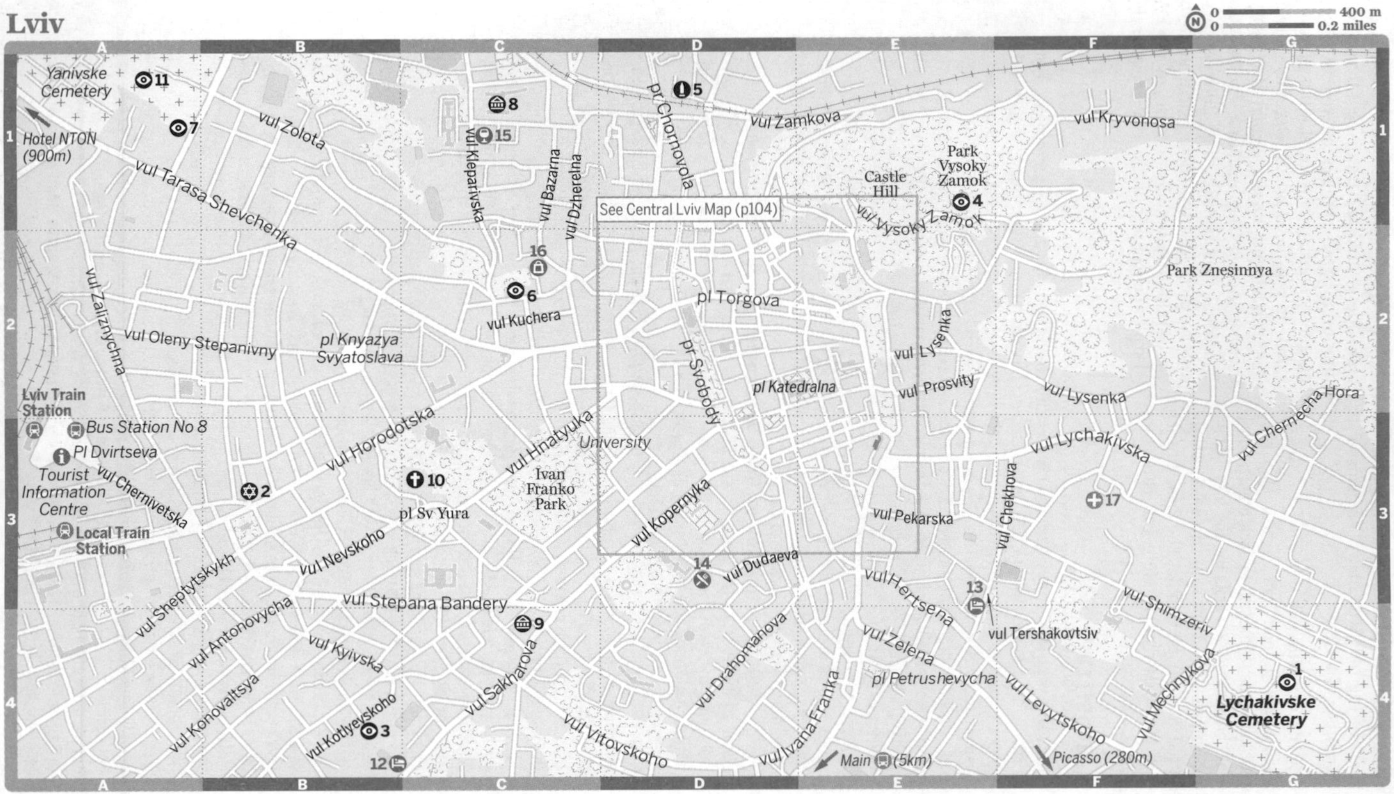

0 400 m
0 0.2 miles

Yanivske Cemetery
11
7
Hotel NTON (900m)
vul Zolota
vul Tarasa Shevchenka
8
15
vul Kleparivska
vul Bazarna
vul Dzherelna
16
6
vul Kuchera
5
pr Chornovola
vul Zamkova
vul Kryvonosa
Castle Hill
Park Vysoky Zamok
4
vul Vysoky Zamok
Park Znesinnya
See Central Lviv Map (p104)
vul Zaliznychna
vul Oleny Stepanivny
pl Knyazya Svyatoslava
pl Torgova
pr Svobody
pl Katedralna
vul Lysenka
vul Prosvity
vul Chernecha Hora
Lviv Train Station
Bus Station No 8
Pl Dvirtseva
Tourist Information Centre
vul Chernivetska
Local Train Station
2
vul Horodotska
10
pl Sv Yura
vul Hnatyuka
University
Ivan Franko Park
vul Kopernyka
vul Lychakivska
vul Chekhova
17
vul Pekarska
vul Sheptytskykh
vul Nevskoho
vul Stepana Bandery
14
vul Dudaeva
9
vul Hertsena
13
vul Tershakovtsiv
vul Shimzeriv
vul Antonovycha
vul Kyivska
vul Drahomanova
vul Zelena
pl Petrushevycha
vul Mechnykova
1
Lychakivske Cemetery
vul Konovaltsya
vul Kotlyevskoho
3
12
vul Sakharova
vul Vitovskoho
vul Ivana Franka
Main (5km)
vul Levytskoho
Picasso (280m)

Lviv

Top Sights

1 Lychakivske Cemetery....................... G4

Sights

2 Beis Aharon V'Yisrael Synagogue......B3
3 Hesed-Arieh Jewish Centre................B4
4 High Castle Hill.....................................E1
5 Holocaust memorial........................... D1
6 Jewish Hospital...................................C2
7 Jewish Section of Yanivske Cemetery... A1
8 Lvivske Museum of Beer & Brewing.. C1
9 National Museum and Memorial to the Victims of Occupation....................................... C4
10 St George's Cathedral.........................C3
11 Yanivske Cemetery.............................. A1

Sleeping

12 Ekotel..B4
13 Eurohotel E4

Eating

14 Kupol D3

Drinking & Nightlife

15 Robert Doms Beer House.................. C1

Shopping

16 Krakivsky Rynok C2

Information

17 Municipal Hospital...............................F3

days. The highlight is an enormous painting depicting the old walled city of Lviv in the 18th century. Pr Svobody was a moat.

Museum of Folk Architecture & Life MUSEUM
(Львівський Музей народної архітектури і побуту; www.skansen.lviv.ua; vul Chernecha Hora 1; admission 10uah; 9am-dusk Tue-Sun) This open-air museum displays different regional styles of farmsteads, windmills, churches and schools, which dot a huge park to the east of the city centre. Everything is pretty spread out here and a visit involves a lot of footwork. As an exhibition, it doesn't hold a candle to Kyiv's Pyrohovo Museum, but it's worth checking out if you're not heading to the capital. To get to the museum, take tram 7 from vul Pidvalna up vul Lychakivska and get off at the corner of vul Mechnykova. From the stop, walk 10 minutes' north on vul Krupyarska, following the signs.

High Castle Hill LANDMARK
(Високий замок; Map p98) Around 30 minutes' walk from pl Rynok, visiting the High Castle (Vysoky Zamok) on Castle Hill (Zamkova Hora) is a quintessential Lviv experience. There's little evidence of the 14th-century ruined stone fort that was Lviv's birthplace, but the summit mound sporting a mammoth Ukrainian flag thwacking in the wind offers 360-degree views of the city and the wooded hills between which it nestles. To reach Vysoky Zamok on foot, head up vul Kryvonosa from Vul Pidvalna until you reach a cafe and toilets where you should take a left. After a few minutes you will see a set of metal steps on the right. If you're feeling lazy, you can take a taxi most of the way up, approaching from the east via vul Vysoky Zamok.

Boyim Chapel CHAPEL
(Каплиця Боїмів; Map p104; pl Katedralna; admission 10uah; 11am-5pm Tue-Sun) Just off pl Rynok's southwest corner, the blackened facade of the burial chapel (1615) belonging to Hungarian merchant Georgi Boyim and his family is covered in magnificent if somewhat morbid carvings. Atop the cupola is an unusual sculpture of Christ sitting with his head in one hand, pondering his sorrows. The interior is dizzying, featuring biblical reliefs with cameo appearances by members of the Boyim family. There are more images of the family patriarchs on the exterior above the door and on the wall flanking vul Halytska. The chapel is now part of the Lviv Art Gallery and hosts temporary exhibitions. Unfortunately it's not always open when it should be.

Dormition Church CHURCH
(Map p104; vul Pidvalna 9; 8am-7pm) This Ukrainian Orthodox church is easily distinguished by the 65m-high, triple-tiered Kornyakt bell tower rising beside it. The tower was named after its Greek benefactor, a merchant who was also the original owner of Kornyakt House on pl Rynok. It's well worth going inside to see the beautifully gilt interior of the church, accessible through the gate to the right of the tower. Attached to the church is the diminutive Three Saints Chapel with its three, highly ornate minicupolas.

Transfiguration Church CHURCH
(Map p104; cnr vul Krakivska & vul Lesi Ukrainky; 7am-7pm) The tall copper-domed church just west of the Armenian Cathedral is the

late-17th-century Transfiguration Church, the first church in the city to revert to Greek Catholicism after Ukrainian independence in 1991. This place is particularly impressive during a service (early mornings and evenings).

Lviv Art Gallery GALLERY

(Львівська галерея мистецтв; Map p104; www.lvivgallery.org; vul Kopernyka 15 & vul Stefanyka 3; admission to each 20uah; ⏲11am-6pm Tue-Sat, noon-5pm Sun) Lviv's main art repository has two wings – one in the lavish **Pototsky Palace** (Палац Потоцького), the other around the corner on vul Stefanyka. The former houses an impressive collection of European art from the 14th to 18th centuries, including works by Rubens, Bruegel, Goya and Caravaggio. The wing on **vul Stefanyka** (Map p104) contains 19th- and early-20th-century art (plus some 21st-century pieces); this includes a superb collection of Polish art, arguably the best outside Poland with some works by Jan Matejko.

National Museum MUSEUM

(Національний музей; Map p104; www.nm.lviv.ua; pr Svobody 20; admission permanent exhibitions 15uah, whole building 45uah; ⏲10am-6pm Tue-Sun) Residing in one of Lviv's grandest 19th-century palaces, this sometimes confusing museum (too many doors, ticket rippers, sections, prescribed routes) has one of the Slavic world's best collections of religious icons, most hailing from west Ukraine and eastern Poland. The earliest examples date from the 12th century and the famous Volyn School is well represented. A seperate section deals with Ukrainian art of the 18th to 20th centuries including a few works by Taras Shevchenko, whose death mask can also be found here.

National Museum & Memorial to the Victims of Occupation MUSEUM

(Національний музей-меморіал жертв окупаційних режимів; Map p98; www.lonckoho.lviv.ua; vul Bryullova; ⏲10am-7pm Mon-Sat, to 5pm Sun) FREE This infamous building on vul Bryullova was used as a prison by the Poles, Nazis and communists in turn, but the small and very moving ground-floor exhibition focuses on Stalinist atrocities in the early years of WWII. Left exactly as it was when the KGB bailed out in 1991, the brutally bare cells, horrific statistics posted throughout and Nazi newsreel from summer 1941 will leave few untouched. Some English explanations.

Lvivske Museum of Beer & Brewing MUSEUM

(Map p98; www.lvivbeermuseum.com; vul Kleparivska 18; admission 15uah; ⏲tours 10.30am-6pm Wed-Mon) The oldest still-functioning brewery in Ukraine turns 300 in 2015, and a tasting tour, which runs roughly every 1½ hours, through the mainly underground facilities is well worth the trek out of the city centre. One old storage vault has been turned into an atmospheric beer hall where you can sample even more frothy Lvivske, one of the most popular brands in the country. To reach the museum, take tram 7 to St Anna Church (where vul Shevchenka peels away from vul Horodotska) then walk north along vul Kleparivska for around 10 minutes.

St George's Cathedral CATHEDRAL

(Map p98; pl Sv Yura 5) On the way between the city centre and the train station stands the historic and sacred centre of the Greek Catholic Church in Ukraine, which was handed back after 44 years of compulsory Orthodox control. Constructed in 1774–90, this yellow building is pleasant enough, especially since a refurbishment for the Pope's 2001 visit. However, it's perhaps not as striking as some of Lviv's less important churches. For many, the most memorable element will be the 3D icon of Christ near the far right corner, if looking from the door. It presents Christ's face from one angle, and the image from the shroud of Turin from another.

Salo Museum GALLERY

(Map p104; www.saloart.com.ua; pr Svobody 6/8; audio guide 40uah; ⏲noon-midnight) For the uninitiated, *salo* is the raw pig fat that Ukrainians love to slip down with vodka and use an an ingredient in national dishes. This 'museum' is more of a gallery in a restaurant where you can pay homage to *salo* at the *salo* monument and wonder at pieces of modern art and sculpture made of the stuff, some of which can be ordered to eat. It's free to wander round or 40uah gets you an audio guide and tasting session involving 14 different types of *salo*.

Apteka Museum MUSEUM

(Pharmacy Museum; Map p104; vul Drukarska 2; admission 8uah; ⏲10am-5pm) This pharmacy museum is located inside a still-functioning chemist's shop dating from 1735. Entrance into the eerie *pidval* (basement) is by re-

DON'T MISS

LYCHAKIVSKE CEMETERY

Don't even think of leaving town until you've seen the amazing **Lychakivske Cemetery** (Личаківське кладовище; Map p98; www.lviv-lychakiv.ukrain.travel; vul Pekarska; admission 15uah; ⌚9am-6pm), only a short tram ride from the city centre. This is the Père Lachaise of Eastern Europe, with the same sort of overgrown grounds and Gothic aura as the famous Parisian necropolis (but containing less-well-known people). Laid out in the late 18th century, when Austrian Emperor Josef II decreed that no more burials could take place in churchyards, it's still the place Lviv's great and good are laid to rest.

Eagle eyes can try to spot the graves of revered nationalist poet Ivan Franko, Soviet gymnastics legend Viktor Chukarin, early 20th-century opera star Solomiya Krushelnytska, and some 2000 Poles who died fighting Ukrainians and Bolsheviks from 1918 to 1920. There's also a memorial to the Ukrainian insurgent army (UPA), who fought for independence against both the Nazis and Soviets. But ultimately you needn't recognise a single soul to be moved by the mournful photos of loved ones, ornate tombstones and floral tributes.

A good strategy is to combine a trip to the cemetery and the Museum of Folk Architecture & Life. The cemetery is one stop past the stop for the open-air museum on tram 7.

quest only. Bottles of medicinal wine with a high iron content can be bought here (temporary tooth discolouration is all part of the fun); just ask for *zalizne vyno*.

Bernardine Church & Monastery CHURCH

(Map p104; vul Vynnychenka) Lviv's most stunning baroque interior belongs to the 17th-century now Greek Catholic Church of St Andrew. The highlight is the long ceiling covered in recently restored frescoes. Sunday masses spill out into the street, filling the surrounding square with song.

Museum of Ethnography, Arts & Crafts MUSEUM

(Map p104; pr Svobody 15; admission 10uah; ⌚11am-5.30pm Tue-Sun) This unimaginatively curated museum has a few interesting pieces of furniture, Czech glass, Art Nouveau posters (Mucha, Lautrec) and various 19th- and 20th-century decorative items from across Europe, the whole caboodle scattered throughout an interestingly run-down palace. The ethnography section is currently in storage awaiting the green light to move into a new home at pl Rynok 10. Due to a lack of funds, this isn't expected to happen anytime soon.

Arsenal Museum MUSEUM

(Музей старовинної зброї; Map p104; ☎721 901; vul Pidvalna 5; admission 10uah; ⌚10am-5.30pm Thu-Tue) The town's former arsenal (1554–56) is now a museum where you can check out suits of armour and various cannons and weapons.

☞ Tours

Tour agencies appeared in the run-up to Euro 2012 like illegal rip-off clothing stalls the day after a police inspection. The biggest and best have survived the post-football hangover.

Chudo Tour TOURIST TRAIN

(Map p104; www.chudotour.com.ua; pl Rynok; tour 50-60uah; ⌚10am-8pm) Ukraine's first and only tourist train leaves every half hour from the right-hand side of the Ratusha on pl Rynok. The one-hour tour with recorded commentary takes in most of the major sights in the city centre. The company also runs themed walking tours.

Kumpel Tour TOUR

(Map p104; ☎067 373 8900; www.kumpel-tour.com; pl Rynok 16) Expert Lviv historian, university lecturer and part-time local radio presenter Ihor Lylo runs the best English-language tours in town for visitors looking to get under the skin of this intriguing city.

Lemberg Tour TOUR

(Map p104; ☎276 5442; www.lemberg-tour.com.ua; vul Vynnychenka 26/1) Quite upmarket tours with historical and cultural themes in and around Lviv.

Just Lviv It! TOUR

(Map p104; ☎067 670 2396; www.justlviv.it; pl Rynok 10) Highly visible operation with an information centre on pl Rynok, its own hostel and tours on every Lviv theme imaginable.

Festivals & Events

No other city in Ukraine does festivals like Lviv – even Kyiv has found itself playing catch-up and you'll find a lot of imitations of Lviv events across the country. There's something going on virtually every week of the year – here are just some of the highlights.

Chocolate Festival FESTIVAL
(www.shokolad.lviv.ua) Beat the mid-February blues at Ukraine's top culinary festival.

Lviv Fashion Week FASHION
(www.lvivfashionweek.com) One of the country's top fashion events held in late March.

Lviv City Day CITY FESTIVAL
(www.cultureandtourism.lviv.ua) Every city has its day in Ukraine – Lviv's is in early May.

Fluhery Lvova MUSIC
(www.dzyga.com) Long-established ethno-jazz festival – early May.

Beer Festival BEER
(www.beerfest.lviv.ua) Held in early May to coincide with other events going on.

Virtuosos MUSIC
(www.philharmonia.lviv.ua) Three-week classical musical festival in late-May or early June.

LvivKlezFest MUSIC
(www.klezfest.lviv.ua) Takes place at tens of venues throughout the summer.

Etnovyr CULTURE
(www.etnovyr.org.ua) Huge folk festival in late August.

Coffee Festival FESTIVAL
(www.coffeefest.lviv.ua) Get the caffeine jitters in late September.

Sleeping

Post-Euro 2012 you'd be hard pushed to find a Soviet-era hotel room in this city, most having rid themselves of the pre-1991 style of hospitality before the football fest began. However, this has left a scarcity of cheap accommodation – expect to pay around twice as much in Lviv as you would elsewhere in western Ukraine.

Lviv's hostel situation seems to be in constant flux, with expats setting up then selling up with alarming speed. Check that a hostel is still running before turning up without a booking. Most hostels seem to have a no-alcohol policy.

Walking Tour Lviv's Historical Centre

START SHEVCHENKO STATUE
END DOMINICAN CATHEDRAL
LENGTH 5.3KM; TWO HOURS

Lviv's relatively compact centre makes for a pleasant walking tour that will get you to most of the major sites. This tour will take approximately two hours – 2½ hours if the Castle Hill loop is included. It starts at the spiritual centre of modern-day Lviv, the Taras Shevchenko statue on pr Svobody, and ends at vul Virmenska in the old city.

With your back to the 1 **Shevchenko statue**, start walking right, glancing up at the interesting cast of stone-carved characters (one resembling New York's Statue of Liberty) on the parapet of the 2 **Museum of Ethnography, Arts & Crafts** (p101). Continue north on pr Svobody towards the 3 **Solomiya Krushelnytska Lviv Theatre of Opera & Ballet**. Skirt right around the theatre, then take a right on vul Horodotska and carry on for about 250m until you reach the 4 **Church of St Mary**, parts of which date from 1340. Carry on past the church then take a right into 5 **vul Chornomorska**, scene of Cold War tragedy. Vibration from Soviet tanks heading to Hungary in 1956 shook several houses to the ground, hence the gap now occupied by a children's playground. A few steps further bring you to pl Stary Rynok, where the 1845 6 **Progressive Jews Synagogue** once stood. Destroyed by the Nazis during WWII, a plaque marks the spot.

Glance up at the old buildings around pl Stary Rynok before performing a quick there-and-back movement up vul Plynikarska to see the 7 **Church of St Nicholas**. Local historians claim this is Lviv's oldest church – elements of the building date back to the 13th century. Back on pl Stary Rynok head east, passing the diminutive 8 **Church of St John the Baptist**, now a book museum, on your left, then bear right on vul Uzhhorodska. Continue uphill about 200m to the corner of vul Zamkova. From here you can easily spot the TV tower that tops 9 **Castle Hill**. High Castle (Vysoky Zamok) is about a 45-minute round-trip

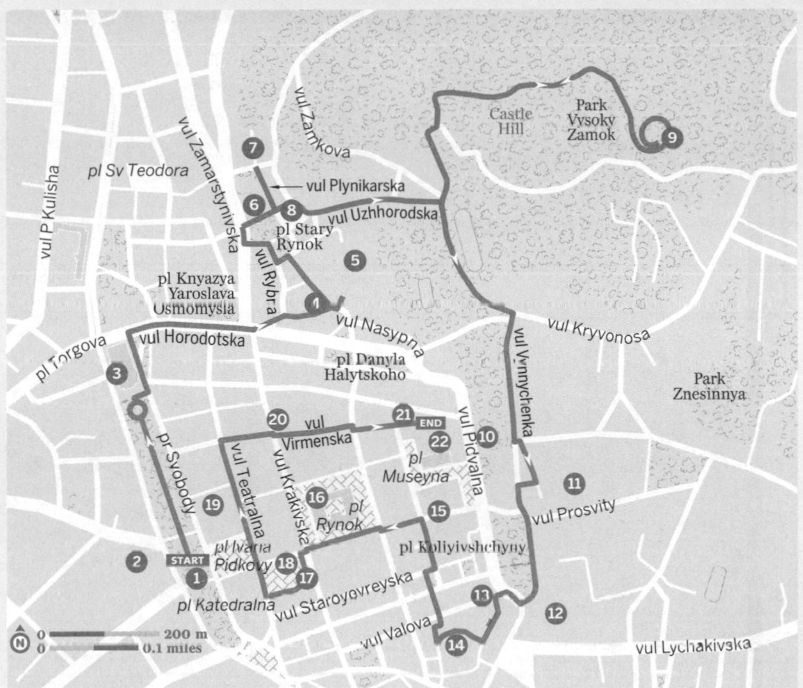

walk from here, and it's worth it for the views across the city. If you're not up for the climb, take a right on vul Zamkova, which leads to the Old Town.

Proceed about 300m on vul Zamkova to a three-way intersection and bear right down vul Vynnychenka. In the park on your right is the 16th-century **10 Gunpowder Tower**, part of the old system of walls and bastions. The twin-spired church looming up the hill on your left is the Greek Catholic **11 St Michael's Church**. It's worth taking a peek inside to see its striking baroque sanctuary. Continue south to vul Valova at the southern end of the park.

If you need a breather, **12 Kabinet Cafe** (p110) is an atmospheric place for a coffee. If not, backtrack about 30 paces and cross the park and tram tracks. You will see No 20 Bapova on your left. Skirt inside the fenced sidewalk and continue along the old brick walls on your right. This is the last standing section of **13 Lviv's medieval fortifications**. Go down the steps and duck right through the arched passageway. You are in the yard of the splendid **14 Bernardine Church & Monastery** (p101).

Head north across the square in front of the church's entrance, cross vul Valova and continue north on vul Fedorova for about 200m until you reach vul Ruska. The **15 Dormition Church** (p99) and its Kornyakt bell tower loom on your right. Go left on vul Ruska, keeping the **16 Ratusha** on your right as you cross pl Rynok. Look for the black facade of **17 Boyim Chapel** (p99), on pl Katedralna, and check inside. When you exit, head straight down the path in front of you, keeping the **18 Latin Cathedral** (p96) on your right, and take the next right on vul Teatralna.

You're now close to where you started, walking north parallel to pr Svobody. Continue past the **19 Jesuit Church**, stopping to admire its interesting baroque and Renaissance facade. Your home stretch, vul Virmenska, is easy to spot – it's Lviv's prettiest street. Hang a right and aim for the eastern terminus of the street, where Dzyga awaits. Before you get there, pop your head into the courtyard of the **20 Armenian Cathedral** (p96). At the **21 Dzyga cafe**, choose an outdoor table with a view of the **22 Dominican Cathedral** (p96) and order yourself a well-deserved Lvivske beer, or a cup of Lviv's legendary coffee.

Central Lviv

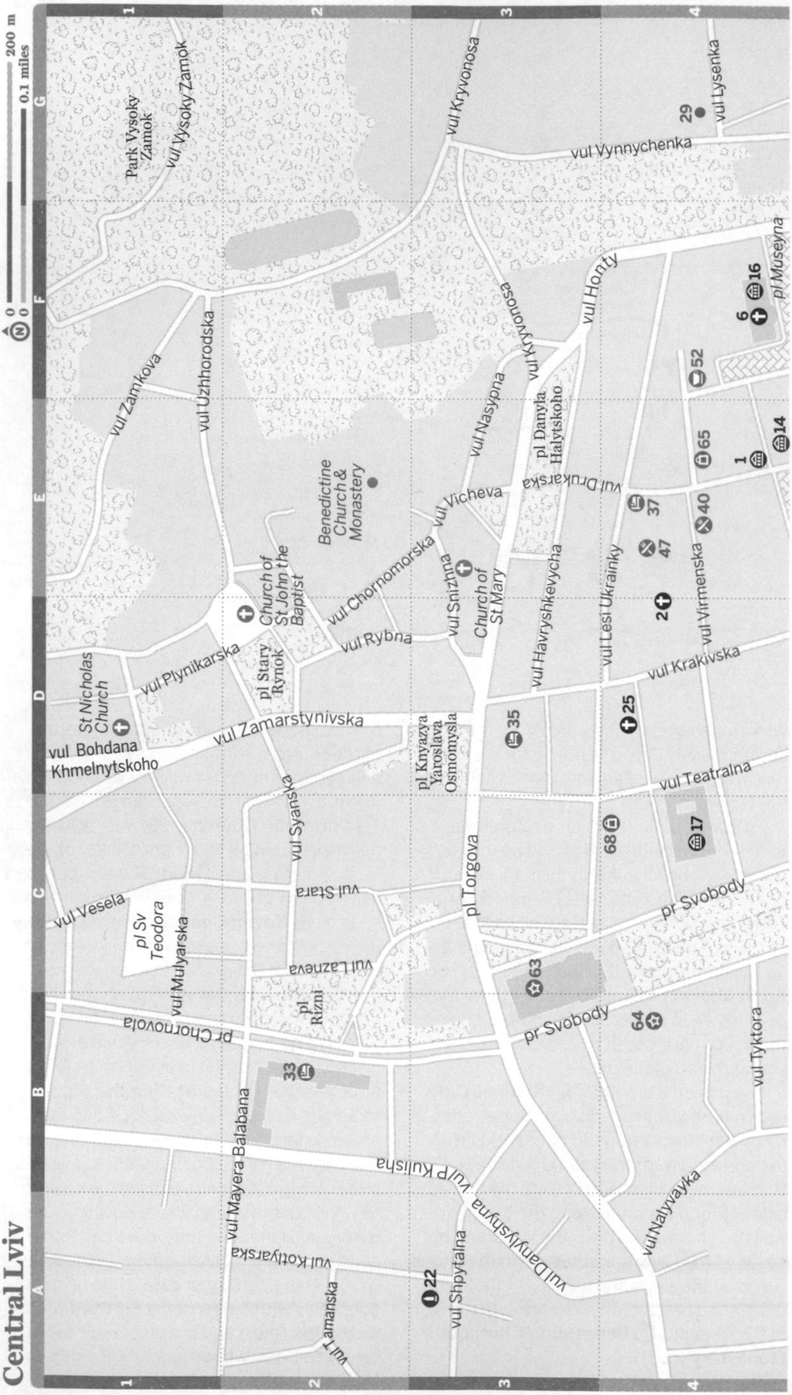

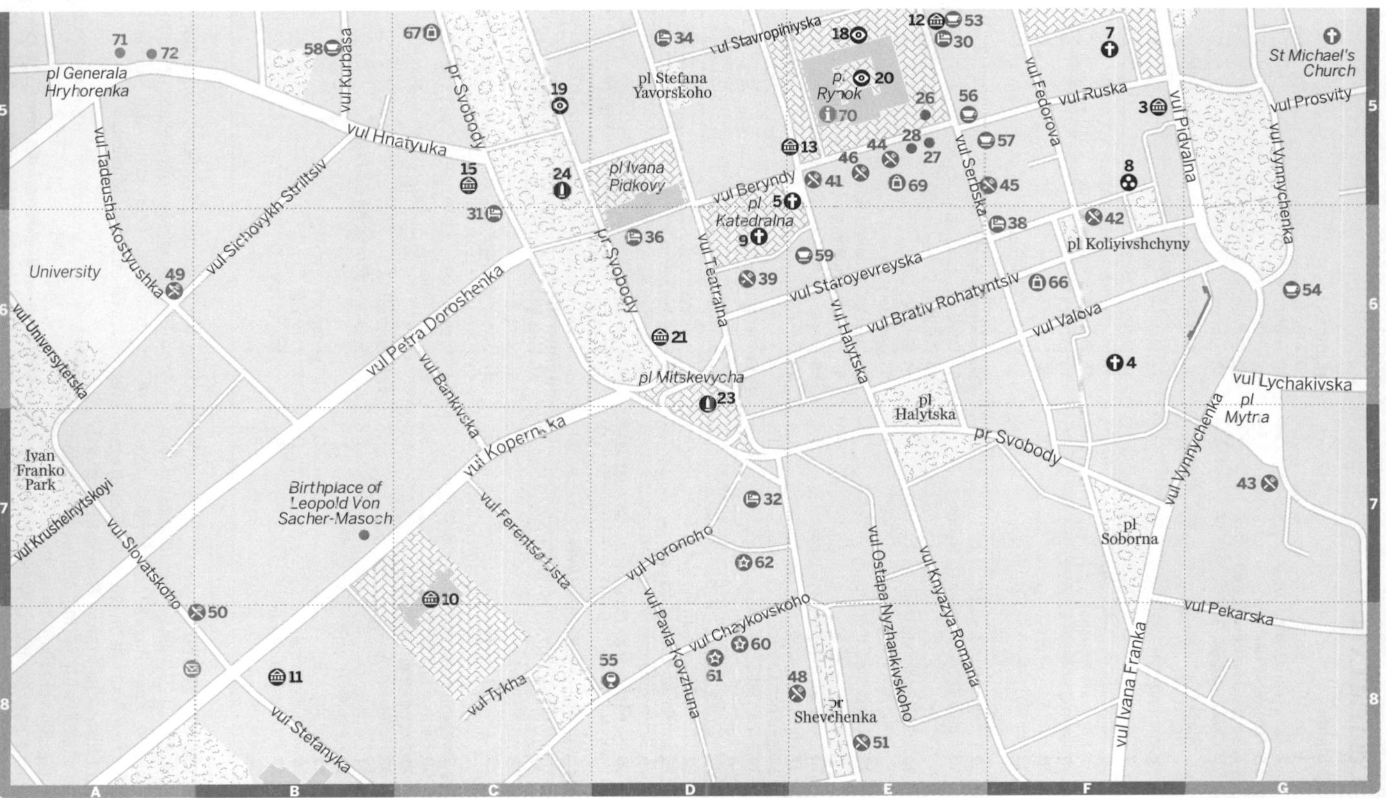

pl Generala Hryhorenka
vul Kurbasa
pr Svobody
pl Stefana Yavorskoho
vul Stavropihiyska
St Michael's Church
vul Prosvity
vul Ruska
vul Pidvalna
vul Vynnychenka
vul Fedorova
vul Hnatyuka
vul Tadeusha Kostyushka
vul Sichovykh Striltsiv
pl Ivana Pidkovy
vul Beryndy
pl Katedralna
vul Serbska
pl Koliyivshchyny
University
vul Teatralna
vul Staroyevreyska
vul Brativ Rohatyntsiv
vul Valova
vul Halytska
vul Petra Doroshenka
vul Universytetska
pl Mitskevycha
vul Bankivska
vul Lychakivska
pl Mytra
pl Halytska
Ivan Franko Park
Birthplace of Leopold Von Sacher-Masoch
vul Krushelnytskoyi
vul Slovatskoho
vul Ferentsa Lista
vul Voronoho
vul Ostapa Nyzhankivskoho
vul Knyazya Romana
pl Soborna
vul Pekarska
vul Chaykovskoho
vul Pavla Kovzhuna
vul Tykha
Shevchenka
vul Ivana Franka
vul Stefanyka

Central Lviv

Sights

1 Apteka Museum ... E4
2 Armenian Cathedral ... D4
3 Arsenal Museum ... F5
4 Bernardine Church and Monastery ... F6
Black Mansion ... (see 53)
5 Boyim Chapel ... E5
6 Dominican Cathedral ... F4
7 Dormition Church ... F5
8 Golden Rose Synagogue ... F5
Kornyakt House ... (see 53)
9 Latin Cathedral ... D6
10 Lviv Art Gallery ... C7
11 Lviv Art Gallery 19th-20th Century Collection ... B8
12 Lviv History Museum ... E5
13 Lviv History Museum (pl Rynok 24) ... E5
14 Lviv History Museum (pl Rynok 2 & 6) ... E4
15 Museum of Ethnography, Arts & Crafts ... C5
16 Museum of Religious History ... F4
17 National Museum ... C4
18 Ploshcha Rynok ... E5
19 Prospekt Svobody ... C5
20 Ratusha ... E5
21 Salo Museum ... D6
22 Sholem Aleichem Plaque ... A3
23 Statue of Adam Michiewicz ... D6
24 Statue of Taras Shevchenko ... C5
25 Transfiguration Church ... D4

Activities, Courses & Tours

26 Chudo Tour ... E5
27 Just Lviv It! ... E5
28 Kumpel Tour ... E5
29 Lemberg Tour ... G4

Sleeping

30 Central Square Hostel ... E5
31 Grand Hotel ... C6
32 Hotel George ... D7
33 Hotel Lviv ... B2
34 Leopolis Hotel ... D5
35 Nataliya-18 ... D3
36 Old City Hostel ... D6
37 Reikartz Medievale ... E4
38 Vintage ... F6

Eating

39 Amadeus ... D6
40 Brudershaft ... E4
41 Celentano ... E5
42 Dim Lehend ... F6
43 Kumpel ... G7
Livy Bereh ... (see 63)
44 Lvivski Plyatsky ... E5
45 Masoch Cafe ... F5
46 Masonic Restaurant ... E5
47 Mons Pius ... E4
48 Puzata Khata ... E8
49 Puzata Khata ... A6
50 Pyrizhky ... B8
51 Veronika ... E8

Drinking & Nightlife

52 Dzyga ... F4
53 Italiysky Dvorik ... E5
54 Kabinet Cafe ... G6
55 Lemberg ... D8
56 Lvivska Kopalnya Kavy ... E5
57 Pid Synoyu Plyashkoyu ... F5
58 Smachna Plitka ... B5
59 Svit Kavy ... E6

Entertainment

60 Kult ... D8
61 Philharmonia ... D8
62 Rafinad People ... D7
63 Solomiya Krushelnytska Lviv Theatre of Opera and Ballet ... C3
64 Teatralni Kasy ... B4

Shopping

65 Iconart Gallery ... E4
66 Nash Format ... F6
67 Opera Passage ... C5
68 Outdoor Arts & Crafts Market ... C4
Ravlyk ... (see 15)
69 Shos Tsikave ... E5

Information

70 Tourist Information Centre ... E5

Transport

71 Kiy Avia ... A5
72 Train Ticket Office ... A5

★ **Old City Hostel** HOSTEL **$**
(Map p104; ☎ 294 9644; www.oldcityhostel.lviv.ua; vul Beryndy 3; dm/d from 80/320uah; @) Occupying two floors of an elegantly fading tenement just steps from pl Rynok, this expertly run hostel with period features and views of the Shevchenko statue from the wraparound balcony has quickly established itself as the city's best. Fluff-free dorms hold four to 16 beds, shower queues are unheard of, sturdy lockers keep your stuff safe and there's a well-endowed kitchen.

Ekotel HOTEL, HOSTEL **$**
(Екотель; Map p98; ☎ 244 3008; www.hotel-ekotel.lviv.ua; vul Sakharova 42; dm 65-140uah, d 220-300uah; @) There are no frills but

plenty of smiles at this spartan but comfortable 94-bed budget hotel and hostel, 2km southwest of the city centre. To keep rates down, rooms do the absolute minimum but are clean and well maintained, though the call-centre furniture could get a touch depressing after a couple of days. The dorms have no bunks, there's a small common room and breakfast is extra.

Central Square Hostel HOSTEL $

(Map p104; ☎095 225 6654; www.cshostel.com; pl Rynok 5; dm/d from 95/320uah;) This hostel may be small, but its location on pl Rynok puts you in the heart of the Lviv action. Free tea and coffee, a pint-sized kitchen and thief-proof lockers, but just one shower.

Reikartz Medievale HOTEL $$

(Map p104; ☎235 0890; www.reikartz.com; vul Drukarska 9; s/d from 595/680uah;) The Lviv link in this 100% Ukrainian chain limits the medieval theme to a few spired bedsteads, the odd tapestry and a bit of chunky furniture. There's also nothing of the Middle Ages about the huge bathrooms, crisp linens and exceptional service. More hryvnya gets you a bigger room, but nothing else.

NTON HOTEL $$

(НТОН; ☎242 4952; www.hotelnton.lviv.ua; vul Shevchenka 154B; s/d from 360/490uah;) Near the terminus of tram 7 in Lviv's western suburbs, this far-flung hotel on the road out to the Polish border may not seem too promising, but this fully renovated place is possibly Lviv's best deal. Rooms are spacious and well furnished, and contain little extras like kettles, sewing kits and hairdryers (these *are* extras in Ukraine!). An entire *Hello* magazine of homegrown celebs has stayed here (Ani Lorak, Via Gra, Valery Miladze), their signed portraits lining the corridors. The breakfast is a bit 'wedding banquet' but there's enough of a choice to satisfy Western tastes.

Hotel Lviv HOTEL $$

(Готель Львів; Map p104; ☎242 3270; pr Chornovola 7; s 220-290uah, d 350-580uah;) This 1965 ugly duckling was transformed into a, well, slightly less unattractive duck in anticipation of free-spending football fans, sending standards and prices higher. It's really the 'updated' singles and doubles you're looking at here, budget rooms that retain a whiff of Soviet lodgings without the nasty pongs and flaky paint. Breakfast is 40uah extra in the 'updated' category.

APARTMENTS

As in most Ukrainian cities, apartments are better bang-for-the-buck than hotels. Try these agencies which should have English-speaking staff:

www.rentinlviv.com (☎067 670 0951; apt from 210uah)

www.inlviv.info (contact@inlviv.info; apt from 350uah)

www.rent-lviv.com (☎238 6193; apt from 400uah)

Hotel George HOTEL $$

(Map p104; ☎232 6236; www.georgehotel.com.ua; pl Mitskevycha 1; s 330-780uah, d 400-850uah;) Seasoned travellers to Lviv will be saddened to learn that the George has been partially renovated and has lost its elusive 'Soviet chic' vibe. A prime candidate for a show-stopping five-star establishment, instead this gorgeous 1901 Art Nouveau building has received a crass, skin-deep makeover, plasticky, faux antique furniture clashing with the high-ceilinged period style in the rooms and cheapo carpets concealing the wonderfully creaky parquet floors. However, communal spaces remain untouched, the English-speaking staff are great and the buffet breakfast is still served in the amazing Oriental-style restaurant.

Eurohotel HOTEL $$

(Map p98; ☎275 7214; www.eurohotel.lviv.ua; vul Tershakovtsiv 6A; s/d from 600/700uah;) This unexciting place is a good example of just what you can do with a surplus Soviet lumpen-hotel. The 90 bog-standard but comfortable rooms are for those who want to sleep, shower and access the web, but little else.

Nataliya-18 HOTEL $$

(Наталія-18; Map p104; ☎242 2068; www.natalia18.lviv.ua; pl Knyazya Yaroslava Osmomysla 7; s/d 500/600uah;) Located on the edge of the former Armenian Quarter, this solid midrange choice features big bathrooms containing Ukraine's softest, fluffiest towels. The 22 odd-shaped rooms are anchored by queen-sized beds draped in fine linens.

★**Vintage** BOUTIQUE HOTEL $$$

(Map p104; ☎235 6834; www.vintagehotel.com.ua; vul Serbska 11; s/d/ste from 760/960/1570uah;) Recently extended, Lviv's first real boutique hotel is this still delightfully intimate 29-room place, accessed through an inconspicuous entrance in the historical centre. Rooms ooze period style with hardwood floors, polished antique-style furniture and Victorian-style wallpaper, successfully blended with flatscreen TVs and 21st-century bathrooms. You'll be looking forward all night to the breakfast, cooked to order and served in the hotel's stylish restaurant. The genuinely friendly staff are glad to help with anything Lviv-related, plus onward travel arrangements and the like.

★Leopolis Hotel LUXURY HOTEL **$$$**
(Map p104; ☎295 9500; www.leopolishotel.com; vul Teatralna 16; s/d from 1100/1300uah;) One of the historical centre's finest places to catch some Zs, the Leopolis comes to you from the same designer who fashioned Tallinn's Telegraaf Hotel. Every guestroom in this 18th-century edifice is different, but all have a well-stocked minibar, elegant furniture and Italian marble bathrooms with underfloor heating. Wheelchair-friendly facilities, a new spa/fitness area in the cellars and a pretty decent brasserie are extras you won't find anywhere else.

Grand Hotel HOTEL **$$$**
(Map p104; ☎272 4042; www.grandhotel.lviv.ua; pr Svobody 13; s/d 880/1150uah;) Having rested too long on its laurels as the only real luxury show in town, the Grand is no longer top dog in Lviv. The rooms, while still holding on to their olde-worlde flavour, are beginning to wilt a bit and the service has been caught flat-footed by other more up-to-speed establishments. Fortunately its prime location on pr Svobody will never fade.

Eating

Lviv is more famous for cafes than restaurants, but the food scene has seen dramatic developments in recent years with some weird and wonderful theme restaurants popping up across the city centre.

Puzata Khata CAFE **$**
(Пузата хата; Map p104; vul Sichovykh Striltsiv 12; mains 11-25uah; 8am-11pm) This super-sized version of Ukraine's No 1 restaurant chain stands out for its classy, Hutsul-themed interior and pure Ukrainian-rock soundtrack. There's another, more tranquil branch at **pr Shevchenka 10** (Map p104).

Celentano PIZZERIA **$**
(Челентано; Map p104; pl Rynok 21; pizza 23-109uah, other mains 12-60uah; 10am-11pm) 'Oh no!', cry those who've picked their way through Ukraine's culinary wilderness via too many Celentano's to reach Lviv's tasty delights, but the new Lviv branch of this popular national chain is a slice above its other stuck-in-the-late-1990s joints. The contemporary interior incorporates chunks of 17th-century architecture and the Apennine fare is delicious and imaginatively presented.

Lvivski Plyatsky CAFE **$**
(Львівські Пляцки; Map p104; pl Rynok 13; strudel 23uah, drinks 15uah; 8am-11pm) Sweet and savoury versions of the strudel, three types of sauce and a simple selection of drinks (this being Lviv, we'd plump for the coffee) – that's the basic idea behind this tiny, 10-seater tucked beneath leaping Gothic vaulting on pl Rynok. The rural-themed interior has cheese graters for lampshades and a definite fixation with the rolling pin.

Pyrizhky PIES **$**
(Пиріжки; Map p104; vul Slovatskoho 4; pyrizhky 3-6uah; 8am-7pm) This blast from the Soviet past has been serving budget *pyrizhky* (pies/turnovers) here for over 50 years.

Dim Lehend UKRAINIAN **$$**
(Дім легенд; Map p104; vul Staroyevreyska 48; mains 30-65uah; 11am-2am) Dedicated entirely to the city of Lviv, there's nothing dim about the 'House of Legends'. The five floors house a library stuffed with Lviv-themed volumes, a room showing live webcam footage of Lviv's underground river, rooms dedicated to lions and cobblestones, and another featuring the city in sounds. A GDR Trabant occupies the roof terrace, the views from which will have you reaching for your camera. From the limited menu, go for the pork chop in berry sauce or the lavash bread stuffed with roast chicken, followed by the delicious apple struddle. It also does a kick-starting breakfast.

Amadeus EUROPEAN **$$**
(Амадеус; Map p104; pl Katedralna 7; mains 100-250uah; 10am-10pm) There's no gimmick at one of Lviv's finest dining spots where the refined interior, peaceful music and perfectly placed patio compliment food that puts this place ahead of its rivals. Fancy European fare like fondue and risotto fill the menu

LEOPOLD VON SACHER-MASOCH

Local historians regularly lock horns on the issue of where the world's original 'masochist' was born. Some claim he came into the world at vul Kopernyka 22 opposite the Pototsky Palace, others assert he must have first seen light of day in a house where the Grand Hotel now stands. Wherever the exact location may have been, the author of *Venus in Furs* was definitely born in Lviv in 1835, although he spent most of his subsequent 60 years begging to be whipped in Austria, Germany and Italy.

If you'd like to experience a light-hearted version of some of Masoch's practices, the waitresses at the **Masoch Cafe** (Мазох-Кафе; Map p104; vul Serbska 7; ⏲ noon-4am) will handcuff and whip you before or after a meal selected from the menu of aphrodisiacs. A bronze of Masoch himself greets 'diners' at the door.

and the drinks menu contains just about every beverage known to man.

Kupol CENTRAL EUROPEAN **$$**

(Купол; Map p98; vul Chaykovskoho 37; mains 40-100uah; ⏲ 11am-9pm) One of the pre-tourism 'originals', this place is designed to feel like stepping back in time – to 1938 in particular, 'the year before civilisation ended' (ie before the Soviets rolled in). The olde-worlde interior is lined with framed letters, ocean-liner ads, antique cutlery, hampers and other memorabilia, and the Polish/Austrian/Ukrainian food is tasty and served with style.

Livy Bereh INTERNATIONAL **$$**

(Map p104; pr Svobody 28; mains 40-80uah; ⏲ 11am-2am) Buried deep beneath the Solomiya Krushelnytska Lviv Theatre of Opera & Ballet, this superb restaurant serves European fare, with a few Ukrainian and Hutsul favourites thrown in. The theme, not surprisingly, is opera, with live broadcasts from the stage above and props throughout, though this sits rather oddly with the wonky walls and crooked door frames. The name, meaning Left Bank, refers to Lviv's underground river which flows under the building, glassed in and crossed by wooden footbridges at the entrance to the restaurant.

Mons Pius UKRAINIAN, INTERNATIONAL **$$**

(Map p104; www.monspius.lviv.ua; vul Lesi Ukrainky 14; mains 40-150uah; ⏲ 9am-11pm; ❄) Well-regimented serving staff dart across the polished brick floors and through the intimate courtyard of this former Armenian bank, a recent and top-quality addition to Lviv's dining scene. Meat dishes anchor the reassuringly brief menu, though there are lots of salads and a few meat-free dishes for non-carnivores. Our only criticism is the small portions, so beef up your beef with a couple of side dishes. Drinks include 'live' Mons Pius beer and lemonade like *babusya* (grandmother) used to make.

Kumpel PUB **$$**

(Кумпель; Map p104; vul Vynnychenka 6; mains 25-80uah; ⏲ 24hr) Centred on two huge copper brewing vats cooking up Krumpel's own beer (1L 29uah), this superb round-the-clock microbrewery restaurant has a low-lit Art Deco theme. The menu is heavy on international meat and two veg combos, with a few local elements included. Locals love it.

Brudershaft CENTRAL EUROPEAN **$$**

(Брудершафт; Map p104; vul Virmenska 16; mains 35-80uah; ⏲ noon-11pm) Austro-Hungary is the theme at this friendly tavern with Emperor Franz Joseph glowering down on diners, a cache of WWI weapons stacked against the bar, and flutters of Habsburg bureaucracy and black spread eagles adorning the walls. This is also reflected in the menu, which is decidedly canivore-friendly and features boar and venison among more common members of the fauna world that regularly make it onto Central Europe's platters.

★ **Masonic Restaurant** EUROPEAN **$$$**

(Map p104; pl Rynok 14; mains before discount 300-500uah; ⏲ 11am-2am) It's hard to know where to start with this place. Finding it is the first obstacle – head to the 2nd floor and open the door of apartment 8 (the number is changed occasionally to throw people off the scent). You'll be accosted by an unshaven bachelor type, into whose Soviet-era kitchen you appear to have inadvertently wandered. Having barred your way for a few minutes, he eventually opens the door to a fancy beamed restaurant full of Masonic symbols and portraits of bygone masons. The next shock is the menu – advertised as Galicia's most expensive restaurant, prices are 10 times higher than normal...so make sure you pick up a 90% discount card at Dim Lehend or Livy Bereh beforehand. The food, by the way, is great and the beer and *kvas* (gingery, beer-like soft drink) come in crystal vases. The toilet is a candlelit Masonic throne. Ukraine's weirdest restaurant experience? Probably.

Veronika INTERNATIONAL **$$$**
(Вероніка; Map p104; pr Shevchenka 21; mains 70-250uah; ⏲9am-11pm) This classy basement restaurant plates up an ambitiously multicultural menu of fish, beef steaks, *shashlyk*, crêpes, *varenyky* (Ukrainian dumplings) and pizzas in a cool, tranquil atmosphere. In addition there's a street-level *konditorei* (central European cake shop and cafe), with criminally delicious desserts.

Drinking & Nightlife

Be careful: Lviv has so many lovely cafes luring you in with olde-worlde charm and the scent of arabica that disciples of the bean risk over-caffeination. Lviv also has a fine and growing selection of watering holes.

★Kabinet Cafe CAFE
(Кафе Кабінет; Map p104; vul Vynnychenka 12; ⏲10am-11pm) The jumble of moth-eaten antique chairs and sofas, book-lined walls and dusty parquet floors are no product of a restaurateur's imagination – this place is real! Evoking prewar (and pre-tourism) Lviv, it would be a shame to sit outside on busy vul Vynnychenka in summer, and in winter this is the perfect spot to curl up with a book, order a warming cup of aromatic Lviv coffee and pretend it's 19-something.

Dzyga CAFE
(Дзига; Map p104; www.dzyga.com.ua; vul Virmenska 35; ⏲10am-midnight; 📶) This cafe-cum–art gallery in the shadow of the Dominican Cathedral has a relaxed vibe. It's particularly popular with bohemian, alternative types, but seems to attract pretty much everyone, really. The summertime outdoor seating is gathered around the city's Monument to the Smile. If it's full, there are other attractive options for a nibble or a cuppa joe nearby on postcard-pretty vul Virmenska.

Smachna Plitka CAFE
(Смачна Плітка; Map p104; vul Kurbasa 3; ⏲11am-11pm) Head down the stairs behind an anonymous wooden door in the facade of the Kurbasa Theatre to find a basement cafe that's everything you want a central European coffeehouse to be – small cafe tables tucked furtively into corners, hard-to-beat coffees and beers, and turtle-necked revolutionaries filling the air with schemes. Hard to find, but one of Lviv's longest established cafes.

Lemberg PUB
(Лемберг; Map p104; vul Chaykovskoho 18; ⏲noon-10pm) The 17 types of mostly Ukrainian beer, the huge burlesque posters adorning the walls, the crude timber floor and smoky, rowdy, local-rockstar-gone-doolally atmosphere make this an entertaining spot to retox, though the service is nonchalant and the miserable cellar is a place to avoid.

Pid Synoyu Plyashkoyu CAFE
(Під синьою пляшкою; Map p104; vul Ruska 4; ⏲10am-10pm) With its nostalgia for the Polish-Austrian past and its dark interior, the tiny 'Under the Blue Bottle' cafe at the back of a courtyard has a cosy, secretive atmosphere. It serves sandwiches and fondues, as well as wine and coffee with pepper. Set well back from the street along a passageway.

Svit Kavy CAFE
(Світ Кави; Map p104; pl Katedralna 6; ⏲7.45am-11pm Mon-Fri, from 8.45am Sat & Sun; 📶) Pick of the bunch on pl Katedralna, with no theme, no gimmicks, just a focus on Lviv's best coffee-making traditions (hence it's always packed with locals). Beans come from almost every continent, and if you like the drink, you can buy the unground raw ingredient in the shop next door.

Lvivska Kopalnya Kavy CAFE
(Map p104; pl Rynok 10; ⏲8am-11pm; 📶) Lviv is Ukraine's undisputed coffee capital and the 'Lviv Coffee Mine' is where the stratum of arabica is excavated by the local colliers from deep beneath pl Rynok. You can tour the mine or just sample the heart-pumping end product at tables as dark as the brews inside or out on the courtyard beneath old timber balconies.

Robert Doms Beer House BEER HALL
(Хмільний Дім Роберта Домса; Map p98; www.robertdoms.lviv.ua; vul Kleparivska 18; ⏲noon-midnight) This fantastic, utterly unique beer hall is located three storeys underground in a centuries-old beer-storage vault once used by the neighbouring Lvivske brewery. It's named after the brewery's founder and features fresh Lvivske served in litre steins,

plus German food and nightly live music in one of the vault's four chambers.

Italiysky Dvorik CAFE
(Італійський дворик; Map p104; pl Rynok 6; ⏲10am-8pm) Even if you decide to skip the Lviv History Museum, it's worth popping in for a coffee in its aptly named inner courtyard. There's a 2uah fee to enter.

Picasso CLUB
(www.picasso.lviv.ua; vul Zelena 88; ⏲from 10pm) Lviv's most atmospheric club, inside a former theatre, has consistently good DJs and a consistently festive crowd paying proper homage to them.

Rafinad People CLUB
(Map p104; www.rafinad-club.com; vul Rudanskoho 1; ⏲from 10pm) If you can get past the face control (no sports shoes, please), this is possibly Lviv's classiest mainstream club with something happening every night of the week.

✩ Entertainment

Advance tickets for most of Lviv's venues are sold at the **Teatralna Kasa** (Theatre Box Office; Map p104; pr Svobody 37; ⏲10am-5pm Mon-Sat).

Solomiya Krushelnytska Lviv Theatre of Opera & Ballet THEATRE
(Map p104; ☎235 6586; www.opera.lviv.ua; pr Svobody 28) For an evening of high culture, and to enjoy the ornate building, take in a performance at this Lviv institution. Closes for most of July and August.

Philharmonia CLASSICAL MUSIC
(Map p104; ☎235 8136; www.philharmonia.lviv.ua; vul Chaykovskoho 7) If classical music is your thing, let yourself be wooed by the sweet strains of Lviv's regional philharmonic orchestra. Things are very quiet here from July through to mid-September.

Kult LIVE MUSIC
(Map p104; www.kult.lviv.ua; vul Chaykovskoho 7; ⏲noon-2am) This superb basement venue next to the Philharmonia reverberates with live Ukrainian rock music every night of the week.

Shopping

Nash Format SOUVENIRS
(Наш Формат; Map p104; www.nashformat.ua; vul Brativ Rohatyntsiv 24; ⏲10am-7pm Mon-Sat, from noon Sun) If *salo* fridge magnets and made-in-Guangdong Hutsul mementos don't have you cracking open your wallet, try this 'nationalist' souvenir boutique selling Ukrainian CDs and DVDs, flags, books and T-shirts emblazoned with Ukrainian/Lviv/nationalist/UPA symbols and personalities (so perhaps not quite the attire for that train trip to the Donbas).

Outdoor Arts & Crafts Market MARKET
(Map p104; cnr vul Lesi Ukrainky & vul Teatralna; ⏲10.30am-6pm) Located opposite the Zankovetska Theatre, this large market sells rugs, embroidered blouses, wooden *pysanky* (patterned eggs), woodcrafts, and lots of Soviet and prewar junk.

Shos Tsikave ARTS & CRAFTS
(Щось Цікаве; Map p104; pl Rynok 13) This tiny emporium is the antidote to Ukraine's souvenir industry and offers one-of-a-kind handmade crafts, some produced by disabled children. It's buried deep behind the facades on pl Rynok's southern flank – enter along the alleyway next to Lvivski Plyatsky.

Iconart Gallery ARTS & CRAFTS
(Map p104; www.iconart.com.ua; vul Virmenska 26) Small shop and adjoining gallery specialising in high-quality modern twists on sacral art, including brightly coloured icons painted on glass and aged lime wood. Many of the artists work as curators and restorers at the nearby National Museum.

Opera Passage MALL
(Map p104; www.operapassage.com; pr Svobody 27) Elite brand shopping mall housing an iStore, a tranquil cafe and a better-than-average supermarket in the basement.

Ravlyk SOUVENIRS
(Равлик; Map p104; pr Svobody 15; ⏲10am-6pm) Located in the Museum of Ethnography, Arts & Crafts, the quality of the souvenirs at Ravlyk is high, particularly the *pysanky*.

Krakivsky Rynok MARKET
(Краківський ринок; Map p98; vul Bazarna) Fans of outdoor markets will enjoy this real, bustling Soviet-style *rynok* (market) with all the fresh fruit, raw meat and cheap junk that entails.

ℹ Information

The glossy English-language lifestyle and listings magazine *Lviv Today* (www.lvivtoday.com.ua) is available at many hotels.

Central Post Office (Map p104; vul Slovatskoho 1; ⏲9am-8pm Mon-Fri, to 4pm Sat, to 3pm Sun)

TRAVEL FROM LVIV TO POLAND

With budget airlines flying into neighbouring Polish cities, Lviv is a popular transit point in and out of Ukraine. However, Poland's EU accession and rampant cigarette smuggling have made border delays even longer.

There are several routes between Lviv and the Polish airports in Kraków and Rzeszow, and different travellers have different preferences. Some recommend the train to and from the Polish border town of Przemysl, where you can at least sit during the average two- to three-hour waiting time. Others prefer to jam themselves on the much quicker *marshrutka* (fixed-route minibus) 297 between Lviv train station and the road crossing at Shehyni/Medyka (20uah, 1½ hours, hourly), where they alight, walk across the border, and then take another *marshrutka* onwards. This can be the quickest route and handy if you need to leave Lviv for Poland after the last train has departed. Beware though; the *marshrutky* are crowded and you have to stand in often long border queues (EU passport holders are sometimes sent to the front of the line).

Municipal Hospital (Map p98; 252 7590; vul Mykolaychuka 9) Hospital with emergency room.

Tourist Information Centre (Map p104; 254 6079; www.lviv.travel; pl Rynok 1, Ratusha; 10am-8pm Mon-Fri, to 7pm Sat, to 6pm Sun) Ukraine's best tourist information centre, which publishes a free, daily what's on schedule. There are branches at the airport (067 673 9194; 10am-8pm Mon-Sat, to 6pm Sun) and the train station (Map p98; 226 2005; Ticket Hall; 9am-8pm Mon-Sat, to 6pm Sun).

Getting There & Away

A cheap way to enter Ukraine is to fly to Poland on a budget airline then proceed overland to Lviv from there.

AIR

Lviv's new **Danylo Halytskyi International Airport** (229 8112; www.lwo.aero; vul Lyubinska 168) stands 7km west of the city centre. The only surviving domestic flight is the Lviv to Kyiv run (1½ hours, four daily). Book through **Kiy Avia** (Map p104; 260 3228; www.kiyavia.com; vul Hnyatuka 20; 8am-8pm Mon-Fri, 9am-5pm Sat, 10am-3pm Sun).

Internationally, Lviv is attracting an ever-increasing number of flights to Western Europe and Russia. There are currently services to/from Vienna, Munich, Warsaw, Timişoara, İstanbul, Dortmund, Venice, Wrocław, Kraków, Naples, Milan, Rome, Tel Aviv, Hurghada and Moscow. Sadly (or maybe not) Ryanair pulled out of planned flights that would have linked Lviv with London Stansted.

BUS

The extremely inconveniently located **Main bus station** (Holovny Avtovokzal; vul Stryska) is a whopping 7km south of the city centre. To reach the city centre take trolleybus 5. Confusing **Bus Station No 8** (Map p98; 032 238 8308), in front of the main train station, is the place to pick up a quick *marshrutka* (fixed-route minibus) if you miss your train or there are no tickets; it also handles a few services to western and southern destinations and is the departure point for the Shehyni border *marshrutka*. **Bus Station No 2** is 3km north of the city centre (take bus 1A from pr Svobody) but is only good for services to Zhovkva (8uah, 45 minutes, many daily), Pochayiv (55uah, 3½ hours, four daily), Olesko (26uah, 1½ hours, many daily) and Kremenets (58uah, 3½ hours, three daily).

From the Main bus station, buses serve most major cities, including:

Chernivtsi 106uah, eight hours, four daily

Ivano-Frankivsk 52uah, 3½ hours, at least two hourly

Kamyanets-Podilsky 106uah, 7½ hours, five daily

Kolomyya 77uah, 4½ hours, 15 daily

Kyiv 175uah, nine hours, up to 10 daily

Lutsk 63uah, three to four hours, many daily (some from Bus Stations Nos 2 and 8)

Odesa 397uah, 16 hours, once daily

Ternopil 50uah, three hours, many daily

Uzhhorod 93uah, 6½ hours, up to 12 daily (some from Bus Station No 8)

International services all leave from the Main bus station. The selection of destinations by and large reflects the number of Ukrainian *gastarbeiter* (guest or foreign workers) a country has, hence the numerous connections to the Czech Republic, Italy, Spain and Germany. Buy tickets at the **International Bus Ticket Office** (Міжнародна автобусна каса; 9am-6pm) inside the Main bus station.

TRAIN

Lviv's main train station is 2km west of the city centre, connected to town by trams 1, 9 and 10.

The quickest way to Kyiv is on the daily Intercity+ express (238uah, five hours), though this leaves at a bleary-eyed 5.50am. There are also at least nine regular trains per day, most of them overnight services (110uah to 150uah, eight to 13 hours).

Other connections from Lviv:

Chernivtsi 81uah, 5½ hours, three daily
Chop 110uah, 5½ hours, four daily
Ivano-Frankivsk 70uah to 104uah, 2½ hours, six daily
Kharkiv 250uah, 18 hours, daily
Kolomyya 72uah, four hours, three daily
Lutsk 15uah, three hours, once daily
Odesa 176uah, 12 hours, four daily
Rakhiv 81uah, 7¾ hours, once daily
Simferopol 432uah, 24 hours, up to three daily
Ternopil 94uah, two hours, 14 daily
Uzhhorod 85uah to 110uah, six hours, up to five daily
Vinnytsya 111uah to 136uah, 6½ hours, nine daily

International trains serve Moscow (25 hours, daily), St Petersburg (28 hours, daily), Bratislava (18 hours, daily) and Minsk (12 hours, daily).

The most painless way to acquire a train ticket is to use the Soviet-era but centrally located **Train Ticket Office** (Залізничні квиткові каси; Map p104; vul Hnatyuka 20; 8am-2pm & 3-8pm Mon-Sat, to 6pm Sun).

Getting Around

To reach the city centre from the airport, take trolleybus 9 to the university (vul Universytetska) or bus 48 to the corner of vul Doroshenka and pr Svobody.

Lviv is riddled with tramlines and trolleybus wires and *marshrutky* dart across the cobbles and into spaces between other vehicles that sometimes turn out to be too small. The Tourist Information Office has comprehensive maps of the entire network (unthinkable in other Ukrainian cities). A useful tram route is the No 7 which trundles from the NTON Hotel to the Lychakivske Cemetery via vul Pidvalna and the Museum of Folk Architecture and Life.

If you must travel by taxi, and Lviv's good public transport network means you can probably avoid it, call **Vashe Taksi** (063 854 8995).

There's a **bike-rental centre** (067 675 6301; www.bicyclerent.lviv.ua; pl Rynok 42; per hr/day 25/90uah) right on pl Rynok. Take your passport or a 1500uah deposit.

Zhovkva Жовква

03252 / POP 13,300

With your own wheels, the most impressive day trip from Lviv is probably Pochayiv Monastery. However, it's too difficult to visit quickly on public transport, leaving the fairly low-key historical town of Zhovkva at the top of the list. Its cluster of pastel-coloured buildings, handful of impressive churches and city-wall remnants will happily occupy you for an hour or two.

Built in the 16th century in an imitation of Italian-Renaissance style, Zhovkva was the birthplace of legendary Cossack Bohdan Khmelnytsky, who reportedly led his men through the 17th-century **Zvirynetska Gate** when liberating the town from the Poles in 1648. Ironically, however, the town's heyday was actually under the Poles, when it became the preferred residence of 17th-century King Jan III Sobiesky. Today roughly a dozen buildings – a monastery, lesser churches, a synagogue and a 'castle' that's not really a castle – cluster around the market square.

Zhovkva is 28km north of Lviv and can be reached by virtually any bus or *marshrutka* leaving Bus Station No 2 (8uah, 45 minutes, several hourly).

Olesko Олесько

03264 / POP 1800

Some 70km east of Lviv, Olesko boasts a French chateau-style hilltop castle visible for miles around. The current castle dates back to the 18th century but it was built on the site of a medieval fortress, destroyed by Tatar attacks in the 15th century. To get to Olesko, take any bus (23uah, 1½ hours, around 25 daily) heading towards Brody from Lviv's Bus Station No 2. Alternatively, travel agencies in Lviv organise day trips.

Drohobych Дрогобич

03244 / POP 77,600

Once home to Jewish-Polish writer and artist Bruno Schulz, Drohobych is of most interest to his fans, who might hope (possibly in vain) to recognise the town from his magic-realist novella *The Street of Crocodiles* (1934). Otherwise this quiet provincial town is mildly diverting if not gripping. There are plenty of historical monuments and some faded Polish and Austro-Hungarian homes. The leafy **Bandera Park** above the town square is lovely today, but it was around here that a vengeful German SS officer shot Schulz in 1942.

Indeed, while up to 40% of Drohobych's 35,000 inhabitants were once Jewish, only a handful remain. The truly enormous **New**

Synagogue (1865) was a Soviet furniture store and has long lain derelict. You pass the building on the left when making the 10- to 15-minute walk from the bus station into town.

Frescoes that Schulz painted for his Nazi 'protector' in WWII were, controversially, taken to Jerusalem's Yad Veshem Holocaust Museum in 2001. But the town schedules a Schulz festival every second November (including in 2014), has plans for a museum and displays a memorial plaque on vul Y Drohobycha.

The town lies some 80km southwest of Lviv. *Marshrutky* (29uah, 1½ hours, at least hourly) depart from Lviv's Bus Station No 8 (in front of Lviv's train station). In Drohobych other frequent *marshrutky* (20 minutes) take you the 10km to Truskavets.

Truskavets Трускавець

☎03247 / POP 30,000

Truskavets is an old-fashioned spa town that in another country and another time might have given the Czech Republic's celebrated spa town Karlovy Vary a run for its money. Unfortunately, that sort of rivalry is a long way off, but the town still makes a fun day trip from Lviv. Its heart is the mineral water *buvyet* (Бювет Мінеральних Вод, spring) in the central park, where locals supposedly once came to drink from the fountain of good health.

Two 'cures' are on tap. Sodova water is reputedly good for the digestive tract; Naftusya for kidney, urinary tract and liver ailments. The springs only run at certain hours and you're supposed to drink the water at a certain temperature, but you can find extensive instructions posted in several languages, including English. Oddly shaped spa cups are used here, with a long spout for sucking. They are so designed because the mineral-rich water is allegedly good for other bodily parts, but not the teeth. You can buy yourself a cup in one of the park kiosks.

Truskavets has thousands of beds in all price ranges but hotels tend to be much of a sameness. However, one hillside hotel stands out if you fancy an overnight stay. The **Rixos-Prikarpatye** (☎032 477 1111; www.rixos.com.ua; vul Horodyshche 8; d & tw from 1000uah;) is an oasis of luxury with a professional medical centre, trendy modern spa treatments, German patients and Ukrainian oligarchs. It even has its own supply of Sodova and Naftusya – drunk elegantly through straws up here.

The simplest way to reach Truskavets is by bus (30uah, two hours, two hourly). Services leave from Lviv's Bus Station No 8 in front of the train station.

TERNOPIL REGION

This triangular-shaped region at the heart of western Ukraine may have some stunning countryside, but it's fairly off the radar for independent travellers. Not many foreigners even make it to the larger population centres, although a couple of the smaller towns like Pochayiv and Kremenets are worth the effort.

Ternopil Тернопіль

☎0352 / POP 218,600

Arrive in Ternopil on the right day, and this town, which lends its name to the wider region, has a laid-back, leafy almost European feel, rather like an anonymous piece of Poland or the Czech Republic. Its signature feature is a huge artificial lake that's pleasant enough to stroll around of an evening, and the tiny Old Town centre has been appealingly renovated, but that's about it. For those with time, the town could be a low-key stop-off between Chernivtsi or Kamyanets-Podilsky and Lviv. Most snore through it on a sleeper train in the early hours.

Sights

Museum of Political Prisoners MUSEUM
(Музей Політичних В'язнів; vul Kopernyka 1; 10am-5pm Tue & Thu-Sun) FREE A block back from bul Shevchenka, this former KGB prison is where several prominent members of UPA and OUN were held, tortured and shot in the years of Soviet repression following WWII. The prison only closed in 1986 and became a museum in the mid-1990s. The dank cells and other spaces contain various chilling exhibitions but have been left in their original state complete with crumbling plaster and barred cellar windows. Access is from the back of the building.

Bul Taras Shevchenko STREET
The town's verdant showpiece, complete with landscaping, fountains and mature trees, is a popular hang-out and a pleasant spot for an evening corso. Heading north

you cannot fail to notice the **Shevchenko Theatre**, one of the region's grandest neoclassical edifices. At the top of the facade is a bust of Shevchenko, who looks as though he has a croissant wedged under his nose. The square in front, maydan Teatralni, is remarkable as it must be the only sizeable piazza in all Europe not to have a single cafe table or brewery-sponsored sun shade occupying its expanse.

Ternopil Lake LAKE
(Тернопільське озеро) Don your best fake D&G, grab a bottle of hop fizz and head to the lake, the place to see and be seen on summer evenings. Created in the 16th century as part of the defence system for the now all-but defunct castle, there are regular boat trips across it, aqua-zorbing on it, a beer-tent strip next to it and a generally jolly atmosphere around it.

Dominican Church CHURCH
(vul Hetmana Sahaydachnoho) At the western end of vul Hetmana Sahaydachnoho, where it opens up into maydan Voli, the dirty-cream and grey Dominican Church and monastery complex hoists the city's finest silhouette. Built in the mid-18th century, its symmetrical twin towers rise from a baroque facade and the interior has an oval nave.

Rizdva Khrystovoho Church CHURCH
(vul Ruska) Ternopil's most attractive ecclesiastical interior belongs to the 17th century Church of the Nativity. Inside this oasis of calm, the nave explodes in gilded colour, musty murals and polished-brass incense burners. Outside stands a very visible monument to the 1932–33 famine (many are hidden in obscure locations).

Sleeping & Eating

Seems like eating out isn't particularly popular among Ternopil folk and public food is hard to come by except in a few fast-food joints. For self-caterers, train carriage gourmets and park-bench diners, the **Barvinok Supermarket** (Барвінок; vul Ruska 5) is a commendable source of bread, cheese and drinking yoghurt.

Hotel Ternopil HOTEL $$
(☎524 263; www.hotelternopil.com; vul Zamkova 14; s/d from 435/530uah; wi-fi) Conveniently located between the lake and the Dominican Church, the Ternopil is a renovated former Intourist wedge with a restaurant and fitness centre. The hotel's unusual slogan is 'Time just never stops here' – you may be glad this is true after a night in one of its garish bedrooms. Rates include a buffet breakfast.

Hotel Halychyna HOTEL $$
(Готель Галичина; ☎533 595; www.hotelhalychyna.com; vul Chumatska 1; s/d standard 335/400uah; wi-fi) Across the lake from the town centre, the Halychyna hasn't quite been transformed from Soviet ugly duckling into 21st-century swan, but the owners have had an OK bash at it. Staff are now courteous and helpful, and rooms have new beds and duvets. However, the USSR still skulks in the jerky lift, on the crumbly balconies and at the proletarian breakfast, the last item now included in the rates, though you'll probably wish it wasn't.

Getting There & Away

Ternopil's frantic bus station, 1km south of the town centre, lives up to its role as a regional hub. Connections include the following:

Ivano-Frankivsk 49uah, three hours, at least twice hourly
Kamyanets-Podilsky 59uah, three hours, up to 10 daily
Kremenets 25uah, 1½ hours, many daily
Lutsk 70uah, 3½ hours, 13 daily
Lviv 45uah, three hours, at least hourly
Pochayiv 23uah, 1½ hours, 14 daily

The train station stands two block east of bul Shevchenka. Connections to/from Ternopil:

Chernivtsi 106uah, six to 7½ hours, three daily
Kyiv 150uah, six to eight hours, around seven daily
Lviv 110uah, two hours, 13 daily plus five slower *elektrychka* (electric train; 12uah)
Odesa 120uah, 10 hours, three daily
Simferopol 280uah, 22 to 23 hours, three daily

Getting Around

Trolleybuses 5, 8 and 9 will get you from the bus station to the train station and the town centre.

Pochayiv Почаїв

☎03546 / POP 17,700

With its ornate golden domes rising up from the surrounding plain, **Pochayiv Monastery** (Pochayivska Lavra; ☎612 18; grounds 24hr, excursion bureau 11am-4pm) FREE is a beacon of Ukrainian Orthodoxy (Moscow Patriarchate) on the edge of a largely Ukrainian Catholic region. Indeed, it's the country's second-largest Orthodox complex

WORTH A TRIP

PIDKAMIN

Known today primarily for its striking natural hilltop standing stone, the village of Pidkamin (Підкамінь) was once most celebrated for its huge fortified monastery. This was founded at the same time as Pochayiv by monks hightailing it from Kyiv before the Mongols hit town in 1240, and was later beefed up to protect the icon of the Blessed Virgin. The icon was spirited away to Wrocław at the end of WWII when most of the region's Polish population was sent packing. The crumbling remains of the monastery rise just a short amble from the 17m-high rock from which Pidkamin, meaning 'under the rock', takes its name. This was a significant place of pagan ceremony, but the graves circling its base probably belong to 17th-century Cossacks.

Pidkamin comes alive once a year during the large **Pidkamin Ethnofestival** (http://pidkamin.ridne.net) in late July, which attracts acts and audiences from across the Ukrainian-speaking provinces.

As the village is in a different region to Pochayiv, there are virtually no 'cross-border' buses between the two. Regular services run from Brody 22km away, which has good connections to Lviv.

after Kyiv's Kyevo-Pecherska Lavra and was founded by monks fleeing that mothership when the Mongols sacked Kyiv in 1240.

Visitors will find the monastery's ornate golden dome and church interiors beautiful and its mystical aura intriguing. The atmosphere is much more devout than at the *lavra* (senior monastery) in Kyiv.

Pochayiv is frequently packed, but tourists are still outnumbered by pilgrims visiting the Mother of God icon (1597) or the 'footprint of the Virgin Mary'. The busiest religious festivals are the Feast of the Assumption on 28 August and the Feast of St Iov, a 17th-century Pochayiv abbot and the *lavra*'s most important monk, on 10 September.

Both of the monastery's famous religious relics are found in the baroque **Uspensky Cathedral** (1771–83), whose entrance is straight ahead and to your left, on the crest of the hill after you enter the main gate. The famed footprint of Mary, reportedly left after the Virgin appeared to a local monk and a shepherd, has a holy spring with purportedly healing waters. The Mother of God icon is imbued with the power to work any miracle. Both are to the right of the central aisle.

The 65m-tall baroque **bell tower** (1861–71) is worth climbing for the view, if you can sneak in with a tour group or monk. Its central knocker weighs over 315kg.

On the far side of the Uspensky Cathedral is a building with a door leading down to the **Cave Church**. Pilgrims come here to pay their respects to the relics (ie remains) of St Iov.

Because this is an Orthodox place of worship, men aren't allowed to wear hats or shorts, and women must cover their head, knees and hands (no trousers, shorts or skirts above the knee, but six-inch heels seem to be fine). This applies to the churches *and* the grounds. Trouser-clad women can borrow a wraparound skirt from the excursion bureau. The souvenir stalls on the way up to the monastery do a roaring trade in headscarves. No photography is allowed anywhere once through the gates, but a snap of the views from the monastery ramparts is possibly worth a ticking-off from a monk.

Tourists almost always visit Pochayiv as a day trip, either from Ternopil, Kremenets, Dubno or even, if they have a car, from Lviv. Little white *marshrutky* shuttle back and forth almost constantly to and from Kremenets (7uah, 30 minutes), from where you can pick up services on the main Lutsk–Ternopil or Rivne–Ternopil routes. They drop off and then wait to fill up at the bottom of the hill below the monastery.

Kremenets Кременець

☎03546 / POP 22,000

The remains of a hilltop **fortress** (admission 5uah) overlook picturesque Kremenets' cluster of pastel-coloured, freshly renovated churches. The Mongols never managed to capture this castle during their sweep through Kyivan Rus in 1240–41 (despite reaching Kremenets' outskirts), but today it's easily breeched by individual hikers and day-trippers. Dating from at least the 12th century, and possibly earlier, the *zamok* (castle) on Bona Hill now lies in ruins, with only a ring of walls and a gate tower remaining. However, it's a surprisingly pleasant spot for longer-term travellers in Ukraine to while away a few hours and the views from the hill are magnificent (see if you can spot Pochayiv glistening in the distance).

Unlike the Mongols, Ukrainian Cossacks did manage to conquer Kremenets 400 years later. During the Khmelnytsky uprising against Poland in 1648, the town was liberated by a band of Cossacks, who principally starved out the Poles. Some 100 or so of the Cossacks who died in the accompanying skirmishes are buried in the remarkable **Pyatnytske Kladovyshche** (Pyatnystke Cemetery), where stubby stone crosses stand lost in the long grass. It's a tranquil spot at any time of day but get up here at dawn or dusk for a bit of Ukrainian magic.

When the Poles regained control of Kremenets, they sealed their victory by building another of the town's main sights, the **Jesuit Collegium** (1731–43), on the main drag through town. In turn the Soviets sealed their triumph in WWII by plonking a bombastic **war monument** right in front of the church.

When you've seen all the above, the obscure **Regional Museum** (vul Shevchenka 90; admission 5uah; ⌚8.30am-5pm Thu-Tue) is worth a spin for its back-to-the-1980s exhibition and light-switch monitors. Highlights include some interesting Cossack and Kievan Rus–era finds, some surprisingly modest folk costumes and photos of prewar Kremenets.

Kremenets was the birthplace of renowned Jewish violinist Isaac Stern (1920). Jewish communities lived here, on and off, from the 15th century until 1942, when the Nazis massacred 15,000 people herded into the ghetto here.

The Old Town centre and fortress both lie 2.5km south of the bus station along the main artery, vul Shevchenko. Turn right when exiting the bus station or bus station office, and walk 30 to 40 minutes to the town, which is strung out along the road. To climb the hill, keep going to just past the edge of the town until you reach a turn-off marked with a yellow sign bearing the words замкова гора. The entire walk from the bus station to the summit takes roughly 1¼ hours. Alternatively, take one of the many buses or *marshrutky* from the bus station to the town centre to halve your journey on foot.

To reach the Cossack cemetery, look for the town market, with the word ринок across an arch. Heading from here back north to the bus station, take the next right opposite a small car park. Bear left then left again where the road forks and walk about 10 minutes uphill.

The most convenient place to stay is **Hotel Vika** (☎238 83; otel_edem@ukr.net; vul Dubenska 57; r 140-190uah; 📶), a big yellow building between the bus station and the town centre with unexciting new rooms containing scratchy carpets, bland office furniture but bathrooms with full-size baths. In the unlikely event it's full, the owners have another hotel with a restaurant. The **Vopak Supermarket** (vul Dubenska 132) next to the bus station is the best source of sustenance in town.

From Kremenets, there are over 40 daily buses to and from Ternopil (25uah, 1½ hours), and a regular service to and from Pochayiv (8uah, 30 minutes). Other destinations include Lutsk (32uah, two hours, at least 10 daily), Lviv (46uah, 3¼ hours, two daily) and Dubno (14uah, twice hourly, 45 minutes).

VOLYN & RIVNE REGIONS

Lutsk Луцьк

☎0332 / POP 202,900

Lutsk is a rare thing in Ukraine – a place that takes tourism seriously. It provides visitors with the genuine Ukrainian experience, but gives them a free map to help them have it. Competing with Lviv isn't easy, but Lutsk is running a definite second, far ahead of any other comparable town in the region.

Volyn's chief settlement has a split personality. The modern town is a relatively successful example of Soviet architecture, with broad boulevards and monumental squares creating a feeling of freedom and space. But the real jewel in Lutsk's crown is its historic conservation area and castle. This small, slowly refurbishing enclave of cobbled streets is lined with architecture from centuries past, harking back to Lutsk's Lithuanian, Polish and Russian history.

Sights

Starting from modern Lutsk's central hub of maydan Teatralny, traffic-free vul Lesi Ukrainky heads southwest towards the picturesque Old Town, which nestles across busy vul Kovelska in a bend of the Styr River.

Lutsk Castle CASTLE
(vul Kafedralna 1; admission 10uah; ⏲10am-7pm Tue-Sun) Lutsk's 14th-century castle stands surrounded by ornate 17th-century churches and homes and is in fairly decent shape for a Ukrainian fortress. Known as Lubart's Castle after the Lithuanian prince who ordered it built, it has sturdy 13m-high ramparts topped with three tall towers, one containing a bell museum. There are also the archaeological remains of a 12th-century church and 14th-century palace, a small dungeon, a museum of books and a small art collection (extra 3uah). The castle's entrance tower features on the 200uah note if you want to get a sneak preview before visiting.

St Peter's & Paul's Cathedral CATHEDRAL
(vul Kafedralna) The Jesuit complex on vul Kafedralna was designed in the early to mid-17th century by Italian architect Giacomo Briano. The stately, newly renovated facade of the cathedral dates from 1640, the renovated interior – painted in pink and yellow tones – resembling a massive Easter egg. Closed following WWII, the building served as a museum of atheism in the 1970s.

Museum of the Volyn Icon MUSEUM
(Музей Волинської Ікони; www.volyn-ikona.at.ua; vul Yaroshchuka 5; admission 15uah; ⏲10am-6pm, to 5pm Sun, closed Wed & Sat) Displaying over 100 painted icons, this museum provides an overview of the celebrated Volyn School of icon-painting from the 16th to 18th century. The highlight is the 'Chelm icon of the Blessed Virgin', which attracts processions of pilgrims to the museum.

Trinity Church CHURCH
(maydan Teatralny) The main Orthodox church in Lutsk dates from 1752 and is a much more atmospheric affair than the Saint Peter's and Paul's Cathedral, not having been stripped of its gilding and icons by the Soviets. The interior is perfumed with beeswax candles and infused with 260 years of worship.

St Bridget's Monastery MONASTERY
(Монастир Бригіток; vul Kafedralna 14) In the 18th century this working monastery was once a convent where the nuns were so strict about their 'no male on the premises' rule that they didn't allow firefighters in when the building was ablaze. The result was a huge fire that destroyed much of the original timber town. Today the derelict courtyard contains a memorial wall with black plaques bearing the names of those shot by the NKVD in 1941 as the Nazis approached Lutsk.

Festivals & Events

Lutsk is a place that takes it festivals and celebrations seriously. Here we list the annual highlights:

Polessian Summer Folk Festival FESTIVAL
Takes place throughout summer at various venues around Lutsk, including Lutsk Castle.

Bandershtat MUSIC, ART
(www.bandershtat.org.ua) Alternative music and modern art festival with a nationalist twist. Held in August.

City Day & Independence Day FESTIVAL
Lutsk city day falls in the third week in August, around the time of Ukrainian Independence day, making this a great time to be in town.

Artjazz Festival MUSIC
(www.artjazz.info) Organised by the Lutsk Jazz Club in mid-September, this is one of Ukraine's best jazz festivals and takes place at Lutsk Castle and in the city of Rivne.

Salo Festival FOOD
Voted Ukraine's No 1 food festival. Held in October.

Sleeping

Sribni Leleky HOTEL $
(Срібні лелеки; ☎757 989; www.leleky.com.ua; vul Chornovola 17; s/d from 330/355uah; ❄📶) The 'sliver storks' may have a bit of an awkward location 1.5km south of the bus and train stations next to a busy road, but this well-designed 'recreation complex' is staffed by friendly and helpful Lutskites, and rooms are fresh and clean. Rates include breakfast.

Hotel Ukraina HOTEL $
(готель Україна; ☎788 100; www.hotel-lutsk.com; vul Slovatskoho 2; s/d from 300/460uah; 📶) A central location overlooking maydan Teatralny, 128 modern rooms offering good standards and reasonable prices make this

the hotel of choice in Lutsk. Rooms are simply furnished, there's a decent restaurant, staff are pleasant enough and there's even a spa. Rates include a buffet breakfast and parking, but not wi-fi.

Station Resting Rooms HOTEL $
(Кімнати Відпочинку; Lutsk train station, 3rd fl; dm/tw 80/160uah) The rooms at Lutsk's immaculately renovated train station would put some midrange hotels to shame, though showers (17uah extra) and toilets are shared. A mere 80uah gets you a bed in a twin, so pay double to avoid having a random stranger tumble into your room at 3am. Some rooms overlook the platform – a trainspotter's dream. Check-in is at the information (ДОВІДКА) window in the main station hall downstairs.

Hotel Zaleski HOTEL $$
(☎772 701; www.zaleski-hotel.com; vul Krivy Val 39; r 350-900uah; ❄ 📶) This super-central, purpose-built hotel just off vul Lesi Ukrainky has immaculate rooms in reproduction antique style, sparklingly clean up-to-the-minute bathrooms and helpful, English-speaking staff. The economy singles are a bit poky, but imagine badly varnished parquet floors and transparent curtains and you'll cheerfully squeeze yourself into these velveted quarters.

Eating & Drinking

Monastyrska Doroha UKRAINIAN $
(Монастирська Дорога; vul Lesi Ukrainky 67; restaurant mains 30-60uah, cafe mains up to 15uah; ⏲8am-11pm; 📶) The ground-floor self-service canteen ladles out Ukrainian comfort food as well as coffee and cakes, but the real treat here comes downstairs in the restaurant where the decor rather risks overshadowing the food. The walls, from floor to ceiling, are plastered in a local artist's astonishingly detailed version of the town's history, a task that took six months to complete.

Korona Vitovta UKRAINIAN $$
(Корона Вітовта; www.kvrestoran.com; pl Zamkova; mains 30-140uah; ⏲noon-midnight; ❄) The idea behind Lutsk's grandest restaurant, which guards the entrance to Lutsk Castle, came from a recipe book – unearthed during an archaeological dig – that belonged to the cook of King Vitovta of Lithuania. The current chef remains as faithful as possible to those 15th-century recipes (though a few tomatoes and potatoes have crept in somewhere) and the menu is as meat heavy as feasting medieval royals would have demanded. The wall in the entrance hall is hung with photos of the rich and good who have dined here, including Viktor Yushchenko (before he was president).

Maska ITALIAN $$
(Маска; vul Dragomana 11B; mains 45-80uah; ⏲11am-11pm) Venice carnival meets Salvador Dalí at this refined and imaginatively decorated place serving what may be Lutsk's most flavour-conscious menu. There's a definite Italian bent here with pizzas, pastas and risottos, but if Volyn's take on the Veneto doesn't tickle your fancio, try the fillet of duck with caremelised pear and plum sauce or Wiener Schnitzel. Very courteous service, a drinks menu the length of a short novel, and views of the Lutsk Castle from the 1st-floor terrace.

Tretyy Kukhol UKRAINIAN $$
(Третій Кухоль; vul Lesi Ukrainky 24; mains 10-90uah; ⏲9am-1am) Well-executed Ukrainian staples are the speciality at this popular subterranean restaurant and pub opposite the tourist office. Roast fish, veal and pork dishes make up the bulk of the menu but there's also green *borshch (*appears as 'sorrel soup' on the English menu) and an international beer card.

Brave Schwejk PUB $$
(vul Lesi Ukrainky 56; mains 25-100uah; ⏲9am-11pm) Named for the famous fictional Czech soldier Švejk (Schweik in German) in *Good Soldier Schweik* by Jaroslav Hašek, this place harks back to the novel's Austro-Hungarian era with its mix of sausages, goulash, pigs'

DON'T MISS

SCULPTOR'S HOUSE

In a quiet spot by the Styr River, sculptor Mykola Golovan is in the process of covering his otherwise modest house with his own flowing works, creating a surreal piece of Gaudí-esque theatre in the most unexpected of locations. It's certainly one of Ukraine's zaniest dwellings and its creator is often around to show visitors his opus. To find it, head along vul Kafedralna from Lutsk Castle to the neo-Gothic, yellow-brick Lutheran church – short vul Lyuteranska starts to the left of here.

THE WORLD OF NIKOLAI GOGOL

Although Taras Shevchenko is the greatest literary figure within Ukraine, one of the best-known Ukrainian writers outside the country's borders must be Nikolai Gogol. He was born in 1809 to impoverished parents in the Cossack village of Sorochyntsi near Poltava. It was here, in deepest rural Ukraine, that Gogol spent his formative years before leaving for St Petersburg in 1828.

Often claimed as a great Russian writer, Gogol was Ukrainian through and through. Many of his stories set in Ukraine are inspired by the supernatural world and the rural superstitions and folk tales of his youth in the Poltavshchina. His tales are set in a land of sun-drenched fields and blue skies, where faded nobles nap in the afternoon heat, Cossacks gulp down bowls of *borshch,* kitchen gardens overflow with tobacco and sunflowers, and shy Ukrainian beauties fall in love under star-dusted skies. Gogol's short novel *Taras Bulba* is a rollicking Cossack tale flush with romantic nationalism, adventure and derring-do.

During his years in St Petersburg, where he was employed in the civil service, his mood changed and his later stories such as *The Nose, Nevsky Prospekt* and *The Inspector General* are darker, gloomier, and riddled with ill health, crime and vice. In fact, the capital had such a bad effect on Gogol that he died in 1852 after burning the second half of his last novel, *Dead Souls,* in a fit of madness.

Gogol is an inspirational companion to pack into your rucksack on long train journeys across the snowbound steppe or midsummer bus trips through Ukraine's endless landscapes.

knuckles, milk veal and similar specialities. The atmosphere is that of a small beer hall, where you'll find the likes of Paulaner and Warsteiner beer from Germany alongside Staropramen and Krušovice from the Czech Republic.

Maydan PUB
(Майдан; www.maydan.com.ua; vul Boyka 2; mains 22-60uah; ⌚9am-2am) The best, most atmospheric watering hole in town boasts a dark tavern-like hall with long benches and a stage for local weekend strummers to perform, two quieter seating areas for daytime imbibing, and a beer menu populated by brews from Western Europe, Russia and Ukraine. The food menu is overambitious so stick to Ukrainian staples.

Information

There's free wi-fi in the top-floor food court of the **Lutsk shopping centre** (pr Voli). Lutsk is well endowed with English-language maps positioned at strategic points around town.

Tourist Office (☎723 419; www.visitlutsk.com; cnr vul Lesi Ukrainky & vul Senatorky Levchanivskoy; ⌚9am-6pm Tue-Fri, 10am-5pm Sat & Sun) Arguably Ukraine's best tourist office offering free walking tours (4pm Sundays), a booking service, heaps of information and free wi-fi in the office.

Getting There & Around

The **bus station** is 2km northeast of the city centre, next to a market; trolleybus 5, plus numerous *marshrutky,* link it to central maydan Teatralny (look for signs like центр or цум).

Scheduled bus connections:

Dubno 18uah, 1¼ hours, at least 10 daily
Kremenets 32uah, two hours, at least 10 daily
Lviv 55uah, four hours, nine daily
Ternopil 60uah, four hours, several daily

The **train station** is just a little south of the bus station, and also northeast of the city centre. Trolleybuses 4 and 7, plus numerous *marshrutky,* shuttle between here and maydan Teatralny. There are two trains to and from Kyiv (117uah, 7½ to 8½ hours); the best service from Lutsk is the overnighter leaving at 10.26pm.

Shatsky National Nature Park Шатський заповідник

The Shatsky National Nature Park lies 160km northwest of Lutsk in the corner between Belarus and Poland, and has some 200 lakes, rivers and streams. However, while fascinating to scientists, Ukraine's wild 'Lake District' and its deep Lake Svityaz is a long way from appealing to all but the most adventurous of (camping and rafting) tourists.

If you are interested in heading to this park, catch one of the frequent buses to Kovel and change for the village of Shatsk. At least eight buses a day also go direct to Shatsk from Lutsk (60uah, three hours). Don't even consider heading this way without lashings of mosquito repellent.

Dubno Дубно

☎03656 / POP 38,100

Some 50km southeast of Lutsk, Dubno is one of several towns in the region with a **castle** (vul Zamkova 7A; admission 10uah; ⏰8am-5pm Apr-Oct, to 7pm Nov-Mar), making it a relatively interesting stopover. This is where Andry, the son of Cossack Taras Bulba, falls in love with a Polish princess in Gogol's famous story, *Taras Bulba,* and crosses over to join the princess and her fellow Poles, while his Cossack brothers are busy trying to starve these enemies into submission. There's not that much to see inside, but the views of the sluggish Ikva River from the ramparts are pretty enough. Dubno's only other attraction is the crumbling 1630 **Church of St Nicholas** (vul D Halytskoho), whose telltale plain interior suggests it was used for secular purposes during the decades of Soviet communism.

Every July, Dubno hosts the popular **Taras Bulba Festival** (www.tarasbulba-fest.kiev.ua) featuring rock music.

Dubno is conveniently located only 41km from Kremenets and 66km from Pochayiv, making it an ideal base from which to explore. The unimaginatively renovated **Hotel Dubno** (☎418 02, 410 86; vul D Halytskoho 9; s/d from 200/300uah; 🚭❄), with its spotless, reasonably priced accommodation, is a good spot if Dubno is your base, though the restaurant seems almost permanently reserved for Dubno's unremitting stream of weddings. If you'd rather not fall asleep to the back catalogue of *Modern Talking,* the five-room, hunting-themed **Antique House** (☎050 579 5905; vul Zamkova 17; s/d from 300/430uah; 🚭❄📶) is an astonishingly well-appointed guesthouse for rural Ukraine and the location at the gates of the castle is superb.

Dubno has bus connections to Lutsk (23uah, one hour 20 minutes, 18 daily), Ternopil (40uah, two hours, 20 daily) and Kremenets (14uah, one hour, twice hourly), from where you can change onto *marshrutky* for Pochayiv. The vast majority of services leave from the bus station on the main drag heading east, though some 'through' buses to Lutsk pick up outside the castle.

The Carpathians
Карпати

POP 3.5 MILLION

Includes ➡

Best Places to Eat

- Reflection (p139)
- Manufactura (p125)
- Cafe-Muzey Pid Zamkom (p142)
- Beer Club 10 (p125)

Best Places to Stay

- On the Corner (p131)
- Smerekova Hata (p135)
- Good Morning B&B (p131)
- Pid Templem (p125)

Why Go?

Clipping the country's southwest corner, the Carpathian arc has endowed Ukraine with a crinkled region of forested hills and fast-flowing rivers that feel a continent away from the flatness of the steppe. This is the land of the Hutsuls, whose colourful folk culture is laced through thin villages stretching languidly along wide valley floors. It's also rural Ukraine at its best, where tiered wooden churches dot hillsides, horse-drawn carts clip-clop along potholed roads, *babushkas* shoo geese, and *marshrutka* (fixed-route minibus) passengers cross themselves as they whizz past roadside chapels.

The 'Hutsulshchyna' may be Ukraine's epicentre of rural folk culture, but this is also a leading holiday spot. The local peaks have been a long-term hit with Ukrainian hikers and skiers; the Carpathian National Nature Park, the country's biggest, lies in this region; and within the park's boundaries rises Mt Hoverla – Ukraine's highest peak at 2061m. It's also home to Bukovel, Ukraine's glitziest ski resort.

When to Go

Ivano-Frankivsk

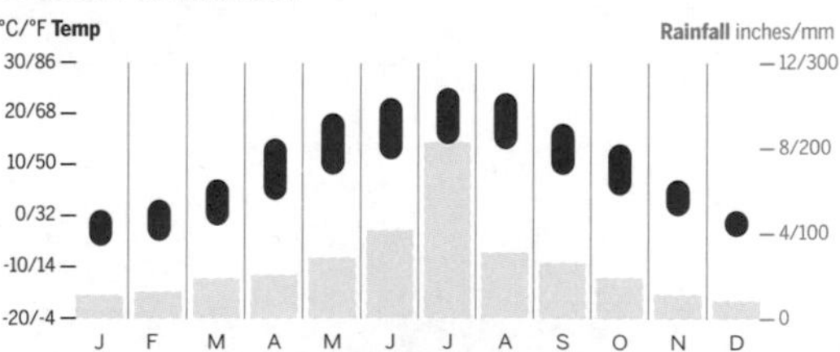

Jul Picnic on flower-filled *polonyny* (summer pastures) as you listen to the tinkle of cow bells.

Sep–Nov Watch local vintners bringing in the grape harvest in the Transcarpathia region.

Dec Enjoy some hearty Hutsul après-ski during the Carpathian ski season.

The Carpathians Highlights

1 Set up base camp in **Kolomyya** (p131) to visit its museums and arrange hikes into the hills.

2 Soak up the easy-going atmosphere of cosmopolitan **Uzhhorod** (p140), a border town with attitude on the frontier with Slovakia.

3 Wander the pastel-coloured heart of **Ivano-Frankivsk** (p124), a pleasant gateway to the mountains.

4 Make an easy-going ascent of Ukraine's highest peak, **Mt Hoverla** (p127).

5 Bargain hard for Hutsul souvenirs at markets in **Kosiv** (p133) and **Yaremche** (p128).

6 Snap on skis for a bit of downhill fun at ritzy **Bukovel Ski Resort** (p130).

7 Join Bukovyna's student population at trippy **Chernivtsi University** (p136), one of Eastern Europe's most mind-boggling places of learning.

History

Formed some 50 million years ago, during the same geological upheavals that produced the Alps, the crescent-shaped Carpathians were the cradle of Hutsul civilisation, and they're still home to this hardy mountain tribe.

A natural barrier between the Slavic countries and Romanised Dacia (Romania), the Carpathians have always provided a refuge from conquest and authority. When the Mongols sacked Kyiv in 1240, many of the city's citizens fled here, and when Poland and Lithuania invaded in the 14th century it's questionable how much control they exercised in the region's higher altitudes. The Poles' lengthy struggle to capture the 'Ukrainian Robin Hood' Oleska Dovbush suggest it was very little.

Signs of 19th-century Austro-Hungarian culture haven't penetrated deeper than Ivano-Frankivsk and Chernivtsi. And when the Soviets rolled up after WWII, locals didn't exactly get out the salt and bread. The Ukrainian Insurgent Army (UPA) survived as guerrillas in the Carpathians well into the 1950s, using the mountains as a stronghold from which to launch attacks on the authorities (the UPA is a controversial entity because of its probable, but unquantified, role in the extermination of Ukrainian Jews during WWII). However, even ordinary Carpathian villagers resisted Russian rule.

The Soviets weren't initially keen on the Hutsuls' folklore and pagan traditions, but came to see their culture as a tourist attraction and largely let them be. However, the Hutsuls have long been integrated into mainstream western Ukrainian culture. Their arts, crafts, cuisine and farming lifestyle all survive, but they reserve their traditional dress, music and dancing for celebrations, ceremonies and other special occasions.

IVANO-FRANKIVSK
ІВАНО-ФРАНКІВСЬК

☎0342 / POP 226,100

A closed Soviet city until 1991, I-F is for many just a gateway to the Carpathians and a popular jumping-off point for the northern peaks. But this once grand city is very much worth a day of exploration in its own right, and with some decent places to stay and surprisingly sophisticated places to eat, you're not likely to regret an overnight stay either.

I-F is a real mixed bag – the city centre is leafy and flaunts almost central European elegance, while the chaotic station strip and third-world market area give visitors a feel for what Ukraine was like 15 to 20 years ago.

Sights

I-F is somewhere nice to wander through, rather than a place offering lots of individual things to see. The main pedestrian drag and the single most attractive street is vul Nezalezhnosti with rows of renovated neoclassical buildings in differing pastel colours.

★Cathedral of the Holy Resurrection CATHEDRAL
(Кафедральний собор Страсного Воскресіння; maydan Sheptytskoho 22) The city's punctiliously renovated Greek Catholic cathedral is a fine example of baroque symmetry crafted in the mid-18th century. Huge bronzes of St Volodymyr and Princess Olga stand by the entrance, solomnly ushering the faithful into the beautiful, dimly lit and mustily aromatic interior.

Main Fountain FOUNTAIN
(maydan Vichevy) The dominating feature on maydan Vichevy is the fountain, a popular meeting spot. If you descend the steps below the fountain's main 'bowl', you can stand beneath the cascading water without getting wet – a little factoid of which locals are inordinately proud, especially those posing for wedding photos.

★Former Armenian Church CHURCH
(vul Virmenska 6) A few steps off pl Rynok stands this eye-pleasingly symmetrical baroque church built by the Armenian community in 1762. Beyond the golden doors the interior is a typically fragrant affair busy with head-scarved *babushkas* lighting beeswax candles and praying before gilt icons.

Taras Shevchenko Park PARK
(vul Shevchenka) Around 20 minutes' walk south from maydan Vichevy, the city's main stretch of green is a great place to shake out the picnic blanket, hire a rowboat on the lake or chill with an ice cream to do a spot of people-watching of a balmy eve. The approaches to the park are lined with refurbished Austro-Hungarian mansions and the grounds have been beautifully landscaped thanks to EU handouts.

Regional Museum MUSEUM
(Краєзнавчий музей; Town Hall, pl Rynok; admission 8uah; ⌚10am-5.30pm Tue-Sun) The city's epicentre is pl Rynok (Площа Ринок, Rynok Sq), at the centre of which rises the 1930s star-shaped town hall, the only one in Ukraine built in the Art Deco style. This houses the Soviet-era Regional Museum, which has displays on various archaeological digs in the region, a worthwhile room of folk art from the Carpathians, exhibitions relating to the history of Ivano-Frankivsk and a whole wing of goggle-eyed taxidermy.

Precarpathian Art Museum MUSEUM
(Музей Мистецтв Прикарпаття; maydan Sheptytskoho 8; admission 10uah; ⌚10am-5pm Tue-Sun) Ensconced in the 17th-century Church of the Blessed Virgin Mary, the city's oldest building, this museum is packed with a jumble of religious sculptures and paintings from around central Europe.

Regional Administration Building NOTABLE BUILDING
(Обласна державна адміністрація; vul Hrushevskoho) This Soviet-realist hulk is worth seeing for its sheer size and bombast. The two glum-looking traditional Ukrainian musician statues that guard the entrance are particularly impressive.

Sleeping

Hotel Auscoprut HOTEL $
(Готель Аускопрут; ☎234 01; www.auscoprut.if.ua; vul Hryunvaldska 7/9; s 240-280uah, d 370-440uah; 📶) Some hotels try to create style, some have style thrust upon them and the latter statement is certainly true of this grand old gem dating from 1912. OK, the breakfast won't win any culinary laurels and the wi-fi is a bit sketchy, but all those towering ceilings, full-length curtains hiding original wooden double windows, parquet floors, pleasantly dated fittings, gracefully ageing pieces of furniture, chandeliers and genuine faded elegance make this a delightfully affordable shabby-chic hideaway.

Pilgrim Hostel HOSTEL $
(☎511 476, 098 606 4545; www.pilgrim-hostel.com; vul Naberezhna 28B; dm 100uah; 📶) Shiny new hostel around 1.7km northwest of the city centre. Ask staff to pick you up at the bus or train station as it's a toughie to track down yourself.

★**Pid Templem** HOTEL $$
(Під Темплем; ☎595 333; www.tempel.if.ua; vul Strachenykh 7A; s 350-600uah, d 400-650uah; ❄📶) Just a few metres separate this new 11-room hotel from the synagogue from which it takes its name (meaning 'Below the Temple'). Rooms are woody and display understated fabrics, there's free tea and coffee, a cooked-to-order breakfast is served in the cosy lobby bar and professionally minded anglophone staff are on hand. Throw in a central location, speedy wi-fi and Jewish-themed museum displays in the public areas and you have I-F's top place to catch some Zs.

Atrium HOTEL $$
(Атріум; ☎557 879; vul Halytska 31; s 300uah, tw & d from 400uah; ❄📶) I-F's most central beds can be found in this new and soothingly well-heeled mini-hotel looking out across pl Rynok. Rooms are studies in leathery luxury, bathrooms dazzle and staff are keen to show off their well-tuned English. Guests receive a 10% discount in the hotel's first-rate restaurant and cafe.

Eating & Drinking

★**Manufactura** HEALTH FOOD $
(vul Mytskevicha 6; mains 25-40uah; ⌚9am-11pm Mon-Fri, 10am-11pm Sat & Sun) Floating cloth lamps, simple timber furniture and a jolly soundtrack (Russian techno-pop is banned) greet you at this cosy, family-friendly place, I-F's most laid-back eatery. The menu is a simple affair of delights you thought you'd never experience in regional Ukraine – how about carrot and ginger soup with bacon, baked trout in white wine sauce, lentil bake, freshly squeezed juices and sweet and savoury waffles, all made with organic ingredients as much as possible. Staff speak English and there are handmade souvenirs on sale.

Beer Club 10 MICROBREWERY $
(Пивний Клуб Десятка; ☎712 121; www.beerclub10.if.ua; vul Shashkevycha 4; mains 12-26uah; ⌚noon-10pm) Good for a light lunch or a night on the house-brewed Klubne beer, this central European–style warren of brick cellars decorated with an assortment of international beer paraphernalia has proved so popular it's even swallowed up a couple of adjacent eateries. Insert yourself at one of the hefty wooden tables, wait for your golden ale to arrive (with free peanuts) then choose from the thirst-inducing

Ivano-Frankivsk

menu. Service is unusually brisk, and the crowd gets more good-natured as the night progresses. Bookings recommended for Friday and Saturday nights.

Bochka UKRAINIAN $
(Бочка; vul Sheremety; mains 18-40uah; ⌚11am-11pm) Seems every post-Soviet city has a pub called 'The Barrel', but they're not always as pleasant as this atmospheric little wood-and-stone faux medieval cellar on pl Rynok. Enter through the barrel-shaped facade or take a summertime seat by the town hall for a pint or two and some cheap soak-up grub.

Franko UKRAINIAN **$$**
(Франко; www.franko.if.ua; vul Halytska 9A; mains 40-180uah; ⌚10am-11pm) Don't be fooled by the unrefined picture menu outside, Franko plates up some of the best gourmet Ukrainian food in the Carpathians and has the door stickers to prove it. The finely tuned *varenyky* (dumplings), *ukha* (fish soup), *deruny* (potato panckakes) and *kotlety* (meatballs) are a world away from their canteen cousins, but there's lots of more sophisticated fare on the extensive menu if you've had your fill of Slavic edibles. The various dining spaces are done out with panache, the cellar Lower Hall (Нижній зал) being our favourite.

Self-Catering

Oazis Supermarket SUPERMARKET
(vul Dnistrovska 26) This supermarket can be found within the Arsenal Shopping mall opposite the main market.

Information

Central Post Office (maydan Vichevy; ⌚8am-7pm Mon-Sat)

Tourist Office (☎502 474; www.rtic.if.ua; Town Hall, pl Rynok; ⌚10am-12.30pm & 1.30-4pm Mon-Fri)

Getting There & Away

BUS

The bus station building is next to the train station on ramshackle pl Pryvokzalna. The following services run into the Carpathians and other destinations:

Chernivtsi 50uah, four hours, at least three daily

Lviv 50uah, three to five hours, nine daily

Kolomyya 21uah, 1½ hours, 15 daily

Kyiv 175uah, 10 to 12 hours, four daily (overnight)

Rakhiv 45uah, four hours, hourly

Yaremche 20uah to 25uah, 1½ hours, at least hourly

Ivano-Frankivsk

Top Sights
1 Cathedral of the Holy Resurrection B2
2 Former Armenian Church C2

Sights
3 Main Fountain B3
4 Precarpathian Art Museum B1
5 Regional Administration Building C2
6 Regional Museum B2

Sleeping
7 Atrium B2
8 Hotel Auscoprut D1
9 Pid Templem C2

Eating
10 Franko B2
11 Manufactura C2
12 Oazis Supermarket C1

Drinking & Nightlife
13 Beer Club 10 .... C3
14 Bochka C2

TRAIN

Ivano-Frankivsk has the following train services:

Kolomyya 60uah, one hour, three daily

Kyiv 200uah, 11 to 15 hours, three daily

Lviv 70uah to 120uah, 2½ to 3½ hours, eight daily

Rakhiv 24uah to 68uah, 4½ hours, daily

CARPATHIAN NATIONAL NATURE PARK & AROUND

This is Ukraine's largest national park and the heart of the Carpathians. However, it's a very different sort of national park – industrial logging occurs here, for example. Only about a quarter of the area is completely protected, but that hasn't detracted too much from the natural beauty of the place...yet.

Founded in 1980, the Carpathian National Nature Park (CNNP; Карпатський Національний природний парк) covers 503 sq km of wooded mountains and hills. Parts of it shelter small numbers of animals and the alpine meadows are carpeted with species of flora. Realistically, however, hiking and skiing are the main reasons to head this way.

The Carpathian National Nature Park straddles the Ivano-Frankivska and Zakarpatska oblasti. From the city of Ivano-Frankivsk, the A265 cuts southwards into the heart of the park. Yaremche, 60km south of Ivano-Frankivsk, sits across the park's northern boundary. Yasinya, 37km further south along the A265, marks the park's westernmost point. Rakhiv, 62km south of Yaremche on the A265, is just outside the southwestern boundary.

Because it stands a little apart from the main CNNP, the adjoining Carpathian Biosphere Reserve is discussed under its main entry point, Rakhiv.

Train services are less frequent and extensive in the mountains than in other Ukrainian regions, so be prepared to ride the crowded buses and *marshrutky* (fixed-route minibuses), and budget for the occasional taxi. Otherwise, agencies and hotels in Lviv, Ivano-Frankivsk and Kolomyya can organise guided tours and transport.

Maps featuring varying degrees of detail have become easy to source and are available from all tourist information centres and souvenir kiosks throughout the Carpathians.

Activities

First, a word of warning: hiking 'trails' criss-cross the Carpathians, but until recently no serious attempt had been made to systematically signpost them. Most Ukrainians rely on a combination of personal family memory, logging roads and Soviet-era maps to find their way. However, the trail to Ukraine's highest peak, **Mt Hoverla** (2061m), is well marked, as is the continuing journey along the Chornohora ridge.

These trails aside, hiking in the Carpathians is usually best done in the company of locals and there is no shortage of guides and tours, official and unofficial, in the area.

Hiking Mt Hoverla

It's hardly the most remote trail in the Carpathians, but the popular ascent to Ukraine's highest peak is relatively easy to achieve. On a clear day, the expansive views from Mt Hoverla are also breathtaking. Initially, the trail follows the Yaremche–Vorokhta–Zaroslyak road, so how much of the way you want to hike and how much you want to cover by *marshrutka* (which go as far as Vorokhta) or taxi is up to you.

About 7km south of Vorokhta (guides know the place as 'sedmoy kilometr'), you will need to take the right fork in the road, heading west to Zaroslyak, where the **Hotel Zaroslyak** (www.zaroslyak.com; r from 210uah) offers convenient accommodation. En route, you will cross the CNNP boundary and pay the entrance fee. From Zaroslyak (20km from Vorokhta) it's about 3.5km to the summit of Mt Hoverla, which is marked with a big iron cross and a huge Ukrainian national flag (and occasionally a provocative EU flag, too).

Along the Chornohora Ridge

The southern Chornohora peak of **Mt Pip Ivan Chornohirsky** (2028m; not to be confused with Mt Pip Ivan Maramorosky) is well known for the abandoned **astronomical observatory** atop it. The Poles completed this observatory just before WWII, and anything of value has been looted, but the place stills retains atmosphere.

One of the easiest routes to Pip Ivan is along the crest of the Chornohora ridge from Mt Hoverla via Lake Nesamovyte. It's hard to get lost this way, as your views are unimpeded, and the route follows the former interwar border between Poland and Czechoslovakia, passing the old boundary markers. At more than 40km return, the hike will take at least three days.

Other routes to Pip Ivan include coming from the village of Verkhovyna via Dzembronya and over Mt Smotrych (requiring at least one night's camping out). Alternatively, you can approach the mountain from Rakhiv.

Chornohora Mountains

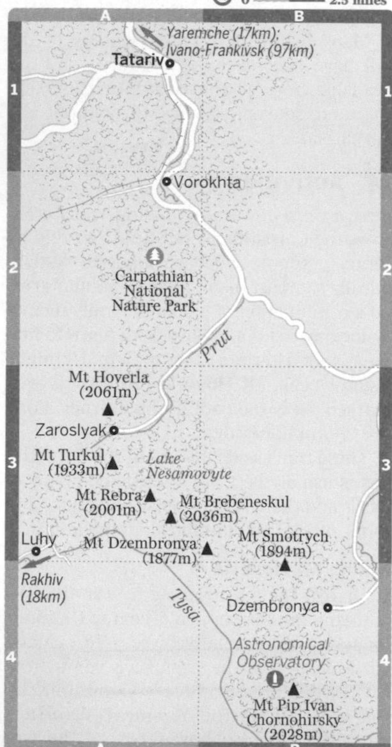

Information

In the unlikely event you'll need it, the **CNNP Headquarters** (☎03434-211 55; www.cnnp.yaremcha.com.ua; vul Stusa 6, Yaremche; ⏰10am-4pm Mon-Fri), the white concrete building with a distinctive stained-glass window, can be reached by heading uphill from the train line in central Yaremche. This is also where you will find the excellent, EU-funded **Ecotourism Information Centre** (☎03434-222 59; ⏰10am-4pm), which includes an exhibition on the culture and natural history of the Carpathians.

Yaremche Яремче

☎03434 / POP 7600

Stretching for around 10km along the valley of the Prut River, your average Carpathian connoisseur shuns Yaremche (also sometimes known as Yaremcha) as too touristy and overcrowded. True, the blitz of Hutsul souvenir markets and naff theme restaurants can be a turn-off, but Yaremche is, in the end, all about heading out into the wilds and not about the town itself. Plus it has more guesthouses than any other Carpathian valley community and is also a good place to look for a guide.

The town is an easily reachable staging point for an ascent of Mt Hoverla. By catching a *marshrutka* or taxi to Vorokhta or beyond you can get to Ukraine's highest peak and back in a day or two, depending on your preferred pace. Yaremche is also one of the best places in the Ukrainian Carpathians to strike out on two knobbly wheels. With more bike-rental places than Kyiv, there are plenty of people around here willing to help you do it.

BIKELAND

Keen mountain bikers should look out for **Bikeland** (Велокраїна; www.bikeland.com.ua), the brainchild of Ukrainian cycling fanatic Viktor Zagreba. This project to construct a network of cycling routes throughout the Carpathians region attracted EU funding as well as an army of eager mountain-biking volunteers who pedalled off into the wilds to create the 1300km of marked trails. Hotels and guesthouses affiliated to the Bikeland project guarantee bike-friendly facilities, such as storage and a place to wash two-wheelers, and the initiative has also spawned a number of bike-rental centres (mountain bikes 90uah to 100uah per day), most notably in Yaremche, meaning there's no need to haul your velocipede through customs at Boryspil International Airport.

Sights & Activities

Souvenir Market MARKET
(vul Petrasha; 9am-dusk) You ain't seen a tacky Ukrainian souvenir market until you've visited Yaremche's. Now reaching absurd dimensions, it's centred around a former beauty spot where a footbridge crosses the river. The rocks below the bridge are still a pretty place to picnic, mainly as from there you can't see the market.

Dovbush Cliffs LANDMARK
(Скелі Довбуша) A popular activity in Yaremche (second only to souvenir shopping) is a hike to the nearby Dovbush Cliffs. To get there, take the not-too-taxing trail that rises on the opposite side of the main road to the turn-off for the exclusive hotel enclave at the far southern end of town, 2.5km south of the train station. The caves are actually a series of boulders, which were pushed off a cliff to form shelters that outlaws once used as hideouts. With several looped trails around here, you could spend anything from half an hour to three hours walking.

Sleeping & Eating

Yaremche has no lack of places to sleep, but addresses can be literally miles from the stations and almost impossible to find on unmarked streets. We encountered several properties that were less than truthful about their locations on popular booking websites. Organising a station pick-up could save you lots of legwork.

For such a tourist magnet, Yaremche has surprisingly few places to eat.

Mriya B&B $
(Мрія; 22168, 067 902 1718; vul Hnata Hotkevych 8A; s/d from 150/250uah;) The nine rooms at this very friendly timber guesthouse are furnished jumble-sale style, but bathrooms are post-Soviet and things are pretty spacious, especially in the loft. There's a guest kitchen in the basement, and the guesthouse has its own riverside pavilion and semi-private stretch of beach. Breakfast is 20uah to 42uah extra, dinner 85uah. To reach Mriya, follow the signposts from the war memorial near the Vopak supermarket.

Tsvit Paporoti HOTEL $
(Цвіт Папороті; 220 52; vul Pidskelna 10; s/d from 180/360uah;) This brand-new 22-room hotel has the advantage of being easy to find and a location close to the stations. Well-proportioned rooms are a touch plasticky with synthetic fabrics, nylon carpets and faux veneer furniture, but everything is spotless and functional and all have balconies with evergreen forest views. Take the first left (vul Pidskelna) after the Vopak supermarket (heading from the bus station) – it's a short walk away on the right. No breakfast outside summer months.

Krasna Sadyba HOTEL $$
(Красна садиба; 222 53, 212 75; www.krasnasadyba.if.ua; vul Ivasyuka 6; r 250-600uah) In a secluded corner yet just minutes from the town centre, this red-brick hotel on the river looks like something from *Hansel and Gretel*. Most of the 15 rooms are spacious and well furnished, and the few more basic rooms are good bargains.

Kolyba Krasna Sadyba HUTSUL $
(vul Ivasyuka 6; mains 15-40uah; 9am-10pm) Krasna Sadyba's *kolyba* (wooden hut) is rightfully considered the best eating spot in Yaremche, serving sumptuous spit-roasted pork, beef *shashlyk* (shish kebab), chicken wings or salmon on a terrace overlooking a leafy, quiet stretch of river. *Borshch*, forest mushroom soup, carp, trout, *kulesha* or *banosh* (two kinds of polenta typical for the Carpathians) are other options.

KIPPING IN THE CARPATHIANS

Several websites advertise homestays and other accommodation in the Carpathians, including www.adventurecarpathians.com, www.greentour.com.ua and www.bikeland.com.ua. However, none is as well maintained, organised and user-friendly as the outstanding www.karpaty.info. Hotels, guesthouses and B&Bs are visited by the website's administrators, who post photos and provide prices, the languages that the hosts speak as well as basic transport information. Most of the website's content is now in English, too.

If you're looking for something a little cheaper still, wild camping is allowed within most of the Carpathian National Nature Park (CNNP), apart from the eastern side of Mt Hoverla. You'll have to pay the CNNP entrance fee, but this is just a few hryvnya.

There are no mountain huts or properly equipped campsites. You will find some well-used fireplaces, even though fires are officially prohibited throughout the park. This rule is now enforced quite strictly in summer due to the heightened risk of forest fires.

★Hutsulshchyna HUTSUL **$$**
(Гуцульщина; ☎223 78; vul Svobody; mains 30-112uah) Quite understandably the backdrop to many souvenir photos, this ornate log cabin, with its central spire and understated sprinkling of Hutsul colour, serves pretty decent food. The menu includes river fish, forest mushrooms, polenta, pancakes and all sorts of other authentically prepared regional fare. It's located near the souvenir market, around 1.5km south of the train station.

Self-Catering

Vopak SUPERMARKET
(Вопак; vul Svobody 257; ⏲8am-11pm) If self-catering, there's a Vopak supermarket between the bus and train stations.

Getting There & Around

The slightly disorganised bus station lies at the northern end of town. There are scheduled services to/from Ivano-Frankivsk (17uah, 1¼ hours, 14 daily) and Kolomyya (16uah, 70 minutes, 10 daily). Yaremche also lies on most routes in and out of Rakhiv (27uah, two hours, hourly), and there's a single daily run to Kyiv (230uah, 15 hours). Nearby *marshrutka* destinations include Bukovel and Vorokhta.

All trains between Kolomyya and Rakhiv, Lviv and Rakhiv and Ivano-Frankivsk and Rakhiv (all one each way daily) stop at Yaremche.

Bukovel Буковель

☎03434

Hard-core regional skiers were sceptical when this ritzy resort opened in 2003–04 and immediately began attracting oligarchs from Kyiv and other 'new Ukrainian' guests. However, as the country's first fully planned ski area, **Bukovel** (www.bukovel.com) soon won some doubters over with its sensible network of lifts and trails, printed trail maps, orderly queues, snow-making machines and 'night-time' slopes. However, environmental concerns have been raised in recent years mainly concerning the use of snow cannons, which are depleting the area's water table.

Here are the numbers: the resort has over 50km of runs ranging from 900m to 1370m in altitude, including 16 lifts, making it one of Eastern Europe's largest ski resorts. However, plans to bid for the 2018 Winter Olympics were scrapped in 2008 when the Ukrainian National Olympic Committee admitted the region lacked the required infrastructure to host such a major event.

As Bukovel is the most expensive ski resort in the country, the major gripe here among Ukrainians (and some foreigners) is the cost of ski passes, but at 336uah on weekdays (slightly more on weekends), they're still cheaper than in most major Western European resorts.

Bukovel is best reached from Yaremche and Kolomyya.

Vorokhta Ворохта

A typical Carpathian sprawl along the Prut River, the village nearest to Mt Hoverla is quite difficult to get a handle on. Apart from the town's very own **Avanhard ski resort** (www.avangard.kurorts.com), the pristine natural surroundings provide the main attraction here. The ever-reliable www.karpaty.info lists countless places to stay in and around the 'village', and if you read Russian/Ukrainian, check out the town's website at www.vorokhta.org.

Regular *marshrutka* and bus services run from Yaremche (one hour) and Verkhovyna (30 minutes). The daily Ivano-Frankivsk-

Rakhiv train also makes a halt here in both directions.

Kolomyya Коломия

☎03433 / POP 61,500

Despite being more than 50km east of the main part of the Chornohora range, pretty Kolomyya is arguably the best base for foreigners looking to discover the Carpathians. English-speaking assistance and good transport links to the rest of the region make getting out into the forested peaks as easy as falling off a log. It's also a centre of Hutsul culture, meaning lots of authentic souvenir material for low prices.

Spruced up in the early noughties, the town has a distinct central European flavour in places, with streets of faded *fin-de-siècle* architecture. This, plus two very worthwhile museums, including the famous Pysanky Museum housed in a monster Easter egg, and Ukraine's best traveller digs (the On the Corner guesthouse) make Kolomyya an essential halt on any tour of the west.

Sights

★Museum of Hutsul Folk Art MUSEUM
(Музей народного Мистецтва Гуцульщини; ☎239 12; http://hutsul.museum; vul Teatralna 25; admission 15uah; ⏲10am-6pm Tue-Sun) This well-curated exhibition of Hutsul artefacts is probably the best of its kind in Ukraine. Decorated stove tiles and other ceramics, musical instruments, carved wooden tools, boxes, furniture, traditional and embroidered folk dress, woven wall hangings and an interesting collection of traditional Hutsul axes fill the museum's grand neoclassical home, which started life in the dying days of the Austro-Hungarian Empire as a Ukrainian cultural institute. Most of the wall texts have been translated into sound English but employing a guide (ask at the town's guesthouses) puts a considerable amount of meat on the exhibition's bones.

★Pysanky Museum MUSEUM
(Музей Писанки; ☎03433-278 91; vul Chornovola 39; adult/child 10/3uah; ⏲10am-6pm Tue-Sun) Kolomyya's most eye-catching attraction is a monster concrete Easter egg, which sits rather self-consciously on the town's main square. Inside and in an adjoining building you'll discover a museum dedicated to the traditional art of egg painting, with examples from Ukraine, Romania, the Czech Republic and as far afield as India, China and Canada. Some of the exhibits, especially those in the main egg building, could do with a little freshening up but nonetheless this remains Kolomyya's star attraction.

Sleeping & Eating

★On the Corner GUESTHOUSE **$**
(☎067 980 3326, 27 437; www.onthecorner.info; vul Hetmanska 47A; dm/s/d 100/160/360uah; 📶) Vitaliy, his mum Ira, wife Anna, and the rest of the extended Pavliuk family, continue to wow guests with their legendary hospitality, making this not only the best place to stay in Kolomyya, but one of the best in all Ukraine. Indeed, this six-room B&B just gets better, with cable TV, wi-fi, laundry, bike hire, planned disabled access and myriad other services that other guesthouses wouldn't even consider. With outstanding cooking and coffee, a multitude of hikes and tours on offer, and assistance and advice provided in English, German, Ukrainian, Russian and Italian, comments praising 'the best place I stayed in Ukraine' just keep on filling up the guestbook. Bikeland-affiliated and motorcycle-friendly.

Good Morning B&B GUESTHOUSE **$**
(Садиба Добрий ранок; ☎547 97, 066 162 9870; www.ranok.kolomyya.org; vul Rankova 4; s/d 150/200uah; @📶) You'll know you're on the right track to this superb B&B as the street is signposted in English from around 200m away. Charming hosts, Maria and Yuriy, speak English and can help with tours, travel and anything else you can think of. The Hutsul-themed room is the most striking of the four immaculate bedrooms, the breakfast menu includes real porridge and they'll pick you up for free from the stations.

DON'T MISS

SEW EARLY!

If you're determined to get your hands on some traditional Ukrainian embroidery, you'll have to get up early to get the best bargains at Kolomyya's embroidery market held near the On the Corner guesthouse. It starts at a bleary-eyed 3am, but as prices are up to five times lower than in Kyiv, it might just be worth setting that alarm clock for the early hours.

Kolomyya

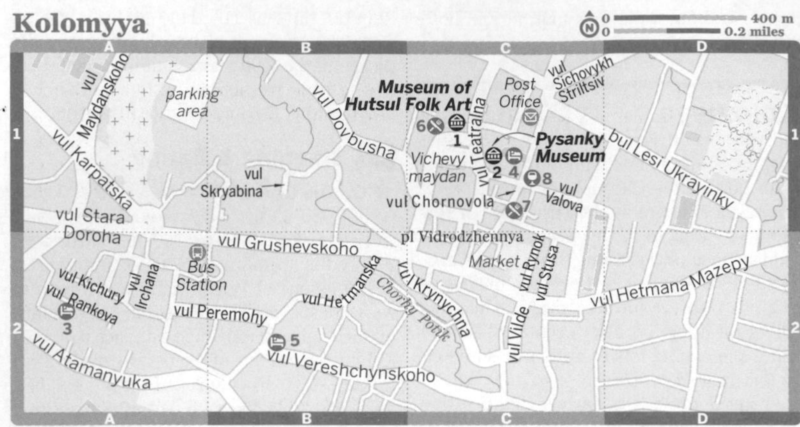

Kolomyya

Top Sights

1 Museum of Hutsul Folk Art C1
2 Pysanky Museum C1

Sleeping

3 Good Morning B&B A2
4 Hotel Pysanka C1
5 On the Corner B2

Eating

6 Kafe Elina C1
7 Malva C1

Drinking & Nightlife

8 Dzhem C1

Hotel Pysanka HOTEL $
(Готель Писанка; ☎278 55; reception@pysanka-hotel.com; vul Chornovola 41; r 252-353uah; ❄📶) Dull but friendly and super-central, it's strange to think the Hotel Pysanka was once the only show in town. The 22 rooms are cheaply furnished and have ageing bathrooms but some hoist pleasingly high ceilings. Ask for corner room 11, which has a balcony extending out towards the Pysanky Museum.

Kafe Elina BEER GARDEN $
(Кафе Еліна; vul Taras Shevchenka; mains 15-50uah) This cafe behind the Museum of Hutsul Folk Art is a typical Hutsul *kolyba* arrangement with tables and knick-knacks in a wooden hut serving Ukrainian stodge. In summer the set-up is reminiscent of a Bavarian beer garden with tables and fairy light–lit gazebos and pavilions nestling under mature trees.

Malva UKRAINIAN $
(Мальва; vul Chornovola 12; mains 7-15uah; ⊙10am-10pm; 📶) For a quick bite between museums this no-fuss cafe has a short menu of simple Ukrainian fare, cheap beer and huge blow-ups of old Kolomyya on the walls. A small streetside dining area is set up outside in summer.

Drinking & Nightlife

Dzhem BAR
(Джем; vul Chornovola 24) Small central bar hang-out that manages to squeeze two cosy levels into its tiny interior as well as sprawling all over the pavement in summer. Lots of Ukrainian beers, a vague sports theme and loud FM radio.

Information

Post Office (vul Drahomanova)

Getting There & Away

BUS

Kolomyya is linked to the following towns by bus:

Chernivtsi 30uah, two hours, 15 daily
Ivano-Frankivsk 20uah, 1½ hours, 14 daily
Kosiv 20uah, 1¼ hours, nine daily (plus many *marshrutky*)
Rakhiv 45uah, 3½ to four hours, six daily
Yaremche 18uah, 70 minutes, 10 daily

TRAIN

Local trains go to and from Rakhiv (four hours, one daily), Ivano-Frankivsk (1½ to two hours, four daily) and Chernivtsi (two hours, four daily).

Kosmach Космач

☎03478 / POP 6000

Few would brave the potholes to this sprawling Carpathian village, 35km to the southwest of Kolomyya, were it not for the privately run **Oleksa Dovbush Museum** (☎03478-576 17; vul Dovbusha 17; ⏲open on request) FREE. Run by the inimitable Mykhailo Didyshyn, this must be one of the oddest sights you'll find among the peaks of Europe's east.

Didyshyn claims the garden hut housing his small museum is the one in which the 'the Ukrainian Robin Hood' was killed and he even shows you Dovbush's very own hat, belt, axe and bag. The rest of the one-room museum is mostly taken up with the strange figures Didyshyn has carved from tree roots, as well as assorted Carpathian junk with a tall story behind every piece. Outside stands Didyshyn's 1988 Dovbush monument, but the museum's most fascinating exhibit is the grandly mustachioed owner himself, an artist and photographer persecuted by the KGB for his Dovbush obsession. Take an interpreter along to hear some of the most colourful tales between Prague and Kyiv. Allow several hours for a visit if Didyshyn is in the mood to talk!

Third-world roads are keeping some tour guides away from Kosmach these days, which is a shame. Combined with Sheshory, it makes an interesting day out from Kolomyya, the best place to pick up a guide/interpreter, but be prepared for a rough ride. Public buses do head this way from Kolomyya but a little local help will save you lots of hassle.

Kosiv Косів

☎03478 / POP 9000

Sitting pretty in a river valley, tiny Kosiv is synonymous with serious, high-quality Hutsul crafts. They're sold at its well-known **craft market** (⏲8am-11am Thu, 6am-noon Sat) and produced in the surrounding hills as well as at the **Kosiv State Institute of Decorative & Applied Arts** (☎212 60; vul Mitskevycha 2) FREE. The latter also has a small **museum** (⏲9am-5pm Mon-Fri Sep-Jun) FREE, but for a much wider overview of the Hutsuls' artistic skills head for the **Museum of Hutsul Folk Art & Life** (vul Nezalezhnosti 55, 1st fl; admission 10uah; ⏲10am-6pm Tue-Sun), which, despite being desperately underfunded, maintains a well-presented display of beautiful 19th- and 20th-century ceramics, carpets, inlaid boxes and embossed leather.

Kosiv is a minor Hassidic pilgrimage destination, though almost all the town's Jews were murdered by the Nazis on the **Miska Hora** (Town Mountain), a hill rising above the town. One side of the hill is peppered with the toppled graves of the former **Jewish cemetery**. Ask locals living around the hill to show you, as the graves are hard to find.

If you want to be here early for the crafts market – and the best buys do go in the first few hours – you could stay at the perfectly comfortable **Hotel Kosiv** (☎229 47; vul Nezalezhnosti 65A; d from 200uah), which has its own cafe.

Kosiv is linked by bus with Kolomyya (15uah, one hour, at least hourly), Chernivtsi (35uah to 60uah, three hours, eight daily) and Kyiv (230uah, 12 hours, three daily).

UKRAINE'S ROBIN HOOD

All around the Carpathians you'll discover cliffs, rocks, trees and caves bearing the name 'Dovbush'. Legend has it that these are spots where the 'Robin Hood of the Carpathians', Oleksa Dovbush, and his band of merry Hutsuls slept while on the run.

Like his Sherwood Forest–dwelling counterpart, Dovbush robbed from wealthy merchants, travellers and nobles and distributed the loot to the poor – in his case Ruthenian peasants and poor Hutsul villagers. Born in 1700 near Kolomyya, he joined and later led a band of *opryshki* (outlaws). Many other bandits operated in the region, but Dovbush's particular generosity to the highlanders led to his legendary status.

Despite the best efforts of a hapless Polish army, which sent thousands of troops into the mountains after him, he was never captured. In the end it was his mistress who betrayed him in 1741 to her husband, a Polish official. Arrested in the village of Kosmach he was executed without trial and his body parts displayed in villages around the Carpathians as a warning to other outlaws.

Western Ukraine continued to have a reputation for banditry until the 20th century. This dubious 'tradition' was even revived for several years in the early 1990s when whole convoys of trucks would mysteriously vanish from the region's highways.

Sheshory Шешори

☎3478 / POP 2000

Sheshory is a Hutsul valley village stretched endlessly along the fast-flowing Pystynka River. In fact, it's the river that's the main attraction here, with many opportunities for wading and plunging in the heat of summer. The most dramatic water features are the **waterfalls**, a loud and impressive sight after rain.

Sheshory used to hold an annual ethnic music festival, but that has since gone walkabout. The only other attraction is the verdant peace and tranquillity of the surrounding hills and mountains. Sheshory is a good base for some easy walks up onto the *polonyny* (summer pastures) where the Hutsuls make their cheese and herd cattle. Ask around in Kolomyya if you a need a guide to help you navigate the trails.

It is possible to stay in Sheshory, as many of the villagers rent out their rooms; check out www.karpaty.info for the latest offerings. Overhanging the river and regarded as one of the best places to eat in these parts, **Arkan** (Аркан; vul Shevchenka 91; ⌚11am-11pm) is celebrated for its authentic Hutsul cuisine and live Carpathian music.

Verkhovyna Верховина

☎03432 / POP 5400

Among the villages in the Ukrainian Carpathians, Verkhovyna is probably the most gorgeously located (alongside tiny neighbour Kryvorivnya). It sits on a wide valley floor ringed by mountains; Mt Smotrych is just one peak visible from here.

Verkhovyna boasts a private **museum** of Hutsul folk instruments. However, you'll almost certainly have to contact a local guide to get the museum to open for you, especially if you don't speak the lingo. As always, to arrange guides in the immediate area, try asking at the hotels in Kolomyya.

Local hiking guide **Vasyl Kobyliuk** (☎096 372 4400; http://kobylyuk.karpaty.info; vul Stus 4A/8) is good at showing people the region, and also has a handful of humble rooms on offer in his apartment. Otherwise www.karpaty.info has plenty of other options.

Bus and minibus services run regularly to Verkhovyna from neighbouring towns and villages such as Kolomyya, Kosiv and Vorokhta.

Rakhiv Рахів

☎03132 / POP 15,240

An international band of brightly clad hikers slurping *borshch* with weather-beaten Hutsuls; mountain bikers competing with horse-drawn carts and clapped-out Ladas for pothole space; wooded mountainsides hoisting a beautiful backdrop as the fast-flowing Tysa River gurgles beneath precariously hung footbridges – this is Rakhiv, chaotically post-Soviet and crudely rural, but the best base from which to explore the southern Carpathians.

While Rakhiv's derelict state in places is shocking even by Ukrainian standards, the place has a raw energy that draws foreigners in their thousands. Some have even settled here to farm and carry on the traditional ways of the Hutsuls. Peace Corps volunteers posted here love the place.

Rakhiv is good for a couple of days to organise supplies, have a chuckle visiting a 'geographical centre of Europe' that's not really and to enjoy a little hiking. A Swiss-Ukrainian project, **Forza** (www.forza.org.ua), is working on regional regeneration, including the marking of trails into the Carpathian National Nature Park.

Sights & Activities

Rakhiv's main attractions lie outside town.

Carpathian Biosphere Reserve NATURE RESERVE

(http://cbr.nature.org.ua; Krasne Pleso 77) Declared a Unesco Biosphere Reserve in 1992, this protected area is made up of six separate locations, four of which can be found around Rakhiv. Some 90% of the reserve is made up of virgin forest, home to rare flora and fauna. About 5km southwest of Rakhiv the main road leads to the **Carpathian Biosphere Reserve headquarters**, which isn't so much of interest for itself as for what's surrounding it.

Museum of Forest Ecology MUSEUM

(Krasne Pleso 77; admission 10uah; ⌚8am-5pm) This old-school museum stands on the hill behind the Carpathian Biosphere Reserve headquarters building. The exhibition is surprisingly informative, rich and colourful as well as slightly kitsch, so inbetween sniggers at the odd moth-bitten, taxidermied sheep, you'll learn a bit from the handy Carpathian Mountains relief map, and the dioramas of forest landscapes and Hutsul festivals.

Geographical Centre of Europe MONUMENT

Fifteen kilometres southwest of Rakhiv lies what Ukraine contends is Europe's geographical centre, just before the village of Dilove. Ukraine is not the only country to declare itself the continent's centre: Germany, Lithuania, Poland and Slovakia have all staked rival claims. Furthermore, Austrian experts, quoted in the *Wall Street Journal Europe* in 2004, say the pillar erected by Austro-Hungarian geographers in 1887, in what is now back-country Ukraine, was never intended to mark Europe's middle; its Latin inscription of simple longitude and latitude was mistranslated.

None of this has dented official Ukrainian aspirations to the honour, although some locals are more sceptical. Today a Soviet-era spire has joined the Austro-Hungarian pillar at the 'geographical centre of Europe', as has a restaurant complex, souvenir stalls and opportunistic photographers equipped with stuffed bears and deer as props.

Sleeping & Eating

★Smerekova Hata GUESTHOUSE $

(Смерекова хата; ☎096 964 7603, 212 92; www.smerekovahata.com.ua; vul Shevchenka 8; r per person from 80uah;) This superb B&B near the market maintains its position as one of the Carpathians' most traveller-friendly halts. Rooms in the new building are fragrant with pinewood and combine traditional Hutsul bedspreads with ultramodern showers. Owners Vasyl and Anna can organise tours and excursions, and even run Hutsul cookery classes (Vasyl is involved in Ukraine's embryonic Slow Food movement). The garden between the two buildings is a lovely spot to relax after a hike.

Sadyba U Frika GUESTHOUSE $

(☎215 63; erwin75@mail.ru; vul Bohdana Khmelnytskoho 86; r per person 80uah; @) The hotchpotch of rooms are more suburban than charmingly folksy here, but there's a friendly, multilingual atmosphere and the hosts like to prepare Hutsul and Hungarian meals. Guests are free to use the kitchen. Three internet-enabled computers, a sauna and a large garden complete the package, but it's a good 20 minutes' walk from the bus station – take the first right just before the bridge and keep going to No 86.

Hotel Evropa HOTEL $

(☎256 53; www.hotel-europa.com.ua; vul Myru 42; d 160uah;) The Evropa offers 15 scuffed, cheaply furnished chambers with bathrooms fitted using the Soviet plumbing

THE HUTSULS

Fiercely independent and individualistic, the Carpathian-dwelling Hutsuls are a mainstay of Ukrainian national identity. They were first identified as a separate ethnic group at the end of the 18th century. According to some accounts, the 'Hutsul' encompass several tribes – including Boiki, Lemi and Pokuttian – so who and what they are is open to some interpretation.

Ethnographers describe Hutsul life as dominated by herding sheep from high mountain pastures *(polonyny)* to lowland fields, with a little agriculture and forestry thrown in. They point to a dialect incomprehensible to other Ukrainians, a canon of pre-Christian, pagan legends and a diet based on mountain ingredients, including mushrooms, berries, *brynza* (a crumbly cow- or goat-milk cheese tasting like feta) and corn-based *mamalyha* (like polenta).

Wooden architecture, particularly churches, and a host of handicrafts, from decorated ceramics and embroidered shirts to woollen rugs and embossed leather, are also totems of Hutsul culture.

But whereas a traditional Hutsul would dress colourfully, carry an ornate *toporet* (hatchet) and play the *trembita* (a long alpine horn), most modern Hutsuls don't bother much with any of these. The few occasions on which they are likely to dust off their folk costumes include dances and weddings. For the former, men wear baggy trousers and women floral hair arrangements. For the latter, guests deck trees with paper flowers and ribbons, eat special flatbreads and consume lots of vodka.

Hutsul souvenirs are touted throughout the region, particularly in Yaremche. To be sure you are getting the real deal, get hold of a copy of the superb *Art Palette of the Prykarpattya* catalogue (available free from the tourist office in Ivano-Frankivsk) which lists individual artists and craftsmen and where to find them.

manual. No breakfast, but a small tour company and info centre lurk somewhere in the building.

Olenka INTERNATIONAL $
(Оленка; vul Myru 48; mains 30-60uah; ⏰8am-11pm) Rakhiv's fanciest dining option is a tranquil island of style and efficient service, and a fine place to grab some post-hike grub (but lose the muddy hiking boots first). Everything on the long menu, from local Hutsul fare to spaghetti Bolognese, was available when we visited, though our food arrived microwaved to the temperature of molten lava. Has a breakfast menu and opens early enough for it to be relevant.

Information

Rakhiv has no tourist information centre, but the small **kiosk** (⏰10am-6pm Mon-Fri, to 3pm Sat) marked with a green 'i' next to the bridge (which once did serve as a centre but is now a souvenir shop) is worth a stab for basic info and maps.

Getting There & Away

BUS

Buses winding over the mountains to and from the north and east connect Rakhiv with Chernivtsi (75uah, five hours, five daily), Ivano-Frankivsk (45uah, four hours, 13 daily) and Kolomyya (45uah, 3½ to four hours, six daily). Most of these services go through Yaremche (27uah, 2½ hours).

Heading west, there are around 15 services to/from Uzhhorod (64uah to 73uah, around five hours) plus at least hourly services to Mukacheve (60uah, three hours). Four services a week go to Prague (540uah); for details, see www.regabus.cz.

TRAIN

Only a handful of daily trains operate to and from Rakhiv's almost completely derelict terminus: one each way from Ivano-Frankivsk (five hours), one overnight service to Lviv (80uah, eight hours) and one service to Kolomyya (4½ hours). All of these pass through Yaremche.

Getting Around

Travelling south from Rakhiv to the Museum of Forest Ecology and the 'Geographical Centre of Europe' there are around two buses an hour heading for Dilove (6uah, 40 minutes). Heading north, there are *marshrutky* to Bohdan (14uah, at least hourly weekdays), which will bring you towards the start of the hiking trail to Mt Hoverla. Four weekday services will drop you in Luhy (7uah), even closer to the trail.

TRAVEL FROM RAKHIV TO ROMANIA

With no cross-border train service, the only way to reach Romania from Rakhiv is via a car-pedestrian bridge across the Tysa River between Solotvyno and Sighetu Marmaţiei. The English-speaking folks at **Cobwobs Hostel** (hostel@cobwobs.com) in Sighet keep abreast of the latest. They recommend foreigners push to the front of the queue as searches of locals and their vehicles (border officials are looking for cigarette and alcohol smugglers) are thorough.

BUKOVYNA

Chernivtsi Чернівці

☎0372 / POP 259,400

Like many cities in the west of Ukraine, energetic Chernivtsi displays the hallmarks of a more elegant past, most obviously in the shape of its star attraction, the phantasmagorical university building. Shabby, leafy and slightly chaotic, this Ukrainian city sometimes has a somewhat un-Slavic flavour, possibly the residue of centuries of Romanian/Moldovan influence. Renovators have been busy with the stucco and whitewash in the city centre, and some of the old Austro-Hungarian tenements are looking pretty dapper, but in general Chernivtsi remains a ramshackle place with a local student population keeping things lively.

Just over six centuries old, Chernivtsi was once the chief city of Bukovyna (Beech Tree Land) in old Moldavia (now Moldova). It belonged to the Habsburg Empire in the 19th century, when much of the city's ornate architecture was built, and after WWI was temporarily drawn into Romania. Today the city remains the 'capital' of the unofficial Bukovyna region, but its past Jewish, Armenian and German communities are now just ghostly presences.

Sights

★Chernivtsi University NOTABLE BUILDING
(www.chnu.cv.ua; vul Kotsyubynskoho) University buildings are often called 'dreaming spires', but Chernivtsi's is more like a trip on LSD.

Chernivtsi

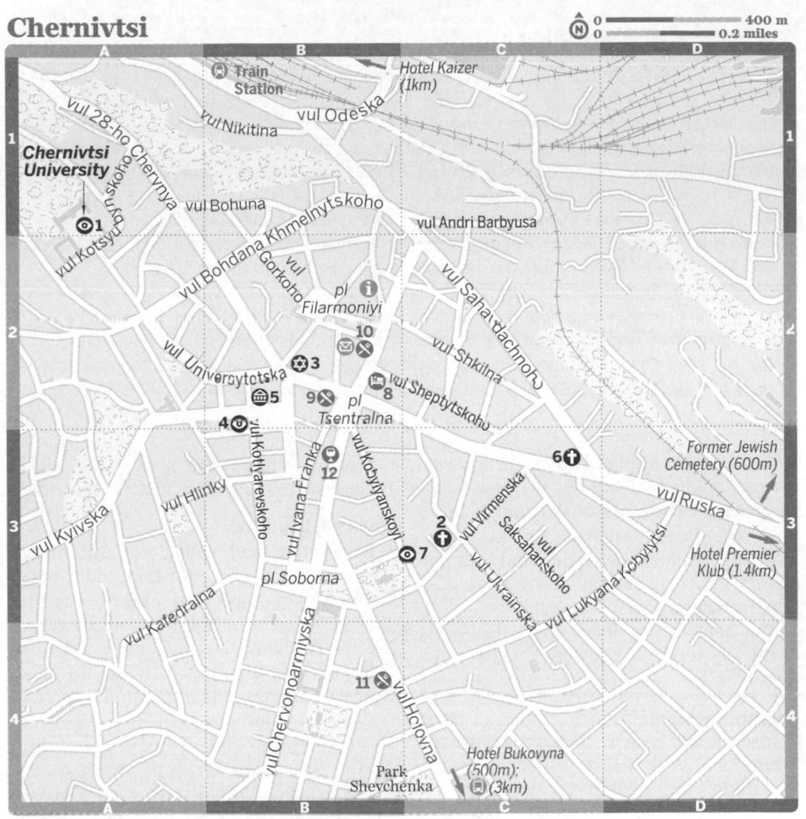

This fantastic, now Unesco-listed red-brick ensemble, with coloured tiles decorating its pseudo-Byzantine, pseudo-Moorish and pseudo-Hanseatic wings, is the last thing you'd expect to see here. The architect responsible was Czech Josef Hlavka, who was also behind Chernivtsi's **Former Armenian Cathedral** (vul Ukrainska 30), as well as large chunks of Vienna. He completed the university in 1882 for the Metropolitans (Orthodox Church leaders) of Bukovyna as their official residence. The Soviets later moved the university here.

The wings surround a landscaped court. To the left as you pass the gatehouse is the **Seminarska Church** (Семінарська церква), now used for concerts and ceremonies. Straight ahead stands the former main **palace residence of the Metropolitans** (Палац-резиденція митрополитів), housing two remarkable staircases and a fantastic, 1st-floor **Marmurovy Zal** (Мармуровий зал;

Chernivtsi

Top Sights

1 Chernivtsi University A1

Sights

2 Former Armenian Cathedral C3
3 Former Synagogue B2
4 Kobylyanska Theatre B2
5 Museum of Bukovinian Jews B2
6 St Nicholas Cathedral C3
7 Vul Kobylyanskoy C3

Sleeping

8 TIU Chernivtsi Backpackers B2

Eating

9 Jidalnya B2
10 Knaus B2
11 Reflection B4

Drinking & Nightlife

12 Pub 34 .... B3

JEWISH CHERNIVTSI

One of Chernivtsi's most famous sons was leading 20th-century poet Paul Celan (1920–70), who was born into a German-speaking Jewish family at **vul Saksahanskoho 5** (formerly Wassilkogasse), when 'Cernăuţi' was part of Romania. His parents died in Nazi concentration camps during WWII and Celan himself survived one to write his most famous 1948 poem 'Todesfuge' (Death Fugue). He later drowned himself in Paris' River Seine. There's also a **Celan monument** (Пам'ятник Паулю Целану) on vul Holovna.

Chernivtsi's **former synagogue** (cnr vul Universytetska & vul Zankovetskoyi) was once famous for its exotic African/Middle Eastern style, but was turned into a cinema in 1954. The **Museum of Bukovinian Jews** (www.muzejew.org.ua; pl Teatralna 5; admission 5uah, audio guide 5uah; 11am-3pm Tue-Fri, to 2pm Sat, 10am-1pm Sun) brings to life the now virtually extinct Jewish culture of Bukovina focusing on the period between 1774 and 1941.

The **former Jewish cemetery** is a melancholic jumble of leaning, overgrown headstones. To get there, follow vul Ruska (or catch trolleybus 2) until you cross the train line. Take the first left, vul Zelena, and continue 500m.

Marble Hall). As a public facility you can wander the buildings at will but the best rooms are usually locked. Ask at the Tourist Information Centre in town about guided tours or look out for guides loitering around the main gates. Security guards may let you take a peek into the main rooms for a small bribe.

The university is about 1.5km northwest of the city centre. Trolleybus 2 will get you there.

Kalynivsky Market MARKET
(Калинівський ринок; www.mtk-kalinka.com; 8am-2pm) With its own police station, bus station and dedicated bank branches, this 33-hectare bazaar is like a town unto itself. As a conduit into Ukraine for goods from neighbouring countries, it attracts tens of thousands of shoppers a day and is a frenetic, wonderful phenomenon. Take any of the numerous *marshrutky* to Калинівський ринок; many leave from in front of the train station.

St Nicholas Cathedral CATHEDRAL
(Собор Св Миколи; vul Ruska 35) Chernivtsi's cathedral is nicknamed the 'drunken church' because of the four twisted turrets surrounding its cupola – painted blue with golden stars, these turrets create an optical illusion. The cathedral is a 1930s copy of a 14th-century royal church in Curtea de Arges (Romania).

Kobylyanska Theatre NOTABLE BUILDING
(театр ім. О. Кобилянської; www.dramtheater.cv.ua; pl Teatralna 1) Set on the exquisitely central European pl Teatralna, Chernivtsi's main drama and music theatre is a beautiful Art Nouveau confection that wouldn't look out of place in Prague or Paris. The ticket office is across the street at vul Lysenka 2.

Vul Kobylyanskoy STREET
When you've had enough of Chernivtsi's barmy traffic, head for the tranquillity of vul Kobylyanskoy, a pedestrianised street running between vuls Holovna and Shevchenka. It's certainly the city's most attractive thoroughfare hemmed with beautiful Art Nouveau facades containing music schools, bookshops, cafes, pizza places and some local government offices. Retro copies of 19th-century gas lamps, freshly planted trees and lots of benches make this the ideal venue for the evening corso and proves that Ukraine can do 'pleasant' when it puts its mind to it.

Sleeping

TIU Chernivtsi Backpackers HOSTEL $
(050 885 7049; tiu.hostels@yahoo.com; vul Sheptytskoho 2, apt 3; dm 100uah;) The English owner's insider tips, nights out, BBQs at Khotyn Fortress and summer excursions into the Carpathians make Chernivtsi's only real backbacker hostel a great base. Beds are limited so book ahead.

Hotel Premier Klub HOTEL $
(Отель Премьер клуб; 554 698; vul Zhasmina 4D; r 200-280uah;) This decent enough semi-budget option has a restful location around 2.5km east of the city centre. Nine rooms have private bathrooms, the three more basic Ekonom classrooms share two showers and two toilets. Staff are friendly enough, but the wi-fi could do with a boost. To get there, take trolleybus 2 along vul Ruska to the Zhytomyrska stop then walk

along vul Zhasmina until you see the hotel signposted. No breakfast.

Hotel Bukovyna HOTEL $$
(☎585 625; www.bukovyna-hotel.com; vul Holovna 141; s/d from 295/335uah; ❄📶) Owing to its convenient location, its relative value for money, and its large number of rooms, this jolly giant has an understandably sizeable chunk of the local market. Rooms range from 'Economy', where the post-Soviet renovation is skin-deep, to 'Comfort', which comes with air-con and furniture from this century. Guests in 'Economy' class are barred from the unexpectedly good buffet breakfast spread unless they cough up 70uah.

Hotel Kaizer HOTEL $$
(готель Кайзер; ☎585 275; www.kaiser-hotel.com.ua; vul Gagarina 51; s & d 300uah; ❄📶) Kyiv, Moscow, New York, Berlin, Rome, Warsaw, Istanbul: the world clocks ticking loudly in Kaizer's empty lobby presage Chernivtsi's nicest rooms, which have an appealing mix of new and retro furniture. They, and the lovely grill restaurant out the back (complete with wooden windmill), are wildly underused though – probably because of the slightly out-of-the-way location on the wrong side of the train station.

Eating & Drinking

Jidalnya CANTEEN $
(Їдальня; vul Universytetska 1; mains 6-17uah; ⏲8am-4pm & 4.40-8pm Mon-Sat) Brightly painted no-frills, no-smiles basement feeding spot with grim dinner ladies ladling out buckwheat, pasta, fried fish and other Ukrainian staples as well as coffees and desserts. Cheap as chips, and they have those too.

★**Reflection** INTERNATIONAL $$
(Рефлекшн; vul Holovna 66; mains 40-60uah; ⏲9am-11pm; ❄) Tea, porridge, English breakfasts – if you're from Blighty you'll love this tranquil retreat with its boutique interior, impeccably polite, English-speaking waiters and a quite un-Ukrainian atmosphere of calm and unobtrusiveness. And if you are from just about anywhere else on the planet, you're gonna love it too for the Caesar salad, fried porcini appetisers, Black Forest gateau, pork in chilli sauce, pannacotta, handmade chocolates and gourmet Ukrainian dishes – treats you probably thought you'd left behind on venturing into the sticks. Surely one of the Carpathians' finest eateries.

Knaus INTERNATIONAL $$
(www.knaus.com.ua; vul Holovna 26A; mains 30-90uah; ⏲noon-4am) Indoors this place teleports you to a kind of Ukrainian Bavaria, but summer is the best time to visit Knaus when you can sit out with a Krombacher beer in the courtyard beer garden. The menu is a mixed bag of Ukrainian staples, German pork knuckle and dumplings, and more exotic dishes such as pumpkin soup with curry. The owners also rent out an apartment on the same courtyard and run a travel company.

Pub 34 PUB
(vul Holovna 34) Keeping to a post-Soviet tradition of naming your business after its building number, this brick cellar pub-club spins cool tracks as you kick back on leather sofas and enjoy the meat-heavy meals and beer. Live music evenings and regular DJ nights.

Information

Post Office (vul Khudyakova 6)
Tourist Information Centre (☎553 684; www.chernivtsy.eu; vul Holovna 16; ⏲9am-1pm & 2-6pm) Free audio guides available (300uah deposit or passport) and staff can arrange guides to the university.

Getting There & Away

AIR

Chernivtsi's airport can now call itself 'international' thanks to the Romanian airline **Carpatair** (www.carpatair.com), which flies three times a week to Timişoara. There are no domestic flights.

BUS

The bus station is 3km southeast of the city centre. Coming from Kolomyya, get off the bus at the roundabout where around half the passengers alight. If you don't, you'll probably end up at the Kalynivsky Market, from where you'll have to haul you luggage through the busy rows of stalls and jam it into a *marshrutka* (No 10) to get to the city centre. Buses to Kolomyya leave from the same roundabout (but start at the market's bus station).

Services leave the bus station for the following destinations:

Ivano-Frankivsk 50uah, 3½ hours, 11 daily
Kamyanets-Podilsky 32uah, 2½ hours, half-hourly to hourly
Khotyn 22uah, two hours, half-hourly to hourly
Kolomyya 25uah, two hours, very frequent
Kyiv 175uah, nine hours, three daily (two overnight)

Lviv 100uah, 8½ hours, five daily
Suceava 71uah, four hours, one daily (7.10am)

TRAIN

Rail connections from Chernivtsi:
Ivano-Frankivsk 67uah, two hours, at least three daily
Kolomyya 12uah, two to 2½ hours, four daily
Kyiv 175uah, 14 hours, two daily
Lviv 80uah, 4½ to six hours, at least three daily
Odesa 195uah, 17½ hours, daily

Getting Around

To reach Chernivtsi's airport take *marshrutka* 38.

Trolleybuses 3 and 5, plus a whole host of *marshrutky*, run between the bus station and the train station. Trolleybus 2 trundles from the university to the city centre then along vul Ruska.

Khotyn Хотин

You might first pass Khotyn on the way from Chernivtsi, but it's closer to Kamyanets-Podilsky and best visited as a day trip from there.

While Kamyanets-Podilsky is awesome taken as a whole, its castle building is upstaged by **Khotyn Fortress** (admission 10uah; ⏲8am-8pm). Eastern European filmmakers love to use this massive fort overlooking the Dnister River as a location; for instance it served as Warsaw Castle in the highly controversial Russian-language 2009 blockbuster movie *Taras Bulba*. With walls up to 40m high and 6m thick, today's stone fortress was built in the 15th century, replacing an earlier wooden structure. Its location safeguarded river trade routes, making it a sought-after prize. The defining moment in its history came in 1621, with a threatened Turkish invasion. The incumbent Poles enlisted the help of 40,000 Cossacks and managed to rout a 250,000-strong Turkish army. This improbable victory made a hero of Cossack leader Petro Sahaydachny, whose huge statue greets you near the fortress' entrance. However, any notion of the fortress' impregnability was dispelled in 1711 when the Turks finally nabbed it. The Russians took over in the 19th century.

Inside the fortress walls there ain't a whole lot to see, but it's really the large riverfront grounds that make the place. Some of the outer fortification walls remain and you can clamber precariously over these. In one far corner, locals even pose for pictures where it appears they're jumping over the fortress. But whatever you do, don't forget to bring a picnic.

Getting There & Away

There are regular buses and *marshrutky* making the 30km journey between Kamyanets-Podilsky and Khotyn (10uah, around 50 minutes) and every Kamyanets-Podilsky–Chernivtsi bus stops en route. The fortress is about 2.5km north of Khotyn town centre and the best strategy is to get off the bus when locals alight near the market (not at the far-flung bus station). Head along the road through the market and you'll pass a blue church on your right and a Soviet war memorial on your left. Stay on this road for a further 20 minutes until you see an old flaking sign marked Фортеця. Take a right here and you'll soon see the ticket office.

TRANSCARPATHIA

Most people are only likely to pass this way if entering or leaving Ukraine via neighbouring Hungary or Slovakia. This is a pity, as this corner of the world, where the Soviet Union once faded out and Europe took over, is a melting pot of Hungarian, Slovak, Ukrainian and Roma cultures and has a fascinating social mix. It's also the home of Ukraine's best red wines and most impenetrable dialects. Transcarpathia is so far west that some old timers still set their clocks to Ukrainian time minus one hour, and it's this independent spirit that makes even Lviv seem a long way away, far beyond the high Carpathians.

Uzhhorod Ужгород

☎0132 / POP 116,400

Formerly known as Ungvar, this border town and main conduit for road traffic into and out of Slovakia and Hungary is a pleasant, if rather untypical, introduction to Ukraine. With its interwar villas, faded Hungarian shop signs, a whole neighbourhood of 1920s Czech-built administrative edifices, pedestrianised streets, a lively vibe and a vibrant tourist industry, it's as if central Europe has forgotten to end at the border and spilt over into the former USSR. With its large Hungarian and Romanian minorities as well as a constant turnover of foreign tourists, this is by far Ukraine's most cosmopolitan regional capital. Kyiv feels a long way away from here in every way, Donetsk and Crimea like a different continent.

Uzhhorod

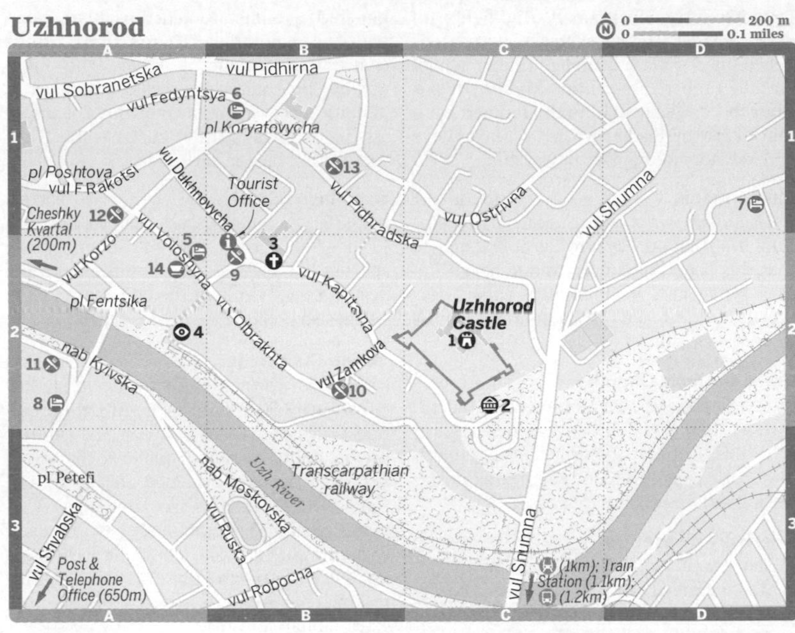

Uzhhorod

Top Sights
1 Uzhhorod Castle C2

Sights
2 Folk Architecture & Life Museum C2
3 Greek Catholic Church B2
4 Philharmonia A2

Sleeping
5 Five Flags Hostel A2
6 Hotel Atlant B1
7 Hotel Ungvarskiy D1
8 Old Continent A2

Eating
9 Cafe Mir B2
10 Cafe-Muzey Pid Zamkom D2
11 Delfin A2
12 Kaktus Kafe A1
13 Vopak B1

Drinking & Nightlife
14 Cafe Verdi A2

Sights

★Uzhhorod Castle CASTLE

(vul Kapitalna; admission 15uah; 10am-6pm Tue-Sun) On the hill overlooking town stands the 15th-century castle with massive walls and beefy bastions built to withstand Turkish assaults. The main palace is home to the **Transcarpathian Museum of Local Lore** (Закарпатський Краєзнавчий музей), which has a good collection of *pysanky* (patterned eggs), regional folk costume, some Hutsul musical instruments including nine *trembity* (the Carpathian didgeridoo) and a section on interwar Transcarpathia – fascinating for those with an interest in central European history.

The tranquil grounds are also fun to wander and the bastion in the northeast corner provides views across Uzhhorod. If you have an urge to try the local plonk, **wine tastings** (6 wines 45uah; 10am-6pm) take place in the castle's atmospheric brick cellars with friendly sommeliers on hand.

Folk Architecture & Life Museum MUSEUM

(Закарпатський музей народної архітектури та побуту; vul Kapitalna; admission 15uah; 10am-6pm Wed-Mon) Next door to Uzhhorod Castle, this is one of the tidiest open-air museums in the country, albeit small. Highlights include several Hutsul cottages with their bench-lined walls, a complete timber school and the timber 18th-century **Mykhaylivska Church** (St Michael's Church), rescued from the village of Shelestovo near Mukacheve and still a working place of worship.

Philharmonia CONCERT HALL
(Філармонія; www.philarmonia.uz.ua; pl Teatralna) Built in 1911, it's pretty obvious at first glance that this beautiful concert venue began life as a synagogue. Its intricately carved terracota facade makes this Uzhhorod's most impressive edifice.

Greek Catholic Church CHURCH
(pl Andreya Bachynskoho) Monumental, recently renovated and built in the neoclassical style, this 18th-century former Jesuit church is worth a peek inside for its huge iconostasis and striking ceiling frescoes.

Cheshsky Kvartal NEIGHBOURHOOD
A short walk west of the immediate city centre, hemmed by the Uzh River on its southern flank, lies the Czech Quarter, an unexpected neighbourhood of 1920s Czech admin buildings and tenements, a treat for architecture fans. The assertive interwar functionalist style, so ubiquitous in Prague and other large Czech and Slovak cities, dominates, the most striking example being the Regional Assembly building. Along the river extends Europe's longest alley of lime trees, a pleasant way to wander into the area.

Sleeping

Bedding down at the **train station** (r 200-300uah, dm 100-150uah; 24hr) is an option for late/early arrivals.

Hotel Atlant HOTEL $
(Атлант; 614 095; www.atlant-hotel.com.ua; pl Koryatovycha 27; s 225-435uah, d 300-485uah;) The 26 European-style rooms are great value, especially the singles, which are on the top floor (no lift) and have skylights and sloping ceilings. As Uzhhorod's best deal it's popular (especially on booking websites), so call ahead if you can.

Hotel Ungvarskiy HOTEL $
(готель Унгварський; 616 565; www.ungvarskiy-hotel.com.ua; vul Elektrozavodska 2; r from 350uah;) With a miserable location on the edge of Uzhhorod's abandonned industrial zone, this plasticky hotel doesn't promise much, but inside rooms are generously cut, clean and well maintained. There's a spa, fitness centre and restaurant, where the high-quality but miserly breakfast (an extra 30uah) is served by burly waiters. Lack of air-con and transparent curtains make for some super-heated early starts.

Five Flags Hostel HOSTEL $
(613 928; www.fiveflagshostel.com; vul Voloshyna 19; dm from 85uah;) Super-central, spartan but spotless hostel on the main pedestrian drag through the city centre. Only 10 beds so booking ahead is essential.

★**Old Continent** HOTEL $$$
(669 366; www.hotel-oldcontinent.com; pl Petefi 4-6; s/d from 690/890uah;) At Uzhhorod's finest digs the choice between 21st-century predictability, baroque opulence or swish Art Deco may be a difficult call, as all the rooms here are immaculate, very well maintained and sumptuously cosy. English-speaking staff are courteous, the location is bull's eye central and there's a decent multitasking restaurant. Our sole complaint – the extra 150uah for breakfast.

Eating & Drinking

★**Cafe-Muzey Pid Zamkom** CENTRAL EUROPEAN $
(Кафе-Музей Під Замком; vul Olbrakhta 3; mains 20-60uah; 9am-11pm) Wistfully celebrating Ungvar's all-too-short decades in the lap of Czechoslovak affluence, this great pub and nostalgia museum rolled into one is packed with chipped enamel signs, radios, typewriters and other assorted interwar junk. Benches are tightly packed, the Czech lager flows freely, and the hand-scrawled menu is a mixed bag of Ukrainian dishes, sandwiches, spaghetti and Czech dumplings.

Cafe Mir CAFE $
(Кафе Мир; vul Kapitalna 5; pizzas 26-49uah; 8am-9pm) Under amiable new ownership, this funky little place serves pizzas, cakes and drinks as you surf the web on chequered sofas. Tibetan prayer flags drape the interior and there's Mizhhirske beer on tap.

Delfin INTERNATIONAL $
(Дельфін; nab Kyivska 3; mains 18-45uah; 11am-11pm) Locals consider this one of the better restaurants in town. European and Ukrainian dishes are served, but it's known for its grilled meats, fish and rooftop terrace with pretty Uzh River views.

TRAVEL FROM UZHHOROD TO HUNGARY & SLOVAKIA

Chop, 22km west of Uzhhorod and 44km northwest of Mukacheve, is the international rail crossing between Ukraine and Hungary or Slovakia. Here, the broader Ukrainian rail gauge meets the narrower standard gauge of central Europe, and there's a delay of anything between one and three hours while your train's carriages are lifted in the air and onto different bogies.

Trains affected are long-distance services like the Budapest–Moscow or Kyiv–Bratislava, but half the time these delays occur barely noticed in the wee hours. The other half of the time, you could use the delay as an excuse to break your journey in Uzhhorod or Mukacheve. As Chop is treated as the last stop on the Hungarian rail system, several additional services (eg Budapest–Chop, Bratislava–Chop) originate from and terminate at its station.

On services heading west from Kyiv and Lviv, domestic trains stop at Chop before reaching Uzhhorod; international services don't stop at Uzhhorod at all (think of it as being on a little rail appendix).

The quickest way between Chop and Uzhhorod is to take a *marshrutka* (fixed-route minibus). It's also possible to catch buses from Uzhhorod to Hungary and Slovakia.

Kaktus Kafe CAFE $
(vul Korzo 7; mains 20-50uah; ⏲10am-10pm; 📶) The vaguely Wild West/Aztec theme may sit incongrously with the Hutsul/Transcarpathian cuisine (try the *kremzliki* – fried pork with potato pancakes in mushroom sauce) but this central joint is a well-run spot for food and international beer on tap, and the atmosphere is welcoming.

Cafe Verdi COFFEE
(Кафе Верди; vul Voloshyna 24; ⏲7.30am-7pm) Located right opposite the Five Flags Hostel, this traditional central European coffee-and-cake halt has prints of old Ungvar on the walls and pleasant service. Good for a sweet-toothed breakfast or caffeine pit-stop.

Self-Catering

Vopak SUPERMARKET
(Вопак; vul Yarotska 2) For self-caterers the only centrally located supermarket is Vopak.

Information

Post and Telephone Office (pl Poshtova 4) There's another tiny branch at the train station.

Tourist Office (☎613 193; www.zakarpattyatourism.info; vul Dukhnovycha 16/1; ⏲9am-6pm Mon-Sun Jul & Aug, closed Sun rest of year) Excellent office offering a booking service, lots of free info and cycle hire (35uah per hour).

Getting There & Away

AIR

Uzhhorod's 'international' **airport** (vul Sobranetska 145), 1.5km northwest of the city centre, has just one flight daily to/from Kyiv's Zhulyany airport (1000uah, 1¾ hours) operated by the obscure **Motor Sich** (www.flymotorsich.com).

BUS

There are long-distance buses to Lviv (93uah, 6½ hours, up to 12 daily). Services also run to Rakhiv (80uah, three hours, 11 daily) and Mukacheve (16uah, one hour, every 15 to 20 minutes).

Marshrutka 145 goes to Chop (10uah, 50 minutes, every 15 minutes) from the side of the bus station facing the train station. Cross-border buses link Uzhhorod most usefully with Košice (110uah, 2½ hours, three daily) in Slovakia. **Regabus** (www.regabus.cz) operates overnight services to Prague (644uah, 14 hours).

TRAIN

Trains to and from Western Europe don't stop in Uzhhorod; you must go to nearby Chop.

Domestic trains go to and from Lviv (104uah, six to nine hours, up to five daily) and Kyiv (200uah, 15 to 18½ hours, three daily). Other services include one middle-of-the-night train to Solotvyno (70uah, 6½ hours, daily) and slow-but-scenic *elektrychky* (electric trains) to Mukacheve (6uah, 2½ hours, seven daily).

Mukacheve Мукачеве

☎03131 / POP 93,700

Echoes of Austro-Hungary, some fine inter-war Czechoslovak architecture, rustic horse-drawn carts competing for cobble space and one of Ukraine's most dramatic castles make Mukacheve a worthwhile stop-off. The town can also serve as an easily reachable, low-key introduction to Ukraine if you're heading into the country by train.

Sights

Mukacheve has a very pleasant, cobblestoned and pedestrianised central zone, anchored by the architecturally distracting Secessionist and neo-Gothic **town hall**.

Palanok Castle CASTLE
(www.zamokpalanok.mk.uz.ua; admission 10uah; 9am-6pm) Mukacheve's highlight is the hilltop castle that pops up from the surrounding plain as you approach Mukacheve from Uzhhorod, like something in a fairytale fantasy. This 14th-century castle, famous as the site where Croatian-Hungarian princess Ilona Zrini held off the Austrian Emperor's army for three years before finally capitulating in 1688, is also popular among Hungarians for its association with Sándor Petőfi (1823–49), the Hungarian national poet, who was held here during the century the building served as an Austrian prison. A couple of ageing exhibits (folk costumes, archaeological finds) with English explanations provide minor distraction, unlike the views which are wonderful. Renovation often gives way to dereliction (or a souvenir shop) here and half the fun is getting lost on the various levels of arcading that surround the courtyard. To get here, board any bus 3 in front of the church on vul Pushkina or take any *marshrutka* heading to Тімірязева.

Sleeping & Eating

'Motel' GUESTHOUSE $
(050 912 8861, 050 501 2040; vul Yaroslava Mudroho 82-84; s/d 160/210uah;) Minutes from the station, but about 15 minutes on foot to the town centre, this friendly guesthouse is Mukacheve's cheapest snooze pad. The 12 rooms are cosy, if a little scuffed, there's a sauna downstairs and an adjoining cafe provides sustenance. No breakfast.

Hotel Star HOTEL $$
(320 08; www.star-ar.mk.uz.ua; pl Myru 10-12; s/d from 397/467uah;) This yellow neoclassical building opposite the town hall has rug-lined, flagstaff halls and dark wooden doors leading to spotless rooms with minibar and international satellite TV. The hotel also has a rather ostentatious restaurant and brews its own beer.

Shchodnya UKRAINIAN $
(Щодня; vul Pushkina 14A; mains 6.50-15uah; 8am-8pm Mon-Fri, to 6pm Sat, 10am-4pm Sun) Modelled on Ukraine's No 1 restaurant chain, Puzata Khata, this self-service canteen cooks up incredibly low-cost Eastern Slavic comfort food – you can easily put together a three-course meal with drinks for 20uah to 30uah – but without the folksy theme. It's at the opposite end of vul Pushkina to the town hall.

Getting There & Away

BUS

Services leave every 15 to 20 minutes for Uzhhorod (16uah, one hour) from the bus station, 1.5km east of the town centre. There are also at least 10 buses a day to Rakhiv (60uah, three to five hours).

TRAIN

The train station is on vul Yaroslava Mudroho, 1.5km southwest of the town centre. Heading eastwards from Mukacheve, four trains a day go to Lviv (90uah, 4½ hours) and three to Kyiv (170uah, 14½ hours). Heading west, there are at least seven daily *elektrychky* (8uah) and mainline trains to Uzhhorod via Chop (where you can pick up international services originating in Chop).

Odesa & Southern Ukraine
Одеса і Південна Україна

POP 4.7 MILLION / AREA 86,300 SQ KM

Includes ➡

Best Places to Eat & Drink

- Klarabara (p154)
- Tavernetta (p154)
- Kompot (p154)
- Bernardazzi (p154)
- Dacha (p155)

Best Places to Stay

- Hotel Londonskaya (p153)
- Frederic Koklen (p153)
- Mozart Hotel (p153)
- Pelikan Tour (p162)
- Babushka Grand Hostel (p152)

Why Go?

This region feels New World much more than Europe. The flat steppe between the estuaries of the Dnipro and the Danube was only properly colonised after Russian empress Catherine the Great wrestled it from the Turks.

It was indeed touted as the Russian California when immigrants from all over Europe poured in to cultivate virgin lands and build the port of Odesa. Greek, Yiddish, Italian and German were all spoken here along with Russian and Ukrainian.

Although less multicultural today, Odesa is still permeated with porto franco spirit, displaying Jewish humour and French conviviality, along with crumbling mansion houses, which line the streets named after settlers' ethnicities.

To the west, colonists' heritage lingers next to the birding paradise of the Danube Delta. In the east, swathes of virgin steppe are preserved on Dzharylhach island and in Askaniya Nova Reserve, which an eccentric German aristocrat populated with wildebeest and zebras.

When to Go

Odesa

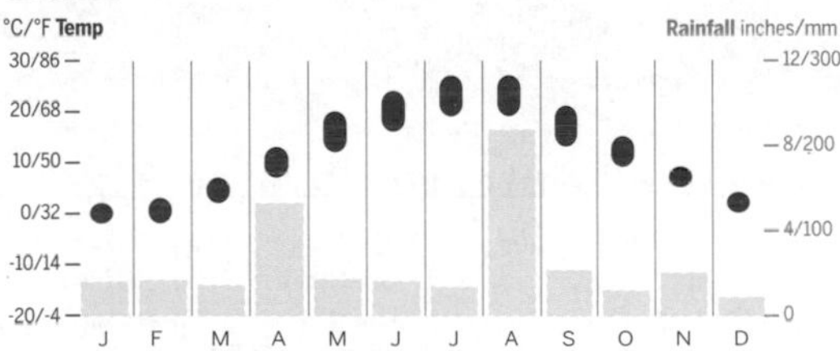

May Smell blooming lilacs and join the vanguard of Odesa's beach-bum army.

Jul Gorge on delicious fruit and watch silent movies on the Potemkin Steps.

Oct Arrive in time for the bird migration in the impressive Danube Delta.

ODESA

☎048 / POP 1 MILLION

Odesa (Одеса) is a city straight from literature – an energetic, decadent boomtown. Its famous Potemkin Steps sweep down to the Black Sea and Ukraine's biggest commercial port. Behind them, a cosmopolitan cast of characters makes merry among pastel neoclassical buildings lining a geometrical grid of leafy streets.

Immigrants from all over Europe were invited to make their fortune here when Odesa was founded in the late 18th century by Russia's Catherine the Great. These new inhabitants gave Russia's southern window on the world a singular, subversive nature.

As well as becoming a duty-free port, Odesa also attracted ordinary holidaymakers with its sunny climate and sandy beaches. True, the city's appearance grows tattier as you head south past half-empty sanatoriums towards its beachside nightclubs. However, this east–west crossroads makes up for that with sheer panache, and Odesans are known across the old USSR for being stylish, funny, savvy and not easily impressed.

History

Catherine the Great imagined Odesa as the St Petersburg of the south. Her lover, General Grygory Potemkin, laid the groundwork for her dream in 1789 by capturing the Turkish fortress of Hadjibey, which previously stood here. However, Potemkin died before work began on the city in 1794 and his senior commanders oversaw its construction instead. The Spanish-Neapolitan general José de Ribas, after whom the main street, vul Derybasivska, is named, built the harbour. The Duc de Richelieu (Armand Emmanuel du Plessis), an aristocrat fleeing the French Revolution, became the first governor, overseeing the city's affairs from 1803 to 1814.

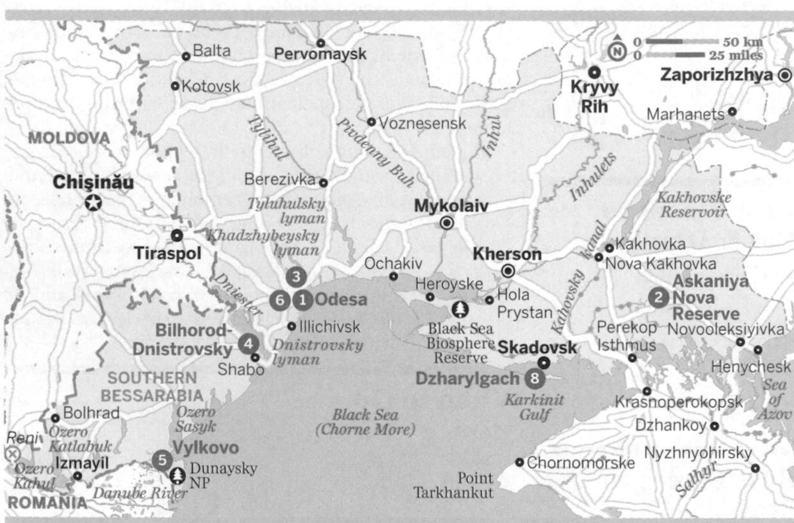

Odesa & Southern Ukraine Highlights

1. Join the tanning and party fest on Odesa's **beaches** (p150).
2. Spot zebra and bison on safari at the **Askaniya Nova Reserve** (p159).
3. Make an ascent of the **Potemkin Steps** (p147) – the setting for one of cinema's most famous scenes.
4. Launch an assault on the beefy ramparts of Bilhorod-Dnistrovsky's **Akkerman Fortress** (p160).
5. Try to keep your feet dry in Vylkovo, epicentre of the **Danube Delta Biosphere Reserve** (p161).
6. Crawl the bars and restaurants in and around Odesa's **vul Derybasivska** (p147).
7. Tuck into a plate of Odesa's endemic and unforgettable **food** (p154).
8. Feel the melancholy of the steppe on the island of **Dzharylhach** (p159).

In 1815, when the city became a duty-free port, things really began to boom. Its huge appetite for more labour meant the city became a refuge – 'Odesa Mama' – for runaway serfs, criminals, renegades and dissidents. By the 1880s it was the second-biggest Russian port, with grain the main export, and an important industrial base.

It was the crucible of the early 1905 workers' revolution, with a local uprising and the mutiny on the battleship *Potemkin Tavrichesky*. Then, between 1941 and 1944, Odesa sealed its reputation as one of the 'hero' cities, when partisans sheltering in the city's catacombs during WWII put up a legendary fight against the occupying Romanian troops (allies of the Nazis). Around 100,000 Jews in the Odesa region were shot or burnt alive by the Romanians implementing the Nazi ethnic purification doctrine.

Odesa was a very Jewish city in the 1920s when many village Jews moved in here, while Russian bourgeoisie and intellectuals were fleeing the Bolshevik revolution. But the Holocaust and emigration fuelled by Soviet anti-Semitism reduced the Jewish minority to almost a shadow. Many Jews moved to New York's Brighton Beach, now nicknamed 'Little Odesa'.

Sights & Activities

Odesa may lack the must-see sights of a Kyiv or a Lviv, but it still packs plenty of charm with its splendid architecture, eye-popping panoramas and quirky monuments. The city centre's shaded avenues are tailor-made for strolling, so lace up your best walking shoes. Just avoid staring at them, as most of Odesa's attractions are overhead in the form of intricate turn-of-the-20th-century facade details, onion-domed church spires and towering statues.

★Potemkin Steps LANDMARK

(Потьомкінські сходи) A woman yells at a tidy line of soldiers as they take aim. Officer commands: 'Fire!' It takes many painful seconds for her to collapse and release a pram with a baby, which starts slowly tumbling down the steps – these very steps. All of that never happened during the real Battleship Potemkin mutiny, but the genius film director Sergei Eisenstein made the world believe it did. The steps lead down from bul Prymorsky to the Sea Port. But pause at the top to admire sweeping views of the harbour. You may avoid climbing back by taking the free **funicular** (⏲8am-11pm) that runs parallel.

★Bul Prymorsky STREET

(Приморский бульвар) Sooner or later everyone gravitates to this tree-lined pedestrian zone with replica 19th-century gas lamps, park benches and more photographers armed with a small zoo of animals with which to have your photo taken. At the boulevard's eastern end, you'll spot the pink-and-white colonnaded **City Hall**, originally the stock exchange and later the Regional Soviet Headquarters. The cannon here is a war trophy captured from the British during the Crimean War. In the square in front of City Hall is Odesa's most photographed monument, the **Pushkin statue** (Памятник Пушкину). The plaque reads 'To Pushkin – from the Citizens of Odesa'.

Continuing along the boulevard, at the top of the Potemkin Steps you'll reach the statue of **Duc de Richelieu** (Памятник Ришелье), Odesa's first governor, looking like a Roman in a toga.

At the western end of bul Prymorsky stands the semi-derelict **Vorontsov Palace** (Воронцовский дворец). This was the residence of the city's third governor, built in 1826 in a classical style with interior Arabic detailing. The Greek-style colonnade behind the palace offers brilliant views over Odesa's bustling port.

★Vul Derybasivska STREET

(Дерибасівська вулиця) Odesa's main commercial street, pedestrian vul Derybasivska, is jam-packed with restaurants, bars and, in the summer high season, tourists. At its quieter eastern end you'll discover the statue of **José De Ribas**. This illustrious gentlemen – half-Catalan, half-Irish – built Odesa's harbour, so they named a central street after him. At the western end of the thoroughfare is the pleasant and beautifully renovated **City Garden** (Gorodskoy Sad), surrounded by several restaurants.

You'll find various touristy knick-knacks for sale here and ex-Soviet tourists standing in two long lines to be photographed with bronze sculptures, one of which is simply a chair – a reference to the Soviet satirical novel *The Twelve Chairs*. The other one is that of 1930s jazz singer Leonid Utyosov.

Across the street, the swanky **Passazh** covered shopping arcade is the best-preserved example of the neo-renaissance

Odesa

0 200 m
0 0.1 miles

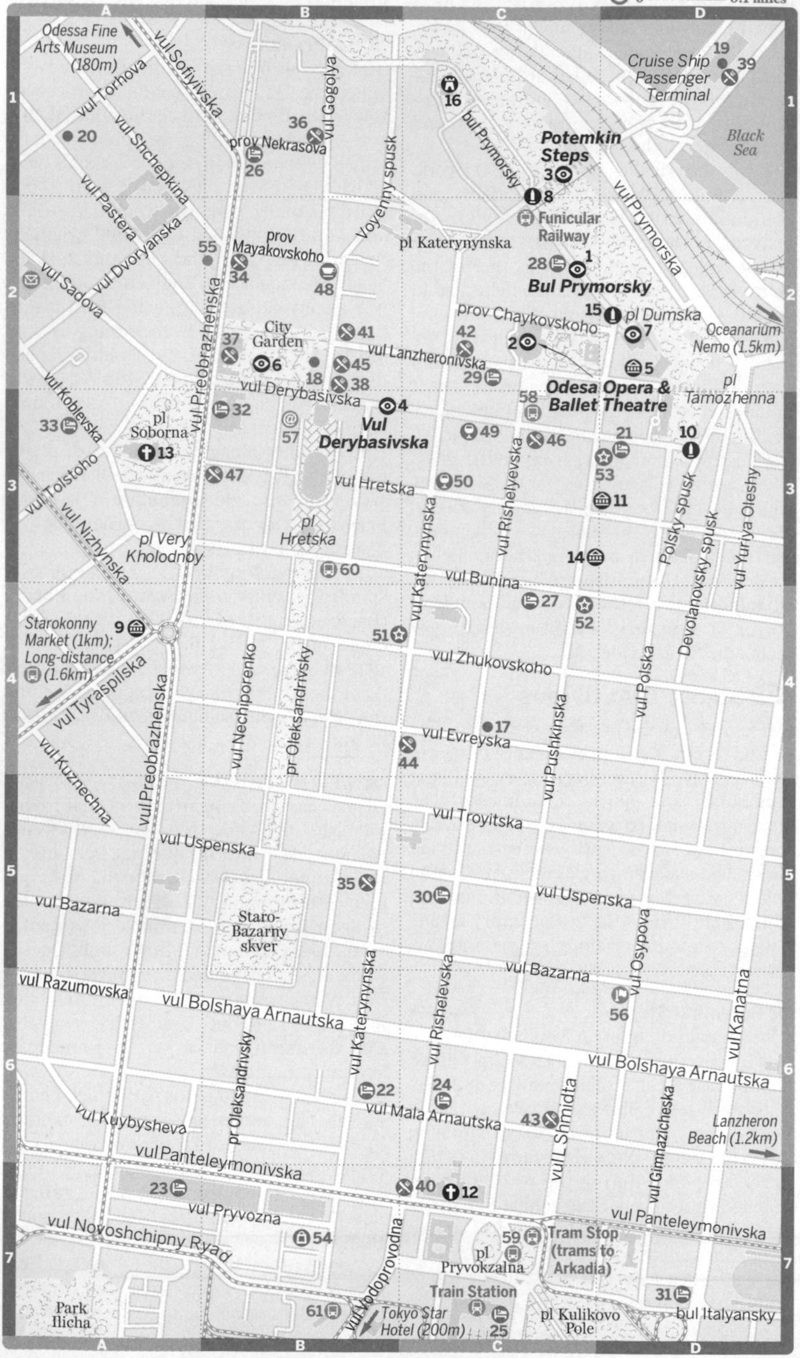
A
B
C
D
1
2
3
4
5
6
7
Odessa Fine Arts Museum (180m)
vul Sofiyivska
vul Torhova
vul Shchepkina
vul Pastera
vul Dvoryanska
vul Sadova
vul Gogolya
prov Nekrasova
Voyenny spusk
bul Prymorsky
Potemkin Steps
Funicular Railway
pl Katerynynska
Cruise Ship Passenger Terminal
Black Sea
vul Prymorska
prov Mayakovskoho
Bul Prymorsky
prov Chaykovskoho
pl Dumska
Oceanarium Nemo (1.5km)
City Garden
vul Lanzheronivska
vul Derybasivska
Vul Derybasivska
Odesa Opera & Ballet Theatre
pl Tamozhenna
vul Preobrazhenska
vul Koblevska
pl Soborna
vul Tolstoho
vul Nizhynska
vul Hretska
pl Hretska
pl Very Kholodnoy
vul Rishelyevska
vul Katerynynska
Polsky spusk
Devolanovsky spusk
vul Yuriya Oleshy
vul Bunina
Starokonny Market (1km); Long-distance (1.6km)
vul Tyraspilska
vul Nechiporenko
pr Oleksandrivsky
vul Zhukovskoho
vul Pushkinska
vul Polska
vul Evreyska
vul Kuznechna
vul Troyitska
vul Uspenska
Staro-Bazarny skver
vul Bazarna
vul Osypova
vul Razumovska
vul Bolshaya Arnautska
vul Rishelevska
vul Kanatna
vul Kuybysheva
vul Mala Arnautska
vul L Shmidta
vul Gimnazicheska
Lanzheron Beach (1.2km)
vul Panteleymonivska
vul Pryvozna
vul Novoshchipny Ryad
vul Vodoprovodna
pl Pryvokzalna
Tram Stop (trams to Arkadia)
Train Station
Tokyo Star Hotel (200m)
pl Kulikovo Pole
bul Italyansky
Park Ilicha
1
2
3
4
5
6
7
8
9
10
11
12
13
14
15
16
17
18
19
20
21
22
23
24
25
26
27
28
29
30
31
32
33
34
35
36
37
38
39
40
41
42
43
44
45
46
47
48
49
50
51
52
53
54
55
56
57
58
59
60
61

Odesa

Top Sights
1 Bul Prymorsky C2
2 Odesa Opera & Ballet Theatre C2
3 Potemkin Steps C1
4 Vul Derybasivska B3

Sights
5 Archaeology Museum D2
6 City Garden B2
7 City Hall D2
8 Duc de Richelieu Statue C1
9 History of Odesa Jews Museum A4
10 José De Ribas Statue D3
11 Museum of Western & Eastern Art D3
12 Panteleymonivskaya Church C7
13 Preobrazhensky Cathedral A3
14 Pushkin Museum C3
15 Pushkin Statue D2
16 Vorontsov Palace C1

Activities, Courses & Tours
17 Eugenia Travel C4
18 Freetours Odessa B2
19 London Sky Travel D1
20 Salix A1

Sleeping
21 American Business Center D3
22 Babushka Grand Hostel B6
23 Black Sea Privoz A7
24 Black Sea Rishelyevskaya C6
25 Central Vokzal Apartment Bureau C7
26 Frederic Koklen B1
27 Hotel Ayvazovsky C4
28 Hotel Londonskaya C2
29 Mozart Hotel C2
30 Odessa Rent-A-Flat C5
31 Palladium Hotel D7
32 Passazh Hotel B3
33 TIU Front Page Hostel A3

Eating
34 Aioli B2
Bernardazzi (see 52)
35 Four Bulgarians B5
36 Gogol Mogol B1
37 Klarabara B2
38 Kompot B2
39 Kompot (Morvokzal) D1
40 Kompot (Panteleymonovskaya) C7
41 Kumanets B2
42 Maman C2
43 Rozmarin C6
44 Tavernetta C4
45 Zakroma D2
46 Zara Pizzara C3
47 Zharyu Paryu B3

Drinking & Nightlife
Friends and Beer (see 46)
48 Kofeynya ZheTo B2
49 Mick O'Neill's Irish Bar C3
50 Shkaf C3

Entertainment
51 Morgan Club B4
Odesa Opera & Ballet Theatre (see 2)
52 Odessa Philharmonic Hall C4
Palladium (see 31)
53 Shede D3
Teatralna Kasa (see 46)

Shopping
54 Privoz Market B7

Information
European Business Center (see 32)
55 Kiy Avia B2
56 Romanian Consulate D6
57 Tsiferblat B3

Transport
58 Buses to Arkadia C3
59 Buses to City Centre C7
Europcar (see 24)
60 Pl Hretska Bus Stop (Buses to Airport) B3
61 Privoz Bus Station B7

architectural style that permeated Odesa in the late 19th century. Its interior walls are festooned with gods, goblins, lions and nymphs. Shabbier but equally ornate representations of this style are huddled around pl Soborna at vul Derybasivska's western terminus, including the Passazh Hotel.

★Odesa Opera & Ballet Theatre THEATRE
(Одеський театр опери та балету; www.opera.odessa.ua; prov Chaykovskoho 1) The jewel in Odesa's architectural crown was designed in the 1880s by the architects who also designed the famous Vienna State Opera, namely Ferdinand Fellner and Herman Helmer. After being closed for several years amid botched reconstruction efforts, the theatre reopened to great fanfare in 2007. You can take a Russian-language tour of the theatre, starting one hour before Friday and Saturday performances (100uah) or, better yet, take in a performance.

Panteleymonivskaya Church
ORTHODOX CHURCH

(Пантелемонівська церква; vul Panteleymonivska 66) Near the train station you can't help but spy the five silver onion domes of this Russian Orthodox church, built by Greek monks with stone from Constantinople in the late 19th century. According to legend, every time the Soviets painted over the church's elaborate frescoes, they would miraculously reappear. While the Soviets eventually succeeded in covering them up, many of the frescoes are once again visible thanks to vigorous restoration efforts.

Museum of Western & Eastern Art
GALLERY

(Музей західного та східного мистецтва; www.oweamuseum.odessa.ua; vul Pushkinska 9; adult/child & student 25/15uah; ⏲10.30am-6pm Thu-Tue) Housed in a beautifully renovated (at least on the outside), mid-19th-century palace, the museum's star turn used to be one of 12 known versions (most likely not the original) of Caravaggio's brilliant painting *The Taking of Christ*. However, in July 2008 the canvas was cut from its frame in Ukraine's biggest art heist and only recovered by police two years later. Lately, the Western collection was kept out of sight because of ongoing renovations, but its highlights have now been returned to the exhibition halls. The Eastern Art section has displays of porcelain and other artwork, mostly from Japan, China, Tibet and India.

History of Odesa Jews Museum
MUSEUM

(Музей історії євреїв Одеси; ☎728 9743; vul Nizhynska 66; admission 20uah; ⏲11am-4.30pm Mon-Thu) Less than 2% of people call themselves Jewish in today's Odesa – against 44% in the early 1920s – but the resilient and humorous Jewish spirit still permeates every aspect of local life. Hidden inside a typical rundown courtyard with clothes drying on a rope and a rusty carcass of a prehistoric car, this modest exposition consists of items donated by Odessite families. Perhaps most touching is the photo of steamship *Ruslan* carrying the first Zionist settlers to Palestine in 1919, along with their immense hopes and terrible fears, both of which would soon materialise. English-language tours of the museum are available, but need to be arranged in advance.

Pushkin Museum
MUSEUM

(Музей Пушкіна; vul Pushkinska 13; adult/child & student 20/10uah; ⏲10am-5pm Mon-Fri) This is where Alexander Pushkin spent his first days in Odesa, after being exiled from Moscow by the tsar in 1823 for mischievous epigrams. Governor Vorontsov subsequently humiliated the writer with petty administrative jobs, and it took only 13 months, an affair with Vorontsov's wife, a simultaneous affair with someone else's wife and more epigrams for Pushkin to be thrown out of Odesa too. Somehow, he still found time while in town to finish the poem 'The Bakhchysaray Fountain', write the first chapter of *Eugene Onegin,* and scribble the notes and moaning letters found in this humble museum.

Odessa Fine Arts Museum
MUSEUM

(Одеський музей образотворчих мистецтв; http://museum.odessa.net/fineartsmuseum; vul Sofiyivska 5A; adult/student 50/25uah; ⏲11am-6pm Wed-Mon) Located in the former palace of one Count Pototsky, this museum has an impressive collection of Russian and Ukrainian art, including a few seascapes by master talent Ayvazovsky and some Soviet realist paintings.

Preobrazhensky Cathedral
CATHEDRAL

(Преображенский собор; pl Soborna) Leafy pl Soborna is the site of the gigantic, newly rebuilt Preobrazhensky (Transfiguration) Cathedral, which was Odesa's most famous and important church until Stalin had it blown up in the 1930s.

Archaeology Museum
MUSEUM

(Музей археології; vul Lanzheronivska 4; adult/child & student 40/10uah; ⏲10am-5pm Tue-Sun) Gold jewellery and coins from early Black Sea civilisations are joined by a few Egyptian mummies at this under-visited museum.

Black Sea Coast

Lots of people swim at Odesa's crowded beaches in summer, but that's not really the aim of going to the beach here. Rather, it's about strolling dishevelled promenades and observing beach life, Ukrainian style. All the beaches we describe are connected by what is known as Trassa Zdorovya – Health Road. Be aware that drinking is now banned on and around Odesa's beaches, so don't give the ever-present police an excuse to extract money from you by carrying a cool one.

Arkadia Beach
BEACH

(Пляж Аркадія) An evening at Arkadia is a must when in Odesa and this is definitely the city's best place to see and be seen. Here

LOCAL KNOWLEDGE

VLADIMIR CHAPLIN: ODESSITE'S SECRETS

Vladimir Chaplin is a guide at the History of Odesa Jews Museum in Odesa.

What's the most inspiring place in Odesa?

There are two. The first is bul Zhvanetskoho because of the splendid harbour view and the 'bribe monument', which they erected there. You can reach it by walking down vul Gogolya. The second is the heart of Odesa – the crossing of vul Bunina and vul Preobrazhenska. There is a touching sculpture of two Odesa boys from Valentin Katayev's book *Petya and Gavrik*.

While in Odesa, you must eat...

- Fried *bychki* fish at Klarabara (p154).
- Aubergine 'caviar' at Dacha (p155).
- Grilled mussels anywhere on the beach where you can make a fire.

What's you favourite Odesa courtyard?

It's definitely the courtyard of our museum, where I know not only all the children by name, but also all the cats. But check out the courtyard on vul Deribasivska 3. Looking from the street, everyone thinks it's the bust of Lenin standing in the middle. But in fact it is Ludvig Zamenhof, who created the Esperanto language. When Esperanto was banned in the USSR, the residents would tell the authorities it was their relative.

What is the best place to swim in Odesa?

Northern Arkadia, where you get into the water from a concrete slab. There are no fussy mums around. There is a nude beach nearby, too.

What do you like about Odesa most?

Odessites know how to enjoy life and take it as it is. Also, everyone knows each other – if not personally, then your aunt from Stepovaya street.

you can play old-school arcade games, dress up like a tsar or tsarina for a photo op, or hang out in a variety of cafes, bars and clubs.

The central part of the beach is almost entirely occupied by beach clubs, which have pools and double as nightclubs after sunset. They usually charge 50uah to 100uah for admission and a sunbed, but a lot more to rent a towel.

Arkadia is easy to reach: take tram 5 from the tram stop near the train station, in front of the McDonald's on vul Panteleymonivska, to the end of the line via the lovely tree-lined bul Frantsuzsky, where the crème de la crème of Odesa's aristocracy lived in tsarist times. Enjoy the views of the old mansions and sanatoriums along the way. Public transport to Arkadia gets extremely crowded in summer, so consider taking a taxi (around 40uah).

The crowds begin to thin out and the water gets cleaner as you head south to the area known as **Bolshoy Fontan**; take tram 18 from the tram stop near the train station.

Otrada Beach BEACH

(Пляж Отрада) This beach can be reached via a primitive **chairlift** (Канатная дорога к пляжу Отрада; kanatnaya doroga; one way 12uah). Like eating *salo* (cured pig fat), riding one of these chairlifts is one of those 'when in Ukraine' experiences that probably shouldn't be missed. To the south of Otrada Beach is a **nudist beach**.

Lanzheron Beach BEACH

(Пляж Ланжерон) Perhaps to copy Brighton Beach, New York – where half of Odesa seems to have emigrated – the authorities built a boardwalk at the beach closest to the city centre. It looks modern and attractive, but it is small and hence often crowded. Lanzheron is reachable on foot via Shevchenko Park, east of the city centre.

Oceanarium Nemo OCEANARIUM

(Океанарій Немо; ☎720 7070; http://nemo.od.ua; admission 50uah, dolphin show 120-180uah; ⏲10am-8pm Mon-Fri, to 11pm Sat & Sun) At Lanzheron Beach, this place puts on four entertaining **dolphin shows** a day.

Tours

The following operators can show you the city, its surroundings and places further afield such as the Danube Delta and Askaniya Nova

Odessa Walks TOUR
(☎063 814 6373; www.odessawalks.com) Inexpensive English-language themed walks of Odesa. You can trace the history of early settlers or stars of the 1920s criminal underworld, or simply join a pub walk.

Freetours Odessa TOUR
(☎725 0024; www.infocenter.odessa.ua/en; vul Havanna 10) It runs a small bureau in the City Garden, where you can arrange a tour, including the catacombs, or rent a bicycle. Enter through the City Garden.

Eugenia Travel TOUR
(☎722 0331; www.eugeniatours.com.ua; vul Rishelyevska 23) Runs a variety of tours.

London Sky Travel TOUR
(☎729 3196; www.lstravel.com.ua) Specialises in ferry tickets but also does the standard city and regional tours.

Salix TOUR
(☎799 0796, 728 9738; www.salix.od.ua; vul Torhova 14) A rare, authentically 'green' Ukrainian travel agency, with responsible tours to Vylkovo and the Danube Delta, as well as Crimea and other southern destinations.

Festivals & Events

Odesa's annual **Carnival Humorina**, celebrated on 1 April, is no joke. The festival fills the streets with carnival floats, music and drunks, and is the biggest party of the year for most Odesans. No less frivolous is **Odesa City Day**, which is held annually on 2 September. The main summer event is **Odesa Film Festival** culminating in a silent film show on Potemkin Steps.

Sleeping

Odesa is popular among Russians and Ukrainians, especially in July and August, but rarely are its hotels and hostels full so turning up without a booking is still feasible, even in the high season. The city's hostel situation is in constant flux, with expats setting up shop, partying for a couple of seasons then moving on. It may be a good idea to check whether hostels are still operating before turning up at 4am unannounced.

Babushka Grand Hostel HOSTEL $
(☎093 984 1356, 063 070 5535; www.babushkagrand.com; vul Mala Arnautska 60; dm from 120uah; ❄@📶) While Odesa's other hostels are decidedly for the young, day-sleeping crowd, the wonderfully named Babushka Grand, occupying a palatial apartment near the train station, has a more laid-back, traveller vibe. The stuccoed interiors and crystal chandeliers are stunning, the staff fun, and at least once a week a real Ukrainian *babushka* comes in to cook up a feast (100uah). It also runs another – more rural-style – outlet outside the city centre and closer to the beach.

TIU Front Page Hostel HOSTEL $
(☎067 183 7347, 096 834 4074; www.tiufrontpage.hostel.com; top fl, vul Koblevska 42; dm 120-130uah; @📶) The current owners inherited the premises from a publishing company that had wallpapered the entire place in magazine front pages, hence the name. Sadly they no longer rent out the private double decorated in Playboy centrefolds. Definitely a party hostel with never a dull moment, so sleep may not come easily here. English proprietor Marcus runs a weekly bus between this and his other hostel in Kyiv (TIU). The bus is free if you book two nights or more in both hostels.

Tokyo Star Hotel BUSINESS HOTEL $
(☎700 2191; http://otel-tokyo-star.ua; vul Vodoprovodna 1A; s/d 150/230uah; ❄📶) This no-frills mini business hotel occupying an old tram depot by the train station is for those who use their room to sleep and wash but little else. The singles have no windows and rooms are so small you'll be constantly climbing over your luggage. With the doubles, make sure you know the person you're travelling with well, as there's very little dividing the bed from the toilet and shower.

Passazh Hotel HOTEL $
(Готель Пасаж; ☎728 5500; www.passage-hotel.com.ua; vul Preobrazhenska 34; s/d from 195/275uah) The Passazh is the epitome of faded glory, but my, how glorious it must have been. Everything here is *big*. A giraffe could preen itself in the enormous mirrors flanking the grand central stairway, and frankly, you could almost swing a giraffe in the cavernous corridors too. The rooms feature lots of Soviet fixtures, bad wallpaper, saggy beds and shoddy tile work, but they are large and come with old-world amenities such as full-length claw-footed bathtubs.

APARTMENTS

As in most Ukrainian cities, many hotels tend to be quite poor value, and apartments offer more bang for your buck. The cheapest flats are offered by the '*babushka* mafia', as locals call it, whose members hang out around the train station (though not in the numbers they once did) and ask around 100uah for a room, or roughly double to triple that for a one-bedroom apartment. Beware: *babushkas* often falsely claim their apartments are located *v tsentre* (in the centre) or *u morya* (by the sea). Carry a map to check. Otherwise contact the following apartment-rental agencies:

Central Vokzal Apartment Bureau (☎727 1381; Odesa train station; r/apt from 200/300uah; ⏰7am-7pm) If you don't want to deal with finicky *babushkas* and haven't booked anything in advance, this is your best walk-in bet. It's across from platform 4 near the train station's rear exit.

American Business Center (☎777 1400; www.odessa-apartment-rentals.com; vul Derybasivska 5; apt from 800uah) Only suitable for long-term visitors, as there's a seven-day minimum-stay requirement.

Odessa Rent-A-Flat (☎787 3444; www.odessarentaflat.com; vul Rishelyevska 11; apt from 400uah)

Odessaapts.com (☎067 708 5501; www.odessaapts.com; apt from 400uah)

Black Sea Rishelyevskaya HOTEL **$$**
(Чорне море Ришельевська; ☎230 0911; www.bs-hotel.com.ua; vul Rishelyevska 59; r from 500uah;) This ugly 1970s concrete tower shelters generic but surprisingly well appointed and spacious rooms, most of which have been smartly renovated (the exception is the shabby and far-from-chic singles). The once-surly staff are now friendly, helpful and speak English. Breakfast is extra.

Black Sea Privoz HOTEL **$$**
(Чорне море Привіз; ☎236 5400; www.bs-hotel.com.ua; vul Panteleymonivska 25; s/d from 500/600uah;) Although in a slightly dodgy area, this hotel stretches your hryvnya a long way at the midrange level. While the decor is hit or miss, the generous size of the rooms, professional service and overall modernity of this 100-room high-rise make up for it.

Hotel Yunost HOTEL **$$**
(Гостиница Юность; ☎738 0412; www.hotel-yunost.com; vul Pionerska 34; r from 495uah;) Occupying a hard-to-miss monolith out towards Arkadia, Yunost has rooms at various stages of transition from Soviet to normal. The more you pay, the better standard you'll enjoy. Economy doubles share bathrooms between two rooms. It's a few stops before Arkadia on tram 5.

★**Mozart Hotel** HOTEL **$$$**
(Готель Моцарт; ☎377 777; www.mozart-hotel.com; vul Lanzheronivska 13; s/tw from 1330/1860uah;) As the name suggests, this top choice epitomises European luxury, with elegant furnishings and a calm, light-filled interior lurking behind its refurbished neoclassical facade. The 40 rooms are individually decorated and the location across from the Opera & Ballet Theatre is perfect.

Hotel Ayvazovsky HOTEL **$$$**
(Готель Айвазовский; ☎242 9022; www.ayvazovsky.com.ua; vul Bunina 19; s/d from 880/1280uah;) From the Chesterfield sofas in the lobby to the spacious, high-ceilinged, European-standard bedrooms to the design magazine perfect bathrooms, this soothing, 27-room sleepery in the heart of the city centre is worth every kopeck. Continental breakfast is delivered every morning to your room, and staff can book tours and countless other services.

Frederic Koklen BOUTIQUE HOTEL **$$$**
(Фредерік Коклен; ☎737 5553; www.koklenhotel.com; prov Nekrasova 7; 1570/2380uah;) Odesa's most sumptuous boutique hotel has guests gushing forth about exceptional service, luxurious period ambience and the great location. Rooms in this renovated mansion are studies in 18th- and 19th-century Imperial-era style and attention to detail, quality of materials and standard of maintenance is outstanding for Ukraine.

Hotel Londonskaya HOTEL **$$$**
(Гостиница Лондонская; ☎738 0110; www.londred.com; bul Prymorsky 11; s/d from 1155/1365uah;) Last refurbished in

the early 1990s, the rooms of Odesa's oldest luxury hotel are becoming slightly dated, but with iron-lace balustrades, stained-glass windows, parquet flooring and an inner courtyard, the place still oozes Regency charm and remains the lodgings of choice for the smart set. Curiously, the 'English' name was invented by the hotel's French founder in 1846. Robert Louis Stevenson and Anton Chekhov both stayed here.

Palladium Hotel HOTEL **$$$**
(Готель Палладиум; ☎728 6651; www.hotel-palladium.com.ua; bul Italyansky 4; r from 865uah; ❄📶🏊) With attractive, pastel-hued rooms featuring minimalist decor and fine-textured carpets, and a wonderful swimming pool, this definitely qualifies as a good deal for Odesa. Admission to the popular downstairs nightclub (closed during summer) is free for hotel guests, as is admission to the summer club Itaka.

Eating

The Odesa restaurant scene easily rivals Kyiv's – not only because of its sophistication or diversity, but thanks to a new phenomena that time has come to call – loud and clear – Odesa cuisine. It's a magic stew of Russian, Ukrainian, Jewish, Moldovan and Levantine cuisines cooked up in Soviet communal kitchens and fishermen's huts. Its main virtue is that it takes full advantage of the region's abundance in vegetables, fruit and seafood.

Zharyu Paryu CANTEEN **$**
(Жарю Парю; vul Hretska 45; mains 20-30uah; ⏲8am-10pm) When lunchtime strikes, going where the local student and office-worker population find nourishment usually makes sense. This clinical self-service canteen of the factory or school variety is such a place, and with cheap and cheerful Ukrainian favourites on the menu board it's ideal for cash-strapped nomads.

Aioli FAST FOOD
(vul Preobrazhenska 22; set lunch 30ah; ⏲10am-7pm; 📶) A hipsterishly designed cafeteria offering a set three-course menu at a dirt cheap price. No *aioli* detected in the ordinary home-style food – it's just a fancy name.

Klarabara INTERNATIONAL **$$**
(Кларабара; City Garden; mains 90-150uah; ⏲9am-midnight) Tucked away in a quiet corner of the City Garden, this classy, cosy, ivy-covered cafe and restaurant is awash with antique furniture and fine art. The menu is inspired by the food people make at home in the broader Black Sea region. That means local fish, delicious vegetable stews and various kinds of *khachapuri* – Georgian cheese pastry. We loved the charcoal-grilled mussels.

Tavernetta ITALIAN **$$**
(Тавернетта; ☎344 621; www.tavernetta.ua; vul Katerynynska 45; mains 70-100 uah; ⏲9am-12pm; 📶) You'd need to hire an army of culinary detectives to find better pasta between here and Italy, but your chances would still be low. The restaurant occupies a large wooden terrace with an open kitchen, which churns out platefuls of magic – try spaghetti with local sardines. Waiters are humorous and if you speak Russian you'll appreciate their Jewish-influenced 'Odesa speak'. Warning: they'll attempt to put a hilarious paper napkin on your neck, which makes serious people look like toddlers.

Kompot EASTERN EUROPEAN **$$**
(Компот; www.compot.ua; vul Derybasivska 20; mains 60-120uah; ⏲8am-11pm; 📶) Odesa's most celebrated restaurateur Savely Libkin conjured this place out of his childhood memories, setting a trend for what is becoming known as Odesa cuisine. The simplest dishes are the best – try cutlets with potato purée and water them down with one of the eponymous *kompoty,* fruity drinks which housewives preserve in jars to consume in winter. The original Derybasivska outlet is way too crowded, so we prefer the other two – at **vul Panteleymonivska 70** (☎345 145; ⏲8am-11pm) by the station and at the **Sea Port** (☎729 3449; Left wing; ⏲8am-11pm). All serve superb French-influenced breakfasts.

Bernardazzi ITALIAN, UKRAINIAN **$$**
(Бернардацци; Odessa Philharmonic Hall, vul Bunina 15; mains 60-160uah; ⏲10am-last customer; ❄) Few Ukrainian restaurants have truly authentic settings but the Art Nouveau dining room of this superb Italian job, part of the eye-catching Philharmonic Hall, is the real deal. In addition to well-crafted southern and Eastern European fare, there's an award-winning wine list, occasional live music and a secluded courtyard for summertime chilling. It's named after the architect who designed the building.

Maman RESTAURANT $$
(Маман; ☎711 7035; vul Lanzheronivska 18; mains 70-90uah; ⊙noon-midnight;) This Odesa mum is a worldly woman who absorbs Asian, Middle Eastern and French influences in her culinary adventures. But emerging before you in the shape of a stout waitress she still forces a napkin on your lap before you blink, as if you are six years old. Her best-kept secret is the outdoor sitting area in Palais Royal gardens, unseen from the street. The *kotlety* (meatballs) section of the menu is worth special notice.

Gogol Mogol EUROPEAN $$
(Гоголь-Моголь; prov Nekrasova 2; mains 70-120uah; ⊙9am-midnight;) From the multi-hued old bicycles and rainbow park benches bolted to the pavement outside to the jumble-sale decor of the quirky interior, this art cafe is an unmissable chapter in the alternative city-centre story. The short menu doubles up as a visitors book, they do a mean cappuccino and it's also a popular evening meeting spot. However, service can be slow and brutal to lone travellers.

Rozmarin JEWISH $$
(Розмарин; ☎347 311; vul Mala Arnautska 46A; mains 70-100uah; ⊙10am-11pm) Ignore the decor, or rather the absence of thereof – this no-nonsense place is all about Jewish food as they made it in a *schtetl* circa 1900. Definitely try *ghefilte fisch* (cold fish cutlets) and *latkes* (potatoes with pike roe). The place is kosher and closed on Saturdays.

Four Bulgarians BULGARIAN $$
(Четверо болгар; ☎784 0410; vul Katerynynska 56; mains 70-100uah;) Since Bulgarians are one of the biggest minorities in the Odesa region, it is only appropriate for their spice- and meat-rich cuisine to emerge on the local culinary stage. Our favourite here is *agneshko po-gergovsky* – mutton rolls with cheese and spinach.

Zakroma INTERNATIONAL $$
(Закрома; ☎728 2972; http://закрома.com; vul Havanna 11; mains 70-90uah; ⊙8am-11pm;) This place is a tribute to all Soviet grannies who spent long Odesa summers stuffing hundreds of jars with delicious garden produce – marinated, pickled, salted, jellified, caramelised – you name it. There are stakes of jars containing all kinds of preserves in the main room which doubles as a shop. On the verandah, people are treated to traditional Odessite and more inventive dishes with international influences.

Kumanets UKRAINIAN $$
(Куманець; vul Havanna 7; mains 40-100uah; ⊙noon-midnight) A kitsch little island of Ukraine in Russian Odesa, this veritable Ukrainian village produces affordable *holubtsy* (cabbage rolls), *varenyky* (dumplings) and *deruny* (potato pancakes) in addition to pricier mains.

Zara Pizzara PIZZERIA $$
(☎728 8888; vul Rishelyevska 5; mains 60-70uah; ⊙9am-midnight) Odesa's best pizzeria has an enviously located summer terrace, real Italian-style thin-crust pizza loaded with toppings, and hefty calzones.

Dacha RUSSIAN $$$
(Дача; ☎714 3119; www.dacha.com.ua; bul Frantsuzsky 85, korpus 15; mains 80-200uah;) *Dacha* – a family summer cottage – is a dreamworld of happy childhood memories for locals. This Odesa institution, perched on a plateau above Arkadia Beach inside Chkalov sanatorium, masterfully re-creates the atmosphere – on a slightly exaggerated scale. Food is homey, Odesa-style, with sumptous portions. You can choose between dining in the garden or inside the house filled with the random bric-a-brac typical of all *dachy*. House policy: women are encouraged to dress down to their bras the way Soviet ladies did on their *dachy*. We haven't seen anyone try it.

Drinking & Nightlife

Just about anywhere along vul Derybasivska is a good place for a drink.

Odesa's raucous club scene has two seasons: summer (June to August) and the rest of the year. In summer the action is at Arkadia Beach, which boasts two huge, Ibiza-style nightclubs that produce heightened levels of madness seven days a week. At other times of the year, the action is closer to the city centre. Unless otherwise noted, the following clubs charge 50uah to 100uah on weekends, and much less on weekdays. Discounted or free admission for women is the norm.

Kofeynya ZheTo COFFEE
(Кофейня ЖеТо; prov Mayakovskoho 1; ⊙8.30am-11pm) If one dessert can save the world, then it is blackcurrant panna cotta from this tiny coffeeshop looking like a cramped antiques shop.

POLICE WARNING

If there is one place in Ukraine where you're likely to be singled out by the cops for a bit of special treatment it's the pedestrian alley leading to Arkadia Beach. Officers occupy strategic sites here, cherry-picking foreigners out of the crowd for a little shakedown. In fact we spoke to one traveller who'd been selected four nights out of eight for the grave offence of looking foreign.

If you're heading this way of an eve, make sure you're carrying your passport (you really should have it with you at all times anyway, but some travellers are afraid of losing their documents while under the influence). If the police want a bribe even after they've seen your papers, stand your ground, don't hand over any money and ask to be taken to the police station. After a certain time the officers will see they're onto a loser and wander off to bother someone else. US visitors could also try calling their embassy in Kyiv, which scares the clappers out of most Ukrainian patrols.

★Shkaf BAR

(Шкаф; vul Hretska 32; beer from 14uah; ⏲7pm-late) It feels like entering a *shkaf* (wardrobe) from the outside, but what you find is a heaving basement bar-cum-club, a surefire antidote to Odesa's trendy beach-club scene and pick-up bars. The inconspicuous, unmarked entrance is always surrounded by smoking/chilling-out patrons, so you won't miss it.

Friends & Beer BAR

(Друзі та пиво; vul Derybasivska 9; ⏲11am-11pm; 📶) This charming re-created USSR-era living room littered with photos of Russian film stars is proof that 'Retro Soviet' doesn't have to mean political posters and Constructivist art. The huge TV screen is possibly not authentic for the period, but it's great for sports.

Mick O'Neill's Irish Bar IRISH BAR

(vul Derybasivska 13; ⏲24hr) This longstanding Irish pub is a great place to start an evening and an even better place to finish it, as it's the only outdoor patio on vul Derybasivska that's open round the clock.

Morgan Club BAR

(vul Zhukovskoho 30; ⏲24hr; 📶) By day Morgan is a pretty benign breakfast or lunch spot or early-evening drinks stop, but at night capable DJs spin till the wee hours and there's a funky downstairs lounge. The crowd of expats, local heavies/beauties and sex tourists never fails to generate a 'colourful' atmosphere.

☆ Entertainment

Theatre, concert and opera tickets can be purchased at the venues or at a **Teatralna Kasa** (Theatre Kiosk; ⏲9am-5pm). There's one on the corner of vul Derybasivska and vul Rishelyevska. The most compehensive listings of events are available on www.today.od.ua, in Russian. You can also buy tickets there.

Odessa Philharmonic Hall LIVE MUSIC

(Одеська філармонія; www.odessaphilharmonic.org; vul Bunina 15; ⏲closed Jul & Aug) Housed in the beautiful building of Odesa's former stock exchange. Unfortunately, the original inhabitants – traders – asked the architects for a building with subdued acoustics, so that their business talks couldn't be overheard. This is a pain, but not an insurmountable obstacle for the **Odessa Philharmonic Orchestra**, led by charismatic American conductor Hobart Earle, a former student of Leonard Bernstein. This orchestra accounts for half the symphonies performed here. Jazz and rock is often played here, too, and it's the venue of the Odessa Jazz Festival.

Odesa Opera & Ballet Theatre THEATRE

(Одеський театр Опери та балету; www.opera.odessa.ua; prov Chaykovskoho 1) In addition to being architecturally magnificent, Odesa's theatre is also known for its marvellous acoustics. Unfortunately, the local opera company does not do justice to the theatre's impressive physical attributes, but performances are eminently affordable and the Odessa Philharmonic Orchestra performs here from time to time.

Clubs

Ibiza CLUB

(Ібіца; www.ibiza.ua; Arkadia Beach; ⏲summer) This white, free-form, open, cave-like structure is Arkadia's most upmarket and most expensive club. European DJs and big-ticket Russian and Ukrainian pop bands often play here. Ticket prices can be high when a big act is in town.

Itaka CLUB

(Итака; www.itaka-club.com.ua; Arkadia Beach; ⌚summer) It's slightly more downmarket than other clubs in Arkadia and consequently often rowdier (in a good way). The Greek columns and statues are a tad much, but you'll hardly care when it's 5am and you are out of your gourd. Like Ibiza, it also draws big regional pop acts.

Plyazhnik CLUB

(Пляжник; ☎700 5522; http://plagenick.com; 13th station of Fontanskaya Doroga; ⌚summer) As it often happens, you'd need to walk an extra mile to find something smarter than clubs on Arkadia. This one attracts a crowd of goatee-bearded, Vespa-driving people and invites Russian/Ukrainian musicians beloved by the young intellegentsia. By day, it is one of the nicest beach clubs on the coast. Plyazhnik can be accessed by stairs from the lower parking lot of the bigger Riviera Club, located under Bolshoy Fontan's 13th station. If that doesn't make sense – take a taxi.

Palladium CLUB

(Паладіум; www.palladium.com.ua; bul Italyansky 4; ⌚Sep-May) The winter headquarters of Itaka takes up the slack downtown when Itaka shuts down in September. There's a nightly show at around 11pm, followed by general debauchery.

Shede GAY

(www.shede-club.com.ua; vul Derybasivska 5) One of Ukraine's best openly gay clubs with Friday and Saturday night shows beginning at 1am.

Shopping

Starokonny Market MARKET

(Старокінний ринок; vul Rizovska & vul Serova) It's like a grungy old-school uncle of all European flea markets – there is nothing neat or touristy about it whatsoever. But it seems like every semi-intact item Odessites throw into garbage bins end up here. There are heaps of junk – if you patiently shuffle through it you may find some gems. The market sprawls around a large neighbourhood near the long-distance bus station. There are no stalls – all merchandise is laid out on the ground. If something catches your eye, pretend you are barely interested, then start bargaining.

Privoz Market MARKET

(Ринок Привіз; vul Pryvozna) Odesa is home to two of southern Ukraine's largest and most famous markets. The centrally located market is possibly the largest farmers market in the country and a must-visit for *rynok* (market) lovers. On hot days you may want to breathe through your mouth in some of the overheated halls. Whatever you buy – always bargain, you'll upset them if you don't.

Information

Central Post Office (vul Sadova 10)

European Business Center (vul Preobrazhenska 34; per hr 6uah; ⌚9am-midnight) Modern internet place on the ground floor of the Passazh Hotel.

Lonely Planet (www.lonelyplanet.com/ukraine/odesa) You'll find planning advice, author recommendations and travel reviews here.

Tsiferblat (Циферблат; vul Admirala Zhukova 3/7; 1st hour 30uah, each subsequent hr 15uah; ⌚11am-midnight) The Moscow-born 'open space' craze has reached the shores of Odesa, so now local hipsters also have a place to enjoy the company of their laptops or real-life friends, play intellectual games, drink free coffee and lemonade, while paying only for the time they spend here. It is a happening place, with cooking classes, acoustic concerts and plenty of other activities. For travellers, it is an unhassled environment to use wi-fi and to meet cool (or nerdy) locals.

Getting There & Away

AIR

Odesa airport (www.odessa.aero) was still an old Soviet affair at the time of writing, but a new terminal might open before this edition expires. Odesa is better linked to Europe than any other Ukrainian airport, with the exception of Kyiv's airport. Lufthansa, Aeroflot, LOT, Air Baltic, Czech Airlines and Turkish Airlines all have regular flights to Odesa, and various regional carriers fly to former Soviet countries. The Ukrainian airline MAU has flights from Odesa to Vienna, Istanbul and Tel-Aviv.

MAU and Utair fliy between Odesa and Kyiv up to eight times daily. **Kiy Avia** (www.kiyavia.com; vul Preobrazhenska 15; ⌚8am-8pm) can sort you out with tickets and timetables.

BOAT

Ferry services to and from Odesa are notoriously unreliable, with services to Derince (Turkey), Constanta (Romania) and Poti (Georgia) ceasing for months on end without explanation. Besides, departure times can be easily delayed by up to 24 hours. Boats are in theory operated by **Ukrferry** (www.ukrferry.com) but planning onward travel around these guys is folly indeed. The only reliable passenger service from Odesa (not run by Ukrferry) is the boat to Crimea (990uah, 20 hours, five to seven sailings a month). For tickets and timetables contact London Sky Travel (p152).

BUS

Odesa has two bus stations that are useful for travellers. The conveniently located, but slightly chaotic, **Privoz bus station** (vul Vodoprovodna), 300m west of the train station, is primarily useful for Vylkovo (67uah, three to four hours, five daily). Minibuses also leave from here for Chişinău (100uah, five to seven hours, eight daily).

Most international and long-haul domestic buses leave from the **long-distance bus station** (vul Kolontayivska 58), 3km west of the train station. Frequent **Gunsel** (☎ 232 6212) buses are the most comfortable and quickest way to travel to Kyiv (200uah to 270uah, six to seven hours, five daily). Its nonstop VIP service has airline-style seats and a stewardess serving free refreshments. Tickets are sold in a separate window. Otherwise speedy *marshrutky* (fixed-route minibuses) leave from just in front of the station building (150uah, six hours). Other destinations include Reni on the Romanian/Moldovan border (120uah, five hours, hourly), Donetsk (375uah, 13 hours, one daily), Simferopol (200uah, 12 hours, six daily) and Chernivtsi (150uah, 13 hours, two daily) via Kamyanets-Podilsky. A dozen buses a day go to Lviv (150uah, 17 hours) and onward to a variety of European destinations.

There are at least 10 buses per day to Chişinău via Tiraspol, and two via Palanka (100uah, five to seven hours). The latter avoid Transdniestr.

TRAIN

Odesa is well connected by train to all major Ukrainian, Russian and Eastern European cities. Despite the addition of 'summer trains' on the most popular routes (eg Kyiv, Moscow, Simferopol and Lviv), seats to/from Odesa fill up fast from June to August, so book ahead.

There are up to seven trains to Kyiv (160uah, nine to 12 hours), three of which are overnighters. Other destinations include Kharkiv (150uah, 14 hours), Lviv (150uah, 12 hours) and Simferopol (125uah, 12 hours). Longer-distance services go to Moscow, Minsk, Rostov and (during summer only) to St Petersburg. There are still no trains to Chişinău.

Getting Around

Odesa airport is about 12km southwest of the city centre, off Ovidiopilska doroha. Bus 129 goes to/from the train station; infrequent bus 117 runs to/from the pl Hretska stop.

To get to the city centre from the train station (about a 20-minute walk), go to the stop near the McDonald's and take any bus saying 'Площа Грецка' (pl Hretska), such as bus 148. Trolleybuses 4 and 10 trundle up vul Pushkinska before curving around to vul Prymorska, past the Sea Port and the foot of the Potemkin Steps.

Tram 5 goes from the train station to the long-distance bus station. From the Privoz bus station to pl Hretska take bus 220.

If you must travel by taxi, **Servis-Taksi** (☎ 234 5077) and **IgAl** (☎ 234 8080) come recommended by the tourist office.

Rental cars are especially useful for exploring Bessarabia or the Kherson area. Try **Europcar** (☎ 777 4011) in the Black Sea Hotel Odessa. Most international car-rental companies are well represented in the airport.

AROUND ODESA

The limestone on which Odesa stands is riddled with some 2000km of tunnels, which have always played an important part in the city's history. Quarried out for building in the 19th century, they were first used to hide smuggled goods. During WWII they sheltered a group of local partisans, who waged a war of attrition against the occupying Romanians and forced the Nazis to keep greater troop numbers in the area.

Most of the catacomb network lies well outside Odesa's city centre. The only tunnels that can be visited are in the suburb of Nerubayske, about 15km north of central Odesa. Here a resident speleologist offers 45-minute **catacomb tours** (☎ 048-725 2874; ⏲ 9am-4pm Tue-Sun) that wend through what was the headquarters of Odesa's WWII partisan movement. Tours cost 10uah per person (plus a 100uah flat fee for the guide) and are in Russian, so you may wish to bring a translator along, although you don't necessarily need one to enjoy the catacombs. Tours exit into the musty Partisan Museum.

Marshrutka 84 to Nerubayske leaves every 10 minutes from Odesa's Privoz bus station (2uah, 35 minutes). Ask the driver to let you off at the 'Katakomby' stop, easily identifiable by the hulking Soviet realist statue depicting five defiant partisans. Tour agencies in Odesa run tours out here for about 600uah per group, or in summer you can look for one of the Russian-speaking guides touting tours in front of Odesa's train station.

WORTH A TRIP

ONE STEPPE AWAY

Most people race through the immense steppe of Kherson Region on their way between Odesa and Crimea without ever stopping to marvel at it.

Meanwhile, herds of buffalo, wildebeest and zebras are roaming in the vicinity. Hey, what zebras? This is not Africa! Well, indeed – but it is the reality inside the 2300-hectare **Askaniya Nova Reserve** (☎055 386 1286; http://ascania-nova.com; vul Frunze 13, Askaniya Nova; adult/child 20/10uah; ⏲8am-5pm 15 Apr to 10 Nov) – the brainchild of a 19th-century Odesa German who acted on his slightly mad idea of importing animals from different continents to this unique natural steppe.

In addition to the above-mentioned species, the reserve boasts Przewalski horses from Mongolia, camels, Central Asian *saiga* antelopes and all manner of birds, from pink flamingos to rare steppe eagles. But perhaps the main attraction here is the virgin steppe – flat as a skating rink and preserved in the same shape as it was at the time of Atilla the Hunn.

As in Africa, the best way to see the animals is on a safari. Alas, that's easier said than done. Apart from its zoo and gardens, the reserve is closed for visitors for most of summer because of (very real) steppe fire danger. So late spring and early autumn are the best times to take a safari (150uah per person) in a horse-drawn cart (which is fun in itself).

Yet, if you are around during a cooler and wetter summer, it's still worth enquiring about visiting. It's a long way, so to avoid disappointment arrange for a Russian speaker to book for you by phone. There are a couple of hotels in Askaniya Nova, the best one being **Kanna** (☎613 37; www.askania-nova-kanna.com.ua; vul Krasnoarmeyska 22; d from 380uah; ❄).

Another large chunk of virgin steppe that you can admire is actually out in the Black Sea. The isle **Dzharylhach** is separated from the mainland by a narrow strait. It is also teeming with all kinds of wildlife – though, admittedly not African, which makes it all the more more authentic. You can reach it by boat from the pier in the resort town of **Skadovsk**.

Dzharylhach is a wild and melancholic place, popular with campers who walk many miles away from the landing point, where chances to spot wild horses or deers inhabiting the island are fairly poor. Note that camping is not officially allowed, though in practice everyone gets away with a small unofficial fee to the rangers – if they ever bother to approach.

If you come on a day trip, definitely board a military truck, which meets larger boats. It takes people across the island to a beautiful sandy beach on the outer side. Riding the truck with other tourists is fun and you might be lucky to spot some wildlife.

Both Askaniya-Nova and Skadovsk can be reached from the regional capital Kherson – a quaint, but otherwise unremarkable town sitting at the mouth of the Dnipro. The local bus station has services to both Odesa (80uah, five hours, every 20 minutes) and Simferopol (115uah, 4½ hours) in Crimea. There are five buses a day for Askaniya Nova (60uah, 2½ hours). Buses for Skadovsk are more frequent (45uah, 2½ hours, half-hourly).

SOUTHERN BESSARABIA

Not too many Westerners venture into the fertile wedge of Ukraine that lies between the Danube and Dnister Rivers. That's too bad because in addition to being beautiful in spots it's also one of Ukraine's most culturally peculiar regions.

Its history is equally peculiar. From the late 15th century until Russia's victory in the Russo-Turkish War of 1806–12, this region was part of the Ottoman Empire. The Turks named it 'Bessarabia' after the Wallachian family – the Basarabs – who controlled the area during the late medieval period. When the Russians took over, they expanded Bessarabia to include most of present-day Moldova (plus a small slice of Carpathian Ukraine). The section of Bessarabia lying south of the Moldovan border in present-day Ukraine was dubbed Southern Bessarabia, or

Budzhak. Between the world wars it was part of Romania before the Soviets annexed it in 1940 and made it part of Ukraine.

Bilhorod-Dnistrovsky
Білгород-Дністровський

☎04849 / POP 58,400

A simple day trip from Odesa, the 'White City on the Dnister' is an ordinary industrial port, but with an impressive **Akkerman fortress** (☎225 96; vul Pushkina 19; admission 15uah; ⏲9am-6pm) built by Moldavians, Genoese and Turks in the 13th to 15th centuries. Today the castle is among Ukraine's largest and best preserved. You can walk along most of the walls, which stretch nearly 2km in total, and admire the views of the Dnister's estuary. Various 'medieval' activities, like bow shooting, are on offer.

Marshrutky departing every 10 minutes or so from Odesa's train station (right side facing the station) cover the 55km to Bilhorod-Dnistrovsky in about 1½ hours (25uah), terminating at the train station. There are also five daily *elektrychky* (electric trains; 7uah, 2¼ hours). To reach the fortress from the train station, walk along vul Vokzalna, and after the park, turn right onto vul Dzerzhinskoho. From here, the fortress is a 1.5km walk.

Shabo Шабо

In 1822 a few dozen francophone Swiss families from Vevey canton, led by botanist Louis Tardane, packed their belongings into horse-driven carts and drove across Europe

MELTING POT ON THE DANUBE

Bessarabia has spent the better part of the past half-millennium getting tossed around like a hot potato by various regional powers. As a result of shifting borders, Moldovans, Romanians, Russians, Turks, Germans and Ukrainians have all called this region home, as have several more obscure groups.

Lipovans

One such group is the Lipovans, Russian 'Old Believers', who were exiled from Russia in the 18th century for refusing to comply with Russian Orthodox Church reforms instituted by Peter the Great. Most of them settled near the Danube Delta, where they still continue to live and practice Old Believer traditions such as crossing themselves with two fingers, and not shaving. Lipovan churches – one example is the St Nicholas Church in Vylkovo – are built in the shape of a boat instead of a cross, and have two spires and separate entrances for men and women. The interior walls are completely devoid of frescoes.

Gagauz

Next up are the Gagauz, an Orthodox-Christianised Turkish group, originally from Bulgaria, who ended up in Bessarabia when the Russians annexed the area from the Turks after the Russo-Turkish War of 1806–12. Today most Gagauz live in Moldova (where they have their own autonomous republic, Gagauzia), but you'll find Gagauz communities throughout Southern Bessarabia, including an active one in Vylkovo. The Gagauz language, Gagauzi, is a Turkish dialect influenced by Russian via the Russian Orthodox Church.

Zaporizhsky Cossacks

From a Ukrainian perspective, the most significant group to settle in this area was the Zaporizhsky Cossacks, who founded the Danube Sich just south of the Danube (in present-day Romania) after being driven out of Zaporizhzhya by Catherine the Great in 1775. Its loyalties split by the Russo-Turkish Wars, the *sich* collapsed in 1828, and most of its inhabitants migrated back east. A few thousand Cossacks, however, remained in the area, ensuring that a dash of hearty Cossack blood would forever be ingrained in the populations of Southern Bessarabia and northern Romania (where a strong Ukrainian community persists to this day).

to the Odesa region, which was touted at the time as Russian California. Taking over old Turkish vineyards in the estuary of the Dnister River, they set up a colony of wine-makers. It ceased to exist 120 years later, with the Soviet occupation of Bessarabia in WWII, when the ancestors of the settlers packed up again and moved back to Switzerland.

Today the newly revived **Shabo winery** (Винзавод Шабо; http://shabo.ua; vul Dzerzhinskoho 10; tour 110uah) is a slick modern operation, but its owners – Georgians from Odesa – are absolutely obsessed with the place's Swiss heritage. Although conducted in Russian, tours of the winery are interesting and fun. You'll see 200-year-old cellars – look out for the Romanian king's autograph on the wall, an entertaining museum which contains objects from Bessarabian-Swiss households, and a great silent movie taking viewers through all stages of wine production.

It all culminates in a wine-tasting session, which is when you can build camraderie with Ukrainian and Russian tourists by giving thoughtful looks before and sharing emotions after each emptied glass. There is a good restaurant across the road from the winery, to which you can repair (be carried to by new friends) afterwards.

Shabo is 9km from Bilgorod-Dnistrovsky, so both places can be easily visited on the same day. You can ask your driver to drop you off at Shabo roundabout on the way from Odesa. From here, it's a 10-minute walk to the winery. Local buses for Bilgorod-Dnistrovsky bus station stop 200m away.

Vylkovo Вилково

☎04843 / POP 8000

A network of navigable canals has earned Vylkovo the nickname 'the Venice of Ukraine'. Frankly, the comparison is preposterous. This sleepy fishing village feels light years removed from Venice – or any other form of civilisation. And while the canals – along which many villagers live – are interesting, you won't spend much time on them unless you take a special tour. But Vylkovo does have one thing going for it that Venice lacks: the heavenly Danube Delta Biosphere Reserve.

The lion's share of the marshy, bird-laden **Danube Delta Biosphere Reserve**, Europe's largest wetland, lies in Romania. Few tourists enter from the Ukrainian side, but those who do are rewarded with extremely affordable half- to full-day boat tours through the delta's unique waterways. You can visit the Danube's terminus (dubbed the '0km mark') or take a birdwatching tour. Guides can drop you off on small islands populated by thousands of terns and their just-hatched chicks. On other islands flocks of cormorants and white pelicans roost (the reserve is home to 70% of the world's white pelicans).

In the centre of Vylkovo you'll find the **Biosphere Reserve office** (☎446 19; reserve@it.odessa.ua; vul Povstanniya 132A; ⏰9am-6pm), with an on-site museum and informational videos (in German and Russian). The staff speak some English and can set you up with a local tour operator to take you into the reserve by boat.

Vylkovo's **canals**, built by the town's original Lipovan settlers, are the other main attraction. The villagers who live along the canals still use traditional, narrow fishing boats known as *chaika* (seagull) to fish and get around. Locals say there are 3000 such boats in Vylkovo, compared with only 600 cars. While touring the canals, drop by a local's house and purchase a bottle of the local wine, known as *novak*.

Booking tours in advance is a good idea, particularly on weekends. There are two local tour operators, but only **Pelikan Tour** (Пеликан Тур; www.pelican-danube-tour.com.ua) has a proven record of catering to foreign tourists. Half-day tours cost 150uah to 200uah per person depending on the number of people in the boat. English-speaking guides cost around 100uah per hour (much more per hour for a professional ornithologist who speaks English). A half day should be enough time to visit both the reserve and the canals. A one-hour canal tour costs about 65uah.

Odesa travel agencies offer Vylkovo as a day trip, but they can charge anything up to 1200uah for transport, a boat trip and lunch. Joining a group can bring the cost down to around 300uah, but it is far more rewarding to spend a night in Vylkovo and use the extra time to absorb some local flavour. In Odesa, we recommend Salix (p152) travel agency. In Vylkovo, you'll find people touting tours by the bus and river stations.

Sleeping & Eating

The following hotels all have catering facilities.

Venetsiya HOTEL $

(Венеція; ☎313 74; http://vilkovo-venecia.at.ua; vul Lenina 19A; r per person from 100uah; ❄) The 'Venice' represents exceptional value for money, with big, bright, comfy rooms and fluffy rugs. Most rooms share pristine bathrooms and there's also a restaurant.

Pelikan Tour GUESTHOUSE, COTTAGES $

(Пеликан Тур; ☎067 483 5207; guesthouse d without bathroom per person 150uah, cottages 500uah) Pelikan Tour runs a homey, 14-bed guesthouse on the banks of the Danube, a short walk from the city centre. You'll have to resist the urge to take up duck hunting when awakened by the loudly frolicking, nocturnal waterfowl in the small marina. The company has also built four comfortable timber cottages in a tranquil spot on the riverbank. They have large glazed verandahs for bird spotting and to let the river views flood in.

Kuba-Daleko GUESTHOUSE $

(Куба-далеко; ☎050 391 0678, 066 731 0850; www.brynzarnya.com; vul Pogranichnaya 2, Primorske; s/d without bathroom 200/300uah) A fun place to stay is the *brynza* (goat cheese) farm, which comes with a little museum of Lipovan Old Believers culture and a hotel, bizarrely themed on a Soviet song about Cuba. The place is on the seaside in Primorske – otherwise known as Vylkovo beach, 10km from town. Book well in advance.

ℹ Getting There & Away

Fast *marshrutky* to Vylkovo leave every two hours or so until late afternoon from Odesa's Privoz bus station (67uah, three to four hours). The occasional buses that depart from Odesa's long-distance bus station are slower, taking up to twice as long to do the run. There are two services a day to Izmayil (20uah, two hours), from where you can continue to Reni (one hour) on the Romanian/Moldovan border.

Crimea Крим

POP 2.3 MILLION / AREA 26,200 SQ KM

Includes ➡

Best Places to Eat

- Café Ostrov (p179)
- Musafir (p175)
- Barkas (p179)
- Izbushka Rybaka (p182)
- Apelsin (p186)

Best Places to Stay

- Dilara Hanum (p173)
- Kichkine (p190)
- Corsair (p186)
- Fazanya Roshcha (p177)
- Dacha Koktebelica (p195)

Why Go?

It might be attached to the mainland by a narrow isthmus, but in every other respect Crimea is an island, with its climate and inhabitants markedly different from the rest of Ukraine. From Romans to Russians, empires tried to grab this tiny gem of a region, but it always slipped away.

In Crimea's south, mountains rise like a sail as if trying to carry it away into open sea. Protected from northern winds, the coast is covered in lush subtropical vegetation. This is where Russian royals built summer palaces, later transformed into sanatoriums for workers.

The mountains are the heartland of Crimean Tatars – a nation of survivors, who brought back from 50-year exile their traditions of hospitality and excellent food. They live surrounded by limestone plateaus – a magnet for trekkers and cyclists who come here for great vistas and to explore ancient cave cities.

When to Go

Simferopol

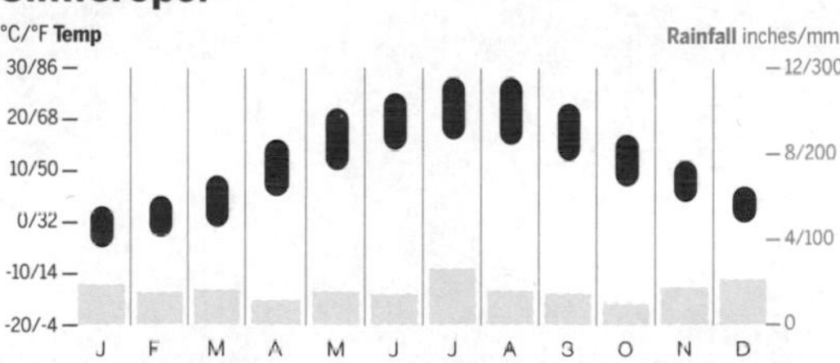

May–Jun Feel the flower power as orchards bloom and mountains are covered in wild tulips.

Jul–Aug Beaches are packed but the sea is warm and the Kazantip rave is underway.

Sep–Oct Crowds wash away. Time for jazz in Koktebel and mountain hikes.

Crimea Highlights

1. Enter a top-secret Soviet nuclear facility in the fjord-like bay of **Balaklava** (p180).
2. Conquer the cave-city of **Mangup-Kale** (p175).
3. Get spooked by thousands of gravestones covered in ancient Hebrew script at **Iosofatova Valley** (p173).
4. Stay with Crimean Tatars, learn their heartbreaking story and sample their food in **Bakhchysaray** (p170).
5. Inspect both the Russian and Ukrainian navy on a cruise of **Sevastopol Bay** (p176).
6. Meet the Karaites – adepts of a little-known religion – at the *kenassa* (temple) in **Yevpatoriya** (p168).
7. Trek through the striking volcanic formations of **Kara-Dag Nature Reserve** (p197).
8. Take a breathtaking cable-car ride to the top of **Ay-Petri plateau** (p189).

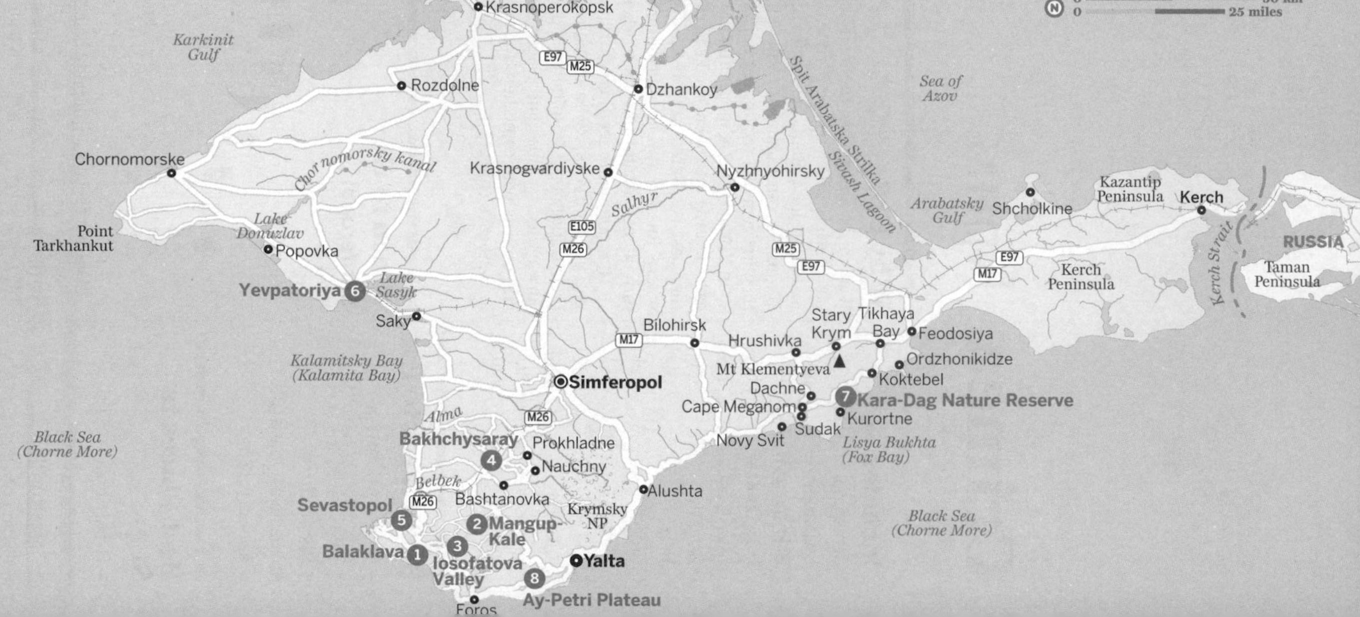

History

The stage is littered with cameo appearances, from ancient Greeks who built Chersoneses (now Khersones) to the 15th-century Genoese merchants behind the impressive Sudak fortress, as well as Cimmerians, Scythians, Sarmatians and Jews. However, the central theme of Crimean history revolves around the struggle between the Turkic and Slavic peoples for control of the peninsula.

This began in 1240, when Mongols conquered Crimea. Two centuries later control passed to their descendants, the Tatars, who held it for centuries. The Crimean Khanate became an independent political entity under Haci Giray in 1428, and after an invasion in 1475 it became a vassal state of the Ottoman Empire. Although advanced in culture and the arts, its main economic activity was trading in slaves, captured during raids into Russian, Ukrainian or Polish territory.

While a Turkish vassal state, Crimea enjoyed much autonomy. The same was not true when the Russians arrived in 1783 and began a campaign of assimilation. Three-quarters of Crimean Tatars fled to Turkey, while Russians, Ukrainians, Greeks, Bulgarians, Germans and even some French were invited to resettle Crimea.

Such Russian expansionism soon began to worry the great powers, Britain and France. As Russia tried to encroach into the lands of the decaying Ottoman Empire, the Crimean War erupted in 1854.

With close ties to the monarchy, Crimea was one of the last White Russian (pro-Tsarist) bastions during the Russian revolution, holding out till November 1920. It was occupied by German troops for three years during WWII and lost nearly half its population. In the war's aftermath, Stalin deported all remaining Crimean Tatars and most other ethnic minorities.

In 1954 Soviet leader Nikita Khrushchev, a self-styled Ukrainian, created the Autonomous Crimean Soviet Socialist Republic and transferred legislative control to the Ukrainian SSR from the Russian Federation.

When the USSR disintegrated, Russia and Ukraine wrestled over the region. They came to a temporary compromise over Russia's Black Sea Fleet, allowing it to stay in Crimea until 2017. Soon after being elected in 2010, President Viktor Yanukovych extended this lease until 2035.

Over 60% of the Crimean population are ethnic Russians and most of the others are Russian speakers. Russian is an official language in Crimea, along with Ukrainian and Crimean Tatar. Locals weren't particularly chuffed by Ukrainian independence, even less so by the Orange Revolution (p236).

Crimean Tatars started returning from Central Asian exile in the late 1980s. Restitution of the property lost in 1944 was out of the question. Penniless and unwelcome by the Russian majority, they resorted to grabbing unused land. Pro-Russian 'Cossack' vigilantes launched a series of violent attacks on Tatar squatters, but by the time of writing tensions have largely subsided.

CENTRAL & WESTERN CRIMEA

Simferopol Сімферополь

☎0652 / POP 345,000

With its odd mixture of Levantine and Soviet, the Crimean capital is not an unpleasant city, but there is no point lingering here, as everything else on the peninsula is much more exciting – and it's only a short bus ride away!

Sights

★Taurida Central Museum MUSEUM

(vul Gogolya 14; admission 70uah; ⌚9am-5pm Wed-Mon) Crimea's largest museum consists of three main sections. The first is a collection of golden artefacts, produced by Hellenized Alano-Goths in the princedom of Feodoro – currently Mangup-Kale (p175). It is located in a guarded premises on the ground floor and can only be accessed with a guide. There is a more conventional history exhibition on the upper floor, with signs in Russian only. At the time of our visit, a separate large hall was occupied by a great exhibition dedicated to the Romanovs in Crimea, where they spent their last happy summers before their demise.

Kebi-Djami Mosque MOSQUE

(vul Kurchatova 4) The restored 16th-century mosque dates back to the Tatar town of Ak-Mechet (White Mosque), a predecessor of Simferopol.

Sleeping

Na Suvorovskom HOTEL $

(www.gostinec.com.ua; Suvorovsky Spusk 9; s/d from 380/420uah;) Occupying a lovely

Simferopol

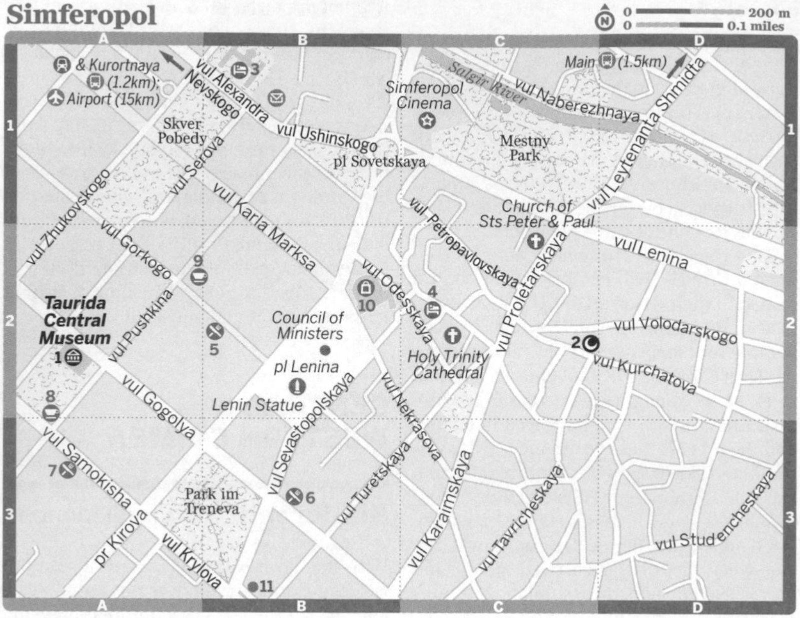

pink low-rise building in a quiet neighbourhood next to a park, this hotel has cosy, well-equipped rooms and nice personnel, though no English is spoken. The place is small and popular, so book ahead. Breakfast not included.

Seven Days HOSTEL $
(☎063 829 8008, 099 912 0173; bul Lenina 15/1, apt 112; dm 120uah; 📶) It's just a converted flat inside a Brezhnevian apartment block, but its location on the train station square makes it convenient for transit purposes. Find entrance 8 in the courtyard and ring 112 for access. These kinds of establishments are often short-lived – check if it is still operating before coming.

Hotel Valencia HOTEL $$
(Валенсія; ☎620 006; www.valencia.crimea.ua; vul Odesskaya 8; s/d from 400uah; ❄📶) Fusing Crimea and Spain, this centrally located, friendly and well-run hotel is justifiably popular, so book ahead. The sole windowless 'economy' single goes for just 250uah, but without air-con it's uncomfortable in summer. Breakfast not included.

Hotel Ukraina HOTEL $$
(Україна; ☎638 895; www.ukraina-hotel.biz; vul Rozy Lyuxemburg 7; s/d from 550/690uah; ❄📶) Admittedly, the baroque public areas of this central, forward-thinking hotel are a bit over the top, but rooms are restrained and well finished – the standard class in sandy ochre and red-earth tones. Staff speak English, plus it has a sauna and *hammam* (Turkish bath).

Eating

Divan CRIMEAN TATAR $
(Диван; vul Gorkogo 6; mains 16-55uah; ⏲9am-11pm) This unassuming cafe serves well as an introduction to Crimean Tatar cuisine. Go for grilled meat – *shashlyks* (shish kebabs) – and make sure you try some traditional sweets.

Vegeteriya VEGETARIAN $
(Вегетарія; vul Samokisha 18; mains 30-40uah; ⏲9am-9pm; ❄📶✍) A cute vegetarian-vegan cafe serving smallish portions of Indian- and Crimean-influenced dishes.

Grand Cafe Chekhov RUSSIAN $$
(Гранд-кафе Чехов; vul Chekhova 4; mains 50-80uah; ⏲10am-11pm) In this beautifully designed oasis of whiteness and coolness, you can just imagine that Anton Pavlovich himself is treating you to classic Russian specialities, such as *ukha* (fish soup) and *blyny* (pancakes), at his Crimean *dacha*

(family summer cottage). We loved pork stir-fried with apples, cooked and served in an iron pan.

Drinking

Ciao CAFE

(Чао; http://dessert.cafe-one.com/; vul Samokisha 7A; ⏲9am-10pm) A large verandah in a little park, Ciao is a great place to while away a few hours waiting for your transport out of Simferopol over a cup of coffee or a sumptuous breakfast meal. Service can be slow.

Kofein COFFEE

(vul Pushkina 8; coffee from 20uah; ⏲24hr;) The 'exoticism' at this trendy African-themed cafe overdoes its appreciation of the female form. But if you can position yourself where your eye's not being poked out by a photographed nipple, you'll find it takes its coffee seriously and turns out a good brew.

Shopping

Silpo SUPERMARKET

(Сільпо; pr Kirova 19; ⏲grocery 24hr, mini-mall 10am-6.30pm) Self-caterers should make a beeline for this conveniently located, Western-style supermarket, located inside Univermag. The grocery section is on the ground floor; the mini-mall is on the 1st floor.

Information

Central post office (vul Alexandra Nevskogo 1)

Getting There & Away

AIR

Every second plane from **Simferopol International Airport** (www.airport.crimea.ua) leaves for Moscow or other Russian cities. Turkish Airways has at least three flights a day to Istanbul. Ukraine International Airlines has at least four flights to Kyiv's Boryspil International Airport, while local Air Onix flies to the more convenient Kyiv International Airport (Zhulyany).

Kiyavia (☎272 167; www.kiyavia.crimea.ua; bul Lenina 1/7; ⏲9am-6pm Mon-Fri, to 5pm Sat) sells both international and domestic air tickets.

BUS

There are three main roads originating in Simferopol. One leads to Sevastopol via Bakhchysaray. Another one crosses the main ridge near Alushta before turning west towards Yalta. The third road heads east to Feodosiya and Kerch, branching off for Sudak.

Buses to pretty much anywhere in Crimea leave from the chaotic **Kurortnaya bus station**, located on the train station square (look out for McDonald's). There are frequent services to Yevpatoriya (20uah, 1½ hours, every 15 minutes), Sevastopol (30uah, two hours, every 20 minutes), Yalta (30uah, 1½ hours, every 10 minutes), Sudak (30uah, 2½ hours, hourly), Feodosiya (40uah, three hours, every 20 minutes) and Kerch (70uah, 4½ hours, five daily).

More buses for Kerch (half-hourly), as well as long-distance buses to the Ukrainian mainland depart from the **main bus station** (☎275 211; vul Kievskaya 4) on the other side of town.

Locals usually catch *marshrutky* (fixed-route minibuses) to Bakhchysaray (10uah, one hour) from the west bus station; they leave every 20 minutes. For newcomers, it's easier to hop on a Sevastopol-bound bus at the Kurortnaya bus station. It will pass Bakhchysaray bus station on the way.

TRAIN

Simferopol is Crimea's main railway junction and has five trains daily to/from Kyiv (300uah, 14 to 17 hours). Daily services by modern Intercity trains have reduced travel time to Dnipropetrovsk (150uah, five hours) and Kharkiv (220uah, seven hours). There are many more slower trains to Kharkiv, which stop at Zaporizhzhya (150uah, five hours). Many Kharkiv-bound trains continue onwards to Moscow. Tickets are often in short supply in summer, especially at the end of August.

SLOW PROGRESS

A fun if slow method of getting to Yalta from Simferopol is by trolleybus. Powered by electricity, those ancient dinosaurs used to be the pride of Soviet Crimea, since they began plying the world's longest trolleybus route long before clean transport became an issue in the West. They have no other virtues we can think of. Seats are cramped and trolleybuses get jam-packed as drivers collect passengers, stopping every 50m in central Simferopol. Yet looking at the long queues at the Kurortnaya bus station, you might be really tempted to get a ticket from a booth across the road and board the trolleybus with no hassle. Trolleybus 52 serves Yalta (15uah, 2½ hours, every 20 minutes from 5.30am to 8pm). Trolleybus 51 only goes to/from Alushta (9uah, 1½ hours, every 20 minutes). Both buses stop at Luchistoye (6uah, one hour). Large bags need a separate ticket.

Local *elektrychky* (electric trains) run regularly along the Crimean peninsula to/from Yevpatoriya (12uah, two hours, seven daily) and Sevastopol (12uah, two hours, seven daily). The latter service stops en route in Bakhchysaray (7uah, 40 minutes).

Getting Around

Trolleybus 9 goes from the airport to the train station. Many more *marshrutka* do the same route and continue to the centre. Look out for 'Сельпо' (Silpo) signs on their side. From the train station, trolleybuses 2 and 5 also go to the city centre. *Marshrutka* 60 and 65 connect the train station and the city centre with the main bus station.

Yevpatoriya Євпаторія

06569 / POP 103,000

Of all Crimean towns, the underrated Yevpatoriya is the only one that has preserved an Ottoman-era medina in the town centre, filled with traces of ethnic and religious groups that once inhabited it. At the time when the peninsula was controlled by the Crimean Tatars and the Turks, it was the largest trade centre where slave traders exchanged Slavs captured in the north for goods from Europe and the Orient. In its turn, it was repeatedly raided by Zaporizhzhya Cossacks, who robbed it of all goods with the noble excuse of freeing Christian slaves. Legend says that in one of those raids they invented what became known as Cossack submarines by upturning their small boats and using reeds to breathe under water. This way they approached the harbour unnoticed and then wreaked havoc all over the town. Left intact, despite decades of Communism, the medina contains Muslim, Christian and – most intriguingly – Karaite places of worship. The rest of the town is a dense grid of sanatoriums, built in the Soviet period when the town was proclaimed USSR's main resort for children.

For history buffs, it is also worth knowing that the Anglo-French-Turkish Allied forces landed here at the start of the Crimean War before moving on to besiege Sevastopol.

Sights

All major sites are located near or inside the medina.

Karaite Kenassas TEMPLE
(Караитские кенассы; vul Karaimskaya 68; adult/child & student 15/7uah; 10am-8pm Sun-Mon, 12-8pm Sat) This beautiful whitewashed colonnaded complex became the main place of worship for Karaites in the aftermath of the Russian takeover of Crimea, when they were allowed to abandon cave cities and live where they pleased. Tsar Alexander I inaugurated the main *kenassa* in 1807. Staunch monarchists, the Karaites later erected his statue on the premises. During the Crimean War (1854–56), the allies converted the *kenassas* into stables, which were targeted by Russian artillery – look out for a cannon ball left in the *kenassa* wall.

Dzhuma-Dzhami Mosque MOSQUE
(Мечеть Джума-джами; 10am-3pm Sat-Thu) Built in 1552, this landmark mosque is attributed to Mimar Sinan, the architect of Istanbul's famous Blue Mosque. Although not in Backhysaray, it was considered the main mosque of Ottoman-ruled Crimea. It served as a venue for enthroning Crimean khans, who disembarked in Yevpatoriya after an obligatory inauguration visit to Istanbul. From the port, they proceeded straight to the mosque, where they presented the sultan's *firman* (licence to rule) to the citizens. For a symbolic donation (say, 20uah) you can join a Russian-language tour of the mosque, which sets off every hour on the hour.

Dervish Tekiye MONASTERY
(Текие дервишей; vul Karayeva 18; admission with guided tour in Russian adult/child & student 15/10uah; ⌚10am-5pm) Early 20th-century travel guides to Crimea still touted dervishes whirling in a breathtaking shamanic dance as one of the peninsula's main attractions, but today unfortunately this site is about the only legacy left by the once-influential Sufi mystics. The 15th-century monastery served as a retreat for the wandering monks of the Mevlevi order, who slept and meditated inside the arched niches of the main building. Sadly today there are no dervishes here – only tourists and nostalgic Crimean Tatars. Women are required to wear a scarf.

Yegiya Kapay Synagogue JEWISH
(Синагога Египя Капай; vul Prosmushkinykh 34/27) Once the heart of a thriving Jewish community, this synagogue was closed by the Bolsheviks, then pretty much all the Crimean Jews were exterminated by the Nazis. Now revived, it once again serves as a spiritual and cultural centre, which runs an excellent Jewish restaurant and occasionally turns itself into a venue for musical festivals.

Gezlev Firewood Gate HISTORIC BUILDING
(Odun-Bazar Kapusi; http://odun-bazar.com/; vul Karayeva 13A; guided tour 10uah; ⌚9am-9pm) Apart from an excellent cafe, the restored gates of the medieval Gezlev (Yevpatoriya's Turkish name) house a small museum with a new, skillfully created 3D model of the walled medieval city.

Tours

Odun Bazar TOUR
(☎095 850 3738, 433 33; http://odun-bazar.com/; vul Karayeva 13A; tours 20uah; ⌚tours 10am, 4.30pm May-Sep) Located inside the Firewood Gate, this little travel agency offers a Russian-language tour of Yevpatoriya that may save you time since it takes in most major sights in the medina and its environs.

Sleeping

TOK Yevpatoria HOTEL $
(ТОК Євпаторія; ☎516 61, 515 48; www.tokevp.com.ua; vul Moskovskaya 29; r incl all meals from 280uah) Buzzing like a beehive, this old Soviet dinosaur has hundreds of musty rooms and a swimming pool. Hot water is switched off at 10pm until 6am next morning.

Krym HOTEL $$
(Крим; ☎544 999, 709 111; vul Revolyutsii 46; r from 460uah) This historic (since 1890) no-frills hotel is good value for the price, considering its location in the Old Town, close to Dzhuma-Dzhami Mosque.

DEATH DEBATE

At the height of WWII, the Nazis summoned three Jewish professors who were imprisoned in the Warsaw and Vilnius ghettoes and told them to voice their opinion on the subject they had studied all their lives. The question was – are Crimean Karaites Jewish or not? In a series of debates with leading scholars, each of them independently gave a negative answer, which largely contradicted everything they had said before in their long, scholarly careers. Their names were Meyer Balaban, Yitzhak Schiper and Zelig Kalmanovich. None of them survived the Holocaust. But the Karaites did – following the debate, the Nazis classified them as 'impure' but not warranting extermination. They even reopened the *kenassa* (temple) in Yevpatoriya, which had been closed by the Bolsheviks, allowing services in Hebrew! All Crimean Jews captured by the Nazis were killed.

Today the Karaites number about 2000, with 650 living in Crimea, mostly in Yevpatoriya and Feodosiya. Although their leaders deny it – perhaps a legacy of their survival tactics – the name of the people probably derives from the ancient Hebrew word for 'reader'. Initially, it was an early medieval Jewish sect in Baghdad, which rejected the Talmud, believing the Old Testament to be the only source of holy wisdom. No one is sure how this teaching spread to Crimea, but by the Middle Ages it became the second most important religion for the Turkic population of Crimea after Islam. It mixed with shamanism and the pagan beliefs of the ancient Turks. To this day the Karaites worship sacred oak groves and call their god Tengri, as did their pre-Judaist ancestors. Speaking a pure version of ancient Turkic, the Karaites even donated 330 words to the modern Turkish language when Kemal Ataturk was getting rid of Arabisms in the 1920s.

Ukraine Palace HOTEL **$$**
(☎94 111, 94 110; cnr pr Lenina & ul Frunze; s/d from 655/865uah; ❄📶🏊) With its large open-air pool, modern and tastefully decorated rooms, Ukraine Palace is about the best place to stay in Yevpatoriya, but you need to book two or three weeks in advance during the high season.

Eating

Kezlev Kyavesi CRIMEAN TATAR **$**
(Кезлев Къявеси; vul Karayeva 13; coffee 20uah) The gorgeous looking and tasting Tatar sweets and Turkish coffee served in this cafe, inside Gezlev gate, alone justify a visit to the town. The adventurous may try *kypchak* tea made with milk, pepper, salt and sugar. For more substantial Crimean Tatar meals, head to the excellent Dzheval restaurant across the road, run by the same people. We also have high expectations of the hotel they are due to open in the vicinity.

Karaman KARAITE **$**
(Караман; Karaimskaya 68; mains 35-55uah; ⏲noon-10pm) The former charity canteen in the *kenassa* houses this excellent cafe, which gives you a chance to sample Karaite cuisine. Similar to Crimean Tatar food, it's arguably more Levantine than Central Asian. Try meat or cheese and paprika *chirchir* (the Karaite version of *chebureki* – fried-meat turnovers) and *yazma* (similar to the Greek *tsatsiki*). Wash it down with *buza* (a minimally alcoholic drink made of wheat).

Yoskin Kot JEWISH **$$**
(Йоскин кот; http://sinagoga.info/; vul Prosmushkinykh 34/27; mains 45-70uah; ⏲11am-9pm; 📶) In the courtyard of Yegiya Kapay Synagogue, this place touts itself as a museum of Jewish gastronomy. It's a long shot, but we loved *ghefilte fisch* (carp cutlets), while carrot *tsimes* (sweet stew) is a pure delight.

Getting There & Around

BUS

In summer buses travel to Yevpatoriya approximately every 15 minutes from the bus station adjoining the Simferopol train station (20uah, 1½ hours).

TRAIN

In summer there are seasonal trains to Kyiv and Moscow.

TRAM & MARSHRUTKA

The bus and train stations are next to each other on vul Internatsionalnaya, northwest of the Old Town, and you can buy a map at the stalls in front of the train station. Then take tram 3 south down vul Frunze to the Ukraine Palace hotel and pr Lenina. Trams and *marshrutky* heading east (left away from the hotel) will take you to the Old Town and waterfront.

Bakhchysaray Бахчисарай

☎06554 / POP 27,500

More a village than a town, the former capital of Crimean Tatar khans is cradled in a narrow valley squeezed between two limestone escarpments. Its name means 'garden-palace', and it's a garden that needs a lot of tilling after 50 years of neglect, when its owners lived in exile. Now the Crimean Tatars are back and, although lacking resources, they have already orchestrated a minor renaissance, which benefits travellers more than anyone else.

Forget the nouveau-riche tackiness of seaside resorts! This is the place to stay with local families, drinking Turkish coffee on their verandahs and gorging on homemade Tatar

BLACK SEA RAVE

Most people west of Berlin have yet to hear of it, but long-term attendees complain that the annual rave **Kazantip** (www.kazantip.com) in July/August has become too commercial. Launched in the early 1990s as an après-surf party near a half-finished nuclear reactor on the northeastern Kazantip peninsula, the five-week-long festival moved, because of local pressure, to Popovka, north of Yevpatoriya. Today 'the republic of Kazantip' is a huge Ibiza-style operation with enormous stage sets, international DJs and thousands of punters, many of them half-naked (or naked), along with dodgy food, deliberately humorous rules and lots of serious security.

Too commercial? Probably, but the only way you'll make up your own mind is to visit. Once you book, the organisers can arrange to pick you up, but for the duration of the festival *marshrutky* meet major services arriving in Simferopol and also leave from outside Yevpatoriya's bus station, on vul Internatsionalnaya.

CRIMEAN MOUNTAIN GUIDES

Crimea has some fantastic hiking and cycling opportunities. Routes are better marked these days, but complicated logistics and a total lack of English signs means that Westerners will find the going more challenging than usual.

If you're still determined to strike out by yourself, read the tips on camping restrictions, registration and mountain rescue at www.tryukraine.com/crimea/hiking.shtml beforehand. If you'd prefer to go with a guide, the following are highly recommended:

Sergey Sorokin (067 793 9100; www.mt.crimea.com) Excellent hiking and bicycle tours.

Outdoor Ukraine (067 915 1257, 097 327 8698; www.outdoorukraine.com) A highly recommended Kyiv-based operator.

Marat Pavlenko (095 528 7232, 067 306 7318; www.bashtanovka.crimea.ua) Marat's well-established operation runs bicycle tours from his base in the village of Bashtanovka.

Mountain Rescue Service (065 544 7740; vul Vostochnaya 11, Bakhchysaray) Best experts in Crimean trekking, but they don't speak English; located in Bakhchysaray.

sweets. But that's not all – the place is full of remnants of past civilisations and is a great base for outdoor adventure in the Crimean mountains.

Sights

Bakhchysaray's sights are strung on the town's main axis, vul Lenina, like pieces of mutton on *shashlyk* skewers served in local restaurants. The Khans' Palace is 3km away from the bus and train stations. Continuing along the road for another 2.5km, you'll get to the parking lot before the ascent to Uspensky Monastery begins. Walk another kilometre from the monastery and you'll reach Iosofatova Valley at the foot of Chufut-Kale.

★ Khans' Palace PALACE

(Ханский дворец; www.hansaray.org.ua; vul Lenina 129; adult/child & student 60/30uah; 9am-5.30pm) When she was busy ordering the mass destruction of Bakhchysaray's mosques in the 18th and early 19th centuries, Catherine the Great spared the Khans' Palace. Her decision was reportedly based on the building being 'romantic', and it is sweet. While it lacks the imposing grandeur of Islamic structures in, say, Istanbul, this is a major landmark of Crimean culture and history. Erected in the 16th century under the direction of Persian, Ottoman and Italian architects, it was rebuilt a few times, but the structure still resembles the original.

Passing through the back of the finely carved, Venetian Renaissance **Demir Qapi Portal** (also called Portal Alevizo after its Italian designer, who also authored parts of Moscow's Kremlin), you enter the west wing and the dimly lit **Divan Hall**. This was the seat of government, where the khan and his nobles discussed laws and wars.

Through the hall lies the inner courtyard, containing two fountains. With its white marble ornately inscribed with gold leaf, the **Golden Fountain** (1733) is probably the more beautiful. However, the neighbouring **Fountain of Tears** (1764) is more famous, thanks to Alexander Pushkin. It's tradition that two roses – one red for love and one yellow for chagrin – are placed atop the fountain; Pushkin was the first to do this.

Behind the palace is the only surviving **harem** of the four that were traditionally attached to the palace and belonged to the khan's wives. Across the yard you can see the **Falcon Tower**.

The **Khans' Cemetery** is beside the mosque, and way back in the grounds' southeast corner is the **mausoleum of Dilara Bikez**, who may or may not be the Polish beauty who bewitched the khan.

Usta CRAFTS WORKSHOP

(www.usta.crimea.ua; vul Rechnaya 125; 10am-5pm; P) Ten years ago Crimean Tatar handicrafts were on the verge of extinction, but Ayshe Osmanova resolved to rescue her people's culture from the precipice. Retrieving old manuals from the Khans' Palace, she taught herself the ancient art of Crimean embroidery and was soon teaching the craft to other Tatar women returning from exile. A veteran silversmith and other artisans joined in.

Bakhchysaray

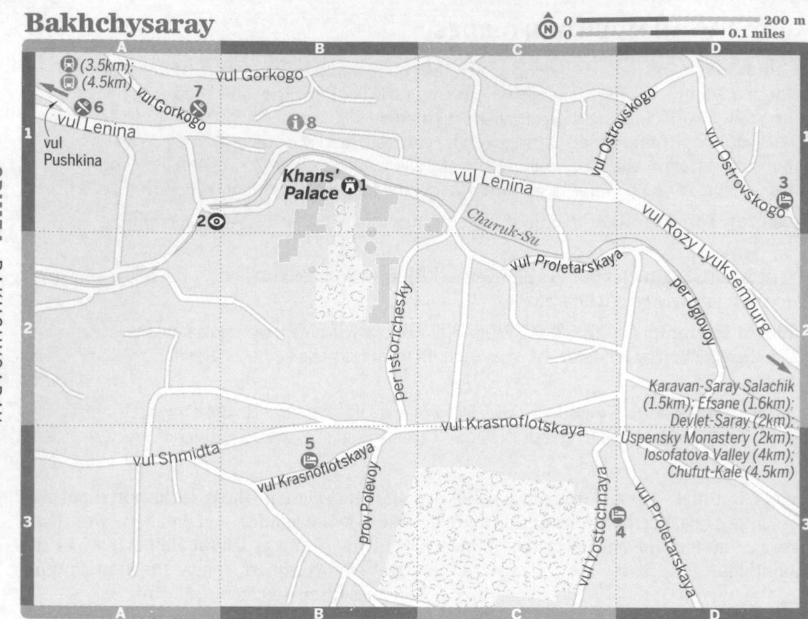

These efforts culminated in a small workshop, where you can watch artists at work and buy embroidered shawls and tablecloths, woven rugs and hangings, pottery and filigree jewellery. The turn-off to vul Rechnaya is just before the palace when coming from the train station.

Uspensky Monastery MONASTERY

(Успенский монастырь) Stop for a moment and say 'aah!' at possibly the cutest little church in a country absolutely jam-packed with them. Part of the small Uspensky Monastery, the **gold-domed church** has been built into the limestone rock of the surrounding hill, probably by Byzantine monks in the 8th or 9th century. Whitewashed monks' cells, a 'healing' fountain and tiled mosaics cling to the hillside too. Of course, the Soviets closed the place down, but it's been operating again since 1993.

★Chufut-Kale HISTORIC SITE

(Чуфут-кале; adult/child & student 50/25uah; ⏲9am-6pm) Rising 200m, this long and bluff plateau houses a honeycomb of caves and structures where people took refuge for centuries. It's wonderful to explore, especially (gingerly) the burial chambers and casemates with large open 'windows' in the vertiginous northern cliff. These are truly breathtaking, as is the view into the valley below.

First appearing in historical records as Kyrk-Or (Forty Fortifications), the city was settled sometime between the 6th and 12th centuries by Christianised descendants of Sarmatian tribes. The last powerful ruler of the Golden Horde, Tokhtamysh, sheltered here after defeat in the 1390s, and the first Crimean khanate was established at Chufut-Kale in the 15th century, before moving to nearby Bakhchysaray. After the Tatars left, Turkic-Jewish Karaites occupied the city until the mid-19th century, which won the mountain its current name of 'Jewish Fortress'.

Following the track from Uspensky Monastery, the best idea is to keep bearing right. The main entrance is not under the flat tin roof to the left of the Chufut-Kale sign, but further up the hill to the right. At this, the 14th-century main **South Gate**, you'll usually be hit for a 12uah entrance fee.

Soon after the gate, you enter a Swiss-cheese composition of carved-out rooms and steps. Behind this a stone path heads along the top of the plateau, past two locked **kenassas** (Karaite temple) in a walled courtyard to the right. There is a **Karaite cultural centre and cafe** (mains 30uah) in the adja-

Bakhchysaray

Top Sights
1 Khans' Palace B1

Sights
2 Usta A1

Sleeping
3 Dilara Hanum D1
Meraba Guesthouse .... (see 2)
4 Nagayevsky-Romm House-Museum D3
5 Villa Bakhitgul B3

Eating
6 Aliye A1
7 Musafir A1

Information
Mountain Rescue Service .... (see 4)
8 Tourist Information Centre B1

cent former house of the city's last resident, Karaite leader Avraam Firkovich.

To the left of the first intersection stands the red-tile roofed **Muslim mausoleum** (1437) of Dzhanike-Khanym, daughter of Tokhtamysh; to the right is an archway. Head left behind the mausoleum towards the cliff edge and enjoy the view into the valley below. To the right (east), a grassy track leads to two **burial chambers** in the northern side of the cliff.

From here it's hard to get lost; there are more caves until you reach the locked **East Gate**, where the road loops back on itself towards the main gate.

Iosofatova Valley CEMETERY

(Иософатова Долина) The forested Iosofatova Valley beneath the Chufut-Kale plateau hides a breathtaking and spooky sight. Thousands of moss-covered gravestones covered in Hebrew script stand, lie upturned or lean at precarious angles in the shade of ancient oak trees. For over a millennium the Karaites brought their dead to the sacred grove, which they called Balta Tuymez, meaning Axe-Don't-Touch in ancient Turkic. The scene is straight out of Michael Jackson's 'Thriller' and at sunset it's hard to escape the chilly sensation of being watched by thousands of empty eye sockets.

Devlet-Saray HISTORIC SITE

(Девлет-Сарай; vul Basenko 57; admission 20uah; 10am-4.30pm) The site where Crimean Tatar khans originally settled in Bakhchysaray now consists of a modest museum, ruins of a public bath, a mausoleum where 18 members of the khan dynasty were buried, and the main highlight – Zyndzhyrli (Chain) Medrese. The eponymous chain is hanging at the school's entrance, placed here to ensure that even the khan humbly bows his head when entering the house of god. To get here, bear left shortly after the parking lot on the way to Uspensky Monastery.

Activities

Bakhchysaray is Crimea's best base for trekking, with beautiful mountains surrounding you on all sides. Owners of many hotels listed here will happily assist with planning routes and often accompany their guests on the treks. Maps of trekking routes are available at the tourist information centre. Rangers from Mountain Rescue Service (p175) are the most experienced guides in town, but you'll have to devise a way of overcoming the language barrier.

If you are into cycling, hook up with the Hotel Koleso owners. They can deliver a mountain bicycle to wherever you are in Bakhchysaray or you can join one of their cycling tours.

Sleeping

Thanks to Crimean Tatars' entrepreneurial skills, Bakhchysaray is now a great base for budget travellers. However, guesthouses are rarely signposted and hard to find, so it's better to call ahead and arrange a pickup. Otherwise, drop by the tourist information centre and ask for directions. Budget travellers, watch out for a new hostel, which the eminent owners of Villa Bakhitgul are planning to open at vul Lenina 100, near the palace.

Villa Bakhitgul B&B $

(050 174 3167; www.bahitgul.com.ua; vul Krasnoflotskaya 20; r with/without bathroom 470/310uah;) People are absolutely raving about this stylish little place, which comes with individually designed rooms, a pool and smashing views of the valley – the closest to a boutique hotel you can find in Bakhchysaray. With a new menu each day, breakfast is a definite highlight. The place is hard to find, so opt for free pickup from the train station.

★**Dilara Hanum** B&B $

(099 535 8070, 050 930 4163; www.bahchisaray.net; vul Ostrovskogo 43; dm 80uah, r from 320uah;) Almost under the escarpment at the

end of vul Ostrovskogo, which branches off vul Lenina, this little guesthouse is 'managed by two grannies and a grandson', as their ad goes. However, Dilara is only a part-time granny and hotel manager – she is also the leader of the Crimean Tatar teachers' union and a mine of knowledge on all Tatar-related issues. Rooms are modern and have private bathrooms. There is a large dining area on the 1st floor with a kitchen, a library and a ping-pong table. Dilara's daughter speaks English.

Hostel Koleso GUESTHOUSE $
(Колесо; ☎050 155 7368; http://meganom.info; vul Pervomayskaya 7, Bashtanovka; dm/d 70/400uah) Cycling enthusiasts are entitled to their own secluded paradise in Bashtanovka, 8km from Bakhchysaray. it's a bit like an old-school hippie hang-out with simple amenities, great ambience and hearty home-cooked meals dispensed three times a day. Bicycles are available for rent (per day 120uah) and you can join the hostel's cycling tours. It is a good base for trekking. Bashtanovka can be reached by bus heading to Sinapnoye from Bakhchysaray's bus station (four daily). Tell the driver you want to get off there, or he won't stop! Taxi costs around 70uah.

Nagayevsky-Romm House-Museum HOSTEL $
(☎477 40; vul Vostochnaya 11; r per person 60-80uah) An artistic couple from Moscow made this place their home many decades ago. Their paintings hang in a downstairs room, which passes as a museum. The place is currently run by rangers from the Mountain Rescue Service and is popular with young artists who stay here for weeks. Rooms are tiny and spartan, with three to four beds each. Once you find the street, look out for a garden filled with vintage Soviet army jeeps, lovingly maintained by the rangers.

Meraba Guesthouse GUESTHOUSE $
(☎067 731 5235; www.meraba.crimea.ua; vul Rechnaya 125B; s/d/tr/q 250/320/400/430uah; Wi-Fi) This nine-room guesthouse just 200m from the Khans' Palace is a long-time favourite among travellers, though it lacks the personal welcome of the town's homestays. Rooms are fairly austere, but bathrooms are post-millenium and there's a pleasant garden for summer barbecues.

Efsane B&B $$
(☎478 61; vul Basenko 32-32A; r from 500uah) Like other hosts in Bakhchysaray, Shevkiye is a bit of a cultural ambassador for the Crimean Tatar people, but unlike most she

THE STRONG LINK

When you disembark from an *elektrychka* (electric train) in Bakhchysaray, you might notice a plaque on the left side of the station building. It commemorates Crimean Tatars who were herded here on 18 May 1944, forced into cattle cars and sent on an arduous journey to Central Asia. Stalin had decided to punish a whole people for collaboration with German occupiers, ignoring the fact that 9000 Crimean Tatars fought in the Soviet army and thousands more joined Soviet partisans.

Ayder Asanov, 82, is one of the few who lived to return from the exile in the 1990s. Sitting in the Usta Workshop, he is only 50m away from the place he was born. 'It was a jeweller's district,' he explains. 'My father, my grandfather and my great-grandfather all were filigree silversmiths.' Aged 16 when he was deported to the desert known as Famine Steppe, Asanov had already mastered the craft, but there was little chance to develop his skills in exile. He faced punishment for making jewellery and there were no materials anyway. Still, from time to time he worked secretly, procuring little pieces of wire at the machinery plant, where he was forced to work.

By the time he returned, Asanov was the only person who knew the secrets of Crimean Tatar filigree. But this last link to the past proved very durable. 'I am amazed how my hands remembered it after all these years. Tatar filigree is much finer than, say, Russian, but I could still do it,' says the old man. Nowadays he has about a dozen students, guaranteeing that the craft will not be facing extinction again anytime soon.

A total of 180,000 Crimean Tatars were deported from Crimea, followed by 37,000 members of smaller minorities – Greeks from Balaklava, Italians from Kerch, Bulgarians from Koktebel, Armenians from Feodosiya and all ethnic Germans. They were usually given only a few minutes to take vital belongings and very few of them lived to see their homes again.

speaks impeccable English, having taught the language to generations of local children. Cultural immersion starts at breakfast – each day it is a presentation of a new Tatar dish. Tours, mountain treks and free cooking classes are on offer. Call ahead for free pickup from the train station.

Eating

★Musafir CRIMEAN TATAR $

(Мусафир; vul Gorkogo 21; mains 30-60uah; ⏲8am-11pm; 📶) A *plov* (a variation of pilaf) master is conjuring a magic stew in the *kazan* (traditional wrought-iron bowl), while patrons spread comfortably on Oriental rugs. Apart from the usual Tatar dishes, they make excellent *yantyk* (a pie-like pastry) and Bakhchysaray's best Turkish coffee. The latter is served with lumps of sugar that you are expected to put straight into your mouth, rather than in your cup.

Aliye CRIMEAN TATAR $

(Алие; vul Lesi Ukrainki 1; mains 25-70uah; ⏲8am-10pm) Popular with locals and tour groups, this super-friendly cafe on the main drag has Turkish-style rugs on the upper terrace surrounded by a garden, and European tables on the lower terrace, which features an artificial waterfall. The *shashlyks* are superb and we also loved the small *yerash* (dumplings with walnut paste).

Karavan Sarai Salachik CRIMEAN TATAR $$

(Караван-сарай Салачик; ☎452 220; vul Basenko 43A; mains 50-80uah) Hookah pipes replace alcohol at this restaurant, in which individual gazebos with *topchans* (low Turkish-style seating) are dotted across a landscaped lawn. There are all the usual Crimean Tatar dishes, including *sheker keyeks* (a little bit like traditional Turkish baklava) for dessert.

Information

Mountain Rescue Service (☎477 40; vul Vostochnaya 11) If you or someone in your group speaks Russian, you can organise treks with the help of mountain rangers based in Nagayevsky-Romm Museum-House. They are also the people to make an SOS call in the mountains.

Tourist information centre (☎066 100 6022; www.infocentre.crimea.ua; vul Lenina 102; ⏲9.30am-6pm May-Oct) USAID-funded office opposite the Khans' Palace handing out hiking and town maps.

Getting There & Away

BUS

Bakhchysaray's bus station is just off the Simferopol–Sevastopol road. Here, you can a catch a bus to both Simferopol (10uah, 30 minutes) and Sevastopol (18uah, 50 minutes). Frequent direct *marshrutky* go to the inconveniently located western bus station in Simferopol. Buses originating in Sevastopol terminate at Simferopol's train station.

ELEKTRYCHKA

Local trains shuffle back and forth between Sevastopol (8.35uah, 1½ hours) and Simferopol (6.90uah, 50 minutes) seven times a day in each direction.

Getting Around

Marshrutka 2 shuttles constantly between the bus station, train station, Khans' Palace and Uspensky Monastery.

Mangup-Kale Мангуп-Кале

If you liked Chufut-Kale and want more, head to **Mangup-Kale** (admission 15uah), the peninsula's most spectacular cave city. Located 22km south of Bakhchysaray, this remote plateau is in the shape of a hand with four fingers. Allocate at least three hours for the return hike from the base of the plateau.

Formerly the ancient capital of Feodoro, the principality of the 6th-century Goths and Alans, this was an excellent fortress due to its sheer cliffs. It was finally abandoned in the 15th century.

The village at the base of the trail is called Khadzhi-Sala, reached from Bakhchysaray by *marshrutka* bound for Rodnoye (Родное; 8uah, five daily) or by taxi (150uah). There are several guesthouses where you can overnight in case you are stuck. The large village Zalisne (Zalesnoye in Russian), 2km before Khadzhi-Sala (coming from Bakhchysaray), has more transport options.

In Khadzhi-Sala, there is a booth selling tickets (20uah) and useful Russian-language maps of the cave city. A trail leading up the plateau between two fingers of land begins about 100m to your right. At the top of the ridge follow the trail to the furthest finger of land until you see a large stone gateway and a long wall. Beyond are carved-out chambers and caves. The most impressive is the final cave room, carved out of the very tip of the cliff with stairs leading down the west side to a burial chamber.

Sevastopol Севастополь

☎0692 / POP 330,000

It is easy to understand why the Russians are lamenting the loss of Sevastopol more than any other chunk of their vast empire. Orderly and clean as the deck of a ship, with whitewashed neoclassical buildings surrounding a cerulean bay, it has everything most Russian cities badly lack.

Not that the loss is complete – an agreement hastily signed by President Yanukovych stipulates that Sevastopol will remain the base of the Russian Black Sea fleet for another 25 years. Most locals are linked to the navy in one way or another and maintain a strong allegiance to Russia. This results in a peculiar cultural microclimate, similar to Gibraltar.

A favourite playground for military history fans, Sevastopol is also attractive to those with no interest in weapons and uniforms. Simply put, it is the most pleasant Crimean city – civilised, easy-going, but largely bypassed by the recreational mayhem of Crimea's southern and eastern coasts.

History

Sevastopol has much to say about the irony of fate. Purpose-built as an impregnable sea fortress to shelter the imperial fleet, it fell three times after being attacked from land. Anglo-French-Turkish allies were the first to lay siege and capture it during the Crimean War. In 1920 the city became the last stronghold of the retreating White Russian army. It saw steamships carrying away the cream of Russian society into a lifelong exile before surrendering to the Bolsheviks.

History repeated itself in 1942, when the Germans captured Sevastopol after a devastating 250-day siege. There was hardly a building left standing when they entered. But very soon Sevastopol was rebuilt by the Soviets with an atypical regard for its historic outlook.

Sights

★Primorsky Boulevard PROMENADE

The city's bay-facing showcase greets seafarers with an array of whitewashed colonnaded buildings. Fresh from a Russian-funded spruce-up, the boulevard is also a pleasant place to walk or hide from the scorching sun in the shade of trees. It begins at **Grafskaya Pristan** (Графская пристань; Count's Jetty) – the city's official gateway, marked by a colonnaded arch. Here you can hop on a **bay cruise** (50uah, 1½ hours). The square behind is dominated by the **Admiral Nakhimov monument** (Памятник адмиралу Нахимову; 1959), dedicated to the man who led the city's defence during the Crimean War. Walking further along the seafront, you will soon spot the **Eagle Column** (Памятник затопленным кораблям; 1904). Set atop a rock in the sea, it commemorates Russian ships deliberately scuppered at the mouth of the harbour in 1854 to make it impossible for enemy ships to pass. The boulevard ends at **Artbukhta** (Artillery Quay) – the city's main nightlife area.

Panorama of Sevastopol's Defence WAR MEMORIAL

(http://sev-museum-panorama.com; bul Istorichesky; adult/student 65/35uah; ⏲9am-5pm, last entry 4.30pm Tue-Sun Jun-Sep, Wed-Sun Sep-May) The focus of Sevastopol's wartime memories, this is a circular building, its inner wall covered in a mammoth-sized painting. Supplemented with 3D props, it brings to life the 349-day siege of Sevastopol. Entry is only as part of a group tour, leaving at allotted times. English- or German-language tours cost 600uah per group.

Black Sea Fleet Museum MUSEUM

(Музей Черноморского флота; ☎542 289; vul Lenina 11; admission 20uah; ⏲10am-5pm Wed-Sun) Full of ship models and Crimean War snippets, this small museum is visually impressive, even though all inscriptions are in Russian. The upper-floor exhibition is less interesting and reflects the Soviet view of the Russian Civil War and WWII.

Khersones RUIN

(Херсонес; ☎241 304; www.chersonesos.org; ul Drevnyaya 1; adult/child & student 25/25uah; ⏲grounds 9am-9pm, museum 9am-9pm May-Oct, to 5pm Nov-Mar) The ruins of the ancient Greek city founded in 422 BC are of great significance to local visitors. This is the place where Volodymyr the Great was famously baptised into Christianity in AD 988, launching what would become the Russian Orthodox Church. Earlier that year, he sacked the city, helping the Byzantine emperor to put down a local rebellion. Today the best-preserved structure is the **ancient theatre**. There's also the restored **Vladimirsky Cathedral** and an interesting **museum** displaying items excavated on the site. History apart, Khersones provides a nice photo opportunity, particularly with the **stone**

arch, whose bell comes from a Crimean War cannon. In May, the place is ablaze with blooming poppy flowers.

Local bus/*marshrutka* 22 goes directly to Khersones. Or catch trolleybus 2 or 6 westwards to the Rossiya (Россия) stop, turn back to the first street (vul Yeroshenko; Ерошенко) and walk for 15 minutes.

★Mikhaylovskaya Battery MUSEUM
(Михайловская Батарея; ul Gromova 35; adult/child & student incl tour 40/15uah; ⏲10am-6pm) A massive piece of fortification seen across the bay from central Sevastopol, the battery served as a hospital when the Russians withdrew to the northern side of the bay during the Crimean War. It has recently been transformed into a museum dedicated to Sevastopol's military history with the emphasis on the Crimean War. Original uniforms, weapons, photos and tons of other memorabilia are on display, but if that's not enough you can listen to old military marches and speeches by historic figures. English-language tours are available – ask for Danil. To get there, take a ferry bound for Radiogorka from Artbukhta (2uah, half-hourly).

Cape Fiolent BEACH
(Фиолент) The southernmost tip of Sevastopol municipality is a spot of a rare, *Le Grand Bleu* type of beauty. But this aesthetic pleasure comes at a cost – an 800-step descent from the cliff-top Georgievsky monastery to the city's most scenic beach – Yashmovy. Reaching Fiolent is not easy, either. You have to transfer to the often-crowded *marshrutka* 3 at the 5km terminal. In summer, there are boats to Balaklava (from 25uah).

Tours

Manita Mishina TOUR
(☎098 313 0891; www.funnydolphin.hostel.com/) Funny Dolphin owner's wife is a professional English-speaking guide and the brain centre of the local Anglophone travel industry. She runs tours of her own and can put you in touch with other colleagues who do the same.

Ostroffroad ADVENTURE
(☎098 313 0891; http://ostroffroad.com; tours 500-700uah) A fleet of shiny new Suzuki Jimny 4WDs regularly sets off to explore Crimean sights that are otherwise difficult to reach. Guides speak English. Vehicles are also available for rent. There is no office – use the website to book.

Festivals & Events

Tourists flock to Sevastopol and hotels greedily raise prices during the last weekend of July, when the city celebrates **Russian Navy Day** with an impressive show of battleships manoeuvring in the bay, planes flying overhead and marines landing on Grafskaya Pristan. This show of force is largely symbolic. With half of the Black Sea and the straits controlled by NATO member-countries, the Russian fleet has no strategic role to play, apart from guarding the coast of Georgia's breakaway Abkhazia.

Sleeping

The shortage of decently priced accommodation in Sevastopol is acute, so renting an apartment deserves extra special consideration. English-run **Travel 2 Sevastopol** (☎050 757 5952; www.travel2sevastopol.com) responds promptly and is knowledgeable and remarkably helpful.

Funny Dolphin HOSTEL $
(☎050 146 4194, 095 501 3343; www.funnydolphin.hostel.com; vul Vasiliya Kuchera 5, apt 2 ; dm/d 140/300uah; ❄📶) A fan of military history and vintage Soviet cars, Yury converted a small flat in a quiet part of central Sevastopol into a modern-looking hostel with bunkbeds in two brightly coloured rooms. On a cobbled road veering uphill from vul Lenina, the place is unsigned, so call ahead to be met by the owners. Two rooms with double beds, shared bathroom and kitchen are in a separate flat a short walk away.

Fazanya Roshcha HOMESTAY $
(Pheasant Grove; ☎050 906 8701; fazanya@mail.ru; vul Fermerskaya 1, Mekenziyevy Gory; s/d from 180/220uah; 📶🏊) Outside the city, in MacKenzie Heights, this place is ideal for motorists because of its proximity to strategic roundabouts, from which roads lead to central Sevastopol, Balaklava and Bakhchysaray, and to the uncrowded beach in Lyubimovka. It is a classic *dacha* with very simple rooms for rent, a tiny pool and gallons of hospitality poured on you by the kindly hosts, including peaches and grapes from the garden. The hosts don't speak English, but they are used to foreign travellers. It's a short ride or 20-minute walk from Mekenziyevy Gory train station on the road leading to Severnaya ferry terminal, across the bay from central Sevastopol. *Marshrutky* 62 and 64 ply the route; ask to be dropped off at

Sevastopol

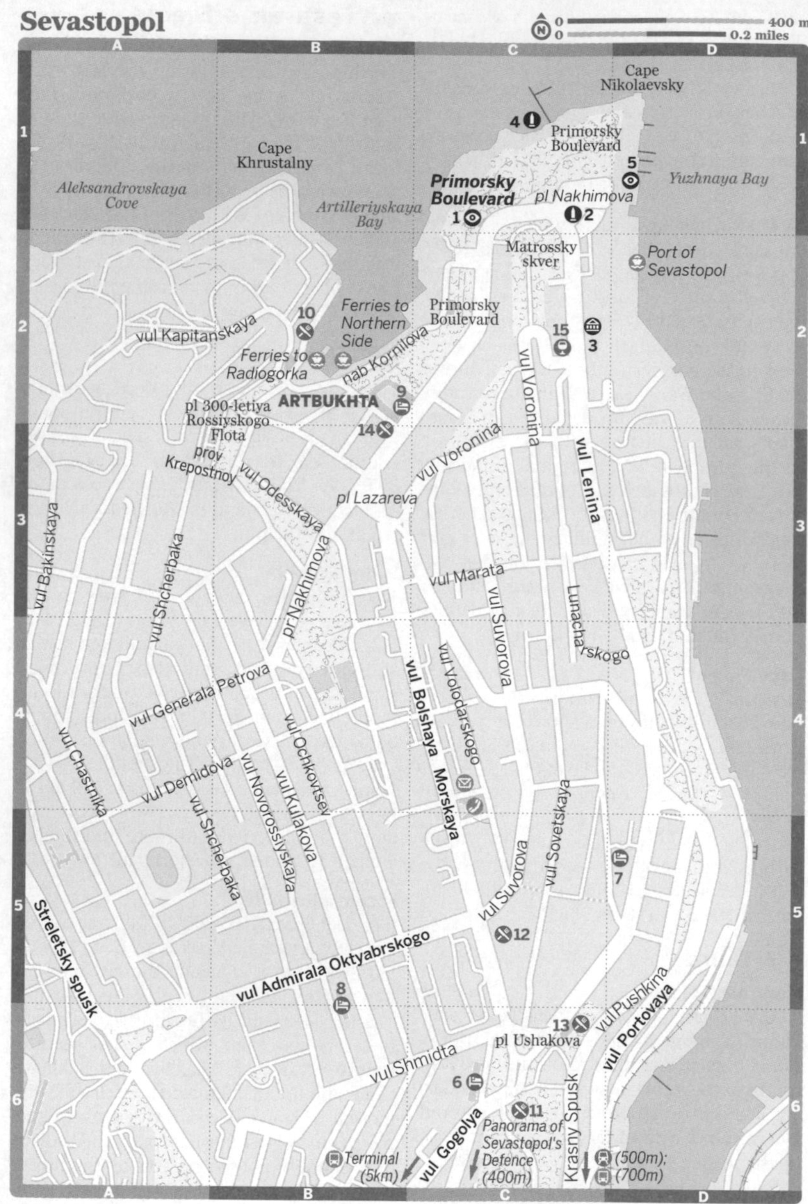

Kolbasny Tsekh stop. The turn-off is marked with a Fermerskaya St sign.

Gostevoy Dom K&T GUESTHOUSE $
(Гостевой дом K&T; ☎553 228; www.ghkandt.com; vul Chertsova 2; s/d from 280/380uah; ❄) The drive leading towards this pretty little hotel is jokingly called an 'ecopath'. In fact, it is a dirt track cutting through a *dacha* sprawl in a ravine close to Khersones. Despite the slightly unfortunate location, the place is favoured by Russian rock and cinema stars whose photos adorn the lobby.

Sevastopol

Top Sights
1 Primorsky Boulevard C1

Sights
2 Admiral Nakhimov Monument C1
3 Black Sea Fleet Museum C2
4 Eagle Column C1
5 Grafskaya Pristan D1

Sleeping
6 Art-Hotel Ukraina C6
7 Funny Dolphin D5
8 Olymp B8
9 Sevastopol B2

Eating
10 Barkas B2
11 Café Ostrov C6
12 Injir Cafe C5
13 Kofein C6
14 Varenichnaya Pobeda B3

Drinking & Nightlife
15 Qbar C2

There is a neat-looking garden with a small pool. Take a taxi – the place is hard to find on your own.

Art-Hotel Ukraina HOTEL $$
(Отель Украина; ☎542 127; www.ukraine-hotel.com.ua; vul Gogolya 2; economy r without breakfast from 440uah, standard s/d 500/600uah;) What makes it call itself an art-hotel we can't fathom, but it is a friendly place with a blackwood interior so favoured by former Intourist establishments. Without an expensive renovation, it somehow succeeded in making even the cheapest rooms look homey. Only standard rooms have air-con.

Sevastopol HOTEL $$$
(Отель Севастополь; ☎539 060; www.sevastopol-hotel.com.ua; pr Nakhimova 8; s/d from 780/1070uah;) Designers at Best Western must have been overexcited when the chain took over this landmark building overlooking the bay from Primorsky Blvd. Thick carpets mute sounds in the high-ceilinged corridors and the neoclassical lobby, which seems suitable for an opera performance. But nothing can protect the bay-facing rooms from pop-music blasted by seafront bars.

Olymp HOTEL $$$
(Отель Олимп; ☎455 789, 097 021 1414; www.olymp-hotel.com; vul Kulakova 86; r from 650uah;) Very helpful staff, a location on a quiet street and comfy pistachio-coloured rooms are Olymp's main virtues. But the lobby could do without those faux-Greek motifs.

Eating & Drinking

Hungry, thirsty or in desperate need of a Segway ride? Head straight to Artbukhta, Sevastopol's Soho, where many restaurants and fast-food outlets are located. Some of the sleaziest nightclubs and bars are also to be found here.

Varenichnaya Pobeda RESTAURANT $
(Вареничная Победа; pr Nakhimova 10; mains 25-40uah; 9am-12am;) Here is the original retro-Soviet dumpling shop, which has exploded into the pan-Ukrainian Katyusha chain. The menu features Ukrainian *varenyky* and Russian *pelmeni* dumplings with all conceivable fillings. The interior, coupled with some vodka shots, may induce nostalgic sobbing among older customers.

★ **Café Ostrov** RESTAURANT $$
(Кафе Остров; ☎099 543 8383; Istorichesky bul 3; mains 85-130uah; 9am-1am;) Its name inspired by *The Island of Crimea* – a celebrated novel by dissident writer Vassily Aksyonov – Ostrov displays an elegance unseen elsewhere on the peninsula. The chef plays a virtuoso game with homegrown products – from sweet Yalta onions and goat cheese to Crimea's extrordinary figs and peaches. Book ahead if you want a bayview table on the balcony.

Barkas SEAFOOD $$
(Баркас; vul Kapitanskaya 2A, Artbukhta; mains 65-150uah;) The motto – 'we store our fish in the sea' – suggests that only the fresh catch is served in this naval-themed restaurant with a blue-coloured interior and waiters dressed as sailors. This is also the place to sample all kinds of Crimean wine.

Injir Cafe PIZZA $$
(Инжир Кафе; vul Bolshaya Morskaya 35; mains 50-70uah;) A local hipster fave, this pizzeria-cum-bar exudes positive vibes, musically and gastronomically speaking. Totally unpretentious, it is equally good for eating and social drinking. Pizzas are properly thin and served on wooden plates by friendly waiters clad in uniform jeans shorts, while the DJ spins summery tunes.

Kofein BREAKFAST, COFFEE $$
(Кофеин; vul Lenina 55; coffee from 20uah; 24hr) No other Kofein outlet in Ukraine

can boast such a scenic location – with a terrace perched above Yuzhnaya (Southern) Bay, where Russian navy ships are moored. The smartly designed picture menu makes it easier to choose from the extensive list of coffee drinks, salads, main courses and cocktails. But the unnecessary 'exotic' ingredients in iced teas and milkshakes are slightly annoying.

Qbar BAR

(vul Lenina 8; mains & cocktails 40-60uah) Qbar has played down the gay theme, though drag queen shows still occasionally take place. But they keep their promise not to let anyone leave hungry, sober or sad. This Rhodes-styled courtyard is the place to hang out with Sevastopol's gilded youth – gay and straight alike. It's supposed to be a pre-party DJ bar, but it is heaving till early morning.

☆ Entertainment

Khersones Theatre THEATRE

(☎544 330; http://hersonesteatr.org.ua; vul Drevnaya 1; tickets 50uah) Sevastopol's Russian theatre stages costumed historical dramas amid the ruins of ancient Khersones. Tickets are sold on the day at the entrance to Khersones from around 4pm.

ℹ Information

Central post office (Почтамт; ☎544 881; vul Bolshaya Morskaya 21; internet per hr 4.5uah; ⏲counters 9am-7pm Mon-Fri, to 2pm Sat, internet centre 8am-6pm Mon-Fri, to 5pm Sat & Sun) Internet available too.

Telephone office (Укртелеком; ⏲9am 10pm) In the side street next to the post office.

ℹ Getting There & Away

AIR

Sevastopol's Belbek airport, once used by Soviet leaders travelling to their Crimean *dachas*, is now catering to ordinary folks, with several Dniproavia flights to Kyiv and Moscow, in summer only.

BUS

There are buses to Bakhchysaray (15uah, one hour, every 15 minutes), Yalta (27uah, two hours, half-hourly) and Simferopol (27uah, two hours, every 15 minutes). There are two services a day for Odesa (210uah, 14 hours)

FERRY

Boat services to Turkey were suspended when we visited.

TRAIN

There are two trains a day from Kyiv direct to Sevastopol (200uah, 17 hours), as well as *elektrychka* to/from Simferopol (12uah, two hours, seven daily in each direction). The latter service stops en route in Bakhchysaray (1½ hours).

ℹ Getting Around

To reach Balaklava and Cape Fiolent, the chaotic 5km terminal comes into the equation. To reach it, hop on any *marshrutka* marked 5KM in the town centre. Once there, look for a large square where trolleybus routes terminate. Walk to its far edge – you'll have apartment blocks on your right and market stalls across the street on your left. You'll find Fiolent *marshrutka* 3 on the same side of the street as the trolleybuses. *Marshrutka* 9 for Balaklava stops across the street and around the corner.

TO/FROM THE TRAIN STATION

The train station is south of the town centre and main seafront. To get into town, cross the metal pedestrian bridge over the tracks and hop on any bus or *marshrutka* – all of them trudge uphill to the centre. Main central streets (vul Lenina, pr Nakhimova and vul Bolshaya Morskaya) form a circle with one-way anti-clockwise traffic movement.

TAXI

To reach Balaklava and Fiolent it is more sensible to catch a taxi, but you will need someone to call for you in Russian. The reliable **Taxi Metro** (☎050 424 1558, 050 424 1556) charges around 50uah in both directions.

Balaklava Балаклава

☎0692

From the bloodthirsty pirates featuring in Homer's *Odyssey* to the Soviet nuclear submarine fleet, everyone used this beautiful curving fjord, invisible from the sea, as a secret hideout.

The British army wintered here during the Crimean War when a storm destroyed many supply ships moored outside the bay. Reading about it in the *Times*, concerned women back home began knitting full-cover woolly caps for the freezing sailors. These garments became known as balaclava helmets, or simply balaclavas.

Today the bay's turquoise waters surrounded by arid, scrub-covered hills shelter an armada of yachts, while pretty much the entire Ukrainian navy is tucked in the bay's far corner.

INTO THE VALLEY OF DEATH

Unquestioning loyalty, bravery and inexplicable blunders leading to tragedy – these ingredients turned an engagement lasting just minutes into one of the most renowned battles in military history. The action in question is the ill-fated charge of the Light Brigade, which occurred during a Russian attempt to cut British supply lines from Balaklava to Sevastopol during the Crimean War.

The battle began northeast of Balaklava early on 25 October 1854. Russian forces based on the east–west Fedioukine Hills wrested control of Allied (Turkish-held) gun positions lining the parallel southern ridge of Causeway Heights. Then they moved towards Balaklava itself.

Initially the Russians were blocked by the 'thin red line' of the British 93rd Highlanders, and repulsed by Lord Lucan's Heavy Cavalry Brigade. But four hours later, they appeared to be regrouping at the eastern end of the valley between the Fedioukine Hills and Causeway Heights. British army commander Lord Raglan sent an order for the cavalry 'to try and prevent the enemy carrying away the guns'.

The order was vague – which guns exactly? – and misinterpreted. The Earl of Cardigan headed off down the wrong valley, leading his Light Cavalry Brigade into a cul-de-sac controlled on three sides by the enemy. The numbers are disputed, but nearly 200 of 673 were killed.

'C'est magnifique, mais ce n'est pas la guerre,' exclaimed a watching French general. ('It's magnificent, but it's not war.') Later, romantic poet Lord Alfred Tennyson would lionise the 'noble six hundred' who rode into 'the valley of death'. His poem 'The Charge of the Light Brigade' did more than anything to mythologise the event for posterity. On its 150th anniversary, the charge was even re-created in front of British dignitaries, including Prince Phillip.

The 'Valley of Death' is now a vineyard, just north of the M18 road from Sevastopol to Yalta. You can look down on it from the hill of Sapun Gora (Сапун-гора), where there's a WWII **diorama** (9.30am-6pm Tue-Sun Apr-Oct, to 4pm Nov-Mar) and memorial. *Marshrutka* 107 (1.50uah) will get you there from central Sevastopol.

History

The 2500-year-old settlement became a Genovese trading post in the medieval period. In 1475 it fell to the conquering Turks, who gave Balaklava its current name, which means Fish's Nest. After the Russian takeover of Crimea, the area was settled by Greek refugees escaping Ottoman rule.

During the war Florence Nightingale ran a field hospital on one of the plateaus above the village, and the infamous charge of the ill-fated Light Brigade took place in a valley north of the city.

Stalin deported Balaklava Greeks to Central Asia in 1944. Few of them returned to their hometown, which was turned into a top-secret Soviet submarine base.

Sights & Activities

Genovese Fortress of Cembalo RUIN
(Генуэзская крепость Чембало) FREE All that remains of the 15th-century Genovese fortress are three semi-ruined towers on top of a strategic hill, guarding the mouth of the harbour. But the view of the bay and the sea coast, stretching to Cape Aya, is breathtaking. The fortress was the site of the last stand of Balaklava's garrison, composed of local Greek fishers who defended their town from the Allied troops during the Crimean War.

Cold War Museum NUCLEAR BUNKER
(Музей Холодной Войны; Tavricheskaya nab 24; adult/student 40/15uah, by boat 60uah; 10am-6pm, ticket desk to 4.45pm) The town's quirkiest sight lurks across the bay from the main promenade. The concrete opening in the harbour wall is the mouth of a natural underwater cave that the Soviets turned into a secret nuclear submarine factory officially known as Facility-825. Today you can breach the huge nuclear-blast-proof doors and wander through parts of the facility, which features repair docks, mess rooms and, thankfully, an arsenal that is now empty. You can take a one-hour Russian-language walking

tour or a ½-hour boat tour, leaving on the hour and at 4.45pm. Take a jumper: it gets chilly inside.

Balaklava Beaches BEACH

In summer, there are frequent boats to beaches with names such as Golden and Silver (15uah). About five boats a day go to Cape Fiolent and Vasili beach (25uah and 15uah respectively).

Sleeping

Listrigon Motel HOTEL $

(Мотель Листригон; ☎637 169, 067 692 1179; www.listrigon.com; vul 7th Noyabrya 5D; economy s/d/tr 85/165/185uah, standard from 455uah; ❄) This Lego-like motel curving around a hillside offers great views, reasonable accommodation and decent prices. The cheapest economy rooms (April to October only) are dormitory-style with shared bathrooms, no windows and breakfast not included; however, there's a cafe where you can pay for breakfast. More expensive accommodation includes a private bathroom and is open year-round.

Kefalo Vrisi PENSION $$

(Кефало Вриси; ☎050 398 7147; www.kefalo-vrisi.com; vul Istoricheskaya 15; d from 500uah; ❄) Flower and fruit trees cover every patch around this pension set in a secluded valley, about 15 minutes' walk along a footpath from the embankment. All rooms face Cembalo fortress. The first of Balaklava's beaches is about 30-minutes' walk from here. Book well in advance in summer and call to arrange a pickup – not all taxis will agree to take you there and carrying luggage uphill to this place is quite an exercise.

Eating

Izbushka Rybaka SEAFOOD $$

(Избушка Рыбака; Fisherman's Hut; ☎455 049; www.isbushka.net.ua; nab Nazukina 33; mains 40-100uah) We heard people calling it the best fish restaurant in Crimea. Located on a floating platform at the far end of the main promenade, it's specialty is *shkara* – a style of cooking once favoured by local Greeks.

Kharchevnya Dreyka SEAFOOD $$

(Drake's Inn; ☎050 278 4116; ul Mramornaya 17; mains 70-100uah) Near the entrance to the Naval Museum, this is an excellent fish restaurant with waiters dressed as *Peter Pan* pirates. All kinds of Black Sea fish are on offer, which is no wonder, since the Fish's Nest is just around the corner.

Getting There & Around

Marshrutka 9 for Balaklava (2uah, every 20 minutes) departs from Sevastopol's chaotic 5km terminal. In Balaklava, boat operators will take you across the harbour to the Cold War Museum for 20uah. Otherwise it's a 30-minute walk around the bay.

SOUTHERN COAST

Sevastopol to Yalta

The drive between Sevastopol and Yalta is one of the most scenic in Crimea. The road twists and turns along a coastal escarpment, with the Black Sea far below and the sheer cliffs of the Crimean Mountains rising behind. Vineyards and cypress trees line the route.

Thirty kilometres from Sevastopol is the small village of **Foros**, notable for three things. First, this is where Gorbachev was held under house arrest during the 1991 coup attempt in Moscow. Locals will happily point out his *dacha,* which has a terracotta roof.

Second, there's the small, gold-domed Resurrection Church, also known as the **Church on the Rock** for its dramatic perch on a precipitous crag overlooking the sea. The 19th-century tea tycoon Alexander Kuznetsov built the church in thanks for the survival of his daughter, whose runaway horse stopped at the edge of the cliff.

Third, Foros is popular with rock climbers because of the left-hand face of Mt Mshat-Kaya, the **Forosskiy Kant**, which rises above the village. The face lies above today's Sevastopol–Yalta road, near the Baydarsky Vorota pass. For details, contact mountain guide Sergey Sorokin (p171).

Yalta Ялта

☎0654 / POP 80,500

Yalta's air – an invigorating blend of sea and pine forest sprinkled with mountain chill – has always been its main asset. Back in the 19th century, doctors in St Petersburg had one remedy for poor-lunged aristocrats: Yalta. That is how the Russian royal family and other dignitaries, such as playwright Anton Chekhov, ended up here. Old parts of Yalta are still full of modest and not-so-modest former *dachas* of the tsarist-era intelligentsia, while the coast around the city is dotted with the luxurious palaces of the aristocracy. But back in 1913, a Russian travel guide remarked that Yalta was a long way from the Riviera in terms of comforts and civilisation. And it hasn't got any closer, despite the extremely beautiful setting in the shade of the chalk-faced Mt Ay-Petri.

A workers' paradise in the Soviet times, Yalta was badly hit by the wild commercialisation of the 1990s, but it is undergoing a visible gentrification. The view from the spruced-up seaside promenade, lined with swaying palm trees, is no longer obscured by the rusting carcasses of sunken boats in the harbour. And a very happy-looking granite Lenin seems particularly pleased when *babushkas* gather at sunset to dance the waltz and polka on the plaza that still bears his name.

Sights & Activities

Chekhov House-Museum MUSEUM
(Дом-музей Чехова; www.chekhov.com.ua; vul Kirova 112; adult/child & student 40/20uah; 10am-5pm, last entry 4.30pm Tue-Sun Jun-Sep, Wed-Sun Sep-May) With many of Yalta's attractions a short distance away, the Chekhov House-Museum is the only must-see in town. It's sort of *The Cherry Orchard* incarnate. Not only did Anton Chekhov (1860–1904) pen that classic play here, but the lush garden would also appeal to the most horticulturally challenged audience.

A long-term tuberculosis sufferer, the great Russian dramatist spent much of his last five years in Yalta. He designed the white *dacha* and garden himself, and when he wasn't producing plays like *Three Sisters* and *The Cherry Orchard,* he was a legendary host and bon vivant, welcoming the Russian singer Feodor Chaliapin, composer Rachmaninov, and writers Maxim Gorky and Leo Tolstoy.

After the exhibition at the entrance, you head down the path to the *dacha,* where all nine rooms are pretty much as Chekhov left them upon his departure from Yalta for Germany in May 1904. Explanation sheets are available in several languages.

Take *marshrutka* 6 from Veshchevoy Rynok bus station or *marshrutka* 8 from the Spartak Cinema bus station to the Dom-Muzey Chekhova stop. It takes 15 to 20 minutes to walk from the Spartak Cinema.

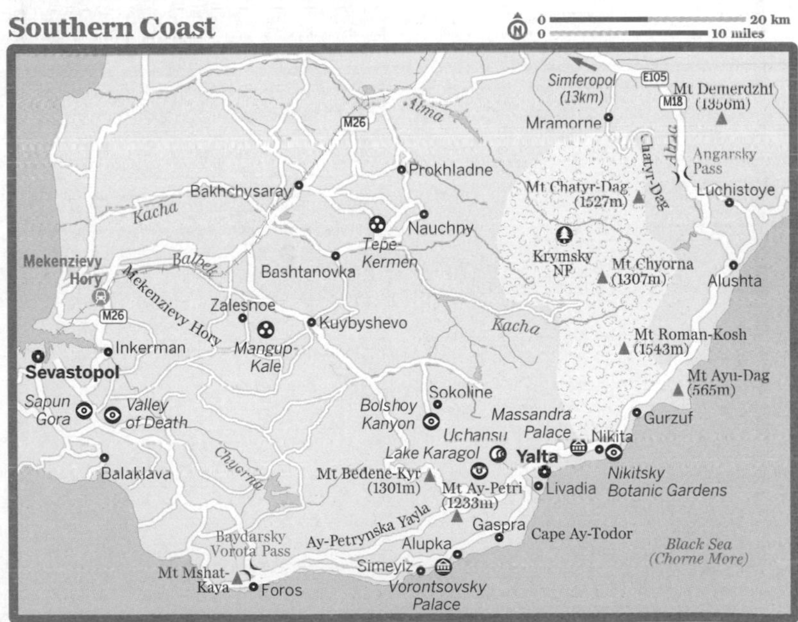

Yalta

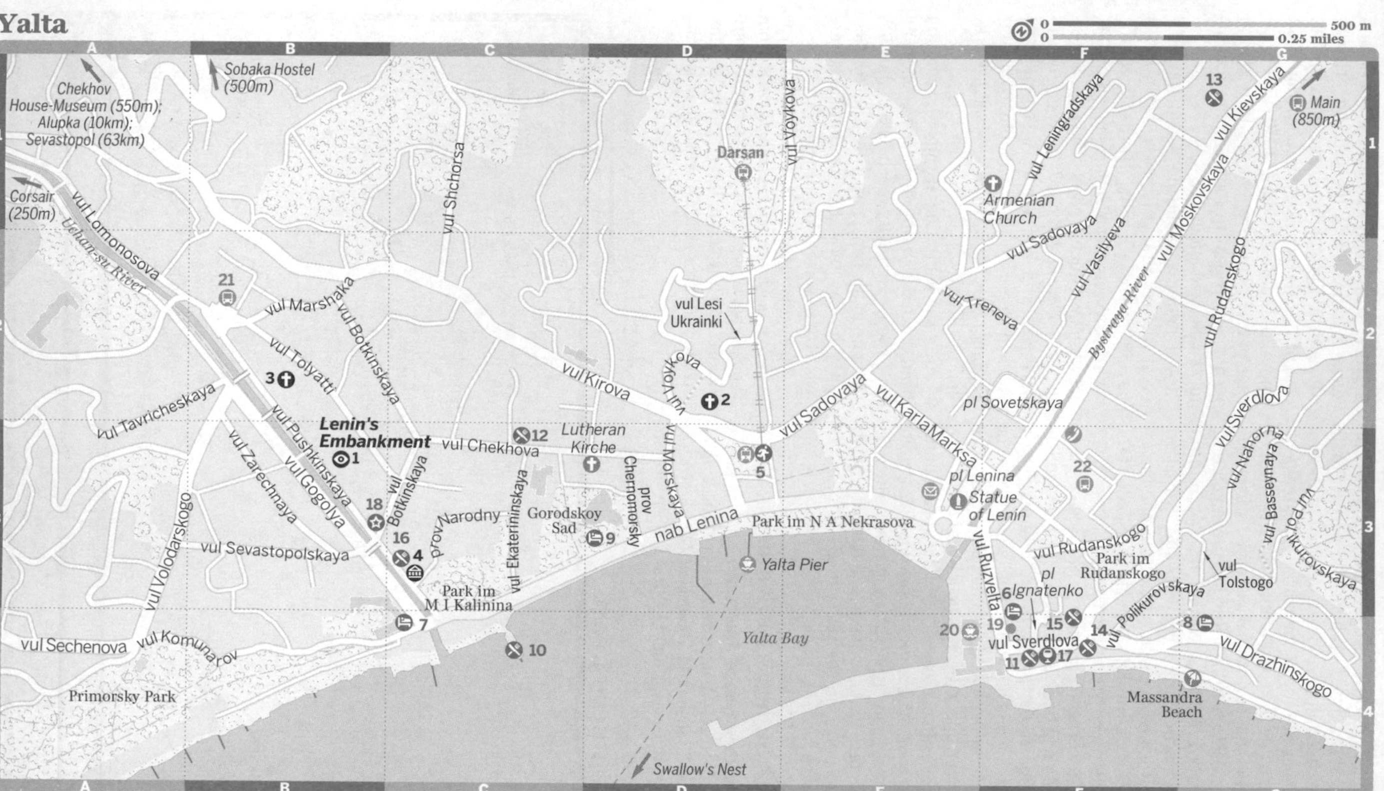
0 500 m
0 0.25 miles
A
B
C
D
E
F
G
1
2
3
4
Chekhov House-Museum (550m); Alupka (10km); Sevastopol (63km)
Sobaka Hostel (500m)
Corsair (250m)
vul Lomonosova
Uchan-su River
21
vul Marshaka
vul Botkinskaya
vul Tolyatti
3
vul Tavricheskaya
vul Pushkinskaya
vul Zarechnaya
vul Gogolya
Lenin's Embankment
1
vul Chekhova
12
Lutheran Kirche
18
vul Botkinskaya
16
4
prov Narodny
vul Ekaterininskaya
Gorodskoy Sad
9
prov Chernomorsky
vul Morskaya
vul Volodarskogo
vul Sevastopolskaya
Park im M I Kalinina
7
10
vul Sechenova
vul Komunarov
Primorsky Park
vul Shchorsa
Darsan
vul Voykova
vul Lesi Ukrainki
vul Voykova
2
vul Kirova
5
vul Sadovaya
nab Lenina
Park im N A Nekrasova
Yalta Pier
Yalta Bay
Swallow's Nest
vul Leningradskaya
Armenian Church
vul Sadovaya
vul Vasilyeva
vul Treneva
Bystraya River
vul Moskovskaya
vul Kievskaya
13
Main (850m)
vul Rudanskogo
pl Sovetskaya
vul Karla Marksa
vul Sverdlova
vul Nahorna
vul Basseynaya
vul Polikurovskaya
22
pl Lenina
Statue of Lenin
vul Rudanskogo
Park im Rudanskogo
vul Tolstogo
pl Ignatenko
vul Ruzvelta
6
20
19
15
14
vul Polikurovskaya
8
vul Sverdlova
11
17
vul Drazhinskogo
Massandra Beach

Yalta

Top Sights
1 Lenin's Embankment ... B3

Sights
2 Alexander Nevsky Cathedral ... D2
3 Catholic Church ... B2
4 History Museum ... C3

Activities, Courses & Tours
5 Chairlift ... D3

Sleeping
6 Bristol ... F3
7 Oreanda ... C4
8 Otdykh ... G4
9 Villa Sofia ... D3

Eating
10 Apelsin ... C4
11 Belaya Dacha ... F4
12 Blinoteka ... C3
13 Central Market ... G1
14 Khutorok La Mer ... F4
Lilia ... (see 13)
15 Pelmennaya ... F4
16 Smak ... C3

Drinking & Nightlife
17 Pinta ... F4

Entertainment
18 South Cafe ... B3

Information
19 Kiyavia ... F4

Transport
20 Passenger Port ... E4
21 Spartak Cinema Bus Station ... B2
22 Veshchevoy Rynok Bus Station ... F3

★ **Lenin's Embankment** PROMENADE
(набережная имени Ленина) Everyone's favourite pastime in Yalta is walking up and down the seafront nab Lenina and the pedestrian zone along the **Uchan-su River**, where you'll find a small **History Museum** (Pushkinskaya 5A; admission 15uah; ⏲10am-5pm Wed-Sun) and a **Catholic church** (vul Pushkinskaya 25). A popular attraction here is a flimsy plastic-bucket-style **chairlift** (vul Kirova, behind nab Lenina 17; return trip 20uah; ⏲11am-5pm Apr-Sep, to 11pm Jul & Aug; cable car) that swings above the rooftops to the Darsan hill. To see **old dachas**, venture into the quiet neighbourhood along vul Botkinskaya and vul Chekhova.

Massandra Winery WINERY
(Винзавод Массандра; vul Vinodela Yegorova 9; tours with/without wine tasting 160/100uah; ⏲five tours daily) Memoirists claim that Tsar Nicholas II would always keep a flask of Massandra port hidden in his high boot during his daily **Sunny path** walks, while his wife sipped the very same drink listening to Rasputin's prophesies. The imperial court's winery is now open to visitors. On a mandatory Russian-language tour (leaving every two hours from 11am to 7pm), you get to see the tsar's wine cellars, which contain over a million dust-covered bottles, including a 1775 Spanish Jerez de la Frontera claimed to be the oldest preserved wine in the world. The tour itself might seem a little boring, if you don't understand Russian. Subsequent wine-tasting sessions are more fun, but you must have a sweet tooth to appreciate local wines. There is a shop selling bottles for collection at modest prices. To reach the winery, take *marshrutka* 40 from Veshchevoy Rynok bus station. Ask the driver to stop at Vinzavod Massandra.

Alexander Nevsky Cathedral CATHEDRAL
(vul Sadovaya 2) A beautiful piece of neo-Byzantine architecture with fantastic detailing.

Sleeping

The entire city seems to be for rent in summer. Apartments come in all shapes, from four walls and a bed for 200uah to fully furnished multi-bedroom cottages that may cost up to US$500 a night. Prices drop drastically in the low season – you can get a nice apartment in the town centre for as little as 60uah in winter. The biggest concentration of holiday houses and apartment dealers carrying signs like Жилье, Квартиры or Сдается can be found at the beginning of vul Drazhinskogo above Massandra Beach.

Yalta Apartment APARTMENT $
(☎050 970 9446; www.yaltapartment.com; apt from 300uah) English-speaking Lyudmila operates several nicely furnished flats in the heart of Yalta, at the beginning of vul Karla Marksa. Our favourite is the cheap unrefurbished Soviet-style flat with ornamental ceilings.

Corsair HOSTEL $

(Корсар; ☎099 474 2421, 063 650 9636; www.corsair-hostel.com; vul Biryukova 14; dm from 160uah, d 450uah) Instantly popular, this new hostel occupies the upper floor of a house, which belonged to the architect responsible for Livadia palace. Its large balconies and shady courtyard make it a place where you want to hang out and meet people, not just sleep. Reception staff have good info on where to eat, drink and dance your night away in Yalta.

Sobaka Hostel HOSTEL $

(Хостел Собака; ☎063 317 0056; www.sobaka-hostel.com; vul Chernova 29A; d/tw 350/120uah; @ 📶) Located in a riddle of old streets around 800m up the hill from the seafront, this year-round hostel offers two dorms and three private rooms in a three-storey new building. Clean rooms, fresh bunks, a kitchen and a washing machine make this a magnet for budget nomads. See the hostel website for directions.

Otdykh HOTEL $

(Отдых; ☎276 027; www.otdyh-yalta.ru; vul Drazhinskogo 14; standard d 700uah, r without bathroom from 350uah; ❄) Hotel 'Relaxation' was a 19th-century brothel; now it's a decent enough budget pension. Some of the bathrooms are a bit whiffy and there's some street noise, but staff speak OK English and the location is convenient.

Bristol HISTORIC HOTEL $$$

(Бристоль; ☎271 603, 271 606; http://bristol.ua/; vul Ruzvelta 10; s/d from 925/1030; ❄ 📶 🏊) Few of us ever really need more comfort than this central, three-star establishment provides. The town's oldest hotel is in a heritage-listed, 19th-century building, but its rooms have been thoughtfully renovated, many in yellow and blue hues. Throw in a good breakfast buffet and reasonable service, and your stay will usually be straightforward and uncomplicated.

Villa Sofia BOUTIQUE HOTEL $$$

(Вилла София; ☎262 525; www.villasofia.com.ua; nab Lenina 31; d from 4000uah; ❄ @ 📶) It once housed public baths built for the city by a Karaite millionaire and more recently was the studio of Soviet pop diva Sofia Rotaru (hence the current name). Now this exquisite Franco-Moorish building has been turned into a high-class boutique oasis for Yalta's richest visitors. Book well ahead as this place is almost always full.

Oreanda HOTEL $$$

(Ореанда; ☎274 250/274; www.hotel-oreanda.com; nab Lenina 35/2; s/d 1745/2020uah; ⊖ ❄ @ 🏊) The crème de la Krim is favoured by oligarchs, expense-account bunnies and others who wish their wealth to be seen. Rooms are elegant and tasteful – which is more than can be said for the hotel's casino and club. However, the rooms are also small and only superior accommodation enjoys sea views. No matter which way you look at it, this place is wildly overpriced.

Eating

Belaya Dacha INTERNATIONAL $

(Белая Дача; ☎067 147 0009; http://belayadacha.com/; vul Sverdlova 3; mains 35-50uah) Here is proof that a nice modern restaurant in Yalta doesn't have to be ridiculously expensive. Food is international with the emphasis on homegrown produce. We loved Turkish-style lamb served with pita bread. Belaya is on the upper floor of a neo-classical building at the beginning of vul Sverdlova.

Pelmennaya DUMPLINGS $

(Пельменная; ☎323 932; vul Sverdlova 8; mains 14uah) This is the best workers' cafe in town because they make your order fresh. *Varenyky, blyny* (pancakes), *borshch* and good, crisp salads all join the namesake dish of *pelmeni* (Russian dumplings).

Blinoteka PANCAKES $

(Блинотека; vul Chekhova 9; mains 40uah; ⏲9am-11pm) Cool, quiet, beige-brown-hued cafe specialising in Russia's favourite comfort food – *blyny* – filled with just about anything you might wish to find within a rolled sheet of gently fried dough. Some Crimean wines and decent coffees available, too.

Lilia CRIMEAN TATAR $

(Лилия; Central Market, vul Kiyevskaya 24; mains 20-30uah) Popular with locals, Lilia is a no-nonsense Crimean Tatar eatery in Yalta's market – located left from the entrance. A typical lunch here would consist of *lagman* (Uzbek noodle soup), *lyulya-kebab* (barrel-shaped kebabs) and *lepyoshka* – flat bread straight from the *tandyr* (tandoor) oven.

Apelsin INTERNATIONAL $$

(Апельсин; http://apelsincafe.com; nab Lenina 8; mains 85-120uah; ⏲24hr; 📶) It used to be just one 'Orange' in the park, now there are three – the best outlet has occupied a pier shaped as a Greek galley (built for a Soviet film about Argonauts). Definitely the best place for an early breakfast, when you can watch sleepy beach bums taking a hesitant morning swim. The extensive menu has a bit of everything – from standard international meat and poultry dishes to Black Sea fish and sushi. Taking pictures of hilarious seagull shadows on the tent above you is an easy way of earning a few zillion likes on Facebook.

Smak CRIMEAN TATAR **$$**
(Смак; vul Pushkinskaya 7A; mains 35-100uah) This simple open-air eatery and takeaway makes more than 10 different kinds of mouthwatering *chebureki* (10uah), an impressive array of Crimean Tatar dishes, great *shashlyks* (25uah to 30uah for 100g) and Black Sea fish – the latter about half the price of upmarket restaurants albeit of the same quality.

Khutorok La Mer UKRAINIAN **$$$**
(vul Sverdlova 9; mains 65-200uah; ⌚11am-2am; 📶) If this is a *khutorok* (a traditional Ukrainian farm), then designers must have salvaged it from the bottom of the sea. The menu is also a wild fusion of rural Ukrainian and marine themes. Nothing prevents you from ordering fried *barabulka* (surmullet) and cabbage *varenyky* at the same time. The terrace overlooks Massandra Beach.

Self-Catering

Central Market MARKET
(Центральный рынок; vul Kiyevskaya 24; ⌚10am-5pm) Definitely the prettiest market in Crimea displaying an abundance of seasonal fruit – from grapes and figs to peaches and watermelons. There are also some nice Crimean Tatar cafes in the premises.

Drinking & Nightlife

Nightclubs tend to gear towards main hotels such as Yalta-Intourist and Oreanda, but in a way all of Yalta turns into a sleazy nightclub after dark.

A LA TATAR

When in Crimea, you may often find yourself staring at a menu with a 'what the hell is it?' expression on your face. Most problematic are Crimean Tatar and Black Sea fish restaurants where people find nothing but endemic Crimean dishes they've never heard of.

Crimean Tatar cuisine is similar to Turkish, but half a century in Central Asian exile left a significant imprint. Here is the list of the most ubiquitous eats:

Cheburek (Чебурек) A fried turnover filled with minced meat and onions.

Plov (Плов) A variation of the Asian pilaf rice dish, usually with pieces of mutton, carrots and raisins.

Qashiq ash (Кашик Аш) Small, ravioli-style, meat-filled dumplings, usually served in broth.

Manty (Манты) Large Central Asian dumplings filled with minced mutton.

Sarma (Сарма) Grapevine leaves stuffed with minced meat.

Dolma (Долма) Green paprika stuffed with a mixture of minced meat and rice.

Studying the menu at a Crimean fish restaurant, you'll be confronted by two questions: which fish to choose and how it should be cooked. For the latter, you can have your fish grilled, fried or cooked in the Greek-Jewish *shkara* style, where fish and vegetables are boiled in a frying pan until most of the liquid evaporates. For the former, here are the most common types of fish.

Barabulka/sultanka (Барабулька, Султанка) Surmullet, small fish that locals often swallow whole, although the fillet is easy to separate from the bones.

Sargan (Сарган) Garfish, small needle-shaped fish rolling itself into neat-looking rings when fried.

Lufar (Луфарь) Bluefish, medium-sized fish.

Kefal (Кефаль) Mullet, the best-known Black Sea fish, mentioned in classical Odesa songs.

Katran (Катран) A small (and totally harmless!) Black Sea shark.

Kambala (Камбала) Sole.

Pinta BEER
(Пинта; www.pub-pinta.com/; vul Sverdlova 7A; ⌚9am-2am) Beer drinkers, you are not forgotten in this sweet-wine kingdom! Two Pinta pubs are strategically located on both sides of the promenade. International beer brands, such as Belgian Leffe and Czech Staropramen, are on tap. Meat dishes dominate the menu.

South Cafe BAR
(☎099 911 2225; vul Botkinskaya 28; ⌚12am-12pm) If overexposure to ex-Soviet pop music makes you feel lobotomised, here is a place to escape. DJs, sometimes accompanied with a live bass player, strive to please more sophisticated and cosmopolitan ears. As ever, the place doubles as a restaurant, so for a touch of post-Soviet kitsch it has a long sushi menu.

Information

Dozens of tourist booths line the waterfront and surrounding area, selling reasonably priced Russian-language day trips and, occasionally, maps. Remember, some attractions don't need much commentary. Many hotels can also help with information.

Black Sea Crimea (☎093 574 7393; www.blacksea-crimea.com) This UK-based operator runs an online guide to Crimea's southern coast and can help find an apartment.

Kiyavia (☎231 210; vul Ruzvelta 10) Book your air tickets here.

Post office (pl Lenina 1; ⌚7am-8pm Mon-Sat, 9am-4pm Sun)

Ukrtelekom (vul Moskovskaya 9; internet per hr 6uah) Telephone and internet centre.

Getting There & Away

BOAT

Some international cruise ships now stop here but Yalta's **Passenger Port** (Morskoy Vokzal; vul Ruzvelta 5) is largely underused. There were no regular services to other Black Sea countries at the time of publication.

BUS & TROLLEYBUS

Buses depart from Yalta's **main bus station** (vul Moskovskaya 8) to Sevastopol (26uah, two hours, every 20 minutes), Simferopol (27uah, two hours, every 15 minutes) and Sudak (24uah, four hours, seven daily). Long-distance buses go to Kyiv (270uah, 18 hours, twice daily) and Odesa (210uah, 15 hours, four daily).

Getting Around

There are several bus/*marshrutka* stations in town. You'll arrive at the main bus station, which is about 1.5km from the waterfront. From here, trolleybuses 1, 2 and 3 go down the hill along vul Kievskaya to the town centre.

Behind the main bus station, on the lower level, you'll find the buses and *marshrutky* going to the sights around Yalta, but perhaps more useful are Veshchevoy Rynok and Spartak Cinema bus stations.

There are several metered taxi firms and they're definitely cheaper for journeys within the city. **Akva-Trans Taxis** (☎067 563 0444, 231 085) is good, but you can generally find some sort of metered cab at the intersection of vul Ruzvelta and nab Lenina.

West of Yalta

☎0654

Yalta's most popular attractions are lined up like ducks in a row several kilometres west of the city. Many *marshrutka* routes (most notably 32 and 27) pass them all. From piers 7 and 8 in Yalta in summer there are eight boats daily to Alupka via Miskhor (for Ay-Petri Cable Car) and Swallow's Nest. Additional boats go to Swallow's Nest only.

Sights & Activities

Livadia Palace HISTORIC BUILDING
(Дворец Ливадия; adult/child & student 70/25uah; ⌚9am-6pm) It's not the most sumptuously furnished Crimean interior, but Livadia Palace reverberates with history. It's the site of the 1945 Yalta Conference, where dying US president Franklin Roosevelt and heat-allergic British prime minister Winston Churchill turned up to be bullied by Soviet leader Josef Stalin. While here, Churchill declared steamy Crimea 'the Riviera of Hades'. No wonder, given the high temperatures and the company he was keeping. Stalin's insistent demands to keep Poland and other swathes of Eastern Europe shaped the face of postwar Europe. Even as huge tour groups nearly trample you in a race to the overflowing souvenir shops in the furthest rooms, it's hard not to be awed by these corridors of power.

In the enormous **White Hall**, the 'Big Three' and their staff met to tacitly agree that the USSR would wield the biggest influence in Eastern Europe, in exchange for keeping out of the Mediterranean. The crucial documents, dividing Germany and ceding parts of Poland to the USSR, were signed on 11 February 1945 in the English billiard room. The most famous Yalta photograph of Churchill, Roosevelt and Stalin is hung on a wall, along with the awkward out-takes, which bring history to life.

It's upstairs, however, that Livadia's other ghosts genuinely move you (yes, even complete antimonarchists). This Italian Renaissance-style building was designed as a summer residence for Russian Tsar Nicholas II in 1911. But he and his family spent just four seasons here before their arrest by Bolshevik troops in 1917 and execution in Yekaterinburg the following year. Photos and some poignant mementos of the doomed Romanovs are still in their private apartments.

From the row of souvenir stands at the entrance, a signposted path leads to the palace's former power station (800m away), which has been transformed into an **organ hall**. In summer, concerts take place daily at 4pm and 8pm.

Marshrutka 47a from Veshchevoy Rynok bus station and *Marshrutka* 5 (3uah, summer only) from the Spartak Cinema bus station drop you right in the palace grounds. A taxi to Livadia will cost around 20uah.

Swallow's Nest HISTORIC BUILDING

(Lastochkino Gnezdo; admission 15uah; ⌚9am-9pm) Like many movie stars, Swallow's Nest is shorter in real life than it appears in pictures. This toy-town castle is a favourite subject for Crimean postcards, but it's only big enough to house an expensive and exceedingly disappointing Italian restaurant.

Instead, it's the castle's precarious perch on the sheer cliff of Cape Ay-Todor, 10km west of Yalta, that elicits a minor thrill. On the surrounding walkway, you realise that the castle actually overhangs the cliff. Although the castle looks medieval in style, it was built in 1912 for German oil magnate Baron Steingel, as a present to his mistress.

The most spectacular approach to the castle is over the water, via the ferry (adult/child 20/10uah, up to 20 daily in high season, four in October), which heads from Yalta Pier to the beach and jetty just below the Swallow's Nest.

Buses 26, 27 and 32 also pass this way, stopping directly in front of a row of souvenir stalls above the castle. Stairs, leading to the castle, are on the left side of the row.

Ay-Petri Cable Car CABLE CAR

(one way 65uah; ⌚10am-6pm, services every 20min to 7pm) On the coastal road in Mishkor, behind a little cluster of market stalls, is the cable car up the cliff of Mt Ay-Petri. It's a truly dizzying ride across the foothills and up the mountain's sheer face, during which you overlook the coast and the sea. Views from the top are stunning, while Mt Ay-Petri's dry plateau itself feels otherworldly, or at least Central Asian. There are also several nice Tatar eateries. Buses 27 and 32 shuttling between Yalta and Alupka stop here; cable cars depart every 20 minutes.

Vorontsovsky Palace PALACE

(Воронцовский дворец; Vorontsovsky dvorets; adult/student 70/35uah; ⌚9am-8pm May-Sep, to 4pm Oct-Apr) Crimea's most exotic palace-park complex is wedged between the coast and Mt Ay-Petri, in a stunning setting 16km west of Yalta at Alupka. The palace was designed by English architects for the English-educated Count Mikhail Vorontsov, the immensely rich regional governor, and it's a bizarre combination of Scottish castle on its landward side and Arabic-Asian fantasy on its seaward side. Its towers are said to repeat the contours of the Ay-Petri plateau looming above it. Vorontsov brought serfs from his estates all over Russia to build the palace and park in 1828 to 1846. A century later Winston Churchill stayed here during the 1945 Yalta Conference.

Tours take you firstly into the palace's luxurious interior, which includes an imitation Wedgwood 'blue room', an English-style dining hall and an indoor conservatory. However, the best views are from the lush gardens behind the palace, where six marble lions flank the staircase framed against the backdrop of Mt Ay-Petri. Churchill joked that one of the lions looked like him – minus the trademark cigar.

Bus 32 from Yalta's Veshchevoy Rynok bus station and bus 27 from Yalta's main bus station shuttle back and forth to Alupka (7uah).

Sunny Path WALKING

(Солнечная тропа) Starting in Livadia Palace's lush coastal gardens, this scenic trail was built on the recommendation of Tsar Nicholas II's doctor, who believed that regular outdoor exercise would improve the royal family's tuberculosis. The tsar typically walked the route with a rifle and in full soldier's gear, his adjutants following him at a respectful distance. The trail stretches for nearly 7km to Rozy Lyuksemburg

FIT FOR A TSAR

Livadia and Vorontsovsky Palaces are the only easily accessible aristocratic estates on Crimea's southern coast, but there are at least a dozen more. They were converted into Soviet-styled sanatoriums, which are hard to visit unless you've booked your stay there with a local tour agency. But you can check yourself into at least one of them. Well, almost. A short walk from the Lastochkino Gnezdo bus stop in the direction of Yalta, **Kichkine** (☎099 205 4000; www.hotel-kickine.ru; d with/without sea view from 990/840uah; ❄ 🏊) is the former cliff-top residence of tsar's nephew, Grand Duke Dmitry Romanov. Unfortunately, you can visit but not stay at the Mauritanian-styled palace. Accommodation is in a modern building, but the spruced-up palace park is all yours. A pool on the cliff edge is the highlight.

About 500m in the opposite direction, **Sanatorium Dnepr** (☎0654-247 230; http://dnepryalta.com; Alupkinskoye shosse 13, Gaspra-2; d from 1230uah) occupies the former Harax estate of Grand Duke Georgy Romanov. Here you can actually get a (very bland) room at the grand duke's Scottish-style house. For 20uah it's possible to walk around the estate and use the relatively uncrowded beach, reached by an elevator – quite an amazing feat of Soviet engineering constructed by experts from the Moscow metro.

Sanatorium in Miskhor. From there, you can catch bus 26 either further to Alupka or back to Yalta. Shortly before the end of the trail, there is a turn-off to **Gaspra/Miskhor** and Ay-Petri Cable Car station. Although the trail is generally well signposted, some stretches are disturbed by new development. If you lose it, keep walking in the same direction and you'll find the trail again.

Uchansu Waterfall to Grand Canyon

Heading northwest from Yalta, bus 30 from the main bus station takes you within walking distance of two beauty spots in the mountains off the Bakhchysaray road. From the Vodopad (Waterfall) stop about 11km out, you can walk to a platform (20uah) beside the 100m-high **Uchansu Waterfall**. From the Karagol stop, 3km further up the road, a track leads to forest-ringed **Lake Karagol**. Both spots have a restaurant.

Continuing past the Karagol stop by car, the road winds spectacularly up to the top of the range 13km on; the summit of **Mt Ay-Petri** (1233m) sits to the left. This route, and several others up Mt Ay-Petri, are ideal for **mountain biking** (for more details, see www.mountainbiking.velocrimea.com).

On the inland side of the range is Crimea's so-called Grand Canyon, **Bolshoy Kanyon** – not very big, really, but a pleasant enough walk. There are several tourist lodges in nearby **Sokoline**, which can only be reached by taxi from either Yalta or Bakhchysaray – buses are not allowed on this derelict road.

East of Yalta

☎0654

Sights

Massandra Palace PALACE

(Дворец Массандра; Dvorets Massandra; ☎321 728; adult/student 70/35uah; ⏰10.30am-6pm Tue-Sun May-Oct, to 3.30pm Nov-Apr) A cutesy hunting lodge built to resemble a French chateau, the turreted palace was completed by Tsar Alexander III in 1889. It's better known, however, for what it became: Stalin's summer *dacha*.

The restored palace contains paintings and antique furniture, although the surrounding parkland is probably more beautiful. Outside there are sphinxes with female heads guarding a pretty pond with water lilies and an Art Nouveau power-station building.

The palace is best visited by taxi (30uah). Otherwise, take trolleybus 2 or 3, heading uphill opposite the Yalta main bus station and ask the driver to drop you at the turn-off to the palace. Cross the road (carefully!) and walk uphill for about 20 minutes.

Nikitsky Botanic Gardens PARK

(Никитский Ботанический Сад; adult/child & student 30/15uah; ⏰8am-6pm) These gardens let you sample a wide range of the world's flora, just wandering around the 3 sq km of their hillside (and seaside) grounds. Founded under the order of the tsar in 1812, they were designed by British gardener Christian Stephen to collect and then disseminate the planet's species throughout Russia. Today 'Nikita', as they're nicknamed, house up to 28,000 species, including olive trees and roses, cacti, ancient yews and pistachios. An on-site cafe only improves the experience.

From Yalta's Veshchevoy Rynok bus station take bus 29 or 34 to the Upper Gate bus stop. For a pleasant tour, boats also sail from the Yalta waterfront to the gardens. Walk to the right of the entrance taking in the bamboo grove and the rosarium then follow the steps to the lower and older part of the park. There are several refreshment stalls on the premises.

Gurzuf Гурзуф

Gurzuf's steep, winding streets and old wooden houses, backed by Mt Roman-Kosh (1543m), were traditionally a magnet for artists and writers. Today they're a site for more inquisitive travellers. The village, 18km northeast of Yalta, is built around a picturesque bay with the rocky Genovese Cliff (Skala Dzhenevez) at its eastern end. Mt Ayu-Dag (Bear Mountain or Gora Medved; 565m) looms along the coast to the east, protruding into the sea.

Overhanging wooden balconies, a few cafes and the odd shop adorn the curving, picturesque main street.

Sights

Gurzuf Park ARISTOCRATIC ESTATE

Two local recreational dinosaurs, sanatoriums Gurzufsky and Pushkino, occupy what used to be the *dacha* of the Duc de Richelieu, governor of Odesa (1803–14). The word *'dacha'* is a serious understatement, especially if you compare it with Chekhov's modest dwelling in Gurzuf. It really is a large coastal estate with a vast subtropical park and palatial buildings, including the one housing **Pushkin in Crimea Museum** (inside Pushkino Sanatorium; 11am-5pm). The exiled Russian poet stayed here after being rescued by Governor Rayevsky from the life of misery in what is now Dnipropetrovsk. By all accounts, he had a great time trekking in the mountains and courting all three of his host's daughters. You can visit the estate on tours of the museum that take place every hour on the hour between 11am and 5pm. Tickets are sold at the booth located under a blue bridge connecting the park and the beach. Tours begin at the gates 100m away.

Chekhov's Dacha MUSEUM

(Дача Чехова; vul Chekhova 22; adult/student 20/10uah; 9am-7pm) Tired of being a local celebrity in Yalta, Chekhov sought refuge in this little Tatar farmhouse tucked in a solitary cove under the Genovese Cliff. The melancholy of this place inspired him to create one of his best plays – *The Three Sisters*. There is nothing much to see apart from the original furniture and photos of actors playing *The Seagull* and *Uncle Vanya,* so sit or lie back on the rocky beach and Chekhov's muse might decide to pay you a visit.

Sleeping & Eating

Hotel Marina HOTEL $$

(Марина; 067 620 4419, 067 654 3291; www.hotel-marina.crimea.ua; vul Leningradskaya 68A; polulyusk 700uah, lyuks 900uah;) A reasonable distance from Gurzuf Beach, on the way to the Artek children's camp, Marina has large and airy *lyuks* (luxury) rooms that come with balconies and a sea view. The slightly cramped *polulyuks* (standard rooms) face the mountains.

Motel Bogema PENSION $$

(Богема; 363 802, 095 526 0788; www.bogema.crimea.com; vul Leningradskaya 9; economy d from 300uah, standard from 700uah;) The Motel Bogema features large, bland rooms with linoleum on the floor and an odd choice of furniture. Standard rooms come with air-con and sea view. Economy rooms have fans and face the square.

Meraba TATAR, ITALIAN $$

(Мераба; nab Pushkina; mains 70-150uah; 11am-11pm) A combination of Crimean Tatar and Italian on the menu at this excellent restaurant is an apt representation of Gurzuf, a place where these two peoples rubbed shoulders for centuries. Black Sea fish is also available. To wash it down, try the *makhsma* (a tonic drink made from wheat).

Getting There & Away

Bus 31 (every 30 to 45 minutes) links Gurzuf with Yalta's main bus station. There are also buses for Alushta (half-hourly). In summer there are boats from Yalta and Alushta.

Alushta Алушта

06560

Dusty and crowded, Alushta is the second-largest resort on the southern coast, but lacks a hint of Yalta's elegance. In fact, it epitomises all the worst things about post-Soviet recreation. Beaches are dumpy and hotels are laughably overpriced. Perhaps the only reason to visit is an excellent hostel, which can serve as a base for exploring Crimean mountains.

Sleeping

KRM Hostel HOSTEL **$$**
(063 692 79 90; www.krm-tour.com; vul Oktyabrskaya 4; dm 130uah, d 500-600uah) Run by a major adventure tourism operator, which primarily caters to ex-Soviet tourists, this is an atypically large and modern hostel with a rooftop lounge zone, dorms dedicated to Western pop idols, and festivities enhanced by regular live concerts and DJ sets. Films are also screened.

Getting There & Away

Alushta lies on the Simferopol–Yalta trolleybus route, but buses are more convenient. There are services to Simferopol (20uah, every 15 minutes) and Yalta (15uah, every 15 minutes). Buses also ply the beautiful winding coastal road to Sudak (25uah, every hour).

Around Alushta

Although the following natural attractions are closest to Alushta, they can also be visited from Yalta (on organised tours) or Simferopol (if hiking from the Simferopol–Alushta road).

Sights

Mt Demerdzhi MOUNTAIN
(Гора Демерджи) The **Valley of the Ghosts** under Mt Demerdzhi (1356m) contains some stunning rock formations created by the wind erosion of sandstone. The freaky pillars have vaguely human features and are certainly memorable. The nearby village of **Luchistoye** (Лучистое) has a couple of lodges boasting spectacular views of the coast below. The friendly young people who own **Dolina Prívideny Lodge** (067 115 8614, 067 945 5058; http://demergi.com/; vul Severnaya 11, Luchistoye; beds per person from 60uah) offer inexpensive mountain treks varying in length, including a two-day trek to their other base on Karabi-Yayla plateau in eastern Crimea.

Luchistoye, from where you can hike to the Valley of the Ghosts, can be accessed from Alushta bus station by *marshrutka* (2uah, every 40 minutes). A taxi from Alushta should cost around 60uah. You can also walk from the Luchistoye bus station on the Simferopol–Yalta road. Travelling from Simferopol it is after Angarsky Pass – get off when the sea comes into view.

Two other options include taking an organised **mountain-bike tour** (www.mt.crimea.com) or booking an organised tour from a stall in Yalta.

Mt Chatyr-Dag MOUNTAIN
(Чатир-Даг) Mt Chatyr-Dag (1527m) lies west of the Alushta–Simferopol road and is renowned for the numerous caves that lie beneath it. The most famous are the **Mramornaya Cave** (Marble Cave; 1hr tour 50uah) and the **Eminé-Ba'ir-Khosar** (Well of Maiden Eminé; 1hr tour 50uah). They're not world-beating, but maybe are worth seeing if you're staying longer in Crimea.

Mramornaya Cave is long and shallow (68m deep and nearly 2km long) and full of strangely shaped stalactites and stalagmites, nicknamed after various animals, objects, fairy-tale characters and international buildings, such as the Leaning Tower of Pisa.

Eminé-Ba'ir-Khosar spirals down to 120m, with jade-like stalagmites, crystal flowers and a lake. According to legend, Eminé threw herself to the bottom of the cave after her lover was killed by her father's family.

Unless you're hiking in the region, the simplest way to reach the caves is via a day trip from one of the tour stalls in Yalta (95uah). 'Extreme' tours of the lower level of the Mramornaya Cave (three hours) are organised by Onyx Tour (p255).

EASTERN CRIMEA

Sudak Судак

06566 / POP 14,500

As an important stop on the Silk Route from China, Sudak was a major and well-defended trading centre run by the Genovese. Its central claim to fame is the fortress that survives from that era, but that's not quite all in this overcrowded resort. Just a few kilometres away lie the popular beaches of Novy Svit.

Sights & Activities

Genovese Fortress MEDIEVAL CASTLE
(Генуэзская крепость; adult/child 80/50uah, photo/video 10uah; 9am-10pm Jun-Sep, to 5pm Oct-May) Its vertiginous location is one of

the major appeals of Sudak's fortress. This once-impregnable complex is perched on a massive seaside cliff, and in true Ukrainian fashion you're allowed to clamber all over it, at times perhaps unsafely.

Built during the 14th and 15th centuries, the fortress still cuts a magnificent silhouette. The remains of its crenulated walls (6m high and 2m thick) extend for 2km, encircling more than 30 hectares of dry, sloping terrain.

Ten original towers remain, most of them bearing the grand-sounding names of Genovese nobles who ruled the city: Francesco di Camilla or Cigallo Corrado, for instance. Open for visitors are the sea-facing **Consul's Tower** and **13th-century temple**. Originally a mosque, it was at different times used by Italian Catholics, German Lutherans and Russian Orthodox Christians.

Every summer the fortress plays host to the medieval festival **Genovese Helmet** (http://festival-sudak.com), held on set days between mid-July and the end of August, where you can watch actors dressed as knights fight with swords or 'storm' the fortress on horseback. Stalls offer blacksmithing, crafts from the Middle Ages and, erm, AK-47 shooting.

Sleeping & Eating

Pretty much every room and house in the city is for rent in summer. You'll find yourself a bed for 60uah, but expect to pay 300uah to 400uah for a hotel-quality room with hot water during high season. There is a cluster of pensions on vul Morskaya and nearby streets that skirt the fortress hill. Cheaper accommodation is found along vul Ayvazovskogo and elsewhere around town.

Solnechny Zamok GUESTHOUSE **$$**
(Солнечный замок; http://sunny-castle.info; prov Kolkhozny 11; r 180-740uah) We'd stay in this tiny cute microcosm for the rest of our lives. Hidden from the street, a tiny Oriental garden with a mountain view is surrounded by tastefully decorated cottages. There is a common kitchen and the owner does his best (even though he speaks no English) to organise your life in hectic Sudak, advising on uncrowded beaches and cheap eateries. Take a taxi as it's hard to find.

Hotel Bastion HOTEL **$$**
(Бастион; 223 88, 945 24; www.hotel-bastion.info; vul Ushakova 3 & vul Morskaya 3B; s/d from 430/505uah;) Spread across five buildings below the fortress, with excellent amenities and prices targeted at differing budgets, this hotel is often fully booked, so plan ahead. Relatively tasteful modern rooms join an alfresco restaurant, outdoor heated pool and jet skis for rent.

Perchem HOTEL **$$**
(Перчем; 067 283 0607, 099 756 4710; http://sudak-perchem.com; shosse Tutistov, kvartal Perchemny 13; r from 720uah;) Designed to resemble a Turkish caravanserai, this Tatar-run establishment stands behind Perchem (Sugarloaf) mountain, on the road leading to the Genovese Fortress. There is a large outdoor pool, which comes as a blessing considering the overcrowding on the beach.

Kunesh GUESTHOUSE **$$**
(Кунеш; 095 358 2517, 099 084 4416; http://kunesh.at.ua; vul Yuzhnoberezhnaya 86; r from 500uah;) This place is good value for money and popular with foreign travellers, largely because of the friendly English-speaking host Elzara. You may not find the street on a map, but it is located on an unpaved street leading inland behind Sudak's aquapark, about a 10 minute walk from the beach.

Tok Gorizont RESORT **$$**
(ТОК Горизонт; 223 78, 211 79; www.tokgorizont.com.ua; vul Turistov 8; s/d from 320/620uah;) This large Soviet *pansionat* (resort) is undergoing a slow transition to normality, but it is still far from modern standards. Rooms look a little Soviet, but the furniture and bathroom equipment are new. Breakfasts are heavy on greasy main courses, so don't expect any muesli. But sea-facing rooms come with an excellent view of the fortress.

Arzy TATAR, INTERNATIONAL **$**
(Арзы; vul Morskaya 5; mains 50-80 uah; 24hr) This Tatar-run place with wicker chairs on a beachside terrace is popular for its relaxed, almost Goan ambience and stunning views of the illuminated fortress in the evening. Italian and Japanese food on the menu are hilariously inauthentic, but all the Crimean Tatar dishes are competently cooked and delicious.

Getting There & Away

There are frequent bus services to both Simferopol (32uah, 1¾ hours, every 15 minutes) and Feodosiya (20uah, 1½ to 1¾ hours, every 15 minutes) via Koktebel (15uah, one hour). There are also four daily buses going along the coastal road to Yalta (32uah, three hours).

Getting Around

The town centre is 1.2km south of the bus station. It's another few hundred metres ahead to the beachfront *naberezhnaya* (promenade) and a further 2km right (west) to the fortress. At the bus station, *marshrutky* bound for the town centre stop under the sign Город, for Novy Svit – Novy Svit, for Dachne – Дачное. All Novy Svit buses pass the town centre and the fortress on the way.

Around Sudak

Novy Svit — Новий Світ

06566

Its name meaning New World, the beautiful bay of Novy Svit used to be the realm of Prince Lev Golitsyn – an idealistic aristocrat turned winemaker. Obsessed with changing Russian drinking culture, he spent all his fortune selling wine and sparkling wine at cheaper prices than vodka. This was a noble but rather hopeless cause – innovative drinkers soon realised they could achieve stunning results by mixing champagne with vodka. The resulting killer-cocktail became known as Northern Lights.

Financially broke, Golitsyn was rescued by Tsar Nicholas II, who appointed him the royal winemaker and commissioned him to build the Massandra winery.

Today buses and *marshrutky* wind regularly across the slightly hairy but breathtakingly gorgeous mountain road connecting Sudak with this popular satellite. Each bus is jam-packed with day-trippers coming to do Golitsyn's favourite walk and sample some bubbly from his winery.

Activities

Golitsyn's Path WALKING

(Тропа Голицына; Tropa Golitsyna; admission 30uah) Starting at the far (western) end of the beach, this trail takes you on a picturesque, if rather slippery, seaside walk through Novy Svit Botanic Reserve. Winding around the base of Mt Orel, the path leads to a seaside grotto where local Prince Golitsyn used to hold high-society parties. You can plunge into the crystal-clear water of the Blue Bay before ascending the headland for the view of Tsar's Beach, once favoured by Nicholas II. It is, however, off-limits to visitors (what else can you expect from such a VIP beach?) and there is a surly police officer to enforce this arrangement.

Novy Svet Winery WINERY

(www.nsvet.com.ua; ul Golitsyna 21; tour & tasting 110uah; at least five tours per day) As in Massandra, the tour through the winery's museum may seem boring if you don't understand Russian (and even if you do), but champagne sampling sessions in the chilly wine cellar, accompanied by live classical music and a hilariously sombre presentation, are fun. Since five small glasses of the bubbly that you get during the sampling session seem extremely insufficient to some visitors, you can buy bottles in the local shop and open them right in front of the winery. Here is your chance to have a tipple with total strangers.

Sleeping

As everywhere in Crimea, if you speak basic Russian you can shop around and find a much better deal than any hotel can offer. Rooms for rent are all over the place.

Knyaz Golitsyn LUXURY **$$$**

(Князь Голицын; Prince Golitsyn; 33359, 050 583 5949; www.hotel-golitsyn.com; vul Lva Golitsyna 5; d mountain view/sea view 1000/1100uah;) A chalet-styled building under a red-tiled roof set on the Sudak road away from the sea, this brand-new luxury hotel has large, tastefully decorated rooms, cool, marble-clad corridors and a wonderful garden with gazebos.

Dachne — Дачне

Lying in the foothills of green mountains, 7km inland from Sudak, Dachne is a sprawling village of fruit gardens and many old wells with the clearest and tastiest mountain water. The population is mixed – Russian, Ukrainian and Crimean Tatar. Several households here are united in a rural tourism project, which gives a totally different perspective on life in Crimea.

The deal is that you can stay in one of the Russian-Ukrainian households, which provide decent and cheap accommodation in relatively modern village houses, while more traditional Crimean Tatar households offer tons of delicious food as well as cooking and handicrafts classes. All of this can be organised through the **Dachne Information Centre** (050 646 9576,

050 761 8122, 095 143 0288; vul Mindalnaya 1; ⌚8am-5pm), run by a hyper-enthusiastic librarian.

The highlight is **the home of Ayshe-abla** (☎095 440 5416), an octogenarian Crimean Tatar weaver, who returned from a 50-year exile to her native village she knows as Taraqtash and, atypically, managed to buy her family's house from Ukrainians who lived there. She spends all day working at her loom next to the 100-year-old adobe house, under a mulberry tree her grandfather had planted. You can arrange a visit either directly or through the information centre. If you ask really nicely, it's possible to stay with them, too.

To get to Dachne, take *marshrutka* 6 from Sudak's town centre or bus station.

Cape Meganom — Мис Мегамон

Holiday-makers flood Sudak's beach like a pack of suicidal lemmings, so more intrepid travellers escape to the clean and less crowded beaches around Cape Meganom, east of the town. Camping is allowed here for a small fee (typically 15uah per day). The easiest beach to access is also called Meganom. Take a bus bound for Solnechnaya Dolina (Солнечная долина) from Sudak's bus station (every 20 minutes) and get off at Kapsel stop, then walk 500m towards the sea. More distant beaches offer more elbow room, while the crowd becomes a bit esoteric. Meganom attracts a lot of alternative and New Age types.

Koktebel — Коктебель

☎06562 / POP 2500

A merry band of Russian bohemians led by the gregarious bearded artist Maximilian Voloshin descended in the 1900s on what was then a small and remote village of Bulgarian refugees, transforming it into a favourite playground for the intelligentsia. This boho atmosphere lingered for a century, but the tide of wild capitalism has largely washed it away. Still, with two major jazz festivals, a couple of good musical venues and a naturist beach on the eastern side of the bay, Koktebel is not your average Crimean resort town, even though the majority of Ukrainian and Russian youngsters who flood it in summer are so very mainstream and provincial.

Sights & Activities

Voloshin's House — MUSEUM

(Дом Волошина; www.voloshin.crimea.ua; adult/student 35/15uah; ⌚10am-5.30pm Tue-Sun) Poet Maximilian Voloshin came to live on this bay beneath the anthropomorphic shapes of the Kara-Dag mountains (which his friends claimed looked like him), and his home turned into a meeting place for intellectuals of all professions and political convictions. He stayed here even while the Civil War was raging in Crimea, 'waiting for the Reds to shoot me for being White, or for the Whites to hang me for being Red', as he noted in a letter.

Aquapark — WATER PARK

(Аквапарк; adult/child from 240/140uah; ⌚10am-8pm) Max Voloshin's big jaw would drop at seeing this symbol of Koktebel's commercialisation, but heck – this is a ruddy great aquapark with multicoloured slides like liquorice and many pools.

Festivals & Events

Every September, when students leave and the village reverts to being the relaxing idyll it once was, it hosts the **Koktebel International Jazz Festival** (http://jazz.koktebel.info), which is attended by major musicians from Eastern Europe and beyond. Jazz is in the name, but there is a strong rock and world music element.

Sleeping

Most people stay in rooms for rent and numerous private pensions that come in all shapes and sizes. Look for Есть свободные номера (Rooms available) signs. None of these places have receptions as such, so you normally need to dial a mobile number posted at the entrance. That's obviously bad news for those who don't speak Russian.

There are several overpriced hotels, but one good-value establishment is **Talisman Hotel** (☎244 80/76; vul Lenina 97; high season s/d from $56, superior d $70, winter s/d $12/24, superior d $36), across the road from the bus station.

Dacha Koktebelica — GUESTHOUSE $

(Дача Коктебелика; ☎050 535 7173, 095 216 9118; www.koktebelika.com; prov Klubny 16; d from 160uah; ❄📶) This one is the most peculiar black sheep in Crimea's dull guesthouse family. Accommodation is in tube-shaped mobile houses, once used by oilers in

SOARING ABOVE CRIMEA

The Soviet aviation and aerospace industries were born in the hills outside Koktebel, and paragliders still come here to enjoy the thermal uplifts where sea breezes meet the sun-drenched, long mountain ridges and steppes beyond. In the 1920s and '30s aircraft designers Sergey Korolyov (father of the Soviet space program), Sergey Ilyushin and Oleg Antonov tested gliders on the 180m tall, 6km-long ridge of Mt Klementyeva (Uzun-Syrt in Tatar). Koktebel was initially called Planerskoye because of this (*planer* meaning 'glider' in Russian).

Today there are still paragliding, hang-gliding and speed-flying schools up here, complete with a landing strip, museum, accommodation and competitions. If you speak Russian, stalls in Feodosiya and Koktebel sell paragliding (about 250uah), hang-gliding (350uah to 800uah) and microlight (400uah) flights, or you can contact the paragliding school **Breeze** (www.paragliding.crimea.ua/; ⏲ Apr-Nov). The mountain ridge is off the Feodosiya–Koktebel road, signposted полеты.

For flights elsewhere in Crimea with an English-speaking guide, visit www.paragliding-crimea.com.

Siberia, which a young polyglot couple from Simferopol installed in their garden in the foothills of Karadag. It's quite amazing how they keep a cool temperature during the hottest day. We also like the computerised solar-battery powered garden shower. Away from the mad crowds, the place is 20 minutes' walk or a quick bycicle ride from the beach. The owners can hook you up with mountain trek operators. Phone to arrange a pickup, or you'll never find it.

Eating

You will not get hungry in Koktebel. *Shashlyks,* Tatar pastry, fruit and *churchkhelis* (nut-based sweets) will almost jump into your mouth from the myriad food stands that line the beachfront. There are dozens of modern *stolovaya* (Russian-style self-service canteens) and cheap restaurants, but you will be hard-pressed to find anything more sophisticated.

Bogema INTERNATIONAL **$$**
(Богема; vul Lenina 110; mains 60-100uah) This unpretentious place hidden behind Pansionat Goluboy Zaliv serves great lamb and seafood dishes, but it is perhaps better known as a music (primarily jazz) venue, with concerts taking place almost every evening. The place is associated with Enver Izmaylov, a Crimean Tatar virtuoso guitarist of international fame, who plays here once in a while.

Getting There & Around

Koktebel's bus station is at the far end of vul Desantnikov – the main drag leading to the beach. From here you can catch a bus to Simferopol (40uah, two hours, half-hourly), Sudak (15uah, one hour, half-hourly), Feodosiya (7uah, 40 minutes, half-hourly) and Kurortne/Kara-Dag Nature Reseve bio-station (5uah, every 20 minutes).

Around Koktebel

Kurortne Курортне

☎06562

Kurortne is one of those rare places in Crimea where you can still relax on a relatively uncrowded beach. Besides, it is the gateway to the striking volcanic formations of Kara-Dag Nature Reserve.

Another local attraction is the nearby **Lisya Bukhta** (Fox Bay). For the full libertarian experience, you can pitch a tent at this long, sandy beach about a 2.5km walk west of Kurortne. Clothing is optional here and the place is isolated. There are several Tatar beach restaurants with a Jamaican twist.

The easiest way to reach Kurortne is on a биостанция (bio-station) *marshrutka.* These travel from the central Feodosiya bus station via Koktebel to central Kurortne (13.50uah), before continuing to the Kara-Dag Nature Reserve. Travelling from Sudak, get off at Shchebetovka on the Sudak–Feodosiya road, then change for the bio-station *marshrutka.*

Sleeping & Eating

Seit-Nebi Baza Turist CAMPGROUND **$**
(Турбаза Сеит-Неби; ☎050 827 7064, 26 235; www.nebi-hotel.com; vul Pionerskaya 14; d without breakfast from 280uah; ❄) Slightly incongru-

ous low-rise buildings surround the grass-covered courtyard of this Tatar-run establishment. Rooms are clean, though unremarkable. There is a large, cheap cafeteria on the premises.

Kolybel Koktebelya HOTEL **$$$**
(Колыбель Коктебеля; ☎067 541 3838; www.kolibel-koktebelya.com; vul Morskaya 2; d/ste from 800/1200uah; ❄ ✱) Opened in 2009, this is as modern as it gets in Crimea. Large rooms with eye-catching, red-and-black furniture are in two-floor cottages with glassy front walls that you can open to catch the breeze at night, if you prefer it to the air-con.

Café Rushana CRIMEAN TATAR **$$**
(Кафе Рушана; vul Morskaya 1; mains 50-80uah) An upmarket beachside restaurant with wall carpets, tablecloths and armchairs covered in Oriental floral ornaments. A creative take on traditional Central Asian food.

Kara-Dag Nature Reserve Природний заповідник Кара-Даг

☎06562

The Kara-Dag Nature Reserve is a true Jurassic Park. Its dramatic landscape is the work of an extinct volcano (Kara-Dag, or 'Black Mountain' in Tatar) that spewed lava and debris over land and sea during the Jurassic period. Over millennia, the elements have moulded the volcanic rocks into striking shapes, with names like 'The Devil's Finger', 'The King and the Earth', and the most striking, 'Golden Gate' (Zolote Vorota), a freestanding arch in the sea. These all circle the 575m craggy Mt Kara-Dag.

The Kara-Dag Nature Reserve **bio-station** (☎262 87; ⏱9am-8pm Wed-Mon May-Sep) is on the outskirts of Kurortne. Anyone is free to visit the aquarium, dolphinarium and botanic gardens, but for environmental reasons you're not allowed in the main part of Kara-Dag territory without a guide.

The park administration offers several **group hikes** a day (except Tuesday), which cover 7km and last four hours (per adult/child 70/35uah).

An alternative is a **boat trip** around the Kara-Dag coast from Koktebel or Feodosiya. The three- to four-hour journey on the deck of a tug-sized ship doesn't get as up close and personal to the reserve as a hike. However, it's less strenuous and your boat does sail through the arch of the lava-formed Golden Gate. Bring your swimwear for one of the most pleasant dips in Crimea, when the boat stops for 20 to 30 minutes in a deep, clean stretch of the Black Sea. In very hot or rainy weather the Kara-Dag administration may cancel all hikes and then a boat trip will be the only option.

Tikhaya Bay Тиха бухта

Amid an astonishing, almost Mongolian, landscape lies a long sandy beach where people escape from Koktebel's maddening beat. Many pitch tents and sleep here, others come for a day or just a few gorgeous sunset hours. There is no regular transport, but it is an easy hike or dirt-track drive from Koktebel's cognac factory located on vul Yunge, on the eastern outskirts of the town. From the factory, a dirt track veers left towards Tikhaya Bay.

Feodosiya Феодосія

☎06562 / POP 72,000

Neighbourhood names like Chumka (Plague) and Quarantine are not exactly romantic, but they hark back to the city's illustrious past. Founded by the Greeks in 6th century BC under its current name, it was rebranded Kaffa by the Genovese, who took over the city in 13th century AD, turning it into a meeting point for caravans from the Orient and European merchants. Mutual interest in silk and slaves brought together people of all nationalities, notably Armenians, who left a significant imprint on the city.

Kaffa's fortress, still partly intact, protected it from plundering nomad armies but not the biological weapon used by the Mongols during one of the sieges. They started catapulting bodies of people who died from bubonic plaque, which was devastating their camp. It is believed that the fleeing Genovese subsequently brought the disease to Europe, which led to the worst epidemics in the continent's history.

Imperial Russians built opulent sea-facing palazzos that they modestly called *dachas*. Some of them survived the Soviet period and still soar above the myriad tacky souvenir stands and fast-food joints, which look like flotsam washed ashore by a recent storm, and seem destined to be swept away by the next one.

Sights

The city centre's tiny axis, vul Galereynaya, abuts the sea, with the promenade beginning on your left. For Sub-Sarkis Church and the Genovese Citadel, walk right past the fenced-off port.

Ayvazovsky Gallery ART MUSEUM
(Галерея Айвазовского; vul Galereynaya 2; adult/student 60/30uah; 9.30am-8pm Thu-Mon, to 1pm Tue) Born in 1817, the most celebrated son of Feodosiya and of its Armenian community, Ivan Ayvazovsky became the official painter of the Russian Navy, assigned with recording all of its victories and defeats on canvas. Mesmerised by the sea, he seemed obsessed with cataloguing all of its conditions. During his long and happy life Ayvazovsky produced thousands of paintings, which is why you can hardly find an ex-Soviet museum that doesn't own at least a couple of them.

Prospekt Ayvazovskogo PROMENADE
(Проспект Айвазовского) With the cacophony of tourist agents touting their services through loudspeakers, along with terrible music, junk-food smells and a train line right on the beach to complete the picture, Feodosiya's seaside promenade is not exactly relaxing. Once it was lined with opulent palazzos. Standing next to each other are **Villa Victoria** (pr Ayavazovskogo 31) and **Villa Milos** (pr Ayavazovskogo 31). But those are easily outshone by the Ottoman-style **Dacha Stamboli** (pr Ayavazovskogo 47) – an Arabesque fantasy straight out of *1001 Nights* built by a Karaite tobacco merchant.

Sub-Sarkis Church ARMENIAN
(Церковь Суб-Саркис; vul Armyanskaya 1) FREE Small and almost literally down to earth, the town's main Armenian church was built in 1363. Its walls are adorned with numerous *khachkar* – stone plaques with crosses marking historic events. Ivan Ayvazovsky got christened and married in this church. His large **tomb** is also here in the garden, almost overshadowing the ancient temple. To get there, walk west along vul Gorkogo past the ornate **Ayavazovsky fountain**, which the painter built for his fellow citizens. The church is hiding behind a small park that will appear on your right.

Genovese Citadel FORTRESS
(Генуэзская крепость) FREE Not nearly as spectacular as its Sudak counterpart, and neglected by the authorities, this is still a beautifully melancholic place where you can get away from the crowds and check out several medieval Armenian churches scattered around the premises. The fortress is in the western part of the city known as Quarantine. To reach it, walk to the end of vul Gorkogo and turn left to vul Portovaya.

Beaches

There is a good stretch of sandy beach east of town, most of it taken over by private establishments, which provide sunbeds, showers, food and night-time entertainment. To get here, take *mashrutka* 4 (4uah) from the downtown bus station.

Club 117 BEACH CLUB
(http://club117.com/; Km 117, Kerch–Feodosia road) Locals unanimously put this beach club ahead of the others for cleanliness, good service and tasty Asian-influenced food in the restaurant. It functions as a beach club by day and turns into a popular nightlife spot after sunset.

Tours

Crimeatours.com TOUR
(www.crimeatours.com; tours from 400uah per person) The owners of Rentmyflatinfeodosia.com also run day trips around Crimea geared for small, English-speaking groups.

Sleeping

Sunflower GUESTHOUSE $
(Подсолнух; 050 769 3421, 432 881; www.lidiya-hotel.com; vul Fedko 59; r from 320uah;) A budget subsidiary of the more upmarket Hotel Lidiya, Sunflower is lovely in a spartan sort of Ikea fashion, and there's a kitchen. Only its location is a wee bit inconvenient.

Roza Vetrov GUESTHOUSE $
(Роза ветров; 315 30; fiord06@mail.ru; vul Kuibisheva 28A; r incl all meals from 350uah;) Cute as a button, this private hotel's most eye-catching feature is its tiny atrium, with slit windows, oleanders, tea roses, a marble floor and a curved staircase. The seven cosy bedrooms and equally snug bathrooms are well cared for and comfortable. But low pipe pressure sometimes makes you abandon the idea of taking a shower.

Rentmyflatinfeodosia.com APARTMENT $$
(067 652 4418, 068 911 8800; www.rentmyflatinfeodosia.com; r from 480uah;) As elsewhere in Ukraine, it makes a lot of sense to rent a flat in Feodosiya, rather than get ripped off by hotels. These incredibly helpful peo-

ple – a Turkish-Latvian couple – operate three tastefully decorated flats with internet connection and lots of books. They also run Crimeatours.com.

Hotel Alye Parusa LUXURY $$
(Алые Паруса; ☎295 29; www.a-parusa.com; pr Ayvazovskogo 47B; high season s/d 690/1070uah, winter 490/750uah;) Far from the habitual post-Soviet tackiness, this is a nicely designed and professionally run top-notch hotel with friendly and very attentive staff. The sea view is complemented by that of Dacha Stamboli. There is an excellent bar-restaurant on the rooftop terrace.

U Sestry HOTEL $$
(У сестры; ☎302 35; www.sister-hotel.com.ua; vul Russkaya 2; r from 400uah;) Aqua walls and brownish furniture somehow conspire to give this humble, central hotel, which used to be the house of Ayvazovsky's sister, a vaguely Art Deco feel. Decent bathrooms too.

Hotel Lidiya HOTEL $$
(Лидия; ☎309 01, 211 12, 211 11; www.lidiya-hotel.com; vul Zemskaya 13; s/d from 520/840uah;) Rub shoulders with visiting Russian celebrities in this upmarket hotel that's still quite affordable for Western tourists. Built in 2001, its rooms are a tiny bit disappointing for the price, but the swimming pool on the 3rd floor (yes, really) is fantastic and the location is good, too.

Eating & Drinking

Mercury CRIMEAN TATAR $
(Меркурий; ☎343 83; pr Ayvazoskogo 1; mains 20-40uah) Behind the Krym Kino Teatr, this popular Tatar restaurant is just as famous for owner Sakine's ability to read your future in the grounds of your Turkish coffee as it is for its excellent cuisine. The *basturma* (pork steak) comes highly recommended and the 1kg 'Kazan kebab' (100uah) will feed four or five people.

Black & White COFFEE
(vul Zemskaya 1; ⏲10am-10pm) A tiny and friendly coffee shop on the main pedestrian street, where staff know how to make the brew and there are great desserts to come with it.

Information

Crimeatours.com (www.crimeatours.com) Offers detailed museum, restaurant and bar listings for Feodosia. Also offers tours and apartment rentals at its website www.rentmyflatinfeodosia.com.

Kiyavia (☎30 132; www.kiyavia.crimea.ua; ul Voykova 5) Buy your air tickets for onward travel through this nationwide agency.

Getting There & Away

BUS

Feodosiya has two bus stations. The main bus station, serving long-distance destinations, is 4km north of the town centre. Buses go to/from Simferopol (from 40uah, 2½ hours, every 15 minutes), Sudak (20uah, 1¾ hours, half-hourly) and Kerch (30uah, two hours, half-hourly).

There's also a downtown bus station where *marshrutky* and smaller buses leave for Koktebel (7uah), Kara-Dag Nature Reserve bio-station (10uah) and the beaches east of town.

Local bus 2, or indeed any *marshrutka* leaving from just outside the main outlying bus station (same side of the road), will take you into the town centre.

TRAIN

Rail services are less useful, although in summer there are services to Moscow and Kyiv.

Kerch Керчь

☎06561 / POP 151,000

Many people feel grateful when the holiday tsunami, which engulfs the rest of Crimea in summer, throws them on this quiet shore. A decidedly untouristy town of ramshackle low-rise buildings, Kerch is the place to chill out and dream of new frontiers. Looming across a narrow strait, the Russian coast invites a Eurasian adventure. Unfortunately, only visa holders can embark on it straight away.

Stuck out on a 100km limb from Feodosiya, Kerch is one of Ukraine's oldest cities. As the ancient Greek colony of Panticapaeum, it was the capital of the Bosporan Kingdom from the 5th to the 2nd centuries BC. Today Kerch is a mecca for archaeologists, who arrive in droves each year, hoping to unearth Greek and Scythian treasures.

Sights

Mithridates Hill HISTORIC SITE
The first thing to do in Kerch is to take the 432 stairs up the central Mithridates Hill. The view from the summit is brilliant, and on the lee side the ruins of the ancient city of **Panticapaeum** have been revealed in an ongoing archaeological dig.

Back on the central pl Lenina, check out the candy-striped **Church of St John the Baptist**. Dating back to 717, this Byzantine building is officially Ukraine's oldest surviving church.

Adzhimushkay Defence Museum CATACOMB
(tour adult/child 50/25uah; ⏲9am-5pm Tue-Sun) Catacombs in the Kerch suburb of Adzhimushkay (Аджимушкай) have been a source of construction material for the city from time immemorial. Early Christians held their clandestine services here in the 2nd century AD. When the Germans sacked Kerch in May 1942, 10,000 Soviet troops and civilians (many of them Jewish) descended into the catacombs and held them for 170 days until all of them were gassed or captured. You can relive their experience on a tour of this museum, which takes you through the unlit caverns turned by the defenders into barracks, hospitals, classrooms and cemeteries. The tour is in Russian, but the scenery speaks for itself. Take something warm to wear – it gets chilly underground. To get here, catch bus 4 for the 'Muzey' stop from the bus station.

Tsarsky Kurgan BURIAL MOUND
(☎547 13; admission 15uah; ⏲9.30am-6pm Tue-Sun) Eight hundred metres from the Adzhimushkay Defence Museum, there is a monument from a completely different epoch. This empty, 4th-century-BC burial mound is thought to be the grave of a Bosporan king. Its exterior is Scythian, but its symmetrical interior was built by the Greeks. The grass-covered mound surrounded by electric pylons is visible from the bus stop. Just walk straight in that direction along the tarmac road until you find a fairly anatomical slit in the hill – when you see it, you'll know what we mean! Once inside, look out for small crosses and the name Kosmae left on the walls by the 2nd-century AD Christians.

Melek-Chesmensky Kurgan BURIAL MOUND
(Мелек-Чесмеский Курган; bus station; admission 5uah; ⏲10.30am-6pm Tue-Sat) Hardly any bus station in the world can boast a Scythian burial mound on the premises, but there is one in Kerch. Much smaller than Tsarsky Kurgan, it was the grave of a small boy, thought to be a Bosporan prince.

TRAVEL FROM KERCH TO RUSSIA

Regular **ferries** (www.pereprava.com.ua; Port-Krym; adult/child/vehicle 37/19/270uah) travel from Port Krym near Kerch to Port Kavkaz in Russia's southern Krasnodar region. Boats take 35 minutes and leave every 1½ hours, day and night, but services can be considerably reduced in low season. EU, American, British and Australian nationals all need visas for Russia. Israelis and most South Americans don't. Customs procedure can be atrociously slow, if you travel by car. *Marshrutka* 1 gets you from Kerch's bus station to the port in about 45 minutes.

Sleeping & Eating

Meridian HOTEL $
(Меридиан; ☎615 07; avers@kerch.com.ua; cnr vul Marata 9 & vul Sverdlova; d from 330uah; ❄📶) Although far from perfect, this is easily the best choice for most Westerners. It's a hard-to-miss high-rise not too far from the town centre with plenty of modern, clean and well-priced rooms. There's also a good supermarket in the same building. Take *marshrutka* 3, 5, 6, 19 or 20 to the Bosforsky stop.

Penguin Brewery BREWERY $$
(Пивоварня Пингвин; vul Lenina 32; mains 50-90uah; ⏲10am-2am) Pop in to sample local brews that go well with the meaty Central European dishes and Black Sea fish featured on the menu. Service is so-so.

Inki Bar MEXICAN $$
(prov Kooperativny 3; mains 50-100uah) A large and happening place that serves faux-Mexican food and all kinds of alcohol.

Getting There & Around

BUS

All west-bound buses go via Feodosiya (35uah, two hours, frequent). Most of them continue to SImferopol (80uah, 4¾ hours, half-hourly). Four buses a day pass on the way to Krasnodar (120uah, 8½ hours) – the nearest large city in Russia.

MARSHRUTKA

Marshrutka 5 is the most frequent of many services between the bus station and the town centre, leaving whenever full. *Marshrutka* 16 plies just one of several routes between the bus and train stations.

TRAIN

Kerch's small train station is a lot quieter than its bus station. All regular trains are bound for Moscow via Kharkiv (120uah, 15 hours).

Eastern Ukraine
Східна Україна

POP 19.6 MILLION

Includes ➡

Best Places to Eat

- Stargorod (p212)
- Fishcafe (p224)
- Yuzovskaya Pivovarnya (p215)
- Café Myshi Blyakhera (p221)
- Sto Dorih (p208)

Best Places to Stay

- Liverpool Art Hotel (p215)
- Hotel 19 (p211)
- Hotel Cosmopolit (p211)
- Menorah Hostel (p221)

Why Go?

In many ways a continent away from the folkloric west of Ukraine, the territory east of the Dnipro is often dismissed as 'not Ukrainian enough'. But from an economic and political point of view this vast region is the country's power source. The industrial metropolises of the east have sent more than their share of presidents and prime ministers to Kyiv as well as providing both leaders of the 2004 Orange Revolution. It's also spawned most of the country's billionaires, who, when the region's mines and steel works were up for grabs in the 1990s, did much grabbing.

But Ukraine's east isn't all about slag heaps, oligarchs and high-ranking kleptocrats. It also includes places that are key to understanding Ukraine, such as the Zaporizhska Sich, Gogol's Poltava region and Unesco-listed Chernihiv. Even Ukraine's second city Kharkiv has its moments, as do dynamic Dnipropetrovsk and Donetsk, the latter possessing Eastern Europe's finest football stadium.

When to Go

Kharkiv

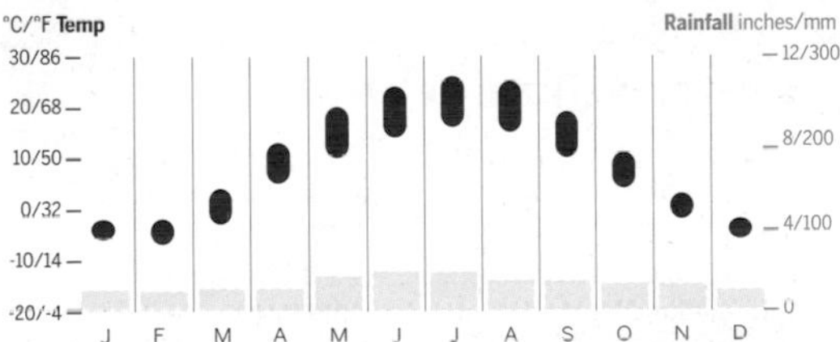

May The region is aflame with blooming lilacs and fruit trees.

Jul The heat builds in the eastern countryside. Pumpkins ripen and sunflowers bloom.

Aug Shop at the annual Sorochynska farmers' fair, made famous by local writer Gogol.

Chernihiv Чернігів

☎0462 / POP 296,000

Modestly receding into provincial obscurity for the past millennium, Chernihiv, Ukraine's most northerly city, was once a a Kyivan Rus (the first eastern Slavic state) heavyweight frequented by 11th-century royalty. The residue of those glory days is a tight cluster of churches on a green bluff in the city's historical core, now a Unesco-listed site and one of the highlights of Polissya. Otherwise, this northern outpost is laced with a slow, provincial charm, the inert

Eastern Ukraine Highlights

1 Dip in and out of ancient churches and monasteries in sleepy **Chernihiv** (p202).

2 Go full circle in pursuit of Ukrainian literary heritage on the **Gogol Circuit** (p206).

3 Don your widest trousers and grow a ponytail to visit the Cossacks on Khortytsya Island in **Zaporizhzhya** (p223).

4 Play football in the **Soledar salt mine** (p219), 300m underground.

5 Visit the pretty cave monastery burrowed into dazzling chalk cliff at **Sviatohirsk** (p218).

6 Sleep, eat and dance at the Beatles-themed alternative universe of Liverpool in **Donetsk** (p217).

7 Watch Shakhtar's home games at the technologically advanced Donbass Arena in **Donetsk** (p214).

8 Take Ukraine's fastest express train to the lively spa town of **Myrhorod** (p205).

Desna River seemingly having given up on ever meeting the Dnipro, the population still deeming foreigners worthy of a stare on the dusty streets. The town makes for an easy day trip from the capital or book ahead for a night out in the cuds and a bit of deeper exploration into this seldom-visited corner of rural Ukraine.

Sights

Dytynets FORT

(Дитинець; enter from vul Preobrazhenska) From Krasna pl it's a three-minute walk southeast along pr Myru to the old historic core, known as the Dytynets ('citadel' in old Russian). Today it's an informal park dotted with domed churches overlooking the Desna River. The highlight is the 12th-century **Boryso-Hlibsky Cathedral** (admission 15uah; 10am-6pm, 9am-5pm winter), which displays the same short, squat style as the St Paraskevy Pyatnytsi Church. The building is now a worthwhile museum where the star attraction is a pair of intricate silver **Royal Doors**, commissioned by the famous Cossack leader Ivan Mazepa. An oil painting at the start of the exhibition shows the extent of the Dytynets at its zenith.

The building next to the cathedral is the 18th-century **collegium** (10am-6pm), built in a style known as Ukrainian baroque. It houses interesting changing exhibitions.

Nearby is the **Spaso-Preobrazhensky Cathedral** (Transfiguration of the Saviour; 1017), with its two distinctive, missile-like corner bell towers. Within its dark interior are the tombs of several members of the Kyivan Rus royalty, including the younger brother of Yaroslav the Wise. Lining the southwestern edge of the Dytynets is a row of 18th-century **cannons**, from where you get a prime view of the five sparkling golden domes of **St Catherine's Church** in the immediate foreground.

At the southern tip of the Dytynets stands a **Shevchenko monument**, or should that be 'sits' as this one has an unusually young Shevvy chilling gloomily on a park bench, momentarily distracted from his view of the sluggish river below.

Krasna Ploshcha SQUARE

Life in Chernihiv revolves around the huge Krasna pl (Red Sq). As with its Moscow namesake, there is nothing remotely bolshie in the word 'red', which simply meant 'beautiful' in old Slavonic. In the park extending southeast of the square along vul Shevchenko rises the **St Paraskevy Pyatnytsi Church**, named after the patroness of the large outdoor market that once occupied Krasna pl. Despite its sturdy, fortress-like appearance, only about one-third of the church survived WWII. With its imposing brick wall and slender single cupola, it reflects the style that was popular when it was built in the 12th century.

Antoniy Caves, Illynsky Church & Trinity Monastery CAVE, MONASTERY

(bell tower admission 5uah; bell tower 10am-7.30pm) About 2km southwest of St Catherine's Church you'll spot the 58m bell tower of the **Troyitsko-Illynsky Monastery** (Trinity Monastery). The **Antoniy Caves**, Chernihiv's answer to Kyiv's Kyevo-Pecherska Lavra, lurk beneath the ground a short walk north of this monastery, under the early 11th-century **Illinsky Church** (admission church & caves 10uah; 9am-5pm Sat-Thu, to 4pm Fri). The caves consist of 315m of passageways, galleries and chapels constructed from the 11th to the 13th centuries. These are very different from those in Kyiv in that they both lack dead mummies and, for the most part, live tourists. The conditions here were too cold and humid to support mummification. Instead, the bones of monks killed during the Mongol invasion are preserved in a windowed sarcophagus; touching the sarcophagus is considered good luck. The cave's benefactor and namesake, St Antony of Pechersk, also helped burrow the Lavra caves.

While you're out here, it's worth checking out the monastery and climbing the **bell tower**, which looks right down on the 17th-century **Trinity Church**, an important pilgrimage site that is often mobbed with worshippers.

It's about a 3km walk to the monastery from the Dytynets, or you can jump on trolleybus 8. To get to Illynsky Church get off at the stop before the bell tower and follow the dirt path downhill through the park across the street from the bus stop.

Tours

Explore Chernihiv TOUR

(063 262 4894, 097 284 8068; www.explorechernigov.narod.ru) Canoe trips on the Desna with overnight homestays or camping in rural villages. A good route is the three-day trip from Novhorod-Siversky to Chernihiv.

WORTH A TRIP

NOVHOROD-SIVERSKY

Life in the sleepy town of Novhorod-Siversky (Новгород-Сіверський), which hides in the deep forest in Ukraine's extreme north, may seem uneventful, but back in Kyivan Rus times it was a happening place. It was from here that Prince Igor set out on his ill-fated expedition against the Polovtsy, which became immortalised in *The Tale of Igor's Campaign*, the 12th-century epic later made into an opera by Alexander Borodin.

Dating back to Igor's era (but rebuilt several times since) is the idyllic **Spaso-Preobrazhensky Monastery** (dawn-dusk) FREE, a complex of wood-shingled buildings and golden-domed churches perched over the leafy banks of the Desna River.

Strolling around the quiet grounds, you'll definitely feel like you're in another era. A wooden walkway atop the monastery fence provides prime views of the forested Desna Valley, and it's an easy walk down to the riverbank should you care for a swim or a picnic.

The town's history can be safely fast-forwarded from Kyivan Rus times to 2004, when President Kuchma, who hails from a local village, hosted Putin and Lukashenko at a trilateral summit. This resulted in several significant improvements. One came in the shape of the top-end **Hotel Slovyansky** (046 583 1801; vul Lunacharskoho 2; r from 400uah; P) which is a remarkable deal considering what you get – four-star comfort, albeit without the four-star service. Budget travellers can still bed down at the **Pasvyrda Hotel** (046 582 1225; vul Karla Marksa 3; r from 180uah) in the town centre.

The other improvement was a railway line with new trains that look space age by Ukrainian *elektrychka* (electric train) standards, though it is a *Star Trek* kind of space age. Three such trains link Novhorod-Siversky to Shostka (one hour) on the main line, from where there are numerous trains for Kyiv.

Buses for Chernihiv (40uah, four hours) depart hourly from the nearby bus station.

Sleeping & Eating

Hotel Ukraina HOTEL **$$**
(готель Україна; 699 036; www.hotel-ukraina.com.ua; pr Myra 33; s/d 330/520uah;) The lurid fabrics draped through the rooms at Chernihiv's best digs would be hotel-style hara-kiri in many other countries but represent a great leap forward in rural Ukraine. Big, relatively well furnished and sound of plumbing, the rooms are a pretty good deal and there are even smiles at reception if you wait long enough. Located right opposite the stops for *marshrutky* (fixed-route minibuses) to/from Kyiv.

Sharlotka/Varenichna CAFE **$**
(Шарлотка/Варенична; pr Myru 21; mains 20-35uah; 10am-11pm) Sharlotka is a laid-back coffeehouse, good for snacks and light lunches; the adjoining Varenichna is an unexpectedly sophisticated but inexpensive cafe serving a refreshingly limited menu of Ukrainian dishes in a dining room decorated in red plates and flashes of traditional style. The staff in both establishments cut new ground for Chernihiv in friendly service.

Falvarek CENTRAL EUROPEAN **$**
(Фальварек; pr Myru 20; mains 30-50uah; noon-midnight Sun-Thu, to 1am Fri & Sat;) A vaguely Central European cellar pub with chatty waiters who like to show their proficiency in foreign languages (mostly German). Meat in all shapes dominates the menu. Just off Krasna pl.

Senator EUROPEAN **$$**
(Сенатор; vul Magistratska 1; dishes 30-60uah; 11am-1am) *Shashlyks* (shish-kebabs), steaks and beer are great in this vaguely Wild West–themed restaurant, but while no one complains about the food here there are those who grumble about the prices and service. Actually on Krasna pl.

Information

Chernihiv has yet to take the intrepid step of opening a tourist office, though it does have a snazzy tourism logo and a Russian-language **tourism website** (www.chernihivtourist.com.ua). Useful pocket atlases (12.50uah) are available from the news kiosk at the *marshrutka* stop opposite Hotel Ukraina. These include a map of and information on the Dytynets, but only in Ukrainian.

Getting There & Around

BUS

The best way here from Kyiv is on a *marshrutka* from Lisova metro station (40uah, two hours, around every 15 minutes), which drop off outside Hotel Ukraina (on pr Pobedy). The departure point is across the road. Buses for Novhorod-Siversky leave hourly from the central bus station (40uah, four hours), located next to the train station.

LOCAL TRANSPORT

The train and bus stations are right next to each other, 2km west of pl Krasna, on pl Vokzalna. Take trolleybus 3 or 11 or just about any *marshrutka* to the 'Hotel Ukraina' stop in the city centre.

TRAIN

The train station comes in handy if you are heading to Belarus, with at least three daily trains to Gomel (from 63uah to 260uah, three hours) and one or two trains daily to Minsk (420uah, eight to 12 hours).

Myrhorod Миргород

05355 / POP 42,000

The relaxing spa town of Myrhorod is the place most closely associated with the writer Gogol and a major halt on the Kyiv–Kharkiv railway line. It makes for an easy-going base from which to explore the surrounding countryside, immortalised in some of the works penned by the region's most famous literary son.

Luring visitors from across the ex-USSR, the top attraction is the leafy, Soviet-era **Kurort** (spa) centred around the angular **Byuvet** (mineral water tap room; 6.30am-10.30am, 11.30am-3.30pm & 4.30-8pm) with its fish-scale roof and folksy, 1970s stained glass. Various spa buildings dot the surrounding area, but if you haven't come to soothe an ailment, there's pedalo hire on the seemingly static Khorol River and wide white-sand beaches on which to work up a tan.

From the river you'll have views of the **Assumption Church** (vul Gogolya 112) with its golden domes dusted with blue stars. Nearby lies the town's famous 'puddle', a pond that was once the focus of the main square and which features in some of Gogol's tales. Bronzes of some of Gogol's characters (Taras Bulba, the two Ivans) ring the pond and the man himself looks out across the main road named in his honour.

The **Hotel Myrhorod** (525 61; www.hotelmirgorod.com.ua; vul Gogolya 102; s/d from 410/520uah;) just along from the gates of the spa is the obvious place to snooze, though it receives mixed reviews. As in all Soviet spa towns, locals often rent out rooms to those taking the waters – the best street to try is vul Troitska at the back gates of the *kurort* where beds can be had for as little as 35uah a night (look out for кімната and житло signs). **Grand Pizza** (vul Gogolya 116; pizzas 20-50uah; 9am-midnight;) at the gates of the spa has been around for years and offers free wi-fi.

The train station lies 2.5km south of the town centre. The Intercity+ express is by far the best service for Kyiv (160uah, two hours), Kharkiv (160uah, 2½ hours) and Poltava (130uah, one hour), but only runs around five times a day in each direction. Buses to Poltava (33uah, 1½ hours, many daily), Kharkiv (50uah to 70uah, four hours, three daily), Velyki Sorochyntsi (7uah, around 10 daily) and Opishnya (26uah, three daily) leave from the central bus station across the street from the spa gates.

Poltava Полтава

0532 / POP 298,600

Quaint and leafy Poltava is all about one particular turning point in history. Had Russian Tsar Peter I lost the decisive battle on the town's outskirts in 1709, he wouldn't have become Peter the Great and Ukraine could have celebrated the 300th anniversary of its independence in 2009. But the Russians defeated a joint Swedish and Cossack force, marking this event a century later by rebuilding the city's centre as a mini St Petersburg imitation. As if avenging the lost battle and architecture imposed from the north, Poltava became a centre of Ukrainian cultural renaissance in the 19th century.

Sights

Poltava Battlefield HISTORIC SITE

(www.battle-poltava.org) The famous battle was fought over a large area around what's now vul Zinkivska, about 7km north of the city centre. The best starting point is the **Poltava Battle Museum** (Shvedska mohyla 32; admission 10uah, audio guide 20uah; 9am-4pm Tue-Sun May-Aug) by the Peter I statue. Inside are displays relating to the battle, including maps, paintings and Peter I's original uniform. English signs that appeared during President Yushchenko's term curiously refrain from mentioning Russia, instead using the term 'Moscow Realm'. Aside from the museum, the battlefield contains numerous monuments and various redoubts of the old fortress, many of which have been restored.

WORTH A TRIP

THE GOGOL CIRCUIT

North of Poltava lies Gogol-land: textbook Ukrainian countryside in which lived writer Nikolai Gogol (1809–52) – who authored *Dead Souls* and *The Nose* – and which he populated with his characters. Witty, humorous, imaginative and very laid-back, locals still have very much in common with Gogol's contemporaries.

Travelling with them in overcrowded village buses is part of the fun if you are doing the circuit of Gogol-related sites. However, this method is exhausting and time-consuming – you'll need at least two days to see everything. One day is probably enough if you rent a car. All crucial turns are marked with English-language signs with the writer's trademark long-nosed profile.

To fully appreciate the trip, you may procure Gogol's *Evenings on a Farm near Dikanka* – a collection of funny and surreal stories inspired by the customs and superstitions of local villagers.

Dikanka

In *Evenings on a Farm near Dikanka*, the red-haired beekeeper Panko starts narrating his macabre tales to a group of eager listeners whiling away a summer evening at a farm near this large village, 30km north of Poltava. Once in the town centre, look out for signs pointing to **Troitska Church**. If we are to believe Gogol, its frescoes were painted by the local smith Vakula, who underwent a hair-raising trial while guarding a coffin of a beautiful witch inside this church. Troitska Church is tucked in a small lane diagonally across the square from the **Regional Museum** (vul Lenina 68; admission 8uah).

Opishnya

Not directly related to Gogol, this potters' village, 20km north of Dikanka, has an excellent interactive **Museum-Preserve of Ukrainian Pottery** (www.opishne-museum.gov.ua; vul Partizanska 102). A pottery class is included in the price and you can buy some great souvenirs here. From Opishnya, road P42 goes west towards Velyki Sorochyntsi and Myrhorod.

Hoholeve

Away from the main roads and reachable from Poltava via Dikanka or from Myrhorod/Velyki Sorochyntsi, Gogol's family estate is surrounded by a tranquil park with a pond, and houses a lovingly curated, old-fashioned **museum** (admission 10uah; ⏲8.30am-4.30pm Tue-Sun).

Velyki Sorochyntsi

This sleepy village comes to life in August during the annual **Sorochynska farmers' fair**, masterfully described by Gogol in *Evenings on a Farm near Dikanka*. The writer himself was born here in 1809. Outside the fair period, the main sight is the **Spaso-Preobrazhenska Church**, with its unique seven-tier wooden iconostasis. Frozen in time, the local **regional museum** (vul Hoholya 28) could easily be rebranded as a Soviet-era village museum.

Myrhorod

The circuit's main halt. For details, see the Myrhorod section (p205).

Bus 4 from outside the Kyivsky shopping mall, near Avtovokzal 3 (bus station 3) runs to the museum. The museum stands next to Shvedska Mohyla station, one stop away from Poltava's Kyivska station. A taxi should cost around 30uah one way from the city centre.

Korpusny Park PARK

The focal point of the city centre is the circular Korpusny Park, laid out in the early 19th century in an attempt to emulate the grand planning ideals of St Petersburg. Eight streets radiate off the plaza, and in its centre rises the **Iron Column of Glory**, topped by a golden eagle. Southeast of Korpusny Park, the city's main pedestrian drag – vul Zhovtneva (better known by some by its Russian name, Oktyabrskaya) – leads down to verdant Zhovtnevy Park.

Poltava Museum of Local Lore MUSEUM
(www.pkm.poltava.ua; vul Konstityutsii 2; admission 5uah; 10am-5pm Mon, 9am-5pm Tue-Sun) Located on the southeast edge of Zhovtnevy Park, the museum exhibits random archaeological and cultural artefacts, its collection almost overshadowed by its gorgeous Art Nouveau building (1903), adorned with the ceramic crests of each district capital in the Poltava oblast. Outside stands an impressive cubist Shevchenko monument, which has the national poet emerging from angular blocks of grey concrete.

Maydan Soborny SQUARE
(Cathedral Sq) Vul Zhovtneva terminates on a bluff at Cathedral Sq, the prettiest little spot in Poltava, with sweeping views of Khrestovozdvyzhensky Monastery across the valley to the northeast. The square is dominated by the rebuilt **Uspenska Church**. A footpath leads to the dramatic neoclassical **Friendship Rotunda** on the edge of the bluff, a great place for photographs. On the way to the rotunda look out for the *halushky* monument on the left, which pays due homage to the tasty local dumplings.

Kotlyarevsky Museum MUSEUM
(admission 8uah; 10am-5pm Tue-Sun) Just behind Uspenska Church, surrounded by a lovely flower garden, this is the lovingly restored former home of Ivan Kotlyarevsky (1739–1838), one of the fathers of Ukrainian literature. The museum provides a glimpse into traditional Ukrainian life in the early 19th century.

Spaska Church CHURCH
A block northwest of maydan Soborny up vul Parizskoyi Komuny is the quaint Spaska Church (1705), with its rebuilt bell tower. It's faced by an odd monument to Tsar Peter I (Peter the Great) across the street on vul Parizskoyi Komuny. Further up vul Parizskoyi Komuny is another monument, this time to fallen Cossacks – it's topped with a typical chubby cross often found on Cossack graves.

Khrestovozdvyzhensky Monastery MONASTERY
(Хрестовоздвиженський монастир) About 3km east of Korpusny Park is the early 18th-century Khrestovozdvyzhensky Monastery (Elevation of the Cross). The main cathedral is one of only two in the country with seven cupolas, rather than five (the other is St Michael's Monastery in Kyiv). The complex is a long (30-minute), straight walk east on vul Radyanska (Sovetskaya) from Korpusny Park.

Tours

Mikhail Ishchenko GUIDED TOUR
(☎066 710 4145, 067 401 2069; m.ishchenko@mail.ru; walking/car tours per hr 200/250uah) A popular private English-speaking guide doing tours of Poltava and the Gogol circuit.

Vilmat TOUR
(☎096 235 4499, 596 960; www.travel.poltava.ua; ul Rozy Lyuksemburg 63) Tours of Poltava battlefield and the Gogol circuit. They can also organise your stay in village houses in Dikanka (60uah to 100uah per night) and elsewhere in the region.

Sleeping

Mini-Hotel Sinay GUESTHOUSE $
(Міні-готель Сінай; ☎508 313; www.hotel-s.poltava.ua; vul Zinkivska 11/31; s/d from 140/220uah;) Six-room guesthouse a short walk from Kyivsky train station offering small, European standard rooms for Ukrainian countryside prices. Rooms are kept sparkling, breakfast costs an extra 20uah and bathrooms are shared.

Palazzo Hotel HOTEL $$
(☎611 205; www.palazzo.com.ua; vul Gogolya 33; s/d from 580/780uah;) This is the place for people travelling on a medium-range budget to enjoy four-star luxury (well, almost). The attractive king-size beds have firm mattresses that will have your back feeling like butter after a lengthy snooze. That and the suave, tawny-toned design almost make up for the small size of the allegedly smoke-free rooms.

Hotel Galereya HOTEL $$
(готель Галерея; ☎561 697; www.hotel.pl.ua; vul Frunze 7; s/d 430/640uah;) Slap bang in the city centre, Galereya's location is not the only thing that makes this friendly sleepery worth checking out. Rooms are of a recent ilk, perfectly dust free and modestly furnished. Bathrooms are large and some even have bidets, objects which must have a few members of Ukraine's nouveau riche scratching their heads. Breakfast can be taken in bed and is included – there's even an English menu.

Eating & Drinking

Be sure to sample the local delicacy, *halushky* – unfilled dumplings with various rich toppings. The Hotel Palazzo's restaurant does a good rendition.

Sto Dorih PUB $

(Сто Доріг; vul Parizkoy Komuny 18; snacks & mains 8-20uah; ⏲10am-10pm) Studenty watering hole and live-music venue, with weekend rock bands, a long beer menu, and a big and busy summer beer garden.

Zefir UKRAINIAN, RUSSIAN $$

(Зефір; vul Zhovtneva 24; mains 30-80uah; ⏲11am-11pm; 📶) With limited success, Zefir is trying to evoke the ambience of imperial-period Poltava. It is nonetheless a good place to taste Poltava *halushky* and *varenyky* (dumplings). Attentive service and a tranquil atmosphere.

Koffishka COFFEE

(Коффишка; vul Zhovtneva; ⏲24hr) Tiny but chirpy coffeehouse at the top of the main drag (near the entrance to the underpass leading to Korpusny Park) fashioned in the shape of a coffee bean mill. Open round the clock for those who require Arabica at 3am.

Poltavske Pivo PUB

(vul Zhovtneva 26; ⏲8am-10pm) Fresh local brews, snacks and outdoor seating on the main drag – ideal for a spot of Poltavan watching. The service here can be very poor.

Self-Catering

Brusnichka SUPERMARKET

(Брусничка; Zhovtneva 43) The best supermarket in the city centre, located on the left as you head from Korpusny Park towards Kyivsky train station.

Shopping

Ukrainian Souvenir SOUVENIRS

(Український сувенір; www.vushuvanka.pl.ua/en_main.php; vul Komsomolska 19) Excellent souvenir shop offering beautifully embroidered traditional shirts, blouses and tablecloths, all handmade by villagers from the Poltava region.

Information

Ukrtelecom (vul Kuybysheva 5; internet per hr 6uah; ⏲9am-8pm Mon-Fri, 10am-5pm Sat, 10am-3pm Sun) Internet access right off Korpusny Park. Also has telephones and a handy ATM.

www.tourism.poltava.ua Official tourism website in English.

Getting There & Around

BUS

Buses go pretty much everywhere from distant **Avtovokzal 1** (Bus station 1; vul Velikotyrnivska), about 5.5km east of the city centre and reached by any bus or *marshrutka* marked кільцевий. The most useful are to Myrhorod (34uah, two hours, at least hourly), Kharkiv (50uah, 2½ to three hours, many daily) and Dnipropetrovsk (57uah, four hours, hourly). Avtolyux and many other operators run buses to Kyiv (75uah to 100uah, six hours, at least twice hourly). On the Gogol circuit, Hoholeve can be reached by taking any bus to Velyka Bagachka (Myrhorod and Kremenchuk services; 26uah, 1½ hours, many daily), where you should change to local *marshrutky*.

Avtovokzal 3 (Bus station No 3; vul Zhinkinvska 6B) just outside Kyivsky shopping mall and close to Kyivsky train station has services to Dikanka (10uah, at least hourly).

New fast *marshrutky* leave when full from outside the Kyivsky train station for Kharkiv (50uah).

CAR

Try **Rentcars.Poltava.ua** (www.rentcars.poltava.ua) if you need a car for the Gogol circuit. Bookings are taken online.

TRAIN

Poltava has two train stations – Pivdenniy Vokzal and Kyivsky Vokzal – the duo conveniently located on complete opposite sides of the city, around 6.5km apart.

Poltava is a stop on the Intercity+ service between Kyiv (174uah, three hours, five daily), Kharkiv (135uah, 1½ hours, three daily) and Donetsk (185uah, four hours, two daily). The Kharkiv train stops at Kyivsky Vokzal while the Donetsk service makes a halt at the Pivdenniy Vokzal. Make sure you go to the right one! All of these express services stop in Myrhorod (124uah, one hour, five daily) en route to/from the capital.

Other connections from Poltava:

Kyiv 140uah, five to six hours, nine daily (Pivdenniy and Kyivsky stations)

Kharkiv 110uah, three hours, at least six daily (Pivdenniy and Kyivsky stations)

Odesa 173uah, 11 hours, daily (Pivdenniy station)

Trolleybus 1 links the two stations via the city centre. Trolleybuses 2, 4, 6 and 11 run from Pivdenniy Vokzal to the city centre.

Kharkiv Харків

☎057 / POP 1.43 MILLION

Kharkiv (Kharkov in Russian) is one of those ex-Soviet cities that has much to say about itself, but fairly little to show. Wars and Soviet development reduced its historical centre, boasting some pretty fin de siècle buildings, to a narrow triangle between vul

Sumska and Pushkinska. The rest is Soviet monumentalism in all its glory – a perverse delight for architecture buffs, but hardly exciting for the uninitiated.

In the 1920s Kharkiv was the seat of the Ukrainian Soviet government, which orchestrated a short-lived renaissance of Ukrainian culture and language. But Stalin accused its members of nationalism and launched purges that eventually led to the Holodomor (Ukrainian famine; p233).

Today it's home to Russian-speaking intelligentsia – scientists and engineers who turned Kharkiv into the brain centre of the Soviet defence industry in the 1960s. It's perhaps a lingering nostalgia for the good ol' days that keep the streets clean, the parks neatly trimmed and the metro rumbling, all lending Ukraine's second city a pleasant if rather sterile ambience.

Sights

★Ploshcha Svobody SQUARE

(Площа Свободи; M Derzhprom) Locals claim that this huge expanse of cobbles is the second-largest in the world after Beijing's Tiananmen Sq. At 750m long it's indisputably huge and is certainly Kharkiv's most unique sight.

Planned as an ensemble of Ukrainian government buildings when Kharkiv was the republican capital, it was laid out between 1925 and 1935. The late-1920s **Derzhprom** (Держпром) at its western end was the first Soviet skyscraper, a geometric series of concrete and glass blocks and bridges. On the southern side of the square is the **university** (early 1930s), formerly the House of Planning, which displays classic Soviet aesthetics. **Lenin** still proudly stands in the midst of it all, looking as though he's just about to take a bow – perhaps someone should tell him the show ended way back when.

★Ploshcha Konstytutsiyi SQUARE

(Площа Конституції; M Istorychny Muzey) If you are looking for a meeting point in Kharkiv, nothing beats the spot under the **giant thermometer** that adorns Istorychny Muzey metro exit to pl Konstytutsiyi. Just west of the square, the gleaming domes of the **Pokrovsky Monastery** (Intercession of the Virgin; vul Klochkovska) are visible from miles away. The predictably peaceful grounds (enter from pl Konstytutsiyi) have two attractive churches. The smaller and more important of the two is the blue, three-domed 1689 **Pokrovska Church** (Покровська церква). As in all Orthodox churches, the altar is under the east-pointing dome, and there's another altar hidden in the basement, which the attendant may show you if you ask. The church is almost always open for services. The yellow church next to it is the **Ozeyansky Church** (Озеяньська церква).

Back on the square, you can't miss the large granite **sculptural ensemble** commemorating Kharkiv's designation as the first capital of Soviet Ukraine on 24 December 1917. Tongue-in-cheek Kharkivites nicknamed it 'five men carrying a fridge' – the resemblance is far from passing. Nearby the **Kharkiv History Museum** (Харківський історичний музей; ☎731 1348; www.museum.kh.ua; pl Konstytutsiyi; admission 8uah; ⏲9.30am-5pm Tue-Sun; M Istorychny Muzey) was receiving a major facelift at the time of research – this involved hoisting a huge glass and steel facade onto the red-brick building. Staff were unclear as to how this would affect future exhibitions.

★Shevchenko Park PARK

(M Universytet) Central Shevchenko Park is one of those post-Soviet parks where you can sit for hours watching families boarding the kiddy train, listening to some remarkably talented buskers, and pondering the shortness of some skirts and height of most heels. Not sure what the national poet might have made of all that flesh on show – from the expression on the face of the **Taras Shevchenko statue** (vul Sumska; M Universytet) it doesn't look as though he approves.

★Kharkiv Art Museum MUSEUM

(Харківський Художній музей; www.artmuseum.kharkov.ua; permanent collection vul Radnarkomivska 11, exhibit hall vul Radnarkomivska 9; admission per bldg 7uah; ⏲10am-6pm Wed-Sun; M Arkhitektora Beketova) Kharkiv's most famous museum owns one of many versions of Ilya Repin's *Zaporizhsky Cossacks Writing a Letter to the Turkish Sultan,* which is found in a room full of Repin paintings in the museum's permanent collection. The entire collection of romantic paintings here is of a high standard for Ukraine, but the neighbouring exhibit hall is hit or miss.

Uspensky Cathedral CATHEDRAL

(Успенський собор; Assumption Cathedral; vul Universytetskaya; M Radyanska) This cathedral with its landmark mid-19th-century bell tower (89.5m tall) is now used only as a concert hall. The ticket office in the entrance is open in the afternoons only.

Central Kharkiv

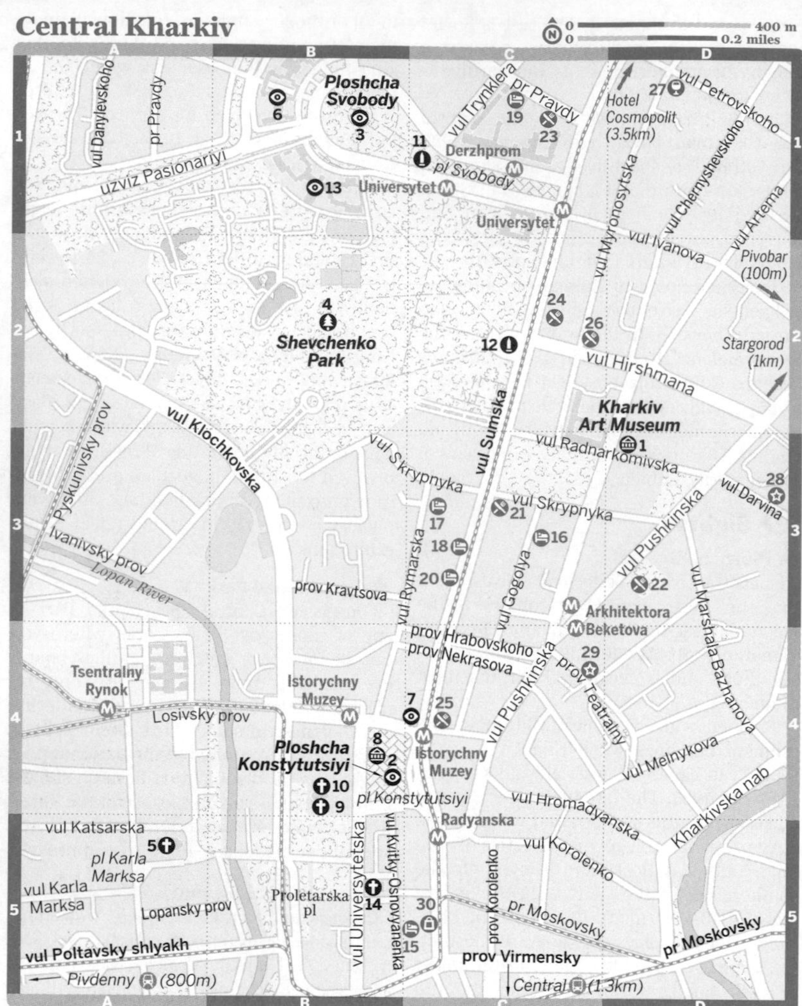

Blahoveshchensky Cathedral CATHEDRAL
(Благовещенський собор; pl Karla Marksa; Ⓜ Tsentralny Rynok) The park across the street from Uspensky Cathedral offers the best vantage point of the striking red-and-cream striped cathedral down in the valley, built in 1881 to 1901. Based on Istanbul's Hagia Sophia, it has a beautifully proportioned bell tower resembling a stick of candy.

Sleeping

If you don't fancy bagging a bunk in one of the city's itinerant hostels, budget beds are hard to come by in business-oriented Kharkiv.

Pushkin Hostel HOSTEL $
(☎057 756 6373; www.hostelpushkin.com; vul Sumska 17, entrance 3, 2nd fl, apt 25; dm from 70uah; @ 🛜; Ⓜ Istorychny Muzey) Spacious, 30-bed hostel on the main drag with parquet floors, huge common room and kitchen, and just enough bathrooms to keep the morning queues moving. Owners are planning to stick around at this address for the foreseeable future.

Hotel Kharkiv HOTEL $$
(Готель Харків; ☎758 0153; www.hotel.kharkov.com; pl Svobody 7; s/d from 350/400uah; 🛜; Ⓜ Derzhprom, Universytet) Kharkiv's textbook

Central Kharkiv

Top Sights
1 Kharkiv Art Museum ... D3
2 Ploshcha Konstytutsiyi ... B4
3 Ploshcha Svobody ... B1
4 Shevchenko Park ... B2

Sights
5 Blahoveshchensky Cathedral ... A5
6 Derzhprom ... B1
7 Giant Thermometer ... C4
8 Kharkiv History Museum ... B4
9 Ozeyansky Church ... B4
10 Pokrovska Church ... B4
Pokrovsky Monastery ... (see 10)
11 Statute of Lenin ... C1
12 Taras Shevchenko Statue ... C2
13 University ... B1
14 Uspensky Cathedral ... B5

Sleeping
15 Apartments-in-Kharkov ... C5
16 Chichikov Hotel ... C3
17 Hostinny Dvir ... C3
18 Hotel 19 ... C3
19 Hotel Kharkiv ... C1
20 Pushkin Hostel ... C3

Eating
21 Adriano ... C3
22 Bukhara ... D3
23 IT Café ... C1
24 Metropol Park ... C2
25 Puzata Khata ... C4
26 Shoti ... C2

Drinking & Nightlife
27 Irish Pub ... D1

Entertainment
28 Churchill's Music Pub ... D3
29 Jazzter ... C4

Shopping
30 Ye ... C5

Soviet behemoth looms over pl Svobody, providing adequately equipped, though unremarkable, rooms in the heart of the city. It's really the cheaper, barely renovated rooms that those on a budget will be interested in. If you've hryvnya to squander, there are more characterful sleeps in town.

AN-2 HOTEL $$
(☎732 4954; www.antwo-hotel.com.ua; vul Plekhanivska 8; s/d from 350/475uah; ❄📶; Ⓜ Prospekt Gagarina) This new, very reasonably priced hotel, a short walk from both the main bus station and Prospekt Gagarina metro station, is named after a famous Soviet-era aircraft but won't have you heading for the emergency exit. The 34 contemporary, box-ticking rooms are spotless and well designed, staff speak English and rates include Ukrainian-style breakfast on the 7th floor.

★ **Hotel 19** BOUTIQUE HOTEL $$$
(☎754 4061; www.hotel19.com.ua; vul Sumska 19; s/d from 1050/1200uah; ❄📶; Ⓜ Istorychny Muzey) This freshly minted, extravagantly fashioned boutique hotel hides away on a tranquil courtyard just off traffic-plagued vul Sumska. The 24 rooms are a soothing antidote to the remnants of the proletarian utopia outside, all done out in wistful 19th-century antique-style furniture and boasting stuccoed ceilings and libraries (books are in Russian so just nice to look at for most). En route to breakfast stop to admire paintings of Kharkiv that line the plush corridors. Guests can swim for free at the 19's sister hotel Nasha Dacha, outside the city centre. Ask the extremely professional staff how to get there.

Hotel Cosmopolit LUXURY HOTEL $$$
(☎754 6886; www.cosmopolit-hotel.com; vul Akademika Proskury 1; r from 990uah; ⊖❄@) This sets the standard for contemporary design in Kharkiv, with flatscreen TVs and loads of extras like plush robes and 24-hour room service. The theme is Italian, and breakfast in swanky Da Vinci restaurant is divine. The huge 'king' rooms are worth the splurge (1500uah). If you're here on business, this is your top choice even if it is a short taxi ride from the city centre.

Chichikov Hotel LUXURY HOTEL $$$
(Готель Чічіков; ☎752 2300; www.chichikov-hotel.com.ua; vul Gogolya 6/8; s/d from 570/1140uah; ❄📶; Ⓜ Arkhitektora Beketova) You may feel you'd like a bit more space in the rooms for the prices this relatively new (2006) epicentral hotel charges, but overall this is a commendable place to kip. Rooms are elegantly furnished, kitted out with all those things you never use, and bathrooms are spotless.

Hostinny Dvir BOUTIQUE HOTEL $$$
(Гостинний двір; ☎705 6086; www.hotel-gd.com.ua; vul Rymarska 28; s/d from 740/850uah; ❄@; Ⓜ Arkhitektora Beketova) This pretty little

APARTMENTS

As is the case elsewhere in Ukraine, apartments often represent a better deal than cheap 'n' fusty hotel rooms.

Apartments-in-Kharkov (719 0879, 050 343 3787; http://apartments.inkharkov.com; pl Konstytutsiyi 1, Dvorets Truda, entrance No 7, office 72-12; 9am-10pm; M Istorychny Muzey) Proprietor Dima offers outstanding service and lets clients use the office internet.

Kharkov Apartment (093 405 6600, 755 0367; www.kharkovapartment.com) Managers Svetlana and Anna speak English.

hotel set in a courtyard behind the posh Chateau restaurant only really becomes boutique as you summit the room scale at junior suite and suite level. Otherwise quarters are business standard, very comfortable, and boast minibars and sound-proof windows.

Eating

IT Café EUROPEAN $
(760 3060; pr Pravdy 10A; mains 30-50uah; 24hr; ; M Universytet) This circular, wrap-around, open-all-hours cafe is the place to whip out your wi-fi-enabled device of choice and get connected, while sipping great milkshakes, smoothies and lemonade. But if you need none of that, this is still an excellent breakfast or lunch option. It also sells bizarre-looking souvenirs designed by Russian designer Artemy Lebedev. Strangely enough, none of the staff speak English. ISIC discount offered.

Puzata Khata UKRAINIAN $
(Пузата хата; cnr vul Sumska & Konstytutsiyi; 8am-11pm; M Istorychny Muzey) This city-centre branch of Ukraine's most celebrated fast-food chain is incongruously styled as a warren of thatched cottages bedecked in bucolic knickknackery, but the food is cheap as you like and it can be elbow to elbow at feeding time.

Adriano ITALIAN $
(vul Sumska 10; mains & pizzas 35-60uah; 10am-11pm; M Istorychny Muzey) Brand-new Italian job in the Ave Plaza shopping centre complete with faux Roman columns, Venetian-themed frescoes, loud Ukrainian FM radio and affordable Appenine edibles, plus sushi.

Stargorod CZECH PUB $$
(Старгород; 700 9030; vul Lermontovska 7; mains 50-110uah; 24hr; M Pushkinska) Rivers of beer cut through mountains of meat to the sound of um-pah music in this Kharkivite version of a Czech pub. There is a microbrewery on the premises pumping out fresh lager and ale, which contributes to the overall happy party atmosphere and triggers wild, table-crushing dances slightly more often than you need. A full-sized sheep or pig is grilled on an open fire each Saturday and Sunday.

Shoti CAUCASIAN, UKRAINIAN $$
(Шоти; vul Myronosytska 12; mains 24-70uah; 10am-11pm Mon-Thu & Sun, to midnight Fri & Sat; M Universytet) Don't be fooled by the plain, though pleasant, interior of this place – here the focus is firmly on well-crafted food from Ukraine and the Caucasus with a menu of *kachapuri* (Georgian cheese-filled bread), grilled meats and syrupy desserts infused with authentic flavour. Takeaway dishes (from the counter in the entrance) are 20% cheaper.

Bukhara UZBEK $$
(Бухара; 716 2045; vul Pushkinska 32; mains 35-125uah; 10am-11pm; ; M Arkhitektora Beketova) The chef here fries up a mean *plov* (pilaf) and other Uzbek treats you won't recognise by name but by ingredients. Most stick to the exotic-sounding salads and grilled meats, the staples of ex-Soviet Central Asia. The service here is very polite.

Metropol Park EUROPEAN $$$
(720 0555; vul Sumska 50; mains 80-190uah; M Universytet) Expensive and exclusive Metropol dedicates itself to gourmet European cuisine. Its popular outdoor terrace brings you eye to eye with the Taras Shevchenko statue across the street.

Drinking

Irish Pub PUB
(Ірландський Паб; vul Myronosytska 46; 1-11pm; M Derzhprom, Universytet) Offers exactly what you'd expect: plenty of beer (fine imports and inexpensive domestic lagers), sports on TV, a few strange Irish dishes and the chance to hobnob with Kharkiv expats.

Pivobar PUB
(vul Frunze 3; 11am-11pm; M Pushkinska) Beloved English ales like Owd Rodger and Riggwelter, as well as its own numbered beers plus an encyclopaedic food menu.

✩ Entertainment

Kharkiv is one of the cradles of Russian-language rock and indie music, with major bands, such as Piatnizza, hailing from here. Check Russian-language http://kharkov.nezabarom.com.ua for entertainment listings.

Churchill's Music Pub LIVE MUSIC
(vul Darvina 9; Ⓜ Arkhitektora Beketova) A well-concealed spot within the building of the National Architects Union supplying an excellent program of live music to an eager, bohemian crowd.

Jazzter LIVE MUSIC
(www.jazzter.com.ua; prov Teatralny 11/13; admission 30-100uah; ⏲ 11am-11pm; Ⓜ Istorychny Muzey) Surprisingly sophisticated bar and lounge for backstreet Kharkiv with smooth local acts and a foot-tapping, tie-loosening after-work crowd.

Shopping

Barabashova Market MARKET
(www.barabashka.com; Ⓜ Akademika Barabashova) For the ultimate post-Soviet bazaar experience, cheap jeans and Vietnamese food, head to this market, which rivals similar bazaars in Odesa for the 'biggest in Europe' title. It's really a mind-bogglingly huge affair, run by Africans and Vietnamese who sell cheap Chinese clothes and all sorts of ripped-off junk.

Ye BOOKS
(€; vul Sumska 3; ⏲ 9am-9pm; Ⓜ Radyanska) This modern bookshop on a seemingly hopeless crusade to Ukrainianise a Russian-speaking city serves as a club for Kharkiv's Ukrainian speakers and cosmopolitans. English speakers are welcome to participate in regular meetings with students of the language – a great way to find local friends.

ⓘ Information

Post office (pl Pryvokzalna; Ⓜ Pivdenny Vokzal) Provides internet access.

ⓘ Getting There & Away

AIR

Kharkiv's **Osnova airport** (☎ 657, 090 031 6571; www.hrk.aero) handles international flights to/from Vienna, Warsaw, Moscow, Dubai, Barcelona and Kutaisi in Georgia, as well as a single domestic service to/from Kyiv (one hour 20 minutes, two daily).

BUS

The most useful services from the **central bus station** (☎ 732 6502; pr Gagarina 22; Ⓜ pr Gagarina) are to Poltava (46uah to 75uah, 2½

Kharkiv Metro

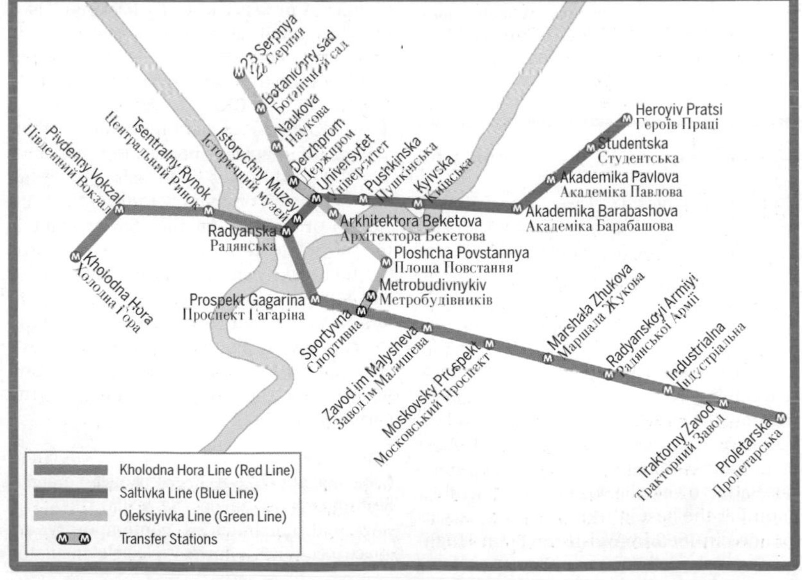

hours, hourly), Dnipropetrovsk (77uah, 4½ hours, hourly) and Donetsk (80uah to 140uah, 4½ hours, six daily).

Autolux (www.autolux.ua) and **Gunsel** (www.gunsel.com.ua) run several buses a day to Kyiv, including some overnight services.

TRAIN

The main station is **Pivdenny Vokzal** (Ⓜ Pivdenny Vokzal). Foreigners should head straight to the Міжнародні Каси (open 7.30am to 8.30pm), on the right as you walk from the main hall to the ticket booths as it has English-speaking staff and no queues.

By far the fastest way to get to/from Kyiv is aboard the Intercity+ service (230uah, 4½ hours, three daily), which does the run twice as fast as the normal passenger trains (181uah, nine hours, four daily). Intercity+ trains stop in Poltava (135uah, 1½ hours).

Other connections from Kharkiv:

Donetsk 90uah to 100uah, four to eight hours, three daily

Moscow 1000uah, 12½ to 14½ hours, up to 13 daily

Odesa 160uah, 14 hours, daily

Simferopol 220uah to 280uah, seven to 10 hours, three daily

Sviatohirsk 70uah, 2½ hours, two daily

Getting Around

The airport is 8km south of the city centre, off pr Gagarina – take trolleybus 5 and *marshrutka* 115E from the Prospekt Gagarina metro stop.

The train station has its own metro stop, Pivdenny Vokzal. Metro tokens cost 3uah. There are no cashiers selling tokens – only machines that don't accept notes with denominations higher than 10uah.

Donetsk Донецьк

☎062 / POP 969,000

Donetsk is a peculiar case of a coal troll working hard to become Ukraine's Prince Charming. Although industrial and Soviet to its core – mines and slag heaps in full view – it has a pleasant southern feel thanks to nicely redeveloped pedestrian promenades, parks and the city's trademark rose beds. The capital of the Donbass coal-mining region, Donetsk is associated with money, power and football. President Viktor Yanukovych and Ukraine's richest man, Rinat Akhmetov, both hail from here. The latter owns the local football club – naturally, the best in Ukraine. Donetsk was founded in 1869 by Welshman John Hughes and originally named 'Yuzovka' after him – hence the local obsession with all things British, reflected in the names of restaurants and hotels.

Sights & Activities

Donbass Arena STADIUM

(vul Chelyuskintsev 189E) Yes, the football arena that hosted one of the Euro 2012 finals is the main attraction in the relatively young and industrial Donetsk. It's home to the country's best team – Shakhtar Donetsk, oligarch Akhmetov's favourite toy. At the clearly marked **Shakhtar Museum**, you can arrange a tour of the arena (adult/student 80/40uah, every hour on the hour 11am to 5pm), including dressing rooms, which saw Wayne Rooney kicking the hosts out of Euro 2012 after he scored the single goal in the England–Ukraine match. Next to the museum, there is a **shop** selling clothes in Shakhtar's stylish black and orange colours. If you want to see Shakhtar in action, drop by the **ticket office** (pr Miru; tickets adult/student from 70/40uah; ⏰9am-8pm).

The arena is surrounded by the manicured **Lenin Komsomol Park**. To the right of the main entrance is the striking WWII **Liberators of Donbass memorial** (Lenin Komsomol Park) set against the backdrop of mines and picturesque *terrikony* (slag heaps). They seem to change colour depending on the season and the time of the day.

Vul Artyoma STREET

(вулиця Артема) The city's backbone is a broad avenue that runs from the train station to the Old Town. It is lined with monuments dating from the Soviet era. The most striking one is **Glory to Miners' Labour** (Shakhterskaya pl) – a giant miner holding out a piece of shapeless black substance, presumably coal, in his open palm. You can't help spotting it on the way to/from the train station or airport. Another Soviet giant is the inevitable **Lenin** (pl Lenina), who adorns the namesake central sqaure and seems to cast an approving sideways glance at revellers on the Golden Lion terrace. Completing the communist pantheon, the square-chested figure of local Bolshevik hero **Artyom**, whose name the street bears, looms at the corner of pr Mira.

Izolyatsia ARTS CENTRE

(Ізоляція; ☎477 26 20; www.izolyatsia.org/en/; 3 Svetlogo puti; ⏰10am-6pm Sat & Sun) FREE The new and much-lauded contemporary art space occupies a former electric insulator factory standing at the foot of a particularly picturesque slag heap. It hosts a number of international resident artists who draw inspiration from the industrial dystopia of Donbass. Musical and educational events are held regularly. The centre's curator conducts a tour of the premises at 11am most Saturdays. Unfortunately, true to its name, it is so isolated from the rest of the city, one can only reach it via a bus station, which itself is on the outskirts. So invest 40uah or so in a taxi ride. An additional complication is that it is only open on weekends.

Sleeping

Red Cat Hostel HOSTEL **$**
(Рыжий кот; ☎050 422 0928/050 470 1089; http://theredcathostel.com.ua; pr Mira 3/1; dm per person 110uah, s 150uah; ❄📶) The city's pioneering hostel is a classical converted flat affair run by a friendly family. It's been getting consistently positive reviews since it was inaugurated by England fans during Euro-2012. It only consists of a four-bed dorm and a single room, so don't expect to put up a football team here!

Hotel Velikobritaniya HISTORIC HOTEL **$**
(Великобритания; Great Britain; ☎305 1951; vul Postysheva 20; s/d from 290/400uah, s without bathroom from 175uah) About the only building left of the tsarist-era Donetsk, the Great Britain – built in John Hughes' times to house Western engineers – oozes heaps of olde-worlde charm. However, the location is crummy and it gets stiflingly hot in summer. A few notable Russian writers passed through a century ago, leaving unflattering comments in their memoirs, and there was a brothel for German officers here during WWII. Breakfast isn't served on weekends.

★**Liverpool Art Hotel** HOTEL **$$**
(☎312 5475, 312 5474; www.liverpool.com.ua; vul Artyoma 131A; s/d from 420uah; P❄📶) Gilded figures of John, Paul, George and Ringo greeting you in the archway may not be a good sign, but there is much more to Liverpool than belated provincial Beatlemania. In fact, this is one of the city's funkiest alternative universes, which, apart from the hotel, includes a great cafeteria and one of the best musical venues in eastern Ukraine.

Azania Boutique Hotel BOUTIQUE HOTEL **$$**
(☎349 3314; www.azaniahotel.com; pr Teatralny 3; s/d ste 650/720uah; 🚭❄@) When you enter your suite in this extraordinary boutique hotel, you might feel you are dreaming already, your body swallowed by one of the California king-size beds. It only gets better: *two* flatscreen TVs in each cavernous suite, DVD collection, kitchen, furniture worthy of a *Home & Design* cover, Jacuzzi etc. Pinch yourself when you look at the price – it's real.

Eva HOTEL **$$**
(Ева; ☎348 4848; http://hotel-eva.com/; vul Shchorsa 29; s/d from 480/530; 🚭❄📶) The decor is slightly on the macabre side – corridors are lined with faux antique busts of Greek gods and Roman emperors – but rooms are very well appointed, making this human sized hotel a perfect midrange choice in Donetsk. It is located on a quieter street within walking distance of vul Artyoma. Breakfast isn't included.

Donbass Palace LUXURY HOTEL **$$$**
(Донбасс Палас; ☎343 4333; www.donbasspalace.com; vul Artyoma 80; s/d from 2800uah; 🚭❄@🏊) The country's first five-star property when it opened in the mid-1990s, the Donbass Palace has a lot more competition of late, but it remains the No 1 choice among well-heeled *biznesmeny*. It boasts four superb restaurants if you're entertaining, and a casino if you're feeling lucky.

Eating

Liverpool Foodmarket CAFETERIA **$**
(vul Artyoma 131A; mains 15-25uah; ⏰7am-11pm) With walls draped in Union Jacks and the Beatles for the soundtrack, this food factory churns out tons of European and Asian meals that are immediately devoured by a horde of hungry students. Payment is with a deposit card, which you get at the cash office near the entrance. You can cash the unspent money on the way out.

★**Yuzovskaya Pivovarnya** CENTRAL EUROPEAN **$$**
(Юзовская пивоварня; John Hughes Brewery; ☎208 9800; http://juz.dn.ua/; vul Artyoma 129B; mains 55-150uah; ⏰11am-1.30pm; 📶) A tribute to the city founder, John Hughes, this place is full of shiny brass – that of the mini-brewery pumping fresh brew into the pipes that take it straight to your table. All you need is to open the tap. A large, airy hall is divided into compartments with red-leather couches seating about six people. Meaty Central European dishes dominate the menu.

Donetsk

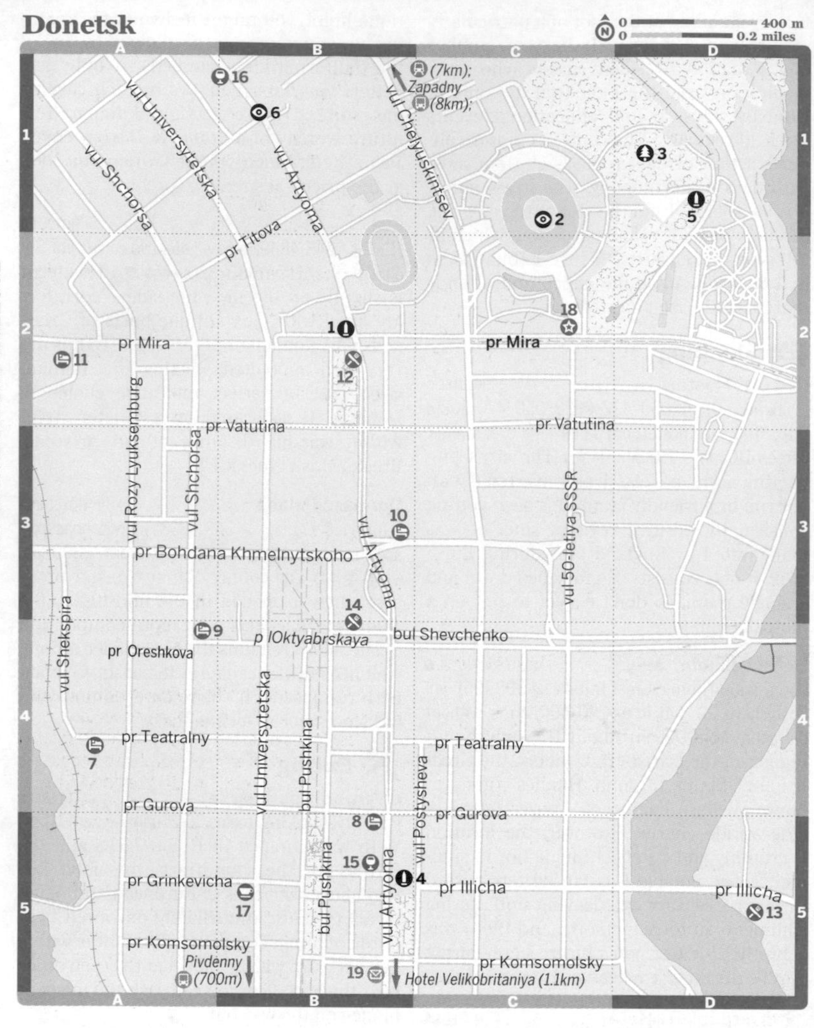

Yo-moyo RESTAURANT $$
(Ё-моё; ☎385 9567; http://emoe.in.ua; pr Ilyicha 15D; mains 80-150uah; ⏰11am-1am; 📶) This hard-to-miss wooden lakeside terrace brands itself an 'ethnic' restaurant. In fact, its only real 'ethnic' component is the Georgian part of the menu, which is the main reason to dine here. Definitely go for cold appetisers, such as *mkhali* (vegetable and walnut paste), and compliment your *shashlyk* with delicious *khachapuri* (cheese pastry).

Sun City Terrace EUROPEAN $$
(Терраса Сан Сити; vul Artyoma 96A; mains 45-70uah; ⏰24hr; 📶) This strategically located open-air place (in summer) is always full of people. If two Donetsk residents need to meet for a chat, it will probably be here. In a classic post-Soviet tradition, it serves a bit of everything – pizzas and pasta, *shashlyks,* Black Sea fish and the inevitable sushi.

Donetsk

Sights
1 Artyom Monument B2
2 Donbass Arena C1
3 Lenin Komsomol Park D1
4 Lenin Statue B5
5 Liberators of Donbass Memorial D1
6 Vul Artyoma B1

Sleeping
7 Azania Boutique Hotel A4
8 Donbass Palace B5
9 Eva A4
10 Liverpool Art Hotel B3
11 Red Cat Hostel A2

Eating
Liverpool Foodmarket .... (see 10)
12 Sun City Terrace B2
13 Yo-moyo D5
14 Yuzovskaya Pivovarnya B4

Drinking & Nightlife
15 Golden Lion B5
16 Izba-Chitalnya B1
17 Kayut-Kompaniya B5

Entertainment
18 Donbass Arena Ticket Office C2
Liverpool Live Music Bar .... (see 10)

Information
19 Post & Telephone Centre B5

Drinking & Nightlife

Kayut-Kompaniya COFFEE
(Кают-компания; vul Grinkevicha 9; 9am-11pm;) Descend to the bottom of the sea in this little cellar coffeehouse-cum-cocktail bar designed to look like Captain Nemo's submarine. A striking example of local escapism.

Golden Lion PUB
(vul Artyoma 76A; 11am-1.30am;) Far from your run-of-the-mill Irish pub, and not just because it's spacious enough to hold a rugby game and stays open after midnight. Here you'll also encounter 9uah Sarmat beer to go along with the standard selection of imported brews. Meals are available for 60uah to 100uah.

Izba-Chitalnya BAR
(Изба-читальня; 110 vul Artyoma; 11am-11pm or later;) Young literati meet here for coffee, cocktails, poetic evenings and DJ sets. It's a small cellar place with many bookshelves and cosy armchairs. Live-music events take place most weekends.

Entertainment

Liverpool Live Music Bar LIVE MUSIC
(vul Artyoma 131A; cocktails 50uah; 12pm-2am or later) This imaginatively designed place claims to have the longest bar in Eastern Europe. The catwalk stage is placed so that musicians find themselves in the middle of the crowd. Some major Ukrainian bands play here.

Information

Post & telephone centre (Почтамт; vul Artyoma 72; internet per hr 4.24uah; 9am-8pm)

Getting There & Away

AIR

The shiny new **Sergey Prokofyev International Airport** (344 7322; http://airport.dn.ua) receives flights from Moscow, Istanbul, Warsaw and Munich. Budget airline Wizz Air flies to five destinations in Europe, including London, plus Kutaisi in Georgia. The most useful domestic service is Utair to Zhulyany airport in Kiev.

BUS

Buses to Sviatohirsk (50uah, hourly) and Artyomivsk (30uah, hourly) were leaving from the distant Zapadny bus station when we visited, but that was due to change with the opening of a new bus station by the airport.

To head towards Crimea, Odesa and the Azov Sea use the more centrally located **Pivdenniy Avtovokzal** (South bus station; 266 5119; pl Kommunarov).

TRAIN

The new Hyundai Intercity train reduced the journey to Kiev (320uah, seven hours, twice daily) by half. There are also two slower overnight trains. For Dnipropetrovsk, the most convenient are fast *elektrychka* (electric trains, 70uah, three hours, twice daily). Another useful train is the daily Scoda Intercity for Simferopol (90uah, seven hours) via Zaporizhzhya (72uah, three hours). For Kharkiv, there are two Intercity trains daily (80uah, four hours).

Getting Around

The airport is 8km north of the city centre, accessible by bus 73A heading up vul Universytetskaya.

A little further south is the train station, a straight shunt down the city's main axis, vul Artyoma, on bus and trolleybus 2. Tram 1 plies the parallel vul Chelyuskintsev.

Sviatohirsk Святогірск

06262

Built into a dazzlingly white chalk cliff above the dreamy Siversky Donets River, the Sviatohirsk (Svyatogorsk in Russian) cave monastery is a heavenly sight, complemented rather than spoilt by the gigantic statue of the Bolshevik hero Artyom, which tops an adjacent hill. All that contrasts sharply with the hellish sprawl of *pansionaty* (Soviet-style workers' resorts) and tacky outdoor cafes on the other bank of the river. The reason is that apart from being the holiest Orthodox site in Eastern Ukraine, Sviatohirsk is also the main recreational zone for the Donbass region. Vacationing miners find time for the spiritual and for the mundane, putting candles in the monastery by day and washing down their *shashlyk* with beer and vodka by night.

Sights & Activities

Sviatohirsk Lavra MONASTERY

(Svyatogorskaya Uspenskaya Lavra; admission 20uah 10am-5pm, after hours free, monastery's excursion bureau tours 10uah) One of only three *lavra* (super monasteries) in Ukraine, Sviatohirsk monastery obtained this status in 2004. It is not nearly as ancient as Kyevo-Pecherska Lavra (p43) founded in 1051 – monks moved in here in 1620, burrowing into the chalk cliff, which they transformed into a five-storey dwelling, complete with several chapels and monk cells. These **caves** now form the monastery's upper part. In the following years it grew to become a prominent religious centre, but in 1790 Catherine II decided to close it, handing the surrounding lands to her lover Grygory Potemkin. The monastery reopened in 1844 when its lower, riverside section was built. In 1920 the Bolsheviks shot the monks and set up a hospital on the premises. But the clergy was back in 1992, taking over the entire *lavra* by 2004. You can check out the riverside section of the *lavra* on your own. Dress appropriately – no shorts or miniskirts are allowed. To visit the caves in the upper part of the monastery, join a group of pilgrims organised by the **monastery's excursion bureau** (9am-noon & 1-4pm), located at the far end of the monastery's riverside section.

Artyom Monument SCULPTURE

On top of a forested hill, the 27m monument of local Bolshevik leader Artyom was designed in an unusual Cubist style by Ivan Kavaleridze, who created some of the worst monuments in Kyiv. Fortunately, this early (1927) work is nothing to be ashamed of. As dazzlingly white as the Sviatohirsk Lavra underneath, it looks like (and in many way is) an idol of a rival religion, but together with the monastery they create a wonderfully bizarre ensemble. The monument is a short hike or 30uah taxi ride from Sviatohirsk Lavra.

Sleeping

Zeleny Gai RESORT $

(55 888, 55 844; www.zeleniy-gay.dn.ua/; vul 60 let Oktyabrya; s/d from 295uah; P) One of the better and friendlier Soviet *pansionaty* in the area. It's on the main road, about 700m from the bus station.

Roche Royal HOTEL $$$

(533 05, 050 701 7272; www.rocheroyal.com.ua; vul 60-letiya Oktyabrya 21; r from 1010uah; P) Right by the bus station, Roche Royal sets new standards for Sviatohirsk's hospitality scene with huge, stylish rooms, a spa and all the amenities a coal mogul might dream of. It also boasts the best restaurant for miles around.

Getting There & Around

TRAIN

Sviatohirsk train station, 5km away from the town and reached by a fairly frequent bus, is convenient for Kharkiv, with at least two fast *elektrychka* a day (45uah, 2½ hours).

BUS

From the bus station, buses leave for Donetsk at least hourly (60uah, 2½ hours). There are also frequent buses to Artemivsk (30uah, 1½ hr).

Dnipropetrovsk Дніпропетровськ

056

POP 1.08 MILLION

With its portly 19th-century houses, trams trundling along leafy boulevards and beautiful river vistas, Dnipropetrovsk has the

WINE IN THE MINE

In the land of mines, you might find yourself urged to descend into the bowels of the earth. But coal mines are unsafe due to deadly methane explosions. Yet the subsoil of Donbass has other treasures you can safely prospect for – namely salt and sparkling wine, or *shampanskoye* – as they call it in the former USSR. North of Donetsk, two industrial towns – Artemivsk and Soledar – lying next to each other offer a perfect underground experience.

Artemovsk Winery (☎062 748 0013, 062 332 2300; www.krimart.com; vul Patrisa Lumumby 87) dug itself into a huge underground cavern, which has an eerily Bondian feel about it, with vehicles whizzing by at dangerous speeds and green bottles moving on conveyer belts like missile warheads. Or perhaps an Austin Powers feel since for some reason the rocks are painted in vivid psychedelic colours. Every day it churns out thousands bottles of *shampanskoye*. A guided tour takes visitors through all stages of the wine-making process and straight into the sampling hall, where you can assess the resulting product.

On a more sombre note, the tour stops by a modest memorial marking the tunnel where the Nazis shot and buried 3000 Jews during WWII. Their bodies were discovered by the Soviets after they liberated Donbass.

The tour costs 100uah and takes place twice daily (usually at 10am and 2pm, but check). It's best booked in advance by phone or via an online form on its website. Artemivsk can be reached by bus from Donetsk's Zapadny bus station (30uah, 10 daily). There are also two morning *elektrychka* leaving from the train station (25uah, 2½ hours). Bus and train stations in Artemivsk are within 200m from each other. Take a taxi (20uah to 30uah) to the winery (say 'Vinzavod' to the driver), as there is no direct public transport.

Across the road leading to Kharkiv, the town of Soledar offers a chance to penetrate Europe's largest salt crystal. It is ironic that the place lies right on the route of the *chumaki* (medieval salt traders), who walked through the dangerous steppe all the way to Crimea, while a huge deposit lay almost on their doorstep. **Soledar salt mine** (☎0627-442 573, 050 608 9070; http://artyomsalt.dn.ua; vul Oktyabrskaya 2B; excursion 100uah; ⏲tours 11am, 1pm & 3pm Tue-Sun) is the gateway to it.

Three hundred metres below the surface, there is salt everywhere – you are actually encouraged to lick the walls, as guides are adamant no bacteria survive at this depth. Licking the mine's protector gnome brings you luck, they will surely add. The atmosphere in the mine is ideal for people suffering from asthma, which is why there is a sanatorium inside the mine, where people stay for days.

There are a few more salt statues in the wide, high-ceilinged galleries. You are unlikely to feel claustrophobic at the end of the tour when they bring you into a giant hall decorated with a Christmas tree – so that guests can have a New Year party here at any time of the year. There is also a football pitch where you can practise your strikes while listening to Bach and Chopin records. The acoustics are stunning. While here, some visitors choose to walk (or play football) barefoot – it is a strange and rather pleasant sensation and they say it's good for your health, too.

It is advisable to book tours (100uah) by phone in advance. No English is spoken, so ask your hotel reception to assist you. The mine can be reached by *marshrutka* (fixed-route minibus; 2.5uah) from Artemivsk bus station, 13km away. A taxi will cost around 100uah. The same *marshrutka* continues to Sil train station, which you will need if you are heading to Sviatohirsk.

potential to become an attractive city. But, unfortunately, its fathers (and godfathers) are too preoccupied with opening new boutiques and shopping emporiums, while heritage buildings are crumbling away and whole blocks are bulldozed, giving way to yet another glassy rectangle. A major centre of the space and aviation industry, Dnipropetrovsk became a springboard for such political heavyweights as ex-president Leonid Kuchma and Orange Revolution leader Yulia Tymoshenko. The city also has a strong

Dnipropetrovsk

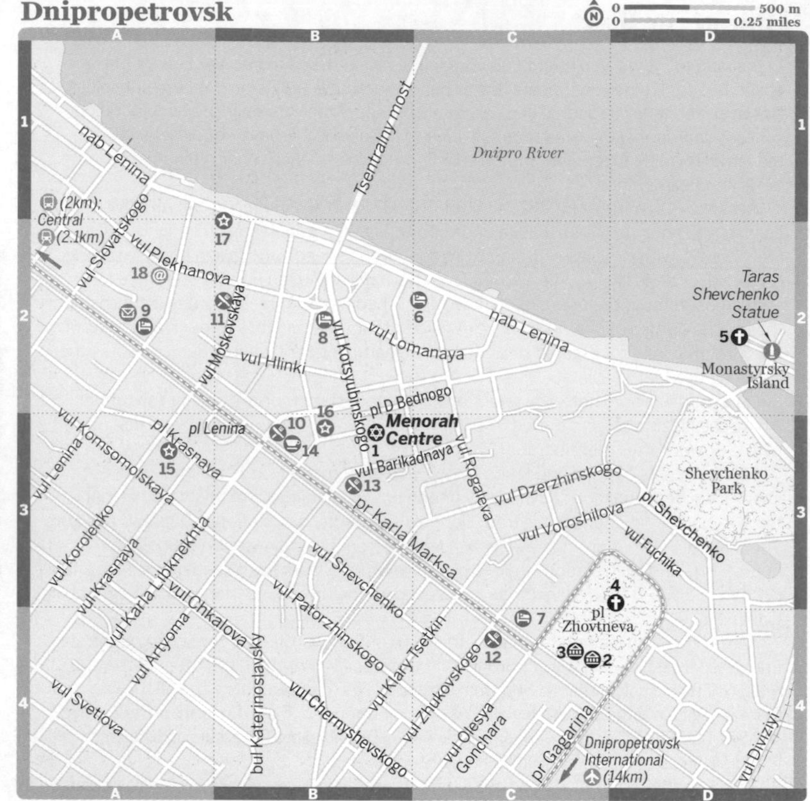

Jewish heritage and boasts the best museum of Jewish history in Ukraine.

Sights & Activities

Window shopping is one pleasant Dnipropetrovsk experience. Another favourite activity is wandering the riverfront promenade.

★ Menorah Centre JEWISH

(050 452 2163; http://menorah-center.com; vul Sholom-Aleykhema 4/26; museum 10am-7pm Tue, Thu & Sun) FREE Vaguely reminiscent of MI6 headquarters in Vauxhall, this giant structure looming over the remains of the Old Town is the slick new heart of the city's Jewish community. It was built over the city's old synagogue, of which only the original facade remains – the interior is completely new. The compound also contains a shopping arcade, an excellent hostel and the main attraction – the **Museum of Jewish Heritage and Holocaust in Ukraine**. Its 1st floor covers the history of Ukrainian Jews till WWII. The 2nd floor is all about the Shoah. Around 70% of Jews who lived in Ukraine before the war were shot, gassed, burnt alive or thrown into coal mines as the Nazis prepared *Lebensraum* (literally 'living space') for 'pure-blood' settlers from Germany.

History Museum MUSEUM

(Исторический музей; pr Karla Marksa 16; adult/student 17/8uah; 10am-5pm Tue-Sun) South of Shevchenko Park is pl Zhovtneva (pl Oktyabrskaya), site of the excellent History Museum, which has large, visually attractive rooms dedicated to the Cossacks, the Russian Empire, the Civil War and Holodomor. Adjoining the museum is a **diorama** (Диорама; adult/child 8/4uah), an 840-sq-metre painted canvas depicting the WWII Battle of the Dnipro, which was fought near here.

Dnipropetrovsk

Top Sights
1 Menorah Centre B3

Sights
2 Diorama C4
3 History Museum C4
4 Preobrazhensky Cathedral D3
5 St Nicholas Church D2

Sleeping
6 Dnipropetrovsk C2
7 Hotel Academy C4
Menorah Hostel .... (see 1)
8 Most-City Apartments B2
9 Mystay.org A2

Eating
10 Café Myshi Blyakhera B3
11 Osyamvalg B2
12 Papa Karla C4
13 Reporter B3

Drinking & Nightlife
14 DoubleDecker Cake & Co B3

Entertainment
15 Art-Kvartira A3
16 Labyrinth B3
17 Neizvestny Petrovsky B2

Information
18 Fish Andriy A2

Preobrazhensky Cathedral CATHEDRAL
(Спасо-Преображенский кафедральный собор; Transfiguration) With its glistening gold spire and dome, Preobrazhensky Cathedral is a classical structure dating from 1830. This is Dnipropetrovsk's holiest church, so don't barge in wearing beach clothes.

Sleeping

As elsewhere in Ukraine, it is totally reasonable to rent an apartment. **Mystay.org** (☎067 563 5906; www.mystay.org; pr Karla Marksa 60/16; apt from 350uah) not only secured a prime internet domain, but provides a good choice of inexpensive apartments in the city centre to primarily foreign clientele.

Menorah Hostel HOSTEL $
(www.menorahostel.com; vul Sholom-Aleykhema 4/26; dm 140uah; wi-fi) Cramped it is not. After all the converted-apartment hostels it is a sheer delight to enter the immaculately white corridor with high ceilings and large wooden doors on the 5th floor of the Menorah Centre (elevator is inside the shopping arcade). Perhaps too sterile and business-like, it is still one of the best hostels we've seen in Ukraine.

Dnipropetrovsk HOTEL $
(Готель Дніпропетровськ; ☎377 9577; www.dnipro-hotel.dp.ua; nab Lenina 33; s/d from 300/360uah; air-con) Located on the river about a 15-minute walk from the city centre, this 11-storey concrete block is not a bad option for the price. Look past its Soviet husk and the loud furniture and you'll find surprises like toothbrushes, colourful soaps, minibars and comfy foam mattresses, even in the economy rooms. Air-con is by request.

Most-City Apartments APARTMENT $$
(☎098 825 3162; vul Hlinki 2; studios 500-800uah) It is not really a hotel but a set of nicely furnished studio apartments in one of the city's highest business towers. More expensive ones comes with great views of the river and city. Considering the central location, it is very good value. Breakfast isn't included. Enter from vul Plekhanova.

Hotel Academy HOTEL $$$
(Гостиница Академия; ☎370 0505; www.academya.dp.ua; pr Karla Marksa 20; s/d from 1000/1700uah; air-con) Fans of Soviet-realist art need look no further than this museum-like hotel. The walls in the lobby and corridors are covered in brilliant paintings epitomising the best of the genre. While the service is outstanding, the rooms (which, curiously, bear Cézanne prints) are simply average. Breakfast in the Deja Vu restaurant downstairs is a highlight.

Eating

Osyamvalg EASTERN EUROPEAN $
(Осямвалг; http://osyamvalg-kafe.com; vul Moskovska 21; mains 30-50uah; 24hr) Designed to resemble a Soviet communal flat, this fun place is filled with all kinds of communist-era bric-a-brac and serves a gentrified version of Soviet canteen food.

★ **Café Myshi Blyakhera** RESTAURANT $$
(Кафе Мыши Бляхера; ☎377 3377; pr Karla Marksa 46; mains 60-120uah; 8am-11pm) There is an over-complicated pun in the name

involving mice and a retired Jewish gangster who allegedly left a handwritten book of recipes in this cellar place. If we are to believe the legend, this hardened man had a soft spot for Italian pasta, Azov Sea *bychki* fish and Danubian frogs. A cool place full of old books and local bohemians. To find the entrance, look out for a blue door on the side of the block.

Papa Karla EASTERN EUROPEAN **$$**
(pr Karla Marksa 27A; mains 40-70uah; ⊙8am-11pm) An uber-cute 20th-century nostalgia place without hammers and sickles – think visiting a Soviet granny back in the 1970s. Savour your beetroot and prune salad or steam cutlets made of pike to the soundtrack of Soviet pop divas, like Alla Pugacheva and Sofia Rotaru.

Reporter EUROPEAN **$$**
(Репортёр; ☎056 233 7575; cnr pr Karla Marksa & vul Barikadnaya; mains 70-120uah; ⊙24hr) Reporter has three wings: a ground-floor coffeehouse serving breakfasts and possibly the plumpest, tastiest homemade *varenyky* in the land; a chichi restaurant upstairs; and a superb basement 'warm-up bar' with a great in-house DJ getting the city's hipsters fired up for a night on the town. You'll find at least one of the three open at any time of the day and night.

Drinking

DoubleDecker Cake & Co CAFE
(pr Karla Marksa 46; ⊙8am-10pm) It looks tiny when you enter, but the upper floor (or deck, rather) has a spacious sitting area with comfy armchairs and a large common table invitingly fitted with plugs for your gadgets. Best desserts we've tried in the region.

Neizvestny Petrovsky CLUB
(Unknown Petrovsky; nab Lenina 15A; admission 30-60uah; ⊙1pm-7am) Run by the same people as Fish Andriy, this is a place where young Bohemians meet for a beer, inexpensive food, and some jazz or alternative live music.

Labyrinth CLUB
(Лабиринт; cnr vul Kharkovskaya & vul Hopner; admission Sun-Thu free, Fri & Sat 50-100uah) True to its name, this is an underground maze of corridors and halls, each with its own bar and soundtrack. Don't buy the full ticket for 100uah unless you are desperate to see a striptease show in the upstairs 'VIP' lounges.

Entertainment

Art-Kvartira ARTS CENTRE
(http://artkvartira.dp.ua/; pl Krasnaya 3/1; ⊙Wed-Sun) A busy modern arts centre with theatre performance, concerts, dancing and yoga classes happening almost daily. English-language movies are shown on Monday.

Information

Check out http://gorod.dp.ua for the latest hotel, restaurant and club news.

Fish Andriy (Риба Андрій; http://ryba.dp.ua/; vul Plekhanova 13A; per hr 15uah; ⊙24hr) A pay-for-time 'anti-cafe', like those in Kyiv, this is primarily a comfortable environment to fire up your gadget and Skype away with friends. Help yourself to free coffee and lemonade. This is also a venue for cultural and educational events organised by the K12 youth initiative, which aims to gentrify the urban environment and local politics. Most notably, it organises excursions to the city's Airspace Centre, old Soviet plants and an abandoned Cossack village it wants to revive as an arts venue. There is a smallish hostel in the premises.

Post office (Почтамт; pr Karla Marksa 62; internet per hr 6uah; ⊙8am-8pm Mon-Fri, to 7pm Sat) Handle both your snail-mail and email needs at the post office.

Getting There & Away

AIR

International carriers Austrian Airlines, Turkish Airlines and Aeroflot all have flights to **Dnipropetrovsk International Airport** (☎395 209), which is about 15km southeast of the city towards Zaporizhzhya (the airport is also convenient for that city). There are at least 10 flights a day to Kyiv.

BUS

Dnipropetrovsk has the country's largest **bus station** (☎778 4090; www.dopas.dp.ua; vul Kurchatova 10), west of the city centre, about a 10-minute walk from the train station.

To save time take *marshrutky*, not buses, to Zaporizhzhya (40uah, 1½ hours, every 15 minutes). 'Luxury' bus operators **Autolux** (☎371 0353) and **Gunsel** (☎778 3935) have overnight trips to Kyiv (170uah to 210uah, seven to eight hours), and you'll find plenty of buses to Poltava, Kharkiv, Odesa and Simferopol.

TRAIN

From the **central train station** (☎005 395 209; pr Karla Marksa 108) the fast Stolichny Express (108uah, six hours) to Kyiv runs early in the morning and late evening, plus there are other services to Kyiv (112uah, eight hours). Trains also rumble to Odesa (120uah, 11½ hours, at least daily), Simferopol (90uah, seven hours, five daily) and all other major cities.

There are daily fast *elektrychky* to Kharkiv (70uah, 4½ hours) and Donetsk (31uah, 4½ hours), plus a few slower passenger trains to both destinations. Some slow trains pass through nearby Zaporizhzhya, but it's much easier and quicker by *marshrutka*.

Getting Around

From the airport, take bus 60 or 109 to the central train station, from you where you can catch tram 1 into the city centre. A taxi should cost about 100uah.

Tram 1 runs the length of pr Karla Marksa, originating at the train station. The metro line currently connects the train station with outlying districts. It will become more useful for travellers once the construction of two stations is completed in the city centre.

Zaporizhzhya Запоріжжя

☎0612 / POP 815,000

So, so Soviet! For a visitor, Zaporizhzhya is essentially one avenue lined with sometimes-imposing Stalinesque architecture. Named after its Moscow equivalent, pr Lenina runs from Avtozaz, the birthplace of the Zaporizhets (USSR's most ridiculed car model) to the Soviet industrial icon, Dniproges power station. Neither of which are the reason people come here on holiday. The reason is Khortytsya – a rocky forested island where Cossacks set up their all-male free-rule republic, which prospered from raids on neighbouring empires and duties levied on anyone who used the river trade route. Today it is the place to learn about Cossack culture and history, admire beautiful river vistas and spend a day hiking or cycling.

Sights

Khortytsya Island HISTORIC SITE

(Острів Хортиця) The Zaporizhska Sich on Khortytsya Island was the most important cradle of Ukrainian Cossackdom, where *hetman* (Cossack cheiftan) Dmytro Baida united disparate groups of Cossacks in the construction of a *sich* (fort) in 1553 to 1554. The island was perfect: strategically located below the Dnipro rapids and beyond the control of Polish or Russian authority. Any man could come to join the Cossack brotherhood, irrespective of social background or indeed criminal record. But no women were allowed entry.

At the height of its power the community numbered some 20,000 fighters, under the authority of one *hetman*. On the battlefield they were formidable opponents; off it, formidable vodka drinkers. The *sich* was eventually destroyed in 1775, on the order of Russian empress Catherine the Great.

Today you can visit the informative **Historical Museum of Zaporizhsky Cossacks** (adult/child & student 18/9uah; ⏰10am-7pm Tue-Sun), which includes painted dioramas and various Cossack weaponry and bric-a-brac excavated from the island. Nearby, a prime spot on the cliff edge is now occupied by the **Sich Reconstruction** (adult/child & student 18/9uah; ⏰9.30am-4.30pm Tue-Sun), a wooden fortress complete with churches and about a dozen thatched-roof *khaty* (dwellings), built for the epic movie *Taras Bulba* in 2007.

With its network of forest paths and tarmac roads, Khortytsya Island is a haven for hikers and cyclists. You can usually find a **bicycle-rental stand** (25uah per hour) at the museum's parking lot.

Dniproges Dam HYDROPOWER STATION

At 760m – two and a half times longer than the famous Hoover Dam – the wall of the USSR's first dam certainly represented a monumental engineering feat when constructed under US supervision in 1927 to 1932. It's still impressive, although stained by years of local pollution. It is best viewed from the Historical Museum of Zaporizhsky Cossacks.

Sleeping

Venetsia HOTEL $$

(Венеция; ☎289 4512; http://venecia-hotel.com.ua; vul Nizhnedneprovskaya 1B; r from 490uah) Right by the river, Venetsia has rooms with faux-Victorian furniture, unexpectedly luxurious for the price. Annoyingly, you need to order breakfast the night before and tell staff exactly when you want it. A sandy beach is across the road and there is a great sauna inside the hotel.

Four Points by Sheraton HOTEL $$

(☎766 0001; www.fourpointszaporozhye.com; bul Shevchenko 71A; r with/without river view from 800/630uah) Located in newly built twin towers with splendid river views, Four Points provides comforts previously unseen in Zaporizhzhya. Most rooms come with floor-to-ceiling windows and balconies.

Eating

The main restaurant row is on bul Shevchenka, but you'll find a few good places along pr Lenina.

Bosfor TURKISH **$$**
(Босфор; vul Yakova Novitskogo 3; mains 40-80uah;) Turkish expats run this pleasant eatery just off pr Lenina. The convenient picture menu features lots of *shashlyks* and appetising Turkish snacks. Patrons smoke *shisha* (hookah) on an open-air terrace.

★ **Fishcafe** UKRAINIAN **$$**
(pr Lenina 107; mains 70-120uah; 11am-11pm) This lovely restaurant with a wood-filled interior and many multicoloured fish-shaped objects adorning the walks could have easily become our favourite in a more sophisticated city than Zaporizhzhya. The main speciality is Black Sea fish, but there are more intriguing dishes inspired by Ukrainian cuisine. Try *svekolnik* – a cold beetroot soup. Fishcafe is on the main road in the old part of town – take any transport heading towards the train station and get off after you pass a large ravine filled with summer cottages.

Entertainment

Khortitsa Equestrian Theatre CIRCUS
(701 2481; http://zp-kazaki.com/; Khortytsya Island; tickets 60uah) Standing on top of a horse, attached to the side of a horse, hanging upside down on a horse – Cossacks defy fear and forces of gravitation in this captivating (and humorous) show. The venue resembles a Ukrainian village, complete with an inn and shops selling crafts. It is unreachable by public transport, so arrange a taxi from your hotel.

Information

Post office (pr Lenina 133; internet per hr 4.50uah; post office 7.30am-8pm, telephone centre 8am-9pm) Besides postal services, an internet and telephone centre, there is also an ATM.

Getting There & Away

BUS

Marshrutky for Dnipropetrovsk (40uah, 1½ hours, every 15 minutes) leave from the bus station or from pl Lenina near Dniproges Dam. The **bus station** (642 657; pr Leninaya 20) is near Zaporizhzhya-1 train station. There are services to Simferopol (140uah, seven hours) and Donetsk (85uah, four hours, hourly).

TRAIN

Zaporizhzhya-1 train station (224 4060; pr Leninaya 2) is at the southeastern end of pr Lenina. New fast services are available to Crimean and major eastern cities: Kyiv (300uah, seven hours), Simferopol (220uah, 3½ hours), Donetsk (170uah, three hours) and Kharkiv (180uah, three hours). There are many more slower trains going to the same destinations. Most of these trains pass Dnirpropetrovsk, but buses are more convenient.

Getting Around

The main street, pr Lenina, stretches for 10km from Zaporizhzhya-1 train station at its southeastern end to pl Lenina overlooking the Dniproges Dam. Between them, bul Shevchenka descends from pr Lenina to the section of the river where both listed hotels are located. Most trolleybuses and *marshrutky* run the length of pr Lenina between Zaporizhzhya-1 train station and pl Lenina, but you can bank on trolleybus 3.

Khortytsya Island lies in the Dnipro, 2km southwest of the Dniproges Dam wall. To get there, take the infrequent *marshrutka* 46 from anywhere on pr Lenina. It goes across the dam and then south along the riverside bul Vintera. Get off as soon it turns right, away from the river, and walk. Return to bul Vintera and walk for another 700m before the road turns left to Khortytsya's northern bridge. Once you have crossed it, find a footpath leading to the museum on your left.

Alternatively, take a *marshrutka* marked Хортица (eg 87 or 58), leaving from the corner of pr Lenina and pr Metallurgov, and get off after it crosses Khortytsya's southern bridge. From there, it is a 30-minute walk north to the museum.

Understand Ukraine

Ukraine Today

In November 2013 Ukraine erupted in mass demonstrations against the government when president Viktor Yanukovych, under pressure from Russian president Putin to join a customs union with Russia, refused to sign an Association Agreement with the EU, a first step to membership. Thousands of protesters set up a round-the-clock camp in central Kyiv in sub-zero temperatures. But underlying the Euromaidan protests are deeper issues than just EU membership.

Best on Film

Shadows of Forgotten Ancestors (1964) Shaggy Hutsul customs and symbolism.

Za Dvumya Zaytsami (Chasing Two Hares; 1961) Diverting romp through early 20th-century Kyiv.

The Battle of Chernobyl (2006) Detailed documentary on the Chornobyl disaster and its aftermath.

Orange Revolution (2007) Steven York's documentary on the events of 2004.

Evenings on a Farm near Dikanka (1961) Technicolor film version of Gogol's most Ukrainian tales.

Best in Print

Evenings on a Farm near Dikanka Nikolai Gogol's stories, mostly set in his native Poltava region.

Borderland Anna Reid's journey through Ukrainian history.

Death and the Penguin Andrey Kurkov's Kafkaesque tale set in the troubled early 1990s.

Everything Is Illuminated Jonathan Safran Foer searches for the lost west Ukrainian *shtetl* (village) of Trachimbrod.

Taras Bulba Gogol's swashbuckling Cossack tale.

The White Guard Bulgakov's portrait of Kyiv during the Russian Civil War.

Dictatorship?

The protests of 2013 are seen by many as a repeat performance of the Orange Revolution of 2004, a popular pro-Western uprising that forced a rerun of disputed elections. The man behind the alleged electoral fraud was Viktor Yanukovych, who was finally elected the country's president in 2010. Many at the time feared Yanukovych and his oligarch-backed Party of the Regions would curtail press freedom and dismantle democracy in the country. So, a few years down the line, has Ukraine descended into dictatorship? Well, not quite. Opposition parties function quite freely (if occasionally hassled by police), protests are still permitted on Kyiv's squares (then normally broken up by riot police), and a few newspapers and TV channels still attempt investigative journalism. But in general, Ukraine feels less free than it did in 2009, with journalists experiencing intimidation and sometimes violence, members of protest groups (such as Femen) effectively exiled, and any successful businesses under threat of confiscation by the Yanukovych family. And as long as ailing opposition leader Yulia Tymoshenko languishes in jail, the overriding atmosphere in the country will be one of pessimism and fear of what the regime and its associates might do next.

Divided Nation

Even the most optimistic Ukrainians would admit that theirs is a divided nation. The opposition is led by Ukrainian-speaking politicians with their support base in the west of the country, but President Yanukovych represents the interests of the Russian speaking east and south. East of the Dnipro River the Orthodox Church rules supreme; west Ukrainians observe a mishmash of faiths. The east bathes in a very selective nostalgia for the Soviet Union, while west Ukrainian nationalists rename streets after Stepan Bandera (controversial WWII leader of the Ukrainian Nationalist Organisation) and hanker to be enveloped in the EU's Russia-proof bubble. The Carpathian Hutsuls quip ominously of insurgency while the Donbas middle class expresses relief that 'their bandit' (as a tongue-in-cheek saying now goes) is in power. West Ukrainians march on Kyiv to protest against the regime while the regime buses in Crimeans and Donetskites to march 'against fascism' (as the banners in summer 2013's marches read). 'How do these people live together?' you might ask yourself – but somehow they do. Of course it's very much in all local politicians' interests to keep the country divided into their power bases and many of the differences are exaggerated. But a divisive history still makes waves here, and Yanukovych's regime and its tactics are just the latest to crash onto Ukraine's troubled shores.

Trouble Ahead

Having taken Ukraine in their grip, Yanukovych and the Party of the Regions are not likely to let it go again without a fight, and most expected that fight to be the 2015 presidential elections. However, throughout 2013 tensions had been rising and Yanukovych's about turn on the Association Agreement saw emotions boil over, especially in the country's west. From behind the barricades on Maydan Nezalezhnosti (Independence Square) the protesters are calling for the resignation of the president and government, the release of political prisoners (former prime minister Yulia Tymoshenko) and an end to 'corrupt rule' by the Party of the Regions. If and when new presidential elections are held, the opposition has promised to field a single candidate, possibly world heavyweight boxing champion Vitaly Klytschko, who recently gave up life in the ring. Whatever the future holds, Ukraine faces a crucial few years, a period that will certainly decide its long-term fate and direction.

Should I Go?

Whatever the outcome of the Euromaidan revolution, the answer to the above question is definitely yes. However, by staying in small, privately run guesthouses, shopping in Ukraine's many markets and generally spending money in local businesses, travellers will be doing their bit to support the Ukrainian people.

POPULATION: **44.6 MILLION**

OFFICIAL UNEMPLOYMENT: **7.5%**

POPULATION BELOW POVERTY LINE: **24%**

NATIONAL ANTHEM: **'UKRAINE HAS NOT YET DIED'**

if Ukraine were 100 people

77 would be Ukrainian
17 would be Russian
6 would be Others

belief systems

(% of population)

Ukrainian Orthodox (Kyiv Patriarchate)

8 Greek Catholic

7 Ukrainian Autocephalous Orthodox

26 Ukrainian Orthodox (Moscow Patriarchate)

9 Others

population per sq km

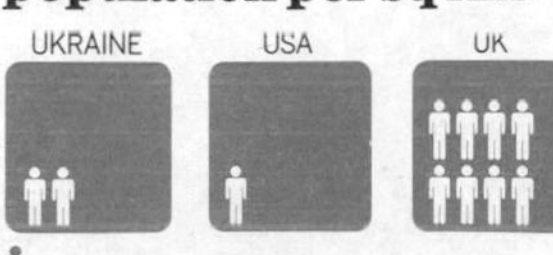

≈ 30 people

History

Although their northern neighbours disparagingly refer to Ukrainians as 'little Russians', it was Ukraine that was home to the first eastern Slavic state. So historically Ukraine is the birthplace of Russia rather than vice versa. Another irony is that this initial state, Kyivan Rus, was founded in the 9th century by neither Russians nor Ukrainians, but by Vikings – an indication of just how much foreigners have meddled in the region's convoluted history.

Leading 20th-century artist Joseph Beuys was rescued by Crimean Tatars when he crash landed on the peninsula during WWII, and his oeuvre of sleds, felt and honey recalls their healing methods.

Invaded by Mongols from the east, encroached upon by Poland and Lithuania from the west and requisitioned by Russia from the north, Ukraine's national culture was principally forged in the wild, Cossack-held steppes in the middle. The baton of nationalism was taken up again in the 19th century by western Ukrainians under Austro-Hungarian rule, but it took the 1991 collapse of the Soviet Union for a centuries-old dream of an independent state to be realised.

Cimmerians to Khazars

Before Kyivan Rus, Ukraine's prehistory is tribal. First came the Cimmerians in the 12th century BC. Then, fierce warrior Scythians from Central Asia settled the steppe in the 7th century BC, while Greeks from western Asia Minor established city-states around the Black Sea. The two groups formed a symbiotic relationship. The famous gold work found in Scythian tombs is believed to have been commissioned from Greek artisans; a fine collection is found in Kyiv's Kyevo-Pecherska Lavra.

Successive waves of nomadic invaders (Sarmatians from the east, Germanic Ostrogoths from northern Poland and Huns from Mongolia) continued to sweep into Ukraine. However, the Slavs, thought to originate from near the borders of present-day Poland, Belarus and northwestern Ukraine, remained untouched by these invasions. Turkic-Iranian Khazars from the Caucasus were probably the first to bring the Slavs under subjugation, in the 8th century AD.

TIMELINE

482

One of Eastern Europe's oldest settlements, Kyiv's origins aren't crystal clear. Legend has it that Slavic brothers Ky, Shchek and Khoriv and their sister Lybid founded it.

879

Nordic King Oleh travels to Kyiv. Taken by its strategic position on the Dnipro River between Scandinavia and Constantinople, he wrests it from his own emissaries Askold and Dir – by murdering them.

989

With Kyivan Rus now established as the first eastern Slavic state, Volodymyr the Great adopts Orthodox Christianity. A mass baptism in the Dnipro River seals this early pro-European decision.

Kyivan Rus

Meanwhile, Scandinavians – known as Varangians or Rus to the Slavs – had been exploring, trading and setting up small states east of the Baltic since the 6th century AD. Travelling south from the Rus power centre of Novgorod (near modern-day St Petersburg) in 879, King Oleh stopped just long enough to declare himself ruler of Kyiv. The city handily lay between Novgorod and Constantinople on the Dnipro River, and under Oleh's urging it became capital of a huge, unified Rus state. At its largest, under the rule of Volodymyr the Great (978–1015), this empire stretched from the Volga to the Danube and to the Baltic, its prosperity based on trade along the Dnipro. Despite Nordic rule, the territory's underlying culture remained essentially Slavic.

As well as consolidating Rus territory, Volodymyr firmly established Orthodox Christianity as the pre-eminent religion. By accepting baptism in 989 and marrying the Byzantine emperor's daughter (at Khersones outside Sevastopol), he opened the door to Byzantine artistic influences and cast Kyivan Rus as a European, rather than Islamic Asian, state. St Sofia's Cathedral in Kyiv is still testament to Kyivan Rus' greatness and the importance of Orthodox Christianity within the state.

After the death of Kyivan Rus' last great ruler, Yaroslav the Wise, in 1054, the empire began disintegrating into separate princedoms. When Mongol warriors sacked Kyiv in 1240, it largely ceased to exist. According to Russian and Western historians, who believe present-day Russia, Ukraine and Belarus all stem from Kyivan Rus, the centres of power then simply shifted north and west, with Russia evolving from the northern princedoms of Novgorod and Vladimir-Suzdal. Some Ukrainian historians, however, prefer to treat Russia as a distinct civilisation – emanating from and returning to Novgorod after 1240.

ROXELANA

Roxelana, the powerful wife of Ottoman emperor Suleyman the Magnificent, was originally a Ukrainian slave from near Lviv, who was sold at Kaffa (today's Feodosiya) and taken to 16th-century Turkey.

Mongols, Tatars & Turks

The Mongol invasion that sounded the death knell for Kyivan Rus in 1240 was led by Genghis Khan's grandson Batu. As a result of his handiwork, a large swathe of the Rus empire was subsumed into the so-called Golden Horde ('horde' meaning region) of the Mongol Empire. This encompassed much of eastern and southern Ukraine, along with parts of European Russia and Siberia, with the now vanished city of Sarai, on the Volga, as its capital.

Over time, Mongol leaders were gradually replaced by their Tatar colleagues and descendants, and when the horde began to disintegrate in the 15th century, it divided into several smaller khanates.

One of these – the Crimean Khanate – eventually became a client state of the Constantinople-based Ottoman Turk Empire in 1475. The Crimean

1199

West of Kyiv, Prince Roman Mstyslavych merges the regions of Galicia and Volynia into one Grand Duchy. Although landowners continue to rebel against his rule, a thriving agricultural society emerges.

1240

A pivotal moment in Kyivan Rus history is reached, as Mongols sack the capital. The already fragmented empire's eastern regions are absorbed into the Mongolian Golden Horde. Many Kyivanhells s flee west.

1349

Ukraine comes under attack from the opposite direction, as Poland overruns Galicia and its capital Lviv. Nearly 40 years later, Poland teams up with Lithuania as both states look east.

1475

The Crimean Khanate, which succeeded the Mongolian Golden Horde in 1428, becomes a client state of the Ottoman Empire, remaining so until 1772. Crimean Tatars frequently take slaves from mainland Ukraine.

Tatars, as the people of the khanate were known, made frequent slave raids into Ukrainian, Russian and Polish territory until the 18th century. When Russia overran Crimea in 1783, it retaliated. The Tatars suffered dreadfully and often have ever since. Reminders of their once-powerful civilisation can be seen in Bakhchysaray, which since independence has become one of Crimea's most interesting tourist attractions.

Neal Ascherson's *Black Sea* is a fascinating tale of the civilisations – and barbarians – that jostled for supremacy around this coast, from prehistory's Scythians to multicultural Odesa's 19th-century founders.

Galicia-Volynia

Meanwhile, from 1199 under the rule of Prince Roman Mstyslavych, the region of Galicia-Volynia (most of present-day western, central and northern Ukraine, plus parts of northeastern Poland and southern Belarus) became one of the most powerful within Kyivan Rus. This enclave's geography differentiated it from the rest of the empire. It was far enough west to avoid conquest by eastern invaders like the Mongols and more likely to fall prey to its Catholic neighbours Hungary and Poland – or, later, Lithuania. More densely populated than any other part of Kyivan Rus, it developed a rich agricultural society.

Until 1340 Galicia-Volynia (also called Halych-Volhynia) enjoyed independent rule under Roman, his son Danylo, grandson Lev and descendants, who kept the Mongols at bay and helped Lviv and other cities to flourish. Political control was wrested from this local dynasty by the Poles and Lithuanians in the 1340s, who split the kingdom between them and used it as a base to expand eastwards into other areas of Ukraine, including Kyiv. However, its brief period of early self-determination seems to have left Galicia-Volynia with a particularly strong taste for Ukrainian nationalism, which is still evident today.

Terry Brighton's *Hell Riders: The True Story of the Charge of the Light Brigade* interweaves participants' accounts and factual reports to unravel the Crimean War's greatest blunder.

Cossacks

Later lionised – perhaps overoptimistically – by nationalist writers such as Taras Shevchenko and Ivan Franko, the Cossacks are central to the country's identity. They arose out of the steppe in the country's sparsely populated mid-south. In the mid-15th century, this area was a kind of no-man's-land separating the Polish-Lithuanian settlements in the northwest from the Tatars in Crimea.

However, the steppe offered abundant natural wealth, and poorer individuals in Polish-Lithuanian society began making longer forays south to hunt or forage for food. The area also attracted runaway serfs, criminals, bandits and Orthodox refugees. Along with a few semi-independent Tatar bands, the hard-drinking inhabitants formed self-governing militaristic communities and became known as *kozaky* (Cossacks in English), from a Turkic word meaning 'outlaw, adventurer or free person'. The people elected the ruling chieftain (hetman). The most famous group of

1554

Some 60 years after Cossacks first appear in the historical record, the fiercest and most famous band of warriors – the Zaporizhska Sich – sets up on an island in the Dnipro River.

1569

The Union of Lublin builds on existing links to establish the Polish-Lithuanian Commonwealth. This monarchical democracy includes parts of Belarusia, Estonia, Latvia, Russia and Ukraine.

1648

Central Ukrainian Cossacks become weary of foreign rule and, under the leadership of Bohdan Khmelnytsky, rebel against the Poles.

1654

Cossacks enter into a military alliance with Russia against Poland. The Cossacks form their own fledgling state – whose initial success is shortlived – called a Hetmanate.

Cossacks was based below the rapids *(za porozhy)* on the lower Dnipro, in a fortified island community called the Zaporizhska Sich.

Although they were officially under Polish-Lithuanian rule from 1569, and sometimes joined the commonwealth army as mercenaries, the Cossacks were, for the most part, left to their own devices. They waged a number of successful campaigns against the Turks and Tatars, twice assaulting Istanbul (in 1615 and 1620), and sacking the Black Sea cities of Varna (in today's Bulgaria) and Kaffa (modern-day Feodosiya). While millions of peasants in the Polish-Lithuanian state joined the Uniate Church, the Cossacks remained Orthodox.

As Poland tried to tighten its control in the 17th century, there were Cossack-led uprisings to try to win greater autonomy. In 1654 the Cossacks formed their own so-called Hetmanate to assert the concept of Ukrainian self-determination. While initially successful, ultimately the Cossacks' military uprisings only led to a change of overlord – from Polish to Russian.

Mikhail Bulgakov's novel *The White Guard* brings to life the confusion reigning in Kyiv during the 1918 Civil War – and better explains the competing factions than most history books do.

Russian Control

It's safe to say (though possibly not in Russia) that without Ukraine and its abundant natural wealth, Russia would never have become such a powerful nation. Ukraine also offered access to the Black Sea, so after a series of wars with the Turks in the 18th century, Russia was keen to expand into southern Ukraine. Catherine the Great led the charge to colonise and 'Russify'. In 1775, the same year she destroyed the Zaporizhska Sich, she annexed the region to the imperial province of 'New Russia' and charged governor Grygory Potemkin with attracting settlers and founding new cities. Potemkin helped establish today's Dnipropetrovsk, Sevastopol and Simferopol, but died before Odesa was completed.

In 1772 powerful Prussia, Austria and Russia decided to carve up Poland. Under the resulting Partitions of Poland (1772–95), most of western Ukraine was handed to Russia, but the far west around Lviv went to the Austrian Habsburg Empire. The Ukrainian nationalist movement was born in Kyiv in the 1840s, but when the Tsarist authorities there banned the Ukrainian language from official use in 1876, the movement's focus shifted to Austrian-controlled Lviv.

New York Times journalist Walter Duranty is a very controversial Pulitzer Prize winner because of his denial of the Ukrainian famine when reporting from the 1930s USSR.

Civil War

Following WWI and the collapse of the Tsarist monarchy, Ukraine had a shot at independence, but the international community was unsupportive and none of the bewildering array of factions could win decisive backing. In Kyiv, the first autonomous Ukrainian National Republic (UNR) was proclaimed in 1918 under president Mykhailo Hrushevsky. Meanwhile, Russian Bolsheviks set up a rival Congress of Soviets in Kharkiv.

1709

Cossacks seize another chance to throw off the colonial yoke, by joining Sweden in its 'Northern War' with Russia. But the Battle of Poltava doesn't go their way and victorious Tsarist forces execute them.

1772

During the three Partitions of Poland, Russia, Prussia and Habsburg Austria divvy up the weakened Polish-Lithuanian Commonwealth.

1775

As her army moves south, and her lover Grygory Potemkin follows, blithely building film-set villages, Catherine the Great orders the destruction of the Zaporizhska Sich.

1783

Russia establishes its sovereignty over Crimea by demolishing mosques. Many Crimean Tatars flee. The Khans' Palace at Bakhchysaray survives because Empress Catherine finds it 'romantic'.

Civil war broke out, with five different armies – Red (Bolshevik), White, Polish, Ukrainian and Allied – vying for power, while various anarchist bands of Cossacks (the most famous led by Nestor Makhno) roamed the land. Author Mikhail Bulgakov estimated that Kyiv changed hands 14 times in 18 months.

Just as any UNR victories in Kyiv proved short-lived, so too did the West Ukrainian National Republic (ZUNR) in Lviv. Proclaimed in October 1918, it was overrun by Polish troops the following summer. Under the 1919 Treaty of Versailles negotiated after WWI and the following Treaty of Riga in 1921, Poland, Romania and Czechoslovakia took portions of western Ukraine, while Soviet forces were given control of the rest. Nationalist leader Semyon Petlyura set up a government in exile, but was assassinated in Paris in 1926.

Soviet Power

Thus handed to the Soviets, Ukraine was at the founding of the USSR in 1922. Behind Russia, it was the second largest and second most powerful republic in the union, but despite – or perhaps because of – that 'little brother' status, it came in for some particularly harsh bullying from the top. When Stalin took power in 1927, he looked upon Ukraine as a laboratory for testing Soviet restructuring while stamping out 'harmful' nationalism. In 1932–33 he oversaw a famine. Executions and deportations of intellectuals and political 'dissidents' followed, along with the destruction of numerous Ukrainian palaces, churches and cemeteries. During the great purges of 1937–39, an estimated one million people in the USSR were executed and a further three to 12 million (the numbers are difficult to quantify) sent to labour camps, a high proportion of them from Ukraine.

MASS GRAVE

The 'Ukrainian Katyn' (mass grave) was revealed globally in 2007, when authorities reburied 2000 victims of the Soviet Secret Police (NKVD). The deaths at Bykovyna, near Kyiv, occurred in the 1930s and '40s.

WWII

Even by the standards of Ukrainian history, WWII was a particularly bloody and fratricidal period. Caught between Soviet Russia, Nazi Germany and an ongoing struggle for independence, some six to eight million Ukrainians, at least 1.6 million of them Jews, were killed. Entire cities were levelled. The Red Army rolled into Polish Ukraine in September 1939, the Germans attacked in 1941, and the Nazis and their Romanian allies occupied most of the country for more than two years. Two million Ukrainians were conscripted into the Soviet army and fought on the Russian side. However, some nationalists hoped the Nazis would back Ukrainian independence and collaborated with Germany. This was a source of much postwar recrimination (and a very ill-informed 'debate' still occasionally flares up today when its suits the political aims of one group or another), but many partisans in the Ukrainian Insurgent Army

1825

Many of the Decembrists behind a doomed St Petersburg coup hail from Ukraine. The most famous of the Decembrist wives, Maria Volkonskaya, also has close links to the country.

1854

France and England have watched Russia's moves south with unease and decide to put a stop to it. The Crimea War sees Sevastopol come under 349 days' siege.

1861

Tsar Aleksander II abolishes serfdom across the Russian Empire. That same year the first railway on Ukrainian soil is opened between Lviv and Przemysl (in today's Poland).

1876

With a new Ukrainian nationalist movement bubbling up since the 1840s, Tsar Aleksander II issues a decree banning the use of the Ukrainian language in public.

(UPA) fought both German and Russian troops in a bid for an independent state. The catacombs just outside Odesa sheltered a celebrated group of partisans.

In the end the Soviet army prevailed. In 1943 it retook Kharkiv and Kyiv before launching a massive offensive in early 1944 that pushed back German forces. In the process any hopes for an independent Ukraine were obliterated. Soviet leader Stalin also saw fit to deport millions of Ukrainians or send them to Siberia for supposed 'disloyalty or collaboration'. This included the entire population of Crimean Tatars in May 1944.

EUROPE'S HIDDEN FAMINE

Between 1932 and 1933, some three to five million citizens of Ukraine – 'Europe's breadbasket' – died of starvation while surrounded by fields of wheat and locked government storehouses full of food. How did this happen? Stalin collectivised Soviet farms and ordered the production of unrealistic quotas of grain, which was then confiscated.

Many historians believe this famine was part of the Soviet leadership's wider plan to solve the 'nationality problem' within several troublesome republics, especially Ukraine. Undoubtedly the agricultural collectivisation of the time was ideologically driven. However, as the USSR's leading farmlands, Ukraine was particularly hard hit, and documents released in 2006 suggest that Ukrainians were deliberately targeted in the 'Great Hunger'. For example, Ukraine's borders were reportedly shut to prevent people leaving.

A total of seven to 10 million people died throughout the USSR. (It's difficult to quantify, partly because those who took the next census were, in Stalin's inimitable style, immediately ordered shot.) Yet the true scale of the disaster has rarely been appreciated in the West.

As Soviet collectivisation began in the 1930s, combining individual farms into huge state-run communes, wealthier peasants (*kulaks*, or *kurkuli* in Ukrainian) who resisted were deported or starved into submission. By 1932 Communist Party activists were seizing grain and produce from collectives and houses. Watchtowers were erected above fields. Anyone caught stealing was executed or deported. As entire villages starved, people committed suicide and even resorted to cannibalism.

At the time Soviet authorities denied the famine's existence, but damning facts have emerged since Ukrainian independence. In 2003 Kyiv designated the Holodomor (Ukrainian famine) as genocide, and a handful of other governments followed suit. In 2005 president Viktor Yushchenko declared 26 November as official Holodomor Remembrance Day, and called on the international community to recognise the famine as genocide. Critics, however, continue to argue that the famine was aimed at certain social, rather than ethnic, groups. The Council of Europe adopted this stance in 2010. Russia remains firmly opposed to any 'genocide' description and new president Viktor Yanukovych has declared the events of the early 1930s a tragedy, but not genocide.

1918

In the chaotic aftermath of WWI, Ukrainians try to form an independent republic but are hamstrung by internecine fighting. Fourteen different factions control Kyiv in 18 months.

1917–34

The capital of the Ukrainian SSR is moved to Kharkiv by the Soviets. The city is still often referred to as Ukraine's 'first capital'.

1928

Stalin's first Five Year Plan sees rapid and brutal industrialisation and massive immigration from the countryside into cities across Ukraine. Industrial output subsequently increases fourfold.

1932–33

Millions of Ukrainians die in a famine caused by Stalin's farm collectivisation. Some historians believe that other grain-grabbing, border-closing measures deliberately targeted its people.

Towards the war's end, in February 1945, Stalin met with British and US leaders Winston Churchill and Franklin Roosevelt at Yalta's Livadia Palace to discuss the administration of post-war Europe, among other things. The fact that the Red Army occupied so much of Eastern Europe at the end of WWII helped the USSR hold onto it in the postwar period.

The Battle for Chernobyl is an in-depth documentary which tells the story of the world's worst nuclear accident and the truth about the clear up.

Postwar Period

For most, WWII ended in 1945. However, the Ukrainian Insurgent Army (UPA) continued a guerrilla existence well into the 1950s, taking pot shots at the Soviet authorities, especially in the Carpathian region. A government in exile was led by former partisan Stepan Bandera, until he was assassinated in Munich in 1959.

Elsewhere, Ukraine rapidly developed into an important cog in the Soviet machine. Eastern regions became highly industrialised, with coal and iron-ore mining around Donetsk, arms and missile industries in Dnipropetrovsk, and Dniproges, a huge hydroelectric dam near Zaporizhzhya.

Ukraine acquired strategic technological and military importance during this era, and at least one Ukrainian rose to become Soviet leader. Leonid Brezhnev graduated from metallurgy engineer to Communist Party General Secretary from 1964 to 1982. Brezhnev's predecessor, Nikita Khrushchev (Soviet leader from 1953 to 1964) was born just outside Ukraine but lived there from adolescence and styled himself as a Ukrainian. Khrushchev's post-Stalin reformist agenda led him to create the Autonomous Crimean Soviet Socialist Republic in 1954, and transfer legislative control over Crimea to the Ukrainian Soviet Socialist Republic.

It's generally agreed that Winston Churchill was saved from execution during the Boer War by Ukrainian writer and journalist Yury Budyak, though neither man mentions the incident in their memoirs.

Nationalism Reappears

The rotten underbelly of Soviet high-tech was cruelly exposed by the nuclear disaster at the power plant Chornobyl on 26 April 1986. Ukrainians weren't just killed and injured by the radioactive material that spewed over their countryside, but also appalled by the way the authorities attempted to cover up the accident. The first Kremlin announcement wasn't made until two days after the event – and only then at the prompting of Swedish authorities, who detected abnormal radiation levels over their own country. However, by then Kyiv was awash with rumour that something was afoot and many promptly decamped to the Carpathians and Crimea as fast as they could.

As more information came to light, discontent over Moscow's handling of the Chornobyl disaster revived nationalist feeling. Ukrainian independence had become a minority interest, mainly confined to the country's west, but slowly, the hardcore in the west started to take the

1941

During WWII Ukraine becomes a blood-soaked battleground for opposing Nazi, Soviet and nationalist forces and some six million locals perish. The death toll includes almost all of Ukraine's Jews.

1943

The Red Army liberates Kyiv from the Nazis on 6 November. Earlier, retreating Soviets had dynamited buildings along the main street of Khreshchatyk; these were replaced postwar with Stalinist structures.

1944

Stalin deports the entire 250,000-strong Crimean Tatar population in just a few days, beginning 18 May. He accuses them of 'Nazi collaboration'. Thousands die during this genocidal journey of 'Sürgün'.

1945

Winston Churchill and an ailing Franklin Roosevelt travel to 'the Riviera of Hades' so Stalin can bully them. At the Yalta Conference, the Soviet leader demands chunks of Eastern Europe.

rest of Ukraine with them. In 1988 marches rocked Lviv, and the Uniate Church, banned by Stalin in 1946, emerged from the underground as a pro-independence lobby. In 1989 the opposition movement Rukh (Ukrainian People's Movement for Restructuring) was established. By 1990 protest marches and hunger strikes had spread to Kyiv.

SEARCHING FOR LOST ANCESTORS

Brought to the reading public's attention by Jonathan Safran Foer's 2002 novel *Everything Is Illuminated*, for the last two decades countless descendents of Ukrainians, Jews, Germans and Poles who left the region in the 19th and 20th centuries have been returning to Ukraine to research their family history. However, as Foer discovers, this is not always an easy task! The secret of finding records, locations and survivors is to do your research before you leave home and hire a reliable guide (especially if you don't speak the language and/or are not familiar with the culture/history/geography of Ukraine). Here we list some helpful resources, contacts and general good places to start.

Web Resources

Federation of East European Family History Societies (www.feefhs.org)

JewishGen (www.jewishgen.org)

Ukraine Geneology Forum (http://genforum.genealogy.com/ukraine/)

East European Genealogical Society (www.eegsociety.org)

State Archives Geneology Section (www.archives.gov.ua/Eng/genealogia.php)

Family Search (www.familysearch.org)

Routes to Roots Foundation (www.rtrfoundation.org)

Memory Book (www.memory-book.com.ua)

Jewish heritage of Galicia & Bukovyna (http://jgaliciabukovina.net)

German geneology resource (www.genealogienetz.de)

Galicia geneology resource (www.halgal.com)

Ukrainian Genealogical & Historical Society (http://ukrainiangenealogist.tripod.com/)

Guides

Active Ukraine (www.activeukraine.com)

Lviv Ecotour (www.lvivecotour.com)

West Ukraine Tours (www.west-ukraine-tours.com/)

Alex Dunai (www.alexdunai.com)

1959

Stepan Bandera, the exiled Ukrainian Insurgent Army (UPA) leader, is killed in Munich by the KGB. Ukrainian partisans had continued ambushing Soviet police until the mid-1950s.

1986

Reactor No 4 at the Chornobyl nuclear power plant explodes, after a failed safety test. More than 90 Hiroshimas are spewed out over the Ukrainian and Belarusian countryside.

AMOS CHAPPLE / GETTY IMAGES ©

➜ Chornobyl monument

1991

President Gorbachev is held prisoner at his country retreat in Crimea while a coup led by hardliners takes place in Moscow.

Independent Ukraine

With the nationalist movement snowballing and the USSR disintegrating, many politicians within the Communist Party of Ukraine (CPU) saw the writing on the wall. After the Soviet counter-coup in Moscow in August 1991 failed, they decided that if they didn't take their country to independence, the opposition would. So, on 24 August 1991, the Verkhovna Rada (Supreme Council) met, with speaker Stanyslav Hurenko's wonderfully pithy announcement recorded by the *Economist* for posterity: 'Today we will vote for Ukrainian independence, because if we don't we're in the shit.' In December some 84% of the population voted in a referendum to back that pragmatic decision, and former CPU chairman Leonid Kravchuk was elected president.

As the new republic found its feet, there were more than the usual separation traumas from Russia. Disagreements and tensions arose, particularly over ownership of the Black Sea Fleet harboured in the Crimean port of Sevastopol. These were only resolved in 1999 by offering Russia a lease until 2017, controversially extended by the new government in 2010 to 2042.

Orest Subtelny's 700-page *Ukraine, A History* is widely considered the definitive work on the subject, narrowly edging out Paul Magosci's equally long *History of Ukraine*. Both have been updated to cover the Orange Revolution. However, the most readable account of Ukraine's history is Anna Reid's *Borderland*, which neatly divides events into digestible chunks.

Economic crisis forced Kravchuk's government to resign in September 1992. Leonid Kuchma, a pro-Russian reformer, came to power in July 1994 and stayed for 10 years.

During Kuchma's tenure, the economy did improve. The hryvnya was introduced and inflation was lowered from a spiralling 10,000% in 1993 to 5.2% in 2004, by which time GDP was growing at a rate of 9%. Kuchma's reign is also remembered for its extreme cronyism. Foreign investors complained that companies being privatised were often sold to Ukrainian ventures with presidential connections, sometimes for well under market value, and international watchdog Transparency International named Ukraine the world's third most corrupt country.

One major scandal surrounded the mysterious beheading of campaigning opposition journalist Georgiy Gongadze in 2000. Kuchma was widely rumoured to have ordered the killing. Although this was never proved, Gongadze became a posthumous *cause célèbre*.

The last working reactor at Chornobyl, No 3, was finally shut down in 2000.

The Orange Revolution

Former central banker Viktor Yushchenko had proved too reformist and pro-European for his masters when he was Leonid Kuchma's prime minister from 1998 to 2001. However, in 2004 as Kuchma prepared to stand down, Yushchenko re-emerged as a strong presidential contender.

1991

As the Soviet Union falters, Ukraine's parliament votes for independence. Some 84% of the population figures that's about right and backs the decision in a referendum.

1994

Former rocket scientist Leonid Kuchma becomes president. With inflation running at 10,000%, he moves to reform the economy, but his popularity wanes when he's implicated in a series of corruption scandals.

2000

After opposition journalist Georgiy Gongadze is murdered, a recording emerges of President Kuchma asking his staff to 'deal with' the journalist. Kuchma later claims the tape has been selectively edited.

2004

Thousands take to the freezing streets to protest that vote rigging has robbed Viktor Yushchenko of the presidency. The 'Orange Revolution' leads to a fairer second election, which Yushchenko wins.

Kuchma's anointed successor, the Kremlin-friendly Viktor Yanukovych, had expected an easy victory and the popularity of Yushchenko's Nasha Ukraina (Our Ukraine) party looked threatening. During an increasingly bitter campaign, and seven weeks before the scheduled 31 October election, Yushchenko underwent a remarkable physical transformation – disfiguration that Austrian doctors later confirmed was the result of dioxin poisoning.

After an inconclusive first round, a second vote was held on 21 November. A day later, contrary to the exit polls and amid widespread claims of vote rigging by overseas electoral observers, Yanukovych was declared the winner.

Over the next few days and weeks Yushchenko supporters staged a show of people power unlike any Ukraine had ever seen. Despite freezing temperatures they took to the streets, brandishing banners and clothes in the opposition's trademark orange. They assembled to listen to Yushchenko and his powerful political ally Yulia Tymoshenko at mass rallies in Kyiv's maydan Nezalezhnosti (Independence Sq). They surrounded parliament and established a demonstrators' tent city along Kyiv's main Khreshchatyk boulevard to keep up pressure on the authorities.

The Yanukovych camp refused to respond to a parliamentary vote of no confidence in the election result and his eastern Ukrainian supporters threatened to secede if Yushchenko was declared president. Despite this, on 3 December the Supreme Court annulled the first election result, and the way was paved for a second poll on 26 December, which Yushchenko won. The tent city was dismantled just in time for Yushchenko's swearing in on 3 January 2005.

ORANGE REVOLUTION

A highly individual, entertaining and quite moving short photo-essay, www.theorangerevolution.com looks back at the false dawn of 2004.

The Orange Glow Fades

Alas, the course of true reform never did run smoothly in Ukraine (to paraphrase a *Time* magazine observation on Russia) and anyone hoping for a fairy-tale ending would be swiftly disappointed. Less than a year after they had stood shoulder to shoulder on the maydan in Kyiv, the Orange Revolution's heroes had fallen out with each other.

Anyone able to follow the ins and outs of Ukraine's political scene after the Orange Revolution probably should have got out more. In the late naughties the blonde-braided Yulia Tymoshenko, a weak president Yushchenko and a resurgent Viktor Yanukovych engaged in an absurd political soap opera featuring snap elections, drawn-out coalition deals, fisticuffs in parliament and musical chairs in the prime minister's office. Russia turned off the gas at opportune moments and the West got bored and moved on. The upshot was complete disillusionment with the Orange Revolution among the population and Viktor Yanukovych's victory in the April 2010 presidential elections.

2006

Russia cuts off gas supplies on 1 January. Kyiv suspects punishment for becoming more pro-European. Moscow says it just wants a fair price – nearly five times the existing level.

2007

Some 100 people die in the worst mining accident in Ukraine's history. The disaster at Zasyadko, eastern Donetsk, highlights safety concerns about all of the country's ageing coal mines.

2007

The Ukraine-Poland bid to host the Euro 2012 football (soccer) championships is successful. Immediately, doubts about Ukraine's ability to hold the event are voiced.

2009

Russia once again turns off the gas on 1 January as Moscow claims Kyiv has failed to pay its bills. This time the EU steps in to resolve the dispute.

The Yanukovych Years

Many feared that upon coming to power Yanukovych and his oligarch-backed, east-based Party of the Regions would begin to gnaw away at democracy, press freedom and human rights. Allegedly behind the electoral fraud that sparked the Orange Revolution, these guys had form. The new president confirmed everyone's misgivings in 2011 when Yulia Tymoshenko was put on trial for abuse of office (basically for signing a 2009 gas deal with Russia that annoyed a few wealthy regime string pullers). This was seen in the West and by most commentators as nothing short of a political show trial and a successful attempt by the new regime to rid itself of any meaningful opposition. Intimidation of critical journalists, provocative language laws sceptically brought to parliament just two days after the Euro 2012 final (ensuring the country didn't stay united for too long), jailing of other members of the previous government, inaction on corruption and a whole list of controversial laws and provocative campaigns have followed.

For an easy-to-absorb, chronological listing of Ukrainian events from the 9th to the 20th centuries, set alongside those in the rest of the world, head to www.brama.com/ukraine/history.

In late 2013, president Yanukovych's refusal to sign an Association Agreement with the European Union (EU) led to huge protests in Kyiv and Lviv (as well as other West Ukrainian cities), which became known as the Euromaidan. See Ukraine Today (p226) for more on current issues.

2010

Despite allegations of a fraudulent election in 2004, Viktor Yanukovych becomes president in a closely fought February poll. Many Ukrainians fear press freedom and democracy will suffer under his rule.

2011

Opposition leader Yulia Tymoshenko is jailed for abuse of office while prime minister. Many see this as a political trial and a sign that president Yanukovych is pushing the country towards dictatorship.

2012

In partnership with Poland, Ukraine hosts the Euro 2012 Cup, the largest sporting event the country has ever witnessed. However, matches are boycotted by EU governments over the Tymoshenko affair.

2013

Protests erupt when president Yanukovych refuses to sign an Association Agreement with the EU. Kyiv's Euromaidan protests endure brutal police attacks and subzero temperatures.

The People

From the Tatars of Crimea to the miners of the Donbas and the hipsters of Lviv, Ukraine is arguably Eastern Europe's most diverse country. Poverty, heartfelt hospitality and a love of nature are the few things they share but little really unites this country's 45 million people. Only sport sees the nation genuinely come together as it does whenever the Klytschko brothers pull on their gloves or the national football team takes to the pitch.

The National Psyche

Having endured centuries of many different foreign rulers, Ukrainians are a long-suffering people. They're nothing if not survivors; historically they've had to be, but after suffering a kind of identity theft during centuries of Russian rule in particular, this ancient nation that 'suddenly' emerged some 20 years ago is well on the road to forging a new personality.

Traditionally, many patriots would unite behind a vague sense of free-spirited Cossack culture and the national poet Taras Shevchenko. This is a religious society, a superstitious society, and one in which traditional gender roles, strong family and community ties still bind. It's a culture where people are friendly and sometimes more generous than they can really afford to be. Paradoxically, it's also one in which remnants of the Soviet mentality – of unofficial unhelpfulness and suspicion of saying too much – remain. As in Russia, many people lead a kind of double life – snarling, elbowing *homo sovieticus* outside the house, but generous, kind and hospitable Europeans around their kitchen tables.

However, Ukraine is also a patchwork nation – city dwellers and peasants, east and west, young and old, Russian-speaking and Ukrainian-speaking, Hutsul and Tatar have very different attitudes. Broadly speaking, Russian-speaking easterners look towards the former Soviet Union, while Ukrainian-speaking westerners gaze hopefully towards a future in Europe. But for every rule, there's an exception too.

IDENTITY

In *The Ukrainians: Unexpected Nation* academic Andrew Wilson examines Ukraine's founding myths, how its history and culture have shaped its national identity and what it all means for this ancient but young nation.

Lifestyle

Just as there is no one 'typical' Ukrainian, so there is no single average lifestyle. This is still a relatively poor, second-world country. However, it's fair to say that daily life has become marginally easier for most households since the turn of the millennium, despite the economic woes caused by the recent international financial crisis. Officially the average monthly gross salary is around 3000uah (US$380, €290), though most Ukrainians will tell you this is way too high, a more realistic figure being between 1000uah and 1500uah (US$120 to US185, €90 to €140). As across the world, prices, particularly of food, have shot up since 2008, meaning a decrease in many people's standard of living.

Middle-class Ukrainians have always had ways of getting by, holding down several jobs, pursuing a number of money-making schemes and looking out for each other. Outside big cities, it's also been common for people to grow food in their back gardens and for extended families to share domestic duties. *Baba* (grandma) is frequently a respected household member, very often in charge of the kids while parents go off to work.

Old Soviet apartments are quite compact and old-fashioned, but most have undergone some *remont* (refurbishment) since 1991. Despite low earnings, Ukrainians always seem to have a new washing machine and the latest flat-screen TV – perhaps as the average family enjoys few other luxuries.

Amid the old housing stock and creaking public transport infrastructure, young Ukrainians are avid users of new technology and media. Everyone has at least one mobile phone (usually more), internet cafes are usually packed and social networking sites are as popular as they are in the West. Even 4G technology is catching on and wi-fi buzzes through all but the cheapest of hotels, cafes and restaurants.

Mind the Gap

Buying produce such as milk, honey and vegetables from old ladies on the street means you are contributing directly to the local economy, and not funding a minigarch supermarket owner's lifestyle in the Bahamas.

Even after two decades of 'reforms', there's still a mammoth gap between average Ukrainians and the super-rich elite. It's the country's oligarchs and 'new Ukrainian' businesspeople you see driving the black Mercedes SUVs and shopping in Kyiv's designer boutiques. Had the aspirations of the 2004 Orange Revolution been fulfilled, this gap might have narrowed, but under President Yanukovych the situation has remained pretty much the same.

At the lower end of the scale are the elderly and other pensioners. Although the basic pension has increased to around 1200uah per month (2012), over 24% of Ukrainians remain below the poverty line. Due to losses in WWII, industrial accidents, deadly roads, vodka and general bad health among males, many of the elderly are women. They can often be seen selling their home-grown produce on the street to make ends meet.

Population

As a crossroads between Europe and Asia, Ukraine has been settled by numerous ethnic groups throughout history and has a fascinating underlying mix. However, most people still describe themselves as Ukrainians and, hence, of Slavic origin. According to the last census (2001), 77% of the country's population are ethnically Ukrainian. The other large ethnic group is Russian, who account for 17% of the population and are mainly concentrated in the south and east. However, these figures are not reflected in the language people speak: many claiming to be Ukrainian use Russian as their first language.

Minorities

Only nine countries in the world have a lower birth rate than Ukraine, with 2013 estimates putting the average number of children born per woman at just 1.29. The world average is around 2.5.

Ukraine's ethnic minority groups include, in order of size, Belarusians, Moldovans, Tatars, Bulgarians, Hungarians, Romanians, Poles and Jews. Almost all of the country's 260,000 Tatars live in Crimea. No one measures the size of western Ukrainian Hutsul communities, which in any case are seamlessly integrated into the wider community.

Dying Nation

Since independence in 1991 Ukraine's population has fallen more dramatically than that of any other country not affected by war, famine or plague. The number of citizens plummeted from 52 million in 1993 to around 44.5 million in 2013, as birth rates and life expectancy dropped concomitantly. This demographic trend has slowed in the last few years, and there's even been a mini baby boom, but the overall situation has only improved slightly with population growth figures for 2013 estimated at −0.6%. Also, due to the bureaucratic system of registering citizens at a certain address, population figures include a huge chunk of the nation that has emigrated in search of a better life, but still officially resides in Ukraine for legal reasons. This means the actual population figure may be as low as 35 million.

A large Ukrainian diaspora of some 2.5 million people exists. Many live in North America, particularly Canada.

Multiculturalism

The 'ethnic' schism between western and eastern Ukraine has been under the spotlight since the Orange Revolution, when there were brief but serious fears the country might split. With Russian immigration into Ukrainian territory from the late 17th century, some Russian Ukrainians still feel their allegiance lies more with Moscow than with Kyiv. This immigration is the single reason Ukrainian nationalists refuse to see an east–west split as a solution to the country's ethnic strife. Though the cause of countless problems, the divisions are neither as clear-cut nor as intractable as some politicians like to suggest.

Former Israeli prime minister Golda Meir and film star Milla Jovovich were both born in Kyiv, Bolshevik Leon Trotsky hailed from outside Odesa, and both Dustin Hoffman and Sylvester Stallone have Ukrainian roots.

Crimea

Extra tensions exist in Crimea, where some 260,000 Tatars have resettled since the 1990s. After early clashes, 14 Tatar seats were granted in the Crimean parliament and the situation quietened down. Over the past decade there have been occasional attacks by skinhead 'Cossack paramilitary' groups on Tatars and their property, and Tatar leaders have also expressed concerns over Ukraine's shift towards a more Russia-friendly policy in Crimea since Yanukovych took over in 2010.

Religion

As the sheer number of churches in Ukraine attests, religion in this country is pivotal. It has provided comfort during many hard times and even shaped Ukrainian identity, as by accepting Orthodox Christianity in 989, Volodymyr the Great cast Kyivan Rus (the first eastern Slavic state) as a European, rather than Islamic Asian, state.

For the low-down from Tatars themselves on their history, culture and contemporary issues, visit www.tatar.net.

Ukraine's Many Churches

Today the country's sizeable Christian population is confusingly splintered into three Orthodox churches and one major form of Catholicism.

In the 17th century, when Ukraine came under Russian rule, so did its Orthodox Church. Even now, over two decades after independence, the largest Orthodox congregation in the country belongs to the Ukrainian Orthodox Church, the former Ukrainian section of the Russian Orthodox Church that still pays allegiance to the Moscow Patriarch. There are also two smaller, breakaway Orthodox churches, which are both more 'Ukrainian' in nature. Another Ukrainian Orthodox Church was formed in 1992 after independence to pay allegiance to a local Kyiv Patriarch.

TEMPLE DOS & DON'TS

Religious Ukrainians are a pretty tolerant lot, but women should cover their heads when entering Orthodox churches. There's an even stricter dress code (no above-knee skirts for women and no hats for men) when visiting particularly holy sites such as the Kyevo-Pecherska Lavra and Pochayiv Monastery. Taking photos during a service, touching the icons and affectionate hand-holding may incur the wrath of the church's elderly custodians.

Crimean Tatars are Muslim, but only a few are really devout and many others even drink alcohol. Nevertheless, women should dress modestly when entering mosques. A scarf to cover the head and shoulders is definitely needed when visiting Yevpatoriya's Dervish Tekiye (Whirling Dervish Monastery), possibly the strictest Muslim site in Ukraine.

Meanwhile, the Ukrainian Autocephalous Orthodox Church, formed during the 19th century in western Ukraine and suppressed by the Soviets, has bounced back since independence.

To complicate matters, another five to six million Ukrainians follow another brand of Christianity entirely. In 1596 the Union of Brest established the Uniate Church (often called the Greek Catholic Church). Mixing Orthodox Christian practices with allegiance to the Pope, this essentially Catholic church was, and is, popular in the western part of the country once controlled by Poland.

Religious Rivalry

For a detailed portrait of all Ukraine's major and minor religions, head to the excellent www.risu.org.ua, which also offers relevant news and statistics.

The two main Orthodox churches – Moscow Patriarchate and Kyiv Patriarchate – have had territorial disputes in the past. The Ukrainian government's 1995 refusal to allow Kyiv Patriarch Volodymyr Romanyuk to be buried inside Kyiv's St Sophia's Cathedral, for fear of reprisals from Moscow, is a good example. They have since confined themselves to more low-level bickering about how many adherents each has.

Tensions between these two churches have been rising recently, especially as the Moscow Patriarch Kirill has made several controversial visits to Ukraine since 2010. The Russian-backed Ukrainian Orthodox Church favours close ties with Russia and is very closely aligned with the regime. All other denominations welcome stronger Western ties.

Other Faiths

Minority faiths include Roman Catholicism, Judaism and, among Crimean Tatars, Sunni Islam. Ukraine's religious freedom means Evangelical, Buddhist, Jehovah's Witness and neo-pagan communities have also emerged since independence from the atheist USSR.

Sport

Every Ukrainian will tell you his or her country is sports mad but, as with most ex-USSR countries, you'll hardly ever see anyone actually engaging in sporting activities, especially outside the big cities.

A MIDSUMMER NIGHT'S DREAM

It involves fire, water, dancing, fortune-telling and strong overtones of sex. No wonder the Soviets tried to quash the festival of Ivan Kupala, a pagan midsummer celebration. Indeed, leaders since the Middle Ages – including Cossack *hetmans* (chieftains) – have tried to outlaw it, but all without success. The festival is still marked across Ukraine and beyond.

To ancient pre-Christians, Kupala was the god of love and fertility, and young people would choose a marriage partner on this midsummer eve. Today's rituals vary, but typically begin with folk singing and a maypole-style dance performed by young women wearing white gowns and floral wreaths in their hair. After this, the women float their wreaths (symbolising virginity) down the requisite nearby river or other body of water. A wreath that sinks indicates bad fortune in love for its owner.

Later a bonfire is lit, around which young couples dance. Couples will also jump over small fires, holding hands, to test whether – if they maintain their grip – their love will last.

After Kyivan Rus adopted Christianity, the festival became mixed up with the birthday of John the Baptist. This not only means the festival has largely been shifted from the summer solstice on 22 June to 7 July, it sometimes means people walk in the fire or jump in the river as a 'cleansing' act. A good spot to join Kupala celebrations is Pyrohovo in Kyiv, or head to the countryside for more traditional rituals.

Football

Dynamo Kyiv is no longer the only well-known Ukrainian team, with now rather more successful Shakhtar Donetsk and Metallist Kharkiv regularly appearing in European competitions (Shakhtar won the UEFA Cup in 2009). The biggest name in Ukrainian football (soccer) was, until his retirement in 2012, Andriy Shevchenko, who played for Dynamo Kyiv, AC Milan, Chelsea and the national team. After kicking his last ball he made a highly ineffective attempt to enter politics.

In 2012 Ukraine successfully co-hosted the Euro 2012 football championships with Poland. The final between Spain and Italy was played at Kyiv's Olympic Stadium and watched by over 63,000 spectators.

Follow the domestic Ukrainian league at www.ukrainiansoccer.net.

Other Sports

Ukraine also enjoys ice hockey (though the national team brings little joy) and has an international presence in boxing with the brothers Vitaly and Volodymyr Klytschko. Vitaly in particular gained prominence as the world heavyweight champion. Injury forced him to retire in November 2005, when he was still the titleholder, and this staunch backer of Viktor Yushchenko announced a desire to become involved in politics. After running unsuccessfully for mayor of Kyiv, Klytschko announced a boxing comeback and now holds the World Boxing Council (WBC) heavyweight title. In politics he's tipped by many to become Ukraine's next president – who says sport and politics don't mix?

Tennis has also gained popularity since independence, and Ukraine now has two men and two women in the ATP and WTA top 100 rankings. A decade and a half ago there were virtually no bicycles on Ukraine's roads, but all kinds of cycling has since gained in popularity, especially mountain biking in the Carpathians and Crimea.

Boxer Vitaly Klytschko's political party is called Ukrainian Democratic Alliance for Reform (UDAR), which in Ukrainian means 'hit' or 'punch'.

Women in Ukraine

Cynically speaking, women have been one of independent Ukraine's biggest tourist attractions. Combine their legendary beauty, devotion to personal grooming and sometimes outrageous, sexualised fashion sense with a relatively impoverished society and you were always going to have fertile ground for online 'dating agencies', 'marriage agencies' and straight-out sex tourism. Sex trafficking of Ukrainian women remains a serious problem, too.

Gender Roles & Discrimination

Traditional gender roles are quite entrenched in Ukraine's paternalistic society. Even the country's many young career women unashamedly place greater emphasis on their looks than some of their Western counterparts would. Ukrainian women face job discrimination, with age, appearance and family circumstances often excluding them from roles they are professionally qualified for.

Sextremism – the Femen Phenomenon

Founded in 2008 in Kyiv by former economist Anna Hutsol and a group of student activists, the Femen movement has become Ukraine's most controversial political export, known to many around the world. This group of radical feminists engages in topless protest, an approach which certainly caused a kerfuffle and much tabloid sensation on the streets of Kyiv in the late noughties and early teenies. Early targets for their naked wrath included Euro 2012, the Orthodox Church, Party of the Regions MPs, prostitution, people trafficking and sex tourists.

According to local superstition, women should never sit down on steps, walls or anything concrete, lest their ovaries freeze and they can't bear children.

In 2012 Femen went international, opening loosely affiliated branches in several countries and a European headquarters in Paris (established

GENDER GAP

There are over 3½ million more women in Ukraine than there are men, despite slightly more boys being born on average than girls.

by group member Inna Shevchenko, who was forced to seek asylum in France after death threats in Kyiv). The group stripped off at the World Economic Forum meeting at Davos, protested against the imprisonment of Pussy Riot, got very close to President Putin, went topless against Belarus president Lukashenko (which nearly ended very badly for some members of the group) and prepared a bare-breasted welcome at Boryspil International Airport for Moscow Patriarch Kirill.

Though activists were regularly arrested and fined (and occasionally served short jail sentences) for the Soviet catch-all offence of 'hooliganism', the Femen phenomenon was perhaps seen in Kyiv as a harmless, slightly naive protest movement, tittilatingly attention-grabbing but generally ignored by the Ukrainian regime (Party of the Regions MPs often referred to members as 'prostitutes'). However, in summer 2013 things got nasty. It's thought the Ukrainian secret police (SBU), possibly under pressure from the Russian FSB (formerly the KGB), were responsible for a series of attacks on Anna Hutsol and other members, putting several, including Anna, in hospital. Things really came to a head in late August 2013 when SBU agents allegedly planted explosive material and firearms in the organisation's Kyiv offices, then arrested the leadership. Accused of illegal possession of weapons, Anna Hutsol, along with prominent members Sasha Shevchenko and Yana Zhdanova, fled Ukraine in fear of their lives.

For more information on the group's activities and the fate of its members visit www.femen.org. A film called *Ukraine Is Not a Brothel* (www.ukraineisnotabrothel.com) by Australian filmmaker Kitty Green, herself interrogated by the Belarusian KGB following a Femen protest there, was shown at the Venice International Film Festival in 2013.

The Ukrainian Table

Ukrainians admit theirs is a cuisine of comfort – full of hearty, mild dishes designed for fierce winters – rather than one of gastronomic zing. And yet, while it has suffered from negative stereotypes of Soviet-style cabbage slop and pernicious pickles, Ukrainian cooking isn't bad these days. In recent years chefs have rediscovered the wholesome appeal of the national cuisine.

Plenty of Ukrainian-themed restaurants offer the chance to sample *varenyky* (stuffed, ravioli-like dumplings), elaborately stuffed fish dishes or red-caviar pancakes, washed down with chilled vodka or freshly pressed cranberry juice. Successive invaders and immigrants have also left their mark on a menu heavily reliant on local produce. So while Ukrainians love the carp, pike-perch and salmon found in their rivers, the pork and game roaming their lands, and the wheat and barley from their fields, they're also familiar with Siberian *pelmeny* (filled pasta-like ravioli) and Jewish-style dishes.

According to some enthusiasts, *borshch* is imbued with all kinds of magical powers, including the ability to melt the hardest heart.

BORSHCH

Staples & Specialities

Many of the country's specialities stem from down-to-earth peasant dishes based on grains and staple vegetables like potatoes, cabbage, beets or mushrooms, seasoned with garlic and dill.

- **Borshch** Locals would have you know that *borshch* (борщ) is Ukrainian – not Russian, not Polish, but Ukrainian – and there's nothing better than a steaming bowlful in winter. A typical version of the national soup is made with beetroot, pork fat and herbs, but there's also an aromatic 'green' variety, based on sorrel. There sometimes seem to be as many recipes for *borshch* as there are Ukrainian cooks but all add a dollop of sour cream before serving.
- **Bread** Dark and white varieties of *khlib* (хліб) are available every day, including the white *pampushky* (soft rolls rubbed with garlic and oil and then fried) occasionally served with *borshch*. Bread is often used in religious ceremonies and on special occasions. Visitors are traditionally greeted with bread and salt.
- **Cabbage Rolls** *Holubtsy* (голубці) are cabbage rolls stuffed with seasoned rice and meat and stewed in a tomato and sour cream sauce.
- **Kasha** Pretty much any grain is called *kasha* (каша) in Ukrainian, and while the word might be used to describe what Westerners would call porridge, more commonly it turns out to be buckwheat. The latter appears as a side dish, as stuffing or as an unusual but filling breakfast gruel.

RESTAURANT PRICES

Price categories used per main course:

- **$** less than 50uah
- **$$** 50–150uah
- **$$$** more than 150uah

➡ **Pancakes** Three types of pancake might land on your plate. *Deruny* (деруни) are potato pancakes, and are served with sour cream and vegetables or meat. *Nalysnyky* (налисники) are thin crepes; *mlyntsy* (млинці) are thicker and smaller, like Russian *blyny*.

➡ **Varenyky** Similar to Polish *pierogi*, *varenyky* (вареники) are to Ukraine what dim sum is to China and filled pasta to Italy. These small half-moon-shaped dumplings have more than 50 different traditional vegetarian and meat fillings. They're usually served with sour cream.

A series of updated and adapted traditional recipes from American-Ukrainian homes is brought together in *Ukrainian Recipes* (1996), edited by Joanne Asala.

Drinks

On street corners in summer, you might see small drink tankers selling *kvas* (квас), a gingery, beer-like soft drink, which is made from sugar and old black bread and is mildly alcoholic. *Kvas* is proffered in plastic beakers, the communal mug on a chain having mostly disappeared. In winter you can buy *kvas* in plastic bottles at the supermarket, but it's over-carbonated and lacks that zingy 'live' taste.

The situation with Ukrainian wine is not very rosé, with production still suffering after Gorbachev's 'dry law' saw many vines pulled up in the late 1980s. Crimea still produces wines, but most of them are sugary dessert wines akin to Madeira or sherry. Some Koktebel-label whites and Inkerman reds are probably the best you will drink in Ukraine. Wines are also produced in the Transcarpathian region but, sadly, the best wines available in Ukraine still come from neighbouring Moldova.

The biggest name in Ukrainian vodka is undoubtedly Nemiroff. However, although Ukrainians seem to imbibe an awful lot of the stuff, surveys show they don't drink anywhere near as much as Russians – which is probably a good thing.

Ukraine produces some very quaffable beers, most more than able to compete with international brands. In fact, the beer market is booming, with many young people turning their backs on vodka for it. Breweries produce various light, dark, unfiltered and flavoured lagers; there are at least 40 different domestic varieties, the leading brands being Chernihivske, Lvivske, Obolon and Slavutych.

Okroshka is a kind of Slavic gazpacho. Eaten cold in summer it's a thick concoction of cucumbers, spring onions, boiled eggs, meat and herbs, diluted with *kvas*.

Celebrations

Ukrainian food truly comes into its own during Christmas, Easter and wedding celebrations. Marta Pisetska Farley's *Festive Ukrainian Cooking* (1990) has the low-down.

At Easter, certain foods are taken to church in a covered basket to be blessed. These usually include hard-boiled eggs, baked cheese and Easter breads like round *paska* (паска; decorated with crosses) or tall, cylindrical *babka* (бабка; a sweet egg bread).

On their wedding day, the bride and groom break a spectacular round bread called a *korovay* (Коровай) – whoever gets the bigger half will be the dominant partner in the marriage.

FAT OF THE LAND

Eating raw pig fat (*salo* in Ukrainian; сало) is a centuries-old tradition that runs deep and thick, quite literally, in the Ukrainian blood. Songs and poems are even dedicated to this product, which long provided a cheaper and more preservable alternative to meat. Some Ukrainian doctors even recommend 30g each morning for a long and healthy life! You'll find it on most menus flavoured with garlic and salt and occasionally smoked, and occasionally you'll even alight on the 'Ukrainian Snickers bar' – *salo* in chocolate. Never suggest to a Ukrainian that eating *salo* could be unhealthy.

Where to Eat & Drink

Restaurant (ресторан) and cafe (кафе) sound similar in English and Ukrainian. Some Ukrainian restaurants specialise in a particular dish, such as a *varenychna* (варенична), which serves only *varenyky*. A *stolova* (столова) is a Russian-style self-service canteen. Theme restaurants aren't as popular as they once were, though new ones, especially in Lviv, do still appear.

When eating out, be aware that prices for many meat and fish dishes are listed on the menu by weight. For example, the *shashlyk* that looks good value at 10uah might actually be 10uah per 100g, so read the menu carefully and, if in doubt, ask.

Tipping is virtually unheard of except in big-city places where waiters have become used to foreigners adding something to the bill. Out in the cuds, a tip may even be returned – the staff believing you've overpaid by accident.

For details of more than 450 great restaurants, with reviews and ratings, log on to www.chicken.kiev.ua/eng.

Quick Eats

Food kiosks selling drinks and snacks sprout up on every spare inch of pavement in Ukraine, especially around train and bus stations. These sell pastries or warm snacks, including newcomers such as hamburgers and hot dogs, as well as Soviet favourites such as *shashlyky* (шашлик), *perepichky* (перепічки, fairground-style frankfurters deep-fried in dough) and *chebureky* (чебуреки, fried meat turnovers). The bottles on the shelves range from water and soft drinks to beer, which is also considered a soft drink by most Ukrainians but is now illegal to drink in most public places.

If you're self catering, head to the local market *(rynok)*, which always provides a colourful experience. Old-style food stores *(gastronomy)* tend to be reminiscent of the USSR, but these are becoming less common as modern supermarkets take over.

Vegetarians & Vegans

While most Ukrainians are carnivores by nature, vegetarians won't find eating out too trying, especially in the larger cities where pizza joints and international restaurants abound. Even Ukrainian cuisine can be meat-free if you stick to a fairly bland diet of *deruny* or potato-and-mushroom *varenyky*. However, it's always a good idea to specify that you want a meat-free salad; *borshch* is, sadly, best avoided if you're strict about your diet. Even 'vegetarian' versions are often made using beef stock.

Vegans are much worse off. In a land that adores *smetana* (sour cream) and slathers its salads in mayonnaise, dining out will prove a trial. The best thing to do is stay in apartments and visit the local markets for cooking ingredients. While most Ukrainians have heard of vegetarianism, veganism is an unknown concept and will seem to most like abstinence from rice would to the Chinese.

You can learn how to cook everything from different types of *borshch* to delicious *medovyky* (honey cakes) with Hippocrene's *Best of Ukrainian Cuisine* (1998) by Bohdan Zahny.

Art & Architecture

Ukraine may not be immediately synonymous with art and architecture, but that means there's a lot to discover in this corner of Eastern Europe. It's not all Soviet realism and drab Soviet blocks as any visitor to the country will quickly learn.

Painting & Sculpture

Few would associate Ukraine with the arts and architecture, but as anyone who's been to the country will tell you, the country's museums and galleries showcase exquisite local art and traditional crafts, much of it with a folksy rural theme, and Ukrainian architecture is not all about USSR-era concrete blocks and Stalinist pomp.

Ukraine's most celebrated sculptor is Oleksandr Arkhipenko (1887–1964), who was born in Kyiv but spent most of his life abroad. His works are scattered across many galleries, mostly in the US.

Icons

Icons are small holy images painted on a lime-wood panel with a mix of tempera, egg yolk and hot wax. Brought to Ukraine from Constantinople by Volodymyr the Great in the 10th century and remaining the key religious art until the 17th century, icons were attributed with healing and spiritual powers. Icon painters – mostly monks – rarely signed works, and depicted only Christ, the Virgin, angels and saints. Many of the oldest examples can be seen in museums, the best being Lviv's National Museum and Lutsk's Museum of the Volyn Icon. Church murals, mosaics and frescoes, as well as manuscript illuminations, developed at the same time as icons. Some of the oldest frescoes are found in Kyiv's St Sophia's Cathedral.

Pysanky

Painted Easter eggs *(pysanky)* are an ancient Slavonic art found across Eastern Europe. Designs are drawn in wax on the eggshell (emptied beforehand), the egg is dyed one colour and the process continually repeated until a complex pattern is built up. Different symbols represent varying natural forces – a circle with a dot in the middle is the sun and so on – but each Ukrainian region has its own traditions. The place to see them is Kolomyya's Pysanky Museum housed in a purpose-built structure that looks like an Easter egg.

One of the finest renovation projects in Kyiv since independence must be the main train station, which received an opulent makeover in 2001.

Romanticism

The first break from religious art occurred during the Cossack Hetmanate. A secular, romantic trend of folk painting slowly developed, common themes being the *Kozak Mamay* (a Cossack playing a *bandura* or *kobza*), country life and folk traditions. Most of these paintings remained unknown, but Ukrainian-born Ilya Repin gained international fame. His famous *Zaporizhsky Cossacks Writing a Letter to the Turkish Sultan* and other Romantic paintings are found in the Kharkiv Art Museum.

Ivan Ayvazovsky is regarded as one of the world's best seascape painters. Ethnically Armenian, he was born and lived in Feodosiya, Crimea, where hundreds of his works populate the Ayvazovsky Gallery.

Soviet Era & Beyond

Socialist realism propagated Soviet ideals – the industrialised peasant, the muscular worker and the heroic soldier. Take, as an example, the sculptural reliefs near Kyiv's Museum of the Great Patriotic War. Ukrainian nationalism asserted itself through the age-old tradition of folk art, leading the Soviet authorities to ban folk embroidery.

After independence, Ukrainian art enjoyed a reawakening, with art schools in Kyiv producing new stars, like painter Maxim Mamsikov (b 1968), sculptor Zhana Khadyrova (b 1981) and multimedia artist Kyril Protsenko (b 1967). One of the most important artists to emerge at this time was the Ukrainian photographer Boris Mikhailov (b 1938).

Since 2006 art lovers in Kyiv have been making a beeline for the PinchukArtCentre. This gallery not only has major international exhibitions and pieces by the likes of Damien Hirst, Anthony Gormley and Andreas Gursky, it's also a good place to see works by leading local artists.

Some of Kyiv's most impressive Soviet architecture can be found underground in the shape of its ornate metro stations.

SOVIET ARCHITECTURE

Architecture

Church design has wrought a vast influence on Ukrainian architecture. Byzantine layout has at various times been merged with traditional wooden Hutsul churches (colonnaded porches and freestanding belfries) and 17th-century baroque to produce unique styles. 'Ukrainian baroque', with its trademark green, helmet-shaped dome, is typified by St Andrew's Church in Kyiv.

Otherwise various styles have come in and out of vogue. After St Petersburg proved such a success in Russia, its planned layout and neoclassical architecture was copied in Odesa and Poltava. In the 19th century there were revivals of Byzantine design (as seen in St Volodymyr's Cathedral in Kyiv) and Renaissance style merged with baroque – for example, in the opera houses in Kyiv, Odesa and Lviv. A modern Ukrainian style based on Art Nouveau featured in the Regional Museum in Poltava and the eclectic Metropolitan Palace, now the university, in Chernivtsi.

The Soviets had a penchant for pompous 'monumental classicism', with enormous temple-like state edifices. Extensively rebuilt after WWII, Kyiv is full of such buildings. The Soviets were also responsible for the most widespread architectural style seen in Ukraine's big cities – the apartment block. Even these can be divided into periods, starting with the so called Khrushchyovka, a normally five-storey brick or concrete tenement built in the 1960s during Khrushchev's tenure at the Kremlin. However, most of Kyiv and Kharkiv's housing stock was erected in the 1970s and '80s. The acres of shabby blocks that ring the capital are made of prefabricated concrete panels that could be locked together in a matter of weeks. Despite their dilapidated appearance, most Ukrainian apartments are very comfortable inside and warm in winter, but not terribly cool in summer. These have now been joined by plasticky high-rises, often thrown up cheaply and with general disregard for what may be around them and the capacity of local amenities to cope with more residents.

Music & Literature

From whooping folk ensembles to cable TV chick pop, dreamy Soviet masters of the *chanson* to post-Soviet rock, music in all its forms flows in every Ukrainian's blood. They're also a well-read nation, though most might know more about French and English literature than their own.

Music

Folk Music

Ukrainian folk music developed as a form of storytelling. The guardians of Ukrainian folklore, *kobzary* were highly respected wandering minstrels who travelled from town to town spreading news through an extensive repertoire of songs. These included *bylyny,* epic narrative poems relating the courageous deeds of the heroes of Kyivan Rus, and *dumy,* lyrical ballads glorifying the exploits of the Cossacks.

The online music shop www.umka.com.ua offers anything from Transcarpathian folk to the latest Donetsk hip-hop.

Traditionally, *kobzary* were required to be blind and they used the lute-like *kobza* to accompany their historical narratives. In the 18th century the *kobza* was replaced by the *bandura,* a larger instrument with up to 65 strings. Popular *bandura* choirs accompanied Ukrainian national songs and folk dances, and this unparalleled instrument soon became a national symbol.

The Ukrainian Bandurist Chorus (www.bandura.org) was founded in Kyiv in 1918 and still performs worldwide today (mainly in the US). To find a *bandura* concert in Ukraine, check listings magazines. The National Philharmonic in Kyiv is a reasonable bet.

Traditional *kobzary* themselves suffered the all-too-familiar and miserable fate of many who lived under Stalin. During the Soviet era, they kept Ukrainians apprised of collectivisation, famine and repression. When Stalin heard about them, he immediately ordered a national *kobzary* conference, feigning great interest – and then had all the attendees shot.

Classical Music & Opera

Bandura 'buskers' can often be seen strumming in Kyiv and Lviv for the tourists. In Lviv, look outside the Grand Hotel.

The most notable local composer remains Mykola Lysenko (1842–1912). The 'father of Ukrainian national music', he applied the logic of Ukrainian folk songs to piano-based classical music. Ukrainian operettas combine more acting and dancing than typical operas.

Contemporary Music

Ukraine's active rock scene provides a welcome antidote to the Russian pop streaming in over the border. Broadly, the scene can be split into four categories: the legends, the nationalists, mainstream alt rock and hip-hop.

The legends are Vopli Vidopliasova (VV) and Okean Elzy. Both have been going since the 1990s and have charismatic front men – Oleh Skrypka and Svyatoslav Vakarchuk respectively – who seek to promote the Ukrainian identity through music. Both tend towards the progressive: VV is more uptempo, Okean Elzy more melancholic.

The nationalists, from Lviv and the west, are defenders of Ukrainian heritage. This category, including Plach Yeremiyi, Mertvy Piven and Mandry, might also fit into the category of folksy alt rock, alongside the edgier but higher profile Druha Rika.

Next up are popular hip-hop acts, like TNMK, Tartak, Boombox and Vova z Lvova. Acoustic reggae duo 5'nizza and ska band Haydamaky boast large followings thanks to their often exceptional arrangements.

Ukrainian chick pop follows the tried-and-tested formula of scantily clad singers belting out studio-driven pop. Ukraine's Eurovision entries – including Tina Karol (2006) and even 2004 winner Ruslana – tend to hail from this group, as do high-profile video stars Ani Lorak and all-girl band Via Gra (geddit?). The vast majority of what you see on Ukrainian MTV and other music channel start-ups, usually porno-pop highlighting the physical attributes of female singers, hails from across the border in Russia.

Ukraine's 2007 Eurovision entry and the overall runner-up – cross-dressing comedian-singer Verka Serduchka – occupies a category all of his/her own. The same is true of NYC gypsy punk outfit Gogol Bordello, whose eccentric singer, Eugene Hutz, is originally from Boyarka, near Kyiv. Another unusual hit is the hard-rock Death Valley Screamers, fronted by a Yorkshireman, Sean Carr, who is married to Evgeniya Tymoshenko, daughter of jailed opposition leader Yulia Tymoshenko.

Literature

Taras Shevchenko is *the* figure towering over all Ukrainian literature. Literally. Statues of Shevchenko now stand on pedestals vacated by Lenin across the entire west of the country. Shevchenko (1814–61) embodied and stirred the national consciousness, while achieving literary respectability for a Ukrainian language then suppressed under tsarist Russian rule. Born a serf and orphaned as a teenager, Shevchenko studied painting at the Academy of Arts in St Petersburg, where in 1840 he published his first work, *Kobzar* (The Bard), a book of eight romantic poems. It was a great success and his epic poem *Haidamaky* (1841) and ballad *Hamaliia* (1844) followed soon afterwards. Later works, such as *Son* (The Dream), *Kavkas* (Caucasus) and *Velyky Lokh* (The Great Dungeon), were not immediately published but are now held in great affection.

Through Shevchenko's prolific work, Ukrainian was elevated from a peasant tongue to a vehicle of eloquent and poetic expression. Combining vernacular expressions and colloquial dialects with Church Slavonic, he formed a unique voice. He passionately preached social justice, in universal terms as well as to the downtrodden peasant and the Ukrainian nation, referring to 'this land of ours that is not our own'. A staunch anti-tsarist, the poet was banished to Siberia for 10 years, which led to his premature death in 1861. In 1876 Tsar Alexander II banned all Ukrainian books and publishing, but Shevchenko's message remained. He was, and is, a Ukrainian hero.

In addition to Shevchenko there are three other Ukrainian writers who rate a mention. Ivan Franko (1856–1916) is another hero who promoted the

PUSHKIN

Alexander Pushkin spent some of his scandal-filled 20s in Ukraine, most notably in Odesa and Crimea. He was also friends with Gogol and some of the Ukraine based Decembrists.

SOFIA ROTARU

The most famous Ukrainian songstress of the last 40 years, bar none, is Sofia Rotaru (b 1947), an ethnic Moldovan born near Chernivtsi. Dubbed the 'Nightingale of Bukovyna' her voice is as familiar to Ukrainians as it is to music followers in Riga, Irkutsk or Vladivostok. Indeed, across the ex-USSR, only the immovable Alla Pugacheva comes anywhere near her profile. Rotaru began her career in the early 1970s, gaining many 'People's Artist of…' and 'Hero of…' titles before making a successful transition to the new order of the 1990s. Singing in three languages (Russian, Ukrainian and Romanian), she still has huge appeal among the over 40s.

Ukrainian language. His better-known writings include *The Turnip Farmer, The Converted Sinner* and *During Work;* he was also a prolific poet.

Equally distinguished was Larysa Kosach (1871–1913), known by her pen name, Lesia Ukrainka. Her frail health inspired her to compose deeply moving poetry expressing inner strength and inspiration – symbolic beatitudes for the Ukrainian people. Her *Forest Song* inspired a ballet, an opera and a film.

Greatly influenced by Taras Shevchenko, Mikhailo Kotsyubinsky (1864–1913) was probably the finest Ukrainian literary talent around the turn of the century. His novels are a snapshot of Ukrainian life in the late 19th and early 20th centuries and some, including the famous *Shadows of Forgotten Ancestors*, were made into films during the Soviet era.

The star of the Ukrainian contemporary literature scene, Andrey Kurkov has had his works translated from Russian into no less than 25 languages – including Ukrainian.

There are several other proudly Ukrainian authors, but none of their works have been translated into English. On the other hand, two internationally renowned authors usually claimed by Russia are Ukrainian-born. Mikhail Bulgakov's (1891–1940) first novel, *The White Guard,* is set in his native Kyiv. Nikolai Gogol's (1809–52) novels *Evenings on a Farm near Dikanka* and *Dead Souls* and short story 'Taras Bulba' (about a Cossack hero and included in the collection *Mirgorod,* in Ukrainian *Myrhorod*) all have links to his country of birth. Odesa-born Isaac Babel (1894–1939) was the most famous chronicler of that city.

Contemporary Writers

As far as contemporary writers go, Kyiv-based author Andrey Kurkov (b 1961) has been called Bulgakov's heir. That might be taking things a bit far, but Kurkov is widely known abroad and his *Death and the Penguin, Penguin Lost* and *The President's Last Love* do indulge in the same flights of fancy as Bulgakov's classic *The Master and Margarita.* In *Death and the Penguin,* for example, would-be novelist Viktor is eking out a miserable existence with his pet penguin Misha, when suddenly he gets a great gig writing stock obituaries for still-living prominent people. Then suddenly, one by one, the subjects of his profiles all start dying.

More for the Ukrainian cognoscenti are the works of Yuri Andrukhovych (b 1960), a western Ukrainian and co-founder of the Bu-Ba-Bu (loosely 'burlesque, side-show, buffoonery') poetry group. Andrukhovych's *Recreations* is a burlesque retelling of four poets' time at a pagan festival cum orgy of excess, while *Perverzion* presents a twist on *Death in Venice.*

Oksana Zabuzhko (b 1960) is another major contemporary name, best known for her 1990s Ukrainian-language novel *Field Research on Ukrainian Sex.*

TOP 10 READS

- *The White Guard* (1925) by Mikhail Bulgakov
- *Street of Crocodiles* (1934) by Bruno Schulz
- *Taras Bulba* (1835) by Nikolai Gogol
- *Dead Souls* (1842) by Nikolai Gogol
- *Death and the Penguin* (1996) by Andrey Kurkov
- *Borderland* (1998) by Anna Reid
- *Recreations* (1998) by Yuri Andrukhovych
- *Everything Is Illuminated* (2002) by Jonathan Safran Foer
- *Complete Works* (reissued 2005) by Isaac Babel
- *A Short History of Tractors in Ukrainian* (2005) by Marina Lewycka

Survival Guide

Directory A–Z

Accommodation

- Accommodation will be your single biggest expense in Ukraine.
- Rooms are slightly more affordable than they once were due to favourable exchange rates.
- Kyiv, Lviv, Crimea and eastern Ukrainian cities are the most expensive places to stay.
- Room prices in rural towns can be as low as 100uah to 200uah a night.
- Rates are normally listed in hryvnya, but you may still come across places where US dollars or euros are quoted.
- Water supply problems are generally a thing of the past, though they do still arise even in big cities.

B&Bs

Just a handful of Ukrainian establishments truly fit this description, but they're often the most wonderful places to stay in the country. Kolomyya, Rakhiv and Bakhchysaray have particularly good options.

Camping

If you intend to camp in Ukraine note the following:

- In Crimea camping is officially permitted in *turstoyanki* (campsites with basic facilities).
- Wild camping is tolerated in most areas of the country (including Crimea and the Carpathian National Nature Park) but is not recommended.
- Lighting fires in national parks is officially forbidden.
- In summer never light a fire in woodland, as Ukraine is prone to forest fires.
- Most so-called campsites are really former Soviet holiday camps, and slightly more formalised than most Western campers prefer. Facilities are usually poor.

Homestays

Crashing with a local is not only cheap, but also a great way to get to know individual cities. There are several ways you can do this.

HOSPITALITY CLUBS

Couch Surfing (www.couchsurfing.com) Surprisingly, this stay-for-free club has over 4000 Ukrainian hosts.

Global Freeloaders (www.globalfreeloaders.com) Mostly Kyiv-based hosts.

Hospitality Club (www.hospitalityclub.org) Hook up with thousands of Ukraine-based hosts.

ONLINE PROJECTS

The best current option is Carpathian-based **Karpaty Info** (www.karpaty.info), which offers details on B&Bs, homestays and hotels in the Carpathians.

PRIVATE RENTALS

In parts of Ukraine, you will still find people standing outside train or bus stations offering rooms in their houses or private apartment rentals. Look for signs reading кімнати (*kimnaty,* Ukrainian) or комнати (*komnaty,* Russian), садиба (*sadyba,* Ukrainian, seen mainly in the Carpathians) or житло (*zhilyo,* Russian, seen mainly in Crimea). This is still common in summer holiday spots like Crimea and Odesa. Although the numbers of *babushky* (grannies) doing so are dwindling, it's also still possible in Kyiv. Prices are usually quite reasonable at around 250uah per night for a one-room apartment (more in Kyiv).

Hostels

Hostelling is now a well-established sector in Ukraine's

BOOK YOUR STAY ONLINE

For more accommodation reviews by Lonely Planet authors, check out http://lonelyplanet.com/ukraine/hotels You'll find independent reviews, as well as recommendations on the best places to stay. Best of all, you can book online.

accommodation market, especially in tourist hot spots such as Kyiv, Lviv and Odesa. However, many hostels are run by expats who open up, party for a couple of seasons, then move on. Check out the following websites:

Hostelling Ukraine International (www.hihostels.com.ua) Gathers all of Ukraine's hostels in one place. Online booking available.

Hostelworld (www.hostelworld.com) Still the best international website for booking a hostel in Ukraine.

Youth Tourism & Hostels of Ukraine (www.hostels.org.ua) Hostels listed tend to be in rather odd locations.

Hotels

As in most countries of the former USSR, Ukraine has a bewildering array of hotel and room types. At the bottom are Soviet-era budget crash pads for less than 100uah, at the top 'six-star' overpriced luxury in over-the-top surroundings. Everything in between can be very hit-and-miss and there are no national standards to follow, so forget any star ratings you might see.

Things to know when choosing a hotel in Ukraine:

- In big cities unrenovated Soviet-era hotels are now rare in city centres.
- Older Soviet hotels often offer the full range of rooms, from semi-luxurious to downright grotty.
- At reception you'll often be presented with a baffling list of room prices and types. Pick your price, then view the room to see if it's acceptable.
- Single rooms in miserable unrenovated or partially renovated Soviet-era hotels cost around the same as a hostel dorm bed.
- Communal heating systems, to which Soviet-era hotels are linked, aren't switched on until early autumn, long after things have got nippy.

SLEEPING PRICE RANGES

The following price ranges refer to a double room in high season. Unless otherwise stated breakfast is included in the price.

$ less than 400uah

$$ 400uah–800uah

$$$ more than 800uah

- It's only worth booking ahead in Odesa and Crimea in summer, in big cities in late December and early January, and in the Carpathians from November to March.

Renting an Apartment

Even if you never normally think of renting an apartment when abroad, you should consider it in Ukraine. With insufficient midrange hotels available, these help fill the gap. Single-night stays are perfectly acceptable, and for longer sojourns you not only have the benefit of a washing machine and a kitchen, you can save up to half the cost of a hotel.

Things to check before you commit to renting:

- Does the apartment have its own hot-water supply (the only guarantee of 24-hour, year-round availability)?
- Does it have its own central heating? Communal heating systems are turned on in October and go off in April/May.
- Does the building have a concierge?
- Is the entrance well lit at night?
- How close to a metro station/city centre/beach is the apartment?
- Who should you call at 3am when the fuse box blows/key snaps in the lock/neighbours flood you out?

Other Options

- **Train stations** Many Ukrainian train stations have a small 'hotel' or *kimnaty vidpochynku* (Кімнати відпочинку; resting rooms) designed for late-night arrivals or those departing early.
- **Turbazy** Simple holiday resorts, most common in the Carpathians; some haven't changed from the Soviet era.
- **Sanatoriums** These health resorts can be found on the Black Sea coastline. Minimum stay conditions apply.

Activities

The following outfits will get you active in Ukraine:

Active Ukraine (www.activeukraine.com) West-based agency specialising in hiking and cycling, primarily in the Carpathians.

Aero-Kiev (www.aero-kiev.com) Paragliding outfit based in Kyiv, but it does most of its flying in Crimea.

Bikeland (Велокраїна; www.bikeland.com.ua) Ukrainian cycling initiative.

Onyx Tour (☎0652-256 348; www.onixtour.com.ua) The only tour company specialising in caving in Crimea.

Outdoor Ukraine (www.outdoorukraine.com) Arranges hiking tours in Ukraine's outdoor hot spots.

Paragliding Crimea (www.paragliding-crimea.com) You will soon be gliding high above Koktebel in Crimea.

Sergey Sorokin (☎067 793 9100; www.mt.crimea.com) Crimea-based guide Sergey can arrange any kind of outdoor activity you choose.

Velocrimea (www.velocrimea.com) Crimea is perfect for mountain biking, and these guys will help you hit the right trail.

Velokosiv (www.velokosiv.if.ua) Bike trips into the Carpathian Mountains.

Children

Ukraine is not the world's most child-friendly destination, so if you're travelling with young children, it's advisable that you have previous experience of the country, or limit yourself to a short break in a major city like Kyiv.

- Levels of hygiene are still low even in big cities. Attitudes to children's health are outdated and finicky.
- Playgrounds are common but very often slides, swings and other equipment are downright lethal.
- Generally speaking, Ukrainian museums have yet to come up with activities for children.
- Long and hot *marshrutka* (fixed-route minibus) rides with kids are no fun.
- Children's car seats are rare and very few people use them.
- Ukrainians adore kids and often show it.
- With a child in tow even the old will give up seats for you on public transport.
- Bureaucratic obstacles may suddenly melt away and you're probably less likely to be hassled by the police if accompanied by a child.
- Kiddies will love Ukraine's easily accessible animal population.

Customs Regulations

You are allowed to carry up to €10,000 when entering Ukraine without having to sign any documentation. You are also permitted to bring in the following items duty-free:

- 1L of spirits
- 2L of wine
- 5L of beer
- 200 cigarettes or 250g of tobacco
- €50 worth of food (not exceeding 2kg)

If you exceed these limits, you'll have to sign a *deklaratsiya* (customs declaration). Be careful not to lose this completed form – you will need to present it when departing the country. See http://www.iatatravelcentre.com/UA-Ukraine-customs-currency-airport-tax-regulations-details.htm for information in English.

It's prohibited to export antiques (including icons), works of art or cultural/historical treasures without special written permission from the **Ministry of Culture** (http://mincult.kmu.gov.ua; vul Ivana Franka 19, Kyiv).

Electricity

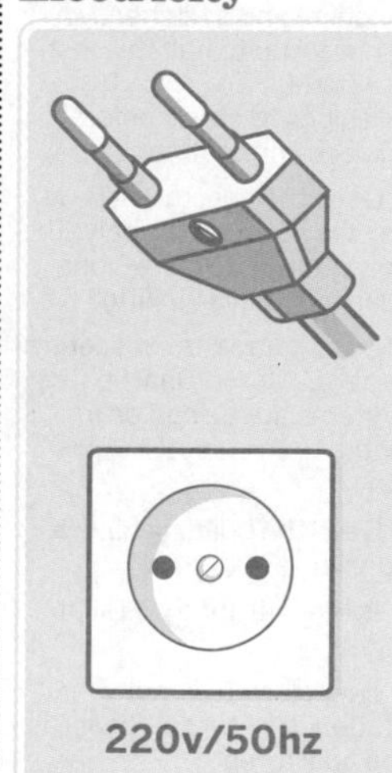

220v/50hz

Embassies & Consulates

The following are located in Kyiv unless otherwise noted. Call your embassy if you need emergency help. Consulates issue visas and can help their own citizens if there is no embassy.

Australian Consulate (☎044 246 4223; vul Kominterna 18, Apt 11; MBoryspilska)

Belarusian Embassy (☎044 537 5200; vul Mykhayla Kotsyubynskoho 3; MBoryspilska)

Canadian Embassy (Map p38; ☎044 590 3100; www.canadainternational.gc.ca/ukraine; Yaroslaviv Val 31; MZoloti Vorota)

Dutch Embassy (Map p44; ☎044 490 8200; pl Kontraktova 7; MKontraktova pl)

French Embassy (Map p38; ☎044 590 3600; www.ambafrance-ua.org; vul Reytarska 39; MZoloti Vorota)

Georgian Embassy (☎044 451 4353; vul Melnikova 83D, Section 4; MLukyanivska); Consulate (☎0482 726 4727; vul Tolstoho 21, Odesa)

German Embassy (Map p38; ☎044 247 6800; www.kiew.diplo.de; vul Bohdana Khmelnytskoho 25; MZoloti Vorota)

Hungarian Embassy (Map p38; ☎044 230 8000; vul Reytarska 33; SZoloti Vorota); Consulate (☎0312 616 179; vul Pravoslavna 12, Uzhhorod)

Moldovan Embassy (☎044 521 2280; www.ucraina.mfa.md; vul Yagotinska 2; MLybidska)

New Zealand Honorary Consulate (☎044 537 7444; vul Bagovutivska 17/21; MLukyanivska)

Polish Embassy (Map p38; ☎044 230 0700; vul Yaroslaviv Val 12; MZoloti Vorota)

Romanian Embassy (Map p38; ☎044 234 5261; http://kiev.mae.ro; vul Mykhayla Kotsyubynskoho 8; SUniversytet); Consulate (Map p148; ☎048 725 0399; http://odessa.mae.ro; vul Bazarna 31, Odesa); Consulate (☎0372 545 414; vul Skilna 16, Chernivtsi)

Russian Embassy (☎044 244 0961; www.embrus.org.ua; pr Povitroflotsky 27; Ⓢ Vokzalna); Consulate (Map p50; ☎044 284 6701; vul Kutuzova 8; Ⓜ Pecherska); Consulate (☎048 784 1542; Gagarinskoe Plato 14, Odesa)

UK Embassy (Map p44; ☎044 490 3660; http://ukinukraine.fco.gov.uk/en/; vul Desyatynna 9)

US Embassy (Map p38; ☎044 521 5000; http://kyiv.usembassy.gov; vul Yuriya Kotsyubynskoho 10)

Food

For information about eating in Ukraine, see p245.

Gay & Lesbian Travellers

Ukraine is generally more tolerant of homosexuality than is Russia, but that's not saying much. Out-and-proud gay views mix badly with those of the Orthodox Church, hence most people's outwardly conservative attitudes.

- Homosexuality is legal in Ukraine.
- Few people are very out here and attitudes vary across the country – what's acceptable in Lviv may not be in Donetsk.
- Ukraine's gay scene is largely underground.
- Young people and city dwellers are much more tolerant of homosexuality.
- Displays of affection between two men (and perhaps two women) in public could create hostility.
- The biggest scene is in Kyiv, but Kharkiv and Odesa have one or two clubs.
- Simeyiz in Crimea is also reportedly a gay mecca in August and early September.

Following are useful gay websites:

- www.gayua.com
- www.gay.org.ua
- www.gaylvov.at.ua

Health

Ukraine's health system is under-resourced and decidedly primitive by Western European standards, so it's important to come prepared. Ukraine has reciprocal agreements with most countries (including the UK and most of the EU), which in theory guarantee foreign citizens free emergency care. However, heading to Ukraine without medical insurance would be foolhardy indeed.

Recommended Vaccinations

No jabs are mandatory to enter Ukraine, but the following are recommended:

- diphtheria
- hepatitis A
- measles
- polio
- rabies
- tetanus
- tick-borne encephalitis (if hiking in summer)
- typhoid.

Medical Facilities

State hospitals and clinics are very basic affairs with limited supplies and facilities. Patients are expected to supply everything from food to syringes, and doctors expect (unofficial) payment for every stage of treatment. Avoid admittance to this type of hospital if you can by contacting the

MEDICAL CHECKLIST

Pharmacists in Ukraine are the first port of call for many people suffering minor complaints, and they will usually make a diagnosis if you can explain or point to the problem. It's always a good idea to bring extra supplies of any medication you are taking and familiarise yourself with the Latin name if it's not on the label. In Ukraine this is often written in the Roman alphabet alongside any medicine's local name. Most common medicines are available, but it might be handy to bring at least some of the following:

- adhesive tape
- antibacterial ointment (for cuts and abrasions)
- antidiarrhoeal drugs (eg Loperamide)
- antihistamine (for hay fever and allergic reactions)
- anti-inflammatory drugs (eg Ibuprofen)
- aspirin or paracetamol
- bandages, gauze rolls
- DEET-based insect repellent for the skin
- tick-removal kit
- eye drops
- insect spray containing pyrethrin, for clothing, tents and bed nets
- oral rehydration salts
- scissors, safety pins, tweezers
- sunscreen
- thermometer.

HIV & AIDS

- Ukraine is the site of Europe's worst HIV epidemic.
- The country is thought to have 230,000 people living with HIV – far more than any other European state.
- The virus continues to spread faster here than elsewhere on the continent.
- The worst-hit areas are Crimea, Dnipropetrovsk, Donetsk, Odesa, Mykolayiv and Kyiv.
- The message is clear: always practise safe sex.

following Kyiv clinics where Western standards of care are maintained:

American Medical Centre (emergency hotline 044 490 7600; http://amcenters.com; vul Berdychivska 1; 24hr; M Lukyanivska)

Dobrobut (044 495 2888; www.med.dobrobut.com; vul Pymonenka 10, Kyiv; 24hr)

Tap Water

Drinking tap water is not recommended anywhere in Ukraine. Bottled water is cheap and comes both still and fizzy.

Insurance

Make sure you are fully insured before heading to Ukraine. Worldwide travel insurance is available at www.lonelyplanet.com/travel_services. You can buy, extend and claim online anytime – even if you're already on the road.

If you're staying longer than 90 days in the country (and therefore will need a visa), you might also be asked to show you have appropriate health insurance, as decided by the Department of Citizenship, Passport & Immigration.

Internet Access

Internet service in Ukraine has improved immensely in recent years.

- Most hotels now offer free wi-fi internet access.
- Restaurants and cafes are rapidly installing wi-fi technology.
- Upmarket hotels often have a business centre with a couple of terminals hooked up to the internet.
- Internet cafes are not as common as they once were but there's usually at least one in every town.
- Internet cafes often double up as noisy gaming centres.
- Ukrtelekom offers web access at its city-centre offices.
- Surf the net at so-called 'open spaces' where you pay for the time you are there, not individual drinks and web access.

Legal Matters

- Carry your passport with you at all times; if stopped by the police, you are obliged to show it.
- If you are stopped by the police, ask to see their ID immediately.
- The police must return your documents at once.
- Do not get involved with drugs; penalties can be severe and the process leading up to them labyrinthine.
- The US embassy in Kyiv maintains a list of English-speaking lawyers.

Maps

Accurate city maps *(plan mista)* are widely available for all reasonably sized cities. They're available from bookshops and news kiosks.

Bikeland (www.bikeland.com.ua) The Bikeland project produces excellent maps of the Carpathians showing cycling trails. These can also be used as hiking maps.

Easyway (www.eway.in.ua) Detailed online maps of Ukrainian cities including public transport.

Freytag & Berndt (www.freytagberndt.at) Austrian company producing a comprehensive *Ukraine-Moldova* (1:1,000,000) map. Order online.

GPS Server (www.navigation.com.ua) Download very detailed maps of Crimea, the Carpathians and other parts of Ukraine to your Garmin GPS device.

Stanfords (www.stanfords.co.uk) This UK travel bookshop sells a wide range of Ukraine road atlases and city maps. Everything can be ordered online.

Topograficheskaya Karta Keep an eye out for this highly detailed Russian-language series, based on former Soviet army mapping, which covers the entire country in 286 maps.

Ukrainian Map Server (www.ukrmap.net) Downloadable detailed regional maps.

Money

- The Ukrainian hryvnya is divided into 100 kopecks.
- Coins come in denominations of one, five, 10, 25 and 50 kopecks, plus the rare one hryvnya.
- Notes come in one, two, five, 10, 20, 50, 100, 200 and 500 hryvnya.
- Kopecks have become virtually worthless and prices are often rounded up or down.

- There is a chronic shortage of change throughout the country – try to give the correct money whenever you can.
- In Russian-speaking regions people may still quote prices in roubles instead of hryvnya from force of habit.
- It's virtually impossible to buy any hryvnya before you get to Ukraine.

ATMs

- Cash machines/ATMs are more common than in some Western countries and can be found in the same sorts of places.
- The best way to manage your money here is to take it out of your account in hryvnya.
- Cirrus, Plus, Visa, MasterCard/EuroCard and other global networks are all recognised.
- ATMs are often slow and the English translations of the instructions can be unclear.
- Your own bank will charge you a small fee for taking out foreign currency.
- Some ATMs also distribute euros and US dollars.

Cash

Exchanging currency is still very much a part of everyday life for many locals. Hoarding hard currency is common.

- US dollars, euros and Russian roubles are the easiest currencies to exchange.
- The British pound is harder to exchange, except in Kyiv.
- In western Ukraine, Polish złoty and Hungarian forints are widely accepted.
- Banks and currency-exchange offices will not accept old, tatty notes with rips or tears.
- US dollar bills issued before 1990 cannot be exchanged.

Credit Cards & International Transfers

Ukraine remains primarily a cash economy. Credit cards are increasingly accepted by upmarket hotels, restaurants and shops inside and outside Kyiv. But be alert to possible credit-card fraud.

With so many ATMs, asking a bank for an advance is unnecessary unless you've forgotten your PIN. The process can be long and rather bureaucratic.

Western Union will receive money wired from anywhere in the world.

Moneychangers

Some hotels have an exchange office and there are numerous exchange kiosks (обмін валюти) scattered along main streets and dotting markets (though not as many as there once were). Some upmarket shops have their own exchange offices, as do department stores and train stations. Rates are usually exactly the same in every one and none charge commission.

Tipping

Tipping is not common in Ukraine.

Travellers Cheques

- Travellers cheques should be avoided or brought only as a backup.
- It's relatively hard to find banks that will accept travellers cheques and the process is lengthy, involving lots of paperwork.
- If you must use them, take Thomas Cook, American Express or Visa cheques in US dollars.
- Cheque-friendly establishments include branches of the nationwide chains Raiffeisen Bank Aval or UKRExim Bank.
- Expect to pay a commission of 1% to 4%.

Opening Hours

Business hours can be hard to pin down in Ukraine. A rule of thumb is that unless an establishment has anything to do with the state, it's normally open when most people are around.

PRACTICALITIES

- **Newspapers** Include *Fakti i Kommentarii* (www.fakty.ua), *Segodnya* (www.segodnya.ua), *Ukrayina Moloda* (www.umoloda.kiev.ua), *Holos Ukrayiny* (www.golos.com.ua) and *Vysoky Zamok*. News weeklies include *Korrespondent* (http://korrespondent.net) and English-language *Kyiv Post* (www.kyivpost.com).
- **Radio** Hundreds of FM radio stations broadcast in Ukrainian and Russian; BBC World Service (www.bbc.co.uk) and Radio Liberty (www.rferl.org) broadcast in English.
- **TV** Channels include Inter TV (www.inter.ua), 1+1 (www.1plus1.ua), 5 Kanal (www.5.ua), state-run UT-1 (www.1tv.com.ua), and pop-music channels M1 (http://m1.tv/ua/) and MTV (www.mtv.com.ua). For English information see www.ukrainatv.com.
- **Weights & Measures** The metric system is used throughout the country.

Lunch breaks (1pm to 2pm or 2pm to 3pm) are an all-too-common throwback to Soviet days. Sunday closing is rare.

Banks 9am–5pm Monday to Friday

Shops 9am–9pm

Restaurants 11am–11pm

Cafes 9am–10pm

Bars & Clubs 10pm–3am

Sights 9am–5pm or 6pm, closed at least one day a week

Post

The national postal service is run by **Ukrposhta** (www.ukrposhta.com).

- Sending a postcard or a letter of up to 20g costs 4uah to anywhere outside Ukraine.
- Major post offices (*poshta* or *poshtamt*) are open from around 8am to 9pm weekdays, and 9am to 7pm on Saturday.
- Smaller post offices close earlier and are not open on Saturday.
- Outward mail is fairly reliable, but you should always send things *avia* (airmail).
- Mail takes about a week or less to reach Europe, and two to three weeks to the USA or Australia.
- Take packages to the post office unwrapped, so their contents can be verified.
- The state-run International Express Mail (EMS) is available at most main post offices.
- Incoming post is still quite unreliable.
- DHL and FedEx have offices throughout Ukraine; rates are astronomical.
- The privately owned **Nova Poshta** (www.novaposhta.ua) is an efficient branch-to-branch alternative to the state-run Ukrposhta.

Addressing Mail

- Traditionally, addresses were written in reverse order (eg Ukraina, Kyiv 252091, vul Franko 26/8, kv 12, Yuri Orestovich Vesolovsky), but the continental European fashion (Yuri Orestovich Vesolovsky, vul Franko 26/8, kv 12, Kyiv 252091, Ukraina) is now common.
- The return address is written in smaller print in the top left-hand corner on the front of the envelope (not on the back).
- When addressing outgoing mail, repeat the country destination in Cyrillic if you can. Incoming mail addressed in Cyrillic, rather than Roman, characters will reach its destination sooner.

Public Holidays

Currently the main public holidays in Ukraine are the following:

New Year's Day 1 January

Orthodox Christmas 7 January

International Women's Day 8 March

Orthodox Easter (Paskha) April/May

Labour Day 1–2 May

Victory Day (1945) 9 May

Constitution Day 28 June

Independence Day (1991) 24 August

Safe Travel

Despite what you may have heard, Ukraine is not a dangerous, crime-ridden place. The infamous mafia are not interested in tourists – in fact, you are infinitely more likely to be knocked down by a *marshrutka* than to be gunned down by the mob.

Crime

Ukraine is normally as safe as most Western European countries; however, petty theft is a serious problem.

Avoiding becoming a victim of theft is a matter of common sense:

- Don't flash your money around.
- Watch your wallet and belongings, particularly on public transport and in crowded situations.
- Stay low-key in appearance and have more than one place on your body where you stash your cash.
- Avoid being alone at night in parks or secluded places.
- In hostels stash your gear away in lockers – traveller-

UKRAINE'S HAZARDOUS HIGHWAYS

You don't need to travel very long in Ukraine to realise that this country has some of the most perilous driving conditions in Europe. The country's mix of poorly lit, potholed roads, an idiotically aggressive driving style and the poor state of many (seatbelt-less) vehicles is a lethal cocktail indeed. Accidents are the norm, and in 2012 over 5000 people died on the country's roads (compare that to just over 1700 in the UK).

In a bid to stop the carnage and stimulate at least a basic instinct for self-preservation in local drivers, Ukrainian TV channels broadcast daily and weekly programs detailing horrific road traffic accidents, most of which are caused by mindboggling stupidity and/or drunkenness.

Driving Ukraine's rutted highways will also bring you into contact with the bane of motorists' lives, the traffic police (Derzhavna Avtoinspektsiya; DAI). Foreign cars come in for special attention.

on-traveller crime is all too common.

➡ Lock your compartment door on overnight trains.

CREDIT-CARD FRAUD

Some embassies have warned of a rise in credit-card fraud. They suggest you use your card only as a last resort, and only in reputable locations. Take all the usual precautions to make sure no one sees or copies your PIN.

THE DROPPED-WALLET SCAM

This well-known rort starts with you suddenly noticing a wallet or a large wad of cash on the ground nearby. If you pick it up, you'll be approached by someone saying it's theirs. They'll thank you… and then say that they had *two* wallets or wads of cash and accuse you of stealing the other. Alternatively, they'll directly accuse you of stealing the first wallet. Accomplices might be brought in as witnesses or 'police'. Don't get involved and walk away quickly.

Racist Attacks

Ukraine has tended to be more welcoming to people of African, Asian and Caribbean appearance than neighbouring Russia, though that's not saying a lot. There have been attacks on non-Europeans but the situation is nowhere near as bad as it is in, say, St Petersburg or Moscow. If you're black, Asian or Middle Eastern, stay alert and exercise extreme caution if going out alone at night.

Solo Travellers

More independent travellers are making their way to Ukraine and, though the rest of the country still doesn't exactly cater to their needs, the growing network of hostels does. Apart from a few well-trodden international train routes (eg Przemysl, Poland to Lviv), these are the only places you can really bank on meeting other travellers.

However, if you're moving around, rather than staying in one city, you'll never feel alone in Ukraine. Whether pressed against local people on a crowded, long-distance bus seat or sharing a train compartment with them, they will often want to chat – regardless of your respective language skills. It's a good incentive to learn at least a little Ukrainian or Russian.

Similarly, you won't feel particularly alone in restaurants. With eating out considered such a treat here, almost no locals would do so alone; everyone will immediately realise you're foreign and chalk your solitude up to that.

GOVERNMENT TRAVEL ADVICE

The following government websites offer travel advisories and information on current hot spots:

Australian Department of Foreign Affairs and Trade (www.smarttraveller.gov.au)

Foreign Affairs and International Trade Canada (www.dfait-maeci.gc.ca)

UK Foreign and Commonwealth Office (www.fco.gov.uk)

US State Department (http://travel.state.gov)

Telephone

Ukraine simplified the way numbers are dialled a few years ago, banishing the confusing system of Soviet-era prefixes and dialling tones. All numbers now start with ☎0. If you see a number starting with ☎8, this is the old intercity and mobile prefix and should be left off.

Phone Codes

➡ Ukraine's country code is ☎+38. To call Kyiv from London, dial ☎00 38 044 and the subscriber number.

➡ There's no need to dial the city code if dialling within that city, unless you're calling from a mobile.

➡ To call internationally, dial ☎0, wait for a second tone, then dial ☎0 again, followed by the country code, city code and number.

Telephone Offices

Almost every large town and city has a Ukrtelekom telephone office (many open 24 hours), where you can make international *(mizhnarodny)*, intercity *(mizhhorodny, mizhmisky)* or local calls.

Mobile Phones

European GSM phones usually work in Ukraine; double-check with your provider before leaving. However, if you're going to be making a few calls, it's more economical to get a prepaid SIM card costing as little as 10uah. Top up credit using vouchers available from mobile-phone shops and news kiosks, or use the special touch-screen terminals found in busy places such as bus stations, markets and shopping centres.

Mobile numbers start with 050, 067, 066 or similar three-digit prefixes.

The main pay-as-you-go mobile providers:

Djuice (www.djuice.com.ua)

Life:) (www.life.ua)

MTC (www.mts.com.ua)

Public Phones

➡ Public phones on the street can be used for local calls only.

- Most require a phonecard, sold at post and telephone offices.
- Phones in each city require a different brand of card.
- Using a Utel card phone is another way to make international and national calls.
- Cards can be purchased at post offices.
- The cards have printed instructions in English.
- Only Utel phones can be used to make calls with these cards.

Time

Ukraine is located in one time zone – GMT plus two hours. During daylight-saving time, from the last Sunday in March until the last Sunday in October, it's GMT plus three hours.

When it's noon in Kyiv, it's 5am in New York, 10am in London, 11am in Paris, 1pm in Moscow and 8pm in Sydney.

Ukraine generally uses the 24-hour clock (for instance, 8pm is 20:00).

Toilets

A women's toilet *(tualet)* is marked with an upwards-facing triangle or ж (for *zhinochy*); men's are marked with a downwards facing triangle, ч or м (for *cholovichy* or *muzhcheny*).

Tourist Information

Reliable tourist information is not as hard to come by as it once was.

Local Tourist Information

You can obtain tourist information in several ways:

Hostels Hostel staff and owners are sometimes very up to date on what's going on locally, and they speak English.

Hotel receptions Due to the lack of tourist offices, reception staff have become used to fielding travellers' queries.

Internet There's a lot of information on the net if you know where to look. Sadly, much of it is out of date.

Tourist information offices Most large towns in the west of the country have tourist offices; the east lags way behind.

Tourist Offices Abroad

Ukraine has no tourist offices abroad, and the information stocked by its consulates and embassies is very general and basic.

Travellers with Disabilities

Even Kyiv, the best-equipped Ukrainian city, isn't that friendly to people with disabilities. The rest of the country is worse. Uneven pavements, steep drops off curbs, holes in the road, lack of disabled access to public transport and very few wheelchair-accessible hotel rooms mean the only way to have an enjoyable time would be to come on a tour catering specifically for travellers with disabilities – and these don't exist.

The following companies and organisations can give advice on travel for those with disabilities, though their knowledge of facilities in Ukraine will be very limited.

Access Travel (☎01942 888 844; www.access-travel.co.uk)

Holiday Care Services (☎0845 124 9971; www.holidaycare.org.uk)

SATH (Society for the Advancement of Travelers with Handicaps; ☎212 447 7284; www.sath.org)

Visas

An attempt by Party of the Regions MPs to force through a law which would have seen the reintroduc-

CALL OF NATURE

There's a Ukrainian saying: 'Where's the toilet? The toilet is everywhere!' When you see some of the public toilets, you'll understand why. To be fair, vile, stinky, clogged holes with foot markers on either side are far less common than they once were, but when you encounter one, you realise why people so often prefer to go behind a bush.

Where it's not possible to consult nature, pay toilets are the most bearable. An attendant will demand 2uah and proffer an absurdly small amount of toilet paper in exchange. Public facilities in Crimea are generally much better than elsewhere in the country. The toilets at newly renovated train stations are quite acceptable, too, if a bit smelly. Avoid free blue Portaloos, which often stand unemptied for days and can be categorically vile.

The bathrooms on the trains are another mucky subject. By the end of a journey, they are usually awash in liquid – but be consoled that it's usually nothing but water that's been splashed around from the tap.

Toilet paper in Ukraine is no longer so bad or so rare that you need to carry a major stash. That said, it's a good idea to always keep a little on hand.

tion of visas for those who currently don't need them seems to have fizzled out. Citizens of the EU, Canada, the USA, Iceland, Japan, Norway, Switzerland, Andorra, Liechtenstein, Monaco, San Marino, South Korea and the Vatican can stay without visas for up to 90 days, for now at least. Citizens of most other countries, and anyone intending to work, study, take up permanent residency or stay for more than 90 days, will require a visa.

Other matters related to visas:

Ministry of Foreign Affairs of Ukraine (www.mfa.gov.ua) Offers a complete list of embassies.

Letters of invitation These are technically needed for all visas, although this is more of a formality these days.

Validity Single- and double-entry visas can be bought for one to six months. Multiple-entry visas are valid for three to 12 months.

Visa types Business, tourist and private, with single, double and multiple entries available.

Visa Extensions

Department of Citizenship, Passport & Immigration (044 224 9051; bul Tarasa Shevchenka 34, Kyiv, 9am-5pm Mon-Fri) If you're staying for longer than three months on a tourist visa or six months on a business visa, or if you want to extend your visa, you'll need to visit this office. The process is a bureaucratic ordeal that's best avoided if at all possible. Take a friend or helper along if you don't speak Russian or Ukrainian.

Volunteering

Volunteers for the US Peace Corps and Soros Foundation have a long history with the country, as do religious missionaries.

Bikeland (www.bikeland.com) If it expands across the country, the Bikeland project may at some point be on the lookout for experienced cyclists to mark out trails. Contact the organisers through its website.

Life2Orphans (www.life2orphans.org) Volunteers are sorely needed in Ukraine's desperately underfunded orphanages. Life2Orphans is an excellent place to start if you're looking for volunteer opportunities in this sector.

Svit Ukraine (www.svitukraine.org) This NGO organises various volunteer camps and placements for young people with the aim of promoting issues such as sustainable development, human rights and democracy.

Volunteer in Ukraine (www.volunteerinukraine.com) NGO dispatching volunteers to orphanages, children's hospitals and disabled children's homes.

Women Travellers

- Old-fashioned attitudes towards women of all ages still reign in Ukraine.
- The likelihood of being harassed in public is pretty slim.
- Local men tend to be either wary of, or protective towards, foreign women.
- Young Ukrainian women dress to kill and deflect most sexual attention away from travellers.
- If you're very cautious, always travel 2nd class on trains. Sharing the compartment with three other passengers, rather than just one, offers safety in numbers.
- Pregnant women get reduced fares on some public transport, but you'll probably need more than just a big bump (such as a certificate from your doctor) to prove you are with child.

Work

Since independence, English teachers and a few adventurous entrepreneurs have been attracted to Ukraine to work and do business. Kafkaesque bureaucracy puts many off registering legally. To get a work permit you have to show that a Ukrainian could not do the job you're being hired for.

Online jobs are advertised on the following websites:

www.cicerone.com.ua Kyiv language school.

www.go2kiev.com/view/jobs.html Jobs and work permit info in English.

job.ukr.net Type 'English' into the search field.

www.joboast.com.ua Type 'English' or 'Teacher' into the search field.

www.tryukraine.com Advice and help finding English-teaching positions.

www.rabota.ua Lists a limited number of jobs for English speakers.

Transport

GETTING THERE & AWAY

The majority of visitors fly to Ukraine – generally to Kyiv. However, low-cost flights to neighbouring countries mean many travellers enter the country overland. Flights, tours and rail tickets can be booked online at lonelyplanet.com/bookings.

Entering the Country

- Your passport must be valid for the duration of your intended stay in Ukraine (obviously). It must be stamped with a visa if you need one.
- Entry is usually trouble-free and border officials ask few questions these days.
- Immigration cards were scrapped for most nationalities in September 2010, so anyone claiming you still need one is up to no good or thinks you need one because *they* do.

Air

Low-cost airlines have struggled to find their way into Ukraine. Even the construction of new terminals in Lviv, Kyiv and Kharkiv has failed to attract budget operators offering direct connections to/from major cities in Western Europe.

Airports & Airlines

Ukraine's international airports:

Boryspil International Airport (☎711, 044 393 4371; www.kbp.aero) Most international flights use Kyiv's main airport, 30km southeast of the city centre.

Lviv International Airport (LWO; www.lwo.aero)

Odessa International Airport (ODS; www.airport.odessa.ua)

Ukraine's last remaining major international operator is **Ukraine International Airlines** (PS; www.flyuia.com). It's always worth checking this airline's rates against your country's national carrier.

The following airlines also fly to/from Ukraine:

Aeroflot (www.aeroflot.ru)

Air Baltic (www.airbaltic.com)

Air France (www.airfrance.com)

Austrian Airlines (www.austrian.com)

British Airways (www.ba.com)

Carpatair (www.carpatair.com)

Czech Airlines (www.czechairlines.com)

El Al (www.elal.co.il)

Estonian Air (www.estonian-air.ee)

Germanwings (www.germanwings.com)

KLM (www.klm.com)

LOT (www.lot.com)

CLIMATE CHANGE & TRAVEL

Every form of transport that relies on carbon-based fuel generates CO_2, the main cause of human-induced climate change. Modern travel is dependent on aeroplanes, which might use less fuel per kilometre per person than most cars but travel much greater distances. The altitude at which aircraft emit gases (including CO_2) and particles also contributes to their climate change impact. Many websites offer 'carbon calculators' that allow people to estimate the carbon emissions generated by their journey and, for those who wish to do so, to offset the impact of the greenhouse gases emitted with contributions to portfolios of climate-friendly initiatives throughout the world. Lonely Planet offsets the carbon footprint of all staff and author travel.

FLYING FROM THE USA & CANADA

With the demise of Aerosvit, there are now no direct flights between Kyiv and North America. The best indirect routings are through the European hubs of London, Frankfurt and Vienna. Istanbul and Moscow are also worth a shot.

Lufthansa (www.lufthansa.com)

Transaero (www.transaero.ru)

Turkish Airlines (www.turkishairlines.com)

Wizzair (www.wizzair.com) Not a Ukrainian airline, but does operate one handy domestic flight between Kyiv and Simferopol.

Land

- Crossing the border into Ukraine is a fairly straightforward, if slightly drawn-out, affair.
- Expect customs personnel to scrutinise your papers and search your vehicle.
- Heading out of Ukraine into the EU and Schengen zone, be prepared for delays.
- The Poland–Ukraine and Romania–Ukraine borders are popular smuggling routes, hence the thorough customs checks.
- When heading for Belarus or Russia, ensure you have the right visa.
- You might need special medical insurance for Belarus, purchasable at the border.
- In the unlikely event you are hitchhiking into Ukraine, it may be a good idea to take a local bus or train across the border, as drivers are generally reluctant to take hitchhikers over the line.
- When leaving Ukraine, a train is preferable to a bus or car.
- You are permitted to walk across the country's borders.

Belarus

Be aware that to even pass through Belarus you will need a transit visa.

BUS

In most cases, you're better off going between Ukraine and Belarus by train.

CAR & MOTORCYCLE

Only two crossings are official:

M01 The road north from Chernihiv to Homel crosses just north of the Ukrainian village of Novy Yarylovichy.

M19 The road between Brest and Kovel crosses just southeast of the Belarusian village of Makrany.

TRAIN

Kyiv–Minsk 390uah, 13¼ to 15¾ hours, up to two daily

Lviv–Minsk 414uah, 13¼ hours, three or four weekly

Hungary

BUS

One Vienna-bound bus a day leaves Kyiv's Dachna bus station, stopping in Budapest (600uah, 19 hours) en route.

CAR & MOTORCYCLE

The main road crossing is between Zahony and Chop. Follow the E573 (M06) from Debrecen and Nyíregyháza. Other major crossings are Beregsurány–Luzhanka and Tiszabecs–Vylok.

TRAIN

Chop, 22km southwest of Uzhhorod, is the international junction for trains between Ukraine and Hungary. Because the two countries use different rail gauges, services have a long stop while the carriage bogies are changed to a different gauge. Note that if coming from Budapest, you'll generally save money by buying a domestic ticket as far as Zahony, then a short international ticket to Chop, and purchasing a domestic train ticket onwards.

- **Kyiv–Budapest** 24 hours, one daily
- **Chop–Budapest** six hours, one daily
- **Lviv–Budapest** 14 hours, one daily

Moldova

The unofficial republic of Transdniestr bordering Ukraine for some 500km causes only minor irritation to travellers these days. The 24 hours you have to cross into Moldova proper are more than enough time. It's another matter if you want to hang around in the 'capital' Tiraspol, which has become an odd kind of I've-been-there tourist attraction in recent years.

EU and US citizens, Canadians, Swiss and Japanese

FLYING FROM AUSTRALIA & NEW ZEALAND

As yet, there are no direct flights linking Australia and New Zealand with Kyiv. Vienna is probably the most efficient transit hub between Ukraine and these countries, although many travellers choose London for its familiarity. Check whether it's cheaper to book a separate Sydney–London flight with one airline and the London–Kyiv leg with another (such as budget airline Wizzair).

BUDGET FLIGHTS TO NEIGHBOURING COUNTRIES

A cheap way of getting to Ukraine is to take a budget flight to a neighbouring country, then cross the border by land. Poland has the most flights from Western Europe, but Hungary, Romania and Slovakia also provide a handful of options.

Ryanair (www.ryanair.com) This Irish budget airline connects six cities in the UK with the Polish city of Rzeszow (90km from the border) and two with Lublin (just over 70km from the border). There are also daily flights to Budapest and Bratislava (Slovakia), from where you can continue by train

easyJet (www.easyjet.com) This no-frills airline links the UK, France and Germany with Budapest and Kraków.

Wizzair (www.wizzair.com) Wizzair has popular direct flights to Kyiv and Donetsk from London Luton, but also connects the UK with Katowice and Warsaw (Poland), Košice (Slovakia), Cluj-Napoca (northern Romania) and Debrecen (northeast Hungary).

Jet2 (www.jet2.com) Links cities in northern England and Scotland with Kraków and Budapest.

Check the websites www.flycheapo.com and www.skyscanner.net for the latest flight information.

don't need visas for Moldova. However, Australians, New Zealanders, South Africans and others do.

BUS

There are at least 10 buses per day from Odesa to Chişinău via Tiraspol, and two via Palanka (100uah, five to seven hours). The latter avoid Transdniestr.

CAR & MOTORCYCLE

Most of the dozen border crossings between Ukraine and Moldova enter Transdniestr. To get into Moldova without going through the breakaway republic, you'll need to come up from the south. The most obvious route is the M15/E87 to the crossing at Palanka – a 280km-long diversion.

TRAIN

There are around five trains a day from Kyiv to Chişinău (14 to 17 hours), all of which originate in Russia. One evening train a day makes the Odesa–Chişinău run (105uah, five hours).

Poland

Most overland travellers enter Ukraine from Poland heading to Lviv. It is possible to get to Ukraine cheaply by combining budget flights with overland travel to Ukraine's western border.

BUS

Cross-border services to Warsaw, Lublin, Łódź and a few other destinations leave from Lviv's main bus station.

Between Przemyśl and Lviv it's quickest to take the *marshrutky* (fixed-route minibuses) from outside each city's train station to the border, walk across and hop onto an onward *marshrutka*. Leaving Lviv, *marshrutka* 297 runs between Lviv train station and the road crossing at Shehyni/Medyka.

CAR & MOTORCYCLE

There are several crossings, of which the easiest in terms of both distance and formalities is Shehyni on the M11 between Lviv and Przemyśl. Travelling from Kyiv to Warsaw via Lutsk, you cross over the border at the Buh River before stopping in the Polish town of Okopy Nowe.

TRAIN

Poland has an online **train timetable** (www.rozklad.pkp.pl) in English. The following is a list of direct connections, but there are plenty of other services if you are prepared to change. The following are direct trains between Poland and Ukraine:

- **Kyiv–Warsaw Wschodnia** 18 hours, one daily
- **Lviv–Przemyśl** 2½ hours, one daily
- **Lviv–Kraków** 8½ hours, one daily

Romania

BUS

There's only one bus a day from Chernivtsi to Suceava (71uah, four hours, 7.10am). The short journey is drawn out by a lengthy border stop, as it's a popular smuggling route. You may be able to catch an unofficial *marshrutka* from near Chernivtsi bus station.

CAR & MOTORCYCLE

There are three Ukraine–Romania road crossings, only two of them important. The main crossing is 40km south of Chernivtsi, where the E85 (A269) crosses between Porubne in Ukraine and Siret in Romania. The other is the bridge between Solotvyno in Ukraine and Sighetu Marmaţiei on the Romanian side.

TRAIN

The only connection between Ukraine and Romania is the Kyiv–Bucharest Nord trains

(25 hours, one daily). Some local *elektrychky* (electric trains) from Chernivtsi stop at the border.

Russia

CAR & MOTORCYCLE

The main route between Kyiv and Moscow starts as the M01 (E95) north of Kyiv and becomes the M8 after the border.

TRAIN

Many major Ukrainian cities have daily services to Moscow, all passing through either Kyiv or Kharkiv. There are many extra services in summer for Russians heading to/from Crimea, though these sell out quickly.

- **Kyiv–Moscow** 14 to 16 hours, many daily
- **Kyiv–St Petersburg** 24 hours, four daily
- **Lviv–Moscow** 24 hours, up to five daily
- **Lviv–St Petersburg** 30 hours, three or four weekly
- **Kharkiv–Moscow** 14 to 17 hours, many daily

Slovakia

BUS

Three buses a day go from Uzhhorod to Košice (110uah, 2½ hours), from where you can catch regular trains and buses to Prague and Bratislava, and daily coaches to London.

ONWARD BUSES

Bus operator **Regabus** (www.regabus.cz) has services from several (mostly Western) Ukrainian towns to Prague and other locations in the Czech Republic. **Ecolines** (www.ecolines.net) travels between a handful of Ukrainian cities and many Eastern and Western European destinations.

CAR & MOTORCYCLE

The E50 from Košice crosses at Vyšné Nemecké on the Slovak side to Uzhhorod in Ukraine, becoming the M08 afterwards.

TRAIN

As with services to Hungary, Chop is the gateway to/from Slovakia. Carriage bogies are changed there, which takes a couple of hours.

- **Kyiv–Bratislava** 29 hours, daily
- **Chop–Bratislava** 10 hours, daily
- **Lviv–Bratislava** 18 hours, daily

Sea

Cruise and cargo ships are the main users of Ukrainian ports but some useful scheduled ferry services do exist. As across the ex-USSR, boat services are erratic to say the least, and if the cost of docking and fuel rises, sailings are cancelled without notice. Basing your travel plans around sea or river travel is probably not advisable.

To/from Ilychevsk

Ukrferry (www.ukrferry.com) is the main operator from Ilychevsk, outside Odesa to Poti and Batumi (Georgia), Derince (Turkey), Varna (Bulgaria) and Constanţa (Romania). Be aware that services are regularly cancelled for months on end without explanation. Check its website for the latest sailing times and days (if there are any).

To/from Kerch

Regular ferries (35 minutes) shuttle between Port Krym near Kerch to Port Kavkaz in Russia's southern Krasnodar region. Boats leave every 1½ hours, day and night, but services can be considerably reduced in low season.

To/from Odesa

London Sky Travel (Map p148; ☎729 3196; www.lstravel.com.ua) sells tickets for summer ferries and cruise ships from Odesa and Ilychevsk.

To/from Yalta

In the past there have been boat services to Novorossiysk on Russia's stretch of the Black Sea coast and Sinop in Turkey, but none were running at the time of research.

Tours

The following agencies provide package tours to Ukraine. Remember that train tickets are much cheaper at Ukrainian train stations than via booking agents.

Australia

Gateway Travel (www.russian-gateway.com.au) Offers escorted group tours.

Canada & USA

Black Sea Crimea (www.blacksea-crimea.com) Small operator with an informative and up-to-date website.

Meest Travel (www.meest.net) This delivery and travel service has over 400 representatives throughout Canada, the USA and Ukraine.

Scope Travel (www.scopetravel.com) Tours from the major cities to the Carpathian countryside and southern regions.

Ukrainetour (www.ukrainetour.com) Ukrainian-run agent based in Canada.

UK

Audley Travel (www.audleytravel.com) Tailor-made tours, often with a history theme.

Regent Holidays (www.regent-holidays.co.uk) Knowledgeable company with varied itineraries.

Ukraine Adventures (www.ukraineadventures.com) Small company capable of organising pretty much anything, including skiing trips.

GETTING AROUND

Air

The national network mainly uses Kyiv as a hub. To fly from Lviv to Donetsk or from Simferopol to Kharkiv, for example, you almost always need to go through the capital. The number of domestic flights and carriers has fallen considerably in recent years and fares are high.

Airlines in Ukraine

Dniproavia (www.dniproavia.com) Domestic airline based at Dnipropetrovsk Airport. Serves Dnipropetrovsk, Kyiv, Ivano-Frankivsk and Sevastopol.

Donbassaero (www.donbass.aero) Based at Donetsk Airport. Serves Donetsk, Kyiv, Odesa and Kharkiv.

Motor Sich (www.flymotorsich.com) Based in Zaporizhzhya. Serves Zaporizhzhya, Kyiv and Uzhhorod.

Ukraine International Airlines (PS; www.flyuia.com) Essentially an international airline based at Boryspil International Airport in Kyiv, UIA is also now the country's largest domestic carrier. Links Kyiv, Kharkiv, Lviv, Donetsk, Odesa, Simferopol, Dnipropetrovsk and Ivano-Frankivsk.

Tickets

Kiyavia Travel (www.kiyavia.com) This useful company has branches across the country. You can buy tickets online to print out or pick them up at a branch.

Bicycle

Although you have to keep an eye out for crazy drivers and keep to the road's shoulder, cycling is a great way to see the real Ukraine. The Carpathians and Crimea – in that order – are particularly pleasant cycling country.

➡ Markets everywhere sell lots of spare parts.

➡ Rental is rare except in Crimea and the Carpathians.

➡ To transport your bike on a mainline train, you must remove the wheels, wrap the bike in plastic, and place it in the luggage niche above the top bunks.

➡ On local *electrychky* trains buy an outsized luggage ticket from the conductor (in the rare event that you are asked to do so).

Boat

Chervona Ruta (Червона Рута; Map p38; ☎044 253 6909; www.ruta-cruise.com; vul Lyteranska 24, Kyiv; Ⓜ Khreshchatyk) is your only port of call if you're interested in Dnipro River and Black Sea cruises. The standard cruise is one week along the Kyiv–Sevastopol–Odesa route. Some cruises go into the Danube delta.

Although unreliable, **Ukrferry** (www.ukrferry.com) offers sporadic Black Sea cruises. Contact **London Sky Travel** (www.lstravel.com.ua) for details.

Bus

Buses serve every city and small town, but are best for short trips (three hours or less), as vehicles are generally small, old and overcrowded. If you're travelling around Ukraine for a longer period of time, bus will be your most common mode of transport. Some stations, especially in the far west, have become quite orderly; others remain chaotic.

Bus Companies

There are literally thousands of tiny transport companies operating services across Ukraine. However, on the main intercity routes large operators use Western-standard coaches.

Autolux (www.autolux.ua) Ukraine's top coach operator. Runs services between Kyiv and most regional centres. The company's nonstop 'VIP' coaches have airline-style seats, acres of legroom and free refreshments.

Gunsel (www.gunsel.ua) Operates mainly between Kyiv and the south and east of the country.

Ukrbus (www.ukrbus.com) Operates services out of Kyiv, Odesa, Donetsk, Reni, Chernivtsi and Yalta.

Bus Stations

Bus stations are called *avtovokzal* or *avtostantsiya*. Some of Ukraine's larger cities have several stations – a main one for long-distance routes and smaller stations that serve local destinations.

Information

Timetables Reliable timetables are displayed near the ticket windows and on board; Soviet-era route maps are unreliable.

Service Information There might be an information window (*dovidkove byuro;* довідкове бюро), but you can usually ask at any window.

Platforms Platforms are numbered and destinations are usually signposted.

Online Timetables etc are listed at www.bus.com.ua, which is hard to navigate without some Ukrainian.

Tickets

➡ Tickets resembling shop receipts are sold at the bus station right up to departure.

➡ Your destination, seat number (*meestseh;* місце) and time of travel is clearly marked.

➡ Tickets from the bus station are valid only for one service. Having bought a ticket, you can't suddenly decide to take a later bus without paying again.

SURVIVING UKRAINE'S BUSES

For the uninitiated, Ukrainian bus travel can be a bemusing and uncomfortable ordeal. Here are our survival tips.

- Bus can mean anything from a lumbering 60-seater 1980s Hungarian coach to a luxury Mercedes minibus.
- Your ticket has a seat number printed on it, but on small buses passengers generally just sit where they like (but not always!).
- Don't sit in a seat that has something on it. This means someone else has 'reserved' it while they go shopping/visit the toilet/call on relatives across town.
- Yes, the bleary-eyed guy stumbling towards the bus – one dose of *salo* (raw pig fat) away from a coronary – is your driver. His job is to drive, not answer questions.
- Luggage should be stored in the *bagazhnyk* (luggage space) under the bus. It's normally free to do so.
- Even if the mercury is pushing 40°C (95°F), all windows will be slammed shut as soon as the bus moves off. The roof hatch may be left open.
- Buses often stop at stations for between five minutes and half an hour. Make sure you know how long the break is, as drivers rarely check if everyone is back on board.
- Buses act as an unofficial postal system, with anything from punnets of strawberries to large car parts transported between towns for a small fee.

- If a bus is passing through a town or village without a bus station, the fare can only be paid to the driver. No tickets are issued.

Car & Motorcycle

Unless you're used to developing-world driving conditions, getting behind the wheel in Ukraine is not recommended. The roads are Europe's worst and there's a tacit, unofficial highway code that only local drivers understand.

Bringing Your Own Vehicle

To bring your own vehicle into the country, you'll need:

- your original registration papers (photocopies not accepted) and certificate of motor insurance
- a 'Green Card' International Motor Insurance Certificate (recommended)
- an international vehicle registration sticker (GB for the UK, D for Germany etc) even if your car has Euro number plates
- warning triangle
- fire extinguisher
- first-aid kit.

Your registration number will be noted, and you'll have to explain if leaving the country without your vehicle.

Driving Licence

Most official sources claim an International Driving Permit is necessary, and given the Ukrainian traffic police's habit of pulling people over for minor transgressions, it would be silly not to have one.

Fuel & Spare Parts

Petrol stations are very common and frequent on main roads. Innovative, shoestring repairs are widespread; genuine spare parts are not quite so unless you have an ageing German vehicle, a Daewoo or a Lada.

Insurance

Third-party insurance is compulsory, which will normally be covered by a 'Green Card' International Motor Insurance Certificate. Hire companies provide their own vehicle insurance.

Road Conditions

Major roads between Kyiv and regional centres tend to be in fairly good condition, but some routes linking towns and cities in the regions, especially in the west (roads in the Carpathians are the worst we've ever seen anywhere) have deteriorated almost to the point of nonexistence. Soviet-era bridges are also beginning to fail, especially across the Dnister River, causing chaos and long diversions. There are no plans or funds to repair any of this essential infrastructure.

Road Rules

- Traffic drives on the right.
- Unless otherwise indicated, speed limits are 60km/h in towns, 90km/h on major roads and 110km/h on dual carriageways.

DAI: TRAFFIC POLICE

Among the biggest road hazards in Ukraine are the traffic cops. The underpaid Derzhavna Avtomobilna Inspeksiya (DAI) officers are infamous for waving drivers down and demanding a 'fine' for some minor violation (eg not carrying a warning triangle), or even an imaginary breach of the road rules.

In 2005 President Yushchenko sacked the entire force in disgust, after being continually pulled over himself while driving an unmarked car from Kyiv to Poland. The DAI was later reinstated by Prime Minister (now President) Yanukovych.

If you're pulled over when not speeding, the DAI are probably just looking for a little cash (say around 50uah). Apparently, officers have to collect a certain amount in bribes per shift to hand over to superiors, and since they don't speak English some expats suggest that nattering away until they lose patience is a good way to escape.

- There's a zero-tolerance policy on drink-driving.
- Believe it or not, it's actually a criminal offence not to wear a seat belt (although everybody completely ignores this rule).
- You must slow down to 50km/h when passing DAI road blocks on the exit roads from towns and cities.
- The DAI have the power to stop you but not to issue on-the-spot fines. Always ask for a *'protokol'* (police report; this normally gets rid of even the peskiest traffic cop).

Hitching

Hitching is never entirely safe, and we don't recommend it. Travellers who hitch should understand that they are taking a small but potentially serious risk.

You simply can't hitchhike around Ukraine for free. Hitching a ride is common, but it's necessary to pay drivers for the privilege. Given the prevalence of unofficial taxis in Ukraine, it's reasonably safe to hitch during the day, within big cities. Obviously, exercise common sense, particularly if you're a woman travelling solo.

You will need to speak Ukrainian to discuss your destination and price, and it's easiest to get a ride where locals are flagging down cars. Put your hand up in the air, palm down.

Local Transport

Ukrainian cities are navigable by trolleybus, tram, bus and (in Kyiv, Kharkiv and Dnipropetrovsk) metro. Urban public-transport systems are usually overworked and overcrowded. There's no room for being shy or squeamish – learn to assert yourself quickly.

- A ticket *(kvytok* or *bilyet)* for one ride by bus/tram/trolleybus costs 1uah to 3uah.
- There are no return, transfer, timed or day tickets available anywhere.
- It's always simplest to pay the driver or conductor.
- Tickets have to be punched on board (or ripped by the conductor).
- Unclipped or untorn tickets warrant an on-the-spot fine should you be caught.
- For the metros you need a *zheton* (plastic token), sold at the counters inside the stations for 2uah to 3uah.
- Metros run from around 5.30am to midnight.
- A metro station can have several names – one for each different line that passes through it.

Taxis

Travelling by taxi anywhere in the ex-USSR can be a decidedly unenjoyable experience for foreigners, so if there's a bus or tram going to your destination, take it.

- If possible, have your hostel or hotel call a cab for you – they generally use trustworthy companies with set fares.
- Always try to call for a taxi. Some companies now send a text message to confirm the booking, exact fare, and make and colour of the car.
- Avoid taxis that tout for business outside airports and stations as these operators are very likely to rip off foreigners (and Ukrainians).
- Calculate the approximate fare between two towns by multiplying the distance in kilometres by two or two and a half.
- Make sure the fare quoted by taxi drivers is the fare to the final destination and not per kilometre (a common scam).
- Never travel in a cab that already has passengers in it.

Train

For long journeys, overnight train is the preferred method of travel in Ukraine. Carriages are old and the network in need of updating, but services are incredibly punctual.

Carriage Classes

All classes have assigned places. Your *vahon* (carriage) and *mesto* (bunk) numbers are printed on your ticket.

SV *Spalny vahon* (SV, sometimes called *Lyux*) is a 1st-class couchette (sleeper) compartment for two people. Perfect for couples but, if travelling alone, sharing with a stranger can be awkward. Not available on many routes and books up immediately despite costing two to three times more than *kupe*.

Kupe *Kupe* or *kupeyny* is a 2nd-class sleeper compartment for four people. The most popular class and also the safest and most fun. Sharing the compartment with two or three others is less awkward and there's safety in numbers. *Kupe* is about twice as costly as *platskart*. Unless otherwise noted, train prices are for *kupe*.

Platskart *Platskart* is a 3rd-class sleeper. The entire carriage is open (no separate compartments), with groups of four bunks in each alcove, along with two others in the aisle.

Zahalny vahon (*obshchy* in Russian) Fourth-class travel means an upright, bench seat for the entire journey. This class of carriage is now rare on intercity trains, but most *elektrychky* have this kind of seating.

1st/2nd class (C1/C2) Carriages on the Intercity+ services have seating divided into two classes (there's little difference between them).

Train Types

There are basically three types of train:

Pasazhyrsky poyizd (also known as *poyizd, skory poyizd* or *shvydky poyizd)* These are mainline services travelling long distances between cities, often overnight.

Elektrychka (*prymisky poyizd,* or *prigorodny poyezd* in Russian) These are slow electric trains running between cities and rural areas. They're often used by locals to reach summer cottages and gardens. *Elektrychky* sometimes leave from a dedicated station set aside for local trains.

Express trains The Intercity+ express trains between Kyiv and Kharkov, Donetsk and Lviv have airplane-style seats, a cafe, functional air-con and pleasant stewards. They make few stops between the capital and regional centres.

Tickets

- Tickets are still relatively cheap.
- Ticket clerks don't speak English, so get a local to write down what you need.
- When buying tickets you need to know your destination, number of tickets required, class of carriage and the date of travel.
- You are supposed to show your passport when buying tickets.
- Several cities, such as Kyiv and Lviv, have advance ticket offices in the city centres.
- So-called 'service centres' are comfortable, Western-style ticket offices found at big-city stations. Tickets cost slightly more here, but there's no queue.
- Never buy tickets from touts.

Information

ONLINE

Ukrainian Railways (www.uz.gov.ua) The official Ukrainian Railway website, now in English.

Poezda.net (www.poezda.net) This online timetable for the entire ex-USSR is available in English. The search facility uses some perverse spellings for town names (eg Ujgorod for Uzhhorod, Harkov for Kharkiv), but is still pretty good.

GIVE ME A SIGN

There are so many varying classifications of desk across Ukraine's non-English-speaking train stations it would be impossible to list them all. However, a few major signs to watch out for, or words to know of, follow:

Довідкове бюро Information desk

інформація Information

Добова каса/каса квиткова Добова Tickets for today (for departures within the next 24 hours)

Продаж квитків Ticket booking/advance tickets

інвалідів та учасників війни Avoid windows with this on the glass, unless you're an invalid or war veteran.

сервіс центр Service centre, where you may or may not be sent if you hold a foreign passport.

міжнародні квитки International tickets

приміський вокзал Station for local or suburban trains (usually part of, or adjoining, the main train station)

приміська каса Local or suburban ticket desk

камера схову/камера зберігання/камера хранення Left-luggage room and/or lockers

Кімнати відпочинку 'Resting' rooms, or rooms for overnight stays, ie train-station hotel

розклад Timetable

прибуття Arrivals

відправлення Departures

LEFT LUGGAGE

Every train station *(zaliznychny vokzal* or just *vokzal)* has a left-luggage counter – which usually goes by the Russian name *kamera khranyeninya* (камера хранения) or *kamera zberihannaya* (камера зберігання) in Ukrainian. Many are open 24 hours except for signposted short breaks. You usually pay when you deposit your luggage and retrieve it with the receipt or metal tag you are given.

Seat 61 (www.seat61.com/Ukraine.htm) Worth checking out, especially if you're planning to enter Ukraine by rail.

AT THE STATION

- Strictly Russian- or Ukrainian-speaking attendants in information booths (*dovidkove byuro;* довідкове бюро) are frequently surly and uncooperative.
- There's a small charge for any information that staff write down.
- Schedules are posted on the wall – once you have mastered some basic words, they're simple to decipher.
- You may find railway timetables in business catalogues, posted in hotels and occasionally at bus stations.

On the Journey

- Each carriage has an attendant called a *provodnik* (male) or *provodnitsa* (female), who collects your ticket, distributes sheets, makes morning wake-up calls and serves cups of tea.
- It's *de rigueur* to change into comfortable clothes in your carriage – tracksuits, slippers, shorts and flip-flops (thongs).
- Dining cars rarely sell anything more than sandwiches, snacks and drinks, so bring supplies.
- Toilets are locked some 30 minutes either side of a station. Bring your own paper.
- Don't drink the water from the tap or even clean your teeth with it.

Language

The official language of Ukraine is Ukrainian, which belongs to the Slavic language family and is most closely related to Russian and Belarusian. It has about 50 million speakers worldwide, including significant Ukrainian-speaking communities in Eastern Europe, Central Asia and North America.

Many Ukrainians speak Russian as their first language and many more know it as a second language; it's predominantly spoken in the east and the south (apart from Crimean Tatar in Crimea). In many places, including Kyiv, you'll hear Russian and Ukrainian intermingled to create a dialect commonly known as *surzhyk*. However, many locals – particularly those in the west who overwhelmingly speak Ukrainian – still see Russian as the language of an oppressor and it's often more politically correct not to use it.

Ukrainian is written in the Cyrillic alphabet (see the following page), and it's well worth the effort familiarising yourself with it so that you can read maps, menus, timetables and street signs. Otherwise, you can simply read the coloured pronunciation guides given next to each Ukrainian phrase in this chapter as if they were English, and you'll be understood. Most sounds are the same as those found in English, and the few differences in pronunciation are explained in the alphabet table. Note that the stressed syllables are indicated with italics.

WANT MORE?

For in-depth language information and handy phrases, check out Lonely Planet's *Ukrainian Phrasebook*. You'll find it at **shop.lonelyplanet.com**, or you can buy Lonely Planet's iPhone phrasebooks at the Apple App Store.

BASICS

Hello.	Добрий день.	*do*·bry den'
Goodbye.	До побачення.	do po·*ba*·chen·nya
How are you?	Як справи?	yak *spra*·vy
Fine, thanks.	Добре, дякую.	*do*·bro *dya*·ku·yu
Please.	Прошу.	*pro*·shu
Thank you.	Дякую.	*dya*·ku·yu
You're welcome.	Добро пожалувати.	do·*bro* po·*zha*·lu·va·ty
Yes./No.	Так./Ні.	tak/ni
Excuse me.	Вибачте.	*vy*·bach·te
I'm sorry.	Перепрошую.	pe·re·*pro*·shu·yu
What's your name?	Як вас звати?	yak vas zva·ty
My name is ...	Мене звати ...	me *ne* zva·ty ...

Do you speak English?
Ви розмовляєте англійською мовою? — vy roz·mow·*lya*·ye·te an·*hliys'*·ko·yu *mo*·vo·yu

I don't understand (you).
Я (вас) не розумію. — ya (vas) ne ro·zu·*mi*·yu

ACCOMMODATION

Do you have any rooms available?
У вас є вільні номери? — u vas ye *vil'*·ni no·me·*ry*

How much is it per night/person?
Скільки коштує номер за ніч/особу? — *skil'*·ky *ko*·shtu·ye *no*·mer za nich/o·*so*·bu

Is breakfast included?
Чи це включає вартість сніданку? — chy tse wklyu·*cha*·ye *var*·tist' sni·*dan*·ku

campsite	кемпінг	*kem*·pinh
hotel	готель	ho·*tel'*
youth hostel	молодіжний гуртожиток	mo·lo·*dizh*·ny hur·*to*·zhy·tok

bathroom	ванна	van·na
double room	номер на двох	*no*·mer na dvokh
shared room	місце	*mis*·tse
single room	номер на одного	*no*·mer na o·dno·*ho*
window	вікно	*vik*·no

DIRECTIONS

Where is ...?
Де ...? de ...

What's the address?
Яка адреса? ya·*ka* a·*dre*·sa

Could you write it down, please?
Могли б ви записати, будь ласка? *moh*·lu b vy za·py·*sa*·ty bud' *la*·ska

Can you show me (on the map)?
Ви можете показати, мени (на карти)? vy *mo*·zhe·te po·ka·*za*·ty me·*ni* (na *kar*·ti)

Go straight ahead.
Ідіть прямо. i·*dit' prya*·mo

Turn left.
Поверніть ліворуч. po·ver·*nit'* li·*vo*·ruch

Turn right.
Поверніть праворуч. po·ver·*nit'* pra·*vo*·ruch

at the corner	на розі	na *ro*·zi
at the traffic lights	біля світлофора	*bi*·lya svi·tlo·*fo*·ra
behind	ззаду	z·*za*·du
in front of	спереду	*spe*·re·du
near (to)	біля	*bi*·lya
opposite	протилежний	pro·ty·*le*·zhny

EATING & DRINKING

Do you have any free tables?
У Вас є вільні столи? u vas ye *vil'*·ni *sto*·ly

Can I see the menu?
Можна подивитися на меню? *mo*·zhna po·dy·*vy*·ty·sya na me·*nyu*

Do you have a menu in English?
У Вас є меню англійською мовою? u vas ye me·*nyu* an·*hliys'*·ko·yu *mo*·vo·yu

I'm a vegetarian.
Я вегетаріанець/вегетаріанка. ya ve·he·ta·ri·a·nets'/ve·he·ta·ri·*an*·ka (m/f)

What do you recommend?
Що Ви порадите? shcho vy po·*ra*·dy·te

I'd like ...
Я візьму ... ya viz'·*mu* ...

Bon appetit!
Смачного! smach·*no*·ho

Cheers!
Будьмо! *bud'*·mo

I don't drink (alcohol).
Я не п'ю. ya ne pyu

Can we have the bill?
Можна рахунок? *mo*·zhna ra·*khu*·nok

The meal was delicious!
Було дуже смачно! bu·*lo duz*·he *smach*·no

CYRILLIC ALPHABET

Cyrillic	Sound	
А, а	a	as in 'father'
Б, б	b	as in 'but'
В, в	v	as in 'van' (before a vowel);
	w	as in 'wood' (before a consonant or at the end of a syllable)
Г, г	h	as in 'hat'
Ґ, ґ	g	as in 'good'
Д, д	d	as in 'dog'
Е, е	e	as in 'end'
Є, є	ye	as in 'yet'
Ж, ж	zh	as the 's' in 'measure'
З, з	z	as in 'zoo'
И, и	y	as the 'ir' in 'birch', but short
І, і	i	as in 'pit'
Ї, ї	yi	as in 'yip'
Й, й	y	as in 'yell'; usually precedes or follows a vowel
К, к	k	as in 'kind'
Л, л	l	as in 'lamp'
М, м	m	as in 'mad'
Н, н	n	as in 'not'
О, о	o	as in 'pot' but with jaws more closed and lips more pursed
П, п	p	as in 'pig'
Р, р	r	as in 'rub' (trilled)
С, с	s	as in 'sing'
Т, т	t	as in 'ten'
У, у	u	as in 'put'
Ф, ф	f	as in 'fan'
Х, х	kh	as the 'ch' in the Scottish *loch*
Ц, ц	ts	as in 'bits'
Ч, ч	ch	as in 'chin'
Ш, ш	sh	as in 'shop'
Щ, щ	shch	as 'sh-ch' in 'fresh chips'
Ю, ю	yu	as the 'u' in 'use'
Я, я	ya	as in 'yard' (when stressed);
	ye	as in 'yearn' (when unstressed)
Ь, ь	'	'soft sign'; softens the preceding consonant (like a faint 'y' sound)

Signs

Вхід	Entrance
Вихід	Exit
Відчинено	Open
Зачинено	Closed
Інформація	Information
Заборонено	Prohibited
Туалет	Toilets
Чоловічий	Men
Жіночий	Women

Key Words

bar	бар	bar
bottle	пляшка	*plyash*·ka
breakfast	сніданок	sni·*da*·nok
cafe	кафе/ кав'ярня	ka·*fe*/ ka·*vyar*·nya
cold	холодний	kho·*lod*·ny
cup	чашка	*chash*·ka
dinner	вечеря	ve·*che*·rya
food	їжа	*yi*·zha
fork	виделка	vy·*del*·ka
glass	склянка	*sklyan*·ka
hot (warm)	гарячий	ha·*rya*·chy
knife	ніж	nizh
lunch	обід	o·*bid*
market	ринок	*ry*·nok
menu	меню	me·*nyu*
plate	тарілка	ta·*ril*·ka
restaurant	ресторан	re·sto·*ran*
salad	салат	sa·*lat*
soup	суп	sup
sour	кислий	*ky*·sly
spicy	гострий	*ho*·stry
spoon	ложка	*lozh*·ka
sweet	солодкий	so·*lod*·ky
with/without	з/без	z/bez

Meat & Fish

beef	яловичина	*ya*·lo·vy·chy·na
carp	короп	*ko*·rop
caviar	ікра	i·*kra*
chicken	курка	*kur*·ka
crabs	краби	*kra*·by
duck	качка	*kach*·ka
ham	шинка	*shyn*·ka
herring	оселедець	o·se·*le*·dets'
lamb	баранина	ba·*ra*·ny·na
pork	свинина	svy·*ny*·na
salami	салямі	sa·*lya*·mi
salmon	лосось	lo·*sos'*
sturgeon	осетрина	o·se·*try*·na
trout	форель	fo·*rel*
tuna	тунець	tu·*nets*
turkey	індик	in·*dyk*
veal	телятина	te·*lya*·ty·na

Fruit & Vegetables

apple	яблуко	*ya*·blu·ko
banana	банан	ba·*nan*
beetroot	буряк	bu·*ryak*
cabbage	капуста	ka·*pu*·sta
capsicum	перець	*pe*·rets
carrot	морква	*mor*·kva
corn	кукуруза	ku·ku·*ru*·za
grapes	виноград	vy·no·*hrad*
kiwi fruit	ківі	*ki*·vi
mushroom	гриб	hryb
olives	маслини	ma·*sly*·ny
onion	цибуля	tsy·*bu*·lya
orange	помаранча	po·ma·*ran*·cha
pineapple	ананас	a·na·*nas*
pomegranate	гранат	hra·*nat*
potato	картопля	kar·*to*·plya
raspberry	малина	ma·*ly*·na
tomatoes	помідори	po·mi·*dor*·i
watermelon	кавун	ka·*vun*

Other

biscuits	печення	pe·*chen*·nya
bread	хліб	khlib
butter	масло	*ma*·slo
cake	торт	tort
cheese	сир	syr
chips	чіпси	*cheep*·si
chocolate	шоколад	sho·ko·*lad*
egg	яйце	*yay*·tse
honey	мед	med
horseradish	хрін	khrin
ice cream	морозиво	mo·*ro*·zy·vo
jam	варення	va·*ryen*·nya
mayonnaise	майонез	ma·yo·*nez*
mustard	гірчиця	hir·*chu*·tsya

oil	олія	o·*li*·ya
pepper	перець	*pe*·rets
salt	сіль	sil'
sour cream	сметана	sme·*ta*·na
sugar	цукор	*tsu*·kor
tatar sauce	соус татарський	*so*·us ta·*tar*·sky
tomato sauce	кетчуп	*ket*·chup
vinegar	оцет	o·*tset*

Drinks

beer	пиво	*py*·vo
coffee	кава	*ka*·va
juice	сік	sik
milk	молоко	mo·lo·*ko*
red/white wine	вино червоне/біле	vy·*no* cher·*vo*·ne/*bi*·le
tea	чай	chai
vodka	горілка	ho·*ril*·ka
(mineral) water	(мінеральна) вода	(mi·ne·*ral'*·na) vo·*da*
yoghurt	кефір	ke·*fir*

EMERGENCIES

Help!
Допоможіть! — do·po·mo·*zhit'*

Go away!
Іди/Ідіть звідси! — i·*dy*/i·*dit' zvid*·sy (pol/inf)

I'm lost.
Я заблукав/заблукала. — ya za·blu·*kaw*/za·blu·*ka*·la (m/f)

There's been an accident.
Там був нещасний випадок. — tam buw ne·*shcha*·sny vy·padok

Call a doctor!
Викличте лікаря! — *vy*·klych·te *li*·ka·rya

Call the police!
Викличіть міліцію! — *vy*·kly·chit' mi·*li*·tsi·yu

I'm ill.
Мені погано. — me·*ni* po·*ha*·no

It hurts here.
У мене болить тут. — u *me*·ne bo·*lyt'* tut

Question Words

How?	Як?	yak
What?	Що?	shcho
When?	Коли?	ko·*ly*
Where?	Де?	de
Which?	Котрий?	ko·*try*
Who?	Хто?	khto

I'm allergic to (antibiotics).
У мене алергія на (антибіотики). — u *me*·ne a·ler·*hi*·ya na (an·ty·bi·*o*·ty·ky)

SHOPPING & SERVICES

I'd like to buy ...
Я б хотів/хотіла купити ... — ya b kho·*tiw*/kho·*ti*·la ku·*py*·ty ... (m/f)

I'm just looking.
Я лише дивюся. — ya ly·*she* dy·*wlyu*·sya

Please show me ...
Покажіть мені, будь ласка ... — po·ka·*zhit'* me·*ni* bud' *la*·ska ...

I don't like it.
Мені не подобається. — me·*ni* ne po·*do*·ba·yet'·sya

How much is it?
Скільки це (він/вона) коштує? — *skil'*·ky tse (vin/vo·*na*) *ko*·shtu·ye? (m/f)

That's too expensive.
Це надто дорого. — tse *nad*·to *do*·ro·ho

Can you make me a better price?
А дешевше не буде? — a de·*she*·wshe ne *bu*·de

ATM	банкомат	ban·ko·*mat*
credit card	кредитна картка	kre·*dy*·tna *kar*·tka
internet cafe	інтернетове кафе	in·ter·*ne*·to·ve ka·*fe*
post office	пошта	*po*·shta
tourist office	туристичне бюро	tu·ry·*stych*·ne byu·*ro*

TIME & DATES

What time is it?
Котра година? — ko·*tra* ho·*dy*·na

It's (eight) o'clock.
(Восьма) година. — (*vos'*·ma) ho·*dy*·na

in the morning	вранці	*wran*·tsi
in the afternoon	вдень	w·*den'*
in the evening	у вечері	u·*ve*·che·ri
yesterday	вчора	*wcho*·ra
today	сьогодні	s'o·*ho*·dni
tomorrow	завтра	*zaw*·tra

Monday	понеділок	po·ne·*di*·lok
Tuesday	вівторок	vi·*wto*·rok
Wednesday	середа	se·re·*da*
Thursday	четвер	che·*tver*
Friday	п'ятниця	*pya*·tny·tsya
Saturday	субота	su·*bo*·ta
Sunday	неділя	ne·*di*·lya

Numbers

1	один	o·*dyn*
2	два	dva
3	три	try
4	чотири	cho·*ty*·ry
5	п'ять	pyat'
6	шість	shist'
7	сім	sim
8	вісім	*vi*·sim
9	дев'ять	*de*·vyat'
10	десять	*de*·syat'
20	двадцять	*dva*·tsyat'
30	тридцять	*try*·tsyat'
40	сорок	*so*·rok
50	п'ятдесят	pya·de·*syat*
60	шістдесят	shis·de·*syat*
70	сімдесят	sim·de·*syat*
80	вісімдесят	vi·sim·de·*syat*
90	дев'яносто	de·vya·*no*·sto
100	сто	sto
1000	тисяча	*ty*·sya·cha

January	січень	*si*·chen'
February	лютий	*lyu*·ty
March	березень	*be*·re·zen'
April	квітень	*kvi*·ten'
May	травень	*tra*·ven'
June	червень	*che*·rven'
July	липень	*ly*·pen'
August	серпень	*ser*·pen'
September	вересень	*ve*·re·sen'
October	жовтень	*zhow*·ten'
November	листопад	ly·sto·*pad*
December	грудень	*hru*·den'

TRANSPORT

Public Transport

I want to go to ...
Мені треба їхати до … — me·*ni tre*·ba *yi*·kha·ty do ...

At what time does the ... leave?
Коли відправляється …? — ko·*ly* vid·pra·*wlya*·yet'·sya ...

At what time does the ... arrive?
Коли … прибуває? — ko·*ly* ... pry·bu·*va*·ye

Can you tell me when we get to ...?
Ви можете мени казати, коли ми доїдемо до …? — vy *mo*·zhe·te me·*ni* ska·*za*·ty ko·*ly* my do·*yi*·de·mo do ...

boat	пароплав	pa·ro·*plaw*
bus	автобус	aw·*to*·bus
metro	метро	me·*tro*
plane	літак	li·*tak*
taxi	таксі	tak·*si*
train	поїзд	*po*·yizd
tram	трамвай	tram·*vai*
trolleybus	тролейбус	tro·*ley*·bus
one-way ticket	квиток в один бік	kvy·*tok* v o·*dyn* bik
return ticket	зворотний квиток	zvo·ro·tny kvy·*tok*
first	перший	*per*·shy
next	наступний	na·*stup*·ny
last	останній	o·*stan*·niy
platform	платформа	plat·*for*·ma
ticket office	квиткові каси	kvy·*tko*·vi *ka*·sy
timetable	розклад	*roz*·klad
train station	залізнична станція	za·li·*znych*·na *stant*·si·ya

Driving & Cycling

I'd like to hire a ...	Я хочу взяти на прокат …	ya *kho*·chu *vzya*·tu na pro·*kat* ...
4WD	чотирьох привідну машину	cho·ty·*ryokh* pry·vid·*nu* ma·*shy*·nu
bicycle	велосипед	ve·lo·sy·*ped*
car	машину	ma·*shy*·nu
motorcycle	мотоцикл	mo·to·*tsykl*

Is this the road to ...?
Це дорога до …? — tse do·*ro*·ha do ...

I have a flat tyre.
В мене спустила шина. — w *me*·ne spu·*sty*·la *shy*·na

I've run out of petrol.
У мене закінчився бензин. — u *me*·ne za·kin·*chy*·wsya ben·*zyn*

My car has broken down.
У мене поламалася машина. — u *me*·ne po·la·*ma*·la·sya ma·*shy*·na

diesel	дізель	*di*·zel
helmet	шолом	sho·*lom*
petrol/gas	бензин	ben·*zyn*
pump	насос	na·*sos*
service station	заправка	za·*praw*·ka
unleaded	очищений	o·*chy*·shche·ny

Behind the Scenes

SEND US YOUR FEEDBACK

We love to hear from travellers – your comments keep us on our toes and help make our books better. Our well-travelled team reads every word on what you loved or loathed about this book. Although we cannot reply individually to postal submissions, we always guarantee that your feedback goes straight to the appropriate authors, in time for the next edition. Each person who sends us information is thanked in the next edition – the most useful submissions are rewarded with a selection of digital PDF chapters.

Visit **lonelyplanet.com/contact** to submit your updates and suggestions or to ask for help. Our award-winning website also features inspirational travel stories, news and discussions.

Note: We may edit, reproduce and incorporate your comments in Lonely Planet products such as guidebooks, websites and digital products, so let us know if you don't want your comments reproduced or your name acknowledged. For a copy of our privacy policy visit lonelyplanet.com/privacy.

OUR READERS

Many thanks to the travellers who used the last edition and wrote to us with helpful hints, useful advice and interesting anecdotes:

Anna Jacenko, Arlo Werkhoven, Artem Myrgorodskyi, Barney Smith, Brian Sherman, Colin Hansen, Damien Tricoire, Danyo Romijn, Diana Maddison, Dimitris Basias, Donald H. Langlois, Edward McPhillips, Evert Bos, Francois Benaroya, George Campbell, Hans Magnus Borge, Helen Haines, Janet Rossmann, Janet van Tubbergh, Jefferry Wong, Jerome Phillips, Jim Rogers, Jo Cook, Karen Davies, Leanne Pupchek, Lennart Davidsson, Lubos Vesely, Marcin Lapinski, Maria Livek, Michal Rudziecki, Monica George, Natasha Martisova, Pamela Stathakis, Sebastian Kelly, Sofiya Papirnyk, Stephen Byrne, Thérèse Remus, Tracey Jeacock, Will Lake, Zeynep Tunc

AUTHOR THANKS

Marc Di Duca

A mammoth *dyakuju* to my Kyiv parents-in-law for all their help during research and for looking after sons Kirill and Taras. Huge thanks to fellow author, Leonid Ragozin, for his professional approach and to Vasyl in Rakhiv; Vitaly and family in Kolomyya; Yarema in Lviv; Olga in Ivano-Frankivsk; Olena and all the guys in Lutsk; Kirill and Lena in the Carpathians; and last, but certainly not least, my wife, Tanya, for her support during my trip and write-up.

Leonid Ragozin

Most of all I would like to thank Dmitry Surnin and Yelizaveta Ovdeyenko for providing shelter in Kyiv and Odesa. My former classmate Nikolay Malinovsky remains my favourite Kyiv expert. Also in Kyiv, many thanks to Vladimir and Viktoria Fedorin for unforgettable evenings and great conversations. Very special thanks to Leonid and Yelena Tsodikov for terrific days at their dacha in Sviatohirsk. Finally in Odesa, my heroes are Alla Belenkova, Yelena Lebedinskaya and Vladimir Chaplin.

ACKNOWLEDGMENTS

Climate map data adapted from Peel MC, Finlayson BL & McMahon TA (2007) 'Updated World Map of the Köppen-Geiger Climate Classification', *Hydrology and Earth System Sciences*, 11, 163344.

Cover photograph: Kyevo-Pecherska Lavra monastery, Kiev, BEW/AWL.

THIS BOOK

This 4th edition of Lonely Planet's *Ukraine* guidebook was researched and written by Marc Di Duca and Leonid Ragozin, who also wrote the previous edition. The 1st and 2nd editions were written by Sarah Johnstone, who was assisted on the 2nd edition by Greg Bloom. Lisa Dunford contributed additional texts.

This guidebook was commissioned in Lonely Planet's London office, and produced by the following:

Commissioning Editors Katie O'Connell, Anna Tyler

Coordinating Editors Briohny Hooper, Kristin Odijk

Senior Cartographer Valentina Kremenchutskaya

Book Designer Jessica Rose

Managing Editors Angela Tinson, Sasha Baskett

Senior Editors Catherine Naghten, Karyn Noble

Assisting Editors Adrienne Costanzo, Gabrielle Innes, Elizabeth Jones, Anne Mason

Cover Research Naomi Parker

Language Content Branislava Vladisavljevic

Thanks to Brendan Dempsey, Ryan Evans, Larissa Frost, Genesys India, Jouve India, Trent Paton, Mazzy Prinsep, Luna Soo

Index

Map Pages **000**
Photo Pages **000**

D

E

F

Map Pages **000**
Photo Pages **000**

N

Map Legend

Sights
- Beach
- Bird Sanctuary
- Buddhist
- Castle/Palace
- Christian
- Confucian
- Hindu
- Islamic
- Jain
- Jewish
- Monument
- Museum/Gallery/Historic Building
- Ruin
- Sento Hot Baths/Onsen
- Shinto
- Sikh
- Taoist
- Winery/Vineyard
- Zoo/Wildlife Sanctuary
- Other Sight

Activities, Courses & Tours
- Bodysurfing
- Diving
- Canoeing/Kayaking
- Course/Tour
- Skiing
- Snorkelling
- Surfing
- Swimming/Pool
- Walking
- Windsurfing
- Other Activity

Sleeping
- Sleeping
- Camping

Eating
- Eating

Drinking & Nightlife
- Drinking & Nightlife
- Cafe

Entertainment
- Entertainment

Shopping
- Shopping

Information
- Bank
- Embassy/Consulate
- Hospital/Medical
- Internet
- Police
- Post Office
- Telephone
- Toilet
- Tourist Information
- Other Information

Geographic
- Beach
- Hut/Shelter
- Lighthouse
- Lookout
- Mountain/Volcano
- Oasis
- Park
- Pass
- Picnic Area
- Waterfall

Population
- Capital (National)
- Capital (State/Province)
- City/Large Town
- Town/Village

Transport
- Airport
- Border crossing
- Bus
- Cable car/Funicular
- Cycling
- Ferry
- Metro station
- Monorail
- Parking
- Petrol station
- Subway station
- Taxi
- Train station/Railway
- Tram
- Underground station
- Other Transport

Note: Not all symbols displayed above appear on the maps in this book

Routes
- Tollway
- Freeway
- Primary
- Secondary
- Tertiary
- Lane
- Unsealed road
- Road under construction
- Plaza/Mall
- Steps
- Tunnel
- Pedestrian overpass
- Walking Tour
- Walking Tour detour
- Path/Walking Trail

Boundaries
- International
- State/Province
- Disputed
- Regional/Suburb
- Marine Park
- Cliff
- Wall

Hydrography
- River, Creek
- Intermittent River
- Canal
- Water
- Dry/Salt/Intermittent Lake
- Reef

Areas
- Airport/Runway
- Beach/Desert
- Cemetery (Christian)
- Cemetery (Other)
- Glacier
- Mudflat
- Park/Forest
- Sight (Building)
- Sportsground
- Swamp/Mangrove

OUR STORY

A beat-up old car, a few dollars in the pocket and a sense of adventure. In 1972 that's all Tony and Maureen Wheeler needed for the trip of a lifetime – across Europe and Asia overland to Australia. It took several months, and at the end – broke but inspired – they sat at their kitchen table writing and stapling together their first travel guide, *Across Asia on the Cheap*. Within a week they'd sold 1500 copies. Lonely Planet was born.

Today, Lonely Planet has offices in Melbourne, London and Oakland, with more than 600 staff and writers. We share Tony's belief that 'a great guidebook should do three things: inform, educate and amuse'.

OUR WRITERS

Marc Di Duca

Coordinating Author, Around Kyiv, Central Ukraine, Lviv & Western Ukraine, The Carpathians, Eastern Ukraine Driven by an urge to discover Eastern Europe's wilder side, Marc first touched down in Kyiv one snow-flecked night in early 1998. Several prolonged stints, countless near misses with Kyiv's metro doors and numerous scary rides in seat-beltless Lada taxis later, he still gets excited about exploring this immense land, fine-tuning his Russian as he goes. Overheated buses and *salo* aside, Marc has a fascination with all things Ukrainian, in particular his favourite two places – Gogol country around Myrhorod and magical Lviv. A long-established travel-guide author, Marc has penned guides to Moscow, Lake Baikal and the Trans-Siberian Railway, as well as the Eastern Siberia chapter of Lonely Planet's *Russia* guidebook. This is Marc's 27th Lonely Planet guidebook.

Read more about Marc at:
lonelyplanet.com/members/madidu

Leonid Ragozin

Kyiv, Odesa & Southern Ukraine, Crimea, Eastern Ukraine Leonid devoted himself to the study of beach dynamics at Moscow University. But for want of really nice beaches in Russia, he helped Australian gold prospectors in Siberia before embarking on a journalist's career in 1998. Since then, he has spent most of the time moving between the TV, radio and online divisions of the BBC. There was also a three-year stint as a foreign correspondent for *Russian Newsweek*. Leonid also co-authored the latest editions of Lonely Planet's *Russia* and *Trans-Siberian Railway* guidebooks.

Published by Lonely Planet Publications Pty Ltd
ABN 36 005 607 983
4th edition – May 2014
ISBN 978 1 74220 205 1

10 9 8 7 6 5 4 3 2 1
Printed in China